Lift Every Voice

ALSO BY PATRICIA SULLIVAN

Days of Hope: Race and Democracy in the New Deal Era

Freedom Writer: Virginia Foster Durr, Letters from the Civil Rights Years

Lift Every Voice

The NAACP and the Making
of the Civil Rights Movement

Patricia Sullivan

THE NEW PRESS

NEW YORK
LONDON

Requests for permission to reproduce selections from this book should be mailed to:
Permissions Department, The New Press, 38 Greene Street, New York, NY 10013.

First published in the United States by The New Press, New York, 2009
This paperback edition published by The New Press, 2010
Distributed by Perseus Distribution

ISBN 978-1-59558-544-8 (pbk.)

LIBRARY OF CONGRESS CATALOGING-IN-PUBLICATION DATA

Sullivan, Patricia, 1950-
Lift every voice : the NAACP and the making of the Civil Rights Movement /
Patricia Sullivan.
p. cm.
Includes bibliographical references and index.
ISBN 978-1-59558-446-5 (hc. : alk. paper)   1. National Association for
the Advancement of Colored People—History.   2. Civil rights
movements—United States—History—20th century.   3. African
Americans—Civil rights—History—20th century.   4. United States—Race
relations. I. Title.
E185.5.N276S85 2009
973'.0496073—dc22   2009009473

The New Press was established in 1990 as a not-for-profit alternative to the large,
commercial publishing houses currently dominating the book publishing industry. The New Press
operates in the public interest rather than for private gain, and is committed to publishing,
in innovative ways, works of educational, cultural, and community value that are often
deemed insufficiently profitable.

www.thenewpress.com

Composition by The Influx House
This book was set in Adobe Caslon

Printed in the United States of America

2 4 6 8 10 9 7 5 3 1

To the memory of
Joe Wood and
John Hope Franklin

Contents

Acknowledgments

Lift Every Voice began with Joe Wood, editor for The New Press. Joe wanted a history of the NAACP and he asked me to write one—not an institutional history, he explained, but one that captured the pulse and life of the association. In short, Joe said, "a book my parents will read." We imagined this book together.

The vast collection of NAACP papers at the Library of Congress made it possible. From the beginning, the association saved and preserved nearly everything—administrative and legal files, field reports, branch correspondence, photographs, and much more—creating the largest and most important archival collection on race and civil rights in the United States of the twentieth century. Thanks to the NAACP and the Library of Congress, these documents are readily available. The library's Manuscript Division has been like a second home. The women and men who staff the reading room create a perfect research environment and I am grateful to them for their generous assistance over the years.

A circle of historians and friends has been close by as I charted a course through an ocean of history. Their knowledge, insights, and encouragement have been formative as I conceptualized, researched, and wrote the book. Each of them has my abiding gratitude.

John Hope Franklin knew several of the leading figures, lived much of the history described here, and was deeply interested in the story of the NAACP. He shared recollections and read chapters, penciling them with edits, questions, and comments. Along the way, there were many conversations about the twists and turns of the history and its meaning.

My deep friendship with Waldo Martin and our longtime collaboration on scholarship and teaching centered on the African American experience in the United States anchors my work as a historian. We discussed approaches to a history of the NAACP from the time I began thinking about the project, and Waldo commented on chapters as the book unfolded. Lewis Steel, a leading civil rights attorney since the early 1960s, read every chapter. He raised penetrating questions, explained legal concepts, and provided editorial suggestions—expanding my knowledge, sharpening my focus, and helping me achieve greater clarity. Lewis and Kitty Steels's steady encouragement and support has been wonderful.

Larissa Smith Fergeson, one of the most talented scholars working in the field of civil rights history, has generously shared her research on the NAACP in Virginia and was always ready to talk through any aspect of the work, from the small details to large interpretive questions. Lara commented on chapters, read page proofs, and helped in other immeasurable ways—she is an amazing friend. Raymond Gavins's work on the NAACP and the Jim Crow South has been a major influence on my work. Ray read several chapters and provided incisive suggestions. Discussions with Kenneth Mack about civil rights lawyers, as well as Ken's comments on parts of the manuscript, helped me fine-tune a major theme of the book.

Henry Louis Gates Jr. has been an enthusiastic and generous supporter—as a friend and as director of the W.E.B. Du Bois Institute for African and African American Research at Harvard University. The book took root at the Du Bois Institute and I have spent most summers there in conjunction with our NEH summer institutes on teaching the history of the civil rights movement, exploring many of the questions that have guided my research.

Steven Hahn read most of the manuscript. Missy Daniel, Eric Bargeron, Michaela O'Neill Daniel, Deborah McDowell, and David Prior read various chapters. *Lift Every Voice* has benefited greatly from their comments, questions, and suggestions. Martha Mae Jones, Leon Litwack, William Preston, and Julius Scott have listened to me talk about the NAACP for almost a decade, shared thoughts and insights and helped me reach further.

A number of scholars have supported my efforts in a variety of ways. The late August Meier laid the groundwork and encouraged me early on. John Bracey, whose knowledge of the NAACP is boundless, has generously shared it with me. I am also grateful to Tony Badger, Elsa Barkley Brown, Mia Bay, Kevin Boyle, Claudia Brinson, Lewis Burke, Margaret Burnham, Bettye

Collier Thomas, Andrew Fearnley, Kenneth Janken, David Levering Lewis, Glenn Loury, Kimberly Phillips, Stephen Tuck and Denton Watson.

Judge Robert L. Carter, NAACP attorney for twenty-five years and top assistant to Thurgood Marshall during the legal campaign against segregation, shared recollections and insights and answered my endless queries. Knowing Bob Carter has deepened my understanding of what it is all about.

Interviews and conversations with men and women associated with the NAACP or the broader movement it shaped helped to illuminate various aspects of the history. I am grateful to: Derrick Bell, Julian Bond, Dorothy Burnham, the late Johnnie Carr, John Doar, Vernon Jordan, Chuck McDew, Bob Moses, Martha Norman Noonan, Reverend Herbert Oliver, Judge Matthew J. Perry, Mildred Bond Roxborough, and Cleveland Sellers.

In 1948, Palmer Weber, then a thirty-four-year-old organizer, wrote from Georgia, "Every day in the field, I thank God for the NAACP." It was my good fortune to meet Palmer when I was a graduate student in history. He turned my attention to the rich history of the NAACP early on.

I am indebted to the institutions whose support provided the resources, time, and space essential to the research and writing of this book. I have enjoyed year-long residency fellowships at the Woodrow Wilson International Center for Scholars, the W. E. B. Du Bois Institute at Harvard University, the National Humanities Center, the John W. Kluge Center at the Library of Congress, and Boston University's Institute on Race and Social Division. I have also been the recipient of fellowships from the National Endowment for the Humanities and the Alphonse Fletcher Sr. Fellowship Program, established to commemorate the fiftieth anniversary of the *Brown v. Board of Education* decision and to support work that furthers its goals.

Beyond my fellowship year at the Woodrow Wilson Center during the initial phase of this study, the Wilson Center provided a place for me to finish the book. Special thanks to director Lee Hamilton, to the Wilson Center's library staff and to the interns who provided research assistance: Federico Sor, Kori Kelley, Kanelle Valton, and Zachery Siegel.

The University of South Carolina has been most generous in its support. I am especially grateful to Patrick Maney, former chair of the Department of History, Cleveland Sellers, former director of the African American Studies program, Lacy Ford, and Dean Mary Anne Fitzpatrick. Pat Maney's active interest and encouragement helped me to keep it all moving forward.

Marc Favreau, my editor at The New Press, brought his red pencil to bear in the shaping of *Lift Every Voice*. Marc's keen editorial eye and fine historical sensibility made him an invaluable ally in my effort to tell the story that emerged from years of research. André Schiffrin, founding director of The New Press, saw promise at the beginning and has been a supporter across the long haul. Sarah Fan and Jason Ng expedited the production process which was brilliantly orchestrated by Cinqué Hicks.

During the years that I have been immersed in researching and writing this book, family and friends in New York, Vineyard Haven, Washington, D.C., and beyond have supported me and the project in countless ways. All have my deep gratitude. I am particularly indebted to: my sisters and brother, Kathleen Basil, Mary Sullivan-Lester, Eileen Sullivan, and Tom Sullivan; the late Joseph Archer; Donna Bohanan; Sheldon and Lucy Hackney; Marge and Jamie Harris; Rhoda Litwack; Bill Preston; Paulette "P.J." Robinson; my friends on The Glen in Chapel Hill; and the "women of 90 Main" on Martha's Vineyard.

Most especially, I thank my father and mother, Thomas and Doris Sullivan. They have long been my most devoted readers and are always an inspiration.

Lift Every Voice is dedicated to the memory of Joe Wood and John Hope Franklin. Thoughts of Joe guided the work. John Hope enriched the journey.

Introduction

*"As we understand it [the NAACP] works against injustice and oppression
directed against our people and seeks to have them accorded ... equality before
the law and fair play everywhere. Surely this is a plane upon which all men,
white and black, may stand."*
                                        —*Wilson Jefferson, February 15, 1917*

In the beginning, the NAACP was an idea. "Equality before the law and fair
play everywhere," as Wilson Jefferson, a postal worker in Augusta, Georgia,
described it. This simple statement of the American creed stood as a bold
challenge to the racial beliefs and practices that defined national life for most
of the twentieth century.

When the National Association for the Advancement of Colored People
was established in 1909, some 90 percent of African Americans lived in the
South under a brutal caste system, sanctioned by the U.S. Supreme Court. A
two-day-long mob attack on the black community in Springfield, Illinois, the
previous summer signaled the spread of southern-style race relations to the
North and stirred a group of whites and blacks to action. In founding the
NAACP, they directly challenged the color line and initiated a national
struggle for full legal and civic equality as guaranteed by the Constitution.

Lift Every Voice tells the story of the NAACP and its role in American life
up through the *Brown v. Board* decision and the passage of the Civil Rights
Acts of 1964 and 1965. The book draws on years of research, primarily in the
NAACP's vast archival collection, including field reports by organizers and

civil rights attorneys, records of local branches, and thousands of letters. It chronicles a history that spans a half-century of far-reaching social and political change—an expanding federal government, the Great Depression, two world wars, the unprecedented economic boom after World War II, the Cold War, and the steady migration of southern-born blacks to the urban North. Across these years, the NAACP functioned as the leading oppositional force to persistent barriers of race.

Launched with scant financial backing, the NAACP developed an improvisational approach at odds with its current reputation as a staid, established institution. It was a lean operation, dependent on the imagination, talent and dedication of a handful of individuals, a growing network of volunteers, and a dues-paying membership. Spirited and often novel efforts to expose and challenge racial injustices and mobilize resistance created a flexible organization, adept at navigating a rugged racial topography and building a movement for change.

The formative years of the NAACP's history have been neglected by a civil rights scholarship that locates the foundational decades of the movement in the New Deal–World War II era. Yet, during the teens and twenties, NAACP activists crafted the "machinery" that would drive the civil rights movement: publicity and protest, litigation and lobbying, community-based organizing and demands for national action. In 1913, for example, the NAACP confronted head-on the deepening segregation of the federal government under President Woodrow Wilson, marking the organization's debut in national politics. After producing an investigative report exposing Wilson's "unofficial" policy, the association staged a mass meeting of several thousand people just blocks from the White House to "Protest Segregation—the New Slavery," orchestrated a nationwide protest, and employed a full-time legislative expert to monitor developments in Washington. Barely a year later, the upstart organization mobilized supporters in cities and towns across the nation to mount targeted protests against *The Birth of a Nation*, the cinematic celebration of the Ku Klux Klan, rallying black Americans in defense of their place in history.

Early organizers of the NAACP—notably W.E.B. Du Bois, Mary White Ovington, Joel Spingarn, May Childs Nerney, Kathryn Magnolia Johnson, and James Weldon Johnson—worked to give the association strong roots through an ambitious program of fieldwork, which made them all the more informed about America's varied racial terrain. After World War I, membership approached one hundred thousand and included teachers, ministers, and other professionals, as well as domestic workers, laborers, and sharecroppers. Organized into branches, local members tackled a range of issues in their own communities—educational inequality, school segregation, housing restrictions, voting rights, violations of labor contracts, and injustices in the legal system—shaping a civic consciousness that defied the badge of second-class citizenship.

The New York–based staff responded to some of the worst atrocities and violations of human and civil rights in ways that gave voice and visibility to the cause. After a murderous assault on African Americans in East St. Louis in 1917, the NAACP organized a "Silent Parade" of ten thousand men, women, and children down Fifth Avenue in New York City to protest mob violence and lynching. In 1920, NAACP officials secured a congressional hearing on the violent suppression of black voting rights in the South during the first major election following World War I and the enactment of women's suffrage. The ensuing showdown between NAACP executive secretary James Weldon Johnson and abusive southern representatives dramatized the viciousness of racism and the will to fight it before an attentive press. In 1926, the NAACP enlisted Clarence Darrow to defend Ossian Sweet, a black man indicted for murder committed during the defense of his Detroit home from a white mob. The case focused national attention on the violent enforcement of neighborhood boundaries in northern cities during the height of the Great Migration. In a dramatic closing argument that explored America's tumultuous racial past, an incredulous Darrow began by asking, "Who are we anyway?"

By the late 1920s, the NAACP could claim a string of legal victories striking down various discriminatory policies in housing, voting, education, and criminal justice. But winning court cases during this period hardly dented harsh conditions on the ground. The movement toward racial segregation and ghetto conditions in the North was unrelenting. In the South, terror reinforced the legal mandates of Jim Crow while Southern Democrats claimed dominance on race matters in Washington. The association's greatest achievement during these first decades, according to Charles Houston, was to keep "the light burning on the lonely peak of absolute equality."

Economic collapse, the rise of radical left politics, and the vast expansion of federal power tested the agility of the NAACP at its quarter-century mark in the 1930s. Black protest and civil rights activism escalated during the Depression and New Deal years, giving rise to alternative approaches to the problems of racial injustice. A heightened emphasis on class-based issues, changing political alignments, and the aspirations of a new generation fostered wide-ranging discussions about strategies and goals.

Other histories of this era tend to emphasize organizational rivalries, personal tensions, and tactical differences, often losing sight of a critical controlling factor: there was no clear path through the mire of American racial oppression. This pervasive reality was manifest in the breadth of the NAACP's reach and the debates centered on its program. Of all the moments when uncertainty prompted discord, W.E.B. Du Bois's 1934 call for a major change was the most poignant and dramatic. Since the NAACP's founding, he noted, segregation in the North had become further entrenched, and white support for the work of the NAACP was minimal. Thus, Du Bois argued for an approach that would concentrate on building up black institutions for what promised to be a long struggle. While his critique of racial conditions was not challenged, the rest of the NAACP's leadership remained committed to pursuing full and equal inclusion in the mainstream of American life.

But how? A sense of urgency rather than possibility informed the NAACP's response to the expansion of federal power under the New Deal and during World War II. In Washington, executive secretary Walter White claimed a place for the organization in the tumult of New Deal politics, institutionalizing the NAACP's presence in the halls of power. He fought to resist federal policies that reinforced widespread patterns of black exclusion and racial discrimination. Backed by an increasingly pivotal northern black vote, White lobbied to bend the emergent liberal-labor coalition toward a racially inclusive legislative agenda and worked to make civil rights a national issue. By the mid-1930s, the NAACP's annual convention had become a major venue for political figures and labor leaders aware of the growing power of black voters in northern industrial states.

Charles Houston joined the NAACP as special counsel in 1934 and sharpened the association's creative edge. A radical visionary and brilliant strategist, he was acutely attentive to organizations and developments aligned with the struggle for black freedom. Houston praised the Communist Party's bold action in the Scottsboro case but was drawn to the NAACP's potential as, in his words, the "crystallizing force of Negro citizenship." At a time when southern segregation seemed impervious, he orchestrated a protracted challenge to Jim Crow and its social and psychological hold—an effort that was carried forward by Thurgood Marshall and a cadre of young attorneys in close association with local NAACP branches. They used the courts and the legal system, long-standing bulwarks of black oppression, as arenas for mobilizing resistance and exposing southern lawlessness. It is rarely noted that in his first case before the U.S. Supreme Court, Marshall represented three black soldiers convicted and sentenced to death in Louisiana on trumped-up rape charges. Battles to access elemental justice in the courts constituted an integral part of an insurgency that aimed to enlist black people in a sustained assault on the legal chains of segregation and disenfranchisement.

During World War II, a time when membership numbers skyrocketed, legendary field organizer Ella Baker described the NAACP's branches as "the life-blood of the association." For historians, they serve as barometers of civil rights activism and race relations in the North and in the West, as well as in the South. NAACP branches in northern urban areas addressed a range of localized incidents and issues, often coordinating with the national office in the fight for equal access to defense jobs and challenges to discrimination in education and housing. Walter White and the leadership of the Detroit branch brokered a major breakthrough with the United Automobile Workers (UAW), opening the union to black workers and creating the foundation for a national alliance with organized labor. After the war, the long-term attack on residential segregation culminated in a U.S. Supreme Court case striking down restrictive covenants. But the amorphous nature of racial segregation made it difficult to gain traction in the fight against the North's informal caste system.

The multi-front efforts of NAACP activists during the 1930s and 1940s revealed, as attorney Robert Carter later observed, that racial discrimination was not only "operative in all aspects of American life but generally accepted as the norm." Major New Deal initiatives accommodated dominant racial practices; public housing and federally assisted mortgage programs, for example, expanded the reach of residential segregation. With the important exception of a hard-won executive order banning racial discrimination in defense industries, the Roosevelt administration bowed to dominant racial practices even as it fought a war against Nazism. Racial segregation prevailed from the Armed Forces to government-sponsored blood banks. Black soldiers flooded the NAACP with complaints about mistreatment and unfair courts martial; the "no discrimination" order for defense industries was fitfully enforced and then abandoned at the end of the war; and racial tensions turned several cities, North and South, into bloody battlefields.

In 1946, a year of explosive racial violence in the South, White leveraged southern outrages and northern black votes to compel President Harry Truman to appoint the President's Committee on Civil Rights. *To Secure These*

Rights, the committee's widely heralded report, offered a blueprint for decisive federal action. Beyond the desegregation of the Armed Forces, however, the report's recommendations were largely ignored for more than a decade. After the 1948 election, southern Democrats strengthened their hold on the legislative process while the domestic Cold War marginalized the racially progressive wing of the New Deal coalition. Liberal Democrats in Congress considered friendly to civil rights yielded to the racial status quo, as was apparent when several actively opposed the NAACP's effort to insert a "no discrimination" provision in the Housing Act of 1949. During the 1950s, NAACP's Washington representative, Clarence Mitchell, soldiered on through the Leadership Conference on Civil Rights to shore up a growing coalition of support for civil rights legislation.

In the decade after the war, the heavy investment of NAACP attorneys and organizers in the South drove the movement forward. When the NAACP won a Supreme Court ruling that struck down the "whites only" Democratic primary in 1944, southern blacks turned out to vote in numbers not seen since Reconstruction, sparking a reign of terror in the Deep South. After being violently barred from the polls in 1946, black Mississippians secured a Senate hearing in Jackson, and hundreds volunteered to testify publicly about the widespread, state-sanctioned violation of voting rights. *Brown v. Board of Education* developed out of these broad-based and well-established efforts in the South. A brilliant exercise in constitutional law that incorporated new insights from social science and history, the famous 1954 ruling rested on nearly two decades of litigation grounded in exquisite lawyering, hands-on fieldwork, and community organizing. It signified a remarkable marriage of intellectual capital and dedicated leadership with the courage and aspirations of countless men and women—people who believed change was possible and were willing to risk everything for it. When they won *Brown* and struck down the legal underpinnings of segregation, the tide of history turned.

Following the *Brown* ruling, the NAACP became a prime target of southern defiance. State legislatures enacted a battery of laws designed to destroy the association, crippling the NAACP in many parts of the South and forcing it to fight for its life in the courts. But other organizations rose up—notably the Southern Christian Leadership Conference and the Student Nonviolent Coordinating Committee—reinforcing the movement and expanding its reach. Mass protests amplified demands for government action to end racial apartheid, ultimately securing the Civil Rights Acts of 1964 and 1965. The legislation strengthened the power of the federal government to enforce the constitutional guarantees of the Fourteenth and Fifteenth Amendments, re-alizing a founding goal of the NAACP. Federal law aligned with the civil rights movement to issue the final blow to the South's overt caste system, while expanding the citizenship rights of all Americans and providing for a more inclusive democracy.

The momentous triumph over Jim Crow laws and practices could not re-dress many of the other forms of racial discrimination and exploitation that divided whites and blacks across the nation. The uprisings that rocked north-ern cities in the later 1960s were emblematic of black frustration over how little had changed in the wake of legislative victories. Long years of systemic discrimination in major areas of life—housing, education, jobs, and the jus-tice system—fostered conditions that proved to be more intractable than the South's legally enforced color line. Today, far-reaching changes generated by the civil rights gains of the 1960s coexist with wide racial gaps in all measures of social and economic well-being, catastrophic rates of black incarceration, and, within society at large, a widespread and often willful ignorance of the nation's racial past and its consequences.

The NAACP emerged at the dawn of the twentieth century, a period de-scribed as the "nadir" of American race relations. The stories of the men and women who created and built the association—what they saw, what they worked to achieve, and the paths they blazed—illuminate the roots of Amer-ica's civil rights movement, tangled deep in the nation's history. In this full accounting, measures of victory and defeat in the incremental and inconclu-sive struggle for racial justice are not easily gauged. It is the struggle itself that commands attention. While shining a harsh light on America's fractured ra-cial landscape, *Lift Every Voice* explores how an unprecedented opening to-ward interracial collaboration and anti-segregationist activism became the vanguard of one of the most powerful social and political movements in mod-ern history.

Lift Every Voice

1

Call to Action

On August 1, 1910, W.E.B. Du Bois arrived at 20 Vesey Street in downtown Manhattan, home of the *New York Evening Post* and headquarters of the newly established National Association for the Advancement of Colored People (NAACP). After more than a decade at Atlanta University, the forty-two-year-old scholar left academic life behind to become director of publications and research for the fledgling organization. Years later, he recalled the sober greeting offered by Oswald Garrison Villard, NAACP treasurer and owner of the *Evening Post*. "I don't know who is going to pay your salary," Villard announced as Du Bois settled into his bare office. "I have no money."[1]

In the summer of 1910 the NAACP remained little more than an idea. Conceived fifteen months earlier, this experiment in interracial alliance failed to attract the support of major philanthropists, leaving its coffers begging. During the earliest days, it was sustained by the sense of urgency that brought founding members together, along with infusions of cash and material support from Villard. The small band of reformers who launched the NAACP represented a broad spectrum of views, but they shared a single-minded commitment to halting the downward spiral of black life and race relations that marked the new century.

By the time the NAACP was founded, white supremacy had triumphed in the South, home to nearly 90 percent of black Americans. Over the previous twenty years southern states enacted a series of laws that effectively stripped blacks of citizenship rights and segregated all phases of public life. The legal underpinnings for a racial caste system earned the endorsement of the U.S. Supreme Court with the *Plessy v. Ferguson* ruling in 1896. Mass terror and violence were essential to establishing and maintaining the new racial order. One of the worst incidents of political terrorism occurred in 1898 in Wilmington, North Carolina, where white Democrats led an armed insurrection against the city's black-dominated government, killing an unknown number of blacks. It was the only recorded overthrow of a government in American history. During the first decade of the twentieth century, there were nearly nine hundred documented lynchings of African Americans.[2]

National sentiment yielded easily to the South's caste system. Social Darwinism and a nationalism steeped in the ideology of Anglo-Saxon superiority crested at the turn of the century with American imperialistic ventures abroad and the influx of dark-skinned immigrants from southern and eastern Europe. Science, history, and popular culture trained new generations of Americans in the catechism of racial difference and black inferiority. While white southerners "redeemed" their region from its brief foray in biracial democracy during the Reconstruction era, historians recast that period of black political freedom as a tragic time and a powerful lesson in the perils of enfranchising the ignorant and socially inferior. The *New York Times* described the Fifteenth Amendment, enacted to secure black Americans the right to vote, as "a blunder in statesmanship" claiming that "it attempted to thwart by legislation a determination which has never been thwarted in the history of the human race—the determination of the white man to rule the land wherein he lives." Booker T. Washington's program of industrial education and deference to "home rule" in the South was widely embraced by most whites as the best way to manage the "Negro problem."[3]

In the years leading up to the founding of the NAACP, black leaders such as Du Bois and Ida B. Wells-Barnett and a handful of white reformers tried to pierce the silence that surrounded the assault on African Americans and on the rights that had been secured under the Fourteenth and Fifteenth amendments. With the publication of *The Souls of Black Folk* in 1903, Du Bois brought the discussion that had been percolating among African Americans about Booker T. Washington into a broader public forum. Du Bois offered recent developments as proof that Washington's widely touted program had failed to halt the deterioration of black life and opportunity in the South. More than a critique of Washington's approach, Du Bois's essay was most concerned with unhinging Washington's grip on public opinion and resurrecting the struggle for political and civic equality as essential for facilitating black advancement and ensuring the health of American democracy.[4]

Oswald Garrison Villard, grandson of abolitionist William Lloyd Garrison and heir to his father Henry Villard's railroad fortune, had been an early supporter of Washington. Yet *The Souls of Black Folk* struck a responsive chord. Villard's *New York Evening Post* and the *Nation*, which he also owned, praised the book and acknowledged that Du Bois's critique deserved "the carefullest consideration." The same year that *Souls* was published, a Justice Department investigation of peonage in the South shook Villard's faith in the policy of accommodation that had characterized his approach to racial affairs. Federal intervention and a vigorous campaign by the northern press were critical in bringing this form of neo-slavery to light and facilitating a grand jury investigation. Subsequent developments in the South convinced Villard that something had to be done to counter the complete betrayal of emancipation and the constitutional guarantees that gave it meaning.[5]

During these years, as racial conditions worsened, ideas germinated and personal networks coalesced to provide the foundation of the early NAACP. W. E. B. Du Bois's efforts in several realms were of critical importance. From his base at Atlanta University, where he joined the faculty in 1898, Du Bois, the first African American to earn a PhD at Harvard, pursued scholarly investigation and publication, leading the empirical challenge to popular notions about racial inferiority. Under his direction, the annual Atlanta University Studies conference series conducted pioneering studies of the lives and social conditions of black Americans, focusing on a different topic each year. Biographer David Levering Lewis describes the "annual processions of scholars, social reformers, religious leaders, university administrators, and public officials" to Atlanta University to participate in these meetings and to meet Du Bois. Visitors included distinguished scholars such as anthropologist Franz Boas and political economist Edwin Seligmann and social settlement workers Jane Addams, Frances Kellor, and Mary White Ovington. While Du Bois became increasingly impatient with the limits of scholarly investigation, the Atlanta conference series created openings toward future collaborations beyond the scholarly realm.[6]

The pressure to act grew. Early in the summer of 1905 Du Bois took the lead in calling together a group of black men who met on the Canadian side of Niagara Falls and founded what became known as the Niagara Movement. The organization gave structure and visibility to anti-Washington sentiments shared by a core group of leading black professionals and began the hard work of organizing widespread dissidence into a movement for racial justice. Its platform claimed for all African Americans "every single right that belongs to a freeborn American—political, civil, and social" and promised that "the voice of protest of ten million Americans" would "never cease to assail the ears of their fellows" until those rights were secured. The group combined publicity, protest, and the organization of local affiliates throughout the country in their frontal assault on racial discrimination. Scant resources, strong opposition from the Washington machine, and a hostile racial climate constrained the possibilities of this ambitious undertaking. Still, though its membership remained small and selective, the Niagara Movement linked blacks from across the nation, forming an incipient vanguard in the struggle for civil rights.[7]

Although he continued to maintain a cordial relationship with Washington, Villard's *Evening Post* provided coverage of the second meeting of the Niagara Movement, held in Harper's Ferry in the summer of 1906 and reported on by Mary White Ovington, a great admirer of Du Bois. Barely a month after the Harper's Ferry meeting, the city of Atlanta erupted in an orgy of antiblack violence. That summer's heated gubernatorial campaign had stoked racial fears to a fevered pitch. Some ten thousand whites rioted, raiding black neighborhoods, assaulting black people, and destroying their homes and businesses. The riot claimed the lives of at least two dozen African Americans. For Oswald Garrison Villard, Atlanta was a turning point. In the aftermath of the riot, he began discussions with Ovington and others about the need for black men and women, north and south, to organize and defend themselves through boycotts and other forms of resistance. He also proposed a national organization devoted to securing and protecting the civil rights of African Americans.[8]

Villard outlined his ideas for what he called a "Committee for the Advancement of the Negro Race" in a speech to the Afro-American Council late in 1906. In what reads like a blueprint for the NAACP, Villard imagined that such an organization would include a research and publicity bureau; a legal division to challenge discrimination in the courts; a special committee to investigate lynching, peonage, and violations of civil rights; lobbyists in Washington and in state capitals; mass protest meetings; and a monthly magazine. His proposal won the interest and support of a small but distinguished cohort of reformers who agreed that the race problem could no longer be left to the South to solve. But it would take another major race riot before sentiment was mobilized into action.[9]

In the summer of 1908, Springfield, Illinois, home to Abraham Lincoln, was the scene of the most harrowing incident of antiblack violence in the North since the New York City draft riots nearly a half century earlier. Suddenly, it seemed as if the violence and brutality that characterized southern race relations were spilling northward. Tensions had been ratcheting up in Illinois as a slow but steady influx of blacks from the South increased the African American presence in urban areas such as Chicago, East St. Louis, and Springfield, places that also attracted southern whites seeking work. Blacks made up 10 percent of Springfield's population in 1908. The rioting, which began on the night of August 14, was sparked by a sequence of events following the arrest of two black men, one charged with murder and the other accused of rape. When the mob's efforts to storm the jail were frustrated by the sheriff, they turned their fury on the black residential area, torching homes and businesses and beating black pedestrians. They lynched two elderly black men, one an eighty-four-year-old cobbler who had been married to a white woman for thirty years. It took nearly four thousand troops two days to finally quell the riot. When it was over, eight black people were dead, scores more injured, and an estimated two thousand blacks fled the city.[10]

William English Walling, a young socialist with southern roots, rushed from Chicago, where he was visiting, to report on the riot. His impassioned article, "The Race War in the North," appeared in the *Independent*, a liberal weekly. Walling expressed near disbelief at the callous satisfaction shared by all of the whites he spoke with save one. For him, the events in Springfield signaled a nation standing at the precipice. "Either the spirit of the abolitionists must be revived" and the Negro treated "on a plane of absolute political and social equality," or, he warned, southern demagogues would succeed in transferring the race war to the North. If that happens "every hope of political democracy will be dead." But, he asked, "who realizes the seriousness of the situation, and what large and powerful body of citizens is ready to come to their aid?"[11]

Upon reading Walling's piece, Mary White Ovington wrote to him immediately expressing her interest and support. In the fall, Walling discussed his idea for a biracial organization with friends at the Liberal Club in New York, particularly Charles Edward Russell, a writer and socialist, whose father had been an abolitionist editor in Iowa. But it was Ovington's persistence that prodded Walling to convene a small meeting at his home to plan for the implementation of his idea. Early in January 1909, Henry Moskowitz, a New

York City social worker, joined Ovington and Walling; Russell, though actively involved, was unable to attend the meeting. The three agreed that a conference of prominent citizens should be convened in New York later in the year, and they invited Villard to join the group and help in organizing support for the meeting. They consulted with Du Bois at once and enlisted the aid of several other New Yorkers, including two prominent black clergymen, Bishop Alexander Walters of the African Methodist Episcopal (A. M. E.) Church and the Reverend William Henry Brooks, minister at St. Mark's Episcopal Church; Dr. W. H. Bulkley, a black public school principal; and Florence Kelley and Lillian Wald, both leading white civic activists and social reformers.[12]

"The Call," written by Villard, was published on February 12, 1909, the centenary of Abraham Lincoln's birth. What would Lincoln find, it asked, if he were to revisit the country at this time? In response, the manifesto described how far the nation had fallen from the promise of emancipation—the routine subversion of constitutional guarantees, the lawlessness and brutality directed against black people, north and south, the silence that meant approval. Borrowing from Lincoln, it warned that "this government cannot exist half slave and half free any better today than it could in 1861." "The Call" concluded with an appeal to all "believers in democracy to join in a national conference for the discussion of the present evils, the voicing of protests, and the renewal of the struggle for civil and political liberty." It was signed by an impressive group of educators, writers, social workers, journalists, and religious leaders, sixty in all. The great majority were from New York; seven of the signers were black. Signatories included W. E. B. Du Bois, Ida B. Wells-Barnett, John Dewey, William Lloyd Garrison Jr., Bishop Alexander Walters, Rabbi Stephen Wise, Lincoln Steffens, Ray Stannard Baker, Jane Addams, William Dean Howells, and Mary Church Terrell.[13]

Walling hosted the planning meetings at his home on West Thirty-eighth Street until the group grew to nearly fifty, causing them to move to the Liberal Club. Over the course of several meetings, the committee made arrangements for what was billed as "A Conference on the Status of the Negro." It would be held on May 31 and June 1 at the Charity Organization Hall, near Union Square. Invited speakers readily agreed to participate and nearly 150 distinguished citizens agreed to serve as sponsors, including the noted constitutional lawyer Moorfield Storey, who would go on to play a major role during the NAACP's early decades. As a young man, from 1867 to 1869, Storey had served as secretary to Senator Charles Sumner, leading opponent of slavery and an architect of the Reconstruction amendments. Working from personal networks and membership lists of organizations like the Niagara Movement, the committee sent out one thousand invitations to the conference. Villard wrote to his uncle, Francis Garrison, who was helping to organize support in Boston, describing a mood of excitement and anticipation in New York. He predicted, "It all ought to be the beginning of something big."[14]

Villard, however, was concerned that their venture not needlessly antagonize or alienate Booker T. Washington. He was surprised by the deep hostility toward Washington expressed by blacks and whites helping to organize the conference. While he himself had privately become increasingly critical of Washington's program, he understood that Washington remained a power broker among philanthropists and foundations that supported race-related causes, and he did not want the conference to be seen as an anti-Washington affair. It was probably with this in mind that Villard sent a personal invitation to Washington just days before the conference began. This was not, he explained in his note, going to be "a Washington movement or a Du Bois movement." Its purpose was to bring men of both races together "to discuss the conditions of the colored people" and to work toward initiating action on legal and political rights. He told Washington that he would understand if he chose not to attend. The organizers of the conference, Villard assured him, "do not wish to embarrass you . . . or seem to ignore you, or to leave you out, or to show any disrespect whatsoever." But they did not want to tie him up with what "may prove to be a radical political movement." For that reason "they have not felt like urging you very hard to join the new movement," but he should know that he would be welcome at the conference. Villard, however, did not want Washington's absence to be "misrepresented" and hoped that the new organization could count on his sympathy.[15]

Washington declined the invitation, claiming a prior engagement, but also allowed that his presence "would probably inhibit discussion." He told Villard that he realized there was work to be done that one in his position and probably no one living in the South could do. On the other hand, he contended, "there is work which those of us who live here in the South can do, which persons who do not live in the South cannot do. If we recognize fairly and squarely this, then it seems to me we have gone a long ways." Washington cautioned his old friend that it "was through progressive constructive work that we are to succeed rather than by depending too largely upon agitation and criticism." While Washington stayed away, he made sure that he had a loyal lieutenant, Charles Anderson, on the scene. Anderson, a prominent black Republican who worked as collector of internal revenue in New York, covered the conference, and began the work of discrediting the affair.[16]

The National Negro Conference, as it came to be called, was by all accounts, an extraordinary affair. Du Bois described it as "a visible bursting into action of long gathering thought and brooding." An estimated three hundred women and men gathered in the United Charities Hall for the two-day-long meeting. Speakers included scholars, social reformers, religious leaders, civil rights activists, and several public officials, including a federal judge, the former attorney general of Massachusetts, and a former Alabama legislator. According to press reports, roughly half of the group was black and half white. The experience of blacks and whites coming together to talk frankly about racial conditions and develop a plan of action was unprecedented and fraught with difficulty. All agreed that bold and innovative action was necessary. The efforts of the past, both by blacks themselves and by whites on behalf of blacks had proven insufficient to meet the challenge. It was time to join forces and try something new. But what form would the enterprise take, who would lead it, and how would it be organized? These were questions that tested the young organization from the beginning.[17]

The conference opened with a robust challenge to "scientific" theories about race long used to justify racial discrimination. Social Darwinism was one of the more popular variants of biological determinism at the time, a body of ideas that loosely applied Darwin's evolutionary theory of natural selection to explain the dominance of whites of European descent and claim the genetically based inferiority of blacks. Frederick Hoffman's highly influential *Race Traits and Tendencies of the American Negro*, published by the American Economic Association in 1896, attributed high black mortality rates to innate racial traits and was used by white-owned insurance companies to deny blacks coverage. Through most of the previous century, the study of brain size and shape had been used to bolster claims about black inferiority. By 1909, such reductive ideas about innate racial difference were slowly being eclipsed in academic circles by the work of Du Bois, cultural anthropologist Franz Boas, and others. A stellar group of social scientists started the meeting off by bringing these new trends in scholarship to the fore and tackling the intellectual foundation of white supremacy.[18]

Livingston Farrand, a Columbia University anthropologist, prefaced his remarks by noting that there was no agreement about what "race" meant. Classification of "so-called 'races'" was purely a matter of descriptions of physical characteristics, and even then, variation was great. Farrand went on to explain that there was no reliable evidence proving any marked differences of mental capacity between blacks and whites. Burt G. Wilder, a neurologist and zoologist, shared a platform with Farrand. A leading expert on the study of the brain, Wilder had served as a surgeon with the black Fifty-fifth Massachusetts Infantry during the Civil War. His "personal experience," Wilder once remarked, demonstrated that blacks had earned full rights "by the general conduct of soldiers of African descent, by their valor, their initiative, and by their deliberate self-sacrifice for the sake of principle." But at the New York meeting, he spoke as a neurologist and came armed with charts and illustrations. He provided a spirited debunking of methodology used in a recent series of articles on the Negro brain, cited in a medical journal as justification for disenfranchisement. Summarizing the broad body of evidence that had been generated around the topic of innate mental capacity over the years, Wilder concluded that "no constant feature" had been found "by which the Negro brain may be distinguished from that of a Caucasian."[19]

John Dewey, the noted educator and philosopher, followed through on the scientific emphasis, drawing attention to the trend in biological science that diminished the significance of inherited traits, and emphasized the importance of environment in individual development and achievement. There was no such thing as an "inferior race" Dewey explained; all points of skill and ability were represented among the members of each "race so called." It was in the interest of society, Dewey argued, from "a strictly scientific standpoint" to ensure that "the environment is provided which will utilize all of the individual capital that is being born into it." Du Bois developed this theme further, challenging the twisted interpretations of Darwin's "splendid scientific contribution." The evolutionary process underscored "the boundlessness and endlessness of possibilities of human achievement," Du Bois explained. In light of Darwin's pioneering work, "freedom has come to mean social self-realization in an endless chain of selves, and freedom for such development is the central assertion of evolutionary theory." Commenting on the "peculiar use of the word 'white,'" Du Bois observed how the South's caste system and the enforced hegemony of the "white races" obstructed this process and threatened "by the means of brute force a survival of some of the worst stocks of mankind."[20]

While these speakers cut through the underbrush of misinformation and pseudoscientific theories that rationalized the color line, most of the comments focused on the legal, political, and economic dimensions of the new racial order and its consequences for the nation. Judge Wendell P. Stafford of the Supreme Court of the District of Columbia announced that "we are confronted today not by a theory but by a fact: the deliberate and avowed exclusion of a whole race of our fellow citizens from their constitutional rights." If the constitution could be suspended in fifteen states, then, the judge warned, it had no meaning at all. Many speakers addressed the disenfranchisement of black southerners and its consequences. Du Bois contended that the Fifteenth Amendment, not emancipation, ended slavery; without the ballot, the way had been opened toward a new slavery of the black man in America. Not mentioning Washington by name, William Monroe Trotter pointed to the bankruptcy of any program of economic uplift and development so long as blacks were denied the vote. "If we are not to have our franchise it has been shown we will lose our industrial opportunity." Du Bois spoke of the larger implications for workers when he described the madness of having two sets of workers side by side, one white, the other black, one set voting, the other set deprived of all participation in government—the conflict it would breed and the oppression it invited. Du Bois, William E. Walling, and Joseph Manning of Alabama all noted that such a situation, while having the direst of consequences for black workers, ensured that all labor in the South would remain divided, cheap, and oppressed.[21]

A major emphasis of the conference proceedings was to define the southern system of racial segregation and disenfranchisement as a national problem with national consequences. Alfred E. Pillsbury, former attorney general of Massachusetts, described how disenfranchisement inflated the political power of the states of the late Confederacy, corrupting the workings of national politics. While the number of voters in these states dramatically decreased as a result of disenfranchisement measures that barred most blacks and many whites from voting, the number of representatives remained constant. As a consequence, a white voter in these southern states had at least twice as much power as those in northern states. Pillsbury claimed that this was even worse than pre-emancipation days when the ⅗ clause provided that only three-fifths of blacks were counted for purposes of representation. Now, all were counted, and nearly all disenfranchised. A provision was included in the Fourteenth Amendment for reduction of southern representation in proportion to the number of voting-age males who were denied suffrage, he noted, but southern leaders acted with little fear that this provision would be enforced. As Walling observed, this was another consequence of the corruption of the system. By virtue of disenfranchisement measures, "the southern reactionary element" maintained a powerful position in Congress. "No greater peril," Walling contended, "stands before democrats of every race. . . . The Negroes' only hope is at the same time the sole safeguard of the nation."[22]

Ida B. Wells-Barnett spoke as a movement veteran, having organized and led a fifteen-year-long campaign against lynching. After many years of exposing the facts surrounding lynchings, publicizing the grim statistics, organizing mass meetings, and passing resolutions, "the butchery continues, in spite of plea and protest." Public sentiment, she concluded, did not measurably decrease the sway of mob law. What, then, was the remedy? The only certain remedy was federal protection of American citizenship. She noted hopeful beginnings in this regard, pointing to a bill drawn by A. E. Pillsbury, then under consideration in the Senate, providing for federal prosecution of lynchers. Wells-Barnett advised the conference to establish a bureau to investigate and publicize the details of every lynching and actively work to influence public opinion. The immediate challenge was to mobilize active opposition to lynching throughout the country, as the critical lever for making it a national issue that demanded the attention and action of federal lawmakers.[23]

After two days of speeches and discussion, the final evening was given over to the open discussion of the resolutions drawn up by the committee headed by William E. Walling. Du Bois described the scene: "The scientific calm . . . and waiting were cast aside. The black mass moved forward and stretched out their hands to take charge. It was their problem. They must name the condition." Ida Wells-Barnett and William Monroe Trotter, militant editor of the *Boston Guardian*, led in puncturing the carefully scripted proceedings. Even though Booker T. Washington was not present, Wells-Barnett reported that Villard's longtime association with Washington caused much concern. There was "the feeling," she wrote, ". . . that [an] effort would be made to tie us to the chariot wheels of the industrial education program." Impatience and anger welled up, mixed with an overall tone of suspicion about the motives of the whites who had taken the lead in this enterprise and seemed determined to control things. How sincere were they? What were they willing to do? Questions, debate, and speeches from the floor went on until nearly midnight.[24]

Villard, a supremely confident man, was unaccustomed to being called to account in this manner. He complained to his Uncle Francis that "their attitude was one of open suspicion [and] ill-conceived hostility." Among the charges was "that the whole proceeding was rigged up in advance." Villard admitted to his uncle that this was the case, as "naturally it had to be." At one point in the evening, he and Walling had considered abandoning their plans for a National Committee and "doing it ourselves as we saw fit." Yet even he had to admit that black people had good reason not to trust whites, having been tricked and betrayed so often in the past. Mary White Ovington was more sympathetic to the suspicions and concerns aired during the final night. "The boasted bond of brotherly love had always a loose strand," she wrote, "and a good pull [often] broke the white from the black." Still, she had a clear idea about the kind of black leadership she felt would be suited to the program at hand. While both Wells-Barnett and Trotter had done courageous work, they were, she wrote, "powerful personalities" and "perhaps not fitted to accept the restraint of organization."[25]

By the end of the evening all of the resolutions had won general approval, and some minor adjustments and additions were made. There was no temporizing, at least on paper, with the program of Booker T. Washington. The resolutions condemned all forms of racial discrimination and called for equal educational opportunities, equal expenditure of public school funds for white and black students, and the strict enforcement of the Fourteenth and Fifteenth amendments. Plans for a permanent organization were also discussed and endorsed during the final session. It was agreed that a conference would be held in one year to formally establish a permanent organization, one that promised to bring racial injustice to the foreground of public attention.[26]

The last order of business was the announcement of the Committee of Forty (also called the National Negro Committee), a group charged with implementing interim plans and calling a national conference in 1910. As midnight neared, Du Bois read the names that had been submitted by the Committee on Nominations. Six black committee members were included among the forty who had been selected. Conspicuously absent were the names of Ida B. Wells-Barnett and Monroe Trotter. In her memoir, Wells-Barnett blamed Du Bois, the only black member of the nominating committee, for ignoring her and her work. If Du Bois had wanted her on the committee, he may have been able to sway the others. But Villard and Ovington were indeed opposed to her inclusion. As Ovington later explained, the nominating committee took a middle course, omitting Booker T. Washington (who plainly would not have agreed to serve), as well as his two most outspoken critics, Wells-Barnett and Trotter. When Wells-Barnett protested her exclusion to committee chairman Charles Russell, he added her name to the Committee of Forty. But hurt and insulted by the treatment she received "at the hands of men of my own race," Wells-Barnett avoided active involvement in the new organization, a move she later regretted.[27]

The white organizers of the conference took some satisfaction that their budding enterprise weathered the final session intact. While they wanted to create an interracial organization, they assumed that they would determine what that meant and how it would be realized. For the next few years, suspicions lingered among leading black figures and opinion shapers, particularly the black press, that the NAACP was a white-run organization. Booker T. Washington fanned these sentiments from the right, and critics on the left like Monroe Trotter leveled similar charges, and in essence, they were correct. Whites dominated the meeting at Charity Hall, and they would continue to dominate in the early years. Yet the small group of reformers who sustained the project were sensitive to the challenge they faced in a society where, as Du Bois noted, "everything tends to break along the color line." Their successful engagement of Du Bois would be critical in creating the new departure that most had hoped for but few were able to imagine.[28]

Du Bois was drawn to the possibilities inherent in this ill-defined undertaking. Reporting on the conference, he described it as the most significant event of 1909, not for any tangible achievement, but for the "vision of future cooperation" it offered. The physical coming together of prominent white reformers and black Americans created an opportunity to breach the wall that separated issues concerning black Americans from the great reform efforts of the day. There was no human problem of advance and uplift in America, Du Bois contended, that did not involve the Negro American and his condition. Integrating the concerns and approaches of the diverse body that gathered in a way that addressed the circumstances of black life in America was essential to addressing the "Negro problem" effectively, as well as the social and political issues that engaged reformers—be it education, suffrage, prison reform, housing, peace, law and order, or distribution of wealth. The New York conference, he hoped, showed "the first fruits" of an awakening toward this realization, the opening toward a new alliance.[29]

In the short term, however, those who took responsibility for carrying the movement forward were less concerned about securing black support and involvement than they were about raising money for the ambitious program that had been proposed at the conference, including the establishment of a permanent organization. As Ovington saw it, "We were primarily a group of white people who felt that while the Negro would aid the committee's work, the whites, who were largely responsible for the conditions and who controlled the bulk of the nation's wealth ought to finance the movement." Villard took the lead on fund-raising. Booker T. Washington, who had the ear of the leading philanthropists with any interest in the race issue, stood as a potential obstacle to tapping the obvious sources, a factor Villard was keenly aware of. Yet the huge success of the conference buoyed Villard's spirits, and he initially remained hopeful that Washington would not actively work to thwart this effort. Early in June he wrote matter-of-factly to his Uncle Francis, "If we get a million dollars we can start right away."[30]

Nine months later, the National Negro Committee (NNC) was on the verge of disintegrating. Villard had little to show for his efforts; the group had a cash balance of less than $100. Walling had resigned as chairman of the committee in November 1909 due to personal problems. Charles Russell, who had served as acting chairman in his absence, was going to be gone from New York for three months, so the job of chairman fell to Villard. Only the dogged efforts of Villard and Ovington kept the project alive. Villard and his mother, Frances Villard, covered the general expenses, which included a salary for Frances Blascoer, who was hired to serve as executive secretary to the group. Blascoer, a white woman who had worked in the social settlement movement, assisted Villard and Ovington in completing plans for the second conference, scheduled for early May. Villard also established a committee to develop a blueprint for establishing an organization. Known as the Preliminary Committee on Permanent Organization, its members included Du Bois, Walling, Russell, Edwin Seligman, John Milholland, and Villard, who chaired the group. Although Du Bois was unable to attend the meetings of the committee, he submitted a detailed plan for a permanent organization, and it guided the group's deliberations.[31]

By the spring of 1910, Villard had abandoned his efforts to bring Washington along and convince him of the importance of the effort being made by the National Negro Committee. While it is not clear how much Villard knew about Washington's efforts to discredit the work of the NNC, Washington remained visibly cool toward the enterprise despite Villard's personal appeals. Meanwhile, racial conditions continued to deteriorate and Villard's efforts to raise money failed to yield even a modest return. In April 1910, he publicly broke with his longtime associate and placed himself squarely in Du Bois's camp. In an editorial titled "Mr. Washington in Politics," he attacked Washington's program of subordinating political rights to the economic betterment of the Negro. Echoing Du Bois's earlier critique, Villard charged that, while advising blacks to eschew politics, Washington himself assumed the mantle of a political boss, and used that position to help silence those who advocated protest and political agitation. Agitation and protest were not only necessary to recover lost ground, Villard argued, but also essential to preventing the loss of more.[32]

The second conference of the National Negro Committee reconvened at Charity Hall on May 12–14, 1910, with public sessions staged at the auditorium at Cooper Union. Du Bois chaired the conference, which was organized around the theme of "Disfranchisement and Its Effect upon the Negro." Former North Carolina congressman George H. White, who served in Congress until 1901, made an appearance at the meeting and was introduced by Villard as "the latest colored congressman, not the last." Speakers followed through on the theme introduced by Du Bois at the first meeting, namely that the vote was essential to securing equal education, protection from mob violence, economic opportunity, and all the other rights and privileges of citizenship. Ida B. Wells-Barnett, Charles Chesnutt, Mary Church Terrell, Franz Boas, Albert Bushnell Hart, and Clarence Darrow were among those who addressed the gathering. Wells-Barnett described a recent lynching in Cairo, Illinois, that, one observer wrote, "sent a shudder through Cooper Union." After a stem-winding speech that skewered the legal profession, the courts, the pulpit, and northern complicity in southern racism, Clarence Darrow predicted that at some time in the distant future racial intermarriage would ultimately solve the race problem, raising a few eyebrows. Villard curtly dismissed Darrow as an "outright demagogue," but admitted his speech "gratified the extreme radicals and Socialists among us, and most of the ardent workers who are really accomplishing something."[33]

During the conference, the National Negro Committee adopted the recommendations included in the final report of the Preliminary Committee on Permanent Organization. The new organization would be called the National Association for the Advancement of Colored People. The use of "Colored" instead of Negro reflected Du Bois's influence and proclaimed the association's commitment to advance the interests of all dark-skinned people. Structurally, it would include a national committee of one hundred citizens to raise funds and give prestige to the organization, and a thirty-member executive committee, elected from the national committee. Half of the members of the executive committee were to be from New York and the rest from other parts of the country. The assembled group elected the following officers of the executive committee: William Walling, chairman; John Milholland, treasurer;

Oswald Garrison Villard, assistant or disbursing treasurer. Moorfield Storey would serve as president of the association.

The committee adopted the broad outlines set down at the 1909 meeting on the objectives of the organization. The NAACP promised a militant campaign on behalf of human rights and for enforcement of the constitution whereby all men are equal before the law and at the ballot box irrespective of their condition or their color. Efforts and activities would be organized around four major areas: investigation, publicity, legal aid, and public meetings. Pointing to cities where the association had already secured a foothold—Boston, Philadelphia, Chicago, and Washington—they urged members to convene a meeting of national committee members residing in those cities and to arrange for general public meetings that would introduce people to the NAACP and get them involved in the work of the association. Annual membership was $1 for associates and $2 for contributors; lifetime memberships were available for $500.[34]

Villard reported that the committee had thus far raised $1,140 and, balanced against expenditures, they were $210 in debt. Over the weeks following the conference, the executive committee debated where the NAACP's scant resources should be concentrated in the short term. Villard argued for giving priority to raising funds and expanding the membership base of the association. Others pressed hard for launching an aggressive campaign of investigation and publicity, under the direction of W.E.B. Du Bois. Villard voted against hiring Du Bois, but Walling and Ovington prevailed, insisting that Du Bois was essential to the future of the enterprise and that this undertaking was perfectly suited to his talents and interests. Du Bois accepted the committee's invitation to serve as director of publications and research, with a promised salary of $2,500 plus expenses for at least a year. With the successful engagement of Du Bois, Ovington wrote, "We nailed our flag to the mast. . . . From that time on no one doubted where we stood."[35]

Walling was careful to remind Du Bois in the letter officially offering him the position that the NAACP offered "work and an opportunity rather than a financially promising or steady position." Du Bois did not hesitate. The NAACP provided a broad canvas for him to continue the work he had pursued fitfully over the previous five years. As he told the readers of the *Horizon*, the small monthly he had edited and published since 1907, at last "we have . . . an organization . . . housed in the metropolis of the nation and devoted to the solution of the Negro problem in accordance with the best ideas of modern philanthropy and democracy." Much of what Du Bois had done during the preceding decade folded into this new endeavor. The Niagara Movement provided the seeds for the NAACP's development in cities around the country, and his early publishing ventures offered a blueprint for *The Crisis*. Second only to Booker T. Washington as a national black leader, he had created an active network of associates and supporters through his teaching, writing, travels, and lecturing, and he lost no time in enlisting their aid. In July he submitted his resignation to Atlanta University and bid farewell to the readers of the *Horizon* in what was its final issue. He urged all to join the NAACP and invited those who were willing to volunteer time and knew something effective they could do for "this great cause" to write to him at 20 Vesey Street, New York.[36]

Housed in a small two-room suite of offices, with borrowed furniture and a single typewriter, the NAACP was a lean operation. Villard's "begging errands" to philanthropists and other well-heeled whites yielded little, putting a high premium on human resources and on the need for an improvisational approach. Reflecting on the early days of the NAACP, Du Bois said, "Few of us realized what an organization of this sort had to be and what changes of form it had to go through." During the first several years, he recalled, it functioned primarily as "a conference of men and women seeking agreement for common action and finally carrying out the work decided upon by a committee of one or more." The early course pursued by the NAACP was dictated by efforts to grasp the totality of the challenge the organization faced, as it responded to some of the most egregious violations of civil rights, while working to build a positive program and secure the support essential to its survival.[37]

The early work of the national office balanced a program of legal work, investigation, protest, and organizational promotion with an uphill effort to raise money and build a membership base. A small constellation of figures at 20 Vesey Street gave form and direction to its incipient program. Primary among them were Du Bois and Villard, along with Mary White Ovington and Joel Spingarn, a literary scholar and political reformer who joined the executive committee in November 1910. While there was not a formal division of labors, the early NAACP developed along two parallel tracks, reflecting different if complementary visions of what the short-term goals of the organization were, who its primary constituency was, and how best to mount an effective campaign. Villard, who replaced Walling as chairman early in 1911, took the lead in setting up the national office, with the assistance of Frances Blascoer and Mary White Ovington, and focused on cultivating financial support while targeting instances of racial injustice where the young organization might intervene. Meanwhile, Du Bois busied himself with plans for publication of a monthly magazine. Three months after his arrival in New York the first issue of *The Crisis* rolled off the press and began the work of connecting the NAACP to the lives and experiences of black people in all parts of the nation.

The legal machinery of the newly formed NAACP was immediately set into motion in response to the case of Pink Franklin, a victim of the peonage system in South Carolina. Franklin had been convicted of murdering a law officer who broke into Franklin's home in the middle of the night, unannounced and with his gun drawn, to arrest Franklin for violating an agricultural contract. On May 30, 1910, the U.S. Supreme Court upheld Franklin's conviction, and the way was cleared for his execution. Villard, who had followed the case closely, described the Court's decision as a "terrible blow" and one that "would encourage the South to go ahead with the peonage business." Advised that the best that could be hoped for in the short term was a commutation of the sentence, Villard worked through every possible contact he had, from Booker T. Washington to members of the Taft administration, to muster support for petitioning the governor. Frances Blascoer traveled to Columbia, South Carolina, where she met with John Adams and Jacob Moorer, the two black lawyers who had represented Franklin, and Reconstruction-era black legislator Thomas Miller. With Miller's aid, Franklin assigned power of attorney to the NAACP and Blascoer enlisted two well-connected white lawyers to bring the appeal to Governor Martin F. Ansel. Just before his term expired and the race-baiting demagogue Cole Blease succeeded him, Governor Ansel commuted Franklin's sentence to life in prison. The association pledged that it would not cease its efforts until Franklin was free. Franklin was finally pardoned in 1919.[38]

From the beginning, the NAACP focused on the law and the courts as a primary arena for exposing injustices, publicizing its cause, and obtaining the enforcement of basic legal and constitutional guarantees—a new and innovative strategy for a national reform organization. During the first year, in addition to the Franklin case, the NAACP got involved with three other major cases: a wrongful arrest and police brutality case in Asbury Park, New Jersey; a Chicago case involving Steve Green, a sharecropper who had shot his landlord in self-defense and was threatened with extradition to Arkansas; and a lynching in Coatesville, Pennsylvania. The NAACP met with a measure of success in the first case and played a supporting role to Ida B. Wells-Barnett's successful effort to stall extradition proceedings long enough to get Green to Canada. In the Coatesville case, the NAACP tried, unsuccessfully, to compel the state of Pennsylvania to prosecute the lynchers. But as a result of the publicity generated by their efforts, an antilynching bill was introduced into the Pennsylvania legislature, and the association established a fund to support the investigation of lynchings.[39]

These cases reflected Villard's concern with peonage and criminal justice issues and served as examples of some of the most brutal and lawless aspects of the racial conditions in the United States. Executive committee member Jane Addams argued for a legal program that focused its resources exclusively on attacking segregation and disenfranchisement laws. While continuing to investigate lynching, peonage, and police brutality cases, the work of the NAACP expanded to address a broader legal agenda. In March 1911, the association established the Legal Redress Committee, headed by Thomas Ewing Jr., a noted New York lawyer, and including Merrill Gates, former head of the New York Legal Aid Society, and Florence Kelley, founder of the National Consumers League. The committee's initial task was to cooperate in several significant legal challenges already under way, including a challenge to Oklahoma's disenfranchisement law and to a residential segregation ordinance in Baltimore. The committee also worked with NAACP supporters in New York and Illinois to test existing state civil rights laws that were routinely violated, particularly segregation in public places.[40]

The NAACP's early emphasis on a legal strategy reflected its interest in nationalizing the race question, both by emphasizing that the routine violation of constitutional rights in the South was a national issue and by exposing patterns of racial discrimination and inequality in the North—an issue that was of deep concern to Joel Spingarn. In January 1911, Spingarn established an NAACP vigilance committee for New York to fight the racial injustices at the association's doorstep. While the city did not experience the sensational outrages common to the South, Spingarn found racial conditions in New York to be perhaps more insidious. "Colored men and women in this city are confronted every day of their lives with the most galling conditions," he wrote. "They are subject to insult, passive or active; they are refused service and courteous treatment even in places where they are guaranteed absolute equality with their white brethren by legal statutes . . . [and they are subject to] actual injustices in the courts of justice." His early work with the New York committee coincided with a major career change, accelerating Spingarn's rise to the top ranks of the association's leadership.[41]

There was little in Spingarn's background to suggest that he would become a leader of the neoabolitionist movement, although he was a rebellious soul and civically engaged. Born on May 17, 1875, Joel Elias Spingarn was the eldest son of Sarah Barnett and Elias Spingarn, Jewish immigrants from Hull, England, and Vienna, Austria, respectively; Elias built a successful wholesale tobacco business. Spingarn was educated at New York City public schools through high school and attended Columbia University, where he earned a PhD in English literature. He joined Columbia's faculty and gained prominence as a cutting-edge scholar of literary criticism as well as an outspoken critic of the corporate culture that infused university life. Politics and public service commanded much of his time and attention. He was prominent in the progressive wing of New York's Republican Party, and in 1908 he made an impressive showing in his bid for a seat in Congress from the Eighteenth District of New York, a Democratic stronghold.[42]

Reflecting on how he came to join the NAACP, Spingarn identified a specific moment. "A great deal of injustice is going on around us all the time," he observed, and one is often at a loss to explain why he or she is ultimately moved to act. For him, the case of Steve Green, the sharecropper who had escaped to Chicago, touched him in a way that nothing else ever had. When he read about Green and his impending return to Arkansas and a waiting lynch mob, he resolved: "I don't care what happens. Steve Green will never be extradited back to Arkansas." He sent a check for $100 to the NAACP to aid in Green's defense and offered to do whatever he could to help. Villard sent word that Green was safely on his way to Canada and promptly recruited Spingarn to join the NAACP's executive committee. Arthur Spingarn, his brother, followed and became one of the association's leading lawyers.[43]

Two months after Spingarn established the New York vigilance committee, a dispute with the president of Columbia over the dismissal of a fellow faculty member led to Spingarn's termination. It was initially a bitter blow, but soon he felt relief that he was no longer "locked up with 700 professors." A man of inherited wealth, Spingarn began devoting much of his time to the NAACP and soon eclipsed Villard as a leading figure in the association. The New York committee took root, making targeted challenges to racial discrimination in theaters and other places of public accommodation and prosecuting cases involving police beatings and shootings of black men. Initially the group met at Spingarn's home and held monthly mass meetings in black churches around the city. They finally established a headquarters in a small one-person office on 135th Street and announced that the office was ready to take reports of "any case of injustice before the law."[44]

As the association worked to establish itself, officials and board members developed programs that often depended completely on volunteer efforts. James F. Morton Jr., a freelance journalist and author of *The Curse of Race Prejudice* (1906), headed up a press committee to write letters responding to racial prejudice and inaccuracies in news stories and reports. (Morton was the grandson of the author of the lyrics of "America.") The thirty-person group included the Reverend Adam Clayton Powell Sr., Mary Church Terrell, John Dewey, Franz Boas, Florence Kelley, and Arthur Schomburg. Education was a major area of concern. Plans for a scientific study of black schools were discussed from the beginning and a committee was established to investigate the issue of national aid to education. Early in 1911, the NAACP endorsed the revival of the Blair Bill, legislation sponsored by Senator Henry Blair of New Hampshire in the 1880s, which provided for federal aid to the states for education, appropriated as a ratio to the rate of illiteracy. The association also marshaled its scant resources to begin what would be a decades-long fight to end lynching. In addition to investigation and exposure, the NAACP sponsored letter-writing campaigns to governors and other public officials protesting each incident they uncovered, and succeeded in getting a ruling from the U. S. Post Office Department banning lynching postcards from being sent in the mail.[45]

Short of any newsworthy achievement, one of the biggest challenges facing the new organization was just getting the word out about the association and the movement it represented. NAACP officials and board members sought opportunities to address other organizations, which represented a wide range of interests and constituencies, including the National Association of Colored Women's Clubs, the National Businessmen's League, the National Elks Convention, a peace conference in Greenacre, Maine, the Association of Friends, and the National Association of Charities and Correction. Friends and members of the association were enlisted to host public meetings in various cities. A lecture bureau was established, and it volunteered to send a representative of the association to meet with small social and community gatherings, to speak to student groups on college campuses, and to address mass meetings in black churches. Early on, the executive committee agreed with Villard's proposal that the annual meeting be held in a different city each year as a way to arouse public interest "and let people know of our

existence." The 1911 meeting was held in Boston and resulted in the establishment of a branch. The following two were held in Chicago and Philadelphia, with very satisfactory results in terms of publicity and attendance.[46]

Through these various events and public meetings, the leadership of the
NAACP promoted their vision of an interracial movement by appealing to
whites and blacks while actively encouraging cross-racial contact. They sponsored interracial parlor meetings, sent black speakers to white college campuses and whites to black campuses, and required that local affiliates of the
NAACP, known as branches, include black and white members. While a
small number of whites did participate in these activities, Villard's tireless
campaign to obtain substantial white financial support for the association
met with little success. Failed efforts to get prominent whites to speak out
against lynching at a meeting organized by the NAACP in New York late in
1911 underscored the enormity of the task at hand. "At no time," *The Crisis*
editorialized, "has the Association realized more clearly the need to awaken
public sentiment."[47]

As director of publicity and research and member of the executive committee, W. E.B. Du Bois worked in tandem with the other leading figures in the
organization. But through his editorship of *The Crisis*, Du Bois carved out a
critical role in defining the challenges facing the association and framing its
mission. Du Bois believed that the future of the NAACP, indeed its very
survival, depended upon securing a firm base among black Americans and
organizing them around a common vision of political and social struggle. He
allowed that it was an enormous task, but an essential one, and he intended
The Crisis to serve as a vehicle for realizing this objective. "We are trying
something which has not often been done," Du Bois explained, and "that is
to spread propaganda over a wide space where there is no territorial unity. We
are trying to bring together people who have never seen each other, but simply have racial discrimination as a point of contact."[48]

Du Bois's determination to launch a monthly magazine overcame the initial misgivings of several board members, concerned about the cost of such a
venture. They authorized a meager $50 per month for a small monthly mag-
azine, leaving it to Du Bois to carry out his ambitious plan. Du Bois recalled
"looking out over the forest of roofs of lower Broadway" as he prepared to
submit the print order for the first issue. The circulation of *Horizon* topped
out at five hundred a month. "In a fit of wild adventure," he said, he ordered
one thousand copies, feeling "like Wellington before Waterloo." Du Bois relied on his extensive network of contacts to aid in mounting a nationwide

distribution effort; these networks also served as sources for local news and information. He compared his agents in the field to "missionaries in a crusade." Monthly circulation of *The Crisis* reached 9,000 by the end of 1911 and climbed to 27,000 in 1912.[49]

The Crisis sank roots into black life in all parts of the nation, profiling black experiences and patterns of racial discrimination against a broad and shifting landscape. It documented conditions around the South and the rising tide of segregation in the North and reported on many other aspects of black life. News items were organized into numerous categories, including politics, education, economics, judicial decisions, social uplift, organizations, science, and art. "The Burden" offered a monthly report on lynching and named the victims. A special section titled "The Ghetto" tracked the growth of residential segregation, particularly in border and northern cities. The first editorial published in *The Crisis* pointed to efforts under way in Chicago, Philadelphia, Columbus (Ohio), and other northern cities to establish separate black schools and appealed to blacks and whites to resist this dangerous trend. There were regular reports of protest and resistance, such as the mass meeting organized by blacks in Stockton, California, to oppose a constitutional amendment that would disenfranchise blacks and Chinese Americans, and efforts by blacks in Mobile, Alabama, to raise money to build a high school for their children.[50]

While connecting the struggles and experiences of blacks in the rural South as well as towns and cities across the nation, *The Crisis* worked steadily to bring African Americans into the orbit of the NAACP. A special section of news from the NAACP was included in each issue, illustrating the many ways in which the association was working to fight racial discrimination. Du Bois continually appealed to his readers to do their part in supporting this effort and "prove that colored people are interested in their own freedom." The machinery was in place that would enable the NAACP to do work of "prodigious importance," he told his readers early in 1912. But unless more earnest support was forthcoming, he warned that the organization would "fail at its moment of achievement." Despite Du Bois's urgings, the growing readership of *The Crisis* did not readily translate into a rise in memberships or financial support for the struggling organization. By the end of 1912, the NAACP had eleven hundred members, organized into eleven branches, and an annual income of just under $12,000.[51]

In three years, laboring under severe financial constraints, the NAACP had created the blueprint, at least, for a nationwide movement. Its small New

York office was a beehive of activity. In June 1912 May Childs Nerney joined the staff as secretary. An energetic and efficient organizer, she supervised the broad range of activities that had taken root over the previous two years, including a legal redress committee, a press committee, a lectures bureau, and a committee on membership and branches. The association sponsored the highest circulating magazine ever edited by an African American. The NAACP had affiliates in nearly a dozen cities, and its representatives traveled and lectured around the country, working to expand the base of membership. As Du Bois observed, the machinery was in place.

Yet the activity of the NAACP had failed to distinguish it as an organization capable not only of defining the problem, but of effectively challenging the growing assault on the lives and opportunities of black Americans. Most of the black press remained cool toward the association, and few African Americans saw it as a vehicle for pushing against the tightening web of racial proscription and discrimination. This, however, began to change when the NAACP rose to meet the spread of Jim Crow in the federal government following the election of Woodrow Wilson and the ascendancy of "Southern Democracy" in the nation's capital.

2

Welding the Hammers

The years leading up to World War I marked a critical testing period for the NAACP. Racial barriers continued to harden in northern and western cities as growing numbers of blacks sought freedom and opportunity outside of the South. Efforts to restrict black access to housing proliferated, local and state officials considered school segregation strategies, and growing numbers of restaurants, hotels, and theaters excluded blacks. Meanwhile, the caste system tightened its hold in the South, and white southerners met little resistance in their efforts to shape racial policies and practices in the national arena, from the federal government to organizations like the American Bar Association, which barred black members in 1912. *The Birth of a Nation*, the cinematic celebration of the "Lost Cause" and the Ku Klux Klan, won national acclaim upon its release in 1915. In a sober reflection on the challenges that lay before them, Du Bois observed that "the forces of hell in this country are fighting a terrific and momentarily successful battle."[1]

Such challenges only illuminated the vital necessity of their enterprise. While NAACP activists claimed the mantle of the abolitionists, they were keenly aware of the pioneering nature of their efforts as they attempted to counter evolving patterns of segregation and the chronic usurpation of constitutional protections. A broad and flexible approach enabled them to recognize and shape opportunities in the face of worsening racial conditions. In response to an aggressive policy of segregation in the federal government, the NAACP established a presence in Washington to contest government's support of racially discriminatory practices and to monitor legislation. At the same time, the association became more deeply invested in enlisting people around the country in their emerging movement through a program of targeted litigation and exploratory fieldwork. These efforts were formative in shaping the identity and future course of the NAACP.

The choices facing voters in the highly contested 1912 presidential election mirrored the growing influence of the white South in national politics. In his effort to build a Republican base in the South, incumbent William Howard Taft deferred to white southerners in making federal appointments in the region. He approvingly noted that "the Negro . . . is coming more and more under the guardianship of the South" and consistently refused to speak out against lynching, which averaged more than seventy-five per year during his administration. Former president Theodore Roosevelt, running on the Progressive Party ticket, allowed southern whites to dictate the selection of delegates to his party's convention, which resulted in the nearly total exclusion of southern blacks. The Democrats offered the Virginia-born Woodrow Wilson as their candidate.[2]

The Republican Party's embrace of a lily-white strategy to woo southern white voters had disregarded black loyalty to the party and argued for a more independent exercise of the ballot. A small but growing and strategically placed black vote in the urban North had encouraged some northern Democrats to practice a liberal approach to black citizens. Moreover, as Du Bois observed, the Democratic Party stood for policies that favored workers and sought to regulate corporate wealth, policies aligned with the economic interests of the vast majority of black Americans.[3]

Blacks, Du Bois wrote, faced "desperate alternatives" in the 1912 election. So far as he was concerned, Taft and Roosevelt were completely unacceptable. In that light, he advised that they test their political strength by supporting the Democratic candidate for president. While allowing that Wilson would probably not be a friend to Negroes, the former governor of New Jersey had not demonstrated the open contempt for black interests evident in the actions of Taft and Roosevelt. Wilson declined to offer specific promises but pledged that black Americans could rely on him for fair treatment and "a justice executed with liberality and cordial good feelings." It was time, Du Bois advised readers of *The Crisis*, to put such pronouncements to the test and see if the Democratic Party "dares to be Democratic when it comes to black men." If the black vote were a factor in Wilson's election, future candidates would pay heed. NAACP chairman Villard, who knew Wilson personally, encouraged these sentiments. An enthusiastic supporter of Wilson, he talked at length with the candidate about establishing a National Commission on Race and felt guardedly hopeful that Wilson would not exclude blacks from the promise of a "New Freedom."[4]

With the election of 1912, Democrats took control of the presidency and the Congress for the first time since before the Civil War. While there are no statistics on the black vote in 1912, black newspapers reported a significant shift of black voters to the Democratic candidate, as large as 30 percent. Du Bois placed the number at one hundred thousand.[5] This, however, failed to blunt the aggressive efforts of white southerners in Congress and in Wilson's administration to put their stamp on federal policy. In fact, the Wilson years were a time of accelerating racial segregation within the federal bureaucracy, a sharp break from earlier practices both in terms of its extent and of presidential sanction. Wilson's betrayal of his promise of elemental fairness drew a swift response from the NAACP, initiating the organization's first effort to mount a nationwide protest, raising its profile among black Americans and resulting in a permanent presence for the association in the nation's capital.[6]

Wilson had barely taken the oath of office when southerners in Congress and within his cabinet launched a campaign to expand Jim Crow practices in the federal government. In the Senate, a triumvirate of Deep South senators—Hoke Smith of Georgia, Benjamin Tillman of South Carolina, and James K. Vardaman of Mississippi—met the president's nomination of Adam Patterson, a black Democrat from Oklahoma, to register of the treasury with a storm of protest. The fact that a black appointee had traditionally held this post meant little. The three senators vowed to derail the appointment of any blacks to positions that put them in a supervisory relationship to white women clerks, and they called for the complete separation of the races in the federal government. Patterson withdrew his name, and Gabe Parker, an Oklahoman of Cherokee descent, was named to the post and confirmed.[7]

Meanwhile, William McAdoo, secretary of the treasury, and postmaster general Albert Burleson, with Wilson's knowledge and approval, quietly instituted a policy of racial segregation in their departments, the two federal agencies with the largest number of black employees. Several other departments followed suit. Under the new policy black workers in the post office building had to climb to the eighth floor to use the one toilet designated for them, and a single restroom for black workers was provided in the corner of the basement of the treasury building. Watchmen policed the white restrooms to ensure the policy was followed. A separate section was set off for blacks in the lunchrooms, and blacks did their work in separate rooms or were set apart by a screen. Burleson explained at a cabinet meeting that the policy was designed to ease racial tension and contended that it was in the best interest of black workers. No one at the meeting raised any objections to the idea. According to Josephus Daniels, secretary of the navy, Wilson said that "he made no particular promises to Negroes, except to do them justice" and that he wished "to see the [segregation] matter settled in a way to make the least friction."[8]

While no official orders were publicly issued, news about segregation in Washington spread quickly. Early in the summer of 1913 Villard sought a meeting with Wilson to discuss this alarming trend and obtained an appointment with Joseph Tumulty, Wilson's chief of staff. Villard told Tumulty that it was time for the administration to show its hand. Was it their intention to take "the Hoke Smith, Vardaman position" and "leave the Negro out of all participation in political life?" Villard warned that if the segregation of federal workers was not promptly stopped, the NAACP would go on the attack. Tumulty, Villard reported, seemed sincere in his own opposition to race segregation, but explained that the president was so driven and overworked that he could not take time to hear both sides of the argument. Villard followed up the meeting with a letter appealing directly to Wilson. He urged him not to betray the hopes of those who believed that his democracy was not limited to race or color. As the first southern president since the Civil War, Wilson had an opportunity to win the confidence of people who asked for nothing but what they were entitled to under the Constitution. Wilson responded, admitting that he had approved the segregation plan and saying that he remained convinced that it was not a move against Negroes, but rather in their best interest. With that, the NAACP proceeded with plans to mount a major protest.[9]

An open letter to President Wilson on August 15 launched the campaign. Signed by Moorfield Storey, W. E. B. Du Bois, and Oswald Garrison Villard, the letter described the administration's segregation policy as a radical departure. The letter charged that the federal government had never before discriminated against civilian employees on the grounds of color, a claim that was not correct. There had been instances of segregation under previous administrations and discrimination in job assignments and promotions, but the scale and scope of the Wilson administration's segregation policy was unprecedented. As the letter noted, black employees were set apart "behind screens and closed doors . . . as if they were leprous." Such a federal policy, the letter warned, would serve as "a warrant for new racial outrages." The letter was widely circulated to the press and members of Congress and to NAACP branches. The association was inundated with requests for copies. William Monroe Trotter wrote asking for twenty-five additional copies, signing his letter "yours for freedom."[10]

May Childs Nerney, who had joined the NAACP as its new secretary a year earlier, orchestrated a major effort to expose segregationist practices in the federal government and mobilize public sentiment. Nerney, a white woman in her mid-thirties, had worked as a reference librarian for the Newark Public Library prior to coming to the NAACP. During the summer, Nerney made two trips to Washington and conducted an extensive investigation of segregation in the federal government, interviewing black clerks and white administrators who spoke freely to her, assuming she shared their racial sentiments. Her findings were published in a hard-hitting report that was widely distributed to newspapers, branches, and members of Congress. She worked closely with NAACP branches, urging them to hold mass rallies and directing a letter writing campaign aimed at flooding the White House and Congress.[11]

Editorial comment in many newspapers outside of the South followed the NAACP's lead, charging the Wilson administration with "officializing race prejudice." NAACP branches in Boston, Baltimore, Detroit, Topeka, Denver, Tacoma, Seattle, and Oakland held mass protests, and thousands signed resolutions that were sent to the president and members of Congress. Several representatives sought additional information from the NAACP, and Villard spent time in Washington meeting with individual congressmen. Yet mounting protests did not sway Wilson. When Villard finally secured a meeting with the president early in October, Wilson basically admitted to a failure of nerve and leadership. According to Villard, Wilson confided, "I say it with shame and humiliation, but I have thought about this thing for twenty years and I see no way out. It will take a very big man to solve this thing."[12]

On October 27 the NAACP called a mass meeting titled "To Protest against Segregation—The New Slavery" at the Metropolitan A.M.E. Church, just five blocks from the White House. The church was filled to capacity with two thousand people an hour before the meeting was scheduled to begin. Thousands more spilled into the streets, blocking traffic. The crowd was so dense that one of the speakers, John Haynes Holmes, had to be lifted over the iron fence surrounding the church so that he could reach a side entrance. Archibald Grimké, the new president of the NAACP's Washington branch, presided, and the Howard University choir sang. Grimké introduced

Oswald Garrison Villard as the reincarnation of his grandfather, William Lloyd Garrison, to a cheering crowd. In his comments, Villard recounted a meeting with high officials in the Wilson administration, telling how they had urged him to use his influence to keep "the colored people in a cool and just equipoise." He responded that he did not have that kind of influence and would not use it if he did. On the contrary, he told the officials that he would "lose no opportunity to preach the doctrine of peaceful rebellion and revolution against discrimination of every kind." When the meeting inside the church concluded, the speakers went outside into a warm, rainy evening and addressed the waiting crowd of some four thousand people. Villard described the evening as "glorious"; around Washington's black community, it was simply referred to as "the great meeting."[13]

The fight over segregation in the federal government galvanized the Washington branch of the NAACP. Founded in March 1913, the branch was on the verge of collapse by July due to factionalism and poor leadership. Nerney intervened and urged the national board to appoint Archibald Grimké, a leader of one of the factions, as temporary president of the branch until an election could be held. Grimké, a member of the NAACP's original executive committee, assumed the leadership of the branch in September and was formally elected the following January.

Riding the wave of public sentiment surrounding the October 27 meeting, Grimké and his associates in the Washington branch launched a campaign to raise money and support for the NAACP. Thomas H. Neval, a history teacher at Dunbar High School who was known locally as "the crusader," wrote a circular on the antisegregation fight that was widely distributed and printed for free in the *Washington Bee*. A Committee of Fifty was established to raise money, with each member pledging to give or raise $25 for the NAACP. A speakers bureau sent men and women out to carry the message of the NAACP "from church to church, from society to society, from secret lodge to secret lodge . . . until they have reached everyone and everyone was willing to give something." Some speakers addressed as many as three meetings a day; one young man made twenty-five talks in a whirlwind campaign. *The Crisis* reported that "the women worked as hard as the men. They . . . gave from their own purses with the greatest liberality . . . and aroused their fathers, husbands, brothers, and friends to the vital importance of the NAACP." Smith Wormley, a teacher in a night school program organized a club with his students; they contributed 10¢ a week, until they raised $35, enough to make them members of the NAACP. Support grew steadily and crossed class lines; the branch "has reached the people," Du Bois declared. By the end of the year, the Washington branch had sent $2,500 to the national office and its membership had grown sixfold to four hundred members. It quickly became the largest branch in the country.[14]

With a presence in Washington, the NAACP moved decisively into the arena of national politics, and the timing was critical. During Wilson's first term, southern Democrats flooded Congress with discriminatory legislation, including bills that would ban interracial marriages, establish residential and transportation segregation in Washington, make blacks ineligible for service in the army or navy, require segregation in the federal government, and bar people of African descent from immigrating to the United States. The NAACP hired two former newspapermen to monitor legislation introduced in the House and the Senate, while the D.C. branch and the national office cooperated in exerting pressure to kill discriminatory legislation. The D.C. branch acted as the association's representative on Capitol Hill and led the local fight against hostile legislation, while Nerney, on receiving word of discriminatory measures, alerted branches and members to telegram their representatives to protest particular bills. *The Crisis* provided extensive coverage of these developments and told readers that "if you want to protest, enroll with us as a new abolitionist in the National Association and do it now."[15]

Washington became a strategic outpost in the NAACP's fight against a tide of segregationist legislation. Small groups from the D.C. branch were prepared to lobby Congress and organize opposition to hostile legislation. Vigilance was essential, as amendments were often buried in bills or tacked on at the last minute. This was the case with a major immigration bill when Senator James Reed of Missouri added an amendment calling for the exclusion of "All Members of the African or Black Race" just before the bill went up for a vote in the Senate. The bill passed the Senate by a close vote (29 to 25) before the branch was able to go into action. A committee including Kelly Miller and Archibald Grimké made a door-to-door canvass of the House Office Building and prepared a brief against the amendment that was distributed to every member of Congress. The bill was defeated in the House by 252 to 75. In the case of much of the discriminatory legislation, defeat was never final; segregationist bills were introduced over and over. During the Sixty-third Congress, no fewer than twenty bills were introduced that would further restrict the rights of blacks.[16]

Archibald Grimké, a prominent member of the city's black elite, moved easily in the world of Washington politics. He had been born a slave in 1849 near Charleston, South Carolina, the son of Nancy Weston and her owner, Henry Grimké. Following emancipation, he attended a school for freedmen and went on to attend Lincoln University. While at Lincoln, he became acquainted with his father's aunts, Sarah and Angelina Grimké, noted white abolitionists. They helped support him through Harvard Law School. Grimké became active in Republican politics and served as U.S. consul to Haiti in the 1890s. Later he distinguished himself as a scholar and writer and served as president of the prestigious American Negro Academy. Grimké participated in the Niagara Movement and had helped to establish the NAACP in the nation's capital.[17]

Grimké became a familiar figure on Capitol Hill. He turned up at hearings on pending legislation, sometimes on a moment's notice and to the chagrin of southern lawmakers. Grimké challenged their assumptions about race and governance, while appealing to fundamental constitutional guarantees and basic principles of democracy. In a hearing before a House committee on civil service reform, Martin Dies of Texas defended a bill mandating segregation in the federal government, arguing that one of the races must rule. Grimké noted that people like him, who had "the blood of both races," confounded Dies's position. He told Dies and other committee members who supported the bill that "the fact that you attempt to keep these people down shows . . . fear" that when given the chance, blacks would show they were equal to whites. In a hearing set up by Massachusetts congressman George Tinkham on an anti-intermarriage bill, Grimké made clear that the "racial amalgamation" that the bill was designed to prohibit was beyond the regulation of law. There had long been, Grimké explained, a double moral standard that countenanced sexual liaisons between white men and black women, one that left black women unprotected from predatory white men. Such a bill would do nothing to prevent race mixing, but would deny black women the one possible sanction they might have should they become pregnant. The national office of the NAACP obtained the printed copies of all such hearings and distributed them widely.[18]

The NAACP claimed credit for the fact that not a single segregationist bill passed. However, efforts to influence legislation that on its face did not discriminate were less successful, as was the case in the Smith-Lever bill. Introduced by Senator Hoke Smith of Georgia and Congressman Asbury Lever of South Carolina, the bill appropriated more than $15 million for agricultural extension work to be administered through agricultural colleges named by the respective state legislature. This meant that the entire appropriation would go to white colleges, making it unlikely that black farmers would receive any support under the program. By the time the bill came to the attention of an NAACP representative early in 1914 it had already passed the House. Charles Brinsmade, the NAACP's newly hired lawyer, immediately drafted an amendment aimed at ensuring that black farmers were included in the program, and Senator Walter Jones of Washington agreed to introduce it. Du Bois and Brinsmade composed a memorandum on the bill for distribution to senators and the press and lobbied individual senators.

Senate debate of the bill went on for two days, and as a result of the NAACP's intervention the racial implications of the legislation were fully aired. Senators sympathetic to the NAACP's position read a letter of protest from the association along with a telegram from the Northern California branch, and prominent leaders of the NAACP were named, including Moorfield Storey, Oswald Garrison Villard, and Jane Addams. The NAACP's role in obtaining the Jones amendment "was made clear to the people of the country," boasted *The Crisis*. In the end, Jones's amendment was defeated by a vote of 32 to 23, and the Smith-Lever bill passed without any provisions to ensure the inclusion of black farmers. Nevertheless, the association claimed a victory of sorts. It had effectively inserted itself into the legislative process, gaining greater visibility for itself and its work. Most importantly, through the debate surrounding the bill, the NAACP had succeeded in placing "the whole race issue squarely before the Congress and the country." The *Washington Bee* reported on how the NAACP had effectively mobilized public opinion behind the effort to secure a fair share of federal funds for black citizens. Formerly a critic of the association, the *Bee* hailed it as "the modern abolition movement."[19]

The campaign against segregation in the federal government and antiblack legislation in Congress gave the NAACP the boost it needed among its key constituents. Villard happily reported to his uncle that "money is coming in from colored people in a very encouraging way." An infusion of financial support from blacks in Washington, D.C., and in other parts of the country lifted the association out of debt and left it with a balance of $1,000 in the treasury as of January 1914. In the fall of 1913, the association was finally able to hire a full-time attorney, thanks to special contributions raised by Nerney from ten branches that covered his salary for a year. By the end of 1913, membership in the association had more than doubled to upward of three thousand organized into twenty-four branches; 80 percent of the members were black. The association continued to encourage the enlistment of white members, but the requirement that branches include black and white members was less rigorously enforced. The annual report for 1913 noted what had become obvious: if the NAACP were to succeed, "it must be increasingly supported by its colored members."[20]

While the prospects in the field looked more promising, tensions within the national office threatened to derail the young organization. By the end of 1913, strained relations between Villard and Du Bois, the two individuals who more than anyone had made the NAACP possible, had reached the breaking point. An undercurrent of animosity, particularly of Villard toward Du Bois, was aggravated by conflicting views about how the association should be managed. For three years Villard had carried the weight of the organization, with little help from board members, as he struggled to raise money and support, often having to borrow funds to meet the payroll. He resented Du Bois's detached and independent manner and wanted him and *The Crisis* to contribute more directly to the promotion of the association, among whites as well as blacks. Du Bois, smarting from "piled up slights and unkindnesses," believed that Villard simply was incapable of working with a black person on a basis of equality. At a board meeting earlier in the spring, long-simmering resentments came boiling up when Villard pressed for greater oversight of *The Crisis*. For starters, he suggested that crimes committed by blacks be reported in the magazine, along with those committed against them. This prompted a heated exchange with Du Bois; the board declined to take up the matter at this point.[21]

In the aftermath of the meeting, Du Bois wrote a somewhat conciliatory letter to Villard. But he made it clear that he viewed himself as Villard's fellow officer and not his subordinate. For the chairman to imply that his independence of action was "a breach of discipline or a personal discourtesy," Du Bois contended, misread the situation completely. He took his orders, Du Bois explained, from the board of directors. Villard, however, saw it differently and warned board members that if he were not given the powers he believed essential to his position as chief executive of the association, he would have to resign as chairman. Mary White Ovington tried to persuade Villard to moderate his approach. Villard's withdrawal from the association, she cautioned, would mean "a confession to the world that we cannot work with colored people unless they are our subordinates." After several meetings failed to resolve the matter to Villard's satisfaction, he resigned as chairman, effective January 1914, and assumed the position of treasurer. While Du Bois was probably relieved to see Villard step down from the top post, he had the highest praise for the former chairman in *The Crisis*, writing that no one had "shouldered more responsibility or done so much downright hard work or raised so much cash" for the movement.[22]

But concerns surrounding the relationship of Du Bois and *The Crisis* to the association persisted, and they would be part of an ongoing discussion about the structure of the NAACP and how to advance its goals. Part of the problem related to different views about the role of the magazine, which raised the larger question of who the association's constituencies were and how best to enlist their support. Some board members complained that *The Crisis* was insensitive to whites and needlessly antagonized potential funding sources. Du Bois did not hesitate to criticize the paternalistic approach of white philanthropists in the pages of *The Crisis*. At times the tone of the magazine appeared distinctly hostile toward virtually all whites, as when Du Bois commented that "it takes extraordinary training, gift, and opportunity to make the average white man anything but an overbearing hog." Even Du Bois's friend and steady supporter, Mary White Ovington, admitted to Du Bois that she thought there was "something wrong with *The Crisis* from the point of view of white readers." Ovington, who viewed the mission of *The Crisis* and the NAACP as one and the same, asked: "Should we preach race consiousness? . . . Is this a work for colored and white people to do together, or is it a work of revolution for the colored people only?"[23]

Joel Spingarn, who succeeded Villard as chairman, was not interested in monitoring the content of *The Crisis*. In the dispute between Villard and Du Bois over editorial control of the magazine, Spingarn held that there should be at least one publication in which a black person could say what he wished without any interference from a white person.[24] He was also sympathetic to Du Bois's emphasis on appealing to black Americans as the primary constituency of the NAACP. Yet Spingarn was deeply concerned about Du Bois's relationship to the rest of the organization. Du Bois's supporters on the board were dwindling, and Spingarn himself began to question Du Bois's ability to work effectively with the rest of the association's leadership. When the NAACP's offices moved to new headquarters at 70 Fifth Avenue early in 1914, Du Bois secured a suite of offices for *The Crisis* that increased expenses by $700 a year. Why, Spingarn asked, when other departments were being squeezed and forced to cut back, did he assume so much additional expense for *The Crisis*? This especially rankled May Nerney, who was responsible for administering most of the association's other programs; Nerney complained that Du Bois was using *The Crisis* to take over the organization. An atmosphere of antagonism surrounded Du Bois, Spingarn told the editor, and it was not merely Villard and Nerney who resented him. The board members generally, black as well as white, viewed him with "a mix of affection and resentment." Many wanted to see him gone. While Spingarn realized that Du Bois was as important as anyone to the association, he cautioned that if Du Bois's talents were not "subordinated to the general welfare of the organization," the whole enterprise was doomed.[25]

In response to the concerns raised by Spingarn and Ovington, Du Bois instructed his colleagues on the fragile nature of their enterprise. To Spingarn, he confided, "I sometimes listen to you quite speechless when you urge easy cooperation and understanding." History, he suggested, was a sobering teacher. "No organization like ours has ever succeeded in America," he told Spingarn. "Either it became a group of white philanthropists 'helping' the Negro like the Anti-Slavery societies; or it became a group of colored folk freezing out their white coworkers by insolence and distrust." A structure whereby blacks and whites could work together on the same level of authority was essential to the ultimate success of the NAACP. But what form would that take? What Du Bois had envisioned from the beginning were, in effect, two branches within the association, one with a white head and one with a black head, "working in harmony and sympathy for one end." While the success of such an approach had yet to be proven, it had to be attempted if the NAACP was to at least have a chance.[26]

The rub of personalities and egos common to most collective efforts, Du Bois advised, should not obscure what he viewed as the deeper challenges that tested the organization. He allowed that his temperament might be difficult to endure. Given his experiences, he told Spingarn, it would "be miraculous if I came through normal and unwarped." To reduce the tensions within the NAACP to simply a matter of personality conflicts and individual rivalries, and not consider the ways of the color line, however, missed the conflict's dynamic. Since assuming his position as the sole black official with the NAACP, Du Bois contended that he had to struggle against "every conceivable effort, conscious, half-conscious, unconscious . . . to force me into a position of submission to some other official." He chafed at the efforts to bind him, the petty criticisms, and the reluctance to give him the opportunity to do the work he needed to do. Indeed, if the association could not invest him, the sole black official in the NAACP, with the same amount of power as

the white executive, how "can we fight a successful battle against race prejudice in the world?" he asked.[27]

Du Bois was attempting to advance "race consciousness" through *The Crisis*. Such an approach, at least to his mind, did not preclude blacks and whites
working together, as Ovington's query seemed to imply. Du Bois envisioned
separate and overlapping arenas of struggle, coexisting within the broad confines of an interracial organization. Black racial consciousness was born from
"the daily fight and eternal vigilance against constant manifestations of racial
prejudice." It was the "cement" that bound black members together in the
struggle to resist and fight assaults on their personal dignity as well as their
citizenship rights. While whites could and should support the struggle, it was
the people who were living it that *The Crisis* spoke directly to, appealing to
their common experiences as a vehicle for organizing a united resistance.[28]

Granting that his vision and plans for *The Crisis* might not be thoroughly
understood by his associates, Du Bois insisted that they allow him to pursue
the work unhampered. In the matter of rent and space, he argued economies
of scale. *The Crisis* needed additional space to meet the growing demand, and
given the trend in circulation numbers, it would not be long before the magazine was completely self-supporting. But even this missed the larger significance of the magazine in relationship to the future of the association. "What
I am working for with *The Crisis*," he told Spingarn, "is to make the NAACP
possible. Today it is *not* possible." He continued, "we can piddle on, we can
beat time, we can do a few, small obvious things, but the great blow—the
freeing of ten million and of other millions whom they pull down—that
means power and organization on a tremendous scale. The men who will
fight in these ranks must be educated and *The Crisis* can train them, not simply in its words, but in its manner, its pictures, its conception of life. . . . With
a circulation of a hundred thousand we shall have begun our work."[29]

A low-grade power struggle centering on Du Bois continued until 1916,
bringing most of the key players involved to the brink of resignation and
threatening to undermine the entire enterprise. May Nerney remained resentful of Du Bois's power to hold the organization hostage to his demands
and agreed with his critique of the racial imbalance at the top of the organization. She lobbied for the hiring of other prominent blacks, also seeing this as
a way to diffuse Du Bois's power over the association. Ovington was willing
to place her faith in Du Bois. He was, she told Spingarn, "the master builder"
while the rest of them were "journeymen doing one day's work to be forgotten

tomorrow." Spingarn was not especially concerned about such distinctions. With his eye toward the short-term health of the NAACP, he continued to insist that Du Bois had to be accountable to him as chairman and commit more time to the work of the NAACP, beyond his editing of *The Crisis*. As the sole black official in a leadership role, and one of the leading black figures in the country, Du Bois operated from a position of strength, knowing that the association needed him as much as, if not more than, he needed it.[30]

Personal tensions and conflicts, however, did not deter the steady growth of the organization. Worsening racial conditions, punctuated early in 1915 by the release of *The Birth of a Nation*, placed greater demands on the national office and pulled energies outward. In the years leading up to America's entry into World War I, the NAACP's leading officials worked feverishly on a number of fronts to counter the ideology of white supremacy while building a program of positive action. A burgeoning legal campaign worked in tandem with an expanding program of fieldwork and branch building, along with a stream of publicity and propaganda.[31]

The NAACP's fight against segregation in the federal government merged into a concerted effort to contain the spread of racial segregation and discrimination outside of the South, providing the association with one of its most effective organizing tools. Even before the Great Migration of the World War I period, a steady migration of blacks to cities in the North and the West, along with the growth of a small but prosperous group of black professionals, activated what Du Bois described as "the American leaven of race prejudice." Increasingly, blacks were barred from restaurants, theaters, hotels, and other places of public accommodation, often in violation of state civil rights laws. Cities, particularly in border states, sought to enact a variety of laws that would limit where blacks could live, while mobs policed the boundaries of predominantly white neighborhoods. The trend toward segregating black children into separate schools steadily increased. Paralleling the flood of discriminatory legislation in the nation's capital, anti-intermarriage bills were debated in the state legislatures of New York, Pennsylvania, Ohio, California, Illinois, Michigan, Wisconsin, Washington, Colorado, Kansas, and Nebraska during 1913.[32]

Through its system of vigilance committees and branches, the NAACP offered the only national structure for fighting this wave of racial proscription. The NAACP provided a mechanism for exchanging experiences, coordinating activities, and systematizing scattered local efforts against race prejudice into "steady, persistent, unwavering pressure." While branches provided the foundation and support for the national office, Du Bois explained, their main purpose was "to federate and organize the local battle against race prejudice." This vision of a national organization with its power rooted in community-based chapters charted an ambitious course for the NAACP. Du Bois and his associates did not promise a quick victory. "We have not even stirred the foundations of disfranchisement and Jim Crow legislation," he cautioned. But he added assuredly, "We are welding the hammers."[33]

Under May Nerney's direction, the NAACP arranged a series of barnstorming tours aimed at electrifying the grass roots and improving the association's knowledge of its constituency. In May 1913, Du Bois took a national tour for the association, visiting eighteen cities in the Midwest, California, Washington, and Oregon, and concluding his travels with a swing through the Deep South. It was his first trip to the West Coast. He delivered twenty-eight addresses to large and small groups, some mixed and others predominantly black, was feted by local black leaders, and met with a smattering of sympathetic whites. While promoting the work of the NAACP, the editor investigated the contours of black life and race relations in the far corners of the country. Reflecting on his seven-thousand-mile journey, Du Bois admitted to being "overwhelmed almost to silence over the things I have seen, the persons I have known and the forces I have felt." In a series of articles for *The Crisis*, he profiled enclaves of prosperous blacks in Los Angeles, San Diego, Seattle, Tacoma, and Portland, including photographs of black homes and business establishments. The "new blood" of Southern California, Du Bois noted, contrasted with the older, easier-going black population of San Francisco, which seemed to have "a less hopeful, pushing attitude." Du Bois delighted in the black community of Tacoma, which he likened to "a place of home coming." With fewer than one thousand black people, this striving group had already established a branch of the NAACP, led by a woman who Du Bois described as "soft-voiced, . . . utterly feminine, and yet an untiring leader of men."

The newer cities of the west, like Los Angeles and Seattle, had experienced a rapid growth in black population over the preceding decade and the color line was steadily tightening. This was evident in the areas of housing, public accommodations, schools, and department stores, where black women were routinely denied service and barred from trying on shoes and gloves. Around the time Du Bois visited Los Angeles, a group of white lawyers had succeeded in driving black tenants from the Copp office building, warning that so long as they were allowed to remain, offices in the building would be "undesirable." Restaurant owners in Los Angeles who wished to bar black customers from their establishments got around a state civil rights act, known as the Shenk Rule, by charging black customers exorbitant prices for food and refreshments. But Du Bois was confident that these trends would be vigorously fought and resisted by the people he had met. They were "pulsing . . . with . . . ambition," he reported, and embraced "the gospel of fight and self-assertion." He contrasted this spirit with the silent almost tragic earnestness that greeted him in the South. Black people who had traveled west, he noted, had found a new kind of freedom and had educated themselves "out of the shackles of dense ignorance" that weighed on their southern brethren.[34]

Du Bois boosted existing branches and encouraged the formation of new ones. E. Burton Ceruti, a black lawyer in Los Angeles, and several associates organized a branch in the wake of Du Bois's visit. Ceruti wrote Du Bois that "problems and grievances" arose constantly and demanded the kind of attention and action that could be provided by a branch of the NAACP. In the early fall of 1913, Letitia Graves, a beautician who was stirred to action by President Wilson's segregationist policies, led the founding of a branch in Seattle. Graves served as the first president, Horace Cayton was vice president, and eight of the twenty-two founding members were women. The Seattle branch joined with the branch in Tacoma in organizing several mass meetings to protest Wilson's policies through petitions, telegrams, and letters.[35]

Traveling under the banner of the "New Abolitionism," Joel Spingarn took three major annual tours for the NAACP from 1913 to 1915. On each of his tours, which he financed himself, Spingarn visited more than a dozen cities, mostly in the Midwest, and as far west as Denver, Colorado. May Nerney worked with an advance team to ensure that a full program of speaking engagements and organizing activity was in place and that newspapers were notified of planned public events. Spingarn addressed a variety of groups, from mass meetings in black churches, to civic groups, men's clubs, chambers of commerce, synagogues, and colleges, both black and white. Often the crowd numbered upward of one thousand; in Cleveland in January 1914, more than 2,500 people gathered to hear Spingarn, reportedly the largest meeting concerning black interests ever held in that city. A passionate and often electrifying speaker, Spingarn frequently advocated the use of self-defense in the face of increasing mob violence, as whites sought to restrict black movement in urban areas. "Rather die now," Spingarn advised, "than live one hundred years in a ghetto." To whites, Spingarn emphasized that there was no "Negro problem," but rather an "American problem," and it would persist so long as segregation and discrimination were substituted for justice. At a luncheon of the City Club in St. Louis, whites walked out during Spingarn's talk until there was only a quarter of the audience left, while waiters listened from the back of the room.[36]

In places where there was an NAACP branch, Spingarn met with its leaders and discussed strategies for increasing membership and strengthening its programs. Where no branch existed, he conferred with the local sponsoring committee and provided guidelines for organizing a branch. Spingarn, like Du Bois, was encouraged by his travels and reported "a profound awakening interest" in the NAACP. His tours garnered wide coverage by the black press, which was especially gratifying, and increasing coverage from white news media, further raising the profile of the association. Following Spingarn's visit to Cincinnati in 1915, the mayor ordered "white" stricken from the required qualifications for members of the city's fire department, a move that stirred greater interest in the NAACP. The Cleveland branch added two hundred members in the wake of Spingarn's visit, and other cities, including Detroit, Chicago, and Quincy, Illinois, reported increased activity and membership; a number of white elected officials were among the new members.[37]

In the years leading up to World War I, organizers for the NAACP made few excursions into the South. This was undoubtedly due to a number of factors, not the least of which was a scarcity of resources and field-workers. The leadership focused its efforts in areas where there was some possibility of success in terms of building up membership and bringing pressure to bear on elected officials, particularly in areas where the black vote was becoming a factor. Archibald Grimké referred to the Deep South as "enemy territory," a place that was, for all practical purposes, beyond the reach of effective intervention. The stark realities of the Jim Crow system also suggested to many that southern blacks would be more inclined to follow Booker T. Washington's program of accommodation rather than engage in the program of civil rights activism promoted by the NAACP.

When a national meeting of social workers gathered in Memphis, Tennessee, Spingarn and Du Bois dared to test this assumption. The National Conference of Charities and Corrections invited representatives of the NAACP to participate in their annual meeting, which was held in conjunction with the Southern Sociological Congress in May 1914. Efforts on the part of NAACP officials to have an open discussion of the race issue included on the program were rebuffed; the topic, conference organizers said, was "too controversial." In response, Spingarn and Du Bois joined forces with William

Pickens, then a dean at Talladega College, and organized an alternative meeting to discuss "the Negro Problem." They secured a church, and Spingarn bought advertising space in all of the local newspapers, announcing that a meeting would be held under the auspices of the NAACP. The half-page ad proclaimed in large letters "All Persons Who Love the Truth and Dare to Hear It Are Cordially Invited."

Reporting on the meeting, Oswald Garrison Villard crowed, "Three evangelists descended upon Memphis [and] told some wholesome truths about the treatment of the Negro." Addressing the large crowd that filled Avery Chapel, Spingarn blasted the social workers who refused to allow any discussion of the fundamentals of the race question for fear of offending white southerners. These organizations of so-called reformers, Spingarn charged, were the modern equivalents of churches and other institutions of the early nineteenth century that remained silent about slavery. He urged his listeners to join in the battle "against the erection of a monstrous caste system" in America. In a conciliatory gesture toward Washington and his supporters, Spingarn explained that the NAACP and Washington's program were two wings of the movement to advance black people and should be thought of as supplementary rather than antagonistic. Acknowledging that Washington worked within the severe constraints of the southern segregation system, Spingarn claimed that this did not preclude Washington's friends from also supporting the struggle being waged by Du Bois and the NAACP. Du Bois agreed, saying "the Negro will need every weapon he can get hold of" in his fight for freedom—"economic resources, higher education, and, above all political power." The crowd greeted the speakers with unrestrained enthusiasm, giving lie to claims that southern blacks were not prepared to fight for their rights. "Memphis Negroes," Du Bois reported, were on their feet in response "to every message of hope and courage." They answered the call to battle for human rights, he said, adding, "The association's work in the South has just begun."[38]

While Du Bois and Spingarn preached the gospel of the New Abolitionism, the NAACP's newly hired attorney, Charles Brinsmade, initiated a legal campaign that bolstered efforts to engage local communities in a national fight against race discrimination. Brinsmade, a recent graduate of Harvard Law School, was hired late in 1913 on a one-year contract with funds raised from a special appeal to the branches. Working closely with May Nerney and the NAACP's Legal Committee, Brinsmade implemented an expanded legal campaign that combined litigation aimed at building up a body of civil rights law with a program of fieldwork. The overarching goal of the Legal Bureau was to secure a series of judicial decisions that would define the law on the matter of civil and political rights, molding it so far as possible to admit no distinction based on race or color. The Legal Bureau also supported and sponsored efforts to secure legislation that would ensure equal access to federally funded programs, as in the case of the Smith-Lever bill, and monitored developments concerning black government workers. Brinsmade filed numerous appeals attempting to stem the spread of racial discrimination in the civil service. For example, he protested the dismissal of thirty postal workers in Atlanta in violation of civil service regulations. This ambitious program was dependent upon cooperation with communities around the country, where the patterns of racial discrimination took form.[39]

Working through branches and membership, the Legal Bureau aimed to establish the NAACP as a central clearinghouse for cases of racial discrimination. Allowing that each locality focused on particular problems—whether they concerned education, residential segregation, police brutality, job discrimination, public accommodations—Brinsmade explained that all should be regarded as manifestations of "the one evil we are fighting, namely, race discrimination." Race discrimination, he emphasized, was a national issue, the principle under which seemingly local problems were harmonized, and the primary focus of the NAACP's legal campaign. In a preliminary effort to coordinate a national program, Brinsmade collected information from each branch regarding their legal program and their arrangements with local attorneys, while also appealing to them and to the large readership of *The Crisis* to contact the national office with information about any cases of race discrimination. In announcing the new Legal Bureau, *The Crisis* stated that its goal was to assist in "any case where a colored person because of color is denied a right to which he is entitled." While they were not in a position to provide financial assistance, they would offer legal advice. Not surprisingly, the office was quickly flooded with requests, through the mail and in person, for advice and assistance on a scale that was impossible for one lawyer to meet.[40]

The scope of the NAACP's legal interests far exceeded the association's ability to offer relief or assistance. Nevertheless, these early efforts expanded the work that had been initiated by the Legal Redress Committee and helped to establish a framework for growth and development. Brinsmade named three areas that defined the broad parameters of the NAACP's work: lynching, denial of civil rights (discrimination and exclusion), and segregation. With regard to lynching, the Legal Bureau continued to emphasize investigation and publicity, urging members and branches to report any cases immediately. Brinsmade followed up on news reports and other leads, and tried to collect as much information as possible, mostly through correspondence with contacts in the South. Victims were named each month in *The Crisis* in a special section titled "The Burden" as part of an ongoing campaign to expose the viciousness and frequency of this horrific ritual.[41]

With "race prejudice running like a prairie fire," the NAACP extended its effort to press for implementation and strengthening of local and state civil rights laws. *The Crisis* continued to spotlight a pattern of increasing racial discrimination in northern and western cities, where blacks were denied access to restaurants, hotels, orchestra seats in theaters, recreational areas, and other public places. Such incidents often sparked the establishment of local vigilance committees and branches, as in Detroit where black and white citizens joined together early in 1912 "to combat the discrimination that has crept into their city." In June 1913, the magazine reported that blacks in the North were becoming more active and more hopeful in pressing for their rights, adding that "the Association is doing no more important work than its encouragement of this attitude on the part of northern colored people." Brinsmade urged local branches to report routine acts of discrimination and volunteered to provide advice on how best to challenge these practices in court. With the encouragement of the national office, local branches pursued these cases and met with some measure of success. It was often difficult, however, to sustain these efforts when, for example, a three-month-long investigation of fifty cases of discrimination in New York City in 1914 yielded no positive outcomes. Still, there were sporadic victories reported in *The Crisis*; in 1915 this included successful challenges to theater discrimination in Detroit, and restaurant cases in Los Angeles, New York, and Cleveland.[42]

When Brinsmade joined the NAACP staff late in 1913, widespread efforts to restrict black access to housing loomed as one of the most urgent problems facing blacks in urban areas. The accelerated pace of black migration from the South dramatically altered the racial composition of major northern cities in the decade prior to World War I. Residential patterns had been relatively fluid up through the turn of the century, given relatively small black populations. But whites responded with alarm as growing numbers of blacks sought adequate housing. Neighborhood groups, landlords, and realtors in Chicago, New York, Minneapolis, and other cities attempted to enforce racial boundaries through a variety of methods. They formed neighborhood improvement associations dedicated to barring blacks from renting or purchasing property in predominantly white areas and experimented with various legal remedies. The Hyde Park Improvement Club raised money to buy back property owned by blacks in this exclusive Chicago community. A *New York Times* editorial in December 1911 observed that "covenants of restriction" provided white real estate owners in upper Manhattan with "an effective means of protecting themselves against the negro invasion," explaining that such agreements were made "solely for the purpose of preventing depreciation of property values."[43]

Whites also resorted to threats and violence in an effort to enforce racial boundaries. *The Crisis* reported on black residents driven from their homes in Denver, Philadelphia, Baltimore, and St. Louis. In Kansas City, Missouri, an organization of white property owners dynamited five homes owned by blacks in an interracial neighborhood, after black families failed to heed white demands that they leave. Appeals by black homeowners to the mayor and the police went unanswered, and local white newspapers remained silent. *The Crisis* included numerous accounts of black resistance to mob terror. In West Philadelphia, for example, a single mother stood down a crowd of "1,000 neighbors" that knocked out the streetlights surrounding the new home she shared with her three children, bombarding it with stones. With the aid of the local NAACP branch, she secured a temporary police patrol outside her house.[44]

Residential segregation ordinances became one of the most widespread legal mechanisms used to enforce the color line. In December 1910, Baltimore became the first major city to enact a residential segregation ordinance after a black lawyer and his wife bought a house on McCulloh Avenue. McCulloh ran parallel to Druid Hills Avenue, which Du Bois described as "one of the best colored streets in the world," but prior to the arrival of the couple, McCulloh was occupied exclusively by whites. Although many of the white residents were renters, they demanded that a law be passed to halt the "invasion" of black people into white residential districts. City councilman George West took up their cause and introduced a law that would divide the city into racially defined districts and zones. The final law, fine-tuned in an effort to deflect legal challenges, made it illegal for any black person to occupy a home on a street where the majority of residents were white and for a white person to occupy a residence on a street where the majority of occupants were black. W. Ashbie Hawkins, a founding member of the NAACP branch in Baltimore, led the legal challenge to the ordinance, and the state supreme court declared it void in April 1913. In his decision, however, the judge indicated that the city could achieve the same objective under its police powers. The city council went on to pass a new measure in September that required residential segregation as a matter of public safety.[45]

As residential segregation ordinances spread, particularly to cities in the Midwest and upper South, Brinsmade and Nerney searched for a case that would provide the basis for a legal challenge. Several factors were critical in making this determination, most importantly a unified black community willing to cooperate, through local counsel, with the NAACP's Legal Bureau. In the spring of 1914, the NAACP agreed to work with the National Urban League to help organize blacks in opposition to residential segregation laws in Richmond, Virginia, and Louisville, Kentucky. Nerney visited Richmond, and Brinsmade traveled to Louisville to meet with local blacks active in the antisegregation fight. Ultimately, they agreed that Louisville, Kentucky, offered the most promising opportunity to mount a constitutional challenge.[46]

Blacks in Louisville had begun organizing against the possibility of a residential segregation ordinance in the fall of 1913, when the idea was first floated publicly. A committee of concerned citizens contacted the NAACP, seeking advice, and had been in correspondence with Brinsmade for several months preceding the passage of the ordinance. Shortly after the ordinance was signed into law on May 11, 1914, Brinsmade visited Louisville and met with local leaders to begin planning a legal challenge, while Nerney planned a mass meeting. On July 5, 1914, Spingarn and Pickens addressed more than eight hundred people gathered in Quinn Chapel in Louisville to protest the segregation ordinance and help raise funds for a legal challenge. Spingarn pledged that the NAACP would carry the Louisville case to the Supreme Court, if necessary. A branch of the NAACP was officially chartered, and funds were raised to hire local counsel. In the aftermath of the meeting, the city's Interdenominational Ministers Union passed a resolution of appreciation for Charles Brinsmade's services and announced that August 9 would be Segregation Sunday, when all ministers would be asked to speak on the subject.[47]

That fall Charles Buchanan, a white realtor who opposed the segregation ordinance, sold property in a predominantly white neighborhood to William Warley, a black postal worker and local NAACP member. In a case engineered by the NAACP, Warley refused to honor the contract, citing the city segregation ordinance, and Buchanan sued him, testing the validity of the ordinance. Clayton Blakey, a member of a prestigious Louisville law firm, represented Buchanan and Pendelton Beckley, the city attorney, represented Warley. A committee of one hundred, with representatives from local churches, schools, fraternal organizations, women's clubs, and secret societies, elected twenty-five captains to sponsor a citywide canvass for funds, raising more than $500. After the Kentucky Court of Appeals ruled to uphold the ordinance in June 1915, Arthur Spingarn, head of the NAACP Legal Committee, announced that *Buchanan v. Warley* would be appealed to the Supreme Court, with Moorfield Storey joining Blakey in preparing and arguing the case.[48]

The NAACP's legal initiative attracted requests for assistance from all parts of the country. Reporting on the large volume of cases referred to the NAACP, Arthur Spingarn commented that it seemed as if "every colored man or woman in the country who has been cheated or wronged or lost a position or wants a promotion assumes that through our association he can obtain the end he desires." Yet, even as the volume of requests increased, the association was forced to eliminate Charles Brinsmade's position as part of a retrenchment plan to meet a debt of $850. Spingarn and his law partner Charles Studin carried the legal work of the association forward on a volunteer basis, with the assistance of Nerney, who took care of correspondence and preliminary interviewing. In response to the varied and increasing number of requests for legal assistance, the legal committee attempted to clarify its policy, emphasizing that it would only take cases that showed actual discrimination because of color. It is doubtful that such a qualification would dissuade the many who appealed to the NAACP for legal counsel since most probably attributed unfair treatment to racial bias. In an effort to further narrow the pool of potential cases, the members of the legal committee embraced the policy promoted by Jane Addams, recommending that the association limit itself to those cases that tested broad legal principles, such as residential segregation ordinances or voting rights.[49]

The Supreme Court's 1915 ruling in *Guinn v. the United States*, striking down the "grandfather clause" as a disenfranchisement tool, elevated the importance of this approach. The Court's ruling was in direct response to a case from Oklahoma but also applied to a similar case from Maryland that was before the Court. The NAACP aided the black plaintiff in the Maryland case and filed an amicus curiae brief in *Guinn*, which was initially brought by the U.S. government during the Taft administration. The case involved an amendment to Oklahoma's 1910 constitution that exempted all persons who had been eligible to vote on January 1, 1866, and their lineal descendants from a newly required literacy test. The blatant racial intent of this exemption pressed the limit of government tolerance for the South's usurpation of constitutional guarantees. U.S. solicitor John W. Davis argued the case for the government, holding that the provision was a "denial of the restrictions imposed by the Fifteenth amendment . . . and recreates and perpetuates the very conditions which the amendment was intended to destroy." Moorfield Storey appeared for the NAACP. Chief Justice Edward White, a former Confederate soldier, wrote the opinion for a unanimous court, declaring that to hold that there was even a possibility for dispute "would be . . . to declare that the Fifteenth amendment . . . [was] wholly inoperative."[50]

"Race Rights Upheld by Supreme Court Ruling," declared the headline of the *Chicago Defender*. "Nothing in recent years," the paper editorialized, "has shaken the solid south so much; they feel themselves slipping." The NAACP greeted *Guinn* as a clear victory, one whose "spiritual effect remained un-impaired" if only because the highest court in the land had finally "committed itself to the proposition" that black citizens could not be deprived of "those rights given them by the 13th, 14th, and 15th amendments of the constitu-tion." Du Bois hailed it as the most important Supreme Court decision that positively affected black people in twenty-five years. In the end, the Court's ruling did little to reverse the widespread disenfranchisement of blacks in the South; states devised a variety of methods less susceptible to legal chal-lenge. But in the wake of this momentous if fleeting victory, the NAACP's intention to work through the courts resonated with many black Americans as an essential and viable path toward securing constitutionally guaranteed rights.[51]

At the time of the *Guinn* ruling, the NAACP was in the midst of a national campaign against *The Birth of a Nation*, a film that showcased the perils of black political empowerment. D.W. Griffith's spectacular production, based on Thomas Dixon's novel *The Clansman*, romanticized the slaveholding South and portrayed the Reconstruction era as a horrific time of vengeful northerners and black political dominance, corruption, and plunder. The groundbreaking film pioneered many cinematic innovations and was hailed as a masterpiece. It was "like writing history with lightning," Woodrow Wil-son reportedly commented following an advanced screening at the White House. *The Birth of a Nation* put Hollywood's stamp on popular stereotypes of blacks—brutish rapists, venal politicians, buffoon-like legislators, faithful servants—just as segregationist movements were cresting around the country. Even before the film opened in New York, the NAACP pressed for censor-ship and laid the groundwork to limit its distribution.[52]

The NAACP and its growing network of branches orchestrated a national protest against the film, which was released in theaters over a span of more than ten months. Following the Hollywood premiere of *The Birth of a Nation* early in February 1915, the Los Angeles branch alerted the national office about the content of the film. The NAACP promptly appealed to the New York–based National Board of Censorship, which had given preliminary approval to the film, urging that all members of the board view the film. Under pressure from the NAACP, the board withdrew its approval. After a screening in New York, a divided board approved the film again. While the NAACP attacked the film's racism and falsification of history, the association argued for its suppression on the grounds that it offended public decency and would incite violence—*The Clansman*, a staged version, had provoked a riot in Philadelphia several years earlier. In New York, the NAACP filed criminal charges against the film's owner and producer. Spingarn, Du Bois, and Villard led a delegation of more than five hundred people to city hall for a hearing with Mayor John Mitchell. These efforts yielded little. The film opened in New York early in April, drew large crowds and was hailed by white critics. This, however, was just the beginning of a rolling protest that spread to cities across the nation.[53]

Major protests in Boston followed swiftly behind New York; Boston mayor James Michael Curley responded by requiring that the most objectionable scenes be cut from the film before it showed in that city. Meanwhile, Nerney sent thick packets of reviews, press clippings, and suggested protest strategies to the association's fifty-four branches, urging them to take action before the movie came to town. The film was not scheduled to open in Chicago until the summer and as late as the fall and following winter in other parts of the country. NAACP branches and members were catalysts in many areas, staging mass protests and securing public hearings to challenge the film's slanderous and provocative portrayal of black people. In Minneapolis, for example, the city council held two days of hearings where opponents and advocates of the film disputed its merits and its "effect on the public mind." Following a bitter debate, the city council voted to grant the theater a permit; the mayor then revoked the permit, and his action was upheld by the state supreme court. Local authorities in a number of cities refused to grant permits to the film, including Chicago, Cleveland, Providence, Denver, Des Moines, and Albuquerque, as well as Gary, Indiana, and Wilmington, Delaware. The NAACP claimed credit for keeping the film out of Kansas and Ohio, where state censor boards barred the film. Officials in New Haven, San Francisco, St. Paul,

Oakland, and Milwaukee required that the most objectionable scenes be cut. Du Bois acknowledged that the very success of their protest may have been neutralized insofar as it served to advertise the film, but added that it was "impossible . . . for the branches of the association to abandon this fight." In his report to the board, Spingarn claimed that nothing to date had helped to "unloosen the energy and to stimulate the support of the colored people of this country as this attack on their character and their place in history."[54]

The protest against *The Birth of a Nation*, the NAACP's aggressive lobbying campaign in Washington and *The Crisis* all helped to bring growing numbers of blacks and whites into the orbit of the NAACP. But May Nerney remained concerned with translating growing interest and support into branches that would carry the work of the association forward. The NAACP was building a movement, and she wanted people in the field who could keep the branches and the national office in direct contact with each other, helping local groups to organize around a constructive program and ensuring that the principles and interests of the national body were adequately represented.[55]

With barely any resources to devote to fieldwork, Nerney relied on her own indefatigable energy and the support of several other NAACP women to mount a sustained effort to build the NAACP from the grass roots. Nerney, who, according to Joel Spingarn, "performed the tasks of three men," traveled for weeks at a time, visiting branches, becoming acquainted with local conditions, working with local leadership, and explaining the NAACP's program to community groups and organizations and at mass meetings. The uninitiated, she observed, could never understand the difficulties encountered by a field organizer for the NAACP. The work required patience and determination, "knowing that one was plowing the ground, and having faith in the future." Efforts were well rewarded in those few instances in which a group emerged "from the welter of personal and factional fights," and people learned to think together and work together toward a common end.[56]

While men dominated executive positions, women played leading roles in fieldwork and local organizing. Nerney recruited several other women to aid in branch building. Prominent among them was Mary Evans Wilson, who, along with her husband, attorney Butler Wilson, was a leader of the Boston branch of the NAACP. Wilson volunteered her time and paid her own expenses and organized new branches in Ohio, western New York, and Pennsylvania. Kathryn M. Johnson, a former high school teacher from Kansas City, Kansas, was the NAACP's first paid, full-time field-worker. Johnson's experience offers a glimpse of early efforts to, in the words of Du Bois, federate and organize "the local battle against race prejudice" under the banner of the NAACP.[57]

Kathryn Magnolia Johnson was an early recruit to the NAACP. As she later recalled, her experience of a race riot in Little Rock, Arkansas, set her in search of a way to fight the scourge of racial terror. After receiving the first issue of *The Crisis* in November 1910, she contacted Du Bois and volunteered her services. Johnson worked as an agent for *The Crisis* in Kansas City and was awarded a prize as one of the top four agents in the country. Early in 1912, Du Bois hired Johnson to travel for the magazine, a job she eagerly accepted. Johnson found teaching "too confining," and she was anxious to travel and broaden her experience. With her parents deceased and only one brother living in Kansas City, there was little to hold her there.[58]

Johnson journeyed through the Midwest and into the Deep South, introducing people to the work of the NAACP while promoting the sale of its monthly magazine. By 1914, she was also helping to establish branches; she organized a branch in Topeka, Kansas, and in Shreveport, Louisiana, the first NAACP branch in the Deep South. Johnson offered an account of her travels at the Sixth Annual Meeting of the NAACP, held in Baltimore in the spring of 1914. She described Oklahoma as "promising," while in Missouri it was so difficult to arouse interest that, she quipped, "we finally decided to take the matter to the Lord in prayer." Johnson reported that blacks in Texas were enthusiastic about the work of the NAACP but feared being publicly associated with an organization that had known ties to "the old abolitionist stock." A man in Waco warned that if she organized a branch there the meeting place would be burned down before she even left town. In Tyler, where three lynchings had recently taken place, a local black man cautioned that she should not expect any protection, adding that if a man came to town and said what she was saying he would be forced "to look up at the first telegraph pole."[59]

Traveling from Texas to Louisiana, Johnson said, was like to moving from one country to another. She was shocked by the desperate conditions there, particularly the widespread lack of schooling. In seventy parishes, there were no schools at all for black children; in New Orleans, fifteen thousand school-aged children were not enrolled in any school. The best school in Shreveport was "a shack and a firetrap." Many of "our people" in Louisiana, she noted, were "densely ignorant" and were simply glad that they were free, though in some places, Johnson added, they were not free at all. Alabama, she reported, was "utterly Booker T. Washingtonized." In Mobile, she met with the ministerial alliance three times before they finally understood the purpose of the NAACP, but they still would not open their pulpits to her.[60]

The challenge was great, and Johnson did not minimize the kind of commitment the work demanded. At the present time the NAACP "meant nothing to the masses of our people," she reported. "This movement will require someone to keep everlastingly at it, going from church to church, explaining to the people what our purpose is" and convincing them that the NAACP must have a foothold in every state. She emphasized that the ministers held the key for introducing the majority of black people to the work of the NAACP. "If you can get to them on Sunday . . . you can enlist their sentiment and help." In conclusion, Johnson said that she had "the greatest hope" for the movement and pledged her willingness "to spend and be spent in anything that is going to help sow the seeds of this propaganda in the country."[61]

Shortly after the annual meeting, Johnson accepted a full-time job with the NAACP as a field agent, with a special emphasis on increasing black membership in the organization. For her efforts, she received a 10 percent commission for memberships she signed up, plus $25 a month in expenses, "providing the treasury contained sufficient funds." Over the next two years, Johnson focused most of her organizing work in the Midwest, though she returned to Texas and Louisiana for several months in 1916. She helped establish branches in places like Des Moines, Iowa; Terra Haute, Indiana; and Galesburg, Illinois. Conditions varied from place to place, and Johnson was successful in enlisting whites as well as blacks. A primary goal, however, guided her efforts: to enlighten black people about their status as citizens and motivate them to take a stand for their rights—by voting, by resisting the steady encroachment of segregation, by challenging civil rights violations, and by organizing a branch of the NAACP.[62]

Johnson's reports from the field revealed the often deep-seated cultural resistance to the fight against segregation within black communities. She disputed a national official who suggested that "the ignorant masses" were the greatest obstacle to building NAACP membership, observing that middle-class and professional people were reluctant to associate with the NAACP. Teachers, postmen, and other civil servants, she noted, were fearful that they would jeopardize their jobs if they joined the organization. She told about a teacher at Sumner High School in St. Louis who refused to speak out against the proposed segregation ordinance there and noted that when he spoke to a white man, he always removed his hat and held it under his arm. In the State Normal School in Texas, after the assembly had gathered to hear Johnson speak, the president canceled the meeting for fear that the state would cut appropriations to the school. John Hodges, principal of the high school that Johnson had taught at in Kansas City, was a notable exception, she wrote, "a teacher with courage." Hodges served as president of the Kansas City branch.[63]

Lethargy, factionalism, and uninspired leadership were among the challenges that Johnson faced, as well as skepticism about the possibility of achieving significant change through the NAACP. In certain areas of the Midwest, such as Kansas City, Missouri, Johnson found that blacks accepted separate parks and playgrounds, although they did mount a protest against *The Birth of a Nation*. It was difficult to keep a branch alive if there were not some type protest or agitation to keep people engaged. And the masses of hardworking black people were reluctant to pay $1 in dues unless there was a likelihood of a tangible gain in the immediate future. When the interest of local people was aroused, personal conflicts and group rivalries could easily undermine efforts to organize a branch as different factions vied for control. Johnson also met her share of men who were eager to curry favor with whites. The Reverend G.W. Brown, pastor of the largest black church in Alton, Illinois, was "a white man's Negro," according to Johnson, and supported the things that the NAACP was fighting against, such as *The Birth of a Nation*. He did allow Johnson to address his congregation, but after introducing her, she noted, Brown descended the stairs behind the pulpit and lit up a cigar, sending smoke up that nearly stifled her.[64]

Johnson succeeded in organizing at least a dozen new branches for the NAACP and revived several existing ones. Her experience in St. Louis, Missouri, which she documented in a series of field reports, sheds light on how the organizing process worked and on the kind of role Johnson played in facilitating the growth of the NAACP during the pre–World War I era. She arrived there late in September 1915 and settled into the Wheatley branch of the YWCA for an extended stay. Her primary assignment was to mediate between competing factions in the local NAACP branch who were in disagreement about how to fight a proposed residential segregation ordinance and get them unified behind a clear plan of action. She reported that the branch was weak and local black leaders, with a few exceptions, were all "in a wild chase for glory, whether the cause suffers or not." There was little agitation among blacks at large about the segregation ordinance; some voiced support for it. People were stirred up, however, about *The Birth of a Nation*, showing at a local movie house, and the branch had mounted a "desperate" and ultimately unsuccessful fight to close the film down. The film served as grist for supporters of the segregation ordinance, who passed out copies of the *Home Defender* to people as they left the theater.[65]

Working with branch president Gustavus Tuckerman and George Vaughn and Homer G. Phillips, two local black lawyers, Johnson mobilized community support against the segregation ordinance while neutralizing the opposing faction, led by the ministers of the four largest churches in town. She took to the stump, speaking in churches, at the high school auditorium, and to a mass meeting of more than seven hundred in a local theater; a local NAACP official followed along, collecting names and addresses. In specially arranged meetings with teachers, pullman porters, and women's clubs, she appealed to them for their advice and support. A.W. Lloyd, grand chancellor of the Knights of Pythias, provided office space for the antisegregation campaign. Within three months, the branch had "forced harmony on the ministers" and united the black community behind the movement. Their efforts encouraged sympathetic whites to establish the Citizens Anti-Segregation Committee. Johnson reported with satisfaction that the people had "awakened to the fact that residential segregation is a calamity."[66]

The branch waged a two-track campaign, challenging the proposed ordinance in the courts, while at the same time planning for the probability of a referendum. The case, which was argued by Vaughn and Phillips, was tried in January 1916 in the same courthouse where the infamous *Dred Scott* case was initially argued in 1847. The district court upheld the ordinance and so did the state supreme court on appeal. Meanwhile, the NAACP branch and the Citizens Anti-Segregation Committee mounted a citywide education and voter registration campaign. Johnson reported that she gave as many as three speeches a night. Representatives of both groups took part in a public forum at Central High School, moderated by the mayor. They also met with editors of the local newspapers to present their position on the issue and lobbied the legislative committee of a citywide organization of labor unions for support. A large number of black people contributed their cars to the effort, and nearly a thousand volunteers covered St. Louis with three hundred thousand pieces of literature. On the Sunday before the election, volunteers leafleted outside churches and theaters and at major intersections.[67]

The Ordinance to Prevent Ill Feeling, Conflict, and Collision between the White and Colored Races and to Preserve the Public Peace passed by a vote of roughly 52,000 to 18,000. There were an estimated 15,000 blacks eligible to vote in St. Louis, where blacks composed 7 percent of the city's population. In the aftermath of the election, the NAACP's executive committee requested that the Citizens Anti-Segregation Committee take steps to block the implementation of the law. Colonel Welles H. Blodgett, a lawyer for the Wabash Railroad and former Union army officer, volunteered to take the lead. Blodgett won a temporary restraining order, effective until the U. S. Supreme Court ruled on the pending Louisville case, *Buchanan v. Warley*, effectively blocking its implementation. It was a victory of sorts. But beyond stalling the implementation of the ordinance, the campaign succeeded in arousing and uniting the black community in St. Louis while also advertising the work of the NAACP. By the end of the campaign, the St. Louis branch boasted five hundred members, making it one of the largest branches in the country. Du Bois singled out Johnson, Vaughn and Phillips, and the branch leadership for praise in *The Crisis*. They set a "standard of service in an uncompromising fight," Du Bois wrote, "sustained through months of heartbreaking struggle."[68]

From St. Louis, Johnson headed south to aid with an antisegregation campaign in Dallas and to visit branches in Shreveport and New Orleans, lonely outposts of NAACP activity. Blacks in Dallas were well organized behind the effort to defeat a residential segregation ordinance that would be on the ballot in that city. Local blacks, she reported, were astonished that an outside organization like the NAACP was interested in their plight and had sent Johnson to aid them. Still, they did not want her to speak as a representative of the NAACP for fear of stirring up local whites and bringing more of them out to vote for the segregation measure. Johnson spoke under the auspices of the local business league. She learned that several prominent whites had volunteered to provide free legal services as well as funding to the leaders of the antisegregation campaign if they would not affiliate with a "northern organization." After the segregation ordinance was approved by a vote of 6,700 to 4,100, however, plans to organize a branch of the NAACP moved forward under the leadership of W. E. King, publisher of the *Dallas Express*. After a few meetings were held peacefully, churches began to open their doors to local NAACP organizers.[69]

When Johnson arrived in Shreveport, she found that the branch she had helped to organize was barely holding on. It had twelve dues-paying members, and all of its officers were from the same church. P. L. Blackburn, the first president of the branch, had worked steadily for a year and a half and enlisted seventy-five members, but felt that little had been accomplished. A plan to petition for better school facilities was undermined by blacks "who had the ear of whites," he told her. So Blackburn resigned his post and advised others to quit the organization as it was "no use." George Lewis, who worked as a porter in a dry goods store, laid claim to the presidency of the branch, since he had brought *The Crisis* to Shreveport. He was full of zeal for the cause, Johnson wrote, but he was not a leader. With the aid of several of the former members, she organized a meeting of the branch, where new officers were elected, many of the old members paid up their dues, and several new ones signed on. Charles Roberson, the first and only black lawyer in northern Louisiana, was elected president, and George Lewis assumed the vice presidency. Johnson was pleased with the results. Roberson was a man of "bull dog tenacity," and popular with blacks and whites. She did note, however, that his "literary raising is woefully deficient," and commented that he never could have passed a written bar examination.[70]

While Johnson was in Shreveport, an incident occurred that she felt begged for action on the part of the branch. A policeman encountered a black man sleeping on a bench in Union Station and poked the man with his billy club to wake him up. As the man woke up, he reached into his pocket. The policeman, Johnson continued, "pretended he thought he was reaching for a revolver and shot him." All the man had in his pocket was a ticket to Nachitoches, where he lived. The man was taken to the hospital, and Johnson did not know whether he had lived. When she advised local NAACP members to pursue this case, since the city or the railroad might be liable, they responded that it was useless; the courts would pay no attention to them.[71]

The most obvious area for work and organizing, she believed, was voting. Blacks composed roughly half of Shreveport's population, or more than fifteen thousand people, yet only eighty of them had registered. A display of guns mounted on the wall of the entrance hall to the city museum greeted visitors, with the following inscription: "These are the guns with which we maintained white supremacy at the polls." Still, Charles Roberson convinced Dr. Wilson, a newly elected member of the branch's executive committee, to go to the polls and vote during the recent gubernatorial election. Wilson admitted that he actually trembled before going to cast his ballot, but, much to his relief and surprise, his reception at the polls was cordial. When Johnson left Shreveport, she was guardedly hopeful about the future of the branch and urged the national office to send Joel Spingarn down to reinforce the groundwork she had laid.[72]

In her reports to the national office, Johnson rarely revealed her personal experiences of the indignities and inconveniences of Jim Crow. Yet occasionally she vented her frustration and anger, particularly regarding travel accommodations. One letter recounted how, while traveling on a steamboat, she did not eat for twenty-four hours because she refused to be segregated to a side table off the main dining room. After several days of exhausting work in Shreveport, she was forced to ride "in a dirty, filthy, colored coach" to New Orleans. The train agent refused to sell her a berth, claiming, falsely, that none were available. "All night long I was furious thinking about paying first class fare for cattle car accommodations. If I had died while I was coming here," she quipped, "I am certain I would have missed heaven."[73]

Johnson demonstrated a tenacity and devotion to the work that yielded a significant measure of success in the field and won the praise of Du Bois and board member Francis Cardoza, who described her as a "jewel." Others, however, found fault with her style and her tendency to speak her mind, revealing unsettled views about the image that the NAACP should project and who it aimed to enlist. Mary Wilson, a member of Boston's black elite, advised that Johnson lacked "the personality and intellect" to interest the "more cultured" segment of the black community or sympathetic whites. Ovington felt that Johnson did not quite represent the NAACP, and several board members claimed that she failed to demonstrate "an ability to reach liberal whites." Johnson countered these complaints with evidence of her success in enlisting whites as well as blacks, including Arthur Capper, the governor of Kansas, who served as president of the Topeka branch. She brushed aside remarks about her intellectual ability, noting her achievements as a teacher, and defended her strategy, which was centered in black communities and relied on local blacks to determine which whites to approach. In the end, "refinement" and "polish" were apparently more important to the East Coast leadership that dominated the NAACP than the skills that Johnson had cultivated during her tenure with the NAACP and her effectiveness in the field. As the board made plans to hire a national field director in the summer of 1916, they terminated Johnson's employment. Johnson continued to work in the field of race advancement. She assisted black troops in France during World War I and later worked as a nationwide representative for the Association for the Study of Negro Life and History.[74]

By the end of Woodrow Wilson's first term in office, the NAACP had established itself as a formidable organization with a foothold in communities around the country. Through its bold attack on Wilson's segregationist policies, its organized opposition to antiblack legislation in Washington, and the nationwide protest it had waged against *The Birth of a Nation*, the NAACP brought the fight for racial justice into the national arena. Tapping into a growing network of members and supporters, the organization mounted a broad challenge to residential segregation laws, and by 1916 had a major case pending before the U.S. Supreme Court. In less than four years, the NAACP had grown from a membership of fewer than five hundred to close to ten thousand members organized in sixty-three branches that stretched from coast to coast, while *Crisis* subscriptions climbed to more than 35,000.[75] Most of the growth in membership was concentrated among African Americans and took place outside of the South, but tentative inroads had been made into that region. The gains made during this period are all the more striking given the financial constraints that the association operated under. May Nerney told the NAACP's annual meeting in January 1916, "We have achieved something that has never been done before. We have built up an organization of colored and white people who stand for equal opportunity regardless of the color line."[76]

Although the growth of the NAACP was impressive and hard won, it paled next to the magnitude of the challenge. Nerney cautioned, "Nowhere are we meeting the situation. Nowhere is the NAACP beginning to cope with the increase in prejudice and discrimination." Following a monthlong tour of the Midwest late in 1915, Nerney reported that in cities with a large population of southern black migrants, the attitude toward the propaganda of the NAACP ran the gamut from "indifference and incredulity to open hostility." Where branches existed, members wanted a definite and practical program. There appeared to be more interest, she observed, in securing economic opportunity than in fighting legal disabilities. For many, "civil rights," "democracy," and "new abolitionism" were phrases only. The association offered lofty principles for which it asked support "in the hope that some day an association will be built to enforce these principles." A major challenge was getting people to sign on to a movement that did not offer any short-term gains. Yet, Nerney contended, by the very nature of the problem, "we cannot hope for very material results" for a long time to come "and certainly not for anything spectacular unless some great crisis arises."[77]

There was a general consensus among the NAACP's leadership that the future of the organization would depend upon expanding and strengthening its membership base. Membership dues and contributions, not philanthropic largesse, as Villard and others had anticipated, had become the association's primary source of income. But local branches and members did much more than generate needed revenue. They were, as Du Bois had emphasized, on the front lines of the battle the NAACP was waging, and their support and active participation was essential to mounting a sustained challenge to racial discrimination in all of its manifestations. The NAACP continued to appeal to all citizens to join in the fight for racial justice and full democracy, but African Americans were the association's lifeline, and efforts to recruit new members and build local support increasingly concentrated on black communities. In the face of severe financial constraints, the board approved a new position for a national field organizer who would devote full time to reviving branches, cultivating new ones, and strengthening the connection between the national office and local communities.

A parallel concern shared by Du Bois and Spingarn was the need to more fully engage black leaders around the country in charting the future course of the association and the broader movement it sought to build. The death of Booker T. Washington in November 1915 offered a critical opportunity to repair long-simmering divisions and to, in Du Bois's words, "bring our tremendous elements of strength into a more . . . solid structure."[78] They organized a meeting at Spingarn's Troutbeck estate outside Amenia, New York, and were careful to include Washington's closest allies in the planning. Tuskegee Institute president Robert Moton and Emmett Scott were among those consulted to develop an invitation list and an agenda. The final roster of fifty men and women who had accepted Spingarn's invitation represented "all phases of Negro thought"—from longtime Washington supporters to veteran Niagaraites and those in between—and included author Charles Chesnutt, educator Lucy Laney, Kelly Miller of Howard University, and Mary Talbert, then president of the National Association of Colored Women.[79]

Held in the waning days of summer 1916, the group gathered at the edge of a pristine lake for three days of talk, fellowship, and recreation. They met "under the pale blue sky" and evening stars, "ate hilariously in the open air," and bedded down in tents at night. A full agenda of discussions on major areas concerning "The Problem" and strategies for moving forward was interspersed with swimming, hiking, rowing, quiet walks in the woods, flower picking, and singing. It was a private meeting. No notes of the proceedings were published, although the group did agree to make public a statement of common goals and principles. "Beautiful and satisfying" was how Du Bois described it. the *New York Age* credited the Amenia conference with creating "a new spirit of united purpose and effort."[80]

It is difficult to measure the tangible consequences of Amenia except for one. The gathering provided the opportunity for Spingarn, Du Bois, and James Weldon Johnson, long associated with Booker T. Washington, to become better acquainted. Du Bois and Johnson shared a tent where, as David Levering Lewis writes, Du Bois's "apprehensions about Johnson's Tuskegee connections had been so well assuaged that the two of them speculated about forming a 'secret organization' to energize civil rights elements represented at the conference." In the aftermath of the meeting, Du Bois and Spingarn set about securing an offer for Johnson to fill the new position of field secretary. Later in the fall, Spingarn wrote Johnson, offering him the position. Du Bois wrote separately, encouraging Johnson to accept, reminding him of their discussions and suggesting that "we might be able to tie a durable knot to insure the permanency of the main organization."[81]

James Weldon Johnson later recalled his genuine surprise upon receiving the offer from Spingarn. At forty-five years of age, Johnson had already had a remarkable career as an educator, diplomat, songwriter, novelist, poet, and journalist. Yet there was no question but that he would accept what was a striking new departure. Reflecting on "the unspoken reactions" between him, Du Bois, and Spingarn at Amenia, he had an awareness that this invitation "was in line with destiny. . . . It at once seemed to me that every bit of experience I had had . . . was preparation for the work I was being asked to undertake." Johnson joined the staff of the NAACP on the eve of America's entry into World War I, a moment when black America and the rest of the nation were facing the most momentous social changes since the Civil War.[82]

3

Going South:
The NAACP in the World War I Era

On the evening of March 7, 1917, the leading black citizens of Savannah, Georgia, crowded into St. Paul's C.M.E. Church to hear James Weldon Johnson, the NAACP's new field secretary. Johnson was nearing the end of a two-month-long tour of the southeastern states, and he was pumped up. "Our race is moving forward," he declared, "and leaving the leaders in the rear." Johnson told how wartime demand for labor had created opportunities for blacks to taste industrial freedom in the urban North and move "towards those centers where they may exercise the ballot." The exodus of blacks from the South elevated the possibilities for those who stayed behind. White southerners, long accustomed to a static and dependent workforce, were waking up to the value of black labor, providing "the Negro race the chance to register its first protest against its treatment in the South."[1]

Johnson described an ongoing social transformation created by the upheavals of the Great War that had engulfed Europe in 1914. Military preparations fueled defense production two years before the United States entered the war in April 1917. The wartime suspension of European immigration created an opening for black workers, who had long been excluded from the industrial labor force. Over a quarter of a million men and women had already left the South by the end of 1916; Johnson predicted that before the wave of migration subsided, two million blacks would go to cities in the Midwest and Northeast. The biblical phrases associated with this movement— "the Exodus," with northern points referred to as the "Promised Land" and "Land of Hope"—told more about what was left behind than the uncertain future that lay ahead. The "economic pull" of northern industries, Johnson emphasized, worked in tandem with an "oppression push," with tens of thousands uprooting their families and seeking relief from the daily brutalities of Jim Crow, the threat of the mob, the lack of justice in the courts—essentially voting with their feet.[2]

Addressing the hundreds who gathered to hear him in churches from Richmond, Virginia, to Jacksonville, Florida, Johnson emphasized the possibilities in the South, where the great majority of blacks would remain. Organization, Johnson insisted, was essential to give voice, direction, and power to the changes released by the war, what an NAACP report described as a "spiritual unloosening" from the constraints of racial repression. Johnson said that the time was ripe for new leadership, and the response to his appeals affirmed this belief. Wilson Jefferson, a postal clerk and the president of the new branch in Augusta, Georgia, was among those who stepped forward. "As we understand it," he reported in the local paper, the NAACP works "against injustice and oppression directed against our people and seek[s] to have them accorded justice [and] equality before the law and fair play everywhere. Surely," he commented, "this is a plane upon which all men, white and black, may stand."[3]

For the NAACP, the war brought new opportunities to translate ideals into action. Over the next two years, the service of more than three hundred thousand black men and women in the armed services further advanced claims to full citizenship rights, while exposing how America's racial caste system undermined the nation's most fundamental values. The association heightened its efforts to expose lynching and some of the most extreme examples of racial discrimination and enlist whites and blacks in countering the drive to consign blacks to a secondary place in the society—through publicity, the antilynching campaign, targeted legal challenges and membership drives. At the same time, the building up of branches during the war rooted the NAACP in the struggles of local communities at a pivotal moment of change and opportunity. With the movement into the South, the NAACP became a national organization, opening on to the main battlefront in the fight for civil rights.

James Weldon Johnson, the second black and the first southerner to serve in an administrative position, brought fresh vision, vitality, and a remarkable range of experience to the NAACP. He was born in Jacksonville, Florida, in 1871 and spent the first thirty years of his life in the South. Following his graduation from Atlanta University, Johnson pursued opportunities and developed his talents in many areas; his accomplishments distinguished him as a leading figure of his generation. He established the first black high school in Jacksonville, was the first black admitted to the Florida bar, wrote the lyrics to "Lift Ev'ry Voice and Sing," which became known as the "Negro national hymn," served as U.S. consul to Venezuela under the Roosevelt and Taft administrations, and authored *The Autobiography of an Ex-Colored Man*—all before he was forty.

Yet, his remarkable achievements did not shield Johnson from his status as a black man in America. In 1902 he was nearly lynched in Jacksonville for socializing publicly with a woman who looked white. As part of a musical trio that included his brother Rosamond, Johnson toured to the far corners of the nation and learned firsthand that racial discrimination knew no boundaries. He recalled a late-night conversation with his fellow musicians after the three were turned away from every hotel in Salt Lake City. Their talk quickly moved "beyond our individual situation and took in the common lot of Negroes in well nigh every part of the country, a lot which lays high and low the constant struggle to renerve their hearts and wills against the unremitting pressure of unfairness, injustice, wrong, cruelty, contempt, and hate." For Johnson, the NAACP offered a way for blacks to push back and mount a concerted fight for their fundamental rights as American citizens.[4]

Johnson began with two major goals: to expand and deepen the NAACP's base of black membership and to take the organization South. When he assumed his position at the end of 1916, the NAACP claimed 348 members in the region that was home to the vast majority of black Americans. As his first order of business, he embarked on a southern organizing trip early in January, starting in Richmond and traveling through the Carolinas and Georgia as far south as Tampa, Florida. In preparing for his trip, Johnson worked through contacts in more than a dozen cities, asking that they convene a meeting of people representative of the community. Johnson met with these groups during his initial swing through the southeast. Together they discussed plans for establishing a branch and scheduled a mass meeting for recruiting members, which Johnson addressed as he doubled back and retraced his ground. As a result, branches were chartered in Richmond, Norfolk, Durham, Greensboro, Raleigh, Charleston, Columbia, Atlanta, Augusta, Athens, Savannah, Jacksonville, and Tampa, and 738 new members joined. Trumpeting the fruits of Johnson's first foray into the field, Du Bois proclaimed that, at last, the NAACP had "a real first line of defense facing the enemy at proper range."[5]

The association's movement into the South coincided with America's entry into World War I, elevating the issue of black service in the armed forces to

the top of the board's agenda. At the April 9 meeting, Mary White Ovington, Oswald Garrison Villard, and William English Walling, avowed pacifists, joined in supporting a unanimous resolution pledging that the NAACP
would work to ensure that black Americans were included in the armed forces
on a full and equal basis. "The uniform of a federal soldier . . . is prima facie
evidence of citizenship," Ovington observed, and "the Negro must demand
this evidence of citizenship on exactly the same terms as other American
citizens." The board sent newly hired secretary Roy Nash to Washington to
lobby against southern efforts to eliminate blacks from the draft. The contentious issue of a training camp for black officers, however, was put off until the
next board meeting.[6]

Two months earlier, NAACP chairman Joel Spingarn spearheaded a controversial effort to secure a separate training camp for black officers. While
emphasizing his opposition to racial segregation in all areas of American life,
Spingarn argued that circumstances demanded that principle yield to the fact
that the U.S. military was completely segregated. In preparation for the likelihood of universal military conscription, the choice was either a separate
camp for training black officers or the exclusion of blacks from officer training. He was careful to insist that he spoke for himself and not for the NAACP,
but it was a distinction that registered with few. The black press led the opposition, lambasting Spingarn and the NAACP for compromising a central
tenet of the fight for equality. Spingarn's proposal, however, found enthusiastic supporters among the individuals most affected, young, college-educated
men. Charles Hamilton Houston, a recent college graduate and instructor at
Howard University, joined with others to form the Central Committee of
College Men to press the War Department for an officers training camp.
With America's entry into the war, black support for the idea grew. In May,
the NAACP's board, while registering its opposition to segregation in this as
in all other cases, voted in favor of the establishment of a separate training
camp "rather than having no officers training camp for colored men" who
were subject to the new draft law. The following month a camp was established in Des Moines, Iowa.[7]

In May, Spingarn and Nash both enlisted in the armed services; several
months later, Nash submitted his resignation as secretary. Mary White
Ovington assumed the position of acting chair and director of branches, and
James Weldon Johnson became acting secretary. With Du Bois, this left only
three full-time administrative officials in the national office. Johnson divided
his time between the field, the New York office, and occasional trips to Wash-

ington, D.C. Under the strains of an organization pushing toward even greater growth, Johnson began working to create a position on the staff for Walter White, a young insurance salesman and recent graduate of Atlanta University whom he had met during his trip to Atlanta. White impressed Johnson as a person of great "mental and physical energy" and as the spark plug behind the organization of the Atlanta branch, the strongest of the new southern crop.[8]

During the last week of May and the first week of June, Johnson traveled to the Midwest, visiting the Chicago branch along with branches in Indianapolis, Louisville, Cincinnati, St. Louis, Detroit, and Cleveland. He addressed several mass meetings and attended the Great Lakes District conference in Detroit, which included representatives from the midwestern branches. The effect of the southern migration was a common concern in these cities, and so were the various manifestations of new segregation practices. Louisville and St. Louis had both been through a protracted struggle against residential segregation laws, with a major Supreme Court ruling pending in the Louisville case. In each place, Johnson and local officials discussed the practical problem of maintaining interest and support for the branch when there was no fight on. They discussed the possibility of a forum program that included lectures and entertainment. The NAACP's dependence on volunteer leadership and the uncertain goals of "racial advancement work" made it difficult to build and sustain strong branches. As a historian of Chicago noted, black leaders during this period were "more interested in the development of community institutions, businesses and political organizations" than in the work of the NAACP.[9]

The racial terror and wholesale violation of citizenship rights in the South created more fertile ground for the NAACP and galvanized its southern growth strategy. Just days after returning to New York from the Midwest, Johnson was off to Memphis to investigate the lynching of Ell Persons. Persons, a woodchopper, had been arrested on May 6 on suspicion of the murder of a sixteen-year-old girl a week earlier. There was no evidence to implicate Persons; a local white paper reported, "Third degree tactics forced a confession from the slayer." With locals vowing to lynch Persons, he was taken to the state penitentiary in Nashville, but he was sent back to Memphis two weeks later for trial. Persons returned in the custody of two deputies, despite the well-publicized plans of the group bent on lynching Persons. Early on the morning of May 22, a mob of men boarded the train outside of Memphis, took the prisoner from the deputies and brought him to the place that had been prepared for the lynching. The press reported that a crowd of fifteen thousand—men, women, and children from counties throughout Tennessee and in Mississippi—gathered after daybreak. They tied Persons to a tree, doused him with gasoline, and lit a fire. His body was consumed by flames as onlookers "fought and screamed and crowded to get a glimpse." A woman protested, "They burned him too quick!" and the complaint echoed across the mob. Two men hacked off the ears of the burnt corpse, another severed the head, and others pinched souvenirs from the remains.[10]

Upon his arrival in Memphis, Robert Church Jr., a prominent black businessman and political leader, drove Johnson to the site of the burning. "A pile of ashes and pieces of charred wood" were all that was left. Johnson reflected on the horror that had transpired there and was struck with the realization that the race question, in large part, involved "the saving of black America's body and white America's soul." Over the next ten days he talked with the sheriff, newspaper reporters, some local whites, and many blacks, and read through all of the relevant news accounts. He learned that a white man was initially the prime suspect, but once Persons was arrested and forced to confess, he was immediately indicted for murder. The failure of local and state officials to resist the will of the mob and the ghastly spectacle were all fully reported in the local press. Du Bois let excerpts from the news clippings Johnson collected tell the story of the lynching of Ell Persons in *The Crisis.*

Johnson found an aroused black community ready to enlist in the work of the NAACP. Robert Church was his host and guide. Church had founded the Lincoln Republican League in 1916, dedicated to organizing blacks to register and vote. Johnson also met B.M. Roddy, a bank clerk who had been working toward establishing an NAACP branch in Memphis ever since Spingarn and Du Bois had hosted their breakaway meeting there three years earlier. Before Johnson left Memphis, he had collected fifty-three paid memberships and nearly thirty-five pledges, and the preliminary work for establishing a branch had been completed. His association with Church developed into a warm friendship, and Church became a critical link in the NAACP's growing southern presence. He served as a source of news and information and lent his considerable contacts and political skills to aid in extending the reach of the NAACP through Tennessee and the Mississippi Delta.[11]

While Johnson worked to root the NAACP in southern soil, Du Bois turned his attention to the migration that was carrying tens of thousands of black workers and their families northward. In one of the first attempts to "give a definite, coherent picture of the whole movement," Du Bois traveled through six southern states in March 1917 and gathered additional information from agents in the field. In interviews across the South, Du Bois found that the immediate causes of the exodus were economic but underlying them all were the conditions in the region, which, as a man in Sumter, South Carolina, explained, "we have had to bear because there was no escape." News of hardships and difficulties in northern cities were not a deterrent. People "were willing to run any risk to get where they might breathe freer," said one informant. Du Bois and his associates estimated that 250,000 had already left the South in what was "apparently a mass movement and not a movement of the leaders." It was too soon to predict what the consequences would be, but it clearly portended "a social change among Negroes of great moment."[12]

Du Bois was preparing for a trip to East St. Louis, Illinois, to study conditions in "a typical community" that attracted southern migrants when that city erupted in a fury of antiblack violence. Trouble had been brewing in this industrial city since the fall election and peaked with a series of labor struggles in the spring of 1917. Since the start of 1916 the black population had increased by 2,400 to slightly over 10,000 in a city totaling roughly 70,000. Democrats charged Republicans with "colonizing Negroes" from the South for their political advantage, and white unionists blamed a growing supply of black workers from the South for taking the jobs of white workers and undermining a series of unionization drives in meat-packing plants and the Aluminum Ore Company. The press fanned racial animosities with sensational stories about "gun-toting Negroes," black crime waves, and an imminent black "invasion" of white residential areas. At the end of May, six hundred union workers marched on city hall to demand that city officials act to stem the influx "of undesirable Negroes." Groups of whites fanned out, assaulting blacks. National Guard troops quelled an incipient riot, but not before several hundred blacks fled to St. Louis. On the night of July 1 whites drove through a black neighborhood, randomly firing into homes. Later a car with police and detectives drove through the same neighborhood. Unable to distinguish this car from the previous intruders, blacks fired on the vehicle, instantly killing one detective and fatally wounding another. Seized upon as evidence that blacks were plotting a massacre, white rage crested into a pogrom that claimed untold black lives and left some six thousand blacks homeless.[13]

On July 8, Du Bois hurried to East St. Louis, now with a very different mission. Accompanied by Martha Gruening, a white social worker and staff member of *The Crisis*, the two conducted an extensive investigation of the riot. Working from an office provided by the Knights of Pythias, Du Bois canvassed the black community and met with city and state officials; Gruening moved around the white community, doing skillful detective work. Together they scoured local papers and collected photographs and other documentary evidence. From the mass of material, Du Bois produced a report excerpting firsthand testimony and exposing the horror and murderous brutality that reigned for two days in this small midwestern city. It was, said one local observer, "a man hunt conducted on a sporting basis. . . . There was a horribly cool deliberateness and a spirit of fun about it." Black men who held their hands up in a sign of surrender were gunned down. An eyewitness "saw a Negro woman begging for mercy set upon by white women who beat her with fists, stones and sticks." Black homes were torched, and men, women, and children were shot as they ran from their burning houses. A mob beheaded a Negro man at the Free Bridge, and threw his head off one side of the bridge and his body from the other. Mutilated corpses bobbed to the surface of the Mississippi River.[14]

The riot's toll in terms of lives lost was impossible to calculate. Municipal records were inadequate, and local citizens contended that many bodies were never recovered. Du Bois estimated that between one hundred and two hundred blacks were killed. The police put the number at one hundred. A congressional investigating committee, acknowledging that an exact number was impossible, concluded that at least eight whites and thirty-nine blacks died. Property damage was estimated at around $400,000. What did East St. Louis portend for the future? Most of the blacks Du Bois interviewed expressed their resolve never to return to the South. Some looked to St. Louis or points farther north. Du Bois encouraged that sentiment and preached a defiant faith in the future. The demand for black labor would not slacken, he wrote, and blacks would continue to come north for the higher wages denied them in "the slave South," despite the determination of white workers and organized labor to keep them out. "Economic freedom for the American Negro is written in the stars," Du Bois insisted; East St. Louis was among the "pools of blood which we must march through, but march we will."[15]

The NAACP's response to the massacre in East St. Louis was a measure of the organization's agility in navigating the turbulent currents of race relations and providing leadership on a broad scale. The association publicized the atrocity; a special twenty-page supplement to *The Crisis* summarized the results of Du Bois and Guerning's investigation and drove the magazine's circulation up to fifty thousand. Through its branch in St. Louis, the NAACP helped organize relief for refugees and provided legal counsel for a dozen blacks accused of inciting the riot, working to ensure that blame for the riot "not be shifted upon the Negro race." Finally, the NAACP led in mounting a mass protest that still stands as one of the most stunning protest marches in the annals of the black freedom struggle."[16]

On Saturday afternoon, July 28, 1917, nearly ten thousand black people marched down Fifth Avenue in New York City in silent protest of the East St. Louis riot and all of the barbarities "practiced against them in the land of the free." Initiated by the NAACP at the suggestion of James Weldon Johnson, an independent committee representing black churches and organizations in New York sponsored what the *New York Times* described as "one of the most . . . orderly demonstrations ever witnessed on Fifth Avenue." An estimated twenty thousand blacks and a scattering of whites lined the route from Fifty-seventh to Twenty-fourth streets and watched in silence. The slow muffled beating of drums accompanied the parade and hung in the warm summer air. Children led the way, followed by women in white, and then men dressed in dark clothes; some wore the uniform of the United States Army, and there were a "few gray haired soldiers of Civil War Days." They carried signs. "We Are Maligned as Lazy and Murdered When We Work," read one. Another proclaimed, "America Has Lynched without trial 2,867 Negroes in 31 years and not a single murderer has suffered." Onlookers were reminded, "We have fought for the liberty of white Americans in six wars; our reward is East St. Louis." A young boy held a placard that said: "Color, blood, and suffering has made us one."[17]

The parade was a visible manifestation of what the NAACP increasingly sought to create—particularly as envisioned by Du Bois and Johnson. While the committee did not specifically exclude whites, the parade was designed to be an expression of black protest. Members of the race representing all conditions and walks of life participated; for once, the *New York Age* observed, Negro Americans, West Indians, and Haitians worked in unison as black men. "The coming together of all classes of Negroes to further a common cause," was the most encouraging sign of all. The American flag swayed over the parade, as did the flags of Haiti and Liberia, the sole black republics. The *New York Call* compared the march to a procession of mourners, while "at the same time [it] gave the impression of outraged dignity with a hint of power to repair the wrongs of centuries." The *Washington Bee* anticipated that this powerful display, evoked by words and photographs, "marched throughout the country in the imaginations of millions of people who will reflect . . . that of all America's shortcomings in trying to live up to her ideals none is more glaring than the treatment accorded the Negro."[18]

In Houston, Texas, barely a month later, the country witnessed a different response to the violence at the core of race relations in the South. A battalion of the all-black Twenty-fourth regiment had arrived in the city late in July to guard federal property while Fort Logan was under construction. Prior to coming to Houston, the unit of 654 soldiers had been stationed in the Philippines and at bases in the western United States, where they experienced little racial discrimination and won public commendations. In Houston, the men faced the humiliations of Jim Crow, an openly hostile white community, and a police force known for brutalizing black people. Skirmishes on streetcars and trolleys, the accumulation of insults and harassment, and episodes of soldiers fighting back, verbally and physically—all stirred a potent brew of racial tension that ultimately gave way to a rebellion by black troops.[19]

On August 23, an encounter between two soldiers and two police officers lit the fuse. When Private Alonzo Edwards saw police officers dragging Mrs. Sara Travers, half dressed, from her home, he intervened and tried to help her. The police beat Edwards and arrested him. Corporal Charles Baltimore, a black military police officer, came upon the scene and tried to inquire about Travers and Edwards. The police attacked him. As Baltimore fled, they shot him in the back of the neck and arrested him. News of the arrests and rumors that Baltimore had been killed filtered back to Camp Logan. Soldiers made plans to attack the police station and seized rifles and ammunition. By early evening, Baltimore had returned to the camp and joined the operation. Sergeant Vida Henry, who had thirteen years of service with the military, took command of the men. More than one hundred soldiers set out for town at around eight o'clock that night. When they encountered resistance along the way shooting broke out. The fighting lasted for two hours until it was suppressed by the National Guard. Sixteen whites were dead, including five policemen. Two black civilians were killed and four black soldiers died from injuries suffered. Sergeant Henry took his own life.[20]

The Houston outbreak exposed the problem faced by the U.S. military when it stationed black soldiers in the South, allowing local custom to dictate the treatment of federal troops. The incident realized white southerners' worst fears about black soldiers and revived southern white protests against stationing black troops in the region. As soon as word of what happened in Houston reached New York, the NAACP dispatched Martha Gruening to investigate. Her detailed report of the "Houston riot" and the events leading up to it identified the "primary cause" as "the habitual brutality of the white police of Houston." *The Crisis* reprinted the report in full. The army moved swiftly to prosecute the soldiers, initially charging sixty-three men with mutiny and murder. They were tried over three weeks in November in the largest military trial in U.S. history. On November 30, after two days of deliberation, the court announced the verdicts and imposed the sentences in a closed session. Fifty-four of the defendants were found guilty of all charges. Thirteen were to be hanged, and forty-one were sentenced to life in prison.[21]

Before dawn on the morning of December 11, 1917, the thirteen men condemned to death were taken under the cover of darkness and secrecy to a clearing on the banks of the Salado Creek. The verdicts had not been publicly announced, nor had they been reviewed and approved by the president and secretary of war, as was military policy in the case of death sentences. During the night, the Army Corps of Engineers hastily built a large wooden scaffold. A bonfire lit the area. The condemned men rode to the execution "singing a hymn, but the singing was that of soldiers on the march." When they saw the scaffolding, they realized that their final request to the army had been denied. The soldiers had asked to face a firing squad, a more dignified end than the army's most severe punishment—death by hanging. Witnesses said that the men displayed "neither bravado nor fear." They refused blindfolds. The order to execute was given at dawn. Later that morning, Major General John Ruckman announced the executions of the thirteen and the verdicts for all of the men convicted during the first trial.[22]

News of the secret hanging and failure to allow for a presidential review of the sentences stirred a wave of grief and anger across black America. "Thirteen young strong men . . . have gone to their death," Du Bois wrote somberly, ". . . soldiers who have fought for a country which never was wholly theirs; men born to suffer ridicule, injustice, and at last death itself." Legal punishment, he conceded, "we cannot protest." But he railed against "this shameful treatment which [they and we] receive all our lives, and which our fathers received and our children await; and above all we raise our clenched hands against the hundreds of thousands of white murderers, rapists, and scoundrels."[23]

The NAACP, working with leading black newspapers, spearheaded the campaign to secure clemency for men condemned to death in two subsequent trials. James Weldon Johnson led a small delegation to Washington and obtained a meeting with President Wilson, to whom they presented a petition with twelve thousand signatures. "The hanging of the thirteen men without the right of appeal . . . was a punishment so drastic and unusual" the petition held, ". . . that the execution of additional members of the 24th . . . would savor of vengeance rather than justice." The petition described the circumstances that fueled the outbreak and also reminded the president of the lynchings and other racial atrocities that had taken black lives in the preceding months. Johnson found Wilson surprisingly interested and engaged. He promised to review each of the cases, and ultimately commuted the sentences of ten of the men to life imprisonment, while affirming the death sentences of six others. The NAACP continued to work for the release of the sixty-one former members of the Twenty-fourth Infantry in Leavenworth Prison, many serving life terms, until the last one was released twenty years later.[24]

On November 5, 1917, a major blow against the legal edifice of segregation offered some psychological relief from the wave of violence that crested on the heels of America's entry into World War I. Ruling in *Buchanan v. Warley*, the U.S. Supreme Court unanimously overturned Louisville's residential segregation ordinance. The justices took note that the Court had previously upheld laws that separated the races on the basis of equal accommodations and equal privileges in transportation and schools. But such legislation had limitations when it exceeded restraints established by the Constitution. The Court held that the Louisville ordinance, clearly designed to limit the rights of blacks to acquire property, was a violation of the Fourteenth Amendment. Moorfield Storey, who argued *Buchanan v. Warley* before the Supreme Court, hailed the ruling as "the most important decision that has been made since the *Dred Scott* case, and happily this time it is the right way." Squeezing hope from a dismal season, the *Chicago Defender* predicted that this "slap" at the South would "lend zest to the millions of our people who are ready to aid and even die for this country in the present great struggle for true democracy."[25]

Buchanan v. Warley did not reverse the trend toward residential segregation in urban areas, North or South. Whites found other ways to achieve similar ends, working through neighborhood associations, cooperative realtors, and perfecting the use of restrictive covenants; harassment and violence often proved most effective in policing and enforcing racial boundaries. Thus, as one battle ended, others loomed. Nevertheless, *Buchanan* was an important victory for the NAACP at a critical moment. It had an immediate impact in Louisville and other cities, overturning residential ordinances in St. Louis, Baltimore, Birmingham, Richmond, and Norfolk, and stimulated growing support for the association. In Louisville alone, NAACP membership climbed from 89 to 1,431 in the aftermath of the *Buchanan* ruling. This victory would be a touchstone in the NAACP's continuing effort to broaden its base and increase membership during the war years.[26]

Two additions to the national staff at the start of 1918 brought the opportunities created by the war more firmly within reach. In January the board appointed John Shillady, a middle-aged white social worker, as executive secretary. "Tall, fine-looking, with gray eyes and graying hair," Shillady's quiet personality and attentive nature enhanced his effectiveness. He was a hardworking and efficient manager and kept a steady rein on the swelling whirl of activity that centered in the national office. Within weeks of taking his new post, he met with Moorfield Storey and devised plans for a major membership drive as a way to commemorate Storey's seventieth birthday—aiming for fifty thousand members, a fivefold increase. He also took an active role in what had become a central concern of the association—the fight against lynching.[27]

The board also acted on James Weldon Johnson's recommendation and hired Walter White for the new position of assistant field secretary. The twenty-four-year-old insurance salesman reluctantly left a promising business career in Atlanta for an uncertain future in race advancement work. It meant "abandonment [of] all the plans of financial security I had made," he recalled. Most everyone he sought advice from agreed, saying he'd be a fool to give it all up for "an almost hopeless cause." His father was an exception, encouraging his son to consider the advantages he had had and his responsibility to help those less fortunate. And maybe there was a deeper desire to fight in a larger arena for a young man whose baptism in racial consciousness came when he was twelve years old, in the heat of the Atlanta race riot. Whatever reservations may have lingered, they vanished as he immersed himself in what would become his life's work.[28]

Walter White was not on the job two weeks when he and Johnson learned of the lynching of Jim McIlherron in Estill Springs, Tennessee—the third burning at the stake to occur in that state in nine months. White volunteered to go undercover and investigate. The blond, blue-eyed Georgian was so fair-skinned that he could slip across the color line and move among whites as if he were one of them. He headed to Tennessee posing as a salesman and carrying press credentials from Villard's *New York Evening Post* as a backup. White talked with a variety of local citizens in this poor, isolated town—

mostly whites, including several who had witnessed the lynching. He learned that Jim McIlherron had a reputation of being a "bad sort"; he had lived in the North for a while, his family owned their own land, and the McIlherrons refused to bend to the will of whites. An altercation with a group of young white men ended when Jim McIlherron allegedly shot and killed two of them. White reconstructed the events leading up to the lynching and detailed the sadistic rituals of torture that slowly extinguished McIlherron's life. Witnesses had complained to him that their victim never cringed or begged for mercy, deriding the mob's efforts to break his spirit. "The Burning of Jim McIlherron," published in *The Crisis*, offered a sample of the intrepid reporting that White would become famous for.[29]

Just three months after the McIllheron lynching, White journeyed to Brooks and Lowndes counties in the southernmost part of Georgia to investigate what he described as "a holocaust of lynchings." The bloody spree was sparked when Sidney Johnson, a black farm-worker, murdered Hampton Smith, a large landowner known for beating and abusing the men who worked his land. Smith's wife was also shot, but survived. A mob quickly gathered to reap revenge, stirred by talk of a conspiracy among blacks to kill Smith. They claimed at least eleven victims, including Hayes Turner. Mary Turner protested the killing of her husband and promised to have warrants sworn out against the guilty parties. The mob then turned its vengeance on her in "a way so revolting and . . . horrible," White wrote, "that it is with reluctance that the account is given." White went on to describe, in gruesome detail, the lynching of Mary Turner, who was eight months pregnant. Hung by her ankles from a tree, they burned the clothes from her body and then, while she was still alive, split open her abdomen. Her baby fell to the ground, and its head was crushed under the heel of one of her executioners. They finished by firing hundreds of bullets into her body. White obtained the names of seventeen members of the lynch mob from an unsuspecting informant. Using his press credentials, he gained access to Georgia governor Hugh Dorsey and personally delivered the names of the seventeen along with a report of what had transpired.[30]

White's reports from Tennessee and Georgia fed news stories across the country. With a national spotlight turning southward, prominent citizens in Tennessee organized a Law and Order League and pledged to end such vigilante activity. Georgia's Governor Dorsey issued a strong statement against mob violence and warned that if state authorities did not suppress it, federal intervention would surely follow. In North Carolina, Governor Thomas

Bickett dispatched troops to Winston Salem to hold back a mob set on lynching a prisoner. Most notably, the NAACP efforts to engage President Wilson finally bore fruit when, in July 1918, Wilson issued a statement denouncing mob violence. He urged that governors, law officers, and "men and women of every community . . . cooperate . . . actively and watchfully to make an end to this disgraceful evil. It cannot live where the community does not countenance it."[31]

Working in tandem with Shillady, White and Johnson invigorated the NAACP's antilynching campaign. The association had established an antilynching committee in July 1916, following the lynching of Jesse Washington in Waco, Texas—a horrific episode that amplified images of the region's depravity. The seventeen-year-old Washington, accused of raping a white woman, was hanged in front of thousands of spectators and his charred corpse was left hanging in the downtown area for several days. The committee pursued a comprehensive program of investigation and publicity and also worked to identify southern leaders who might be allies in the antilynching fight as a "law and order" issue. Shillady assigned two researchers to the Library of Congress to research all of the lynchings that had been documented since 1890, resulting in the publication of *Thirty Years of Lynching*. Published in the spring of 1919, the widely distributed book provided a tally of more than 2,500 lynchings—providing names, dates, location, sex, manner of death, and charges against the victim. Less than 20 percent of the victims had been accused of rape, puncturing a popular mythology regarding the "defense of white southern womanhood."[32]

In addition to pursuing more active efforts to document and expose lynchings, the NAACP turned attention toward securing congressional legislation and working more deliberately to mobilize national opinion. In April 1918, two Republican congressmen, Leonidas Dyer from St. Louis and Merrill Moores of Indianapolis, each introduced an antilynching bill. Dyer had taken the lead in obtaining a congressional investigation of the East St. Louis race riot and had a good working relationship with the NAACP. Based on the Fourteenth Amendment, his bill aimed to guard "citizens of the United States against lynching" when local government failed to act, thus denying victims equal protection of the law. It became the standard for NAACP-supported antilynching measures over the next three decades. That same year, Shillady initiated plans with the Anti-Lynching Committee to organize a national conference on lynching that aimed to bring together influential leaders and public-opinion shapers.[33]

Thus began what would be the long and at times dispiriting effort to use whatever tools were available to mobilize opinion and test American tolerance of ritualistic torture that almost always went unpunished. It was highly unlikely that Congress, dominated by Democrats, would act affirmatively in the near future. But the mere introduction of legislation placed lynching on the national agenda and opened the way toward organizing political support. The most effective course in the short term, as Moorfield Storey noted, was to arouse public opinion in the South in a way that might expand the "law and order" movement that had begun in Tennessee, "and in the North so as to make the southern people feel that what they are doing is done under the eyes of the world and is mere barbarism." The tepid response to the NAACP's initiatives offered a measure of white America's indifference to the crime of lynching, but the association did count small victories—when a local official stood up to the mob; a governor sent troops to safeguard a prisoner; the rare indictment and prosecution of accused lynchers; and the small but growing chorus of legislators in Washington and in state legislatures who joined the voices calling for government action.[34]

A major goal of the NAACP during the war years was to increase its black membership base; this effort energized the organization and fueled a remarkable period of growth. Service in the armed forces, migration, and rising racial tensions all contributed to heightened black claims on citizenship. "The field was ready to be harvested," Johnson recalled. Reporting on a tour through the Midwest and along the eastern seaboard in July 1918, he noted that "everywhere . . . I saw evidence of the fact that people were awakening to the realization that the National Association stands as the most effective means through which the race may voice its protests against unfair treatment and by which it may make known its desires to the whole country." The numbers bore out Johnson's claim. By July, membership had quadrupled from 9,282 to nearly 36,000 with branches in thirty-five states.[35]

The growth of the NAACP outside of the South followed along patterns that had already been established. Branches formed to meet the expansion of racial segregation and exclusion, as whites in northern and western cities sought to contain growing black populations fueled by wartime migration. In some areas, efforts to restrict public places or segregate hospitals and public schools were in violation of local or state civil rights statutes; NAACP branches provided a venue for investigating and challenging these practices. NAACP branches in Michigan, Pennsylvania, and Ohio took the lead in lobbying for a state civil rights law modeled on an amended law enacted by New

York in 1913, which provided "that full and equal accommodations shall be enjoyed by all persons within the jurisdiction of the state at all public resorts, places of amusement, and public accommodations." As racial boundaries tightened around housing and employment, NAACP branches supported protests and legal challenges and lobbied elected officials to hire blacks in public service jobs. Police brutality and criminal justice issues often sparked the organization of a branch, as did efforts to provide support for southern migrants. National campaigns around antilynching and in response to the East St. Louis race riot were also factors in broadening the membership of the NAACP. Beyond specific issues, there was a shared sense of becoming part of something larger. As the secretary of the Denver branch wrote, they established a branch "so that local interests of colored people might be better protected as well as to give added strength to the NAACP."[36]

The expansion of the NAACP into the South was the major development of the war years. After his initial tour of the region early in 1917, Johnson wrote confidently that "when the Association has spread over the entire South, as it is certain to do, and the thinking men and women of the race feel and know they are leagued together with thinking men and women of both races all over the country for one and the same purpose . . . many are the changes that are going to be brought about." Johnson's faith in the willingness of black southerners to enlist in the NAACP was not disappointed. Over the next two years, the NAACP established branches in every southern state, in rural areas as well as urban centers. But this ambitious incursion into Jim Crow territory won few white supporters and ultimately generated widespread resistance and backlash. In the end, the wartime growth of the NAACP in the South succeeded in establishing what Walter White described as "our first line trenches in the fight on prejudice."[37]

Southern branches organized around a variety of issues and created an arena for civic activism and leadership. Atlanta's branch led the new branches in membership and served as an anchor for the early growth of the NAACP in Georgia while providing a recruit, Walter White, for the national office. Founding members included representatives of the city's leading black institutions and churches, such as John Hope, president of Atlanta University; Benjamin J. Davis, editor of the *Atlanta Independent*; A.D. Williams, pastor of Ebenezer Baptist Church (and future maternal grandfather of Martin Luther King Jr.); W.J. Trent, secretary of the Atlanta YMCA; George Towns, Atlanta University professor; and Harry Pace, secretary-treasurer of the Standard Life Insurance Company. Atlanta was unique in that no women were invited to the founding conference. But women did take an active part in the branch's first major campaign to improve public school conditions for the city's 75,000 black youth.[38]

The branch's education campaign began as an effort to halt the city's plan to abolish the seventh grade in the black public schools and over the next two years grew into a major drive to increase appropriations for black education. When the city refused to accommodate their demands, the Atlanta branch sponsored a massive voter registration drive, working through churches and house-to-house canvassing. The all-white Democratic primary thwarted effective black participation in the election of candiates to office, but elections on bond issues were open to all. After a vastly enlarged black electorate helped to defeat several bond issues dedicated to school spending for all of Atlanta's public schools, the city finally pledged over $1 million for black schools, resulting in the construction of Booker T. Washington High School, the city's first public high school for black students. Under the leadership of attorney A. T. Walden, the Atlanta branch developed an active legal redress committee, which provided assistance to a burgeoning network of branches around the state, numbering sixteen by 1920.[39]

Charleston, South Carolina, was among the most active new branches. Its first protest targeted the exclusion of black women from six hundred new wartime jobs for women in the Navy Yard's clothing factory. R. Augustine Skinner, the politically well-connected president of the Minneapolis branch, and Archibald Grimké aided the Charleston branch in bringing pressure to bear on Congress and the secretary of the navy. By November 1918, 250 black women had been hired. The branch mounted a campaign to secure jobs for black teachers in Charleston's black public schools, successfully challenging a long-time policy of hiring only white teachers. Thousands attended mass meetings in support of the effort, and the branch "raised up an army" of volunteers to collect signatures on petitions, including twenty-year-old Septima Clark, who would become a leading activist in the state. Charleston, like most branches, pursued criminal justice cases. Through its dogged efforts, the branch secured the indictment of a white streetcar conductor for killing "a highly respected Negro mechanic." Despite overwhelming evidence of guilt, the man was acquitted by an all-white jury. "We hardly expected a conviction," branch president Edwin Harelston wrote the national office, "[as] such things are unheard of in these parts." Nevertheless, there was great satisfaction in having brought the murderer to trial; it was "the first time in at least twenty years that a white man in Charleston County has been tried by a jury for the murder of a Negro."[40]

The range of activities carried on by the southern branches reflected the kinds of challenges communities faced and could effectively organize around. In Savannah, the branch lobbied the city council to block a plan by the mayor to locate the "red-light district" of unofficially sanctioned prostitution in the black neighborhood near West Broad Street. They succeeded, and as a result "the stock of the NAACP soared." In Columbia, South Carolina, voter registration and participation was a major focus of branch activity; as a result of the increased number of blacks on the registration rolls, four blacks were called to serve on a jury—a rarity in the South. The Memphis branch attempted to follow Atlanta's lead and organized to secure increased appropriations for black schools; in Jacksonville, Florida, the branch petitioned the board of education to obtain summer school opportunities and salaries for black teachers commensurate with what white teachers received. Beyond the importance of particular issues, such efforts helped to advance what Wilson Jefferson of the Augusta branch described as "a healthy public sentiment." Reporting on the impact of NAACP activity in his city, Jefferson told Johnson that "the old spirit . . . of let well enough alone is fast dying out."[41]

The NAACP offered a place where southern blacks could assert their rights under the banner of a national organization dedicated to securing their citizenship, creating a sense of possibility in a society where they lacked access to the traditional levers of political power. "We are hoping for great things through the NAACP for our people," wrote Margaret Downs McCleary, the dynamic secretary of the Jacksonville, Florida, branch. Yet her correspondence to the national office, while mostly brimming with news of a vibrant and growing branch, revealed that McCleary struggled hard to hold on to hope. "In this work we find much that is discouraging," she wrote. "But I suppose nothing more can be expected when we fight against such terrible odds." More support and unity among blacks would enable them to do much more, she noted. However, white arrogance, the daily indignities, and the nature of power in the Jim Crow South tested her fortitude. McCleary reported on the cold-blooded murder of a successful black man by a policeman who had already killed several other black men. "As you know the white man, in most cases, is conscienceless," she wrote Johnson. "[At] the slightest pretext they are instantly transformed into raving, inhuman brutes bent on torturing and killing anyone of our Race." A report that the War Department was planning to use black draftees to work on farms had stirred up much feeling and discussion in the branch and even got the conservative members riled up. If that injustice were permitted, she wrote, "then civil war is directly before us . . . as our men will not submit to what would be, in these Southern states, virtually convict life." Looking toward the long struggle ahead, she asked Johnson, "Is it not true that any race of people who have wrenched from their oppressors their inalienable rights have had to do so with the greatest sacrifices and suffering? Must we not prepare also to pay the price?"

Johnson assured McCleary that he would pursue the issue regarding black troops with the War Department and urged her to stand firm, praising her efforts in Jacksonville. He had great confidence that the growth of the NAACP in the South would cultivate a spirit of resistance and activism essential to undermining the demeaning and dispiriting culture of segregation and establishing a foundation for change in the region. Toward this end fieldwork was critical not only to organize new branches but to support existing ones, helping to counter a sense of isolation and futility. White and Johnson traveled frequently in the South, and they encouraged leaders of some of the stronger branches to visit other branches in their area. Johnson hired George Towns of the Atlanta branch to aid in building up the association in Georgia, South Carolina, and Florida, and in the fall of 1918 he enlisted Mary Talbert to conduct a major organizing campaign in the Southwest.[42]

Talbert, a leading civic activist and president of the National Association of Colored Women's (NACW) clubs, served on the NAACP's national board. Based in Buffalo, New York, Talbert had participated in the founding of the Niagara Movement more than a decade earlier and was one of the NAACP's most devoted supporters, playing an important role in coordinating the work of the NACW and the NAACP. Her trip through the Southwest combined an NAACP/NACW–sponsored tour to sell Liberty Bonds for the war effort with her efforts to promote the NAACP and aid in establishing branches.[43]

In her two-month-long swing through the Southwest, Talbert addressed nearly sixty meetings for the NAACP and an estimated 35,000 people. She told Johnson that Texas was "thoroughly aroused; everywhere they are anxious to join the association." Talbert organized eight new branches in Texas and one in Louisiana and helped to revive existing branches in the region. C.B. Carlton, secretary of the Beaumont, Texas, branch, wrote that Talbert had brought in more than fifty new members, people beyond his reach, and urged the national office to send representatives on a regular basis. Working through her contacts in the Texas Federation of Colored Women's Clubs, Talbert made a special appeal to women and recruited volunteers to continue organizing in Texas after she was gone. Early in 1919, Johnson wrote Talbert that "the Texas branches are coming along splendidly. My opinion is that Texas is going to be one of the strongest states in the association." By summer, Texas could claim the largest statewide membership, with 7,046 members organized into thirty-one branches.[44]

The new organizational power of the NAACP was on display during an intense struggle over black labor rights. In the spring of 1918, a "work or fight" provision was added to the Selective Service Act, authorizing local draft boards to order men of draft age to work at jobs considered essential to the war effort or face induction into the armed forces. This provision was seized upon throughout the South to tighten control over a black labor force that had gained a slight measure of autonomy as the war and the migration broadened employment opportunities. Georgia, one of the first states to act, passed its own version of the law, applying it to all male residents of the state between the ages of seventeen and fifty-five. It held that failure to be "regularly engaged in some lawful, useful, and recognized business, profession, occupation, trade, or employment" was a misdemeanor, which made the accused liable for arrest and imprisonment. The NAACP's Atlanta branch lobbied successfully to eliminate a provision including women in the state law.[45]

Cities and towns in Georgia and throughout the South quickly enacted variations of "work or fight" laws. In August 1918, James Jordan, an NAACP member in Wrightsville, Georgia, reported on the "work or fight" ordinance passed in his town. It applied to all able-bodied persons, male and female, and required that they be in the same occupation at least fifty hours a week. The law required workers to have employers sign a work card each week and then turn cards into the police. Upon investigation, Jordan found that the cards were only being issued to black women. He asked the national office to advise him on the legality of this law, noting that black citizens in Wrightsville were prepared "to fight it out with your assistance."[46]

During the fall of 1918, Walter White conducted a six-week-long investigation of "work or fight" orders throughout the South. After a week in Alabama and Georgia, White reported that the use of such ordinances to control black labor was much more widespread than he had anticipated, particularly in rural communities and smaller towns. Often the orders were directed against women who quit domestic work to earn better wages elsewhere.[47]

White reported on a case in Wetumpka, Alabama, a small town outside Montgomery, where the mayor's cook quit when he refused to increase her wage. The mayor had her arrested the following morning, and the next day she was tried in court before the mayor himself. She was fined $14, a fine the mayor paid before ordering the woman back to work. In Birmingham the city employment agency ordered all black women to "either go to work or go to jail." Twenty black women were arrested on the first day the order went into effect. Several days later Mrs. Andrew Ferguson, wife of "a respectable colored man" was arrested while sitting on her porch paring potatoes for supper and charged with vagrancy. She was held in jail overnight and released after her husband paid a $25 fine.[48]

In some larger towns and cities, blacks succeeded in defeating these measures. In Jacksonville, Florida, when blacks protested the provision targeting women in a "work or fight" ordinance, it was repealed. When the city council of Bainbridge, Georgia, attempted to force married women to work outside their homes under the local "work or fight" law, black men promised to resist with violence if necessary. The law promptly fell into disuse. In Thomasville, Georgia, women were arrested for vagrancy and forced to work on public streets pulling up weeds and cleaning. White reported that through the efforts of a newly organized NAACP branch, this practice was stopped.[49]

White's travels across the South were sobering. Writing from New Orleans on November 16, 1918, five days after the war ended, he confided to John Shillady: "I have become convinced on this trip as never before that the white man of the South is absolutely incapable of practicing democracy so far as any case where the Negro is concerned." He reported on the revival of the Ku Klux Klan as but one indication of how white southerners planned to meet the return of Negro soldiers who may have "new" ideas about democracy. Now, he concluded, "the problem we have confronting us fighting discrimination in the South is ten times as great as it would be if the war lasted two years longer, and we will be forced to work ten times as hard."[50]

A month later, an encounter on a street car in Alabama set in motion a series of developments that illuminated the forces vying to define the South's postwar racial order. Sergeant Edgar Caldwell, stationed at Camp McClellan outside of Anniston, was riding the streetcar in town when the conductor charged that he had not paid his fare. Caldwell insisted that he had but the conductor ordered him off the car. The soldier refused to leave unless his fare was returned. A scuffle ensued and, aided by the motorman, the conductor physically threw Caldwell from the car; they continued to kick and beat him as he lay on the pavement. Caldwell drew his gun and fired, killing the conductor and wounding the motorman. In the publicity surrounding the incident, the white press falsely charged that Caldwell had attempted to sit in the white section of the car, feeding rumors that Caldwell, who was from Atlanta, was a "damn yankee Negro soldier" who had come south to start trouble. There was talk of a lynching.

For the Reverend R. R. Williams, the arrest and trial of Edgar Caldwell was "a test case of what is coming after the war." Shortly after Caldwell's arrest, he sent an urgent appeal to the national office of the NAACP, reporting that the case was being rushed through the courts for fear of mob violence. He requested the association's assistance in obtaining "a fair and impartial trial." John Shillady promptly responded, advising that they secure a good lawyer and explaining that he would write to the Montgomery, Alabama, branch and to Robert Church in Memphis urging them to assist in these efforts. Williams and his associates hired B. M. Allen, a well-regarded lawyer from Birmingham. After a swift trial, before a jury "fully under the influence of race prejudice," Caldwell was convicted of first-degree murder despite overwhelming evidence that manslaughter was the highest offense he could have committed. He was sentenced to be hung.[51]

Blacks in Anniston organized a branch of the NAACP and over the next year and a half worked in conjunction with the national office and James Cobb, head of the Legal Bureau of the NAACP's D.C. branch, to overturn the conviction and save Caldwell's life. The Anniston branch contributed the largest sum toward the defense, with additional support provided by the five other branches in Alabama and aid raised nationally by the NAACP. James Cobb donated his services. Caldwell's attorneys argued that since he was a soldier at the time of the shooting, it was the responsibility of the federal government to ensure that he received a fair trial. The NAACP appealed to the War Department, the Department of Justice, and directly to the president and supported appeals that ultimately brought the case before the U.S. Supreme Court in March 1920. The case hinged on the interpretation of a 1916 revision of the War Articles. According to Caldwell's lawyers, it gave the War Department complete jurisdiction over criminal offenses committed by military personnel, requiring that Caldwell receive a new trial before a military court. The U.S. solicitor general's office submitted an amicus brief in support of Caldwell's case. The Supreme Court ruled on a narrow interpretation of the War Articles, upholding the authority of the state in this case. Appeals to Alabama governor Thomas Kilby to commute Caldwell's death sentence failed. Edgar Caldwell was hung on July 30, 1920.[52]

While he met a tragic end, Caldwell demonstrated that blacks were prepared to fight back—a critical factor in the volatile terrain of postwar race relations. For many soldiers, the struggle over the meaning of wartime service began in France, where they were the targets of racist propaganda, discrimination, and insults by white American officers and troops—much of it documented by W. E. B. Du Bois, who spent three months in France during the winter of 1918–1919 interviewing black troops. Charles Houston's experience as a second lieutenant steeled his determination to study law and fight "for men who could not strike back." Native South Carolinian and army sergeant Osceola McKaine joined with fellow black officers in Le Mans, France, and founded the League for Democracy, vowing to keep the militant spirit fueled by the war alive and to bring it home. P. A. Williams, secretary of the Austin, Texas, NAACP branch, wrote early in the summer of 1919: "The boys that are returning from overseas are telling of their mistreatment by the Americans [and] arousing a racial feeling that is likely to give vent to rioting at any provocation. They have returned to old homes but are not going to submit to old conditions." NAACP branches in Texas became a forum for ex-soldiers, whose accounts invigorated the movement to secure rights "which had been bought by blood." In a May 1919 *Crisis* editorial, Du Bois announced, "We return fighting," rallying blacks to "marshall every ounce of our brain and brawn to fight a sterner, longer, more unbending battle against the forces of hell in our own land."[53]

Early in the summer of 1919, the NAACP held its annual conference in Cleveland, under the banner: "To Make America Safe for Americans." With membership at more than 55,000, this was by far the largest such gathering held in the association's ten-year history, and the most representative. Two hundred eighty-four delegates and members attended, representing thirty-four states; more than a third of the delegates were from the South. The one hundred southern delegates "made themselves heard" and were among the most aggressive and outspoken participants. The weeklong meeting featured overflowing crowds at public sessions on topics from the experiences of black soldiers to the antilynching campaign and the importance of voting. There were daily forums for branch officials from all parts of the country to report on their work and to exchange ideas and strategies. The branch reports and discussions revealed many areas of activity and concern: voter registration drives in a number of southern cities; the successful collaboration of the Michigan branches in securing a state civil rights law, and continuing like efforts in Ohio and Pennsylvania; campaigns against "work or fight" laws; the issues arising from southern migration to northern urban areas; the problems facing industrial workers in the North and rural workers in the South; and protests against the treatment of returning veterans. Delegates also discussed organizational matters, such as obstacles to racial unity, strategies for boosting membership, and the advantages and disadvantages of creating statewide organizations. With all sections of the country represented, Cleveland became a critical part in the process of knitting local concerns and struggles into the fabric of a national movement. At the urging of the southern delegates the conference voted to hold its next annual meeting in the South, in Atlanta.[54]

In the month following the Cleveland convention, major race riots broke out in Longview, Texas, Washington, D.C., and Chicago. In Longview, an interracial love affair triggered the assault by a white mob on a black residential area, where they torched homes and killed at least four black men. The press whipped up white fury in Washington with a series of sensationalized stories implicating blacks in a wave of sex crimes. A crowd of more than a hundred white soldiers in uniform invaded the southwest section of Washington, randomly beating black people, sparking three days of rioting. James Weldon Johnson, who investigated the riot for the NAACP, reported that black "men and women . . . were . . . mobbed, chased, dragged from street cars, beaten and killed within the shadow of the Capitol." Six people were killed outright and hundreds wounded. Arming themselves with guns brought in from Baltimore, blacks fought back. Just days after order was restored in Washington, an assault by whites on a twelve-year-old black swimmer who floated into the "white" section of Lake Michigan resulted in his drowning. Failure of the police to arrest those who had attacked the boy led to fighting between blacks and whites, which escalated into a weeklong riot in Chicago that left thirty-eight people dead, twenty-three blacks and fifteen whites. The fact that blacks fought back, Johnson observed, marked a "turning point in the psychology of the whole nation regarding the Negro problem."[55]

Local NAACP officials were targets of violence and harassment after the war. In Memphis, where the branch was planning a suit to secure equitable distribution of school funds, the white press denounced branch officials as "instigators," dividing the branch leadership and causing the branch to drop the challenge. A mob drove leaders of the NAACP branch in Anderson, South Carolina, from the town; the local paper reported that their advocacy of social equality had contributed to "the increasing insolence of many Negroes in the city."[56] In Tchula, Mississippi, the Reverend E.R. Franklin was arrested for distributing *The Crisis*. Dr. D.D. Foote, president of the Vicksburg, Mississippi, branch, wrote to Johnson from Chicago, reporting that the branch had been suppressed and he and several officers driven from the state. He told Johnson that "under the guise of patriotism, we were called disloyal citizens because we asked for a reform, a real democracy." Dr. J.A. Miller, secretary of the branch, was "given a coat of tar and feathers" before he was able to leave town. In a bold stroke, the Reverend A.J. Browne revived the Vicksburg branch six months later.[57]

The most aggressive campaign against the NAACP was waged in Texas, where memories of the Houston mutiny were still fresh and black veterans infused the activism of new NAACP branches. In July 1919, Governor William Hobby ordered an investigation of the NAACP and the black press in response to rumors, growing out of the Longview riot, that blacks were buying guns and planning an uprising. The NAACP's Austin branch had played an active role in defending twenty-one men jailed as a result of the violence in Longview. Hobby consulted with federal investigators, who had been monitoring black protest activities since the start of the war, telling them that "Bolsheviks" or some other "sinister source" was working to array Negroes against constituted authorities. The following month, Austin branch president P.A. Williams was summoned to appear before the justice of the peace, along with the records and correspondence of the branch, and warned that the branch was not chartered to do business in the state. The national office acted swiftly to support the Austin branch and counter the state's action. "We must stand strongly behind the locals," Johnson told Ovington. "It may be that the whole future of the organization in the South depends on what we do at this moment."[58]

On August 20, John Shillady traveled to Austin to meet with state officials and answer any legal objections to the operation of the NAACP. Armed with NAACP literature, he assured the assistant attorney general and other state officials that the association relied on legal and constitutional methods and insisted that the branches had nothing to do with purchasing arms and planning attacks on whites. Later, a hearing before a "court of inquiry" grew hostile as Shillady met charges that the NAACP promoted racial equality; the presiding county judge advised him to leave the state. The following day, after meeting with officials of the Austin branch, a mob that included the county judge and local constable attacked Shillady outside of his hotel, beating him almost to unconsciousness. Shillady left by train, with a warning not to stop within the state limits. Bruised and battered, he returned to a hero's welcome in New York's Penn Station, where Red Caps (porters) organized a spontaneous demonstration of support. But he was badly shaken by the experience. He resigned within the year, having lost confidence in the ability of "overcoming the forces opposed to Negro equality by the means and methods . . . within the Association's power to employ."[59]

Shillady's assailants publicly claimed responsibility, charging that he "was inciting the negroes against the whites." When the NAACP urged the governor to punish the offenders, Governor Hobby replied that Shillady was the offender and advised that "your organization can contribute more to the advancement of both races by keeping your representatives and their propaganda out of the state." Continued harassment by state and local officials was reinforced by a revival of the Ku Klux Klan in Texas. By 1920, most NAACP activity in Texas had ceased.[60]

In neighboring Arkansas, barely a month after Shillady was assaulted, black efforts to assert freedoms experienced during the war culminated with a massacre. Phillips County, in the Delta region of southeastern Arkansas, was a center of booming economic growth, fueled by the timber industry and cotton production and supported by a black workforce of mostly sharecroppers and tenant farmers. Over one thousand black men from the county served in the war; those who stayed behind enjoyed expanded labor opportunities in the local timber industry, benefited from high cotton prices, and shared in the county's prosperity. After the war, landowners moved to reassert control over the black labor force and were alert to any threat of "unionization" invading the area. The ambitions and expectations of blacks in Phillips County were not easily contained. A primary issue of contention was the right to market their own crops and obtain a fair settlement for the shares they sold to the landlord. Toward this end, sixty-eight black farmers joined the Progressive Farmers and Household Union of America (PFHUA) and hired Ulysses Bratton, a white Little Rock attorney, to represent them. When whites attacked a meeting of the union at a church in Hoops Spur, blacks fired back, killing one white man.[61]

Upon hearing news of the "shootout," the sheriff deputized three hundred men to hunt down union members; planters deputized their own posses. On the following day, more than six hundred landowners, veterans, and law enforcement officials from Arkansas and Mississippi reinforced the "army" to suppress the rumored black insurrection. All phone lines from Elaine, the county seat, were cut. At Governor Charles Brough's request, the secretary of the army sent 583 federal troops to the area, including a machine-gun battalion. Their commander, Colonel Isaac Jenks, ordered the troops to kill any black person who refused to surrender. Indiscriminate shooting and killing over a two-hundred-mile radius took an untold number of black lives; most estimates ranged from two to three hundred. White fatalities registered from five to twenty-five. More than one thousand men and women were arrested; many were interrogated and tortured. The alleged leaders of the insurrection were quickly indicted and tried. Sixty-seven were sentenced to long prison terms, and twelve were sentenced to death.[62]

During the weeklong siege, prominent businessmen and public officials constructed their versions of the events. They reported that blacks were organizing an insurrection under the directions of a union, and planning to murder landowners and plantation managers. Walter White immediately went south to investigate what happened outside of Elaine, Arkansas. Passing as a white reporter for a Chicago newspaper, he interviewed the governor and leading white officials, met with several of the jailed defendants, and pieced together a story that countered the widely publicized claim that the state had promoted. The root cause of the trouble, according to White's investigation, was that whites were determined to suppress any efforts on the part of black sharecroppers to exert control over their labor. His reports on the Arkansas case exposed the system of peonage that reigned in eastern Arkansas and successfully challenged the state's version of events. Soon national newspapers adopted the NAACP's interpretation of what happened—namely that the government officials and landowners would not tolerate a black union and used the full force of the state to crush these efforts. The NAACP led in organizing the defense of the twelve sentenced to death, working with black attorney Scipio Jones and a locally based Citizens' Defense Fund Commission that raised at least $10,000. The case, *Moore v. Dempsey*, ultimately made its way to the U.S. Supreme Court.[61]

During 1919, fear of subversives became a national obsession. That year, a wave of strikes involving 4 million workers from Seattle to Boston marked the greatest period of labor unrest in the nation's history. This massive display of labor activism coincided with a series of anarchist bombings and attempted bombings and amplified warnings that the Bolsheviks who had triumphed in the Russian Revolution had infiltrated the United States. The U.S. Senate and state legislatures initiated investigations of the labor movement for subversive influences, police raided radical centers, and New York state passed legislation making the Socialist Party illegal. Attorney general A. Mitchell Palmer, whose home was the target of a bomb, led a series of high-profile roundups of hundreds of aliens, many of whom were deported. In August 1919, he hired J. Edgar Hoover to head up a Bureau of Investigation to track down radicals, which became the basis for the Federal Bureau of Investigation.[64]

Within this climate, racial conflict loomed as one of the greatest threats to domestic peace. Commenting on the thirty-eight race riots that erupted across the nation during 1919, the *New York Times* observed that "a new ne- gro problem" had come out of the war and that it was arguably "the most grave [problem] . . . facing the country." In a search for causes, the article fo- cused attention on the rise of a militant black leadership that had eclipsed the conciliatory approach advocated by Booker T. Washington. The *Times* ad- mitted there was a difference between revolutionaries sympathetic to bolshe- vism and militants like W. E. B. Du Bois, fighting an uncompromising battle against the color line, but the distinctions blurred in that both approaches stoked racial unrest. The paper voiced a common fear that blacks were some- how more susceptible to revolutionary doctrine. The military surveillance program of the War Department had monitored blacks since the start of the war, paying close attention to black soldiers and veterans, as well as protest organizations. The postmaster general briefly considered suppressing the May 1919 issue of *The Crisis*, which included Du Bois's report on black sol- diers in France and the "We Return Fighting" editorial. In October 1919, a representative of the Justice Department visited the office of the NAACP and inquired about funding sources and whether there was any "Bolshevik talk" or "tendencies" among personnel. Government officials dedicated to promoting social order often linked black protest to subversive elements, en- hancing the challenges facing the NAACP.[65]

Following the state-sponsored assault on NAACP activity in Texas and attacks in other parts of the South, a number of board members expressed reservations about holding the 1920 annual conference in Atlanta. Mary White Ovington polled branches and asked whether they would send a del- egate if the meeting were in Atlanta and inquired specifically of southern branches whether meeting in Atlanta would strengthen their position. Those opposing an Atlanta conference warned that it was too dangerous. The as- sault on Shillady, wrote Boston's Butler Wilson, demonstrated the inability and unwillingness of public authorities to protect citizens engaged in the work of the NAACP. Some argued that a climate of fear and intimidation would compromise freedom of speech. The Philadelphia branch added that declining the invitation to meet in Atlanta would serve as "a strong protest against the attitude of the South toward colored people." Supporters of the Atlanta meeting contended that the NAACP could not give into intimidation. Meeting in Atlanta would demonstrate they had the courage of their convictions. It also offered an opportunity to educate whites to the purposes of the NAACP. The Braddock, Pennsylvania, branch believed it would draw the branches closer together and "make those in the South feel we are greatly interested in doing our part to help better their condition as well as our own." Quincy, Illinois, contended that they would be as safe in Atlanta as anywhere else in the United States. Harry Pace of Atlanta urged that the issue must be fought out in the South and that now was the time. The responses were evenly divided nationally and among southern branches, for and against. After nearly two hours of debate, the board voted to go to Atlanta.[66]

Never before had a national organization dedicated to racial equality sponsored a conference in the South. Atlanta, the self-styled New South city, was the place where Booker T. Washington had sanctioned the new order of "separate but equal" in his famous 1896 speech, often referred to as the "Atlanta Compromise." Ten years later the city was the scene of one of the worst race riots in the nation's history. Now Atlanta's mayor welcomed the NAACP, an organization committed to ending segregation, along with hundreds of black and white delegates from around the country. Such a gesture hardly signaled an endorsement of the organization's goals; racial segregation was an article of faith, even among the region's most liberal whites. Yet Atlanta's desire to host the conference revealed a rare convergence of interests and concerns.

The race riots and lynchings that swept the South after the war had led to the founding of the Commission on Interracial Cooperation (CIC) in Atlanta a year earlier. The CIC, organized by young Methodist minister Will Alexander, established a program for bringing blacks and whites together in a formal organization with chapters around the South dedicated to promoting "better understanding" between the races and defusing the climate of fear and hate that led to violence. NAACP leader Harry Pace described the CIC approach as "a group of white men endeavoring in their own way to reach some sort of working basis with a similar group of colored men." This modest attempt to bridge the color line was a significant development in the South at this time and reflected widespread concern that the "race problem" was reel-ing out of control. A reporter covering the NAACP meeting in Atlanta found that local whites and blacks were in agreement on at least one thing—the South was "sitting on a volcano." The desire to stem racial violence created a common ground of sorts for employers anxious to hold on to black labor, civic boosters concerned with the South's image, white reformers dedicated to taming the excesses of the Jim Crow system, and NAACP activists joined in challenging the foundation of the South's caste system.[67]

The NAACP approached the Atlanta meeting as a historic opportunity and worked to ensure a large attendance and a roster of participants that would take advantage of their southern location. The association made arrangements with the Southern Railway to secure special Pullman cars that would leave from three primary destinations—Washington, D.C., Cincinnati, and Memphis—and carry delegates to Atlanta. Atlanta University agreed to provide housing and breakfast for delegates at the nominal fee of $1.25 a day. The new Butler Street branch of the YMCA served as the registration center. In preparing the program, the Atlanta branch took the lead in securing the participation of the city's leading white business, political, and civic figures—including Mayor James West; Eugene Black, the president of the Chamber of Commerce; Plato Durham, the dean of Emory University's School of Theology; Sam Dobbs, the president of Coca Cola; and the Reverend Ashby Jones, a founding member of the newly established Commission on Interracial Cooperation, headquartered in Atlanta.[68]

Three evenings of public plenary sessions held in the Bethel A.M.E. Church were filled to overflowing. More than three thousand people attended the gatherings each evening, including the 227 delegates who participated in the conference. The NAACP hired publicity experts to ensure that the conference attracted national attention, doubtful that the southern white press was capable of "giving fair and unbiased accounts." The *Christian Science Monitor* and the *New York Times* were among the national newspapers that provided daily coverage of the public proceedings. The *Atlanta Constitution* proudly claimed that nationwide interest was focused on the city as host to a conference of men and women "who express the opinion that the relation between the races will be clarified by frank discussion."[69]

Mayor West welcomed the conference, which he hoped would demonstrate to the country that Atlanta was a "broadminded city, willing to try to solve its problems through cooperation of the races." Arthur Spingarn, substituting for the ailing Moorfield Storey, introduced the NAACP at its first major public forum in the South by saying: "We have no views to present that are so radical that they cannot be found in the Sermon on the Mount or in the Constitution of the United States. Mutual tolerance, mutual sympathy, and mutual respect must be cultivated. All our problems must be solved with justice." Over the next several days, the narrow and indeterminate approach of the Atlanta-based interracial movement competed with a spirited discussion of the inequities at the root of the "race problem" that all agreed existed and specific proposals for change.[70]

The public meetings discussed migration and labor, lynching and segregation, and education and the ballot. In the session dedicated to migration and labor, Plato Durham of Emory University reported on the work of Atlanta's interracial group in bringing "leading citizens" together to advance mutual understanding and promote racial justice. Robert Bagnall, an NAACP leader from Detroit, countered that interracial conferences would do nothing to curtail the exodus of blacks from the South. Reporting on the migration to Detroit, which saw the black population soar from 9,000 to over 55,000 in just three years, Bagnell declared that the "only hope of the Negro lay in his continued migration to the North until the South is forced through economic necessity" to end legal segregation, equalize educational opportunities, and provide full voting rights. Joel Spingarn proposed that southern states establish governor-appointed interracial committees with even representation of blacks and whites to investigate incidents of racial violence and friction and make recommendations for legislation and policy.[71]

Some of the highlights of the public sessions included Charles E. Russell's detailed account of the vast inequalities in public education in the South, which he linked to the problem of illiteracy that had been exposed as a great source of national weakness during the war. Russell offered statistics showing that eight to ten times more public funding was spent on white as compared with black students. Florence Kelley discussed the importance of organizing to advance economic and political rights, offering labor unions and the women's suffrage movement as models. Suffragist and National Women's Party leader Ella Bush Spencer reported on the impending passage of the Nineteenth Amendment. James Weldon Johnson spoke about lynching, offering statistics that debunked the common assumption that rape was its primary cause and noting that more than fifty women had been lynched over the previous thirty years. He introduced five proposals that provided the basis for the resolutions ultimately endorsed by the Atlanta conference: abolition of lynching by federal action, equal access to the ballot, the abolition of "Jim Crow" transportation, equal educational and industrial opportunities, and the abolition of legal segregation.[72]

For Du Bois, the Atlanta meeting was a homecoming of sorts. At an outdoor ceremony in front of Stoner Hall at Atlanta University, he was awarded the NAACP's Spingarn Medal, the fifth recipient of an award created and endowed by Joel Spingarn to focus national attention on black men and women of distinguished accomplishments.[73] On the closing night of the conference, Du Bois reached for a consensus around the issue that concerned a broad spectrum of opinion—from business groups and the Commission on Interracial Cooperation to the NAACP—the desire to end mob violence. Lynching, Du Bois pointed out, flourished in direct proportion to the extent that blacks were disenfranchised. So long as black people were denied the franchise, appeals to racial prejudice and violence would rule the South. "In the Negro's defenseless state," he warned, "[he is] an invitation to every lawless and reactionary movement."[74]

The determination of the white South to keep a lock on the ballot box was on full display in the months that followed the Atlanta meeting. After the war the ballot had become the most contested symbol of the "new" democracy sought by blacks and feared by whites. Wartime service in the cause of democracy and the widely heralded principles of self-determination enshrined in the peace treaty buttressed spontaneous efforts among blacks throughout the South to vote. Early in 1919 a Greenwood, Mississippi, newspaper reported that "a good many Negroes" had shown up at the circuit clerk's office for the purpose of registering to vote. "Such a thing," the paper exclaimed, "is simply unthinkable."[75] Less than three months before the 1920 presidential election, the passage of the Nineteenth Amendment granting women the right to vote further energized black voter registration efforts throughout the South.

The struggle around the right to vote gave coherence and focus to the NAACP's southern organizing work. In the months leading up to the 1920 election, the association received letters from individuals in different parts of the South telling of their efforts to vote and the methods used to bar them from registering. These testimonies revealed the willingness of southern blacks to risk humiliation, physical abuse, and even death to participate in an electoral process that promised few short-term gains. One Oklahoma man explained, after being turned away four times by the registrar, "I am wanting to vote to suit myself." Countless reports tell of individuals returning to the registrar's office multiple times after being turned away. L.W. Fields, a black lawyer in Hampton, Virginia, where the hostile treatment of black women at the county courthouse had invited a special NAACP investigation, told of his nearly fatal encounter after his wife was mistreated by a registrar. "I was ready to die for the way she was treated. We are too weak. Some of us must die."[76]

These bold efforts signaled a civic-mindedness and personal fortitude that was representative of a broader change in expression of black political consciousness. "Black men are determined as never before not simply to vote," Du Bois observed in June 1920, "but to make their vote tell." The Republican Party's efforts to woo southern white voters at the expense of black loyalists along with the emergence of the black vote as a factor of consequence in key northern urban areas encouraged an independence among black voters and a willingness to explore new tactics and political alliances. In discussions around the 1920 election, NAACP officials missed no opportunity to point out that black voters would soon hold the balance of power in key northern industrial states. The association developed a questionnaire that it sent to all of the presidential candidates, as well as candidates for Congress, inviting them to state their position on issues that were of particular concern to black voters.[77]

While the growing number of black voters in the north promised to become a critical lever in developing national policies sensitive to racial issues, the South offered the primary arena of struggle. The great majority of blacks lived in the South and their efforts to secure voting rights and protest the abuses of Jim Crow countered common assumptions about the nature of race relations in the region. The extreme measures southern whites took to keep blacks from voting offered compelling evidence of the flagrant disregard for democratic procedures inherent in the Jim Crow system. Building on inroads that had been made during the war years, the NAACP's national leadership actively encouraged voter registration efforts and suggested ways for individual branches to coordinate their efforts. They worked through contacts to identify patterns of voter discrimination and began building a case for a congressional investigation of disenfranchisement in the South.

Many of the reports sent to the NAACP office highlighted strong turnouts by black women and the arbitrary and legally unsound methods used throughout the South to bar them from registering to vote. In Birmingham, Alabama, where the local NAACP conducted voter education classes for women around the city, the registrar turned down thousands of women "on grounds of color."

Clara Mann reported from New Bern, North Carolina, that the registrar told the black men and women who attempted to register that they must read the state constitution, commit it to memory, and write it out. She and several others insisted on going forward, assuming that the registrar would give in when he saw how determined they were. Exasperated, he told her that if she "was the president of Yale and colored" she could not register. In Americus, Georgia, the registrar avoided registering women by hiding the book, or saying it was in another precinct, or by simply leaving. Local officials in Mobile, Alabama, drove black women out of the registration office, threatening to jail them if they refused to leave. Butler Nance reported that the Columbia, South Carolina, branch had "a very big fight" on its hands. The registrars had invented new educational requirements for black women attempting to register and were turning away college graduates and teachers who had been certified by the state of South Carolina. "Please give this publicity," he advised James Weldon Johnson, "in order to let the world know the kind of 'DEMOCRACY' our sons fought for on the battlefields of France."[78]

Johnson and Walter White advised local branches on how they might proceed, providing examples of how other branches handled similar situations and frequently urging them to hire local counsel to challenge the registrar's actions. Clara Mann replied that "it is impossible for us to employ lawyers here not even for a handsome price. We have two very competent lawyers here but they wouldn't do anything against the white people." Channing Tobias reported a similar situation in Hampton, Virginia, where black women were barred from voting on specious grounds. "No white lawyer would take the case and no colored lawyer dared to." When the Vian branch in Oklahoma responded that "we don't know a lawyer here or anywhere," White contacted several other Oklahoma branches urging them to assist the Vian branch. Ultimately the twelve NAACP branches in Oklahoma joined together and hired counsel to work in their behalf to secure their right to register.[79]

Florida offered some of the most egregious examples of white resistance to black voting. In Ocoee, the determination of Jules Perry to vote led to a white assault on the black section of town. The *New York Times* reported the riot on the front page, describing a shootout between blacks and whites while whites torched more than twenty black homes and businesses. Newspaper accounts said that six black people and two whites had lost their lives, but according to testimony gathered by Walter White, at least thirty-two men, women, and children burned to death in the fires or were shot as they tried to escape burning houses. The mob lynched Jules Perry. In Suwanee County, two brothers who had been active in voter registration were beaten by a white mob and driven from town. In Jacksonville, where blacks made up roughly one half of the total population, voter registration among black women exceeded that of white women, causing the local paper to warn that "Negro washerwomen and cooks" would dominate unless white women turned out. Several nights before election day more than a thousand Klansmen paraded in Jacksonville as a warning to blacks to stay away from the polls. Black voter turnout, however, far exceeded previous years. Polling places were segregated by race and gender, providing four separate entrances. More than four thousand black citizens were left standing in line when the polls closed.[80]

In the aftermath of the election, the NAACP secured a hearing before the House Census Committee, chaired by Isaac Siegal of New York, to investigate the disenfranchisement of blacks during the 1920 election season. With the support of a handful of congressmen, the NAACP aimed to press for enforcement of provisions of the Fourteenth and Fifteenth amendments, which would reduce southern states' membership in the House of Representatives in proportion to the actual voting population. On December 29, 1920, black and white spectators crowded into a small congressional hearing room and heard testimony from four representatives of the NAACP: James Weldon Johnson, the newly appointed secretary of the organization; assistant secretary Walter White; recently hired field secretary William Pickens; and James Cobb of the NAACP's Washington D.C. Legal Committee.

In a remarkable scene, four black men went before a congressional committee to testify about the fraudulent, violent, and state-sanctioned methods used to deny black men and women the right to vote in the South and to request federal action. Southern representatives met each claim "with a storm of denials" and countercharges "that gathered in volume as the session progressed." When Walter White described the lawlessness that pervaded many southern communities, "southern members of the committee," the *Washington Post* reported, "jumped to their feet." Representative W.W. Larsen of Georgia protested the "wholesale charges of slander against one section of the United States." Congressman Carlos Bee of Texas energetically supported his colleague, adding: "Knowing what we have done in upbuilding the Negro race, I cannot sit in silence under a statement made by a witness from New York." As he tried for naught to rein in his colleagues, Chairman Siegel wryly suggested the southern members might like to take the witness stand. Samuel Brinson of North Carolina described ignorant Negro voters as a threat to that state's civilization, while protesting that he and his fellow white southerners were doing everything they could "to help the colored." Bee warned of "the evil agitation that has been fostered among them" and joined his colleagues in peppering White with questions about the NAACP—wasn't it true that the organization sent secret agents south? Where did they get their money? Siegel reminded his colleagues that this was not a trial.[81]

White persisted through the harangue and provided a clear statement of what happened in Florida, even as members interrupted to question the validity of his evidence. William Pickens described the way in which the disenfranchisement of black voters inflated the power of southern white voters as compared with other parts of the country, noting that one white man in the South had four to ten times the voting power of a northern voter. Johnson followed and debunked the accusations and misrepresentations floated by the southern members. "We all know very well," Johnson declared, "that the colored people generally throughout the southern states are not allowed to vote under the same qualifications and requirements of the white citizens." He told of how during a recent trip through the South he had interviewed thirty-five editors of white southern newspapers. While they all opposed lynching and said that the Negro should have a fair deal, all but one expressed the belief that the Negro should not have the privilege of voting.[82]

"The Negro today is not the Negro who was emancipated, illiterate [and] penniless," Johnson explained. They defended the country during the Great War, and their loyalty was well known. Negro men and women were qualifying themselves to vote "and when they are qualified they have the right, and you cannot go on denying them forever." How long was Congress prepared to let this situation continue, he asked? It was a fundamental question at the root of republican government, and it could not be covered up. If Congress shrinks from the challenge, the question will not go away, he cautioned, but will "continue to come up in the future with increasing force." Johnson's appeal did little to quell the southern members in their efforts to twist the purpose of the hearing. They asked what the NAACP was doing to promote the moral uplift of Negroes and whether the association made any effort to prevent Negroes "from doing [the kinds of things] that cause lynching." Midway through the hearings, a newspaper photographer appeared to take a photograph. The southern representatives refused to sit for a photograph with a background dominated by the large group of black men and women who had crowded into the hearing. Representative James H. Aswell of Louisiana stomped out

of the room in protest. In an effort to avoid further disruptions, the committee went into executive session and cleared the room of spectators.[83]

The NAACP's board of directors reported that the organization received
more publicity on the testimony before the House Census Committee than
on any other matter it had handled up until that time. It was front-page news
in many southern newspapers. White took pleasure in reading editorials in
the southern press denouncing the association. "They don't realize they are
giving us thousands of dollars of free advertising," he wrote Butler Nance.
While most editorials in the white southern press attacked the NAACP, the
Memphis *Commercial-Appeal* contrasted the composed approach of the
NAACP's representatives with the humiliating behavior and bullying tactics
of several of the southern congressmen. "From this exhibition it seems quite
clear that the South must improve the quality of its representatives."[84]

The *Washington Bee* echoed the sentiment of the black press at large, praising the presentation made by the NAACP's representatives in the face of
endless harassment. They "put the South on the defensive," the *Bee* reported,
"by supporting a good case with thorough and complete knowledge of the
law . . . and of the facts which make this situation a reproach . . . to the pres-
ervation of law and order." The *Houston Observer* reported on James Weldon
Johnson's assessment of the hearing. Commenting on the behavior of southern committee members, Johnson declared, "It is nothing short of a national
scandal that representatives of the people should actually be opposed to a
congressional investigation to determine whether or not there is representative government in the United States."[85]

The effort to obtain a congressional investigation of disenfranchisement in
the South won scant congressional support. Congressman George Tinkham
of Massachusetts introduced a resolution calling for such a probe. The House
voted it down 285 to 46. Yet, while failing to secure effective congressional
action, the organization had succeeded in focusing attention on the blatant
disregard for citizenship rights at the heart of the southern segregation system. According to the *New York Times*, the brief flurry of activity around the
issue of voter discrimination struck fear in the hearts of southern representatives, who worried that continued agitation would garner sympathetic support among some northern organizations. In 1920 Southern Democrats
wielded enough power to block any federal action that might threaten the
segregation system. But the struggle to frame the public debate around the
issues raised at the hearing was just beginning and would play a critical role
in shaping the course of the civil rights struggle.[86]

The NAACP's support of voting rights efforts and its success in bringing the issue of disenfranchisement before the United States Congress marked a major achievement in the effort to weld the isolated struggles of local communities into a nationally oriented movement. For southern blacks, affiliation with the NAACP amplified their claim to citizenship rights and sustained a sense of possibility. Caesar Simmons, president of the Boley, Oklahoma, branch, articulated sentiments shared by many when he wrote that communications from the national office have "aroused in every individual . . . a new spirit of encouragement and inspiration and hopefulness." Writing from Jacksonville, Florida, in the fall of 1920, Mrs. Janie Lowder put it this way: "Without the help of a most high and just God, and the help of the GREAT NAACP, we here in the South would be completely helpless." Butler Nance of South Carolina assured William Pickens that he had not been completely "swamped by the avalanche of violence" that had engulfed the South. "I am thankful that I am still alive and fighting for what is ours."[87]

Early in 1921, in a testimony to what the NAACP had come to represent in the most repressive part of the nation, fifty sharecroppers formed an NAACP branch in Democrat, Arkansas, not far from Elaine. Correspondence from the branch described slavelike conditions. "We are treated like dogs regardless to the laws that is issued," wrote one member. The mail from the New York office was opened and local whites threatened to break up the branch "and make another Elaine scrape out of it." But the men and women who formed the Democrat chapter persisted and appealed to the NAACP for aid in getting what they knew was theirs. "We pay all of the tax and do all of the work and can't get no protection for our family so we want to know what to do," several members wrote. Letters to the New York office asked them to tell the Department of Labor and other officials in Washington about conditions in Democrat, the stealing and violation of labor contracts and general lawlessness. "We are calling on you up there because we can't get there to ask for ourselves." Walter White forwarded these reports to the Justice Department. The branch held on for two years, until the president was forced to leave the area. While branches often faded, the NAACP maintained a presence in the Deep South because it stood as a national organization representing and affirming rights brutally denied by white southern society. A member from Pine Bluff, Arkansas, wrote that the NAACP "has given the race a second emancipation."[88]

The expansion of the NAACP into the South was at the core of the transformation of the organization that took place during the war years. By working to root itself in the experiences of African Americans just as the massive demographic shift northward began, the NAACP was strategically positioned to give voice and direction to the rising expectations and militancy generated by the war. The association was left fighting a mostly defensive battle, however, as it tested the receptiveness of white Americans to the democratic vision that framed its program. The organization did not notably increase its support among whites and secured few tangible gains in the struggle to reverse the tide of racial discrimination—North and South.

By 1920 the NAACP had established the outlines of a national movement for racial justice and civil rights—a multifront struggle that would be waged in the courts, in legislative arenas, in the realm of public opinion, and anchored in black communities around the nation. Membership reached close to one hundred thousand, a tenfold increase in just three years. However, the viability of the organization and the movement it aspired to lead would be sorely tested in the decade following the war. In the South, inroads made during the war slowly dissipated in the face of white reprisals and the limited ability of the NAACP to aid in countering violence and repression or in securing relief from the injustices embedded in the South's racial order. Outside of the South, aggressive and often violent efforts to contain growing black populations and limit black opportunity suggested that most northern whites embraced racial attitudes that differed little from their southern brethren. As he took the helm of the NAACP at the close of 1920, James Weldon Johnson's primary task would be to hold the ground that had been secured and to develop a strategy for navigating the seemingly barren terrain of postwar America. [89]

4

Making a Way:
The "New Negro" in Postwar America

"The New Negro, who stands today released in spirit," wrote Oklahoma newspaper editor Roscoe Dunjee in 1920, "finds himself in America . . . physically bound and shackled by laws and customs that were made for slaves." The postwar militancy that alarmed whites was "the battle of free men pounding on the walls that surround them."[1]

In Tulsa, Oklahoma, a bold expression of civic activism had dire consequences. In the spring of 1921, several black veterans, intent on preventing a rumored lynching, led an armed group of some forty men to the courthouse to guard a man accused of assaulting a white woman. The violent response of whites to this gesture escalated into a massive assault on the black section of town, known as Greenwood, one of the most prosperous black urban areas in the nation. Blacks defended their lives and property but were overpowered by mobs of whites aided by several National Guard units, whose rampage wreaked the wholesale destruction of businesses, churches, and homes. Estimates of the fatalities ranged from 35 to 150, and property damages topped $1.5 millon. Walter White warned that America ignored the lesson of Tulsa at its peril. Was the nation prepared to enforce the law and protect the rights of all of its citizens, or "was America waiting for a nationwide Tulsa?"[2]

The postwar season of riots and lynchings along with tightening segregation in all parts of the nation tested a central tenet of the NAACP's approach: a faith in the capacity of American democracy to bridge the color line and function equitably. The efforts of black people to assert the full measure of their citizenship met an unyielding determination on the part of many whites to enforce black subordination, in the North as well as in the South. The Los

Angeles branch of the NAACP urged the national office to take a more aggressive approach. Appeals to reason and fairness were worthless; "there should be a veiled threat, a subtle suggestion that the Negro was ready to fight back."[3]

The black migration of the war years continued at a high rate through the 1920s and dramatically altered the racial terrain of urban areas across the nation. The doubling and tripling of black populations in many northern and western cities supported the growth of black churches, businesses, and other institutions, fostering the development of a vibrant social, cultural, and political milieu. White racial intolerance grew apace. Black men and women faced hardening patterns of racial restrictions that limited their access to public places, constrained their opportunities, and fueled a housing crisis that exacerbated urban problems of poverty and crime. Restrictive covenants, discriminatory lending practices, and white neighborhood associations combined to create what one Los Angeles resident described as "invisible walls of steel," confining blacks to marginal residential areas. White-owned businesses, department stores and financial institutions only hired blacks for the most menial positions; most labor unions barred black workers from membership. Restaurants, theaters, and places of public recreation were generally off limits to African Americans. In the years following World War I, an "informal and unofficial caste system" took root in northern cities.[4]

The emergence of large, diverse black communities in northern cities brought a fuller exploration of ways to advance the interests of black Americans. A. Philip Randolph, Hubert Harrison, Cyril Briggs, and other young activists looked toward socialism and labor solidarity as the most promising path for a people who were increasingly urban and industrial and almost completely of the working class. Charles S. Johnson, who emerged as a primary architect of the Harlem Renaissance, promoted the cultivation of black art and literary talent as a more effective strategy for alleviating racial tensions than a direct challenge to discrimination. The Jamaican-born Marcus Garvey amplified the spirit of the "New Negro" with his dramatic appeal to racial pride and uplift, and galvanized what NAACP official William Pickens described as "the first great movement of the masses of [Negro] people." His ambitious plans for a black-run shipping line, his embrace of Africa, and the pageantry of his movement combined to mobilize hundreds of thousands of men and women. Chapters of Garvey's United Negro Improvement Association (UNIA) sprang up across the nation, in some places eclipsing inroads made by the NAACP.[5]

James Weldon Johnson, who assumed the NAACP's top administrative position in 1920, was deeply engaged in the discourse regarding the future of black America and the search for effective strategies and tactics. Racial pride and unity was a theme he continually emphasized, in terms that were compatible with the impulse that drove Garveyism. A rift between Marcus Garvey and the NAACP leadership developed, fueled by Garvey's disdain for what he viewed as the light-skinned, elitist leadership of the NAACP and the NAACP's questioning of Garvey's business practices, his leadership style, and his embrace of black separatism. For black Americans struggling from day to day in an aggressively hostile society, both the UNIA and the NAACP offered tools for self-determination. Yet at a fundamental level, the Garvey movement and the NAACP offered quite different visions of what was possible and desirable for black Americans. While Garvey saw no future for blacks as part of the American mainstream, the NAACP program remained anchored in the fight for full inclusion in the life of the nation. "Since we have [already] paid the price . . . in labor, . . . in loyalty, . . . in blood," said Johnson in a 1922 speech, "let us resolve that we shall get for ourselves and those who come after us . . . the precious things for which the price has already been paid."[6]

The board of directors' appointment of Johnson marked a new departure for the NAACP. Several members had been reluctant to break with the tradition of whites serving as executive secretary. But their doubts gave way to the firm conviction of Du Bois and others that a black person be appointed and, moreover, that there was no one, black or white, better prepared to lead the association than Johnson. His political savvy, diplomatic skills, and leadership abilities were notable, his work in the field invaluable. For three years, Johnson had traveled the country, building the association, establishing personal contact with NAACP branches and observing the varied contexts of black life and race relations. During this time he had become well acquainted with the workings and politics of Washington and had established relationships with liberal and radical reformers in New York. After Johnson served as acting secretary for five months, the board finally appointed him executive secretary in November 1920.

Johnson presided over a period of development and growth that set the future course of the NAACP. The interracial board steadily deferred to his experience and leadership, causing the center of power to shift from the board to the office of the executive secretary, marking the "clear-cut ascendancy of black influence" within the NAACP. Walter White, his ambitious, energetic and brash young assistant, complemented Johnson's cool and even disposition; the two made a formidable team. In addition to William Pickens, who replaced Johnson as field secretary, Johnson expanded the field staff to include Robert Bagnall as director of branches and Addie Hunton as a full-time field organizer. They joined W. E. B. Du Bois and Herbert Seligman, recently hired press official, as the core paid professional staff; Seligman was the sole white member of this group. Johnson's engaging personality and willingness to delegate responsibility enabled him to cultivate his associates in a way that reinforced their collective strength and ability. With the exception of Hunton, they remained together for as long as Johnson served.[7]

By the early 1920s, approximately 85 percent of the NAACP's support came from black people, which Johnson described "as one of the most hopeful signs yet." This base was fertile ground for realizing Johnson's vision for the association and the change it sought to advance. "What we need and must have is power," Johnson wrote an associate early in 1921. "It is time for colored men and women of clear brain and red blood to discredit the weak kneed, compromising teachings that have been so long foisted on the race. We must put up a bold front and let this country realize that we know the things we want, we know the things we are entitled to, and we are determined to have them at any cost."[8] More than any concrete achievements, the foremost mission of the NAACP, Johnson emphasized in a 1922 speech, was "to awaken the American Negro" and not only make him realize what he is entitled to, but to "instill a determination to get it." Determination, however, was not sufficient. "We must have the machinery," Johnson proclaimed. "Individuals amount to very little. . . . It takes mass action."[9]

Johnson was guided by the goals that had informed the association's program since its founding a decade earlier, but the war and its aftermath changed his understanding of the challenges they faced. The spread of segregation in the North along with the nation's continued tolerance of the terror and lawlessness that enforced racial caste in the South defied the hopes that had attended the founding of the NAACP—that publicity, exposure, and agitation would generate an interracial movement dedicated to ending racial discrimination and building an inclusive democracy. While the NAACP continued to seek white support and involvement, it was clear that the power to make change rested primarily with black Americans. Black veterans and a growing black population outside the South amplified demands for full citizenship. During the 1920s, Johnson and White worked in tandem across a broad front of activity—initiating the fight for civil rights legislation in Washington, establishing a permanent legal defense program, leveraging the incipient power of the black vote, and enlisting the arts in the cause of black freedom and racial equality. Connecting all of these struggles was the growing synergy between a nationally focused movement for civil rights and struggles in communities across the country.

The fight against lynching galvanized the association's postwar program. Lynchings were occurring at a rate of more than one per week after the war. In 1920, black demands for legislation to make the crime a federal offense provided the Republican Party with an opportunity to recommit itself to this increasingly important segment of the electorate. The Republican Party plank urged Congress to consider "the most effective means to end lynching," describing it as a "terrible blot on our American civilization," a position publicly endorsed by party nominee Warren G. Harding. A Republican sweep at the polls in November created an unprecedented opportunity for securing anti-lynching legislation, and early signs suggested that the administration was committed to acting on the party's pledge. In a special message to Congress shortly after his inauguration, Harding declared that "Congress ought to wipe the stain of barbaric lynching from the banners of a free and orderly representative democracy." His statement coincided with the revival of the Dyer anti-lynching bill, initially introduced in 1918. Sponsored by Leonidas Dyer of St. Louis, the bill would make lynching a federal crime, allowing for the prosecution of officials who negligently failed to prevent lynchings as well as members of the mob and providing that counties where lynchings took place pay $10,000 to the victims' families. Johnson led the campaign to secure passage of the bill and the NAACP orchestrated the first major congressional debate over federal protection of civil rights since the Reconstruction era.[10]

A convergence of developments created a favorable climate for passage of the Dyer bill. A body of opinion outside die-hard proponents of states' rights had questioned the constitutionality of such an extension of federal power, because lynchings involved the action of individuals who acted independently of the state. By 1921, however, this point of view had yielded significantly to the argument that failure of local law enforcement to protect the lynching victims or to prosecute mob members amounted to a violation of the Fourteenth Amendment's provision that no state shall "deprive any person of life, liberty, or property without due process of law; nor deny any person within its jurisdiction the equal protection of the laws." There were fifty-five lynchings recorded in 1920, and in more than half the cases, victims had either been removed from jails or taken from officers of the law. Furthermore, the

Eighteenth Amendment, ratified with the support of southern states in 1919, imposed federal regulation in barring the sale and transport of alcohol, paving the way, some argued, for the kind of federal intervention provided for in the Dyer bill. Moorfield Storey prepared a brief supporting the constitutionality of the legislation. Attorney general Harry M. Daugherty led the list of eminent officials who supported the legislation early in 1921 and held that its provisions were constitutional.[11]

"The entire machinery of the NAACP, its full organizational strength and all the collateral force it could muster were thrown behind" the Dyer bill, Johnson recalled. During the year and a half that the legislation made its way through the House and the Senate, Johnson spent nearly all of his time in Washington while Congress was in session. Working closely with Dyer and other supporters of the bill, he conducted an intensive lobbying campaign on Capitol Hill while White mobilized public pressure behind the bill at critical points. Theodore Burton, congressman from Ohio, and Senator William Calder of New York provided office space for Johnson. He immersed himself in the legislative process, researching and writing speeches for several congressmen and providing supporters of the bill with essential facts and figures—statistics, for example, demonstrating that less than 17 percent of the victims of lynching had been charged by the mob with rape. "I tramped the halls . . . constantly," he wrote, meeting with every representative who was interested in the legislation and those he thought could be won over. The first victory came when the House Judiciary Committee reported favorably on the legislation in October 1921. Dyer and Johnson strategized successfully on getting the bill to the floor for a vote when Congress reconvened after the holidays.[12]

Several hundred black spectators filled "every available nitch" in the galleries when the bill was debated on the floor of the House. Two days of bitter debate were punctuated by a heated exchange between Congressman Robert Sisson of Mississippi and Henry Cooper of Wisconsin. In his attack on the bill, Sisson bandied the false charge that rape was the main cause of lynchings and warned that mob violence would not be stamped out until "black rascals keep their hands off the throats of white women." When Cooper chided Sisson for openly advocating mob rule on the floor of the House, blacks in the galleries rose up and cheered. "Sit down niggers," Southern Democrats shouted from the floor, to which a voice replied, "We are not niggers, you liar." Republican leader Frank Mondell described lynching as "anarchy in its most abhorrent and degrading form" and insisted that "it is high time that the

Federal government assert its authority, the States having failed utterly to assert theirs." Burke Cochran of New York dismissed southern howls about federal usurpation of state power. "If the Federal government can reach out and snatch a mug of beer from the hand of a peaceable citizen," Cochran said, "surely it has the authority to reach out and snatch a halter from the hand of a lyncher." Republicans cut off delaying tactics by Southern Democrats and brought the bill to a vote at the end of January, easily winning passage by 230 to 119 votes. Eight northern Democrats voted in favor of the bill. The *New York Times* attributed the impressive victory to "an insistent countrywide demand."[13]

Johnson faced a steeper climb in the Senate. In addition to a strong southern bloc of opposition, leading senators claiming expertise in constitutional law, like Republican senator William Borah of Idaho, held that the bill was unconstitutional. Borah charged that those seeking to transfer powers vested in the states by the Constitution to the federal government were "lawless brothers" of those who joined the mob and took the law into their own hands. Congress watchers predicted that the Senate would let the bill die "because it stirred up so much feeling in the House." Johnson and the NAACP pushed ahead with an accelerated campaign of political pressure, heightened publicity and mass protest, while news of shocking atrocities from the South provided continuing evidence of the need for action. Early in May, as the bill languished in a Senate Judiciary subcommittee, Johnson delivered a petition to Republican leader Henry Cabot Lodge, urging action on the bill. It was signed by twenty-four governors, along with leading lawyers, jurists, religious figures, newspaper editors, college presidents, and other influential figures. That same day, three black men were roasted to death in the town square of Kirvin, Texas; Johnson sent copies of the front-page story in the *New York Times* describing the gruesome killing to every senator. Less that two weeks later, in front-page stories, the *Times* and the *Washington Post* reported on the torture and burning "over a slow fire" of fifteen-year-old Charlie Atkins before a mob of two thousand people in Davisboro, Georgia. After he was dead, the crowd fired two hundred bullets into his corpse.[14]

During the late spring and summer, mass meetings, marches, and escalating letter-writing and telegram campaigns engaged people around the country, kept the issue of lynching before the public, and provided Johnson and his allies with added momentum in the effort to get action from the Senate. Hundreds marched in New York and Newark demanding passage of the anti-lynching bill. On June 14 five thousand black men, women, and children paraded around the U.S. Capitol and to the White House to protest; among the marchers, several young boys carried a placard that read "We are Fifteen Years Old. One of Our Age was Roasted to Death." At the NAACP's national convention later that month, Helen Curtis proposed that women mount a campaign in support of the Dyer bill, resulting in the establishment of the Anti-Lynching Crusaders. The group, under the direction of Mary Talbert, launched a nationwide campaign to mobilize "one million women" to aid in securing Senate passage of the bill. Working through women's-club networks at the local and state level, the crusaders raised money and organized letter-writing campaigns targeting the senators from their individual states.[15]

Senator Lodge, who introduced petitions in favor of the bill from his constituents, played a central role in keeping the measure alive. Early in the summer, "to the surprise of the Senate," according to the *New York Times*, the Judiciary Committee reported favorably on the bill by an 8-6 vote. More delay followed. Samuel M. Shortbridge, the junior senator from California, managed to bring the bill to the floor of the Senate shortly before adjournment at the end of September, only to be outmaneuvered by Senators Pat Harrison from Mississippi and Oscar Underwood from Alabama, who blocked the bill from coming to a vote.[16]

The final showdown came during a special session of the Senate in November. Republican supporters ensured that the measure was on the agenda and the NAACP made one last effort to arouse public opinion and win passage of the bill. With the support of a grant from the newly established American Fund for Public Service and funds raised by the Anti-Lynching Crusaders, it ran a full-page ad in the *New York Times* and ten other major newspapers just after the session opened. "The Shame of America" was printed in large letters across the top of the page, and a stark, factual account of the prevalence of lynching followed. The ad reported that "the United States is the only land on earth where human beings are burned at the stake" and noted that eighty-three women were among the nearly 3,500 lynched since 1889. Half of the page was devoted to a description of the Dyer bill: the essential law enforcement mechanism it provided, responses to popular questions about the bill, and a summary of the consensus of legal and scholarly opinion attesting to its constitutionality. It urged readers to telegraph their senators to support enactment of the bill.[17]

In an unprecedented move at the start of the special session, southern senators announced that they were going to block all legislative business "until we get an understanding that this bill won't be passed," previewing a tactic that would become a hallmark in future battles over civil rights legislation. Up until the Dyer bill, the filibuster, an arcane rule of procedure, had been used by the minority to delay a vote, add an amendment, or run out the clock at the end of the session by endless talking and speeches. This was reportedly the first time that a group of senators overtly employed the filibuster in a move targeted to derail a major piece of legislation—and the first time, noted the *Washington Post*, "that filibusterers frankly avowed that they were filibustering." Southerners called the antilynching legislation a "force bill," and described it as the "most daring and destructive invasion of states rights in history." Republicans pledged to bring the legislation to a vote, but their resolve wore down in the face of a determined southern bloc. After a week of deadlock, they surrendered and agreed to drop the Dyer bill.

Editorials in papers around the nation marveled at the power that Southern Democrats were able to wield in the face of a Republican majority of twenty-four seats while also commenting on the "utter absurdity" of rules that "prevent a legislative body from legislating." Republicans eagerly blamed the bill's demise on the Democrats' brilliant manipulation of Senate rules, but the final outcome left little doubt that Republicans were willing to see the Dyer bill go down to defeat. Appeals to President Harding to speak out on behalf of the legislation went unanswered until after it all was over. After the drawn-out struggle in the Senate, Johnson was not surprised by the "betrayal" of the Republican leadership. But his bitter disappointment at the end of the long fight was compounded by the realization that if the Senate had been allowed to vote on the bill, it almost certainly would have passed.[18]

The battle offered its own rewards by serving as a major phase in a national exploration of black political power and alliances. Black people in all parts of the country sent letters and petitions to their representatives and money to the NAACP. They had "shown a power which they did not realize before," Johnson wrote, enlisting the support of whites who would not otherwise have been attracted to the cause. They had "made the United States Congress a trumpet through which the facts of lynching [were] broadcast to the country." The process of educating political leaders and the public about lynching and the need for federal action in the field of racial reform had begun in earnest.[19]

At the same time, the fate of the Dyer bill pushed black Americans further down the road toward independence from the Republican Party. "The lukewarmness on the part of the Republicans," Johnson contended, was as "much resented by the colored people as the aggressive tactics of the Southern

Democrats." The failure of a Republican-controlled Congress to pass the bill confirmed Du Bois's sentiments. Commenting on Frederick Douglass's famous maxim about the Republican Party being the ship, Du Bois had quipped, "For God's sake give us the sea." He continued to patiently chart the steady growth of black voters outside the South; here was the promise of the future. He urged blacks in these states to concentrate on congressional elections, where independent black political power might begin to exert some influence. In the short term, however, blacks remained suspended between the two major parties, with little traction in the arena of national legislative politics.[20]

By contrast, the courts proved to be a more promising arena for the NAACP's efforts. On February 19, 1923, shortly after the Dyer bill went down to defeat, a four-year-long legal struggle growing from the Elaine, Arkansas, riot ended in an impressive Supreme Court victory for the NAACP. In a 7-to-2 decision in *Moore v. Dempsey* the Court overturned the conviction and death sentences of six of the twelve sharecroppers charged with the murder of whites, ruling that the mob spirit attending the trial denied the defendants due process of law. Eventually all were released. *Moore* marked a major turning point in criminal justice proceedings. Prior to this case, the Supreme Court allowed states wide discretion in the conduct of local trials. One of the most noted cases involved the Court's refusal to reverse the conviction of Leo Frank. A mob atmosphere dominated the trial of Frank, a Jewish man who had been charged with murdering a thirteen-year-old girl in Atlanta, Georgia. Frank was subsequently lynched. Louis Marshall, a leading constitutional lawyer who had worked on Frank's case, was so gratified by the NAACP's role in the *Moore* ruling that he joined the NAACP's legal committee and volunteered his services to the organization.[21]

The litigation of the Arkansas case was a critical training ground for Walter White. His investigation exposed the 1919 massacre, and he took the lead in organizing the defense of the condemned men. White engaged local counsel, a remarkable team of lawyers that included Scipio Jones, who had been born into slavery, and Colonel George W. Murphy, a Confederate veteran and former Arkansas attorney general. He consulted with government officials and mediated between the national office and a local civic group that had contributed $10,000 toward the defense. Unfortunately, White's tendency to underestimate local black lawyers and his eagerness to claim all credit for the NAACP at the expense of other organizations were on display here. Yet, despite these flaws, he exhibited talent and skill in navigating a complex social and legal terrain, a preview of the formative role he would play in shaping the NAACP's litigation program.[22]

The *Moore* victory and the well-publicized fight for the Dyer antilynching bill enhanced the NAACP's reputation as a national force in the fight for racial justice. Beyond these high-profile developments, however, the work of securing the future of the NAACP rested on the more mundane chores of increasing membership and sustaining branches—the nuts and bolts of the machinery for carrying the movement forward. Members organized in branches remained the major source of the association's funding. Branches that had multiplied during the war to more than four hundred by the early 1920s served a larger purpose. They were the association's eyes and ears, provided a network of contacts, and served as the front lines in the struggle to resist and reverse the permutations of the color line. The migration northward, which continued apace through the 1920s, saw segregation become more deeply entrenched outside of the South, creating a vital arena for NAACP activism. In the South, a major challenge was holding the ground that had been gained during the war years.

Johnson dedicated three staff members to full-time work in the field—one half of the paid professional staff. William Pickens, who succeeded Johnson as field secretary, had been born in South Carolina and grew up in Arkansas. A hardworking and ambitious young man, he graduated Phi Beta Kappa from Yale University and had most recently served as dean of Morgan State College. Pickens had been among the founding members of both the Niagara Movement and the NAACP. Robert Bagnall filled the new position of director of branches. A native of Virginia, Bagnall was an ordained Episcopal minister and served as pastor of St. Matthew's Church in Detroit. During the war years he worked as NAACP district organizer for the Midwest. Addie Hunton was born and raised in Norfolk, Virginia, and began her career as a schoolteacher. During World War I she went to France with Kathryn Johnson as a YWCA worker to aid black troops, and they co-authored a book about their experience. In 1920, Hunton had investigated voter fraud in the South for the NAACP and remained on the staff through 1923.[23]

After two years of fieldwork covering the Northeast, Midwest, and South, Hunton reported that the NAACP was well known throughout the country and widely "regarded as the strongest, most permanent factor for securing rights and justice." Yet membership numbers sagged, and branches had entered into a steady decline during the early 1920s. The annual challenge of renewing memberships depended upon keeping interest alive at the local level—a task that fell to branch leaders, who worked on a volunteer basis. Hunton's field reports provide a glimpse of the ebb and flow of branch activity and describe problems common to such enterprises. Pittsburgh and Atlantic City, she noted, both needed "an infusion of new blood." She reported on successful membership drives in Chicago and Indianapolis, but found branches flagging in Ohio, which had been a major center of NAACP activity. Lima was "almost expiring for the want of active leadership." The Youngstown branch was dormant and failed to respond to the growth of the Ku Klux Klan in that city. There had been a good branch in Columbus, but "the wrong bunch got a hold of it." In Springfield, however, the local branch was absorbed in the fight against school segregation, and Dayton, "practically dead a year ago," was on the upswing. She reported on a successful effort in Toledo to "penetrate Garvey's ranks" and win back those who had been carried away "by the great wave" of the UNIA that had swept Ohio the year before. Overall, however, she advised that there was a "need for a larger inculcation of the spirit of the NAACP in Ohio."[24]

In the South, the routine problems of leadership and the challenges of organizing were compounded by the danger attached to affiliation with the NAACP and its program. C. Frederick Douglass wrote from Jacksonville early in 1921 that "our leaders are not in evidence" since the revival of Klan activity in the area; the branch existed "only on paper." In Hampton, South Carolina, the police detained the Reverend P. P. Watson after he delivered an Emancipation Day speech in January 1921, charging that it was disruptive of "the general peace and . . . good feeling between the races." Robert Nance, Columbia branch president, reported that the police said Watson had "emphasized 'organization' too much." Charles A. J. McPherson, president of the Birmingham branch, reported in June 1922 that a recent wave of Klan activity in that city made it impossible for the branch to meet their membership goals. "Tension is very high," he wrote. "The police department usually do our lynching for us." He assured the national office, "We are going to continue to give you our moral support as well as our cooperation so much as we feel that we can do with discretion." Following a six-week-long tour through the South early in 1923, Hunton marveled at the fortitude of the membership that held on. "I have had a new realization of . . . some strong forces working for the abolition of injustice as I have not felt . . . in the North and in the West. . . . The National Association has a work that can hardly be ap-

preciated until one has touched and tasted the humiliating conditions imposed upon colored people in this section of the country. Nothing else matters
if one answers to the description of a Negro."[25]

The practical problem of sustaining active local branches had become
chronic by 1923, with dire consequences for the association's revenue flow.
Membership crested in the aftermath of World War I to a high of one hundred thousand; in 1923, the NAACP claimed 450 branches. But the branches
contributed just $25,000 toward the association's annual budget of $55,000 in
1923. An investigation by a board-appointed committee found that 130 of
the branches were dead and 63 more were inactive. In 1924, Robert Bagnall
and William Pickens began an extensive overhaul, revoking the charters of
forty-seven "stone dead" branches and reorganizing others. Johnson and
Bagnall agreed that field-workers should concentrate efforts on raising funds,
soliciting contributions in the $25 to $100 range, and inducing members to
contribute $5 to $10 as an annual membership fee. The $1 fee would remain,
but it was emphasized that this was an exceptional minimum for those who
could not afford to pay more. Well-heeled supporters were invited to purchase a life membership for $1,000. By late spring 1924, the NAACP claimed
363 active branches, but the funds coming in from the branches more than
doubled. In 1926, branches contributed 80–90 percent of the NAACP's operating budget. Still, finances remained tight, and the association, as Johnson
wrote in 1927, continued to operate on a "very, very, very narrow margin."[26]

The NAACP had minimal success in obtaining philanthropic support.
Julius Rosenwald and George Peabody were among a handful of wealthy individuals who provided regular contributions, usually in $1,000 increments,
and Johnson assiduously cultivated their continued support. Johnson's personal connections to a small group of New York reformers, many of whom
had been radicalized by World War I, helped to open new channels of support for the NAACP. Antiwar activist and civil libertarian Roger Baldwin
brought Johnson on to the board of the American Civil Liberties Union
(ACLU) when he established the organization in 1919. It was probably
through Baldwin that Johnson was invited to join the board of the American
Fund for Public Service (AFPS), and this connection would have major implications for the future of the association and its programs.

The American Fund for Public Service was funded by the million-dollar
inheritance of Charles Garland. The twenty-four-year-old Harvard drop-
out embraced the cause of radical social change and initially refused the

inheritance because it was money he had not earned. Roger Baldwin convinced him to establish a foundation that would support socially progressive causes. To this end, the American Fund for Public Service was incorporated in July 1921. The board of the new organization included labor organizers Elizabeth Gurley Flynn, Sidney Hillman, and William Z. Foster, who had recently joined the Communist Party, *Nation* editor Freda Kirchway, Socialist Party leader Norman Thomas, and James Weldon Johnson. The fund would provide seed money for pioneering efforts aimed at building a "new social order." While oriented toward labor issues and radical economic reform, protection of minority groups was also included in the AFPS's policy goals. Shortly after its establishment, the AFPS provided more than $3,000 to fund advertising in support of the Dyer bill. This was the first in a series of grants that would provide support for the NAACP at critical junctures during the 1920s as the NAACP developed its litigation program.[27]

By the mid-1920s, the NAACP's leadership had concluded that the courts offered the most promising avenue for advancing the association's goals. The disenfranchisement of the great majority of blacks limited the possibilities of electoral politics. Moreover, the NAACP had access to some of the top legal talent in the nation, lawyers who provided their services free or for a very low fee. The courts also offered an arena for strengthening the connections between the NAACP, its branches and the larger constituency of black Americans. During 1924, the association received 476 appeals for legal aid, often independently of local branches. Walter White commented on the fact that many seemed to view the NAACP as a "legal aid society" and clarified that there were two major criteria for association involvement: 1) the case had to involve racial discrimination and 2) have the potential of establishing a precedent that would affect the rights of black people. In reviewing the many requests that came into the office, cases that met these criteria were often referred to branches for further consideration and others to the NAACP's Legal Committee, headed by Arthur Spingarn.[28]

The NAACP orchestrated a remarkably ambitious legal campaign during the 1920s, one that married the strength and expertise of its Legal Committee to the efforts being waged in communities around the nation to fight racial discrimination. The broad criteria for association involvement invited a wide variety of legal challenges and brought a growing network of local legal talent into the NAACP's arena. Major areas of litigation concerned criminal justice, voting, housing, and schools. The litigation process helped solidify the NAACP's reputation among black Americans and strengthen local branches.

It also shaped the NAACP's national program, laying the groundwork for the major legal challenges that would provide the foundation for the civil rights movement.

Efforts to obtain elemental justice for blacks caught in the South's criminal justice system was a major focus of NAACP branch activity. Extradition cases provided a high-profile version of what was virtually a modern-day underground railroad. Frequently with the aid of the national office, local NAACP-affiliated lawyers in northern cities and in Canada fought the extradition of fugitives from southern justice in cases where the accused would likely be denied a fair trial or be the target of a lynch mob. They were often successful. More common criminal justice cases spotlighted routine abuses. The dogged efforts of the Houston branch in the defense of Luther Collins, who had been sentenced to death on trumped-up charges for allegedly assaulting a white woman, led, after five years of appeals, to the dismissal of his case and Collins' release from prison. Noting the significance of this case, Walter White wrote, "Every time an innocent man is defended . . . it means that even in the South, court officials will be less likely to railroad innocent Negroes . . . when they know a strong organization is both able and ready to defend [them.]" While the national office provided little if any financial support for such cases, it publicized the work of individual branches in these areas, helping to encourage similar efforts elsewhere and forging a sense of common purpose.[29]

As the evolving "machinery" of the NAACP linked the work of local branches to the resources and expertise of the national office, the opportunity for mounting major legal challenges cohered around several issues. In 1923, L. W. Washington, president of the NAACP's branch in El Paso, Texas, consulted with William Pickens at the annual convention about a law passed in Texas barring blacks from voting in the Democratic primary. Pickens advised Washington to find a plaintiff to challenge the new law. Washington enlisted Dr. L. A. Nixon, a local dentist and founding member of the El Paso branch. On July 26, 1924, Nixon attempted to vote in the Democratic primary and was turned away. The branch hired Fred Knollenberg, a white attorney, to represent Nixon and sent information regarding the case to the national office. The board of directors voted unanimously to support *Nixon v. Herndon* and split the legal costs with the branch. Louis Marshall and Moorfield Storey eventually took the case to the U. S. Supreme Court.[30]

The rapid spread of racial segregation in the North emerged as a galvanizing issue for black America during the 1920s and a formative one for the NAACP. Building on the wartime migration, a million more black southerners migrated north during the twenties. Between 1910 and 1930, major centers of black population growth included Chicago, which saw an increase from 44,000 to 233,900; Philadelphia where the black population grew by two and half times to 219,600; New York whose black citizenry more than tripled, from 91,700 to 327,700; and Cleveland where the black population jumped from 8,400 to 71,900. As black populations swelled in urban centers, the struggle around housing became a major axis of black-white confrontation. In an effort to contain growing black populations, Indianapolis was the only northern city to enact a residential segregation ordinance, in defiance of the 1917 *Buchanan v. Warley* ruling. The fight against the segregation ordinance energized the Indianapolis branch. The branch recruited twelve hundred new members and raised more than $5,400 to challenge the ordinance, which was struck down by the circuit court. Several southern cities enacted residential segregation ordinances during the twenties. The New Orleans branch's challenge to that city's residential segregation law made its way to the U.S. Supreme Court, where the law was overturned.[31]

More commonly, white homeowners associations and real estate interests attempted to make an end-run around the *Buchanan* ruling, which prohibited state action, by developing private agreements not to transfer property to black buyers, a practice known as restrictive covenants. In 1922, Helen Curtis, women's club leader and wife of a Howard University Medical School professor, sought the assistance of the NAACP's Washington branch when she was barred by injunction from taking possession of a house she had purchased from Irene Corrigan. A neighbor, John Buckley, charged that the sale violated Corrigan's agreement not to sell to blacks. James Cobb, chairman of the Washington, D.C., branch's legal committee, brought the case to the attention of James Weldon Johnson, and the NAACP voted to support a legal challenge as its major test case of this growing practice. *Corrigan v. Buckley*, Cobb argued, was probably more important than the Louisville case, for such a policy, if allowed to stand, would permit individual property owners to write segregation ordinances of their own—and, in effect, nullify the victory won in the *Buchanan* ruling.[32]

While neighborhood groups and realtors developed formal methods of exclusion, whites relied on intimidation and violence to enforce racial separation. The revival and growth of the Ku Klux Klan in midwestern and northeastern cities after World War I contributed to the climate of racial intolerance and helped stimulate mob action. In 1925 the NAACP reported on black homes being bombed, attacked, and threatened in cities across the country, including Brooklyn, New York; Cleveland, Ohio; Oakland, California; Kansas City, Missouri; Pittsburgh, Pennsylvania; Roanoke, Virginia; and St. Paul, Minnesota. One of the most widely publicized cases involved Samuel Browne, a mail carrier in Staten Island, New York.

Browne and his wife, Catherine, a public school teacher, purchased a home in a predominantly white neighborhood and moved in with their four children, all under the age of ten, in the summer of 1925. After Browne refused to accept a higher price for his house and move, trouble began. Death threats signed by the Ku Klux Klan arrived in the mail, a mob of white men regularly marched in front of the house, and the Browne home was bombarded with stones on several occasions. Browne obtained a gun permit, and he and his wife took turns guarding their home through the night. The NAACP helped secure police protection and supported Browne's suit against the real estate agent who was behind the harassment. The case was settled out of court. Browne remained in his house and became a leader in the local NAACP branch.[33]

In the same period, Detroit emerged as a center of racial strife. The transformation of this midwestern city into a "modern metropolis of steel, smoke and . . . assembly lines" was one of the major stories of the early twentieth century. The breathtaking growth of Detroit's automobile industry fueled a massive migration of men and women seeking jobs and opportunity; many were recently arrived European immigrants; large numbers came from the South. Overcrowding taxed the city's housing stock and public resources and created a potent brew of class, racial, and ethnic tensions. New voters challenged the dominance of the conservative elite that had long ruled the city. Reform politics clashed with a strain of antiunion, anti-Catholic, anti-Semitic, and antiblack sentiments, stirred by the postwar incursion of the Ku Klux Klan. In 1923, the Klan counted 22,000 members in the Motor City.[34]

Race became a major fault line in the city's evolving social and political order. Detroit had the fastest-growing black community of any major urban area; it reached eighty thousand by the mid-1920s, up from eight thousand a decade earlier. Black settlement concentrated in an area known as the "Black Bottom." Up through the early 1920s, however, residential patterns remained relatively fluid; a small number of black families moved into predominantly white areas and initially met little resistance. But this quickly changed as white Detroiters responded to the growing black presence in the city by actively seeking to enforce racial separation. Neighborhood improvement associations, restrictive covenants, and a cooperative real estate industry combined to restrict black residential mobility. In 1924, the real estate agents trade association barred its members from selling houses in white neighborhoods to black clients. By the mid-1920s, when black families managed to cross these racial boundaries, whites increasingly resorted to violence to enforce the color line.[35]

During the spring and summer of 1925 the west side of Detroit exploded in a series of attacks on new black homeowners. Fleta Mathies fought back, firing into the crowd that stoned her home. She was arrested and, with the aid of two black lawyers, acquitted on the grounds of defending her property against the mob. She remained in her home. In July, three major assaults focused national attention on the Motor City. A mob raided the home of Dr. Alexander Turner, terrorizing the doctor and his wife until he finally agreed to sell the house after living in it for one day. Just weeks later, a rampaging crowd drove John Fletcher from his home after a massive assault broke every window as a crowd chanted "lynch him." Before fleeing, Fletcher fired into the mob and wounded a young man. Vollington Bristol withstood the attack on his home, with the aid of police protection, but lived in a sea of white hatred and resentment.[36]

The battles fought in Detroit that summer dramatized one of the most pressing issues facing black Americans in cities across the nation and begged for a more robust response from the NAACP. In the fall of 1925, Johnson announced that NAACP officials would launch a series of mass meetings starting in Detroit to rally opposition to the wave of violence and segregation sweeping the North. An organized campaign was also critical to tapping into an energized black populace and raising funds for the Washington residential segregation case that was making its way to the Supreme Court, along with the El Paso white primary challenge. Early in September, Johnson began working with NAACP president Moorfield Storey to develop an application to the American Fund for Public Service to help support the establishment of a permanent legal defense fund. But Johnson told black Americans that the NAACP depended upon them to provide "the munitions of war," a war that the association pledged "to fight to the finish if . . . given the means necessary."[37]

On September 11, 1925, as Johnson prepared for the fall campaign, news of a riot at the home of Dr. Ossian Sweet, where a white man was killed and ten black men were arrested on homicide charges, reached the New York office. He wired the Detroit branch for full information. A telegram back from W. Hayes McKinney with details of the incident was followed by an urgent long-distance phone call requesting that Walter White come to Detroit immediately to aid with the investigation. Within twenty-four hours, White was on a train headed to Detroit.[38]

Ossian Sweet epitomized the promise of Detroit's young black professional class. He came from a striving, land-owning family in Bartow, Florida, where his parents' ambitions for him and his siblings blunted the force of Jim Crow. Educated at Wilberforce College in Ohio and Howard University Medical School, Sweet established a medical practice in the Black Bottom section of Detroit, which was heaving under the weight of continuing migration and hardening racial borders. Sweet married Gladys Mitchell, a member of one of the city's most prominent black families. Between 1923 and 1924, the Sweets spent a year in Vienna and Paris, where Ossian took advanced study in pediatrics and gynecology. Their daughter Marguerite was born in Paris. After returning to Detroit, the Sweets, who had been living with Gladys's parents, began looking for a house. The most suitable homes for the young doctor and his family were in predominantly white areas. Several houses that attracted their interest were covered by restrictive covenants, and realtors promptly turned them away. They finally found a bungalow on Garland Street in a modest white working-class area and purchased it in June 1925 at a greatly inflated price. The Sweets planned to move in later in August.

In the intervening month, the riotous attacks on black homeowners rocked the city's west side. One of the targets, Dr. Alexander Turner, was an associate of Ossian Sweet. Ossian and Gladys refused to give in to the fear of the danger that likely awaited them. They postponed their move until the day after Labor Day and arrived prepared for trouble. Ossian's brothers and several male friends accompanied them; they were armed and ready to defend themselves. A mob gathered the first night and did little more than mill around. On the second night, a larger crowd of several thousand gathered and began stoning the house and shouting out racial epithets. Responding to the threats, Ossian's younger brother Henry, a student at Wilberforce University, fired a rifle from the top-floor window of the house, striking two white men, killing one of them. The police arrived and arrested all eleven adults while a crowd of some five thousand whites gathered as news of the shooting spread.[39]

Upon arriving in Detroit on September 15, Walter White met with local political leaders and NAACP branch officials and sized up the situation. He promptly set about orchestrating the defense of the Sweets, elbowing aside a local Garveyite lawyer along with several others who, according to White, were out for a fee and some glory. Biographer Kenneth Janken notes that

White was unnecessarily dismissive of the three local black attorneys who responded to Sweet's initial call and had begun preparing to defend the group; the local attorneys included Cecil Rowlette, one of the lawyers who had won an acquittal for Fleta Mathies after she defended her house from a mob. White nearly caused a complete rupture with local blacks with his impatient, "take charge" approach. He, however, was set on securing the best attorney available to lead the defense team, and in 1925 it was assumed that the "best" would necessarily be white. "The case was bigger than Detroit or Michigan," he wrote. "[It] was the dramatic climax of the nationwide fight to enforce residential segregation." In light of the fact that even the "very best white sentiment" was against Sweet, an eminent white attorney could help educate white opinion and, most importantly, have some chance of winning over a white jury. The defendants were persuaded. Within two weeks of White's first visit to Detroit, they signed full and complete charge of the case over to the NAACP.[40]

White's inspired idea initially fell flat. Only one white attorney in Detroit would consider taking the case, a high-profile lawyer associated with organized crime who required a $7,500 fee. At the suggestion of N. K. McGill, general counsel for the *Chicago Defender*, Johnson sent a telegram to Clarence Darrow, the nation's leading defense attorney, imploring him to take the case. Darrow had just completed his brilliant and widely publicized defense in the Scopes trial, challenging Tennessee's antievolution law, three months earlier. It took little effort to persuade Darrow. The dramatic case appealed to his abiding concern for the plight of black Americans. He agreed to represent the Sweet defendants and, at $5,000, charged one-tenth of his normal fee. As chief counsel the sixty-eight-year-old Darrow was joined by the prominent civil liberties attorney Arthur Garfield Hayes and the three black attorneys who had been involved from the start: Julian Perry, Cecil Rowlette, and Charles Mahoney. With Darrow as chief counsel, the Sweet story suddenly became news in the white press, and coverage in the black press became even more vigorous.[41]

The day that Darrow joined the Sweet defense team, the NAACP announced that the American Fund for Public Service had awarded the association $5,000 toward the establishment of a permanent legal defense fund and pledged $15,000 more as soon as the association raised $30,000. Normally, this would have been a tall order. But the Sweet case stirred black Americans like no case in recent memory and quickly became a potent symbol of the struggle the association was waging. The *Detroit Independent* asserted that the entire colored citizenry of Detroit, indeed of the country, was on trial. "Negroes the country over," wrote the *Pittsburgh Courier*, "await breathlessly the outcome of this case. . . . If . . . favorable to the defendants it will be a signal to other Negroes to hold their own against all odds." Commenting on the "heroic defense of their homes" by "those brave and fearless Detroiters," the *Philadelphia Public Journal* claimed: "The time has come when it is more glorious to die for principle than for some high sounding meaningless phrase coined during the war only to be forgotten after the war is over." It must not be left to the NAACP to undertake their defense alone. "Every Negro in the United States should pay the debt we owe them."[42]

The People v. Sweet began on October 30; Henry Sweet, who had confessed to the shooting, was tried first. Judge Frank Murphy, a young Democratic Party activist and progressive jurist, presided. Walter White remained deeply involved in what he described as "the biggest legal battle we have ever handled." He spent long days in the courtroom, seated at the reporters' table thanks to a press pass from the judge, followed by late-night sessions with Darrow and his entourage, squeezing in fund-raising swings through the Midwest. As a packed courtroom looked on, prosecutor Robert Toms built his case claiming the murder of an innocent white man at the hands of violent blacks. There was no mob in his version of events; just a dozen or so people standing around. But the prosecution's case collapsed under Darrow's cross-examination. As he artfully probed, witnesses wove a powerful narrative that told of a stone-throwing mob, numbering five hundred to six hundred people, bent on driving the Sweets from their home. It was capped by Ossian Sweet's dramatic testimony. Darrow guided Sweet through an account of his life, highlighting his efforts to get an education, working his way through college and medical school, and his experience of racial violence, including the 1919 Washington race riot. All of this was preparation for Sweet's account of the night of September 9, which effectively brought his listeners into the house with his wife and daughter, where they saw, through his eyes, the surging mob. By the time the jury adjourned, the defense could taste victory. The jury of twelve white men, however, deadlocked, and Murphy declared a mistrial.[43]

A disappointed Walter White wrote a friend that the jury's stubbornness "is going to cost us about $25,000 more." Yet, the fact that the Sweet case remained alive helped to sustain a very successful fund-raising campaign. The rallies for the Sweet defendants continued, and early in January Gladys and Ossian, who had been released on bail, spoke in New York and took a six-day

tour of NAACP branches. By the end of December, the NAACP had surpassed the $30,000 mark required for AFPS matching funds, with almost all
of the money coming from black people. A month later the legal defense fund
had climbed to $76,000.[44]

The second trial began toward the end of April and covered previous territory. The trial was highlighted by Clarence Darrow's soaring six-hour closing
argument, which began by his asking, "Who are we, anyway?" He explored
the soul of America, stained by racial prejudice, the sordid history of slavery
and race discrimination, the corrosive power of hatred, the fanaticism of the
mob. He "unrolled," recalled James Weldon Johnson, "a complete panorama
of the experience, physical and spiritual of the American Negro, beginning
with his African background, down to the present—a panorama of his suffer-
ings, his struggles, his achievements, his aspirations." He talked about the
debt that white America owed black Americans. He spoke of Detroit and of
Michigan and the future. He appealed to the jurors' humanity and belief in
progress. Darrow's oration brought Johnson to tears and struck the chord he
aimed for. "Not guilty" was the verdict from the all-white jury. The effect,
Johnson wrote, was "electrical," marking the end of "the most dramatic court
trial involving the fundamental rights of the Negro in his whole history in
this country."[45]

For the NAACP, the *Sweet* case was a major breakthrough. Du Bois noted
that by all counts, the decks were stacked against blacks: the police lied, the
press was biased, the prosecuting attorney appealed to the community's basest
racial antipathy. Indeed, the jails and penitentiaries were "full of black men
just as innocent as these eleven defendants." What was different in Detroit?
First and foremost, Du Bois noted, was the fact that "the American Negro
went down in his pocket and . . . put into the treasury of the NAACP an
amount of money that meant these defendants would have a chance for a fair
trial." In the end, the trials cost $37,489, three-fourths of which was paid by
the NAACP. "Justice in the United States costs money. No pauper need apply
at the barred gates of our criminal courts," Du Bois averred. Secondly, they
found in Clarence Darrow a brilliant attorney and a man of great moral courage, unafraid to stand up and defend unpopular causes. Active black support
and first-rate legal talent was, Du Bois observed, "the combination that is
going to win throughout wide futures."[46]

On May 24, 1926, just two weeks after the dramatic culmination of the
Sweet case, the U.S. Supreme Court dealt a major defeat to the battle against
residential segregation. The court dismissed *Corrigan v. Buckley*, the Wash-

ington, D.C., restrictive covenant case, holding that it had no jurisdiction. Nonetheless, the Court issued an opinion, rejecting claims by James Cobb, Moorfield Storey, and Louis Marshall that restrictive covenants were unconstitutional. Because courts would be responsible for enforcing these private agreements, the NAACP lawyers contended, state action was involved and thus violated constitutional guarantees of equal protection under the law. Writing for a unanimous court, Justice Edward Stanford referred to the issues raised by the case as "unsubstantial" and "frivolous." Concurring with the rulings of the lower courts, the opinion stated that restrictive covenants and their enforcement were solely a matter of private action and thus beyond the scope of the "equal protection clause" of the Fifth and Fourteenth amendments. With the Supreme Court's ruling, pending cases in Kentucky, Oklahoma, Maryland, Wisconsin, Missouri, and New York were disposed of, and restrictive covenants became standard practice in many communities. The NAACP attempted to bring several other cases forward, but it would be twenty years before the Supreme Court revisited this issue, allowing racial boundaries to expand in cities across the nation.[47]

In less than a year, the Texas white primary case came before the U.S. Supreme Court with a more encouraging outcome. Ruling in *Nixon v. Herndon*, a unanimous court struck down the Texas law as a violation of the equal protection clause of the Fourteenth Amendment, handing the NAACP a significant victory. Hailed by the NAACP as striking a deathblow to the white primary, the ruling was less ambitious than that. By failing to apply the Fifteenth Amendment, as urged by Louis Marshall's brief, the Court left open the possibility for private action to dictate access to primary elections. Texas Democrats immediately set about circumventing the Court's ruling, replacing the 1923 law with a bill that allowed the party to determine qualifications for membership and voting in party primaries. The state executive committee of the Democratic Party promptly adopted a resolution limiting participation in primary elections to whites, which was identical to party procedures in Arkansas, Florida, and Virginia. Blacks in each of these states brought challenges to the party-sponsored white primary, with varying degrees of assistance from the NAACP. Over the next two decades, Texas would remain the principal site for a series of Supreme Court challenges to the determined efforts of white Democrats to bar blacks from participation in the South's most important electoral arena.[48]

* * *

Educational inequality was one of the most vexing issues facing black Americans. Failure to provide black children a decent education, Du Bois warned, threatened "to fasten slavery permanently upon the colored people of the United States." In the South, the blatant inequity of Jim Crow education, he wrote, revealed "discrimination so fundamental and so calculated to perpetuate ignorance, crime, prejudice, poverty, and disease." The trend toward segregated education accelerated in the North during the 1920s, nationalizing the problem of unequal schooling. During the twenties the national office of the NAACP worked with local branches to develop strategies for exposing and challenging the various permutations of racial discrimination as manifested in the public education of black children. Its efforts in the North, however, met with a mixed response, reflecting divisions within northern black communities regarding the value of "mixed" as opposed to separate schools in the face of intensifying white racism.[49]

With the first issue of *The Crisis* in November 1910, Du Bois observed that northern cities such as Chicago, Philadelphia, Atlantic City, and Columbus, Ohio, had begun to establish separate colored schools in response to newly arrived southern migrants. Due to vastly inferior Jim Crow schooling in the South, southern children were often poorly prepared and below "average" in comparison with their northern classmates. The move toward segregation, Du Bois observed, was an effort on the part of the public to shift to black northerners a community-wide responsibility for educating these newcomers. Once established, the provisions for segregated institutions were always worse, therefore compounding the problem. Beyond the unfairness of segregation, Du Bois warned that it also undermined the democratic mission of schools. "Human contact, human acquaintanceship, human sympathy is the great solvent of human problems. Separate school children by wealth and the result is class misunderstandings and hatred. Separate them by race and the result is war. Separate them by color and they grow up without learning that it is impossible to judge the mind of a man by the color of his face." In the end, he wrote, "the argument for color discrimination in schools . . . is an argument against democracy."[50]

Efforts by whites to impose school segregation increased dramatically in the 1920s, paralleling the move toward residential segregation and a broader effort to enforce racial barriers in the face of growing black populations. The poor preparation of southern black students led to charges that they were "backward" and reinforced stereotypes of black inferiority, providing a primary rationale for segregation. While most northern states had adopted laws in the late nineteenth century prohibiting segregation, cities and towns across the region employed a variety of tactics and policies to separate black and white students. (Indiana permitted school segregation by local option, and Kansas authorized cities with a population greater than fifteen thousand to segregate schools.) In some places, residential segregation resulted in segregated schools, and quite often school officials facilitated the process. Chicago gerrymandered school district lines, employed racially conscious assignment policies, and provided a liberal transfer policy for white children to transfer out of predominantly black schools while denying similar privileges to black students. Philadelphia's school board steadily increased the number of all-black schools during the 1920s. In parts of southern New Jersey and Indiana, dual school systems were established. Some school districts established separate buildings for black students and, more commonly, separate classes were established according to race. Tracking students by academic ability was adopted as a tool for isolating black students. Blacks and whites were often segregated during recreational activities as well. In many instances, schools barred black students from swimming pools. NAACP lawyer Robert Carter, who attended high school in Newark, described how blacks were permitted to use the swimming pool on Fridays; it was then "drained, cleaned and refilled for the use of white students the following Monday."[51]

The NAACP stood ready to encourage and support efforts to fight this trend, but did so in the face of divided black communities. In some instances, blacks petitioned for separate schools, and this was often used by local school boards to support segregation. Arguments for separate schools were driven by a number of considerations. Often, black students were subject to insult, mistreatment, and neglect in mixed schools, which led many to leave school, resulting in low graduation rates. Separate schools provided opportunities for black teachers, offered a positive and nurturing environment, and allowed for a curriculum that incorporated black history and culture. Black teachers, who were generally barred from teaching in racially mixed schools, were among the strongest proponents of separate schools. In some instances southern migrants tended to support separate schools, while middle-class northern blacks were among the strongest supporters of integration. But this pattern varied considerably from place to place.[52]

Du Bois was well aware that black students often suffered discrimination in mixed schools, and he shared the concerns of parents and communities determined to confront and ameliorate this problem. But he insisted that the solution was not separate schools. "Of all the evils," he wrote, "segregation in education is one of the greatest and . . . this evil cannot be outweighed by the few benefits that result from separate schools." Listing his objections to separate public schools, Du Bois noted that they planted race prejudice among the young, tended to foster feelings of black inferiority and white supremacy, and consigned blacks to inferior schools with lower standards "calculated to fit them for the lowest place in society." Du Bois advised that blacks use agitation, political power, and legal methods to stop the segregation of public schools, while pressing for the hiring of black teachers and monitoring the treatment of black students in mixed schools. Still, he acknowledged the paradox facing black communities. "We must oppose segregation in schools; we must honor and appreciate the colored teacher in the colored school. . . . Small wonder that Negro communities have been torn asunder by deep and passionate differences of opinion arising from this pitiable dilemma."[53]

Walter White saw the fight against school segregation as part of a larger battle, with widespread implications. "There must be a nationwide agitation to launch a counter offensive not only where segregation is being attempted but also in those places where segregation exists and where there is a chance of fighting it effectively—that is, in brief, in all northern and border states," he wrote in the fall of 1924. "Unless we can win out in the North, we shall never be able to win in the South and the acceptance of any segregation in the North will lessen immeasurably any efforts against future segregation in the South." But in order to mount an effective challenge, the NAACP relied upon local communities to take the initiative, and black ambivalence regarding mixed schools minimized the number of cases that arose during the 1920s.[54]

There were several notable efforts to resist school segregation. In Springfield, Ohio, the school board established Fulton School as an all-black elementary school in 1922 and authorized the employment of black teachers for the first time in nearly forty years. Prior to the board's action, three hundred black women had petitioned for the establishment of a segregated elementary school in an effort to secure jobs for black teachers, a plan that also had the support of the ministers of two of Springfield's largest black churches. Divisions within the NAACP branch regarding Fulton School led to the founding of the Civil Rights Protective League to mount the fight against the establishment of the all-black school, with the support of leading local NAACP officials. Addie Hunton and Robert Bagnall visited the community several times and aided in the fight that used mass meetings, boycotts, and picketing to mobilize the community. The league won a court injunction barring the assignment of students based on race, effective the following school year. While planning to appeal the decision, the school board, anticipating that Fulton would open in the fall on an integrated basis, dismissed all of the black teachers and hired white teachers to replace them. The board then dropped the appeal, but liberal transfer policies for white students in the Fulton district, denied to black students, siphoned off most of the white students. A decade later, Fulton School was 97 percent black.[55]

One of the most widely publicized protests against school segregation erupted in Toms River, New Jersey. Edgar Fink, supervising principal of the public school, boasted that his eyes had been opened during a visit to Texas about "how to treat the colored people." At his urging, the Dover Township school board leased a local A. M. E. Church in a neighboring town and, at the start of the winter term in 1927, reassigned thirty-five black students from Toms River's modern school building to a primitive one-room structure across the river. The students, ranging from six to fifteen years of age, were the children of recent migrants from the South who had come to work in the clay mines and sand works. Several of the children's fathers organized a protest, and all but five of the students boycotted the segregated school while their parents prepared to challenge the school board's action. "We left the south because of Jim Crow laws and we are not going to stand for that treatment here," announced a statement issued by a committee of the parents. Their protest won attention in all of the major New York papers. The *New York World* noted that "unschooled as [they] may be," these parents expressed "high ideals about education for their children and are as eager to see them taught in the ways of this new land of the North as are the immigrant parents in New York."[56]

James Weldon Johnson learned about the case through the news reports. He immediately shot off a telegram to Governor Harry Moore insisting that Edgar Fink be dismissed and reminded the governor that there were two hundred thousand blacks in New Jersey, a sizeable voting bloc. He sent letters to the NAACP's fifteen branches in New Jersey urging them to publicize the situation in Toms River and organize support to reverse the policy. The national office worked with Eugene Hayne, a lawyer engaged by some of the parents, and provided $500 toward his legal expenses. Later in March Johnson led a delegation including parents and representatives from the New Jersey branches to meet with Governor Moore and state commissioner of education John Logan. The governor assured the group that New Jersey did not stand for segregation and discrimination and urged them to work through legal channels.

Efforts by town officials to force the parents to send their children to the segregated school under threat of fines and prison failed. Judge Harry Newman ruled that the parents were not guilty of keeping their children out of school because the Dover school board had no right to lease a building in another township for the education of the black students. At the end of June, the commissioner of education, noting the New Jersey law barring the exclusion of a child from a public school based on religion, nationality, or color, ordered the reinstatement of the black children at the school in Toms River. Although this case involved a small number of black students in a remote town, it was hailed as a significant victory in the fight against northern school segregation. The *Philadelphia Tribune* heaped praise on the parents for rebelling against a condition "that Negroes in other cities accept quietly." Acknowledging the important work of the NAACP, the *Tribune* underscored that "the courage, the backbone, and moral stamina exhibited by the colored citizens of Toms River when they faced jail by refusing to send their children to the inferior school [were] the main elements that broke the back of the scheme to segregate the children of Toms River."[57]

While there were pockets of resistance and a number of victories in the courts, the trend toward school segregation in the North persisted during the 1920s. In Philadelphia the school board ignored petitions and protests by the local NAACP branch to stop the steady expansion of segregated schools. The board's policy won the support of the Pennsylvania Association of Teachers of Colored Children, which passed a resolution endorsing separate schools. In 1929, the *Philadelphia Tribune*, which had worked during the 1920s with the local NAACP branch to roll back the segregationist tide, conceded, "We have Jim Crow schools springing up like mushrooms." Litigation to enforce state antisegregation laws was generally successful, but relatively few cases were mounted during the twenties. And often successful legal action failed to end the practice in the face of determined efforts on the part of northern school boards to avoid racial mixing—either by ignoring court rulings, as in the case of Dayton, Ohio, and Gary, Indiana, or devising other methods for achieving the same ends. In 1929, black sociologist and Howard University professor Kelly Miller pronounced: "The color line in public education is vigorously asserting itself across the continent from Atlantic City to Los Angeles."[58]

The South posed a different kind of challenge. In the 1920s, a direct attack on segregated education in the South was not considered. The pervasive caste system and extreme racism in the South made "mixed schools" in Du Bois words, "utterly impossible." He continued, "Even if by law we could force colored children into the white schools, they would not be educated. They would be abused, browbeaten, murdered, and kept in something worse than ignorance."[59] The NAACP focused attention on the gross inequities plaguing black schools in the South. In the early 1920s, the specter of federal legislation that would underwrite this blatant and widespread inequality became a catalyst in the effort to expose the condition of black schooling in the South and find a way to improve educational opportunities and conditions for black students.

In December 1921, Florence Kelley alerted the NAACP's board of directors of the Smith-Towner bill, which would appropriate millions of dollars in federal funds annually to the states to help raise educational standards. The bill was a response to the high rates of illiteracy among recruits for the armed forces during the war. It provided for equalizing educational opportunities, enhancing the preparation of teachers for public school service, and promoting physical education. Writing about what later became known as the Sterling bill, Kelley warned that "people who do not personally know conditions of Negro life in the South are attracted by the . . . phrases 'in order to encourage the states to remove illiteracy.'" Yet with no oversight from the federal government, the funds would be "distributed and administered in accordance with the laws of the State" by "State and local authorities," Kelley explained. Thus southern states would in effect apply federal funds to a system of white domination and impoverished black schools, "legalizing discrimination against the public education for Negroes."[60]

Kelley, a long-serving board member of the NAACP, was a prominent figure in social welfare work and children's issues, served as general secretary of the National Consumer's League, and had extensive legislative experience. During her years with the NAACP she had grown into an effective advocate for racial justice and was among the few white progressives whose passion for social justice did not stop at the color line. "By word and pen and personal complaint," Du Bois noted, she led in exposing the dangers inherent in the Sterling bill. She investigated the disbursement of federal funds authorized by previous legislation, primarily the Smith-Hughes and the Morrill acts, which provided examples of how inequitable distribution of funds supported discriminatory practices throughout the nation. In organizing opposition to the Sterling bill, Kelley advocated that standards be established to ensure that federal funds were dedicated to equitable educational opportunity for all children. As a part of this effort the NAACP board voted to begin a campaign of investigation and publicity concerning the education of black children in the South and established the Committee on Public Education of the Negro in the South, which included Kelley and Du Bois.[61]

The Committee on Public Education surveyed southern branches for information on school conditions and collected state education reports, developing a composite of facts on black education in the South and illustrating how the provisions of the Sterling bill would perpetuate these conditions. A brief report, issued in June 1923, outlined the racial breakdown of per-pupil expenditures, average teachers' salaries, length of term, and number of high schools, providing a stark portrait of the racial divide which in some cases saw $8 to $10 spent on each white child for every dollar spent on a black child.[62] Opposed by the U.S. Chamber of Commerce and others aligned against federal spending for education, the Sterling bill failed to come to a vote in the Congress. But the efforts it generated on the part of the NAACP to focus attention on the condition of black education in the South resulted in sustained activity in this area and provided the template for a more ambitious study by W. E. B. Du Bois.

"The average Negro child in the South," Du Bois observed, "was not being given a chance to learn to read and write." Compounding the wretched condition of black schooling in the South was the fact that it was barely commented upon within mainstream society. In appealing to the American Fund for Public Service to support a major survey of black common schools, Du Bois noted the broader social costs of such blatant inequity. As blacks moved north in increasing numbers they were becoming an important part of the labor force in the United States; ignorant and cheap black labor threatened to hinder the development of a strong working-class movement. The first step toward remedying the root cause of the problem was to collect the facts on black education in the South and put them before the public. The states provided very little information on black education, and there had not been any effort to study black schools in the South since 1901, when Du Bois conducted one such study as part of the Atlanta University series. With a $5,000 grant from the AFPS, he directed a survey of black education during 1925 and 1926 in a sampling of southern states with the assistance of several field-workers, including E. Franklin Frazier and Horace Mann Bond.[63]

The results of investigations done in Georgia, Mississippi, North Carolina, South Carolina, and Oklahoma were published in a series of articles in *The Crisis* from September 1926 to July 1928. While admittedly incomplete and fragmentary, the reports documented the base inequity that resulted in inferior facilities, shortened school terms, and poorly paid teachers. In Mississippi, where black children composed 54 percent of the school-age population, the state spent $3.3 million on building and equipping white schools and $350,000 on black schools. North Carolina, a beacon of enlightenment in comparison with its Deep South neighbors, still spent roughly twice as much on white students than it did on black students. It was not too much to say, Du Bois concluded, "that half of the black children in the South today have no chance to receive a thorough education through the grammar grades, and that not one-tenth have a high school education open to them." In open defiance of the U. S. Constitution and state laws, state and federal funds devoted to education were "systematically spent so as to discriminate against colored children." Deep South states were especially "shameless and impudent in their defiance" of law and justice. "There must be a way to bring . . . cases before state and federal court." It was time, he insisted, "to start the crusade."[64]

In the face of such seemingly intractable racial barriers, the literary and artistic flowering of the 1920s created an opening toward a fuller expression of black aspirations. In 1923, James Weldon Johnson confided to Walter White that the development of Negro art "will not only mean a great deal to the Negro . . . but will provide the easiest and most effective approach . . . to the race question," and one that offered "the least friction."[65] Johnson, White, and Du Bois joined Charles S. Johnson and Howard University professor Alaine Locke as leading promoters of what came to be known as the "Harlem Renaissance," an unprecedented outpouring of black literature and art. Expectations that this vibrant expression of creativity and talent would diminish the racial prejudice of white America, "civil rights by copyright," as David Levering Lewis named it, proved elusive. Nevertheless, cultivating the spirit of the "New Negro" provided an arena for the talents and ambitions of the movement's elite and a measure of relief from what Johnson described as "this grueling race-struggle," while infusing the movement with a new level of confidence and determination.[66]

Early in the 1920s *The Crisis* showcased the work of young black writers and poets, including Langston Hughes, Claude McKay, and Countee Cullen, the postwar generation "whose poetry of protest and rebellions," wrote James Weldon Johnson, "expressed what the race felt." It was, however, the famous dinner hosted in 1924 at the Civic Club by Charles S. Johnson, editor of *Opportunity*, the newly established magazine of the National Urban League, that marked the start of a concerted effort to promote black literary talent. Guests included H.L. Mencken, Eugene O'Neill, Freda Kirchwey of *The Nation,* and other noted white artists, publishing luminaries, and opinion shapers, along with prominent black figures. It was a roaring success. A month later, Du Bois's fifty-sixth birthday party offered another venue for showcasing black artists and convening the smart set in black and white. *The Crisis* and *Opportunity* both launched prizes for literature, funded by white patrons, while Charles S. Johnson and Walter White sought out promising black writers and artists across the land and lured them to New York. There were a dizzying array of dinners, parties, and soirees, uptown and downtown, a whirl of interracial mixing. This was the time, as James Weldon Johnson recalled, when "the Harlem of story and song" was born.[67]

Harlem was the hub of the New Negro movement, which echoed in towns and cities across the nation. The massive shift of blacks to the urban North in successive waves of migration created, in the words of Alaine Locke, "a mass movement toward the larger and more democratic chance." Burgeoning black communities, concentrated in cities like Philadelphia, Chicago, and Cleveland, supported a growing black professional and business class, accelerating the process of class stratification. At the same time, segregation enforced self-contained communities that became laboratories "of . . . race welding," further fusing the sentiment and experience of black people in all of their diversity. Young black artists lived the pulse and rhythm of this new dynamic and gave voice and form to the varied contours of black life, defining the aesthetic of the "New Negro" free from "the tyranny of social intimidation and implied inferiority." In this cauldron, black Americans came into a fuller realization "of the great discrepancy between the American social creed and . . . practice [forcing] upon the Negro the taking of the moral advantage which is his." The way was open, Locke declared, toward molding a new American attitude that might hasten the full integration of national life.[68]

The NAACP's leading lights participated as literary figures as well as promoters of the Harlem Renaissance. James Weldon Johnson struggled to keep his artistic side from being completely submerged. He published *The Book of American Negro Poetry* in 1922, the first anthology of African American literature, followed by an anthology of black spirituals and *God's Trombone: Seven Negro Sermons in Verse.* The pages of *The Crisis* promoted black poetry and literature and sponsored a yearlong symposium titled "The Negro in Art" in 1926. Du Bois published two books, *The Gift of Black Folk* (1924) and *Dark Princess* (1928), a novel. With his usual gusto, Walter White immersed himself in the New Negro movement, becoming one of its leading impresarios. His ability to detect talent was matched by the ease with which he moved within the literary world of artists, publishers, and celebrities. According to his biographer, White's exposure to the high life and a restless ambition not easily contained by one calling fostered his own literary pursuits. He published two novels in quick succession and in 1927 won a Guggenheim Fellowship, the first by the new foundation to be awarded to a black person. White took a one-year leave of absence from the NAACP and sailed to France with his family in the summer of 1927 to work on his next book while he pondered a full-time writing career.[69]

Recognition by whites and their support of black artistic talent paid impressive dividends. In 1926, the Harmon Foundation established a half-million-dollar fund to honor black achievement in the arts and literature, and two years later the Rosenwald Fund established a fellowship program that would support the training of southern black scholars, writers, and artists over the next twenty-five years. While hailing such developments, Du Bois cautioned all concerned that they not lose sight of the larger struggle. In his address to the NAACP's annual meeting in Chicago in 1926, he advised that whites should not be lulled into thinking that a growing recognition of individual black artists would stop agitation on "the Negro question." "Do great things, and the reward is there," was an implied message, one that some writers and artists were too eager to accept, "especially those who are weary of the eternal struggle . . . and to whom the money of philanthropists and the alluring publicity are subtle and deadly bribes." The few who won acclaim, Du Bois remarked, were "but the remnants of that ability and genius among us whom the accidents of education and opportunity have raised on the tidal wave of chance."[70]

More important than individual achievements, the blossoming of black creative arts revealed a deepening racial consciousness, the beginnings "of a new desire to create, a new will to be." It was part of "the great fight," Du Bois exclaimed, and represented "a forward and upward look—a pushing onward." As the vistas widened, attention must be trained on the future. What did black Americans want? Of course, "we want to be Americans . . . with all the rights of other citizens." But was that all, "simply to be Americans"? Pushed aside as they had been, blacks had an ability to see America as it really was, and envision what it could be, the kind of world "that we want to create for ourselves and for all America." It was here, Du Bois concluded, "that the National Association for the Advancement of Colored People comes upon the field with its call to a new battle . . . before the old things are wholly won; and to say that the Beauty of Truth and Freedom which shall some day be our heritage and the heritage of all civilized men is not in our hands yet and that we ourselves must not fail to realize."[71]

One of the more tangible consequences of the growing concentration of blacks in the urban North was access to the ballot and the expanding opportunities to press forward in the electoral arena. In 1928, presidential hopeful Al Smith looked to northern black voters as a potentially important constituency and sought the assistance of a seasoned political operator in tapping into this base. In the spring, the Smith campaign offered Walter White a job heading up the effort to organize black support for Smith, a prospect that lured White back from his writing sabbatical in France four months early. As White and his colleagues in the NAACP weighed the merits of his joining the Smith effort, White pursued a study of black voting strength in the North as part of a broader consideration of how the Democrats might cultivate support that could be pivotal in a closely contested election. His findings, contained in a paper titled "Analysis of Possible Effect of Negro Vote in 1928 Election," illuminated the potential power of the black vote in the national political arena. It described how a relatively small number of black voters could tip the balance to the Democratic candidate in those states where white voters were evenly divided between the two major parties. In the end, White did not join the Smith campaign, but he served as an unofficial adviser.[72]

As a Catholic, however, Al Smith was handicapped as a candidate in the traditionally solidly Democratic South, and it was the South that ultimately dictated the racial terms of his campaign. Promised public gestures from Smith toward black Americans failed to materialize. At the national convention in Houston, black delegates were segregated in cages, and Smith selected segregationist Senator Joseph Robinson of Arkansas as his running mate. Even more troubling was the tenor of Smith's southern campaign, as his supporters competed with lily-white Republicans in an unrestrained appeal to white racial hatred. Toward the end of the election season, a statement in *The Crisis*, signed by black leaders representing a broad spectrum of political views, described the 1928 contest as the most antiblack presidential campaign since the Civil War. Titled "An Appeal to America," the manifesto charged "the political leaders of this campaign of permitting without protest, public and repeated assertions on the platform, in the press, and by word of mouth that color and race constitute in themselves an imputation of guilt and crime."

The Democrats' desperate effort to shore Smith up in the South failed to hold on to the region. Herbert Hoover carried Tennessee, Virginia, Florida, North Carolina, and Texas, and an overwhelming number of northern blacks stayed with the Republican candidate.[73]

The "extraordinary spectacle" of the 1928 campaign, Du Bois observed, exposed deep flaws in the American political process. Disenfranchisement of blacks invited blatant appeals to white supremacy that echoed through national politics. The silence that surrounded the exclusion of blacks from the ballot box in the South tested "the honesty of philanthropy in America toward the Negro." He warned that "every advance in the South unprotected by political power was based on chance and changing personalities." The state of black education in the South was proof enough that philanthropy and good will were no substitute for effective democratic control. Hard-won gains in the courts, such as the recent ruling on the white primary in Texas, were "without significance unless they point to fuller political power." While the consequences of the South's corrupt political system fell most heavily on blacks, it dragged down white laborers, deprived the entire region of decent and accountable government, and raised "an insistent question" for the nation—namely "whether the United States of America is going to maintain or surrender democracy as the fundamental starting point of permanent human uplift."[74]

The spread of segregation in the North demonstrated that the ballot was not an automatic check on discrimination, but with free access to the vote, Du Bois noted, blacks in northern cities were beginning to build a "firm . . . basis of permanent freedom." According to Walter White's analysis, given the sizeable and growing black vote in major northern cities, an organized black electorate could hold the balance of power in at least ten states. Political power, however, required that black voters exert their independence and make their ballots "an uncertain quantity." Du Bois anticipated the possibility of alignment with other groups who found themselves "politically homeless: the women, the liberal white South, organized Labor, the Pacifists, and the Farmers [who were] all politically dressed up with nowhere to go." Both he and White advised blacks to focus on local and state elections for strategic as well as practical reasons. Looking beyond presidential politics in October 1928, White wrote that "the choice of members of both Houses of Congress and of state legislatures and of county and city officials means much more to minority groups than who shall sit in the White House."[75]

*   *   *

The NAACP's high-profile work in the *Sweet* case and the Texas white primary ruling aided organizing efforts in the field, which continued to be a high priority. In one year, for example, officers of the association covered 75,517 miles and addressed 449 meetings. Bagnall and Pickens spent months on end in the field. Still Bagnall despaired that it was impossible for them, despite their "elasticity," to effectively cover the entire country. As a consequence many places that may have been organized or revived were not, while others became dormant. He urged that full-time field-workers be hired and assigned to the South, the Midwest, and the West as soon as the funds were available. Both men worked themselves to near physical and mental exhaustion. In 1929, the forty-eight-year-old Pickens reported that after ten years of fieldwork, he had to "be overhauled by two doctors" who prescribed sea-travel and rest.[76]

The North and West were the most dynamic areas of growth, fueled by growing black populations and the ongoing struggle along the color line. Newcomers often helped to invigorate existing branches. Claude Hudson, a native Louisianan who had served as president of the NAACP's Shreveport branch, moved to Los Angeles in 1924 and soon became president of the branch there, providing vigorous leadership into the next decade. Bagnall enlisted the aid of the more established branches to help organize new branches in surrounding communities of recent black population growth. Local NAACP officials pushed for the development of a statewide organization to provide for closer collaboration among branches and with the national office. NAACP branch leaders in Indiana led the way in 1929, holding a conference that brought together representatives from the branches and resulted in the establishment of a permanent state conference of branches. Ohio and New Jersey followed soon thereafter.[77]

The NAACP's victory in the white primary case, *Nixon v. Herndon*, in March 1927 helped to further heighten its profile in the South and stimulate black political activity. Bagnall observed that large numbers of blacks in Savannah and Richmond voted in the Democratic primary. It was "especially gratifying," he wrote, "to find that the Republican Party is no longer a fetish and that [many] realize the importance of voting in the Democratic primary and [in the general] election." During a tour through the Deep South in the spring of 1928, Bagnall found active branches and increased voter registration efforts in Mobile, Alabama, Jackson, Mississippi, and Pine Bluff, Arkansas, where Scipio Jones was challenging the efforts of election officials to bar blacks from voting. After a tour of the entire region in the spring of 1929, Bagnall and Pickens reported that the "old timidity" was gone and enthusiasm for the NAACP was growing, but that a full-time regional secretary was "badly needed" in order to realize the potential of a strong NAACP presence throughout the region.[78]

Bagnall's insistent pleas for additional help bore fruit late in 1929 when the board of directors agreed to hire Daisy Lampkin as a regional field secretary for the Midwest. The forty-eight-year-old Lampkin had recently led the revival of the Pittsburgh branch of the association, helping to secure two thousand new members. Lampkin was a nationally known figure, largely through her long association with the National Association of Colored Women, which included service as NACW's national organizer and chair of its executive board. She was married to William Lampkin; the two had no children. Lampkin devoted herself to civic work and the advancement of the race. She was a seasoned political activist, with wide-ranging experiences as an organizer and fund-raiser. Early in her career she served as president of the Negro Women's Franchise League, led an enormously successful Liberty Bond drive during World War I, and rose to a leading position in the women's division of the Republican Party, serving as a delegate to the 1926 Republican National Convention. After winning a contest for selling the most subscriptions to the *Pittsburgh Courier* in 1913, she began a long association with publisher Robert L. Vann, and in 1929 became a vice president of the paper. Lampkin joined the staff of the NAACP in January 1930, hired at an annual salary of $2,400 for an initial period of six months.[79]

Lampkin's responsibilities included building support among women. For Lampkin, this was a natural part of any organizing strategy; women, she believed, held the key to building strong branches. "Our male leadership is so busy with their private interests that nothing is done unless the women do it," Lampkin told White. A trend toward organizing women's auxiliaries had recently taken hold, and Lampkin agreed to work on strengthening them and increasing their numbers. But she cautioned that women resented "men holding the leadership when [the women] do all the work." Enthusiastic reports on Lampkin's work poured into the national office. "I have never seen such interest manifested before in this community by our women," wrote the branch president in Akron, Ohio. She was especially effective in engaging young women, who dominated the executive committee of the newly formed auxiliary. Lampkin's achievements and personality, he wrote, were an incentive "to the young women . . . for public work for most of them are anxious to become public speakers and lead large organizations." Her organizing ability, he said, was unsurpassed.[80]

The normal challenges of fieldwork were compounded by the growing economic depression. But the immediate day-to-day routine initially obscured the impact of the economic downturn. "It simply means more intensive work," Lampkin wrote. Indeed, she thought that it was having a positive psychological effect upon many black people. "As they face this temporary curtailment they seem to realize the need for the Association." Her early success in the field probably merited this optimistic view. Before the year was out she oversaw the organization of the Ohio state conference of branches. Working with young college-age black men and women in Cincinnati, she developed the idea of establishing what would become the Youth Division of the NAACP. By the end of 1930, however, the magnitude of unemployment and homelessness in cities like Detroit and Chicago became a major focus of her correspondence and tempered her confidence in future prospects.[81]

By 1930, the NAACP had a finely tuned leadership, a nationwide network of branches, and a program that engaged black communities across the land in fighting the varied manifestations of race discrimination. What the organization lacked in resources was made up for, to some extent, by the vision and determination of the individuals who actively participated in the work of the association. As Du Bois noted on the occasion of the NAACP's twentieth anniversary in 1929, the significance of the NAACP's achievements was best measured by "the foundation we have begun to lay" rather than the advancement that had been made.[82]

When President Herbert Hoover nominated John J. Parker to fill a vacant seat on the U.S. Supreme Court early in 1930, the NAACP was prepared to draw on the dynamic elements that made up the association and finally test its muscle in the national political arena. John J. Parker of Charlotte, North Carolina, a federal judge on the Fourth Circuit Court, was not widely known when Hoover announced his appointment on March 21. Walter White, then serving as acting secretary while James Weldon Johnson was on leave, sent out an urgent call for information on the nominee. Dr. A.M. Rivera of the Greensboro branch responded with a news clipping reporting on a 1920 speech Parker gave when he accepted the Republican Party's gubernatorial nomination. Disavowing charges by Democrats that the Republicans would seek black votes, Parker declared that "the participation of the Negro in politics is a source of evil and danger to both races and is not desired by wise men in either race or by the Republican party of North Carolina." White telegraphed Parker asking if he was quoted correctly by the *Greensboro Daily News* and, if he was, whether he continued to hold these views. When Parker failed to respond, the national office contacted NAACP branches in states where blacks voted in significant numbers urging them to telegraph their senators and oppose Parker's nomination and warn that they will "hold their senators accountable for their votes on the Parker confirmation." White wrote directly to the forty-six senators informing them of Parker's statement and soliciting their aid in opposing the nomination.[83]

White secured an invitation to testify on Parker's nomination before a subcommittee of the Senate Judiciary Committee. Parker's 1920 statement, White told the senators, was nothing less than a "shameless flouting of the Fourteenth and Fifteenth amendments of the federal constitution" and a pandering to race prejudice for political advantage. Such actions made him unfit for service on the nation's highest court. Furthermore, White observed that in recent years the U.S. Supreme Court had become the major arena of redress for blacks seeking the rights guaranteed under these amendments. The Court had heard eight major cases in this area and more were pending. Parker's appointment would compromise the Court's ability to provide the evenhanded justice essential to settling the "race problem."[84]

White's pointed testimony rattled North Carolina senator Lee Overman, who challenged White to produce evidence of black disenfranchisement in the Tar Heel State. When White volunteered to collect data and have them submitted for the record, Overman declined the offer. Still, White's testimony did little to influence the debate in the committee. The senators seemed most concerned with the opposition of organized labor and the testimony of American Federation of Labor (AFL) president William Green. Parker had upheld yellow-dog contracts that allowed companies to bar labor unions. Green for his part ignored White, careful not to align his group with the NAACP. While White initially seemed doubtful that Parker could be defeated, he believed that it was important to raise a protest, and he set his sights beyond Capitol Hill in organizing that effort.[85]

Working in concert with Bagnall, Pickens, and Lampkin, White orchestrated a major grassroots campaign to pressure senators in states where the black vote held a potential balance of power. The 250,000-member National Association of Colored Women (NACW) joined the NAACP in the fight, along with some two hundred black newspapers, fraternal organizations, churches, and individuals. A young physician in New Jersey traveled the state visiting with ministers and leaders of civic, fraternal, and welfare organizations to stir them to action. At many of the mass meetings in large cities, telegraph banks were provided to make it easier for individuals to send their protests. Telegrams, letters, and petitions poured into Senate offices. Daisy Lampkin, who organized the anti-Parker movement in Indiana, Ohio, and Pennsylvania reported that "there has been nothing that the Association has ever done that has attracted such wide attention to it as has this fight. . . . To even have an organization whose opinion and protest can be respected by the leaders in American life is more than worthwhile. I have never been so proud of the Association." Du Bois wrote that the campaign "was . . . conducted with a snap, determination and intelligence never surpassed in colored America and seldom in white."[86]

By mid-April, an inside source reported to White that the NAACP's campaign "was raising hell in Washington." Supporters of Parker's nomination shifted attention from labor to a desperate effort to blunt the force of the NAACP's campaign. The *Greensboro Daily News* denied that it had ever printed or heard of such a speech as the one Parker reportedly gave in 1920, an assertion that was repeated in other newspapers. The NAACP made copies of the original *Daily News* article and distributed them to the president, senators, and members of the press. There were reports that the Hoover administration was pressuring black federal officeholders to endorse Parker. Hoover personally appealed to his longtime supporter, Tuskegee Institute president Robert R. Moton, who had actively campaigned for Hoover in 1928. Moton declined. He wrote the president that the overt racism of Parker's statement was such that he "could have nothing less than an uncompromising and everlasting hostility" toward the man. In the end, only one prominent black figure, Dr. James Shepard, president of North Carolina College for Negroes, vouched for Parker. White commented that blacks had not "worked so unitedly" on any issue since the Civil War.[87]

On May 7, 1930, the Senate defeated Parker's nomination by two votes, 41 to 39. Half of the South's Democratic senators voted no; they were more concerned about blocking Republican inroads in the region than bucking the loose black-liberal coalition aligned against Parker. The *Washington Post* expressed a consensus of opinion when it observed that it "was the Negro opposition that gave the commanding position to the movement led by Progressives [to defeat Parker] aided . . . in some degree by organized labor." The mainstream press found no merit in the argument advanced by the

NAACP regarding Parker's promotion of black disenfranchisement in defiance of the Constitution. Rather, there was a palpable tone of alarm upon realizing the potential power exerted by black voters in the North linked with what the *Washington Post* described as "socialistic groups." The *Post* and the *New York Times* opined that such pressure-group politics threatened an independent judiciary, with the *Times* warning that "organized minorities are now in a position to wield a powerful influence over the Senate when Supreme Court nominations are at stake." Hoover, who placed most of the blame on the NAACP for Parker's defeat, had the Justice Department investigate the organization for radical or illegal activities.[88]

In a more positive assessment of the campaign's significance, the *Christian Science Monitor* called Parker's defeat "the first national demonstration of the Negro's power since Reconstruction days." The association would exert that power in the upcoming elections as it attempted to make good on the promise to oppose senators who voted to confirm Parker. Working in conjunction with local branches, the national office concentrated its resources and efforts on two senatorial races in 1930: Henry Allen of Kansas, who had led the fight for Parker in the Senate, and Roscoe McCulloch of Ohio. There was a large constituency of black voters in both states, strong local NAACP leadership, and both men were politically vulnerable. Daisy Lampkin stumped Ohio and was actively assisted by Walter White, while the newly established Ohio State Conference of Branches united around the movement to defeat McCulloch. Roy Wilkins, the thirty-year-old editor of the *Kansas City Call*, cut his teeth on the anti-Parker campaign and helped lead the effort to defeat Allen. Mass meetings frequently attracted more than a thousand people, energizing the campaigns in both states and boosting NAACP membership. The majority of black voters in Kansas and Ohio lined up for the Democratic candidate, contributing to the defeat of both Allen and McCulloch.[89]

The dramatic demonstration of independent political action in the anti-Parker fight as well as the November elections marked a watershed in the maturation of black political power and heightened the national reputation of the NAACP. Walter White used the opening created by the Parker fight to further define and reinforce the NAACP's position in the national political arena. In the aftermath of Parker's defeat White spent several days in Washington forming personal contacts "that might be useful in the future." He met with senators who had expressed opinions regarding the campaign waged by the NAACP and also conferred with AFL leader William Green. The NAACP's pivotal role in the coalition that defeated Parker, White assumed, might have left the union leader more inclined to adopt a favorable attitude toward the association. When Hoover nominated Owen J. Roberts to the seat Parker would have held, a quick review of the nominee's background indicated he was someone the NAACP could readily support. He was a trustee of Lincoln University and had a good relationship with the NAACP's Philadelphia branch. Letters of support were sent to the president and the nominee, in part to indicate that the NAACP was not "a purely anti-organization."[90]

A less-publicized development in 1930 would have even greater significance for the future of the NAACP and the broader movement it sought to create. That summer, after a close vote, the American Fund for Public Service awarded the organization $100,000 to mount a widespread legal challenge to the racial caste system in the South. James Weldon Johnson was a member of the AFPS's Committee on Negro Work that developed the successful but contentious proposal, which initially requested $300,000. Their effort generated a debate that would become more pronounced in the 1930s. Roger Baldwin and several other AFPS board members opposed the group's emphasis on litigation and held that an economic approach, built around the common plight of black and white workers, would be most effective in advancing the interests of the great majority of black people as well as the goals of the Garland Fund. Board members sympathetic to this view supported funding the leftist International Labor Defense and the American Negro Labor Congress.[91]

The Committee on Negro Work urged fellow board members to consider the fact that although black workers carried "the normal burden of workers under capitalism . . . [they] must constantly pay the penalty for their blackness." Black workers and blacks in general, the proposal contended, could best be aided by an "energetic and dramatic program" that fought for rights that "were assumed as axiomatic by . . . white workers [who] even in feudal Pennsylvania . . . [enjoyed] equal rights to go to school, to walk and ride in the streets, to live where they want to when they can afford it, to vote and sit on juries." A systematic and widespread campaign for equal schooling through test cases, the "crusade" that Du Bois had advocated, would be psychologically liberating and help stir "the spirit of revolt" among southern blacks. In addition to schools, the campaign advocated by the proposal included the areas of public transportation, voting, and jury selection. In the end, securing basic citizenship rights for blacks, they held, was essential to realizing black economic independence and creating the conditions for a robust labor movement.[92]

The proposal highlighted "the machinery" that distinguished the NAACP as the one organization capable of implementing such an ambitious undertaking. It had a national legal committee of leading lawyers as well as a nationwide network of more than one hundred black and white lawyers who were prepared to "serve the NAACP at a moment's notice." The NAACP had branches in forty-four states, including every southern state, as well as "correspondents" and contacts in places where branches didn't exist. The proposal emphasized the critical importance of local members and branches not only to initiating cases but to the follow-up critical to securing legal victories. As the NAACP leadership had learned in the *Buchanan* case, the vigilance and active involvement of local communities was essential to the enforcement of court rulings and guarding against efforts to subvert or ignore the law. Finally, the NAACP had proven itself to be a lean operation capable of achieving much on a shoestring budget. In the end, six of the eleven voting AFPS board members were convinced. The actual implementation of this program would be hammered out over the next several years, even as the Depression depleted most of the promised funding and heightened the appeal of a class-based approach to the plight of black America.[93]

The NAACP had tracked a steady upward path during the 1920s. Through its lobbying efforts on Capitol Hill, high-profile legal victories, and a national campaign against lynching, the NAACP had established itself as a major national organization that focused attention on the issue of racial justice. The decline in the number of lynchings from seventy-five in 1909 to eleven in 1929 and the public shame attached to these barbaric rituals was, Du Bois suggested, but one measure of the association's effectiveness, representing "a revolution in public sentiment." Lower-profile developments deepened the association's support among black Americans, including its successful support of black control of the new Veterans Administration hospital in Tuskegee and its quiet leadership of the movement to free the soldiers imprisoned for the Houston mutiny. By the end of the 1920s, nearly all had been pardoned or paroled. Two soldiers remained in Leavenworth Prison, and efforts would continue until they were released. At the same time, as individuals such as Moorfield Storey and Louis Marshall passed from the scene (both died in 1929), the NAACP was able to enlist some of the nation's leading legal talent and political figures in its work. Clarence Darrow and Felix Frankfurter were among those who joined the NAACP's Legal Committee in the late 1920s. By 1930, board members included New York lieutenant governor Herbert Lehman. In contrast to its earliest days, James Weldon Johnson observed, it had become easy for white people, "even liberal southern white people" to think well of the NAACP. Indeed, Du Bois noted, the NAACP "is almost respectable today," adding "that is perhaps its greatest danger."[94]

In December 1930, after a long-term leave, James Weldon Johnson resigned from his position as executive secretary. On the verge of turning sixty, he had devoted fourteen years to the NAACP, working at a grueling pace that took a physical toll while limiting the time for intellectual and literary pursuits. He left with little hesitancy given the magnificent performance of the association during his year of absence, under the leadership of Walter White. Johnson took satisfaction in all that had been achieved during his tenure, sharing credit with his board and his staff, and noting that all of their accomplishments rested upon "the zeal of the men and women active in our branches all over the country and the support that has been . . . generously given by the black press." While the association had come to wield considerable power, he observed that "there exists opportunities and resources sufficient to increase that power ten-fold, fifty-fold, a hundred-fold," a challenge that rested with black Americans. Johnson pledged to remain active in the association. "This work, as it has been, will always remain for me a part of my life, a greater part of my hopes, and in a still high degree, my religion."[95]

The hopeful tone of Johnson's sentiments, the sweet victory around the Parker nomination, and the endorsement of the Garland Fund seemed but a culmination of hard-earned advances and an opening toward a fuller development of the association's program. Yet this moment yielded to a tumultuous period that tested the agility that had been the NAACP's hallmark. The departure of Johnson, a steadying influence, coincided with other institutional changes and a deepening economic depression that sent membership plummeting. Walter White, his successor, was thrust into a position he suddenly seemed ill-prepared for. While other groups rose up to address the deep economic distress plaguing black America, the NAACP struggled to maintain its footing and chart a new direction during the Depression decade.

5

Radical Visions:
The Depression Years

They began arriving in Scottsboro as dawn broke on April 6, 1931, traveling from surrounding towns to the small county seat in northern Alabama. Thousands packed the town square when a contingent of National Guardsmen escorted nine young men, aged thirteen to twenty-one, to the courthouse. A line of soldiers kept the crowd clear of the building and several others guarded the entrance with mounted machine guns. "The town," wrote one observer, "looked like an armed camp in wartime."[1]

After a near lynching, Alabama officials were prepared to contain any violence that might interrupt the trial. Two white women had charged the nine black men with rape after deputies found them traveling on the same Memphis-bound freight train. The women were unemployed cotton mill workers from Huntsville, Alabama; the young men were from towns in Tennessee and Georgia. Poor, adrift, and looking for work, all were suddenly caught in the grip of what would become the most sensational trial of the Depression era.

During the two weeks leading up to the trial, stories of a gang rape at knifepoint filled the local press along with false reports that all but one of the accused had confessed. Stephen Roddy, hired by a group of black ministers in nearby Chattanooga, Tennessee, to defend the young men, met shouts and jeers as he made his way to the courthouse. He had fortified himself with drink in anticipation of such a reception. When the judge summoned the defense counsel to the bench, Roddy denied that he was the counsel of record. He was not familiar with Alabama law, he said, and was in court merely as an adviser. Milo Moody, a "doddering" old lawyer anxious for a fee, volunteered to join Roddy as a court-appointed attorney. The fate of the nine rested with this pair.[2]

The defendants were tried in four separate cases. A confident Victoria Price, aged twenty-one, and a hesitant Ruby Bates, aged seventeen, reconstructed their accounts of what happened on the train. The women differed on key points, but they were spared rigorous cross-examination. Two doctors who examined Price and Bates said that both women had been sexually active during the previous twenty-four hours, but there was no evidence of a violent assault. Ruby Bates recanted her testimony two years later, saying that she and Price had lied about the rape; they had not had any contact with the men on the train.

The jury for Clarence Norris and Charley Weems, who were tried first, took less than two hours to find the men guilty, condemning them to death in the electric chair. When the sentence was announced, the courtroom erupted into applause and cheers, echoed by the thousands gathered outside. The next two trials moved along similarly—the young men were tried, found guilty, and sentenced to death. The final defendant, thirteen-year-old Roy Wright, was sentenced to life in prison. The entire proceedings were completed in three days. The judge set the earliest possible execution date, July 10.[3]

Walter White had assumed the post of executive secretary of the NAACP just a month earlier. The New York press ran a short story about the mass arrests on March 24, and the Montgomery branch sent news clippings, but neither the board nor White did more than take notice. Board chair Mary White Ovington advised waiting to get more information before deciding whether to get involved in the case; the association "did not want to defend boys guilty of rape." But firsthand accounts were not readily available. Chattanooga, the closest branch, had been dormant for several years. Meanwhile, other matters and increasingly dire financial circumstances relegated the Alabama story to the margins.[4]

On April 2, Dr. P.A. Stephens, a black physician in Chattanooga, wrote White that the city's Interdenominational Ministers Alliance had raised "some little funds and retained a lawyer for the purpose of seeing that the boys get justice." He asked if the NAACP might assist them. White referred the letter to William Andrews, the special legal assistant, adding, "You will remember this case previously came to our attention." Andrews wrote Stephens seeking more information; upon reading the next day that eight had been sentenced to death, he asked Stephens to send copies of trial transcripts, still not volunteering what, if anything, the NAACP might do. Several days later, White received a press clipping about the case and an urgent plea from a Mr. Thornhill of Lynchburg, Virginia: "By all means do something to help these poor fellows." White responded that they were waiting to review the trial transcript. William Pickens wrote from the field asking the office to forward information about what the NAACP was doing "in connection with that Alabama horror, where the state is moving to murder those eight Negroes." He drew a similar reply.[5]

White's cautious response to the "Alabama horror" seemed out of character for the man who had exposed the massacre in Elaine, Arkansas, and engineered the defense of Ossian Sweet. While there was no active branch in the area, in the past the NAACP did not hesitate to dispatch an investigator under such stunning circumstances—the mass arrest of black men on rape charges in the Deep South, swiftly tried and sentenced to death. It would be more than two weeks before the ministers' group in Chattanooga sent a copy of the trial transcript. Meanwhile, blacks and whites outraged over the fate of the Scottsboro boys began to rally behind the American Communist Party and its legal arm, the International Labor Defense (ILD) in its no-holds-barred attack on the "legal lynching" that posed as justice.[6]

The Communist Party of the United States (CPUSA) was just beginning to cultivate a base in the South in 1931. Organized in New York a decade earlier, the CPUSA established an outpost in Birmingham in the heart of the Black Belt in 1930. A party resolution held that blacks in this section of the United States constituted "an oppressed nation" entitled to self-determination. While the idea of self-determination resonated with some, party organizers gained more ground when they addressed the concrete economic despair and racial oppression that crippled the lives of blacks in Birmingham and the surrounding area—the unemployed, the working poor, and sharecroppers. But the Scottsboro case provided a stellar opportunity for the party to announce its presence in the South and trumpet its militant and uncompromising opposition to racism.[7]

A Chattanooga-based party organizer immediately contacted New York with news of the arrests and the threat of a mass lynching. Charles Dirba, ILD official in New York, in turn wired Lowell Wakefield, their representative in Birmingham, and instructed him to make a full investigation. Wakefield and an associate attended the trials and after the first day predicted that Scottsboro might well be the equivalent of the infamous Sacco-Vanzetti case. As soon as the verdicts were announced, the party launched a massive campaign through its affiliates, directing telegrams to the governor of Alabama and the judge protesting the "legal lynching" of the nine black "victims of capitalist justice." This was joined by protests from around the country; telegrams and letters "poured into the governor's office." Simultaneously, the ILD set about planning to appeal the cases and immediately tried to enlist Clarence Darrow as its lead attorney.[8]

Darrow contacted White on April 10, the day after the final verdict, suggesting that he join him in meeting with a representative of the ILD. White declined, charging that the ILD was "more interested in . . . propaganda than immediate results." Vastly exaggerating the extent of the NAACP's involvement at this point, he assured Darrow that they were already cooperating with a group in Alabama who had retained a lawyer. Indeed, this would have been news to NAACP official William Pickens. On April 19, Pickens wrote a letter to the *Daily Worker*, the Communist Party's newspaper, praising the party for the fight being waged to "prevent the judicial massacre of Negro youth in Alabama." He included a small donation and concluded by saying that now was the time for "every Negro who has intelligence enough to read to send aid to . . . the ILD."[9]

While awaiting the trial transcript, events and a cresting flood of inquiries compelled the association to break its public silence on the Scottsboro case. On April 24, an NAACP press release announced that it had been at work on plans for the defense "of the eight Negro boys sentenced to death in Alabama after a hasty trial" and had retained Stephen R. Roddy, a claim that surely raised eyebrows among those familiar with his performance during the trial. As the first salvo in the NAACP's effort to assert its control of the case, the press release offered a lackluster summation of the trial and a brief statement about what was at stake. Embarrassingly, it came on the day that the *Daily Worker* published the Pickens letter urging blacks to aid the ILD, which brought Pickens a severe reprimand. Board chair Ovington "condemned the unwisdom—and what might be construed as the disloyalty" of his action."[10]

Two days later, the ILD staged a mass protest in New York, grabbing headlines in the *New York Times*: "Police Clubs Rout 200 Defiant Reds Who Attacked 'Lynch Law' in Alabama." Increasingly identified in the public mind with the case, the ILD moved to consolidate its control. On April 22, the ILD had announced that it had retained George W. Chamlee, a well-regarded attorney from a prominent Tennessee family, to replace Roddy and serve as lead counsel in the appeal. ILD attorneys Allen Taub and Joseph Brodsky sought out the parents of the young men and worked to persuade them that their sons should engage the ILD. On April 24, they arranged for several of the parents to visit Kilby Prison outside of Montgomery for a tearful reunion with their sons. Janie Patterson, mother of defendant Haywood Patterson, attended the New York protest as a guest of the ILD and addressed a rally in Harlem. The *Daily Worker* set the tone of what became a steady harangue, charging that the NAACP was more concerned with maintaining "respectability" among "the liberal white millionaires" and not offending the southern ruling class than it was in "saving the lives of nine children being murdered in Alabama."[11]

Desperate to recover lost ground, White hurried to Alabama during the first week of May. "Public interest is so deep," he told his colleagues, "we cannot afford not to be in this case." In typical whirlwind fashion, White met with his contacts in Chattanooga and NAACP branch officials in Birmingham, visited the defendants in Kilby Prison, and sought out their parents in Tennessee and Georgia. After a conference with Roddy, a "heavy drinker" who was neither "diligent" nor "well trained," White promptly identified a prominent Birmingham lawyer, Roderick Beddow, and enlisted him to lead the defense. In the end, though, all depended upon the young men and their parents, several of whom had already accepted the ILD's offer to appeal their convictions.[12]

With his own credibility on the line and the reputation of the NAACP at stake, White's reports from Alabama conveyed little empathy for the terrifying circumstances of the young men trapped in a cycle of false accusation, incarceration, and impending execution. He rarely mentioned them or their parents without noting their ignorance or stupidity. In a determined effort to win them over, White could hardly conceal his impatience and said that he warned one mother that "when Red prejudice was added to Black," she practically ensured her son's execution. White succeeded in obtaining a signed agreement from four of the boys; two others wanted to consult with their parents; the others preferred to stay with the ILD. This was just the beginning of a dizzying contest between the NAACP and the ILD in a fierce display of organizational rivalry.[13]

Upon returning to New York, White wrote a "confidential" letter to the editors of black newspapers to report on his trip and announce that the NAACP was completing plans "for the most effective defense possible for the nine boys." Sent more than a month after the trial, this was the national office's first word to the black press about the case beyond the April 24 press release. He confided that after a "careful investigation" he was convinced that

the boys were not guilty of the crime—a revelation to few who had been following the case. The letter went on to lambast the communists for "the most
intemperate sort of misstatements, vituperation, and vilification for the sake
of getting into the press" and for their outlandish tactics. They bombarded
the governor of Alabama with ninety-four telegrams demanding that the
boys be freed—"a manifestly absurd and impossible demand," White wrote.
Leading white and black citizens told him that such antics would only wreak
more vengeance upon the young men. White expressed confidence that the
editors would support the NAACP's efforts in the face of the "misrepresentations the communists are spreading for selfish purposes."[14]

White's letter did little to reassure many of the black editors, at best puzzled
by the association's long silence. An obsession with the ILD seemed to trump
the main issue—the impending sacrifice of eight young men to "the hob-
goblin of 'White Supremacy.'" The *Washington World* bemoaned the sorry
spectacle of the NAACP using the same "mudslinging" tactics as the Communist Party, while the party earned praise from the paper for its aggressive
public campaign that aroused the nation to the seriousness of the Scottsboro
cases. White's claim that the association had been involved from the start,
commented Roscoe Dunjee in the Oklahoma *Black Dispatch*, was a further
indictment of the NAACP's failure to take any public stand or action during the weeks following the trial. That White was reduced to splitting hairs
about the communists was further indication of the association's impotency.
"Another NAACP Needed?" asked Eugene Davidson, editor of the *Washington World*. "If [the NAACP] now feels that fighting the spread of communism is more important than fighting white Southerners who will lynch,
massacre and slaughter and expect to get away with it," then "it has outlived
its usefulness."[15]

The Communist Party's bold defense of the Scottsboro boys offered a dramatic contrast to the seemingly staid approach of the NAACP. In his indignant defense of the association, Du Bois chided the ILD for its "ill-considered
and foolish tactics against the powers in whose hands the fate of the Scottsboro victims lie." Others countered that the communists' loud protests challenged that power by exposing Jim Crow justice with mass demonstrations
throughout the country and around the world. Howard University Law
School dean Charles Houston took issue with William Pickens, who had
become an ardent critic of the communists' publicity campaign. "Pickens
seems to think justice for the Scottsboro boys can be obtained in Alabama
without outside pressure. Personally I do not believe it. . . . If the boys are to

be saved, they must be saved by public opinion." Looking back many years later, Robert Weaver compared the effect of the publicity surrounding Scottsboro to the dramatic impact of police turning hoses and dogs on young black protesters in Birmingham in 1963. "It was a great shock . . . and made many people face up to a situation they would not have faced up to before."[16]

The fight for control of the case ended in December 1931 when the ILD secured the written authorization of all of the defendants to take their appeal forward. For White, the experience had been a harrowing introduction to the altered political terrain of the Depression years. The conflict around the Scottsboro case rehearsed issues that would resonate across the decade. In the shorter term, it illuminated broader questions about the future of the NAACP at a critical moment for the association and its new executive secretary.

The NAACP had entered the decade of the 1930s secure in its position as the leading advocate of black civil rights; suddenly it was on the defensive. While it shared blame with the ILD for the bickering that sapped energy from the effort to save the Scottsboro boys, the contest became part of a broader struggle, one that tested the NAACP's ability to meet the new circumstances spawned in the tumult of the Great Depression. In this dramatically altered environment, the legal campaign branched out and emerged as a driving force of the organization's program. It provided the means for challenging the routine violations of legally guaranteed rights and enlisting black communities in a sustained struggle against racial discrimination. Open competition with the Communist Party and its legal arm for cases supported this surge in legal activity, which was largely the result of the forward-looking strategy developed by Charles Houston.

By the end of 1931, the NAACP was perched on the edge of bankruptcy. While the Depression bit into the coffers of similar organizations, the NAACP was dependent upon a segment of the population hardest hit by the economic collapse. Black unemployment was at least twice as high as white, reaching nearly 60 percent in Detroit. NAACP membership fell to twenty thousand, while demands on the association more than doubled. The Garland Fund stock plummeted, making it impossible for the foundation to fulfill its $100,000 pledge to support the anticipated legal campaign. During the early 1930s, William Rosenwald, youngest son of the late Julius Rosenwald, and New York lieutenant governor Herbert Lehman, member of the famous banking family, generated a critical infusion of funds from other, mostly Jewish philanthropists and businessmen through a series of matching fund appeals. Still, unless painful cuts were made, budget chairman Charles Russell feared that "the whole enterprise [would be] on the rocks."[17]

White's elevation to permanent executive secretary in March 1931 intensified the uncertainty that clouded the future. He was a study in contrasts to the widely admired Johnson, whose leadership built the NAACP into an effective, nationwide organization. Some members of the board had their doubts about White. "He had a genius for publicity," recalled Arthur Spingarn, "and knew everybody," but "his vagueness on financial matters" was worrisome. A gregarious man of frenetic activity, White could be arrogant and abrasive. He seemed to have little regard for the challenges facing the field staff; Daisy Lampkin complained that three times White had failed to follow through on a promised visit to the struggling Baltimore branch. Those working in the New York office found White constantly looking over their shoulders. He "tried to supervise everything in connection with the work" the office secretary confided to board chairman Ovington. That included checking up on clerks and reviewing their time cards, which was her responsibility. Executive staff members grew increasingly restive as White sought to assert his authority over them and put his stamp on what had been a more fluid operation.[18]

Du Bois viewed Walter White's ascension to the top post as an unmitigated disaster. Fundamental differences about building and sustaining a movement for black advancement joined a "combustible mixture of age and ego" to create an unbridgeable divide between the two men. Moreover, declining circulation of The Crisis, which had hit a low of nineteen thousand in the spring of 1931, along with a steady decrease in advertising dollars, made Du Bois increasingly dependent upon the financial support of the association, allowing White to push for more oversight. Du Bois insisted that the future of The Crisis and the association were inextricably bound. Hardly any board members shared that assessment. Du Bois's old supporter, Mary White Ovington, was quite matter of fact in telling him that the association had eclipsed The Crisis in importance and advised that "it cannot belong to you as it has in the past." But he worked confidently to shore up his enterprise. In 1930 he attempted to hire Roy Wilkins, the impressive young editor of the Kansas City Call, to help oversee the business side of the operation. The salary was not enough to lure Wilkins east. Less than a year later, when White became the permanent executive secretary, Du Bois led the move to hire Wilkins as assistant secretary and this time Wilkins accepted, joining the staff in August 1931.[19]

The pinch of tightening resources heightened tensions in the national office. At the end of 1931, with White already weakened by his handling of the Scottsboro case, Du Bois seized the opportunity to mount a major challenge to his leadership. That December, with data supplied by White, the budget committee of the board recommended salary cuts between 5 and 10 percent, and that the business operation of *The Crisis* be completely taken over by the association. White's report claimed that neither the field staff nor the editor were bringing in enough money to justify their salaries. With Du Bois in the lead, William Pickens, Robert Bagnall, Herbert Seligman, and the newly hired Wilkins joined in an open revolt.[20]

In a collective letter to the board, Du Bois and his associates accused White of supplying false information to the budget committee and lying to cover his own wastefulness. "The Secretary has absolute domination of these expenditures and practically reports to no one," they charged. Unless White was "going to be more honest . . . with his colleagues . . . and more conscientious in his expenditures of money . . . the question is how long can he remain in his present position and keep this organization from utter disaster?" In a final blow, they stated: "In our several careers, we have never met a man like Walter White who under an outward and charming manner has succeeded within a short time in alienating and antagonizing every one of his coworkers, including all the clerks in the office." Du Bois read the statement to the board at its December meeting.[21]

The revolt was short lived. White easily maintained the support of board chair Ovington and NAACP president Joel Spingarn. Ovington, whose affection for Du Bois had cooled, confided in Spingarn that if the choice was between White and Du Bois, "Walter is worth ten times as much to us." When it became clear that White's position was secure, Wilkins was the first to jump ship. The day after the board meeting he wrote a note to White, confessing his deep regret for his part "in that awful mess" and offering to resign. Pickens followed, announcing that he disavowed any part of the statement that reflected on White's honor. Seligman and Bagnall also disassociated themselves from the statement and sought White's forgiveness. Spingarn, who remained close to Du Bois, implored his friend to drop the charges. Du Bois refused "to retract or change a single word."[22]

The crisis that engulfed the NAACP led to an evaluation of the organization and its procedures, helping to focus attention on the association's weaknesses and strengths at a transitional moment. Spingarn engaged Edna Lonigan, who specialized in examining civic organizations, to audit the association and provide an independent response to allegations of mismanagement. Her report, released in April 1932, provided a comprehensive review of the association's finances, structure, and practices. It noted White's penchant to spend extravagantly on "Pullman tips, taxicabs, valet and laundry service, and . . . rooms and meals" while traveling, and advised that "extreme economy" be employed in all realms. The report cautioned against a tendency to regard branches "merely as sources of revenue," and suggested a fuller integration of the branches into the work of the national office. White's narrow, "bottom line" method for measuring the costs and results of fieldwork was inadequate, the report concluded. Continuous efforts to cultivate "local officers, members and ought-to-be members" were essential, and the report advised that new blood be brought into fieldwork wherever possible. The "walls" should come down, and the whole staff be considered part of the field department. The report also recommended that the association develop a definite and consistent economic program for meeting the problems exposed and intensified by the Depression.[23]

In a parallel effort to orient the association toward new political realities, Du Bois initiated a frank examination on how a major segment of black America viewed the Communist Party. *The Crisis* sponsored a symposium on Communism with seventeen newspaper editors, published in a two-part series in April and May 1932. The majority of respondents were positive in their assessment of the party, on practical rather than ideological grounds. Quite simply, noted Carl Murphy of the *Baltimore Afro-American*, the communists were the only white group to openly advocate "the economic, political, and social equality of Negroes." There were numerous examples of the party's willingness to act on its stated commitment to racial equality and economic justice, from the Scottsboro case to a mass protest of hospital segregation in Philadelphia and rent strikes in New York City. It had seized on the burning economic issues raised by the Depression and promoted black-white working-class unity, which many viewed as essential to advancing economic as well as racial justice. In a departure from the paternalism characteristic of philanthropists and liberal reformers, party activists offered brotherhood, not charity and uplift; they "practiced" equality. One did not need to embrace the ideology or goals of the party to appreciate their role in fighting racial injustice. "When a man is drowning does he ask reasons for the helping hand?" asked W. P. Dabney of the *Cincinnati Union*. The communists had demonstrated the appeal of bold action and courageous leadership. "We are today standing on the brink of revolutionary change in our social and racial attitudes," observed Roscoe Dunjee, editor of the Oklahoma *Black Dispatch*. "Whatever the trend, Negro leadership should not overlook the chance to make the most of this moment."[24]

The discussion over the association's future dominated the 1932 annual convention in Washington, D.C., at the end of May. "A spirit of revolt, of restlessness, and of political independence [was] sweeping Negro America," White declared. Internal divisions subsided, with Du Bois, White, and others united by the belief that the NAACP was needed now more than ever. Du Bois addressed the recent attacks on the association by the communists and their allies and advocated a plan for new directions. "The widest spread criticism within the Negro race" was that it was "a highbrow organization." He acknowledged that the concept of a "talented tenth" had guided the NAACP since its founding, assuming that those distinguished by educational and professional achievement would lead in advancing the race. But then came the question, were the more privileged of the race working merely for their own advancement? Even more compelling, the tremendous change sweeping the nation and the world demanded a complete rethinking of the NAACP's approach. It was not sufficient that the advancement of the masses of people be the object of the association, for "who is to be the judge of what these people want and ought to have?"

The NAACP must develop a positive program that would go beyond just attacking manifestations of racial discrimination, Du Bois insisted. Working through its system of branches, it should provide the structure through which the great majority of black people could be heard, and their struggles should infuse the thrust of the NAACP's work. Du Bois advocated getting away from a tendency for the national office to "send life down" to the branches. NAACP branches should represent a thousand different centers, studying their own problems, and using the national office as a clearinghouse rather than a place "where solutions are made." This would be achieved, Du Bois advised, through some decentralization of authority and power, and a commitment to creating *real* branches—"living cells of activity and ideals," rather than mere appendages of the national office. Here was the starting point for developing a positive economic program, essential to advancing the welfare of black people and testing the possibilities of interracial alliances. Finally, he called for a more deliberate effort to engage youth in the work of the NAACP, for they were the source of new ideas and the strength needed to carry the movement forward. "The link between the generations," Du Bois insisted, "must be made."[25]

Abram Harris and George Schuyler, hailed as voicing the aspirations of "young and insurgent Negroes," called for a more economically driven approach to the problems of black America. The thirty-three-year-old Harris, a professor of economics at Howard, was co-author with Sterling Spero of the pioneering study *The Negro Worker*, published a year earlier. Harris offered a critique of the causes of worldwide depression, rooted in the failure to balance productive outcome with consuming power. Those who suffered the greatest burden of depression and unemployment—workers, black and white—must join together to advance the democratic control of industrial production, he argued. The AFL, a federation of craft unions that generally excluded blacks, was ill-equipped to advance such a movement. "We must begin from the ground up and build a new labor movement," Harris declared, offering a united front for securing their "common welfare" as workers. George Schuyler, a celebrated young writer who was hailed as "the black Mencken," urged the NAACP to help blacks to realize their own economic power through the establishment of black consumer cooperatives.[26]

In this presidential election year, politics was a major convention topic, bringing out an impressive lineup of congressional representatives. Senators Robert Bulkley of Ohio, Arthur Capper of Kansas, and Robert LaFollette Jr. of Wisconsin each addressed the meeting. LaFollette, anticipating the spirit of New Deal reform, gave a stirring address advocating a strong role for the federal government in securing an equal chance in life for every man, woman, and child. Senator Bulkley had won election with the support of black voters galvanized to defeat his pro-Parker opponent. He pledged continued cooperation with the NAACP and praised the growing political independence of black voters as "good for our country." Walter White reminded the convention that blacks now held the balance of power in thirteen states and predicted that this was the year that the black vote "will come into its own." But neither the incumbent Herbert Hoover nor the likely Democratic candidate, New York governor Franklin D. Roosevelt, curried the favor of the black voters. While White recognized that the outcome of the presidential race would be of some significance for blacks, he urged that the NAACP put its energies toward electing a liberal Congress and local and state officials willing to act on measures vital to blacks as well as "other working classes."[27]

The NAACP's new legal campaign was showcased at the Washington meeting by Nathan Margold. A former U.S. attorney in New York City and a protégé of Felix Frankfurter, Margold had been hired the previous October to direct the NAACP's Garland Fund program. In the interim months, the fund's losses reduced the grant to only a fraction of the promised $100,000. Still, the NAACP pressed ahead, adding its own funds to the meager contribution of the Garland Fund and hired Margold on a part-time basis. That spring Margold had produced a major report mapping out a fresh and innovative approach for attacking segregation in education, transportation, and housing, with the major emphasis on education. The vast and well-documented disparity between black and white schools, Margold argued, opened the way toward challenging the constitutional validity of state segregation laws. The Margold Report laid out an ambitious agenda which became a blueprint for the NAACP's legal campaign. In his speech to the conference, however, he offered few specifics about how such a sweeping plan might be implemented. Charles Hamilton Houston, dean of the Howard University Law School, provided a preview of how the legal campaign would be carried forward.[28]

Charles Houston was among the few conference participants who offered a prescription for action. In his speech to the convention, Houston asserted that the black lawyer was central to the next phase of the movement. In outlining a program of cooperation between the all-black National Bar Association (NBA) and the NAACP, he described how the NBA supported Negro legal education as an essential training ground for the "soldiers" who would carry on "the actual battles in the courtroom" and serve "as advisers of the people." Access to justice was fundamental to sustaining faith in "the system," Houston explained, as well as inspiring local efforts on other fronts. The NBA was working to create a legal aid program to ensure that legal assistance was available to poor people regardless of the question of a fee. Yet, the implementation of such a program faced a major obstacle—namely the "distribution of flesh and blood Negro lawyers throughout the country." As of 1930, the census listed 1,230 black lawyers as compared with 159,735 white lawyers. Many of the black lawyers counted were not actually practicing law, and just a fraction of practicing black lawyers were scattered around the South, centered in a few major cities. This was a situation Houston and his colleagues in the NBA were striving to redress as the NAACP prepared to embark on its legal campaign.[29]

While much of the convention was devoted to looking forward, the role of historical memory and interpretation in the struggle for black advancement received significant commentary. The conference included a pilgrimage to Harper's Ferry where the Niagara Movement had met twenty-five years earlier. The NAACP had planned to place a plaque at the building used by John Brown as the fort in his failed antislavery insurrection in 1859, honoring the militant abolitionist who, in Du Bois's words, gave his life "in the cause of human liberation." Brown was tried and hung for murder and treason against the state of Virginia, culminating an episode that had heightened tensions around the issue of slavery. The trustees of Storer College, on whose property the fort stood, had originally approved the placing of a public marker. But upon reviewing the inscription written by Du Bois, they rejected it as too controversial. Nevertheless, the plaque was unveiled at the site, and Du Bois delivered a powerful address about the history and meaning of what happened at that place.

"Here John Brown Aimed a Blow at Human Slavery that woke a guilty nation . . . " began the inscription. Du Bois expressed dismay that the simple facts listed on the small bronze tablet caused such a stir. "It did not occur to me that I was saying anything that anyone in the United States would disagree with." He talked about the lies that students at Storer College and throughout the nation were being taught about the Civil War and its aftermath. "I am sorry for these students . . . and the students that are coming," he said, "because after all it is the Truth, in the long run, that makes us Free." White described Du Bois's speech as a high point of the conference, and "the greatest speech he ever made." At the end of the ceremony, NAACP staff packed up the plaque and took it back to New York, where it would be displayed in the national office.[30]

It was "vital," White wrote James Weldon Johnson, "that this year's conference go over big in view of the attacks upon us . . . during the past year by the communists and the difficulty during this period with everyone being hypocritical." He could not have been more pleased with the results. "I wish you could have been there," he enthused. It would have "thrilled you to have seen the militancy of the Association reach a very high peak." Joel Spingarn, who had been worn down from the internal sniping and bickering, was also relieved and revived by the spirit that prevailed in Washington and at Harper's Ferry. Hoping to channel this energy for the long-term benefit of the association, Spingarn proposed a second Amenia conference at his Troutbeck estate to engage younger black professionals in an open discussion about the future of the NAACP. Du Bois was receptive to the idea, but it would be another year before planning for such a gathering got under way.[31]

In the immediate aftermath of the conference, Walter White appeared to take Houston's admonitions to heart, although other pressures had made White attentive to the association's failure to cultivate black lawyers as part of the NAACP's leadership. The national office had completely alienated a group of black lawyers in the city of Houston, furious with the association's failure to include them in the implementation of its ongoing legal campaign to defeat the white primary in Texas. After James Cobb, the only black to serve on the National Legal Committee, was appointed to a judgeship in 1926, it was two years before T.G. Nutter, another black attorney and a long-time leader of the NAACP's Charleston, West Virginia, branch, joined the legal committee. In the summer of 1932, due to White's efforts, four additional black lawyers were added to the then ten-member national body: Jesse Heslip, who was president of the NBA; N.J. Frederick, the sole practicing civil rights lawyer in Columbia, South Carolina; Louis Redding, the first black lawyer in Wilmington, Delaware; and Charles Houston, boosting black representation on the National Legal Committee to one-third. William Hastie, a young instructor at Howard University Law School, and Homer Brown of Pittsburgh joined the committee the following year. In August 1932, White delivered the keynote address to the National Bar Association's annual meeting in Indianapolis and invited cooperation in all aspects of the NAACP's evolving legal campaign.[32]

Over the next couple of years, Walter White and Charles Houston forged a relationship that would have profound consequences for the NAACP and the direction of the civil rights movement. White would ultimately recruit Houston to lead the NAACP's new legal office and give him free rein in orchestrating a broad-based challenge to racial discrimination and segregation—which became a cornerstone of the NAACP's program. The two were, in some ways, a study in contrasts. Houston possessed a quiet brilliance, was intensely focused on the work, and had an open approach to radical political movements committed to racial advancement. White was the maestro of the NAACP, a man of great personal ambition and well-connected to white cultural and political elites. Born two years apart, both men had traveled a path from secure middle-class upbringings through the gauntlet of American racism and were joined in their commitment to purge the blight of racial injustice and inequality from national life.

Charles Houston, the only child of William and Mary Houston, was born in 1895 in Washington, D.C. He attended the prestigious Dunbar High School, the leading black high school in the nation, and graduated Phi Beta Kappa from Amherst College in 1915. Houston was working as an instructor in English at Howard University when he helped lead the effort to secure a training camp for black officers. Among the earliest recruits to come through the Des Moines camp, Houston's experience as an officer in the U.S. Army during World War I determined his future course. The abuses endured by black soldiers in the segregated armed forces were compounded by Houston's experience as a judge advocate, where he witnessed a blatant disregard for fairness and justice when blacks were the subject of prosecution. The case of a sergeant with an exemplary record, stripped of his rank and sentenced to a year at hard labor on a trumped-up charge of insubordination was one example. Houston later wrote: "I made up my mind . . . that if luck was with me and I got through this war I would study law and use my time fighting for men who could not strike back."[33]

In the fall of 1919, Houston entered Harvard Law School. He was one of the top students in his class and was the first African American elected to the *Harvard Law Review*. While pursuing a demanding course of study, he marshaled the strength and talent of his fellow black students to create venues for mutual support in the white-dominated and racially exclusive environment. Houston was a founder and central figure of the Nile Club, originally called the Harvard Negro Club. It was open to all black students at Harvard. He arranged a luncheon for Marcus Garvey, which brought together twenty black students from the Cambridge/Boston area. Before continuing on to graduate work, Houston indicated his plans for the future in his appeal to the Veterans Bureau for an extension of his vocational training period. "There must be Negro lawyers in every community . . . and the great majority will come from Negro schools . . . [where] the training will be in the hands of Negro teachers. It is to the best interests of the United States . . . to provide the best teachers possible."[34]

After returning to Washington in 1924, Houston married Margaret "Mag" Gladys Moran, his longtime sweetheart, and joined his father's law firm. He also began teaching at Howard University Law School. Two years later, Mordecai Johnson became the first black president of Howard and transformed the university into a vibrant center for black intellectuals and scholars. In 1927, Houston directed a yearlong study for Howard Law School, funded by the Laura Spelman Rockefeller Foundation, titled "The Status and Activities of Negro Lawyers in the United States." Upon becoming vice-dean of the law school in 1929, Houston further developed and applied his ideas regarding the role of the black lawyer in American life.[35]

Houston transformed Howard Law School from a nonaccredited night school into a full-time accredited program. Previously, the law school had depended exclusively on part-time faculty drawn from practicing lawyers and judges in Washington. The newly accredited law school had five full-time professors, who composed the core group, and six part-time instructors. In addition to Houston, the full-time faculty included Leon Ransom, valedictorian of his class at Ohio State University Law School; William Taylor, who graduated at the top of his class at Iowa University School of Law; William Hastie, a graduate of Harvard Law School whom Felix Frankfurter placed in the top 2 percent of his class; and Alfred Buscheck, the sole white full-time faculty member, who was a graduate of the University of Wisconsin Law School and had received a JSD degree at Yale. While Houston technically served as the dean, he would not accept the title until the salary of the law faculty and the staff was raised to a level of compensation equal to the minimum a poor school would pay.[36]

As legal scholar Mark Tushnet has observed, under Houston's leadership, the core faculty developed what was perhaps the first public-interest law school "with an institutional focus of the effects of the legal system on the black community." Houston's approach drew on the innovative theory of social jurisprudence advanced at Harvard by Roscoe Pound, Felix Frankfurter, and others, and was grounded in the belief that through the creative exploration and application of the Constitution, the black lawyer could achieve reforms that were unattainable through traditional political channels. His rigorous and demanding program earned him the moniker "Cement Pants" from his students. But many of those who stuck with him would serve on the front lines of the mounting battle to overturn Jim Crow. The black lawyer, Houston stressed, must "be trained as a social engineer . . . prepared to anticipate, guide, and interpret his group's advancement." Moreover, he believed that the alignment of historical forces favored and even demanded the kind of innovative and ambitious intervention for which he was training his students.[37]

That Americans were living in the midst of a broad economic, social, and political restructuring in the early 1930s was indisputable. But for black Americans, Houston identified changes stretching over more than a decade that informed the challenges and possibilities they faced. There was the First World War, which taught them organization, discipline, "and the unimportance of death," and the accompanying wave of migration of black southerners to the North, where those who escaped the South had their first taste of freedom, and preliminary lessons in politics and trade unionism. The Garvey movement, Houston declared, was "a black man's dream." It was "immaterial whether [Garvey] was a charlatan or a fool." He had "a profound influence on

Negro thought" and made "a permanent contribution in teaching the simple dignity of being black." Finally, Houston observed, the Scottsboro case "has caught the imagination of Negroes as nothing else within a decade." Through their bold and uncompromising intervention, "the communists have been the first to fire 'the masses' with a sense of their raw, potential power, and the first to preach openly the doctrine of mass resistance and mass struggle." They had altered the terrain of black protest, Houston explained, and "made it impossible for any aspirant to Negro leadership to advocate less than full economic, political, and social equality, and expect to retain the respect and confidence of the group."[38]

The Scottsboro case was of critical importance, Houston believed, both for what it revealed about the complete failure of the South's judicial system so far as blacks were concerned and how it demonstrated the necessity of taking the fight beyond the courtroom through public exposure, mass protest, and pressure. The case, Houston wrote, touched "every Negro in the country . . . and demands our complete and undivided support until the last Scottsboro boy is free." Houston contributed money to the ILD on a regular basis, readily provided legal assistance and service, and was frequently in touch with his friend, ILD director William Patterson. He admired the ILD's bold tactics, noting on a press clipping that reported a five-thousand-strong protest in Los Angeles that the ILD was "everlastingly at it. They never let the public forget." One of his most prized possessions was a poster of an open-air Scottsboro protest rally in Amsterdam.[39]

While the ILD and the Communist Party had led the way in arousing mass protest, Houston believed that the NAACP provided the machinery best suited to his vision for securing long-term change. The Communist Party, quite new to the American scene, had yet to work out a philosophy or program suited to the nation's history and conditions, he wrote. Its advocacy of a separate black nation in the Black Belt was a case in point. Houston contended that most blacks did not think of themselves as a separate nation, and, further, "given the history of Civil War . . . any high school student knows this would not be tolerated. It would be race suicide to try." The NAACP was in need of a major retuning along the lines pioneered by the communists, but in Houston's view, it "represented more than any other organization the crystallizing force of Negro citizenship in this country." He lent his efforts to diminishing the rancor between the two groups, imploring the NAACP and the ILD not to waste time fighting each other, but rather to train their ammunition on racial injustices, attacking the "same front by means of convergent movements." Nevertheless, Houston's primary allegiance would be to the NAACP. At a time when Walter White was desperate for a guiding force, he made himself fully available on a volunteer basis as a lawyer, field-worker, investigator, and adviser.[40]

White struggled throughout 1932 to hold his ground under the pressure of events and the constant need to look for funds. The work of the association had trebled over the previous two years, White told Roger Baldwin, but revenue was down $8,000 compared with 1931. As of November, the association owed more than $13,000 and had a balance of $215 in the bank, mandating yet another round of salary cuts and further reduction of the staff, including the dismissal of Robert Bagnall. The NAACP's triumph before the Supreme Court in *Nixon v. Condon* that May was one of the bright lights in a dim season. In a narrow 5-4 decision the Court overturned Texas's clumsy attempt to circumvent the earlier white primary decision. The Court's ruling, however, allowed room for the Texas Democratic Party to perfect its effort to exclude blacks from membership in the party and left disaffected blacks in Houston ready to proceed independently of the NAACP in mounting another challenge. In November, the ILD won a landmark Supreme Court victory in *Powell v. Alabama*, when the Court reversed the Alabama Supreme Court's ruling that upheld the death sentences of the defendants in the Scottsboro cases, on the grounds that they "were not accorded the right of counsel in any substantial sense." Arthur Spingarn provided informal assistance to the noted constitutional lawyer Walter Pollack, who argued *Powell* before the Supreme Court for the ILD. The following year, the NAACP worked out an arrangement to assist in raising money for the Scottsboro defense.[41]

The rise of public work programs under the Hoover administration brought the issue of racial discrimination on federally financed projects to the fore, initiating a struggle that would heighten during the New Deal. The most ambitious project was the Hoover Dam on the Colorado River, a $185 million project administered by the Interior Department. The contracting companies announced a preference for servicemen and veterans, drawing black veterans from Texas and Louisiana to the area. None were hired. In the spring of 1932, the NAACP joined with the National Bar Association to protest the total exclusion of blacks from a workforce that had grown to 3,800. Charles Houston and Walter White were part of a small delegation that met with Interior Secretary Roy Lyman Wilbur. Wilbur assured them that this was not federal policy and promised that the ban on black workers would be ended.

As a result, forty black men were hired and given "the meanest kind of work." By the end of 1932, once again, there were no black men working on the project.[42]

In the summer of 1932 the NAACP launched a series of investigations of the treatment of black workers on the federally financed flood control project along the Mississippi River, which was concentrated in Mississippi, Louisiana, and Tennessee. Helen Broadman's initial survey of the project found that blacks earned an average of ten cents an hour and were forced to work twelve-hour days, seven days a week. When the NAACP presented the Hoover administration with the results of the Broadman Report, Hoover appointed a commission to investigate the treatment of black workers but then neglected to fund it. A $2,500 contribution from Katherine Drexel, the mother superior of the Sisters of the Blessed Sacrament, allowed the NAACP to support an extensive investigation by Roy Wilkins and George Schuyler. Dressed as laborers, they traveled through work camps across the Mississippi Delta, and documented "slavery like conditions," describing the "terrorism, robbery and overwork" that plagued black workers. White discussed the findings of the investigation with New York senator Robert Wagner along with the broad problem of discrimination against black workers in federally funded projects. Later that spring, Wagner introduced a resolution calling for a Senate investigation of the Mississippi flood project.[43]

Early in 1933, the arrest of a black man in Boston for a murder in Virginia initiated Charles Houston's involvement in the work of the association. On March 6, 1933, White wrote a letter to Houston urgently seeking his assistance in a case involving George Crawford, a twenty-eight-year-old man who had been arrested and charged with a sensational double murder in Middleburg, Virginia. White became convinced that there had been a rush to judgment in the murder of Agnes Boeing Ilsley, a popular forty-year-old widow and member of the fox-hunting set, and Nina Buckner, who had worked as her maid. Both women had been bludgeoned to death. Local authorities seemed eager to "pin the crime on a Negro." Crawford, who had occasionally done odd jobs for Ilsley, became the sole target of the police investigation, despite evidence pointing to Ilsley's younger brother as a likely suspect. Unable to find Crawford, authorities concluded that he had escaped to the North.

In January 1933, a year after the murder, local police found him in living in Boston when he was arrested on a minor larceny charge. After three hours of questioning by two Boston police officers and a district attorney from Virginia, Crawford confessed that he was involved in the robbery of Ilsley's home, but that his accomplice, Charley Johnson, had murdered the women. Crawford later denied any involvement and refused to sign a statement. The NAACP sent an investigator to Middleburg, who further confirmed White's suspicions that Crawford was being railroaded. Working closely with White, attorney Butler Wilson, president of the Boston branch of the NAACP, and J. Weston Allen, the former attorney general of Massachusetts, joined to block Crawford's extradition to Virginia. They seized on the issue of black exclusion from the grand jury that indicted Crawford as the means for obtaining a writ of habeas corpus from the U.S. district court, but needed hard evidence in order to make their case.[44]

A week before the scheduled March 13 hearing, White appealed to Houston, asking that he travel to Middleburg and examine the court records to develop the evidence in order to make their case. "Unfortunately," White added, "we are absolutely strapped and have already spent more money on this case than we could afford" but he would cover expenses. Houston left for Virginia the day after receiving White's letter and took along Washington attorney Edward Lovett, a 1932 graduate of Howard Law School. They interviewed several local officials, reviewed taxpayer lists from which the grand jury list was drawn, examined the grand jury panel that indicted Crawford, and secured sworn statements from local black citizens that no blacks had served on juries in recent memory. With the evidence Houston and Lovett collected, the attorneys in Boston were able to secure a continuance of the hearing until March 24. The trip also served to acquaint Houston with the racial situation in and around Middleburg. At the end of a lengthy report, he nudged White, "The people in Leesburg and Middleburg asked me why the association didn't send an organizer up there."[45]

The further he got into the case, Houston wrote, "the more I see its possibilities." Based upon a series of recent cases in which the U.S. Supreme Court broadened the constitutional protections afforded defendants, Houston saw some useful stepping-stones. In the Elaine, Arkansas, case *Moore v. Dempsey*, the Court had ruled that the actions of the mob had denied the defendants a fair trial; *Powell v. Alabama* established the right to counsel in a capital case. "On the question of Crawford suffering prejudice from the grand jury as constituted," evidence of black exclusion from the grand jury was, to Houston's mind, "sufficient."

But the implications of Houston's analysis went beyond the form and content of trials. If Crawford was held in Boston and freed on the grounds that the indictment was illegal and violated due process under the Fourteenth Amendment, "then you have a decision that hits discrimination *wherever* practiced." In the future, when a black person faced indictment in the South and he could make it North, a southern state would be unable to get him back until it abandoned the practice of excluding blacks from juries. This, Houston believed, would go "the greatest distance yet toward breaking up discrimination against Negroes on juries in the South." Finally, there was the public relations value of such a case playing out in a northern courtroom and focusing national attention on the routine denial of basic constitutional rights to black citizens.[46]

Houston advised White to fully consider the consequences of the NAACP's pursuit of the Crawford case, which was "made to order for the ILD." Crawford was unemployed and a member of the unskilled working class, and his case had "certain elements of persecution by members of the idle capitalistic class." Such a thought was hardly far from White's mind. Indeed, the Crawford case provided the perfect opportunity for the NAACP to scoop the ILD on the issue of black exclusion from juries in the South, which was a central issue in the next Scottsboro case heading toward the Supreme Court. But Houston insisted that White be prepared to go all the way once the NAACP committed itself to the case. This required ensuring that the federal question was raised properly and "pressed to the utmost" in Boston. While criminal law was not his specialty, Houston told White that he was available to serve in whatever capacity desired. "If your money is short, we will be glad to raise the question of jury discrimination for you and Crawford." Confident that he could rely on Houston, who would not require a fee, White was ready to put the full weight of the NAACP behind Crawford's defense. "This may be the most important case of this sort ever fought," he told Nathan Margold. At White's request, Houston traveled to Boston in March, accompanied by Lovett and Thurgood Marshall, a twenty-five-year-old former student, then practicing law in Baltimore, to interview Crawford and meet with Boston attorneys Wilson and Allen.[47]

In preparation for the Boston hearing, Houston and Lovett made several more trips to Middleburg and the surrounding area. They documented the qualifications of white jurors who served, took depositions from black citizens with equal or superior qualifications to white jurors, and reviewed census data and tax lists. With a full schedule as a dean and professor, Houston worked nights and weekends at the law school, typing up depositions, preparing reports for White and the Boston attorneys, and composing the brief. At one point, he reluctantly asked White to hire a stenographer. "After the typing," much of which was mere copying, he was so tired that he could hardly get his thoughts together, adding that his time might "be much better spent on thinking." In a prompt response, White commanded, "You must not under any circumstances waste your time doing typing" and authorized him to spend as much money as necessary for stenographic services.[48]

On April 24, black Bostonians packed the small, drab courtroom where federal district judge James A. Lowell heard arguments put forward by the attorney for Loudon County, Virginia, and the NAACP's defense team. Virginia's representatives defended black exclusion from jury service, citing it as "just an old Virginia custom." Crawford's lawyers stated that Virginia could not have it both ways, namely invoking the Constitution in demanding the prisoner's rendition while at the same time violating the Constitution by illegally barring blacks from serving on grand and petit juries. Relying on the NAACP's brief, Lowell granted a writ of habeas corpus, freeing Crawford. The judge declared that Virginia's plea "goes against my Yankee common sense." Why would he "send a Negro back from Boston to Virginia" and "have a case go on for two or three years" when "everybody knows the Supreme Court will say that the trial is illegal." The state of Massachusetts appealed Lowell's ruling, leaving Crawford's fate in limbo for the next stretch of months. Meanwhile, a howl of protest went up from southern representatives in Congress. Congressman Howard Smith of Virginia initiated a move to impeach Judge Lowell.[49]

White immediately turned his attention to raising funds for the appeal, while he and Houston made plans to tour Virginia to build support for the case, stimulate NAACP branch activity, and work to cultivate favorable white sentiment in the event that Crawford was returned to Virginia for trial. Accompanied by Edward Lovett, the three men traveled in Houston's car and visited Richmond, Petersburg, Hampton, Norfolk, Roanoke, and Alexandria during a week in June. They met with branch officials, held public meetings, and secured memberships. Houston, who reported that their best audiences were in smaller towns, found a "new spirit spreading among the younger element." In Richmond, they held a conference with Virginia's leading newspaper editors, Virginius Dabney of the *Richmond Times-Dispatch* (and a special correspondent of the *New York Times*) and Douglas Freeman of the *Richmond News Leader*. Both were "cordial" and expressed the opinion that the Crawford ruling had struck a deathblow to the barring of blacks from juries. At White's urging, Freeman agreed to send a reporter to Loudon

County to pursue a thorough investigation into evidence concerning Mrs. Ilsley's younger brother; Houston volunteered to share the results of his investigations. After returning to New York, White wrote Houston that the "barnstorming trip" was "one of the most delightful experiences in my fifteen years with the Association." White was pleased that Houston had the opportunity to see the inside machinery of the association, especially with regard to the relation between the national office and the branches.[50]

As the Crawford case unfolded in Boston, the possibility of a very different kind of case arose in Durham, North Carolina. Two young black attorneys, Conrad Pearson, a recent Howard Law School graduate, and Cecil McCoy had been working with a group of young blacks in Durham to find a plaintiff to challenge the exclusion of "colored youth from the professional schools of the University of North Carolina." There were no facilities in the state for blacks who chose to pursue studies and training beyond college. Twenty-four-year-old Thomas Hocutt, a graduate of North Carolina College for Negroes who worked as a waiter, agreed to apply to the School of Pharmacy at the University of North Carolina (UNC). Early in February, while Hocutt prepared his application, Pearson and McCoy wrote White informing him of their plans to file a suit, assuming that Hocutt's application would be rejected. In their letter, they wanted to know if they could count on the NAACP for advice and support.[51]

White saw this situation as a godsend. With the Garland Fund project stalled due to lack of funds, the North Carolina case might jump-start the campaign for educational equality. White urged the young attorneys to file suit, and after Hocutt was rejected, he became their intermediary with Nathan Margold and the Legal Committee. As their March 24 court date approached, pressures by white political leaders heightened. The promised "unqualified" support from almost "every influential man of color" evaporated, and the branch voted against aiding the prosecution, McCoy reported to White just days before their trial date. "We now find ourselves almost alone." He urged White to send Margold to appear with the local attorneys in court. Margold, who had just been appointed solicitor of the Department of Interior in the new Roosevelt administration, could not go. On March 20, White wired Houston, who was in Boston for his first visit on the Crawford case. It was impossible for Houston to leave, but he enlisted his colleague and friend William Hastie, then in Cambridge studying for a doctorate at Harvard Law School. Hastie promptly flew to New York, picked up the files on the case and $50 for expenses, stopped over in Washington, and then headed by train to Durham. He arrived on the evening of March 23, ready to join McCoy and Pearson, his former student, in court the next morning.[52]

"Capacity crowd . . . town agog . . . Negroes solidifying behind us," Hastie wired White after his first day in court. "Incalculable good done whatever the outcome." Blacks and whites filled the courtroom. Law students and professors from Duke and the University of North Carolina, UNC officials, and local attorneys were among those drawn to this head-to-head contest between the black attorneys and the state's attorney general in a potentially precedent-setting case. The twenty-eight-year-old Hastie did not disappoint. He "swept the entire courtroom off its feet," Pearson reported. Judge M.W. Barnhill described *Hocutt* as one of "the most brilliantly argued" cases he had heard in more than twenty years on the bench. In the end, Barnhill ruled against Hocutt; the lawyers had not sought the proper remedy, the judge said. The case was also compromised by the refusal of James Shepard, president of North Carolina College for Negroes, to provide Hocutt's transcript, a required part of his application.[53]

A flurry of activity followed in the wake of *Hocutt*. Pearson and McCoy met with Houston in Washington to consider plans for an appeal. There were broader discussions within the NAACP about lessons learned from the *Hocutt* case and discussions with local leaders about how they might be applied through similar challenges in Virginia and Kentucky. Meanwhile, state legislators in North Carolina hurriedly introduced a bill to provide out-of-state scholarships for blacks qualified for admission to graduate and professional schools in North Carolina, modeled on similar laws in Missouri and West Virginia. An editorial in the leading local newspaper, the *Durham Sun*, strongly supported the legislation, warning that unless the state acted, a perfected legal challenge would force open the doors of "white institutions of higher learning to blacks." UNC president Frank Graham publicly supported the "provision of adequate professional training for members of the colored race."[54]

In May, Walter White took a weeklong tour through the Tar Heel State, building on the excitement generated by *Hocutt*. He addressed eighteen mass meetings and was on hand for the establishment of six new branches. White found "an enthusiasm almost amounting to adulation of the NAACP" in wake of the battles fought in the UNC and Crawford cases, and a "tremendous eagerness on the part of young people" to work for the association. C. C. Spaulding, president of the North Carolina Mutual Life Insurance Company, one of the largest black-owned businesses in the nation, offered to quietly support the NAACP's statewide organizing efforts. "We have a golden opportunity to make progress hitherto impossible in the matter of education," White reported to James Weldon Johnson. Some southern whites, fearful of the effect of communist propaganda on blacks, seemed more willing than ever to consider the NAACP's program, even if just as "the lesser of two evils." White made plans to return in October for the proposed founding meeting of a state conference of branches, and that summer Hastie began working with Pearson and McCoy to develop a case to challenge teacher salary differentials.[55]

Hocutt "started something," Hastie recalled some twenty years later.[56] North Carolina had become the testing ground for strategies and approaches that would provide the main focus of the school equalization campaign. The failure of southern states to provide blacks with access to graduate and professional education and the wide racial disparities in teachers' salaries offered glaring examples of the inequities embedded in the Jim Crow system and invited legal challenge. These early efforts offered a means for exploring white reactions, engaging public opinion, and offering a focus for black civic activism. They also provided the kind of on-the-ground experience critical to shaping future efforts. Regardless of the uncertainties surrounding the Garland Fund's support, White, Houston, and Hastie did not hesitate to respond to the efforts of a small group of young black men in Durham. The NAACP's intervention proved essential to igniting black support for the effort and illustrated Houston's vision for the kind of role black lawyers might play in laying the groundwork for change.

Meanwhile, Alabama continued to command attention as the center of "white supremacy in its vilest form." That July, White received a desperate plea from Dr. Charles McPherson, secretary of the Birmingham branch, for aid in the case of another black man sentenced to death under appalling circumstances for a crime he did not commit. Two years earlier, just months after the first trial of the Scottsboro defendants, Willie Peterson was charged and ultimately convicted of the murder of two teen-aged white society girls. Peterson, however, a thirty-year-old man suffering from advanced stages of consumption, did not match the description provided by Nell Williams, a white girl who was with the girls when they were murdered, nor that of one of the victims before she died. While Peterson was being held in jail, he was shot and nearly mortally wounded by Dent Williams, Nell's brother. Peterson's first trial resulted in a mistrial. He was tried again, convicted, and sentenced to death. Dent Williams was subsequently tried for shooting Peterson and was acquitted.

The case aroused the interest and passion of blacks in and around Birmingham. The local branch of the NAACP succeeded in raising more than $2,000 to pay for Peterson's defense, with minimal assistance from the cash-strapped national office. By the time the Alabama Supreme Court upheld Peterson's death sentence, the local branch owed its lawyer $800. McPherson urged that the national office take responsibility for the case and the appeal to the U. S. Supreme Court. "Many of our people are at a crossroads," McPherson told White. "Unless the proper judication of the Willie Peterson case is made as well as the Scottsboro cases they will lose hope. . . . Our organization, especially our Birmingham branch, must keep on the firing line right here in the heart of the South without retrenchment because . . . it is here the battle must be won."[57]

White immediately consulted Houston. Upon reviewing the record of the case, Houston agreed with McPherson's assessment. Scottsboro and the Peterson case marked "a social crisis which may determine future leadership of Negroes in the South," Houston wrote. The struggle centered in Alabama, with the ILD and the NAACP representing two alternative approaches in their efforts to claim leadership. The ILD, in its campaign of uncompromising legal action, backed up by mass pressure, had saved the lives of the Scottsboro boys and might ultimately win their release. On the other hand, the NAACP, through its Birmingham branch, had controlled the Peterson case, and he was condemned to death for a crime that most blacks and many whites doubted that he had committed. Peterson's execution would, Houston warned, "clamp the lid on the Negro's hope of southern justice."[58]

In August, Houston and Edward Lovett traveled to Alabama and made a weeklong investigation, gathering facts for a new trial or for an appeal to the governor if the U. S. Supreme Court refused to hear the case. Houston met with Peterson, whom he described in his report as a "ginger-snap brown, weighted around one hundred pounds—mere skin and bones." Peterson's alibi, that he had been at and around his home when the crime was committed, was supported by his neighbors who testified at the trial. Most significantly, Peterson in no way fit the description of the assailant provided by the two women: a dark-skinned robust man who had lectured them on communism and the race problem, before perpetrating a triple assault and a double murder. It was unimaginable that Peterson was physically capable of this attack on three women, each of them stronger than he was. Moreover, Houston added, "a few minutes contact with Willie Peterson would convince anyone that he would not dream of lecturing white people on the race problem."

Houston interviewed the chief of police, the sheriff, the editor of the *Birmingham News*, leaders of the Alabama Commission on Interracial Cooperation, the attorneys involved in the case, as well as Peterson, and consulted with local NAACP leadership. He proved adept in winning the confidence of whites and identified a consensus of opinion regarding the case. The chief of police, was "perfect" Houston reported, and offered a firsthand account of the Dent Williams shooting. Both the chief and the sheriff were convinced of Peterson's innocence, as was most everyone else Houston spoke with. The only person who attempted to argue Peterson's guilt was Roderick Beddow, the prosecutor and Dent Williams's lawyer, who, ironically, had agreed to represent the Scottsboro defendants for the NAACP. Upon reading Houston's seventeen-page report, White declared, "We are prepared to go the limit in following this up with all possible vigor."[59]

The day before Houston left Alabama, Dan Pippen Jr. and A.T. Harden, aged eighteen and fifteen, were lynched outside Tuscaloosa. The young men and a companion had been accused of murdering an eighteen-year-old white woman. There was no evidence linking them to the crime and each had credible alibis. Following their arrest, rumors of lynching and talk of avoiding another Scottsboro were rampant. At the start of their trial on August 2, Judge Henry B. Foster refused to recognize the three ILD lawyers who had been retained by the young men and their families. The judge appointed local counsel to represent the men and had a militia on hand to escort the ILD lawyers out of town. The case was continued to a subsequent date. In the interim, Sheriff R.L. Shamblin decided to transfer the defendants to Birmingham for safe keeping, not bothering to obtain the requisite court order. He and several deputies accompanied the three men, driving along an unfrequented route. Two cars with a dozen armed men intercepted the group and allegedly forced them to surrender the prisoners. The men shot all three defendants and left them for dead, but Elmore Clark survived. Instead of seeking the killers, the sheriff blamed "the interference of the ILD lawyers in the case" for the lynching. This action, as Houston later noted, aimed to serve notice that any "aggressive organization which insisted on immediate equality of rights for Negroes in the South would be just as violently opposed."[60]

Upon returning to Washington, Houston went immediately to the White House with George B. Murphy of the *Baltimore Afro-American*'s Washington bureau to schedule an appointment for a delegation of representatives from the NAACP, the ILD, and ACLU to meet with the president regarding the Tuscaloosa lynching. This was Houston's first encounter with the recently installed administration of Franklin D. Roosevelt. A secretary advised them to return the next morning, and she would arrange to have their request considered by Louis Howe, the president's secretary. When the civil rights representatives returned at the assigned time, they waited an hour before this same white woman approached them and curtly asked, "What do you boys want?" After waiting another hour, a message relayed from presidential assistant Stephen Early reported that the president was completely absorbed in setting up his new administration and constructing a national recovery program and could not possibly find time to see the delegation.[61]

In a subsequent exchange of letters with Early, Houston gave little quarter to pleas of time and more pressing matters. He objected to the "summary manner in which our request going to the fundamental protection of citizens' rights was disposed of." After having waited several hours, it would not have been a hardship to wait until Early was free to see them, allowing them an opportunity to explain why it was imperative for the president to meet with their delegation. While sensitive to the many demands on the new president, Houston doubted that this was the primary reason that Early rejected their request. Rather, he surmised that the driving consideration was the effect that such a meeting would have on "certain sections of the country, with resultant repercussions on the N.R.A. [National Recovery Administration] program." Houston countered, "The lives and physical protection of American citizens are just as important as any NRA program can be." Indeed, "the traditional policy of temporizing with injustice and disrespect of law is to a great extent responsible for the moral collapse and selfishness exhibited in so many quarters today." He renewed the delegation's request for a meeting with the president, and Early advised him to be in touch after Labor Day to schedule an appointment, following Roosevelt's return from his vacation at Hyde Park.[62]

On August 19, three days after visiting the White House, Houston was at Joel Spingarn's Hudson Valley estate in Amenia, not far from FDR's riverside mansion, for the conference first proposed at the 1932 annual convention. Du Bois and Spingarn took the lead in planning the meeting and selecting the participants, with assistance from Walter White and Roy Wilkins. As the Depression wore on and Franklin Roosevelt prepared to initiate his New Deal, the moment seemed ripe for a brainstorming session. The NAACP leaders hoped to facilitate a fresh "appraisal of the Negro's existing condition" with a view toward integrating "the special problems of the Negro within the larger issues facing the nation." Twenty-seven men and women described as "coming leaders of Negro thought" gathered at Spingarn's estate along with a smaller contingent of seasoned leaders. The group included a broad range of intellectuals, professionals, and organization workers—the epitome of the "talented tenth." At a median age of thirty, nearly all were from cities on the East Coast, with three from the Midwest and one each from Louisville, Kentucky; Nashville, Tennessee; and Hampton, Virginia. Among the participants were Howard University professors Ralph Bunche, Sterling Brown, and Abram Harris along with Houston; YWCA executives Frances Williams and Anna Arnold; Juanita Jackson, head of the Young People's Forum in Baltimore; economist Mabel Byrd; and E. Franklin Frazier from Fisk University. James Weldon Johnson, Walter White, Roy Wilkins, and W.E.B. Du Bois also participated.[63]

The conference was a private affair and produced no major initiatives. It was difficult for "age and youth . . . to find a common language," Du Bois reported. The young participants did not indulge their elders. There was little interest in what the NAACP had done, and some glaring ignorance about what the association was actually doing. Resolute in their desire "to junk the old policies," wrote Louis Redding, he and his cohort were unable nonetheless to develop a clear-cut outline of a new philosophy or program. The conferees appeared more concerned with positioning themselves within the existing order, which "inhibited any real contemplation of the condition of the great Negro mass." The discussions "agitated me deeply," Redding remembered. The meeting was "quite ragged in spots," Frances Williams wrote, but worthwhile because of the people she met and the "new insights" gained "into myself." Houston dubbed it "the anemic conference." After "three days of talk," the group "resolved it could not resolve." Du Bois found a "startling lack of discipline" on the part of some of the conferees. With fond memories of frolicking interludes at the 1916 gathering, he was astonished to discover "these young people could not sing." They wouldn't even try; "too sophisticated."

In the end, however, the gathering appeared to serve its broader purpose. The discussions were wide ranging and explored ideas and approaches that would mature over the next decade. Du Bois's account of the meeting identified economic issues as the most compelling problem discussed. He highlighted Abram Harris and Ralph Bunche's advocacy of a new labor movement, capable of aligning the interests of black and white workers. Du Bois, however, argued that black economic independence was a prerequisite for building black-white working-class unity, creating a fundamental point of disagreement with Harris and Bunche, who insisted that class trumped race as the defining element in the struggle to liberate black people. There were discussions on the nature and role of Black Nationalism, the relationship of blacks to the existing political parties, and the problem of Negro farmers in the South, including the importance of securing black agents under the new Farm Credit Administration. The group formed a continuations committee to consider "the practical implications" of its deliberations. It became the basis for the Committee on the Future Plan and Program of the NAACP, established a year later and headed by Abram Harris.[64]

"At the root of all utterances at the conference lay the desire that the Negro become a full and equal participant in every phase of American life," wrote Louis Redding. While this statement summed up the mission of the NAACP quite succinctly, the Amenia conference revealed that many of the younger black thinkers and activists were ready for something new. The questions raised about the NAACP's relevance to current problems lingered. Yet, during the early 1930s, the NAACP demonstrated its continuing ability to respond to the varied conditions and problems facing black Americans, while representing the interests of the race as state and federal governments expanded their involvement in the economic lives of their citizens. Indeed, even before the Roosevelt administration launched the New Deal, the NAACP had led the effort to fight black exclusion and racial discrimination on federally funded projects, notably the Hoover Dam project in Nevada and the Mississippi Flood Control project. As a direct result of the NAACP's efforts, Senator Robert Wagner introduced a resolution to establish a committee to investigate conditions on the Mississippi Flood Control project.[65]

The greatest strength of the association, and one that many of the young intelligentsia overlooked, was the nationwide structure the NAACP had built up over the previous twenty-five years around an ideal of citizenship that defied the color line. While membership ebbed and flowed and branches often flagged, the organization had created a network linking blacks throughout the country to fight racial discrimination in its many guises. The trend toward establishing state conferences of branches continued, with new ones springing up in Pennsylvania, Missouri, Kansas, Michigan, and Oklahoma, and a region-wide organization in New England. Northern state conferences helped to mobilize the strength of black voters around issues of statewide interest. During the early 1930s, based on a model bill drawn up by the National Legal Committee, NAACP groups in Indiana, Illinois, New Jersey, and New York led successful efforts to secure legislation barring racial discrimination in state-funded public works projects. The Indiana state conference, under the brilliant leadership of Florence K. "Flossie" Bailey, successfully pursued the indictment of five men charged with a double lynching and secured passage of an antilynching bill. In West Virginia, NAACP leader and attorney T. G. Nutter won $5,000 compensation for relatives of a lynching victim under that state's newly enacted antilynching law.[66]

The NAACP was the primary vehicle through which northern communities continued to resist the spread of school segregation. There were protests and legal challenges in Hillburn, New York; Gary, Indiana; Montclair, New Jersey; Mansfield, Ohio; and Berwyn, Pennsylvania. The Berwyn case marked one of the few victories in the fight to halt this trend and demonstrated the power of a unified community as well as the effectiveness of fusing mass protest and litigation.

The Bryn Mawr branch had just recently been organized when the Berwyn school board established separate schools for black students in two adjoining townships in the fall of 1932. After petitions failed, the branch led in organizing a boycott by the families of two hundred children and, on the recommendation of the national office, enlisted Philadelphia attorney Raymond Pace Alexander to sue the school board. Alexander did not charge a fee; the NAACP's national office contributed toward his expenses. The Berwyn boycott lasted for more than a year; only eleven students attended one of the separate schools. Many of the parents paid to send their children to schools in neighboring towns. Fifteen parents were jailed for violating the compulsory attendance law; others lost their jobs at a time when an estimated 25 percent of the parents were out of work. The local chapter of the Red Cross, a major distributor of relief prior to New Deal programs, cut off supplies to blacks. People shared coal, fuel, and other essential provisions and hired tutors to instruct the children. "Nothing dinted the morale of our forces," an NAACP official reported. Meanwhile, Alexander's efforts bogged down when the court ruled that the attorney general needed to bring suit. In an effort to help rally popular support for the case, Alexander joined with several other groups, including the ILD, in the Joint Action Committee. The committee's plan for a mass protest of five thousand people through the streets of nearby Philadelphia was blocked by city authorities. But in the face of heightened public pressure, the attorney general agreed to bring suit, causing the Berwyn school board to integrate its schools in April 1934.[67]

The scope of activity carried on through the branches and the national office reflected the many fronts black Americans struggled along in the years just prior to the New Deal. In the North and the West, the NAACP and its branches led the efforts to challenge racial discrimination and segregation, reinforced by growing black political strength. The national office fought discrimination on Greyhound buses in the Northeast, bringing numerous complaints of black passengers, forced to sit in the rear of the bus, to the attention of the company's national office. When the association refused Greyhound's invitation to charter buses to carry delegates to the 1932 convention in light of this situation, the subtle economic pressure had an effect. A company vice president sent out special bulletins to regional managers instructing them to abide by the company's policy against discrimination on the buses and opened up a direct line for receiving complaints about violations. The Toledo, Ohio, branch led one of the earliest "Don't Buy Where You Can't Work" boycotts, resulting in the hiring of twenty blacks in the city's Kroger food stores. In Denver, the branch won its suit to overturn a new city law barring blacks from municipal pools and beaches.[68]

By the early 1930s, swift intervention from the national office was sometimes sufficient to obtain redress in areas where black voters had become a factor in politics. In New Jersey, when the governor appointed an all-white committee of citizens to survey the school system and make recommendations for reforms, Walter White immediately contacted the governor. Surely, he advised, the committee would want at least one Negro among its members if it were to consider the unique difficulties under which black students labored. The governor admitted that he had never thought about appointing a black person, and with White's approval, appointed Dr. J.C. Love of Montclair to the committee. In New York City, a protest by the national office prevented the segregation of a new Detention Center for Women. Prompt action by the national office also forced the city to abandon plans to designate separate places for black and white women to register for relief.[69]

The South presented a unique challenge, given the tight legal structure of segregation and disenfranchisement, the region's insular politics, and the terror and lawlessness that reinforced the caste system. There were a few isolated initiatives around education, similar to the *Hocutt* case. Blacks in Richmond lobbied successfully for the hiring of black principals in the black public schools, and NAACP activists in Virginia began planning a challenge to teachers' pay inequities. But these efforts were overshadowed by the nearly airtight enforcement of white supremacy, which challenged the courage, re-sourcefulness, and endurance of those working for change. In the voting rights arena, methods of skirting Supreme Court decisions that ran against the grain of racial practices became well-honed in Texas. The narrow but significant victory won in the May 1932 Supreme Court ruling *Nixon v. Condon*, overturned the effort of Texas Democrats to devise an all-white pri-mary that could withstand a court challenge. This victory sparked an upsurge of black voting in the Texas primaries and other southern states and drew positive statements from a number of public officials, including the mayor of San Antonio. But party leaders in Texas immediately went to work perfecting the notion of a "private" party function, free of state regulation. Many blacks, including plaintiff L. A. Nixon, were barred from voting in the 1932 Demo-cratic primary; by 1934, the door had closed once again.[70]

Powerlessness in the face of stark terror was on display in a violent spree in Mississippi, where white vigilantes assaulted black trainmen in an effort to take away their jobs. Attempts by the Illinois Central Railroad officials to intercede failed when local city and county authorities refused to cooperate in stemming the violence. Two men had been murdered and six seriously wounded by the time the black trainmen appealed to the NAACP for help in February 1932. The national office put the matter before the Criminal Pros-ecutions Division of the U. S. Justice Department. The head of the division along with attorney general William D. Mitchell promised to investigate and take appropriate action if they could find a federal statute allowing for the intervention of the Justice Department; they concluded that the federal gov-ernment had no legal authority. Walter White turned to Will Alexander of the Commission of Interracial Cooperation in devising a plan for prominent white and black citizens of Mississippi to issue public statements condemn-ing the violence and to pressure law enforcement officials to end the killings and assaults. The assaults subsided for a time, but erupted again two years later.[71]

In the wake of its slow reaction to Scottsboro, the NAACP had become more vigilant regarding so-called legal lynchings, where black defendants were summarily tried and sentenced to death on flimsy evidence and trumped-up charges, lacking adequate legal defense. The Willie Peterson case was a prime example. Other cases included a father and son, both sharecroppers in Arkansas, convicted in the first-degree murder of their landlord, despite the obvious merit to their plea of self-defense. Another involved Ernest Herring, convicted and sentenced to death for the murder of the postmaster in Kerr, North Carolina, based solely on the testimony of a mentally retarded witness.[72]

A number of these cases involved consensual relations between black men and white women. Ervin Pruitt of Meridian, Mississippi, had fathered a child with a white woman. The woman poisoned the baby and claimed that Pruitt had forced her to do it. Her husband testified that Pruitt was not at their home when the child was poisoned. Nevertheless, the fact that Pruitt had been sexually involved with a white woman was enough to convince the jury of his guilt; they sentenced him to be hung. When Walter White learned of Pruitt's pending execution through a contact in Atlanta, the national office retained S.D. Redmond of Jackson, Mississippi, for $500 to appeal the case. The Mississippi Supreme Court upheld the conviction, with two dissenting votes. Redmond widely publicized the dissenting opinions, and White persuaded the Commission on Interracial Cooperation to organize moderate white opinion in Mississippi and appeal to the governor to spare Pruitt's life. Their efforts succeeded. The governor commuted the death sentence, but Pruitt remained condemned to life in prison.[73]

The case of Jess Hollins in Oklahoma, which would ultimately reach the Supreme Court, brought Oklahoma City branch president Roscoe Dunjee to the fore as a major force for the NAACP in the state. Hollins, a poor farmer living in Creek County, had been intimately involved with Alta McCullom, the white daughter of a tenant farmer. When he ended the relationship, she charged him with rape. On December 27, 1931, law enforcement officials dragged Hollins from his bed, where he was asleep with his wife, took him to the jail in Sapulpa and obtained a confession, which he disavowed later and claimed was coerced. The local judge hurriedly convened a night session of the court in the basement of the jail, pronounced Hollins guilty, and condemned him to be electrocuted. He was transferred to the state prison, where several representatives of the ILD visited him, and Hollins accepted their offer to represent him. The ILD organized protests in Oklahoma City, the state capital, featuring Hollins's wife, raised funds for Hollins's defense, and organized letter-writing campaigns to the governor. But less than a week before Hollins's scheduled execution on August 15, Dunjee learned from M.A. Looney, a local white lawyer who had taken an interest in the case, that no legal procedures had been instituted to prevent the state from going ahead with the execution.

Looney obtained a stay of execution on the grounds that no written record of the first trial had been filed with the governor as required by law; nor in fact did a record exist. Looney also presented an amicus curiae brief to the criminal court, arguing that Hollins had not received a trial according to the due process of the law. The ILD lawyer filed a formal writ, which basically presented Hollins's statement arguing his innocence. The court ordered a new trial based on Looney's brief; the ILD lawyer faded away. Dunjee, president of the Oklahoma City branch, obtained a statement from Hollins giving the NAACP control of the case. With $100 provided by the national office and nearly $300 raised through the state conference of branches, Dunjee hired E.A. Hill and W.N. Redwine, two prominent white attorneys, to represent Hollins. Over the next several years Dunjee worked, through his newspaper, the *Black Dispatch*, and the state's NAACP branches, to keep interest in the case alive and raise money to meet the lawyers' fees, all the while helping to build the Oklahoma state conference into a strong unit. Nonetheless, Hollins was tried, convicted, and sentenced to death by an all-white jury. Procedural irregularities along with exclusion of black jurors provided the basis for the appeal. Charles Houston shared briefs from the Crawford case and was in contact with Dunjee as the case developed.[74]

By 1933, NAACP membership numbers had reached one hundred thousand, organized in 327 branches, though actual contributions through branch memberships continued to suffer under the burden of the Depression. Income from branches hit a low of $16,932 that year. In spite of this, the national office was optimistic. "Never before . . . have our branches in all sections of the country, North and South, East and West exhibited such a militant, alert, fighting spirit," Wilkins wrote Dunjee in spring of 1933. Reports from delegates at the annual conference in Chicago that summer attested to the vitality of the NAACP and the broad range of issues that engaged the branches, including school segregation cases; segregation in parks, theaters, travel, and relief; citizenship schools and voting; the fight for jobs in state and federally funded programs as well as in chain stores; and legal defense work.[75]

A frank review of the aims and methods of the association dominated the annual meeting, along with an airing of criticisms and proposals for change. While some of the younger delegates called for a complete reorientation of the association's program toward economic issues, Charles Houston and Chicago-based attorney Earl Dickerson spoke about the broader process of strengthening the NAACP at its base. If the NAACP was going to be able cope with problems as fast as they arose, Dickerson held, it must actively engage the rank and file in the work of the association and develop "a kind of mass consciousness that is going to enable us at any point of attack" to mobilize a mass group of people to take action. The key challenge, as Houston saw it, was not how "radical" the association could be, but its effectiveness in providing a way for blacks to address and fight the racial injustices manifested in their communities. The two-tiered structure of the NAACP—with a national office and a network of branches—allowed for flexibility that was essential to responding to the array of challenges black people faced in different parts of the nation. Too many branches, Houston said, were dominated by the professional classes. The NAACP could not be "safely a national organization" if it dictated to some people what is best for them. All elements of the community must be involved, and the branches offered this opportunity. "This association for its greatest effect must be of the Negro, by the Negro and once and for all for all the Negroes."[76]

In the late summer and fall of 1933, Houston became more deeply involved in the work of the NAACP and the effort to meet the violence and blatant injustice that anchored the segregation system. "Relief from physical terrorism" was at the basis of all black progress in the South, Houston believed, and essential to all other struggles for equal rights. The convergence of developments in the Tuscaloosa lynching and the Peterson and Crawford cases provided an opportunity to expose conditions in the South and push on multiple fronts for action. Houston appealed to the fledgling interracial movement in the South, focused the strength of progressive groups committed to racial justice, pressured the federal government for action, and reinforced the NAACP's support of local black efforts. As he told White, "My interest is to roll up a wave of public opinion. . . . I have come around to the point that I think the thing is to strike and strike quickly from as many quarters as possible."[77]

Houston's persistent efforts to place the Tuscaloosa lynching before President Roosevelt resulted in a meeting with attorney general Homer S. Cummings on August 24. He led a delegation of representatives from the NAACP, the ACLU, the ILD (including the three lawyers who were run out of Tuscaloosa for attempting to defend the young men), the Women's International League for Peace and Freedom, and the A. M. E. Zion Church. The group sought federal intervention in the case under a Reconstruction-era law holding that any state official who willfully caused a citizen of the state to be subject to the deprivation of any rights, privileges, or immunities secured or protected by the Constitution was subject to federal prosecution. By allowing the mob to seize the young men, Sheriff R. L. Shamblin of Tuscaloosa had violated this law, providing the grounds for a federal indictment. Cummings and Houston argued the points involved in the charge, with Cummings finally requesting that the delegation submit a brief showing a violation of the federal code in Shamblin's case. Houston, Leon Ransom, and Edward Lovett researched and wrote a brief on the case and submitted it to the Justice Department on October 13. Just three days earlier, the grand jury that had convened in Alabama to investigate the lynching adjourned without bringing an indictment, citing "lack of evidence."[78]

In constructing the brief, Houston and his colleagues drew upon southern sources, making "the South condemn itself wherever possible." Regarding the question of state sovereignty, the brief quoted the *Montgomery Advertiser*'s response to the lynching: "A state that does not or cannot offer protection to the most lowly residents does not deserve the right to call itself a sovereign state." The brief also pointed to the international context, which demanded a consistent approach to the issue of human rights, particularly at a time when the crimes of Nazi Germany were becoming apparent to the world a large. "A nation which can raise its hands at the atrocities perpetrated . . . under the Nazi government in Germany cannot, if it be honest and honorable, remain quiescent in the face of barbarities practiced daily within its own boundaries." Beyond making its case to the attorney general, they placed the issue before the public at large. Two thousand copies of the brief were printed in pamphlet form and included a call to action. They were distributed nationally by the NAACP to newspapers and periodicals, every governor, U.S. congressmen and senators, various organizations and universities, and all branches of the association.[79]

Coinciding with the completion of the Tuscaloosa brief, the Alabama Supreme Court upheld the conviction of Willie Peterson and set his execution for December 8. Two days later, on October 15, the U.S. Supreme Court let the circuit court's reversal of Judge Lowell in the Crawford case stand, preparing the way for Crawford's return to Virginia for trial. Both cases commanded the attention of the NAACP for the next several months, taxing its personal and financial resources to the limit. Houston, working under the demands of a full schedule at Howard University, was prepared to devote as much time as he could to both cases—but doubted that he could carry full responsibility for trying the Crawford case.

As soon as he learned of the Supreme Court's decision, Houston advised White to hire an expert investigator and added, "We had better begin looking out for a good Virginia lawyer immediately." White would not hear of it. The Legal Committee instructed him to authorize Houston to take full charge of the case. "Of course, we have no money . . . but are setting the machinery in motion immediately to raise funds . . . [and] know that you will try to get the job done as economically as possible." But, "above all else, we want you as chief counsel and trust that nothing whatsoever will prevent you from being in full charge." Houston would consider going forward with the case if he could head an all-black defense team. He told White, "The men here [at Howard Law School] feel if Crawford could be defended by all-Negro counsel, it would mark a turning point in the legal history of the Negro in the country." White agreed to Houston's condition and promptly arranged a meeting in New York. Houston and Leon Ransom, along with Edward Lovett and James Tyson, both graduates of Howard Law School, attended a meeting at Arthur Spingarn's home in New York on Sunday afternoon, October 22, to discuss plans for Crawford's defense. Roy Wilkins, Walter White, and Columbia Law School professor Karl Llewellyn were also in attendance. The group agreed that Houston would seek a six-week leave as dean and serve as lead counsel with Ransom, Tyson, and Lovett, representing George Crawford in the courts of Virginia.[80]

As he prepared for trial in Virginia, Houston was also the point man in keeping the Peterson case on track. The Birmingham branch already owed John Altman, the white attorney on the case, nearly $700. Houston traveled to Birmingham at the end of October and met with Altman, working out arrangements for him to obtain a stay of execution and take the case on appeal to the U.S. Supreme Court. Houston promised that the back debt would be paid and negotiated a fee of $750 for Altman to prepare the brief and file an application for certiorari by the U.S. Supreme Court. The burden of the fee was shared by the Commission on Interracial Cooperation, which provided 50¢ toward each dollar the NAACP paid for Peterson's defense. Still, White confided to McPherson that the association was forced to sell some stock in a very bad market so that small payments could be made to Altman, hoping it was enough to sustain his active pursuit of the case.

While in Birmingham at the end of October, Houston met with Willie Peterson in prison and followed up with local editors, attorneys, and other white leaders he had met with two months earlier. He included Charles McPherson, the branch president, in these meetings. Houston reinforced the work of the local NAACP leadership and encouraged their critical efforts on the front lines. He was sensitive to the tremendous pressures under which they labored while their efforts often went unrewarded and unheralded. In a letter to McPherson, Houston praised him and his colleague Dr. E.W.

Taggert for "the great work" they were doing. "I clip and paste everything you send me," he told him. "Sooner or later your work is going to be felt in a big way."[81]

Along with a desperate effort to save Peterson's life, Houston approached his work in Alabama as a test of methods and procedures. In a notable contrast to the ILD, Houston appealed to a sense of fairness and justice among southern whites and their own interest in maintaining civil order at a time when, in the words of a local newspaper editor, "bestial anarchy" was on the rise in Alabama. McPherson agreed that their best hope was to crystallize public opinion "against the crime of electrocuting an innocent man." He organized a small interracial meeting during Houston's visit to provide a forum for sympathetic whites to speak out. More than three hundred people attended. Among those who took the floor was the county superintendent of education, who asserted that blacks would never get justice in the courts as long as they were denied the ballot, and, despite the disapproval of his friends, he stood ready personally to help any Negro to qualify to vote. McPherson reported that the meeting and Houston's visit helped to create "a very hopeful and healthful sentiment." Houston urged White to send Daisy Lampkin to Birmingham, noting the time was ripe for a membership campaign.[82]

Just days after the Birmingham meeting, Houston was in Loudon County, Virginia, for preliminary hearings in the Crawford case, the NAACP's cause célèbre, which had held the attention of many black Americans for nearly a year. The association's initial challenge in Boston had already had a salutary effect in the Old Dominion. In the aftermath of Judge Lowell's ruling, blacks began to appear on grand jury lists in several Virginia counties for the first time in thirty years. However, Houston's effort to have the original indictment of Crawford overturned due to the exclusion of blacks from the grand jury in Loudon County was denied by the judge. When reporters queried whether Houston would seek a change of venue, he was unequivocal: "Loudon County and Virginia justice was as much on trial as Crawford," and that is where the case would be argued.[83]

Houston approached the case confident in Crawford's innocence, but as they prepared for the trial, cracks began to appear in Crawford's story. Most damning was the emergence of Bertie De Neal, Crawford's former girlfriend, as the leading witness for the state. She had been the key to his Boston alibi. When Houston confronted Crawford with this and other developments, his client admitted to being in Middleburg at the time of the crime, and to committing the burglary. As the facts shifted, Houston and his co-counsel rested

their strategy on forcing the prosecution to prove their case beyond a reasonable doubt, while "taking advantage of every reversible error made by the
court."[84]

The *Washington Post* described the weeklong trial as "perhaps the most remarkable in the history of Southern jurisprudence." At the start of the trial,
racial feelings were so tense in Leesburg that local blacks dared not offer accommodations to Houston and his colleagues, leaving them to commute seventy miles each day from Washington. Virginia state troopers armed with
submachine guns and tear gas flanked Judge James McLemore. The trial
moved swiftly through three days of "uncontested evidence" that established
Crawford's participation in the double murder. Yet, according to Frank Getty,
who covered the trial for the *Post*, it was Houston who profoundly influenced
the proceedings. Without ever yielding a point of law, he "set a high standard
of gentleness and courtesy for his opponents at the bar." The closing arguments by the Commonwealth's attorneys lacked the fire of "outraged southern chivalry" that routinely attended such cases. They asked for the death
penalty, but the restraint with which they made their closing remarks, along
with compliments paid to the defense counsel, left "hotheads in the audience . . . open-mouthed in astonishment." The judge described the trial as "an
oasis in the desert."[85]

In his appeal to the jury, Houston set his sights on saving Crawford's life.
The evidence surrounding the case had established that two men participated
in the crime. If the Commonwealth's case was to rest on Crawford's Boston
confession, then there was the question of "Charley Johnson" who, according
to Crawford's statement, committed the murders. If Johnson was ever to be
identified, they would need Crawford to do it. Furthermore, Houston argued,
George Crawford was "not the killer type." He pointed to Crawford's personal characteristics that had been on display during the previous week. He
was courteous and respectful, and there was nothing in his record to suggest
that he was capable of such a heinous crime—a thief, yes, but not a killer. According to Virginia law, presence at the scene of a murder, even if one did not
commit the act, warranted the charge of first-degree murder. The jury found
Crawford guilty of murder in the first degree, but recommended life in prison.
Here, wrote Getty, was "Virginia justice . . . tempered with mercy and rare
consideration."[86]

Critics on the left and some leading black editors in the country were less
pleased by the trial's outcome. The ILD stirred doubts about the NAACP.
But many black supporters were deeply concerned about the abrupt turn in

the defense's case, having long believed in Crawford's innocence, an assumption promoted by the NAACP. Du Bois even raised questions in *The Crisis*. When Crawford's alibi dissolved in the midst of trial preparations, there was little room for a public airing of the circumstances that had caused Houston and his associates to shift their tactics, and this contributed to the lingering confusion. After the sentencing, many questioned why the defense did not file an appeal based upon the exclusion of blacks from the grand jury that had indicted Crawford. A jailhouse interview with Crawford by a reporter from the Norfolk *Journal and Guide* fueled rumors that he had wanted to file an appeal, but Crawford later denied that he had made such comments. Houston addressed these various concerns in several public forums and in an article he co-authored with Leon Ransom. The primary reason for not appealing was that Crawford had indicated that he did not want to, and "it was his case and his life." Houston thought this a wise choice, believing that if there were a second trial Crawford would probably get the death sentence.[87]

The essay by Houston and Ransom, published in the *Nation*, identified some of the broader principles that evolved as the NAACP became more deeply involved with the realities of black life and race relations in the South. As an outside organization, the association had to consider the question of local community relations and "calculate carefully how far it was justified in turning the county upside down then walking out on local Negroes, leaving them in their weakness to catch the full force of community resentment." Admittedly, at times "in major social movements" it might be "necessary to sacrifice the peace of a community for the greater interests of the whole, but the decision should be made after great deliberation." There was little to be gained by pressing further the issue of jury exclusion in the Crawford case, and much to be lost. In addition to the issue of Crawford's life and death, one must consider the dramatic change in the racial climate in Leesburg. By the time the trial ended, blacks and whites reported that race relations were better than they had ever been. The NAACP had demonstrated to the larger community that its program was guided by a sincere effort to foster "interracial cooperation, mutual confidence and good will." At the same time, the entire proceeding had served notice that the NAACP would continue to press the jury issue and stay in the fight until every "Virginia Negro enjoys the powers and privileges of every other citizen of the Commonwealth."[88]

The culmination of the Crawford case only deepened Walter White's appreciation of Houston's rare combination of legal brilliance, tactical skill, and unflinching devotion to the cause. White had been lobbying for Houston to assume Margold's former position as the head of the special legal campaign since the previous summer, when the Garland Fund agreed to release $10,000. But the appointment got bogged down in a debate about whether to hire a white or a black lawyer for the position, with Roger Baldwin leading the push for bringing on another prominent white attorney. White contended that a black lawyer would encounter far less hostility than a northern white lawyer and emphasized Houston's superior qualifications. He was well acquainted with the southern situation and had already demonstrated an ability to win the trust of blacks and the respect of whites. Moreover, his appointment would send a strong positive message to black lawyers and also enhance the NAACP's appeal to young black men and women in general. After Karl Llewellyn declined an offer in the spring of 1934, White prevailed upon Arthur Spingarn to nominate Houston. At the end of May the Garland-NAACP committee engaged Houston as special counsel, initially on a part-time basis, for a year at $2,000, with "subsequent compensation to be . . . dependent upon funds available."[89]

Over the previous year, Houston had explored a range of tactics and strategies in his effort to challenge a system that violated human decency as well as fundamental guarantees of American law and democracy. The fate of Willie Peterson and the outcome of the Tuscaloosa lynching tested a major component of Houston's approach. Appeals to moderate southern white opinion resulted in token concessions in the Peterson case. After the Supreme Court refused to hear the case, the governor responded to overwhelming evidence of Peterson's innocence, supported by an impassioned plea from the sheriff and the petitions of leading white citizens of Birmingham, and commuted his sentence to life in prison. McPherson and others pledged to keep up the fight until Peterson was released, but he died in prison four years later. There was no action on the Tuscaloosa lynching. The U.S. attorney general sat on the brief Houston had submitted for more than six months before notifying him that the Justice Department would not bring charges against the sheriff. The failure of the federal government to act in this case, Houston had earlier predicted, would announce to black Americans that the guarantees of the federal Constitution were "For Whites Only."[90]

Houston had tremendous faith in black people, a contemporary recalled, and in the capacity "within the black community to bring about change." This belief was reinforced by his travels through the South at a time of widespread economic despair, shifting political alliances, and the stirrings of a

more militant resistance. In each community, he sought out "heads of fraternal organizations, church and civic leaders and relief workers," met with large
and small groups, and often addressed mass meetings. The work of Charles
McPherson in Birmingham, Conrad Pearson and Cecil McCoy in Durham,
Roscoe Dunjee in Oklahoma City, and J.M. Tinsley in Richmond illustrated
the kind of role the NAACP could play in cultivating the strength of individual communities and in providing a structure for the educational work and
political activity essential to building "a mass movement." In order to realize
its potential, Houston wrote, "The NAACP must win the Negroes primarily
to its program . . . [and] be the great laboratory for developing Negro leadership wherever possible."[91]

Houston was in a position to implement the vision that had guided him
for more than a decade, setting the NAACP on a course that would shape the
burgeoning movement for civil rights in fundamental ways. Largely due to
his influence, the work of the association would be concentrated in the South
for the foreseeable future. More than 80 percent of black Americans resided
in the region, where, as he noted, they suffered "the greatest handicaps and
discriminations." The South's caste system was propped up by an eclectic
system of state laws that defied the intent of the Reconstruction amendments, providing an opportunity for the creative lawyer to help engineer fundamental change. The Constitution, Houston explained, offered "wide room
for experimentation" and would enable black people "to force reforms where
they could have no chance through politics." Experiences in Birmingham,
Durham, and Leesburg had demonstrated that carefully selected cases provided, in the words of William Hastie, an "opportunity to rally dispirited
and discouraged Negroes to fight again for that equality and human dignity
which [they] had been deprived of for so many years." Remembering their
early interventions in the South, Hastie explained that "once the ordinary
black citizen learned that litigation to vindicate his rights was being pursued openly, with determination and some success, community reaction was
electrifying."[92]

When Houston began his work as special counsel in 1934, he calculated
that there were not more than one hundred full-time practicing black lawyers
in the South. There were few incentives to entice graduates of Howard and
other law schools seeking a traditional career to return to the region where
they would be professionally isolated, dependent on a relatively poor client
base, and marginal to the political life of the larger community. Yet Houston's
hopes rested with younger lawyers who saw their futures in a different light,

those who embraced "the opportunity for service" and accepted "the risks . . . [of] working on a social frontier." Conrad Pearson and Cecil McCoy in Durham, J. Alston Atkins and Carter Wesley of Houston, Byron Hopkins in Richmond, Cecil Robertson in Muskogee, Oklahoma, Thurgood Marshall in Baltimore, and a handful of others scattered around the South were already engaged in the work. Many of them had been trained at Howard, and Houston was confident that more would join their ranks. As New Deal programs and the rise of mass-based unionism further loosened traditional relations, the possibilities were limitless for "young Negroes who are willing to make the fight." As Houston saw it, "the Negro lawyer in the South in the next twenty-five years has a chance to reconstruct the entire southern picture."[93]

6

Crossroads:
Protest and Politics in the New Deal Era

Franklin D. Roosevelt's inauguration on March 4, 1933, was a prelude to one of the most far-reaching political realignments in American history, one in which black Americans would play a pivotal role. As the desperation of the Depression years yielded to the creative experimentation of the New Deal, Roosevelt trumpeted the government as a tool for advancing the economic security and welfare of all Americans. Robert Weaver, then a graduate student at Harvard, recalled feeling a mixed sense of possibility and urgency. The dramatic intervention of the federal government in the life of the nation was reminiscent of Reconstruction, reviving the idea of national citizenship and offering a lever for blacks to assert their rights. But the dominance of Southern Democrats in Congress ensured that new federal programs would reinforce the caste system unless there were insistent and effective demands for full and fair inclusion of black Americans in the recovery program. Almost overnight, Washington, a southern, segregated town, became a primary arena in the struggle for civil rights and fertile ground for fashioning alliances that would elevate racial equality to an issue of national consequence.[1]

The New Deal era was a critical period of black political activism and a formative stage in the evolving movement for freedom and civil rights. The unprecedented expansion of federal power, the inclusive rhetoric of the Roosevelt administration, the enactment of labor rights legislation and growth of the industrial labor movement, and the emergence of black-white coalitions on the Left all helped to challenge and disrupt the foundations of the nation's racial divide. In this fluid and dynamic environment, the northern black vote became a significant factor in national politics. The emergence of an activist federal government in response to widespread economic suffering stirred the expectations and political consciousness of African Americans as never before and brought new, younger leaders to the fore. There were wide-ranging debates over ideas and goals, tactics and strategies, and experimentation with different types of protest and political organizing techniques as new and old groups competed for prominence in the struggle for racial justice.

The hopes released by this fusion of change and political activity sought expression in a society where racial segregation and discrimination was the norm, and close to 80 percent of black Americans lived under a racial caste system. What was possible, where to find an opening, how to organize for change—these questions informed the debates within the NAACP and in the larger realm of black political struggle during this yeasty period. Efforts to dismantle racial barriers and secure full citizenship rights continued to guide the NAACP's efforts, although a vastly altered political terrain demanded new approaches and strategies. The proliferation of federal relief and jobs programs brought the NAACP permanently into the realm of national politics under Walter White's leadership as an advocate for no discrimination in federally funded projects and a visible representative of civil rights and racial equality in the broader political process. At the same time, the legal program continued its ascent, as Charles Houston laid the groundwork for prolonged struggle in the South.

Demands for equal treatment under federal recovery and relief policies stirred black America's response to the New Deal, helping to create a new kind of politics amplified by the growing black vote in the urban North. The NAACP's protest of abysmal working conditions on the Mississippi Flood Project under the Hoover administration had already exposed the problem of racial discrimination on federally sponsored programs and made it a national political issue. New York senator Robert Wagner's resolution providing for an investigation of the levee work camps passed just a month before Roosevelt's inauguration. With an investigation looming, White lobbied the newly established National Recovery Administration (NRA) for coverage of levee workers under new federal standards. In July, the Public Works Administration (PWA) received an allotment of $37 million for flood control work and brought many levee workers under its minimum wage and maximum hour regulations. The new secretary of war, George Dern, whose department administered the flood control project, pledged that an NRA code would apply to levee workers on contracts not covered by the PWA. Walter White claimed these developments as a victory, but kept a close watch on enforcement. Yet White and the NAACP were initially ill-prepared to monitor the broad reach of the NRA program and the dizzying burst of legislation that marked the start of the Roosevelt administration.[2]

The National Industrial Recovery Act, passed into law on June 16, 1933, established the National Recovery Administration. Relying on the voluntary participation of business, the NRA was designed to restore purchasing power and moderate competition by establishing maximum hours and minimum wages for nearly six hundred industries. It also included a provision, Section 7a, acknowledging the right of employees to organize and bargain collectively, helping to invigorate the labor movement. Public hearings to set wage and hour codes drew representatives of industries and unions, white officials who had little interest in the racial dimension of economic dislocation. Clark Foreman, newly hired assistant to interior secretary Harold Ickes, tried unsuccessfully to persuade NRA officials to focus special attention on the status of black workers. He reported that there was no check on the political pressure exercised by manufacturers and southern Congressmen "determined to keep Negro labor cheap and amenable." Robert Weaver and John Davis, two young Washingtonians, stepped into the breach, prepared to represent the interests of black workers and insist on a federal standard for fairness and equity.[3]

John P. Davis, twenty-eight years of age, had just graduated from Harvard Law School, and the twenty-six-year-old Robert Weaver was a doctoral candidate in economics at Harvard. They had been part of a small group of students at Harvard, including political science student Ralph Bunche, who had studied and discussed the devastating impact of unemployment and economic collapse on black communities. Upon returning home to Washington in the summer of 1933, Davis and Weaver were alarmed to find no one representing the interests of black workers before the NRA code hearings. Working out of a borrowed office on Capitol Hill, they established themselves as the Negro Industrial League and became regular attendees at the hearings. While young black intellectuals debated the future at Joel Spingarn's estate, Weaver and Davis were making noise on Capitol Hill—testifying on the adverse effect of specific codes and lobbying for equal wages for black workers. "We were something of an oddity," Weaver recalled. "No one expected us, we were literate, and we were contentious." After a visit with the pair, Roy Wilkins reported that they had won the confidence and respect of "official Washington" and of the press. Furthermore, he noted, "They are the only Negroes in Washington who have their hands on the situation. No one else seems to know what it is all about."[4]

Having ignited this ambitious effort on a shoestring, Davis and Weaver appealed to the NAACP, the National Urban League, and other groups to "submerge organizational differences and suspicions" and participate in a coalition that would support the work of soliciting funds, assembling information, "presenting the Negro's cause at the hearings," and continuing to investigate "violations and discrimination against Negroes even after the codes are in effect." Wilkins enthusiastically supported the idea, and in the fall of 1933 the NAACP joined in helping to establish the Joint Committee on National Recovery, a coalition of fifteen organizations that included the Urban League and the Race Relations Department of the Federal Council of Churches. Financial assistance from the NAACP and a small grant from the Rosenwald Fund provided a $5,000 operating budget, which included a small salary for John Davis as executive secretary. Largely due to Weaver and Davis's swift action, race-based differentials were not incorporated into the NRA codes. Southern businessmen, predictably, found other ways to maintain a dual wage through regional codes and simply by ignoring code provisions at the local level. But the indefatigable Davis monitored the NRA and exposed code violations while also investigating other federal programs. The Joint Committee kept the issue of racial discrimination before the public and attracted the attention and interest of Eleanor Roosevelt and interior secretary Harold Ickes, who also directed the $3.3 billion Public Works Administration. At the suggestion of Clark Foreman, Ickes hired Robert Weaver to help implement a no-discrimination policy in the PWA.[5]

Harold Ickes disturbed the highly segregated world of the federal government. A former social worker, Ickes had served as Chicago NAACP branch president in the early 1920s. As interior secretary, he fought for the full inclusion of black Americans in the recovery effort and agreed to house a new position for a special adviser on Negro affairs, funded by the Rosenwald Fund. A storm of black protest erupted when Ickes hired Clark Foreman, a white Georgian, to serve in the post. But Ickes had confidence in Foreman, a strong advocate of black equality, and insisted that at least initially he was the best person to lobby white industrialists, union officials, and heads of agencies on behalf of the needs of black Americans. But both men quickly set about working to see that black professionals were hired throughout the administration, and Foreman hired Lucia Pitts, a black woman, as his secretary. Shortly after Weaver joined the PWA, Ickes brought William Hastie on as an assistant solicitor in the Interior Department and was instrumental in having blacks recruited to work in other agencies and departments. While these officials faced constraints, they influenced policy development in some areas, served as a conduit for black access to the federal government, and helped facilitate a growing black identification with the Roosevelt administration.[6]

The new climate in Washington and a rise in mob violence prompted the revival of federal antilynching legislation. After reaching a low of ten in 1929, there were twenty-one lynchings reported in 1930; the number jumped to twenty-eight in 1933, including the double lynching in Tuscaloosa, Alabama, in August. Three days after Charles Houston submitted his brief to the Justice Department arguing for federal intervention in Alabama, a gruesome lynching occurred in the town of Princess Anne on the eastern shore of Maryland, not far from the nation's capital. On October 17, 1933, a crowd of two thousand witnessed the torture of George Armwood, a mentally retarded black man, charged with raping an eighty-two-year-old white woman. Armwood was taken from the jail, dragged through the streets, and hung from a tree in front of a local judge's home; his body was then mutilated and burned. The *New York Times* described it as "the wildest lynching orgy the state has ever witnessed."[7]

Disgusted by this "throwback," James Weldon Johnson told White that the time was ripe for "another try" to get a bill through Congress. The great change that was taking place "in the national attitude toward government" and the trend toward "greater centralization and an increase in federal power" convinced Johnson that chances for passage of an antilynching law were much improved. White needed little persuasion. Lynching dramatized the lawlessness and brutality that reinforced the Jim Crow system unlike any other phenomenon in American life. With the exception of Ida B. Wells-Barnett, who had died two years earlier, White was the leading investigator of these atrocities and the most prolific publicist. Moreover, the fight for antilynching legislation would give full rein to his talents as a lobbyist, honed in the fight to defeat John Parker three years earlier and on display in his successful effort to focus Senate attention on the plight of levee workers on the Mississippi River. He embraced the opportunity to solidify his position on Capitol Hill amid the rising expectations and fresh infusion of personnel generated by the new administration.[8]

The NAACP's Legal Committee drew up a bill, and White enlisted Senators Edward Costigan of Colorado and Robert Wagner to introduce legislation similar to the Dyer bill at the start of the session in January. It provided that the federal government would prosecute local and state officials who participated in a lynching or proved negligent in preventing one. As he had emphasized in his brief on the Tuscaloosa lynching, Charles Houston contended that the law was already sufficient to permit such action by the federal government. But he supported the move for antilynching legislation as a tool for educating and mobilizing public opinion. The public announcement of the pending legislation in December coincided with a nationally broadcast address by FDR in which he condemned lynching as a "vile form of collective murder" and appealed to a "new generation" to take up the "war for social justice." Roosevelt, however, proved reluctant to publicly endorse federal antilynching legislation in the face of strong southern opposition in Congress.[9]

The antilynching fight became a cornerstone of the NAACP's program in the 1930s and shaped its broader effort to influence the spirit of New Deal reform. In preparing for hearings before the Senate Judiciary Committee, White assembled a coalition of support that included the YWCA, the Federal Council of Churches, the ACLU, the Women's International League for Peace and Freedom, and the Writers League Against Lynching. Notably, the AFL declined to sign on. H. L. Mencken, who had blasted Maryland's tolerance of "the lynching spirit" in his column for the *Baltimore Sun*, became an active supporter of the legislation and aided White in his preparations for the hearing. White's efforts to win the support of southern moderates and liberals yielded mixed results. The Commission on Interracial Cooperation (CIC) and the recently formed Association of Southern Women for the Prevention of Lynching opposed federal antilynching legislation and promoted education along with local and state action to stem mob violence. Cracks, however, began to appear in the wall of white southern opposition to a federal law. Arthur Raper, a leading member of the CIC, testified in support of the legislation and the Women's Missionary Council of the Methodist Church South unanimously endorsed the Costigan-Wagner bill at their annual meeting in Birmingham.[10]

Students from a constitutional law class at Howard University and their young professor, Ralph Bunche, were among the more than three hundred people crowded into the Senate caucus room for the hearings. Senators Wagner and Costigan opened the hearings with statements underscoring the urgent need for legislation to secure the federal government's power to enforce the law when the states failed to. "National citizenship," Costigan emphasized, "is as undisputed as . . . state citizenship." A racially diverse and geographically balanced group of thirty-five men and women testified over the next two days, providing a concentrated look at the horror and history of lynching, documenting the failure of local and state officials to prosecute lynchers and explaining why federal action was essential to ending the barbaric practice. Of the more than 3,500 lynchings recorded since 1900, Arthur Spingarn reported, there were only twelve convictions of sixty-seven indicted offenders. An anonymous supporter used her influence with the National Broadcasting Company and paid for the hearings to be aired over radio coast-to-coast. This was reportedly the first time an entire Senate hearing was broadcast nationally.[11]

The color line in Washington invited challenge as debates over civil rights moved into the corridors of political power. During the lunch break, several of the men and women in attendance at the hearing attempted to dine in the Senate lunchroom. The head waitress turned them away, announcing that "colored" could not eat in the restaurant. Mabel Byrd, who had recently been employed as an economist with the Interior Department, arrived with two white friends and refused to leave. The manager summoned the Capitol police, and two officers dragged Byrd out of the restaurant and down to the police station, where she passed out. A group of Howard students returned to the restaurant several days later and were forcibly ejected by guards. Southern leadership in the Congress would not tolerate any breach of the color bar on the Hill, but the Wilson-era barrier in the executive offices collapsed across town at the Department of Interior. Robert Weaver and William Hastie ignored the protest of the white clerk in the cafeteria when they strode into the lunchroom one noontime. When an agitated group of white women protested to Ickes that "Negroes are eating in the lunchroom" and asked him what he planned to do, he allegedly responded, "Not a damn thing."[12]

In mid-April the Senate Judiciary Committee reported favorably on the Costigan-Wagner bill and sent it to the Senate for consideration. A survey of both houses by White indicated that there were enough votes to enact the legislation, but leading southern senators were set to keep it off the Senate's calendar. White turned his attention to the other end of Pennsylvania Avenue; if President Roosevelt put his weight behind the bill, there was a chance that the Senate would act. Eleanor Roosevelt emerged as an ally, and through her White obtained an appointment with the president. Roosevelt met with White for over an hour and agreed to urge a vote on the bill before the Senate adjourned but said he would not challenge a filibuster. The president, however, proved unwilling to spend any political capital in the face of firm resistance from key southerners in the Senate. The Senate adjourned without considering the bill.[13]

The battle to focus the attention of the federal government on the crime of lynching shifted to the Department of Justice later that year. Attorney general Homer Cummings, after much stalling, rebuffed requests by the NAACP that he put lynching on the agenda of the National Conference on Crime held in December 1934. As a result, the national office, working through the Washington, D.C., branch, organized plans to picket the conference. The police chief refused to provide the group with the necessary permits. A small group went ahead and picketed the opening of the conference with signs denouncing lynching and government inaction; one proclaimed "My Country 'Tis of Thee, Land of the Lynching Bee." Roy Wilkins was among four of the protesters arrested and hauled off to jail for parading without a permit. Charles Houston immediately organized a protest that did not require a permit. With the help of his colleague Ralph Bunche, he enlisted fifty Howard University students along with twenty faculty and NAACP branch members. Kenneth Clark, who would later play a major role in the *Brown v. Board of Education* cases, was among the student protesters; half of them were women. They stood shoulder to shoulder across from Memorial Continental Hall, the site of the conference, in a line that stretched along Seventeenth Street to Pennsylvania Avenue. Houston and Bunche stood with them; all wore a rope tied in "a lyncher's knot" around their necks. Police captain Edward Kelly fumed and threatened but had no grounds for breaking up the protest. The image was picked up by the *New York Herald Tribune* and claimed a prominent place on the front page of many black newspapers.[14]

In January 1934, W. E. B. Du Bois published an editorial on segregation, igniting the long-simmering tensions between himself and Walter White into a public battle over the ideology and future course of the NAACP. As his biographer David Levering Lewis has explained, Du Bois had already begun his withdrawal from active involvement in the NAACP but had no intention of going quietly. Beneath the personal animosities, there was a deep questioning about the prospects for black America in light of what had transpired since the NAACP's founding. While White and many younger activists saw the developments of the early 1930s as creating opportunities for pursuing full integration into American life, the sixty-six-year-old Du Bois brought a different perspective to bear. His analysis of trends in race relations argued for a dramatic change in emphasis. His method of raising his concerns, however, led to a final showdown and would culminate with his resignation from the NAACP.[15]

Du Bois had become increasingly isolated within the NAACP and disaffected with the leadership, with the exception of board chairman Joel Spingarn. He had no confidence in Walter White or in his assistant secretary, Roy Wilkins. The editor chafed under the efforts of White and several board members to exert oversight of *The Crisis* as the magazine's survival became increasingly dependent on the financial support of the association. From 1929 to 1934, the cash-strapped national office contributed more than $35,000 to *The Crisis* to keep it afloat. As in the past, Du Bois threatened resignation to maintain control of the magazine, but his base of support had diminished. In January 1933, he took a visiting professorship at Atlanta University hoping to secure a permanent position. While he carried out his editorial duties long-distance, his protégé, George Streator, and Roy Wilkins shared responsibility for business operations and day-to-day management. During the year that followed, Du Bois put the finishing touches on his seminal *Black Reconstruction in America* and took stock of the current state of black life and race relations. Through a series of essays and addresses, he floated the ideas that would ultimately lead to his break with the dominant opinion in the NAACP.[16]

By the spring of 1933, the vision that had inspired the Niagara Movement and the establishment of the NAACP seemed remote. At the Conference on the Economic Status of the Negro, sponsored by the Rosenwald Foundation, Du Bois observed that the effort of blacks to become an integral part of the United States had failed. "There seems no hope that America in our day will yield in its color or race hatred any substantial ground," Du Bois wrote in an essay on race pride, "and we have no physical nor economic power, nor any alliance with other social or economic classes that will force compliance with decent civilized ideas." That black Americans had made progress since the turn of the century was undeniable—in education, literary and artistic production, and the growth of business enterprises. But this was a function of blacks striving through their own institutions and organizations—churches, businesses, schools, newspapers, and literary publications. Du Bois therefore thought it imperative that black people depend upon themselves for their economic survival and progress during the massive reordering of the nation's economic life under the New Deal.[17]

A. C. MacNeal, president of the Chicago branch, wrote Walter White in October 1933, worried that Du Bois's ideas might encourage segregationists in the Roosevelt administration. A month later, a southern official in the Interior Department cited Du Bois's separatist approach to defend the Homestead Subsistence Bureau's decision to fund segregated resettlement communities as part of the New Deal relief program. An alarmed Walter White promptly telegrammed Du Bois in Atlanta to warn him of how his name was being used and urging, "Please call us collect." Hardly contrite, Du Bois raised the volume, broadcasting his support for black self-determination in an essay on segregation published in the January issue of *The Crisis*. Du Bois reaffirmed his position—namely that while broad human contact was the ideal, blacks could not wait for the "millennium of free and normal intercourse." It was, Du Bois maintained, "the race-conscious black man cooperating . . . in his own institutions and movements who will eventually emancipate the colored race." With apparent reference to the subsistence homesteads, Du Bois held that "groups of communities and farms inhabited by colored folks should be voluntarily formed" and their "only insistence" should be that equal provisions be provided.[18]

The timing of Du Bois's pronouncement could not have been worse as far as Walter White was concerned. After plans for a whites-only homestead colony were announced for Arthurdale, West Virginia, the national office of the NAACP joined the Charleston, West Virginia, branch in protesting the policy and alerting Eleanor Roosevelt. She intervened and plans were made to admit twenty black families to the Arthurdale settlement. According to White, officials in that bureau seized upon Du Bois's editorial to hold up the admittance of the black families. Du Bois thought it all a smokescreen. He argued that most homestead colonies, especially those in the South, would never admit blacks, and in cases where they were admitted, there was no chance that they would be treated equally. Given the stark realities, he wrote, "it would be nothing less than idiotic for colored people themselves to refuse to accept or neglect to ask for subsistence homestead colonies of their own." Indeed, many blacks petitioned for their own homestead colonies. This, combined with the fact that whites would resist any such interracial experimentation, encouraged government officials to leave the separate policy intact.[19]

But the debate did not end there. The response to the editorial compelled the NAACP to consider its policy on segregation, which had never been formally stated. Du Bois opened the pages of *The Crisis* to a discussion on "a new and changing philosophy concerning race segregation in the United States" and went on to develop his own views. He addressed hard truths that brooked no easy dismissal or solution. Beyond the seemingly static Jim Crow

South, racial segregation throughout the nation had "become more insistent, more prevalent, more unassailable by appeal or argument." Where blacks had been welcomed at the best hotels in major northern cities in 1910, in 1934 there was not a single northern city, with the possible exception of New York, where blacks could be guests in a first-class hotel. The successful legal fight against residential segregation ordinances had failed to diminish white determination to confine blacks to urban ghettos in northern cities. Restrictive covenants, upheld by the Supreme Court in *Corrigan v. Buckley* (1926), served that end. The problem of school segregation and black education presented an especially difficult dilemma. As Du Bois noted, a black man born in Boston had a right to protest any separation of schools by color, but what, then, of his helpless child, sent into a mixed school, "where white children kick, cuff, or abuse him, or where teachers openly and persistently neglect or hurt or dwarf his soul"? The dilemma is complete, Du Bois wrote, and there is no escape.[20]

In a sorrowful tribute to William Monroe Trotter, Du Bois bitterly wrote that unbending devotion to principle was not sufficient. Trotter, the great apostle of integration, plunged from the roof of his three-story apartment building in Boston on April 9, his sixty-second birthday. The *Washington Afro-American* expressed a widely held sentiment when it described Trotter's death as his final "protest against color barbarism." It was time to focus attention on reality rather than the hopes that had long guided their struggle, Du Bois instructed. The choice was not between segregation and no segregation, but "given varying degrees of segregation, how do we conduct ourselves so in the end human difference won't be emphasized at the expense of human advancement." Not only will blacks "be compelled to submit to much segregation," he wrote, but by voluntary action separation might be necessary for mounting a long-term attack on discrimination and ultimately breaking down barriers. While he did not dismiss the need to protest state-enforced segregation, such an approach was insufficient to marshaling the strength of the black community for the long fight ahead, Du Bois argued.[21]

For White and many others, any voluntary acceptance of racial segregation undermined the thrust of what had to be the primary focus of NAACP activism in 1934. With the vast expansion of government involvement in the economic and social life of the nation, it was vital for blacks to oppose any attempt to "put the stamp of federal approval" of racial segregation on projects financed by state or federal money. In a letter to White, Du Bois suggested that White's concerns were more narrowly focused than his and merited further thought and explanation. But personal animosity spiced Du Bois's pursuit of the issue, and he publicly discounted White's opinion on the subject by questioning his racial identity and allegiance. "In the first place," he noted, "Walter White is white. . . . He has more white companions and friends than colored. He goes where he will in New York City and meets no color line." White, for his part, did not rise to Du Bois's bait publicly but worked behind the scenes to further document that Du Bois had become a drain on the association. The national office had been paying his salary for nearly five years, and beyond *The Crisis*, he had done little to contribute to the association and the alleviation of its desperate financial situation.[22]

The debate around the issue of segregation and Du Bois's role as editor of *The Crisis* sapped the energy of the association for six months. Rumors of a plot to oust Du Bois generated some protest from the ranks. Several board members stood firmly by the editor. The Reverend William Lloyd Imes asserted that "for one who hates segregation as much as I do, I had rather have Dr. Du Bois's segregation than all the so-called anti-segregation of his opponents." Cleveland attorney Harry Davis found the debate around segregation futile and untimely, but he valued the open discussion and warned against the magazine becoming a rubber stamp for the NAACP. Others vigorously contested Du Bois's position and his use of the editorial page of *The Crisis* to challenge what many assumed to be NAACP policy, while insulting its executive secretary. From his perch inside the Roosevelt administration, William Hastie warned that Du Bois's "puny defense of segregation" was a "powerful weapon in the hands of our enemies." The *Afro-American*'s Carl Murphy had been arguing that *The Crisis* needed a younger editor. Now that board members found it necessary to apologize for editorials in *The Crisis*, patience and forebearance were no longer virtues. He concluded that it was time for Du Bois to resign. The black press, by and large, joined the chorus of opposition, with some editors wrongfully interpreting Du Bois's strategic turn as a retreat to Booker T. Washington's brand of accommodation.[23]

The NAACP had avoided strict pronouncements of policy, particularly regarding the thorny issue of segregation. As one observer noted, improvisation and opportunism were inescapable for the NAACP in light of the irreconcilable contradictions the organization faced. "A program which is rational in Cleveland, Ohio is simply impossible in Savannah, Georgia"—to say nothing of the rural Deep South where plantation culture prevailed. But in April, the board of directors enacted a resolution. Failing to adopt a more nuanced statement, the board responded to pressure from White and issued a short, unequivocal resolution expressing its opposition "both to the principle and practice of enforced segregation . . . on the basis of race or color." In the May issue of *The Crisis*, Du Bois challenged the blanket pronouncement, reciting a litany of questions about what it implied regarding black organizations and institutions. On the same page, he took a swipe at Charles Houston and his legal team and their conducting of the Crawford case and called for a fuller accounting of the circumstances leading to Crawford's conviction and life prison term. Finally, the board agreed to rein in the editor. The next month it voted that "no salaried officer of the Association shall criticize the policy, work, or officers of the Association in the pages of *The Crisis*; that any such criticism should be brought directly to the Board of Directors and its publication approved or disapproved." Unable to abide by such restrictions, Du Bois submitted his resignation from the NAACP, effective June 11, 1934.[24]

By the time the board met in July, Du Bois's resignation was final. He had briefly considered working out a compromise with the board but changed his mind. Apparently unaware that White had threatened to resign, Du Bois likely conceded that efforts to dislodge White and Wilkins were futile. Seeing nothing but continued strife ahead, he severed all ties with the NAACP as of July 1, 1934. In his final letter of resignation he noted that his efforts to work for change within the organization since the start of the Great Depression were "almost absolutely unsuccessful." And now, in light of the limitations set on the freedoms he had enjoyed as editor of *The Crisis*, his position had been completely undermined. There seemed "but one thing for me to do," Du Bois wrote, "and that is to make the supreme sacrifice of taking myself absolutely and unequivocally out of the picture so that the leaders of the NAACP without the distraction of personality and accumulated animosities can give their whole thought and attention to the rescuing of the greatest organization for the emancipation of the Negro that America has ever had." The board accepted his resignation, with regret and appreciation "for the services he has rendered," acknowledging, "no one in the Association can fill his place with the same intellectual grasp." Du Bois would remain at Atlanta University for the next decade.[25]

With Du Bois gone, Walter White solidified his dominance of the NAACP. Roy Wilkins became acting editor of *The Crisis*, and Louis Wright, a longtime friend of White's, succeeded Joel Spingarn as chairman of the board; Spingarn continued in the honorific role of president of the NAACP until his death in 1939. White was energized by the possibilities of the early New Deal era, claiming "we can do more when things are in a state of flux." At home in the corridors of power, he set about establishing a permanent presence for the NAACP in Washington, while assembling an impressive team to press ahead on other fronts. Several months after Du Bois's departure, the board voted to hire Charles Houston as director of the new legal program. The NAACP continued to work through John P. Davis and the Joint Committee on National Recovery to keep tabs on New Deal programs in the field and mount targeted protests against discrimination in locally administered federal programs, aided by local branches. In the fall of 1934, the Committee on Future Plans and Programs issued its report, which grew out of the discussions at the Amenia conference.[26]

The report of the Committee on Future Plans and Programs was an ambitious blueprint that touched on most major areas of NAACP activity. The report reflected the concerns of Abram Harris, who headed the committee, and other young black intellectuals, including fellow committee members Sterling Brown and Rachel Du Bois, who were impatient with the civil rights program that dominated the NAACP. They argued for a radical reorientation of the association, with an emphasis on the plight of workers and the potential of a united, interracial labor movement. The call for such a dramatic shift found little support among board members. The struggles unfolding around New Deal legislation and the early initiatives of the legal campaign in the South hardly merited a relaxation of the NAACP's brand of civil rights activism. Moreover, the possibilities of interracial unionism appeared remote in 1934. At that time, White was lobbying for a provision that would bar racial discrimination by unions in legislation providing for federal protection of labor rights; it faced stiff opposition from organized labor. Nevertheless, many agreed that the association had to find a way to respond more directly to the economic crisis facing black Americans, and several of the reports' recommendations guided efforts toward this end. The kind of economically and labor-oriented program that Harris and his colleagues advocated found outlets in other arenas, particularly with the founding of the National Negro Congress early in 1936.[27]

With the messy battles of the early 1930s behind him, Walter White immersed himself in the dynamic politics and heady atmosphere of New Deal Washington. This was the turf he was comfortable navigating—and he was good at it. White found himself hobnobbing with the likes of Eleanor Roosevelt along with senators, congressmen, and plucky New Dealers, angling for a place at the table and gearing up for what would be a long battle for federal action on civil rights. A revived Costigan-Wagner antilynching bill sparked a major showdown in the spring of 1935 when Senator Costigan brought the bill up for immediate consideration by the Senate. With southerners promising to filibuster "until Christmas," *New York Times* reporter Arthur Krock wrote that the bill hung over the president's second wave of reform legislation "like a poised avalanche." It was widely believed that if the bill came to a vote, it would pass. After an eight-day standoff, a majority of senators voted for adjournment, vacating the bill from the Senate's calendar. A supporter of the bill described the surrender to southern pressure as "Appomattox in reverse." Were it not for FDR's silence, after privately expressing his support for the bill, White believed they could have prevailed over the southern obstructionists. Still, as Houston observed, the fact that the lynching issue could tie up the Senate for more than a week was in itself a victory of sorts.[28]

The struggle around the reform legislation of Roosevelt's "Second Hundred Days" in the spring of 1935 demonstrated the limited political power of blacks in the rough and tumble of congressional politicking. Indeed, FDR's advisers were indignant at White's persistence and his apparent willingness to play the "spoiler" by injecting the explosive issue of race into the fragile arena of reform politics. Southern Democrats were prepared to block any bill that hinted at federal tampering with the racial status quo. Two major pieces of legislation during the Seventy-fourth Congress would have major consequences for blacks, the most economically vulnerable segment of the population. The Wagner Labor Relations Act provided federal protection of the rights of labor to organize and bargain collectively. Pressure by the AFL along with the specter of southern opposition brought elimination of a provision barring discrimination by unions seeking federal protection, thus threatening to lend federal sanction to the discriminatory policy of unions. In a second major defeat of intensive lobbying efforts by the NAACP and the National Urban League, the Social Security Act failed to include domestic and agricultural workers, barring an estimated two-thirds of gainfully employed blacks from coverage. Houston described the final bill as "a direct blow to Negro workers." Such battles previewed the pattern of yielding to southern racial norms that riddled the emerging coalition of liberal and labor groups within the Democratic Party.[29]

Throughout this period, Charles Houston monitored federal programs, frequently testified on legislation, investigated the administration of relief and jobs, and joined in public protests. But as head of the legal program, he dramatically expanded the NAACP's arena of activity, setting out to anchor the association more securely at its base. Litigation, in Houston's mind, served first and foremost as an organizing tool to "arouse and strengthen the will of local communities to demand and fight for their rights." A lean budget, funded by a $10,000 grant from the Garland Fund, required that the campaign narrow its focus. Discrimination in education would initially be the primary target. The abysmal condition of black schooling placed an entire generation at risk. Furthermore, Houston noted, improved educational conditions and opportunities would "change the whole relationship of the Negro to the South," making him "more active and insistent on his rights." He did not minimize the enormity of the task. "It takes a long time to get a mass of people to move" especially "in the face of the open hostility of superior numbers." But, as he brought together a network of black lawyers and became more deeply acquainted with black life in the South, he looked to the future with patient determination. "This is no star performance," he told his young colleagues. The goal was "to make the movement self-perpetuating. . . . Our idea should be to impress upon the opposition and public that what we have is a real program sweeping up from ground influence and popular demand . . . a program that is going to go on without regard to personnel."[30]

The campaign was rigorous, disciplined, and highly improvisational and depended upon first-rate legal talent. In preparing to move forward on the education front, Houston identified several possible areas where the system was vulnerable to legal challenge—unequal apportionment of school funds, differentials in teachers' salaries, and failure to provide black citizens with access to publicly funded graduate and professional education. A goal of the program was to work out model procedures, through test cases, that could be used by local lawyers and communities around the South in cases brought on their own initiatives and with their own resources. But how to proceed and the best points of legal attack would be determined by the given situation in a particular place. The national office could expose rotten conditions and stand ready to back the community in fighting, "but," Houston emphasized, "the will to struggle must first appear in [the] local community."[31]

Fieldwork was a critical part of the legal program; it invigorated the NAACP's effort to build strong, active branches while exposing national staff members to conditions in the South. Houston began working for the NAACP on a part-time basis in November 1934, while still dean of Howard Law School. The first thing he did was embark on a monthlong tour of the southeastern states, combining a recruiting trip for Howard with work for the NAACP. Edward Lovett, a Howard Law School graduate then practicing in

Washington, joined Houston on a barnstorming trip that took them to eleven towns in Virginia, the Carolinas, and Georgia. Houston met with black lawyers in each state, spoke at thirteen black colleges, attended the district Conference of the African Methodist Episcopal Church in Rock Hill, South Carolina, and met with teachers groups, NAACP branches, fraternal organizations, and the North Carolina statewide conference of tobacco workers. On the same trip, they investigated school conditions and the administration of federal relief and jobs. With the assistance of Bishop Jones of the A.M.E. Church in Rock Hill, who provided introductions to local ministers and teachers, Houston and Lovett filmed school conditions in southwestern South Carolina, documenting the inequities between neighboring black and white rural schools. Houston hoped to initiate legal action in the Palmetto State, and enlisted Charles H. Thompson, editor of the *Journal of Negro Education*, to do an extensive comparative study of black and white education in South Carolina.[32]

As an amateur filmmaker, the power of the visual image to arouse interest and shape public sentiment intrigued Houston. A year earlier he had suggested to White that all field-workers carry a pocket camera and document key individuals, scenes, and events so that lectures could be illustrated with slides or motion pictures. In particular, Houston noted, "motion pictures humanize and dramatize the discrimination which Negroes suffer much more effectively than any corresponding amount of speech could do." Based on the filming he did, Houston produced *A Study on Educational Inequalities in South Carolina*, a 30-minute long documentary on the inequities plaguing black education. Footage of black children of widely varying ages crowded on benches in a sparse one-room shack in Chester County was followed by scenes of white children attending a modern brick two-story structure nearby, equipped with a paved basketball area. The camera captured black children walking along a dirt road long distances to school, while school buses carried white children. The schools in several districts were filmed, juxtaposing black and white, as well as highlighting recreational facilities and sanitary conditions. These moving images were interspersed with factual data collected by Charles Thompson, documenting the wide disparities in resources allocated for the education of black and white children. The film concluded with a call to action. "Negroes must . . . protest discrimination in education by publicity, by appeals to friends, by test cases in court, by the ballot, and by every other legitimate means. They must persist until the state offers the identical quality of educational opportunity to all citizens, regardless of race, color or creed." The film had its premiere at the 1935 NAACP annual convention and was shown to community groups, various NAACP gatherings, and liberal supporters.[33]

The South offered a broad canvas for development of the NAACP's legal campaign. During his initial tour through the South, Houston began the process of documenting conditions and introducing the legal program to southern communities. His efforts to encourage a challenge to inequity in teachers' salaries in Columbia, South Carolina, floundered; longtime black civil rights attorney N.J. Frederick proved to be "very evasive on the school issue," Houston reported. Maryland and Virginia offered fertile areas for early test cases. The NAACP had made major inroads in Virginia during the Crawford case, tapping into liberal white sentiment and reviving NAACP activity. In January 1935, the state's seven branches formed a Virginia state conference of branches. But neighboring Maryland took the lead. Two years earlier, responding to the encouragement of Walter White and Carl Murphy, editor of the *Baltimore Afro-American*, a group of black college-age students in Baltimore, led by twenty-one-year-old Juanita Jackson, had begun to systematically apply for admission to the law school at the University of Maryland. Their efforts led to the case of Donald G. Murray, the first major case in the NAACP's education campaign.[34]

The fight to open up the University of Maryland Law School converged with efforts to revive the Baltimore branch of the NAACP and cultivated the talents of a new generation of leadership. In 1931, Juanita Jackson had founded the Citywide Youth Forum, which sponsored regular meetings to address social and political issues of the day and facilitate political action. The group launched a vigorous "Don't Buy Where You Can't Work" campaign in Baltimore to get blacks hired as clerks in chain stores. The lynching of George Armwood in the fall of 1933 further galvanized young people, including Clarence Mitchell, who covered the lynching as a cub reporter for the *Baltimore Afro-American*. Around that time, Walter White enlisted the aid of Juanita Jackson and her youth group to help organize support for the Costigan-Wagner antilynching bill and energize the Baltimore branch. In turn, the national office provided funds when a court injunction barred the Youth Forum from picketing A&P grocery stores, although a higher court sustained the injunction. Thurgood Marshall was a pivotal figure in the converging forces. After graduating from Howard Law School in spring 1933, he returned home to Baltimore to practice law and became legal adviser to the local NAACP branch. Marshall, whose application to attend the University of Maryland Law School had been rejected four years earlier on racial grounds, was eager to participate in overturning this barrier.[35]

Donald Murray's case unfolded swiftly and almost seamlessly. Murray came from a prominent Baltimore family and graduated from Amherst College in December 1934. The following month he submitted his application to the University of Maryland Law School, the only state institution providing legal education. The registrar returned the application and the $2 fee, refusing to consider it. With a strong plaintiff, an aroused community, and his prized former student Thurgood Marshall prepared to take the lead on the ground, Houston was ready to go forward. The NAACP announced on April 21, 1935, that they were filing a suit against the University of Maryland Law School and that it would be the opening shot in the campaign against color discrimination in tax-supported educational institutions. Marshall carried the bulk of the work preparing the case while in constant communication with Houston. The state's efforts to counter the challenge included the establishment of an out-of-state scholarship for black students in 1933, but legislators had neglected to appropriate funds. One hundred seventy-five black applicants exposed the sham and, as Marshall noted, punctured the myth that blacks were not interested in higher education. At the end of May, he wrote confidently to Houston that "all 'barber-shop' lawyers are sure we will win." On June 19, the Baltimore City Court ruled that the University of Maryland could not bar Murray from the law school because of his color and ordered Murray admitted pending the state's appeal. With the appeal tentatively scheduled for later that year, Murray enrolled at the law school in September.[36]

At a time when Jim Crow seemed immutable, the victory in the *Murray* case demonstrated the potential power of litigation and community action in dismantling the legal apparatus that bolstered segregation and second-class citizenship for African Americans. Alaine Locke, the dean of black letters, joined a chorus of voices when he hailed the *Murray* ruling as "a tide turning victory." He told Houston, "More power to your legal elbow." Roy Wilkins enthused that the ruling helped to "restore . . . the prestige of the NAACP in the popular mind." But Houston advised, "Don't shout too soon," cautioning that *Murray* was a small opening toward future opportunities. Beyond the pending appeal, Houston was sensitive to the need to act swiftly and deliberately on multiple fronts in order to reap the full benefits of this initial ruling. He instructed Marshall to make sure a photographer was on hand for Murray's first day of classes, telling him that "there is nothing like a picture to convince." The extensive coverage of the case by the *Baltimore Afro-American*, to Houston's mind, offered an excellent example of the relationship "between court proceedings and the formation of public opinion," and he touted it as a model at numerous public forums. Houston cultivated representatives from the black press as well as sympathetic white journalists, including H.L. Mencken, in an effort to ensure that the publicity value of the case "might be increased to the maximum." On the legal front, he was in contact with attorneys and NAACP officials in Virginia, Missouri, Tennessee, North Carolina, and Kentucky regarding incipient efforts to bring cases to open up graduate and professional education in those states, sharing copies of the petition and ruling in the *Murray* case and visiting with key individuals in each of those states during the summer. Houston emphasized the importance of a collaborative approach. "We are in new territory," he told an associate, "and no one of us or no group of us can afford to stand alone."[37]

Anticipating the challenges that Murray would face as the first black student to attend the Law School, Houston did all he could to ensure he would succeed. He arranged to have the funds to cover the tuition for Murray's first term advanced through Carl Murphy so that Murray could devote himself fully to his studies, without worrying about money. He prodded Marshall to keep an eye on Murray. "Check Murray up and see he is abstracting and taking good notes. Tell him I want to see him." As final exams approached, he arranged for Murray to have several sessions with Leon "Andy" Ransom. "Ship him over to Andy for review," he advised Marshall. "We have got to teach him how to answer questions. . . . Impress upon Murray also that from now on girls are nix until after his examinations." That December, Houston orchestrated a broad appeal to fraternities and sororities when he arranged for Juanita Jackson, William Hastie, Thurgood Marshall, Roy Wilkins, Leon Ransom, and himself to fan out to address all fraternity and sorority conventions that traditionally met over the holiday season. They explained the education fight and sought their support, specifically for funds to aid fellow college students who broke down the color line in graduate and professional schools. Alpha Phi Alpha contributed $500 to cover Murray's spring tuition, and enough funds were raised from the other groups to "practically insure scholarships for all admitted to state universities." Murray completed his first year successfully.[38]

Houston found a brilliant, energetic, and reliable associate in Marshall, who devoted increasing time to the work of the NAACP, to the detriment of his private practice. Houston expressed concern and cautioned Marshall to "keep a finger on your office practice." But Marshall, while frequently commenting on his dire financial straits, was already in too deep to step back. As the *Murray* case unfolded, he had begun investigating school conditions around the state, documenting them with photographs and moving pictures and ultimately brought a suit challenging the failure of Baltimore County to provide a high school for black students, while barring them from the eleven all-white public high schools in the county. He also began laying groundwork for a teacher salary equalization case. His work, in concert with Carl Murphy and a revived Baltimore branch under Lillie Jackson, mother of Juanita, illustrated how a vibrant legal campaign tied to a targeted effort to engage community support could invigorate the NAACP and boost its membership. Late in the summer of 1936, Marshall proudly announced that within a year, their cases had contributed to such a dramatic growth in membership that Maryland's state conference of branches was as large as any other state's "and most likely larger." In October 1936, William Gibbs, a principal in Montgomery County, wrote to Marshall and volunteered to be a plaintiff in a teacher salary equalization suit. Marshall took the case, and it became the bedrock for developing procedures in the teacher salary equalization fight in Maryland and throughout the South.[39]

While Maryland's constellation of NAACP leaders played an exemplary role in launching the legal campaign, success there was hardly a measure of what was possible elsewhere. As a border state, Maryland had a relatively less rigid segregation system. Houston noted that public policy on race was not so crystallized that it would not be affected by court decisions. By contrast, Houston's extensive travels deeper in the South during the first year of his tenure revealed the challenges confronting the legal campaign and the movement it sought to nurture. He described the "lack of knowledge and indifference on the part of the public in general to the question of Negro education" as "astonishing." There was a great degree of apathy within the black community, as well as fear and reluctance on the part of older and more conservative blacks to come out in support of any challenge to educational discrimination. Teachers associations were, by and large, "passive and docile," reflecting the control imposed by county and state authorities. In Virginia, the *Norfolk Journal and Guide*, one of the most influential black newspapers in the nation, initially refused to endorse the NAACP's support of applicants to the University of Virginia's graduate program and its effort to bring a teacher salary equalization case. The difficulty of finding young people willing to be plaintiffs for the graduate and professional school cases was compounded by the need for individuals with impeccable records so that they could not be rejected on academic grounds. The consequences of inequitable education and poorly resourced schools made it all the more difficult to fight this battle. For example, the NAACP declined to pursue the case of an applicant who was denied admission to the graduate program at the University of Virginia due to a weak academic record; another, more promising candidate withdrew under pressure from his parents.[40]

In response to the NAACP's program, trends and patterns of resistance emerged. The white press in Virginia unanimously condemned the NAACP's activity, and employers threatened the handful of potential applicants to the University of Virginia with loss of their jobs. Tennessee's assistant attorney general warned of violence if such efforts were vigorously pursued there. The *New York Times*, while acknowledging "the validity of the protest from the legal point of view," cited the reaction of the white southern press "which called into question the wisdom of rectifying 'the injustices in a manner that ignores the deep-lying . . . forces that have compelled a separation of the races in the South's educational establishments.'"[41]

"I am not only a lawyer, but an evangelist and stump speaker," Houston wrote Marshall in the fall of 1935. During his first year as full-time director of the legal campaign, he traveled more than 22,000 miles meeting with individuals, civic groups, and parent-teacher associations and addressing mass meetings in a tireless effort "to explain and convert the public to the program." These experiences and developments attested to the urgency of the program, revealed some of the obstacles, and began the process of creating a network of local contacts. Houston adjusted his expectations and predicted that it would take at least five years before the campaign gained full momentum. He was guided by a fundamental belief that the legal work "must not go forward any faster than it can carry with it substantial support among the Negro group." He stressed the singular importance of undergirding the effort in the courts with the support of black organizations and institutions—churches, fraternal organizations, labor unions, teachers associations, fraternities and sororities, and the black press. Houston rarely missed an opportunity to visit black college campuses and appeal to college students as potential graduate and professional students as well as teachers, emphasizing their responsibility to black youth coming after them. John Hope Franklin, then a student at Fisk, oversaw Houston's visit to his school, which was sponsored by his fraternity. He recalled how Houston conveyed to them, in the most powerful way, the "very critical disadvantages we were living under" and their consequences. His presence as well as his message, Franklin recalled, "made a deep impression on me."[42]

The campaign slowly yielded returns. In January 1936, the Maryland Court of Appeals upheld the *Murray* ruling, making it the "first case of its kind in the history of American law." By spring, three states in addition to Maryland had established out-of-state scholarships for black students seeking to attend graduate or professional school since the NAACP's legal effort began— Oklahoma, Kentucky, and Virginia. West Virginia and Missouri already had such scholarship programs. While the NAACP did not accept this arrangement as constitutional, it was a measure of the impact of the campaign and provided some temporary relief to students seeking to pursue graduate education.[43]

Promising developments in Virginia paved the way for the legal program to push deeper into the South. Close proximity to Washington allowed Houston and Leon Ransom to make frequent trips through the Old Dominion, where they built upon the visibility and networks they had established during the Crawford case. Two of their former Howard law students worked on the ground with NAACP branches—Byron Hopkins in Richmond and Raymond Valentine in Petersburg. There was a strong cohort of local leadership who provided support for moving ahead on the issue of education. School principal Thomas Dabney of Norfolk had personally campaigned around parts of the state to mobilize support for educational equality, including equal salaries for black and white teachers. Luther P. Jackson, history professor at Virginia State University in Petersburg, aided with studies of school conditions and in identifying potential plaintiffs. Dr. J.M. Tinsley, head of the Richmond NAACP branch, emerged as the moving force behind the formation of the Virginia state conference of NAACP branches.

One of the Virginia state conference's first initiatives was to launch a special campaign to raise $1,500 for a suit to challenge the racial differential in teacher salaries. At the end of 1935, the annual conference of the Virginia State Teachers Association and a meeting of the Virginia state conference of branches coincided in Roanoke over Thanksgiving weekend, indicating the start of a coordinated effort on the part of teachers and the NAACP on salary equalization. In his keynote to the teachers association, Houston urged that a $1,000 scholarship fund be established to provide support for any plaintiff in a teacher salary case, since he or she would almost certainly lose his or her job.

The teachers association voted to make all of its reserve funds available to the teacher salary equalization effort. Houston and Ransom used both forums to discuss the potential problems and logistics as the legal campaign moved forward. Black teachers, ready to fight for equal wages, invigorated the growth of the NAACP throughout Virginia and laid the groundwork for what would be a precedent-making case.[44]

Houston's work in Virginia in the fall of 1935 illustrated how he connected with local people, while working steadily to strengthen the NAACP and broaden its reach. In the month leading up to the Roanoke meeting, he spent an extended period of time in the Tidewater area of the state, coordinating his work with Daisy Lampkin, who was conducting a major membership drive. He supported her successful efforts to enlist postal workers and longshoremen "solidly behind the Norfolk drive" and wrote the budget committee regarding the failure of the national office to provide her with essential resources in the field. In preparation for the Thanksgiving weekend meeting in Roanoke, he traveled the back roads in his car, investigating school conditions, meeting with people, and addressing several mass meetings. Houston cultivated a friendly relationship with William Milner, secretary of the Norfolk branch and employee of the *Norfolk Journal and Guide*. He dined with Milner's family and wrote at one point that he would "be happy to go fishing with you" on his next visit. Acting on a plan he and Milner had discussed, Houston tested dining facilities on the ferry between Norfolk and Washington. Houston refused to sit behind a screen in the dining room, explaining that Virginia's Jim Crow laws did not apply on the high seas; this was federal territory. He took his meal in his room, but insisted on being charged the dining room fee rather than the price for room service, which was twice as high. At first the steward refused, but then conceded to this demand once he understood that Houston was prepared to file a suit against the ferry line upon returning to Washington. The black waiter who brought Houston his meal quietly praised him for his bold stand.[45]

The NAACP's campaign for educational equity was part of a broad effort dedicated to promoting civic engagement and voter participation during a politically tumultuous period. As the 1936 presidential election approached, black voters in the North were emerging as a pivotal constituency in the New Deal–inspired realignment of the national Democratic Party. The ramifications in the South, while subtler, were equally significant. For decades, law, custom, and the threat of violence had barred southern blacks from effective participation in the electoral process. The federal activism of the Roosevelt administration expanded upon the inroads made by the Scottsboro case and stirred the political imagination and activism of southern blacks. As Du Bois observed, New Deal programs aroused "a new and direct connection between the federal government and the individual . . . in the South that had never been experienced before," reviving the concept of national citizenship. The NAACP cultivated these trends, with Houston constantly emphasizing voting as critical to advancing and securing change in the South. "Every educated Negro man and woman is a civic derelict who does not register to vote," Houston told editors of the black press in a memo urging them to hammer away at the importance of voting on every possible occasion. An aroused and active electorate was critical to creating an environment supportive of public officials willing to promote racially fair policies.[46]

During the 1930s, black political aspirations became apparent in a variety of venues. The Democratic Party primary was a major arena of activity as southern blacks increasingly identified with the party of Franklin Roosevelt. While white southerners sought to obstruct the enforcement of the Supreme Court's 1932 ruling that overturned Texas's plan for excluding blacks from the Democratic primary, Houston reported on organized attempts by blacks in South Carolina, Alabama, and Texas to vote in primary elections in 1934. In his field investigation of southern politics, Ralph Bunche reported that "despite the hardships frequently imposed by registrars . . . increasing numbers of Negroes in the South are demonstrating an amazing amount of patience, perseverance, and determination . . . and keep returning after rejections until they get their names on the registration books." Blacks were responsive to appeals by Houston and his associates when they urged greater political participation. In Louisa County, Virginia, at a mass meeting with parents and teachers on school issues in November 1935, Houston stressed the importance of paying poll taxes and voting, and promised to take the case of any qualified citizen who was denied registration. He reported that the people were enthusiastic and "simply wanted to know that they would not be left alone in case a fight started." In the aftermath of the meeting the number of registered black voters in the county doubled.[47]

The NAACP provided encouragement and legal assistance to southern black voters as it extended its presence in the South through its branches and the campaign against racial discrimination in pubic education. In fall of 1934, Professor W. H. Hannun of Livingston College and C. M. Petty of Wilkesboro, North Carolina, contacted Houston regarding John Cashin, a registrar in Wilkesboro who refused to allow fifteen registered black voters to cast a ballot in a close general election. Houston advised them on the procedure for assembling evidence. While he cautioned that the U.S. Justice Department would be "very reluctant to touch the case," he promised that the association would "exhaust every effort to make it prosecute." Signed affidavits by the citizens barred from voting were submitted to the Justice Department, and Houston visited Wilkesboro in August to meet with Hannun, Petty, and local citizens. The Justice Department failed to act for more than a year, but Walter White reported that the NAACP planned to keep the pressure up. Even if it did not produce immediate results, it might lead the Democratic Party "to quietly issue instructions against depriving Negro citizens of the franchise." Finally, in December 1935, Cashin was indicted, tried in federal court, found guilty, fined $300, and put on probation for three years.[48]

This singular victory came in the aftermath of a major setback in the fight for political rights in the South. In April 1935, the U.S. Supreme Court had bolstered the all-white Democratic primary, sanctioning a revised Texas plan designed to remove the primary from any state regulation. White Texas Democrats had gone to work immediately following the Court's narrow 1932 ruling in *Nixon v. Condon*, adopting a resolution at the party's state convention to restrict membership to whites. Challenges by blacks in several cities to the new restriction failed in the Texas Supreme Court, which ruled that "the Democratic Party [was] a voluntary political association" and that its convention had the right to "determine who shall be eligible for membership in the party and, as such, eligible for participation in the primaries." In response to complaints filed by the NAACP and the National Bar Association, the Justice Department concluded that the exclusion of blacks from the primary in Texas was within the bounds of the law. Attorneys Carter Wesley and J. Alston Atkins, along with several other black leaders in Houston who had chafed at the NAACP's reliance on white lawyers in the earlier cases, moved hastily to take a case to the U.S. Supreme Court, independent of the NAACP. In *Grovey v. Townsend* the Court ruled unanimously in favor of the Texas Democratic Party's right to exclude blacks.

Grovey elicited comparisons with the infamous *Dred Scott* decision as a defining blow to black civic aspirations. It eliminated the incremental gains made in the earlier two cases brought under the NAACP and reinforced the most effective barrier to black political participation. Ironically, it also led to the revival of NAACP activity in Texas. In the aftermath of the *Grovey* ruling, the black leadership of Houston sought to mend fences with the national office of the NAACP and build toward the future. Charles Houston's appointment as director of the legal campaign had defused a major criticism of attorneys Atkins and Wesley, who had demanded a more prominent role for black lawyers and emphasized the need to build "the fight" in Texas "around Negro leadership"—objectives Houston actively promoted. Walter White seized the moment and set about strengthening the NAACP in Texas. He enlisted newspaper editor and NAACP leader Roscoe Dunjee in neighboring Oklahoma to coordinate a statewide organizing effort in Texas. Working through his contacts with black editors around the state, Dunjee orchestrated a massive publicity campaign to promote the NAACP, and took a tour of key cities with William Pickens, the director of branches. Their efforts helped to stimulate branch activity and supported the efforts of Dallas NAACP leader Maceo Smith and a handful of others to organize a state conference of branches. In June 1937, delegates from five branches met in Dallas and formed the Texas State Conference of the NAACP, dedicated to renewing the fight against the white primary and supporting the struggle for equal educational opportunity.[49]

As the NAACP made a few dents in the armor of Jim Crow, its southern campaign began to take on form and substance. Charles Houston had demonstrated the ways in which litigation could serve as a tool to organize black people behind the fight for fundamental civic rights. His active presence in the South, along with the small but growing corps of black attorneys, complemented the work of Daisy Lampkin, William Pickens, and other field-workers in making the NAACP a vital and tangible presence. These personal connections were essential to the growth of healthy branches and the development of effective legal challenges. NAACP branches and the emerging system of state conferences helped to break down the fear and isolation that inhibited political activity and provided a structure for joining individuals and communities around a common resistance to the oppressive weight of segregation. Few underestimated the fortitude and courage necessary to mount a long-term attack on the South's segregation system. But its very pervasiveness aided the NAACP's pioneering efforts, under Houston's leadership, to craft a unity of purpose and direction. The vibrant political culture of the 1930s and the reach of federal relief and jobs further enhanced a palpable sense of possibility in the face of enormous odds. While education and voting served as the primary battleground in the South, Houston continually emphasized that these efforts must be bound to "a general attack on discrimination and segregation in all phases of American life."[50]

*   *   *

Racial discrimination and segregation above the Jim Crow South offered a
different kind of challenge, one that was at the heart of Du Bois's critique in
his editorials on segregation. There were no laws mandating racial separation,
and the ballot was unrestricted, yet blacks were steadily losing ground in the
North. Barriers to housing, education, and jobs tightened as black migration
steadily altered the northern urban landscape. The existence of a smattering
of municipal and state civil rights laws along with efforts by the NAACP and
various other groups to fight individual cases of racial discrimination did little
to stem this trend. The Depression further deepened the economic divide
between blacks and white in the urban North. By the time the New Deal
began, the majority of Harlem's population, noted a city-commissioned report, was "on the verge of starvation as a result of the Depression and of an
intensified discrimination that made it all but it impossible for Negroes to
find employment."[51]

On March 19, 1935, black frustration and despair erupted in Harlem. In
the wake of rumors that police had beaten a ten-year-old dark-skinned Puerto
Rican boy held for shoplifting, crowds swelling to an estimated three thousand attacked white-owned stores and businesses. During the uprising, three
blacks were killed, more than a hundred people were wounded, and seventy-
five people were arrested. Property damage reportedly reached $2 million. In
the aftermath, Mayor Fiorello La Guardia established a commission of
prominent blacks and whites to investigate the causes of the disturbance. The
commission concluded that the riot was a spontaneous outburst of anger and
resentment fueled by the entrenched racial discrimination evident in poor
employment opportunities, educational inequalities, overcrowded housing,
unfair rents, and police brutality. Commission member Hubert Delaney, who
served on the NAACP's board, contended that what happened in Harlem
was "by no means a race riot, but an active expression of a resentful community against those who have exploited them" and made it impossible for them
to secure "the necessities that citizens of any civilized community need." Educator Nannie Burroughs warned, "The colored man has reached the endurance limit."[52]

Jobs and lack of economic relief loomed as the major crisis facing blacks
in northern urban areas. A variety of groups channeled efforts to strike
down barriers to employment and secure relief, sometimes using tactics that
went against the grain of the NAACP's restrained approach. Communist
Party–affiliated organizations, including unemployment councils and tenant
organizations, mounted direct-action protests in cities across the country, tar-

geting local and federal relief organizations, employers, and landlords. Among the most widespread and notable protests of the decade were locally generated movements against white merchants who profited from black patronage but refused to hire black employees. "Don't Buy Where You Can't Work" campaigns emerged in at least thirty-five cities, combining boycotts and picketing of targeted establishments. While many were short-lived, more than a half dozen were sustained campaigns that cracked the barrier to black employment in neighborhood stores and won significant concessions from white-owned businesses. Some NAACP branches participated in these protests, but the national office remained ambivalent about the use of such tactics and did not officially endorse this approach. Cleveland's Future Outlook League, an organization dominated by working-class blacks, sponsored one of the most successful campaigns and opened more than a thousand jobs to blacks by the end of the 1930s. The New Negro Alliance in Washington, D.C., led by Howard University students and faculty, mounted a vigorous effort and, with the assistance of William Hastie, succeeded in winning a U.S. Supreme Court ruling in 1938 securing the right of racial groups to picket against job discrimination, a landmark decision that fueled a revival of "Don't Buy" protests.[53]

In the arena of northern black protest, the NAACP began to feel increasingly crowded as it struggled to find a way to address the varied problems that plagued urban communities. For most of the 1930s, many of the NAACP's most prominent northern branches were dominated by professional elites who were not attentive to the needs and desires of the majority of working-class and poor blacks, many of whom were recent migrants from the South. In Detroit, leading members of the branch maintained a mutually beneficial relationship with automobile manufacturer Henry Ford, with prominent black ministers serving as brokers between Ford and blacks seeking work in the industry. When John Hope Franklin, a graduate student at Harvard, spoke to the Boston branch in the mid-1930s and advocated protest against segregation in that city, an older member of the group accused this "outsider" of being a troublemaker. Here, Franklin recalled, was an example of how some elite African Americans could "buy into a system that gives them a sense of belonging without bestowing on them the rights that others enjoy." Chicago boasted a more militant leadership. Its robust Legal Redress Committee made strides in enforcing the state's civil rights law, challenging the exclusion of blacks from restaurants, hotels, and theaters, and mounted a fight against residential segregation led by Carl Hansberry, father of future playwright Lorraine Hansberry. But 90 percent of the individuals represented by the branch in civil rights cases were not members; furthermore, such cases did little to alleviate the desperate economic plight of most black people. Meanwhile, affiliates of the Urban League and locally grown groups such as the Detroit Civil Rights Committee and the Future Outlook League in Cleveland provided venues for seeking economic rights and opportunity. Impatient with the NAACP's approach, young black leaders founded the National Negro Congress (NNC) in February 1936 designed to mobilize black workers around a militant program to fight racial and economic inequities.[54]

The National Negro Congress grew from the concerns aired at the 1933 Amenia meeting and further articulated at a national conference on "the economic crisis and the Negro" sponsored by Howard University and the Joint Committee on National Recovery in May 1935. The Howard conference, organized by Ralph Bunche and John P. Davis, brought together a broad spectrum of opinion and experience. Speakers included New Deal administrators; representatives of the National Urban League, the Socialist and Communist parties, and the southern interracial movement; prominent black social scientists, including E. Franklin Frazier, W. E. B. Du Bois, Charles S. Johnson, and Ralph Bunche; labor leader A. Philip Randolph; and Nannie Burroughs. Commenting on the composition of the participating audience, Charles Houston noted that "the presence of workers gave this conference an impact of reality which was wholly different from the average gab-fest conference." The deliberations took an unvarnished look at the economic status of black America and the patterns of racial discrimination that riddled federal relief and jobs programs and reinforced blacks' disproportionately high representation among the unemployed and underemployed. Bunche and Davis invited a select group of leaders, including Charles Houston, to a small follow-up meeting. As a result, Davis, Bunche, and A. Philip Randolph developed plans for "a national Negro congress" to organize a black, mass-based organization capable of articulating and representing black economic interests in the emerging labor movement and the broader political arena.[55]

The founding meeting of the National Negro Congress in Chicago drew nearly a thousand delegates, mostly from the Midwest and Northeast, and heralded a new departure in black protest. A. Philip Randolph, the highly esteemed founder and president of the Brotherhood of Sleeping Car Porters, served in the honorific role of president, and John Davis served as secretary. The NNC's emphasis on economic and labor concerns, along with its largely northern-based constituency, distinguished it from the NAACP and, Davis contended, offered a complementary component in the struggle for racial justice. But his efforts to enlist the formal support of the NAACP failed to convince Walter White. White had cut the NAACP's support for the Joint Committee on National Recovery the previous fall, arguing tight finances; he undoubtedly viewed the NNC as a competitor for membership and funds. Roy Wilkins, who attended the NNC's founding meeting as an observer, reported to White that rumors of communist involvement attached itself to the enterprise. He was most impressed, however, by the presence of large numbers of young people, black and white, and delegates "from the so-called working class and mass organizations, who came at great personal sacrifice and who owed their allegiance only to organizations committed to a militant fight for the Negro." Wilkins argued for a formal affiliation between the NAACP and the NNC, as did William Hastie, but White refused to budge. Nevertheless, as the NNC established affiliates in northern cities, it often enlisted the active support of NAACP members as it supported unionization efforts among black workers and found common cause with the newly established Congress of Industrial Organizations (CIO), the broad coalition of industrial unions that advocated open recruitment of black and white workers.[56]

Charles Houston was in sympathy with Davis, if doubtful of his abilities, and cautioned that he exposed a major weakness of the NAACP's approach. He warned White that the only way "to keep [John] from running off with the show—unless he breaks his neck in the meantime, which is always possible with John—is for the Association to put on a bigger and better performance of its own." The national office was too narrowly centered on the antilynching fight, Houston said, while neglecting to wage an equally vigorous battle for black economic independence and security. He compared it to fighting "the manifestation of the evil and ignoring its causes." There were not "enough irons in the fire. . . . There should be a three ring fight going on at all times," Houston advised. The limited range of the national program also reflected structural problems with the association, and the frequent refrain of "no money" did not satisfy Houston as an excuse. White's hiring of Juanita Jackson as his special assistant late in 1934 was a case in point. While she was "personally swell," Houston told White, "the thing that bothers me about your own set up and your personal thinking is that it is too white collar. What you need now is strength on the industrial side; and frankly you don't get it in Juanita." The NAACP did not need to engage in labor organizing;

that was beyond its expertise and best left to others. But Houston advised that the organization needed to close the gap between its members and the working class and could begin by organizing "a strong group of lawyers and members to back up Negro labor in its fight to organize, to picket and to strike, freedom of speech and freedom of assembly."[57]

When asked by Wilkins to review a draft of the program for the 1935 annual conference, Houston held Davis's Howard meeting up as a model and told Wilkins that his plans were "weak and timid" by comparison. In order to organize the conference for maximum effect, Houston said, it must appeal directly to the mass of black people, involve them in the proceedings, and illustrate how and why they need the NAACP. The meeting should hear from sharecroppers, industrial workers, people on relief, relief workers, and railroad workers who were being forced from their jobs. "They may not make grammatical speeches, but their very presence is more eloquent than all of the prepared speeches you could present." There was nothing about relief on the program draft, Houston pointed out. Yet the whole question of discrimination under federal relief programs was critical, especially in the aftermath of the Harlem riot, "with the possibility of explosions elsewhere in the country at any time." While the antilynching fight deserved attention, Houston advised that "we don't want to waste an evening listening" to Walter telling about "the change in white Southern sentiment." White's message "should tie up lynching with all of the evils we suffer from; show how it perpetuates political disfranchisement . . . how it keeps down labor organizing [and] keeps down protests against intolerable relief conditions."[58]

Houston's critique echoed "the clamor . . . from isolated places out in the country" directed to the national office for "a new economic philosophy" and a more democratic approach, and Wilkins took heed. The annual conference, Wilkins acknowledged, offered an opportunity to gain exposure to more views during a tumultuous time and to identify a wider variety of contacts with knowledge of local conditions and situations. The 1935 meeting, held in St. Louis, and the annual conference in Baltimore the following year, showcased the role that the NAACP could play in knitting together the diverse strands of the black experience around a common struggle while also serving as a national forum for labor and government officials increasingly solicitous of the economic and political aspirations of black Americans. The annual convention emerged as a crossroads, drawing delegates from every part of the country, with a strong southern representation, to work in tandem with the national staff, including the nascent legal team in assessing the status of black

America, measuring the progress of the past year, and mapping future directions. Increasingly, labor leaders and national Democratic Party figures sought
a platform at the NAACP's annual meeting.[59]

Economic issues dominated the St. Louis meeting. Randolph addressed
the opening session, and urged participation in the trade union movement,
warning black workers not to let prejudice deter them. In a series of other
keynote speeches during the five-day meeting, John P. Davis reviewed the
impact of New Deal programs on black people, lambasting those who barred
blacks from the recovery program. Hubert Delaney exposed the economic
destitution that fueled the Harlem "riot," and Howard Kester shined a harsh
light on the plight of sharecroppers and tenant farmers struggling under vir-
tual slavery conditions while promoting the pioneering efforts of the interracial Southern Tenant Farmers Union. Presentations by a white sharecropper,
a black woman farmer, and a representative of black railway workers gave
depth and voice to the more formal presentations. A screening of a film made
by Charles Houston and John Davis on rural relief conditions in Lauderdale
County, Alabama, provided visual evidence of the struggles blacks faced when
seeking aid from New Deal programs. Houston urged branches to investigate
and protest such discriminatory conditions and refer them to the national
office if appeals to local and state officials failed to secure equal treatment
from federal relief agencies. The creation and articulation of public sentiment
"in favor of equal rights and in opposition to discrimination," Houston emphasized, was essential to progress on all fronts.[60]

Houston introduced the new legal program to a large and broadly representative NAACP audience; the annual convention remained a major forum
in the development and advancement of the legal effort. In his comments, he
talked about the case of Jess Hollins, which he had argued before the Supreme Court with an all-black legal team, a first for the NAACP. He won the
reversal of Hollins's conviction based on the fact that blacks had not been
included on the jury rolls. (This followed on the heels of the Court's ruling in
Norris v. Alabama, one of the Scottsboro cases, which established that failure
to include blacks on the jury rolls was unconstitutional.) Houston explained
that proof of complete exclusion of blacks from a jury now was grounds for
overturning a conviction. He urged branches and local lawyers to monitor
jury lists and attempt to press further to expose token inclusion of just one or
two black citizens as going against the spirit of the law.[61]

Houston completed the editing of *A Study of Educational Inequalities* just in
time for the annual conference, where it had its first showing. This graphic

exposure of the harsh and almost primitive conditions of schooling for black children in the Deep South underscored the critical importance of the NAACP's campaign to compel the states to offer the "identical quality and quantity of education for all citizens." But they were in the early stages of the battle, and Houston looked to the long struggle ahead. In his report to the conference, he highlighted the University of Maryland case and explained the long-term strategy that guided the education campaign. He advised patience, noting that "it takes time to perfect the procedures of attack. . . . In new fields even the best of us are only learners." Houston told the delegates that "the most hopeful sign about our legal defense is the ever increasing number of young Negro lawyers, competent, conscientious, and courageous, who are anxious to pit themselves against the forces of reaction and injustice."[62]

Increasingly, as demonstrated in St. Louis and at the conference in Baltimore the following year, these annual gatherings offered a venue for delegates to report on developments in their communities to a nationally representative group; develop contacts; debate, refine, and develop strategies and tactics; and see their efforts within the full context of NAACP activity. During these meetings, for example, the Reverend Roy Young, president of the Meridian, Mississippi, branch, reported on efforts by the Meridian and Jackson branches to reverse the "frame-up" of three black farm laborers convicted of murdering a plantation owner. The president of the Chicago branch told about victories in a string of civil rights cases, including an extradition case. And the Albany, Georgia, branch described its fight against unequal education. Professor W. H. Hannun of Livingston College and C.M. Petty of Wilkesboro, North Carolina, reported on the hard-won victory in their voting rights case. During both conferences, there was "bitter comment" on the treatment of blacks under the New Deal, and such sentiment caused many delegates to advocate more radical action. While the Chicago delegation opposed any alignment with "left wing movements" John LeFlore, president of the Mobile, Alabama, branch, argued that black people must swing to the left and "use every means to secure the same rights and opportunities as other Americans."[63]

The 1936 conference in Baltimore met in the midst of the presidential election season. The largest delegation traveled for four days in a car caravan from Oklahoma, led by Roscoe Dunjee. More than five hundred delegates attended, including two hundred youth delegates, organized by Juanita Jackson, making it the best-attended conference ever. With the decisive victory in the University of Maryland case earlier in the year, an exuberant Walter White proclaimed to the gathering, "If you are willing to struggle with us . . . who knows but there may be Negroes in the universities of states such as Mississippi and Arkansas?" But politics claimed a primary place at this conference. Just two weeks earlier at the Democratic National Convention in Philadelphia, the courting of black voters had begun in earnest. For the first time, blacks were accredited as delegates to the convention and black reporters were welcomed in the regular press box. The Reverend Marshall L. Sheppard, black Philadelphia minister and Pennsylvania legislator delivered the invocation at the convention, causing South Carolina senator "Cotton Ed" Smith to stomp out of the hall in a widely publicized display of outrage. President Roosevelt and interior secretary Harold Ickes seized the opportunity offered by the NAACP annual conference to promote a vision of inclusion. In his written greeting to the conference, Roosevelt declared that "the questions of legal justice for all, of civic rights, of economic opportunity, of adequate educational facilities, are matters of deep concern to the nation as a whole."[64]

Ickes addressed the opening session of the conference. In a speech broadcast to a national audience, he sought to focus attention on the intent and inherent philosophy of the New Deal, asserting that the "new democracy" promoted by the Roosevelt administration implicitly favored black Americans, who were disproportionately represented among the economically disadvantaged. Federal initiatives designed to advance the social and economic well-being of all citizens replaced the laissez-faire concept of government that had been dominant since the end of Reconstruction. The commitment to equality and full inclusion at the core of New Deal programs gave "the members of the Negro race a standing which they have not enjoyed since they became citizens." Acknowledging the discriminatory administration of job and relief programs at the local level, Ickes observed that prejudices that had "been built up for sixty years cannot be done away with overnight." But the secretary tried to defuse any doubts about the commitment of the Roosevelt administration to ensure the "equality of opportunity under law which is implicit in . . . American citizenship." Indeed, he compared Roosevelt with Lincoln and the departure initiated by the New Deal with the changes set in motion by the Civil War.[65]

Walter White bore in on the shifting political balance and discussed the potentially pivotal role of black voters in securing the program advanced by the New Deal. Southern conservatives were not only committed to derailing antilynching legislation but were among the staunchest opponents of the New Deal's socially enlightened policies for the very reasons Ickes touted them—

fear that they would benefit black as well as white citizens, thus disrupting the racial status quo. The economic concerns of southern elites also fueled fierce southern opposition to the newly won rights of organized labor. Disenfranchisement in the South vastly inflated the power of southern politicians in a way that allowed them to hold the entire reform program of the New Deal hostage. In such a scenario, northern black voters were emerging as a critical element in the political realignment fostered by the initiatives of the New Deal and the rise of organized labor. John Brophy, secretary of the newly established CIO, addressed the Baltimore meeting, promising equality and no discrimination; the conference passed a resolution endorsing black support and active participation in the new industrial union movement. White advised that how blacks used their newly acknowledged political power could be critical in shaping the future course of reform and "bringing about that justice and fair play which the Negro has been so long denied in America."[66]

The political transformation that Du Bois had predicted and Walter White steadily monitored took hold in 1936, when the battle for the black vote emerged as one of the major stories of the campaign season. The steady migration of blacks to the North had spiked during the Depression, boosting the number of potential black voters in eight pivotal northern states by 291,600. These states—Illinois, Indiana, Michigan, Missouri, New Jersey, New York, Ohio, and Pennsylvania—accounted for 202 of 523 electoral votes. For the first time, both parties advertised extensively in the black press, taking out full-page ads. Republican candidate Alfred Landon railed against "the horrible discrimination" in New Deal agencies and the "Southern-controlled" Roosevelt administration—though the candidate refused to commit himself on antilynching legislation or other specific policy initiatives. Meanwhile, the Roosevelt administration had a record to run on and, equally important, powerful symbolic gestures that held out hope for the future.[67]

Despite rampant discrimination, blacks had benefited from New Deal programs. "The struggle to survive took precedence over the struggle for equality," historian Nancy Weiss has observed, "and in the struggle to survive, many New Deal programs made a critical difference." Public testimonies of black recipients of jobs and relief were promoted in campaign literature and featured in a sixteen-minute film, *We Work Again*, screened in movie houses and at Urban League meetings. Mary McLeod Bethune, Robert Weaver, and other black members of Roosevelt's administration, often referred to as the president's "Black Cabinet," actively campaigned for FDR. Local Democratic groups sponsored an extravagant multicity celebration of the seventy-third anniversary of the Emancipation Proclamation, claiming that the "social and economic programs of our great President, Franklin D. Roosevelt," represented "the real spirit of Abraham Lincoln." Barely a week before the election, FDR and Ickes participated in the dedication of a new chemistry building at Howard University, built by the Public Works Administration. In his speech, which was broadcast nationally and claimed front-page coverage in the black press, Roosevelt told the audience that "among American citizens, there should be no forgotten men and no forgotten races."[68]

FDR made his campaign a referendum on the New Deal, in the face of an obstructionist Supreme Court, which had struck down the NRA and the Agricultural Adjustment Administration as an overreach of federal power, and those "economic royalists" who had come to see government "as a mere appendage of their own affairs." Proclaiming that "freedom is no half and half affair," he pledged the continuation of an activist government, committed to the "establishment of a democracy of opportunity for all people." Roosevelt swept 60.8 percent of the popular vote, the largest popular plurality in history, marking a sea change in American politics. His class-based appeals absorbed much of the energy generated by independent movements on the Left, and the 1936 election marked the political debut of the CIO, which coordinated a massive get-out-the-vote effort. But "the real political sensation of the time" wrote longtime political reporter Frank L. Kent, was the wholesale crossover of black voters into the Democratic column. In many places, the black vote for Roosevelt exceeded the national average. He won 81 percent of the black vote in Harlem, 75 percent in Pittsburgh's black neighborhoods, 69 percent in Philadelphia, 65 percent in Cleveland, and 60 percent in Chicago. "It's amazing how overwhelming the President's triumph has been," Walter White told Eleanor Roosevelt.[69]

The response of black voters to Roosevelt was tied in large part to the reach of New Deal programs, however racially compromised, and reinforced by the inclusive gestures of high-profile administration officials. South Carolina civil rights activist Mojeska Simkins put it this way: Roosevelt "took the jug by the handle. He tried to give the people who were down and had nothing something. . . . It was a shot in the arm for Negroes." Howard University professor Rayford Logan, who voted for Roosevelt in 1936, explained that the Roosevelts set a new tone. "Aside from questions of policy, treating Negroes as human beings was a very significant factor," a sober commentary on previous occupants of the White House. Clarence Mitchell wryly observed,

"When you start from a position of zero, even if you move up to a point of two on a scale of twelve, it looks like a big improvement."[70]

Addressing the 1937 annual conference of the NAACP, Robert Weaver, who had assumed the post of special adviser on Negro affairs under Ickes, underscored the challenge that faced black Americans in relationship to the new role of the federal government in the life of the nation. The benefits that blacks received under the New Deal were worth noting, and he provided a brief sketch of how hundreds of thousands of blacks had benefited. But, he advised, "Vastly more important than a factual representation is an interpretive analysis of results . . . and an evolution of techniques for the future. Such techniques," he emphasized, "are survival factors for minorities." The federal government's assumption of responsibility for the social and economic welfare of its citizenry, with many programs "designed to benefit persons of low income and restricted economic opportunity . . . can and should improve the status of the Negro." The problem that continued to face the Negro was "how to influence and respond to federal activity in such a way as to secure equal and just benefits from it." He cautioned that "unless a group like ours is constantly developing . . . such techniques, it will not only fail to advance, but it must rapidly lose such advantages as it inherits from its forefathers."[71]

The political landscape shifted dramatically after 1936, accelerating the struggle for a more inclusive democracy and inviting the kind of strategic engagement Weaver advocated. Initiating his second term with a stirring inaugural address, Roosevelt pledged to fulfill the mandate "to find through government the instrument of our united purpose," namely to advance the security and peace of all citizens through "practical controls over blind economic forces and blindly selfish men." At his back, and at times pushing out ahead, was a new coalition of liberal, labor, and black voters, which served as a strong counterweight to New Deal obstructionists and the long-term dominance of Southern Democrats. In a bold move, he launched his second term with an ultimately disastrous effort to rein in the Supreme Court, which was set to rule on the Wagner Labor Relations Act and the Social Security Act. FDR's "court-packing plan" went down to defeat in Congress, with Southern Democrats moving into open revolt. The Court subsequently upheld the New Deal programs, and a series of retirements soon enabled Roosevelt to secure a majority of justices sympathetic to his philosophy. That left Congress as the primary battleground over the future of New Deal reform.

Pumped up by his electoral mandate and reports of wide support in the South, Roosevelt trained his sights on Southern Democrats, who had become leading opponents of his legislative agenda. He took on three towering figures in the 1938 primary—Senators Walter George of Georgia, "Cotton Ed" Smith of South Carolina, and Congressman Howard Smith of Virginia— publicly urging their defeat and endorsing other candidates in the primary elections. FDR campaigned in the South, appealing to voters who had benefited from New Deal programs, urging them to reject proponents of "a feudal economic system," men whose minds were "cast . . . in the 1898 mold." Senator George called FDR's bold intervention "a second march through Georgia," harking back to General William T. Sherman's devastating attack on the Confederacy. Predictably, the president's enormous popularity in the region did not register on primary day; black voters in many states were barred from the primary, and many white beneficiaries of the New Deal were disenfranchised by the poll tax. Thus, the attempted "purge" was an abysmal failure at the ballot box, but it did stimulate the efforts of white and black southerners joined in a commitment to end voter disenfranchisement, democratize southern politics, and reap the full benefits of New Deal reform—a development that the NAACP would support and actively help to cultivate.[72]

In Washington, Walter White's attempts to parlay black voting strength into positive action met with little success during FDR's second term. The debacle around the Court-packing plan and the failed southern purge paralleled a growing preoccupation with war in Europe. During this time, persistent efforts to broaden the coverage of Social Security and ensure that proposed federal legislation on housing, education, health, and relief included amendments mandating no discrimination reaped little tangible gain. United southern opposition conspired with white liberal indifference and a racially conservative White House staff to sideline the work of White and others lobbying for a robust commitment to fair and equitable policies. Nevertheless, White, Houston, and others increasingly used hearings before Congress and administrative bureaus as a critical platform "in the fight for equal rights," testifying on racial discrimination in federally funded programs, including the armed services; shining a light on patterns of racial discrimination; and working to educate and persuade legislators and broader public sentiment. Working in tandem with the litigation program, Houston observed that the NAACP must be poised "to start the fight before [a] bill even gets to the state of becoming a law."[73]

The struggle for federal sanctions against lynching remained the centerpiece of the NAACP's legislative agenda. To those who had grown weary of the issue, NAACP board chairman Louis Wright underscored that antilynching legislation was central to the "fundamental citizenship struggle in the South." More than anything else, Wright explained, it was the climate of terror and lawlessness that kept citizens in Mississippi, South Carolina, and Georgia from demanding their civic rights. And it was an issue that generated financial support from the base—the sale of antilynching buttons at 10¢ each netted more than $8,000. The continuing introduction of legislation brought a continuing stream of publicity, tested procedures and strategies, and provided entré to the White House. In April 1938, FDR met with an all-black delegation led by White and personally encouraged them to keep fighting for an antilynching bill, while allowing that his support would only hinder their efforts. White thought the best thing to come from the meeting was FDR's exposure to black leadership that represented an important segment of the Democratic Party's newly fashioned reform coalition. At this point, it was doubtful that FDR could be of much use in coaxing southern senators into line. Antilynching bills passed the house in 1937 and 1939, never making it past southern filibusters to a vote in the Senate. It had become clear, Houston noted, that they could not overcome "the reactionary forces of the South and northern indifference" without broader public support. Toward this end, he advised "a closer tie-up with the labor forces," which meant turning attention "more closely to Negroes in the organized labor movement."[74]

As efforts stalled on Capitol Hill, the legal program continued to grow, free of the constraints imposed by southerners in the legislative arena. Houston steadily institutionalized his vision for the legal program, winning support from the board at a time of continuing financial constraints. In the fall of 1936, the board approved the hiring of Thurgood Marshall for a period of six months at a monthly salary of $200. Marshall had been working closely with Houston and the NAACP for over a year on a fee basis, investigating school conditions in Maryland, developing education cases, and building up public support behind the NAACP's program. He told Houston that this was the work he wanted to do but that he needed a more secure financial base. For his part, Houston desperately needed help in New York if the legal campaign was going to sustain its momentum, and to his mind there was no one better suited to the work than Marshall. In October 1936, Marshall temporarily closed his office in Baltimore and moved to New York. His youthful energy and expansive personality was a perfect complement to Houston's more serious demeanor and a tremendous asset in the field. Marshall pushed ahead with cases in Maryland and Virginia, did fieldwork in North Carolina, investigated school segregation in Hillburn, New York, and assisted Houston on the case of Lloyd Gaines, who had been denied admission to the University of Missouri Law School. He quickly proved to be indispensable.[75]

Houston transformed the NAACP's National Legal Committee, "pruning [the] dead weight" and adding lawyers who were actively working with branches in different regions of the country. Under his guidance, the committee became an active network of lawyers working at the grass roots, prepared to advise, support, and implement the legal campaign. Houston worked through the legal committee to provide assistance to black workers in various labor disputes, placing the association more firmly behind efforts to secure and advance the rights of black workers "without much greater effort and cost." Black lawyers from the South had a strong representation on the committee and played a critical role in the development and implementation of campaigns for education equality and voting rights. During the latter part of the 1930s, additions included Leon Ransom of Howard Law School; Louis Redding of Wilmington, Delaware; A. T. Walden of Atlanta; Charles Anderson Jr. of Louisville; Z. Alexander Looby of Nashville; Charles A. Chandler of Muskogee, Oklahoma; James Nabrit of Houston; Thomas Griffiths, president of the Los Angeles branch; and William T. McKnight, chairman of the legal committee of the Ohio state conference of branches. During this period, future U.S. attorney general Francis Biddle of Philadelphia also joined the Legal Committee, and Felix Frankfurter resigned from the committee in 1939 upon his nomination to the U.S. Supreme Court.[76]

The NAACP's legal campaign invigorated the association's presence throughout the South. While methodically laying the groundwork for a sustained legal challenge to Jim Crow, Houston and Marshall functioned as field-workers, aiding in the growth of membership and branches and helping cultivate the local leadership that emerged during the late thirties. Marshall described traveling in the South with Houston in Marshall's "little old beat up '29 Ford," with Houston typing out briefs while Marshall navigated southern roads. "Charlie . . . could type up a storm, faster than any secretary, and not with any two fingers, I mean he used all of 'em." They would stay at friends' homes, Marshall recalled, adding, "We had absolutely no money at all in those days." John LeFlore, a postal worker and president of the Mobile branch, was one of the many inspired by meetings with Houston; he became a powerful force for the growth of the NAACP in the Deep South. In 1936, LeFlore organized a regional conference of southern branches that included Alabama, Mississippi, Louisiana, Georgia, and Florida and, later, Tennessee.

It brought local leaders and members from the participating states together in annual conferences and pooled resources to fight targeted legal battles.[77]

Public support grew behind the legal campaign as news of the campaign spread, legal assistance became available, and victories began to materialize. Lloyd Gaines's effort to seek admission to the University of Missouri Law School was likely headed to the U. S. Supreme Court. Potential challenges to black exclusion from graduate and professional programs were being considered in Georgia, Texas, North Carolina, Virginia, and Kentucky. Largely as a result of the NAACP's efforts, the General Assembly of Maryland passed a law in 1937 mandating equal school terms for black and white students. A Committee of One Hundred Negroes in Prentiss, Mississippi, requested assistance in eradicating the gross discriminations in that city's elementary school and planned to start with an attack on the inequality of the school term. Local groups in communities around the South were investigating expenditures on education, appearing before local and state education boards to protest inequities. In some cases they secured additional funding for facilities and bus transportation; in others, such as Muskogee, Oklahoma, and Baltimore County, Maryland, legal challenges to discrimination at the elementary and secondary level were under way. Local groups in Jacksonville, Florida; Mobile, Alabama; and Atlanta, Georgia, were working to equalize teachers' salaries, and Thurgood Marshall spent time in Virginia and North Carolina at the request of several groups preparing to test salary differentials in those states.[78]

At the end of 1937, Houston cited this impressive record in his appeal to the American Fund for Public Service (the Garland Fund) for a renewal of funding, as the final installment of the initial grant was about to run out. It would be "tragic," Houston told the AFPS board, "that just when its effect is beginning to be felt on a regional scale," the legal campaign "should be cut off from the necessary support to broaden its scope and effectiveness." Houston failed to persuade the board, leaving it to the NAACP to absorb the full cost of the legal effort. The termination of the Garland Fund's contribution was a heavy blow to an organization operating on "a slender financial margin." But there was no question that the board would retain Marshall on a permanent basis and continue to fund the legal program. "So vital is the work of Misters Houston and Marshall," reported the Budget Committee, "that it must be continued at all costs."[79]

In the fall of 1938, the education campaign reaped its greatest victory to date when the case of Lloyd Gaines won a hearing before the U. S. Supreme

Court. The University of Missouri Law School had rejected Gaines's application on racial grounds, and Gaines had declined the offer of an out-of-state tuition grant. Houston and Sidney Redmond, an NAACP-affiliated lawyer in St. Louis, held that the state of Missouri had to either admit Gaines or provide equal facilities within the state, an argument rejected by the Missouri courts. Once the Supreme Court agreed to hear the case, the question of funding asserted itself, and White and Houston managed to wrangle an additional $700 from the AFPS to help cover essential costs at this critical phase. But the promise of funding was not secured until, as fund chairman Roger Baldwin insisted, a legal expert other than Charles Houston vouched for the likelihood of a favorable ruling.[80]

William Hastie, who had attempted to crack open the doors of higher education in North Carolina five years earlier, looked on as Houston presented his argument before the high court. "Never before," Hastie reported, "has the Supreme Court been more effectively used as a forum for presenting the various aspects of the race problem." Drawing on history and the law, Houston emphasized the public importance of the case, noting that sixteen states denied black students admission to their state universities. The state of Missouri, interestingly, had no statutory provision prohibiting the admission of black persons to the state university. "Perhaps," he declared, "the State of Missouri thought colored children would never reach the University of Missouri." Students from out of state, Mexicans, Chinese, and all other people were admitted to the University of Missouri, with the exception of people of African descent. Poking holes in the state's argument, Houston took a shot at the notion that the color bar protected the public interest by guarding against social equality—a code phrase for interracial mixing. The evidence of social equality, Houston told the Court, was written into the features and complexions of colored people. He appealed to the Court to require the state of Missouri to afford black citizens equal protection under the law by admitting them to the university professional and graduate school program, or provide a substantial equivalent. Houston spoke, uninterrupted, for nearly forty-five minutes. The justices listened intently, with the exception of Justice James McReynolds of Kentucky. The Woodrow Wilson appointee, who had served as Wilson's attorney general, ceremoniously swiveled his chair around, turning his back to Houston when he stepped forward to address the Court.[81]

On December 13, the *New York Times* announced the Court's decision in a front-page story headlined "Court Backs Negro on Full Education." In a 6-2 decision, the Court ruled that the state of Missouri was required, under the Fourteenth Amendment, to provide Lloyd Gaines a legal education equivalent to that provided white students. The ruling eliminated out-of-state tuition grants as an acceptable way for a state to fulfill its obligation to black residents who sought graduate or professional education. Gaines, the Court ruled, was entitled to be admitted to the University of Missouri Law School if "other proper provisions for legal training" were not available in the state. Morris Ernst, a member of the AFPS board, hailed the ruling: "Charlie's job is probably the outstanding accomplishment of the Garland Fund. I do not refer only to this case, but . . . to what I find throughout the South." Pauli Murray, whose application to the University of North Carolina Law School had been denied on racial grounds, described *Gaines* as the "first major breach in the wall of segregated education." It was, she said, "the beginning of the end."[82]

By all measures, the *Gaines* decision was a brilliant victory. The NAACP had breathed legal life into the concept of educational equality, elevating the fight to secure full citizenship rights for black people. But white political and educational officials maintained the advantage in dictating the meaning and application of the ruling. Just a month after the decision, Missouri's General Assembly promptly turned its attention to establishing a law school at Lincoln University, an all-black institution. Meanwhile, Lloyd Gaines said he was uncertain about whether he would enroll in the University of Missouri's Law School and then mysteriously disappeared. Considering the significance of *Gaines*, Virginius Dabney, the moderate white editor of the *Richmond Times-Dispatch*, conceded that southern states would be required to make far-reaching adjustments and predicted that the NAACP would ultimately prevail in having unequal teachers' salaries, curricula, and equipment declared unconstitutional as well. But he expressed a common sentiment that "maintenance of separate institutions for Negroes" at the graduate and professional level would remain intact. Black leaders in the upper South, Dabney contended, would be patient while state officials developed adequate facilities for blacks seeking professional and graduate education. In the Deep South, whites would make it "so uncomfortable for any Negro applying to one of their white institutions for admission" that the impact of the decision would be "virtually nil." While Dabney mused, Houston and Marshall hunkered down for continuing battle in Missouri and beyond."[83]

At the end of 1938, Charles Houston moved his base of operation to Washington, D.C., primarily for family reasons. The board promoted

Marshall to the position of co-special counsel, and he assumed responsibility for the New York office. The next year, the NAACP Legal Defense and Education Fund, Inc. was established, allowing the legal arm of the association to receive tax-deductible donations. The NAACP's lobbying program made it ineligible for tax-exempt status. As a separate entity, the "Inc. Fund," as it came to be called, would be devoted "exclusively to educational and legal work." It maintained close ties with the parent organization. They shared overlapping boards, and Houston and Marshall remained co-special counsels to the NAACP. Marshall became director counsel to the Fund.[84]

Barely four months after the *Gaines* ruling, the NAACP enjoyed a major symbolic triumph, one that seemed to crystallize the hopes that had been fermenting during the 1930s. It all started in January 1939 when the Daughters of the American Revolution (DAR) rejected Howard University's request to host their annual spring concert, featuring black opera singer Marian Anderson, at Constitution Hall, the largest concert venue in Washington. The hall's manager responded that the date was booked, but also reiterated its policy of barring black performers. White went into full battle mode, fueling a massive blitz of publicity and orchestrating a protest by leading artists and singers. Even the *Montgomery Advertiser* found the DAR's policy beyond "all human understanding," noting that the world-renowned artist was not only the toast of Europe but had been welcomed in the concert halls of the Deep South. When the DAR refused to reverse their stand, Eleanor Roosevelt famously resigned her membership. A Marian Anderson Citizens Committee, chaired by Charles Houston and including representatives of more than fifty organizations, worked to secure the Central High School auditorium for the Easter Sunday concert, but these efforts faltered when the board of education insisted on intolerable conditions. Meanwhile, the Citizens Committee organized a boycott of Constitution Hall. Houston persuaded Senator Robert LaFollette to publicly denounce the DAR's actions and move a lecture series he chaired to another venue. The next featured speaker was Swedish economist Gunnar Myrdal, who had just been enlisted by the Carnegie Foundation to study race relations in America.[85]

As the April 9 date for the originally scheduled event drew near, White hatched the idea of staging an outdoor concert at the Lincoln Memorial on Easter Sunday. A phone call to his friend Oscar Chapman, assistant secretary of the Interior Department, set things in motion. Chapman easily won approval from Harold Ickes and the support of FDR, who, according to White "is just as excited as the rest of us." The deal was made with just ten days left to make and finalize plans. White, the master impresario, worked with Anderson's manager, Interior Department officials, and Houston's Citizens Committee to make arrangements and ensure a large turnout. He secured a list of more than three hundred sponsors, headed by New York congresswoman Caroline O'Day. Washington notables attorney general Frank Murphy, Supreme Court justice Hugo Black, Senator Robert Wagner, and Mary McLeod Bethune were joined by conductor Arturo Toscanini and Hollywood stars Katharine Hepburn, Tallulah Bankhead, and Frederic March. Broadcast arrangements with the three major radio networks would provide a nationwide audience. By the day of the concert, U.S. senators were angling for seats at the front of the platform.[86]

Marian Anderson stood on the steps of the Lincoln Memorial, facing the Capitol and looking over a sea of 75,000 people, a mix of black and white, stretching to the base of the Washington monument. Her bronze figure, clothed in an elegant gown with a mink coat draped over her shoulders, was framed by the white marble monument, the massive seated figure of Lincoln visible above her; the early shadows of evening softened the sparkling spring day. Anderson opened the program with "America." Her voice, amplified by speakers, echoed "with bell-like purity." "For the first time in the nation's capital the words, 'My country 'tis of thee, sweet land of liberty,' rang true for many who always considered these words a mockery," wrote one observer. It was at once an elegant and defiant protest of the petty, mean-spirited practice of segregation and racial exclusion that marred Washington, D.C., and much of the land, and a glimpse of what was possible. Robert Carter, then a twenty-one-year-old student at Howard Law School, was there. He wept and remembered others also weeping. "It was a very emotional occasion," he recalled more than sixty years later. "It felt like we had reached the point where there was a change in race relations and that it would never be the same."[87]

In its fulsome coverage of a glorious day, the *Baltimore Afro-American* described Anderson's concert as "a message of peace which drowned out the rumblings of war machines."[88] But the rumblings of war soon eclipsed the promise of that moment, and the power of race to dictate the most basic meanings of citizenship boldly asserted itself. As war mobilization primed industrial production, black Americans found themselves largely shut out of the explosion of jobs that finally pulled the country out of the Depression. A segregated United States military, meanwhile, prepared to fight Nazism. Seasoned by a decade of struggle and hard-won gains, the NAACP faced an unprecedented range of demands and challenges as black Americans across the nation enlisted to fight on two fronts for the democracy and freedom consecrated in song at the foot of the Lincoln Memorial on Easter Sunday, 1939.

Figure 1. W. E. B. Du Bois at around the time of the founding of the NAACP in 1909. RE-
PRODUCED FROM THE COLLECTIONS OF THE LIBRARY OF CONGRESS

Figure 2. Archibald Grimké at the legislative advocacy meeting sponsored by the Washington,
D.C., branch of the NAACP in 1914. REPRODUCED FROM THE COLLECTIONS OF THE LIBRARY
OF CONGRESS

Figure 3. On July 28, 1917, a silent parade in New York City protests the East St. Louis race riot and the crime of lynching. REPRODUCED FROM THE COLLECTIONS OF THE LIBRARY OF CONGRESS

Figure 4. NAACP executive secretary James Weldon Johnson in his office during the 1920s. REPRODUCED FROM THE COLLECTIONS OF THE LIBRARY OF CONGRESS

Figure 5. "A Man Was Lynched Yesterday" flag flies outside NAACP headquarters at 69 Fifth Avenue, announcing news of a lynching. REPRODUCED FROM THE COLLECTIONS OF THE LIBRARY OF CONGRESS

Figure 6. Pilgrimage of the 23rd Annual Conference of the NAACP to Harpers Ferry, West Virginia, May 22, 1932. Walter White and Mary White Ovington are seated in the center of the front row. REPRODUCED FROM THE COLLECTIONS OF THE LIBRARY OF CONGRESS

Figure 7. Walter White (left) with NAACP chief legal counsel Charles Houston, ca. 1935.
REPRODUCED FROM THE COLLECTIONS OF THE LIBRARY OF CONGRESS

Figure 8. NAACP officials picketing National Crime Conference in December 1934; Charles Houston stands by with his camera. REPRODUCED FROM THE COLLECTIONS OF THE LIBRARY OF CONGRESS

Figure 9. Thurgood Marshall (left) with Donald Gaines Murray (center), who was denied entry into the University of Maryland Law School, and Charles Houston rehearsing for court proceedings in 1935. REPRODUCED FROM THE COLLECTIONS OF THE LIBRARY OF CONGRESS

Figure 10. NAACP special assistant Juanita E. Jackson (left) visits the Scottsboro boys, January 1937. REPRODUCED FROM THE COLLECTIONS OF THE LIBRARY OF CONGRESS

Figure 11. African American school on Spring Hill AME church property in Clarendon County, South Carolina, 1938. JOSEPH DELAINE COLLECTION, SOUTH CAROLINIANA LIBRARY

Figure 12. Elisha Davis, a founder of the NAACP branch in Brownsville, Tennessee, with his wife Nan Davis and their children in 1940, shortly before whites forced Davis to leave the state. REPRODUCED FROM THE COLLECTIONS OF THE LIBRARY OF CONGRESS

Figure 13. Detroit branch office of the NAACP during World War II. REPRODUCED FROM THE COLLECTIONS OF THE LIBRARY OF CONGRESS

Figure 14. Ella Baker joined the staff of the NAACP as a field worker at the start of World War II and served as Director of Branches from 1943 to 1946. REPRODUCED FROM THE COLLECTIONS OF THE LIBRARY OF CONGRESS

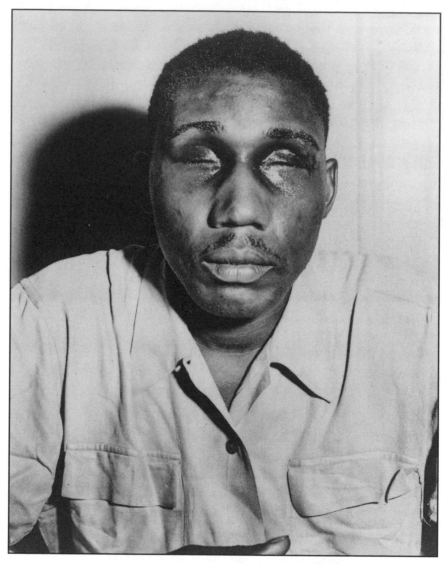

Figure 15. Isaac Woodard, World War II veteran, after he was beaten and blinded by police officer Leonard Shull in Aiken, South Carolina, in February 1946. REPRODUCED FROM THE COLLECTIONS OF THE LIBRARY OF CONGRESS

Figure 16. State highway patrolmen register and search a group of black citizens arrested in Columbia, Tennessee following a police raid on the black community there in February 1946. REPRODUCED FROM THE COLLECTIONS OF THE LIBRARY OF CONGRESS

Figure 17. Men waiting to testify about voter harassment and intimidation before the Senate Campaign Investigating Committee in Jackson, Mississippi, December 5, 1946. BETTMAN ARCHIVE

Figure 18. Walter White (right) with President Harry Truman and Eleanor Roosevelt on June 19, 1947, prior to Truman's address to the NAACP's 38th Annual Conference from the steps of the Lincoln Memorial. YALE COLLECTION OF AMERICAN LITERATURE, BEINECKE RARE BOOK AND MANUSCRIPT LIBRARY

Figure 19. On August 10, 1948, men and women in Columbia, South Carolina, wait to vote in the Democratic primary for the first time. JOHN H. MCCRAY COLLECTION, SOUTH CAROLINIANA LIBRARY

Figure 20. George W. McLaurin, plaintiff in *McLaurin v. Oklahoma State Regent*, seated in an anteroom, separate from white students, at the University of Oklahoma. REPRODUCED FROM THE COLLECTIONS OF THE LIBRARY OF CONGRESS

Figure 21. Texas students from nearby colleges marched toward the steps of the state capitol in Austin, Texas, on April 27, 1949, protesting segregation. REPRODUCED FROM THE COLLECTIONS OF THE LIBRARY OF CONGRESS

Figure 22. Roy Wilkins addresses the opening meeting of the National Civil Rights Mobilization in Washington, D.C., January 15, 1950. REPRODUCED FROM THE COLLECTIONS OF THE LIBRARY OF CONGRESS

Figure 23. Heman Sweatt (center), plaintiff in the University of Texas Law School case, with Roy Wilkins (left) and Robert Carter during press conference interview at NAACP's New York office. REPRODUCED FROM THE COLLECTIONS OF THE LIBRARY OF CONGRESS

Figure 24. The attorneys in *Brown v. Board of Education of Topeka*. COURTESY OF THE NAACP LEGAL DEFENSE AND EDUCATIONAL FUND, INC.

Figure 25. George B. Morris, vice president of the Philadelphia branch, explains the NAACP program at a neighborhood meeting held in north Philadelphia, early 1950s. REPRODUCED FROM THE COLLECTIONS OF THE LIBRARY OF CONGRESS

Figure 26. Thurgood Marshall arrives on the Silver Meteor in Charleston, South Carolina, May 1951, for the trial of *Briggs v. Elliot*, challenging racial segregation in Clarendon County schools. CECIL WILLIAMS

Figure 27. Ruby Hurley, director of the NAACP's southeast regional office, addresses a mass meeting at a church in Charlotte, North Carolina, in 1957. REPRODUCED FROM THE LOOK MAGAZINE PHOTOGRAPH COLLECTION, LIBRARY OF CONGRESS

Figure 28. Ruby Hurley at a late night meeting at Tampa, Florida, NAACP headquarters, 1957. REPRODUCED FROM THE LOOK MAGAZINE PHOTOGRAPH COLLECTION, LIBRARY OF CONGRESS

Figure 29. Tennessee NAACP officials inspect the tent city in Fayette County in 1960, set up to aid blacks evicted by white landowners after they attempted to vote. REPRODUCED FROM THE COLLECTIONS OF THE LIBRARY OF CONGRESS

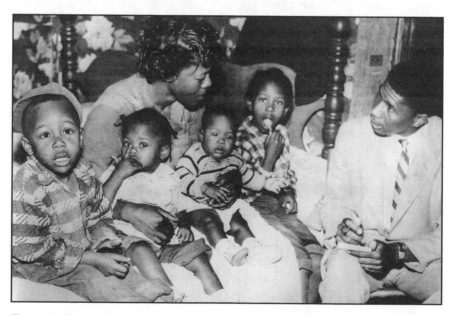

Figure 30. In 1955, Mississippi field secretary Medgar Evers interviews Mrs. Beulah Melton, 29, widow of Clinton Melton, murdered by a cotton gin owner during a dispute over a purchase. REPRODUCED FROM THE COLLECTIONS OF THE LIBRARY OF CONGRESS

7

In the Shadow of War: Battlefields for Freedom

On the morning of June 23, 1940, two fishermen found the mutilated body of Elbert Williams floating in the Hatchee River outside Brownsville, Tennessee. Williams, the thirty-three-year-old secretary of the local NAACP chapter, had been missing for several days. Ropes around the neck and ankles anchored his badly decomposed body to a sturdy log. There were stab wounds in the chest, and Williams's battered head was twice its normal size.[1]

A lifelong resident of Brownsville, Williams was last seen alive on the evening of June 20. He and his wife, Annie, had just finished listening to the Joe Louis–Arturo Godoy fight on the radio when Tip Hunter, a city police officer, arrived at their door. He insisted that Williams come outside to a waiting car, where there was some discussion with other men. Hunter then forced him into the car. Williams, who was barefoot and clothed in pajama bottoms and an undershirt, must have anticipated an interrogation similar to the one experienced by his friend Elisha Davis, another founding member of the NAACP branch. Four days earlier a mob of sixty men took Davis to the Hatchee River bottoms at midnight, forced him to reveal names of NAACP members, and promised to kill him if he remained in Brownsville. Davis walked eight miles to the town of Alamo and called Milmon Mitchell, head of the NAACP branch in Jackson, Tennessee, who met Davis and brought him to Jackson.[2]

The murder of Elbert Williams capped a reign of terror in the seat of Haywood County, a place where, in the words of a former resident, "King Cotton" was supreme along with "pellagra, malaria and ignorance." The trouble began when NAACP branch president the Reverend Buster Walker and executive committee member Elisha Davis led a group to the office of the county registrar early in May so they might register to vote. Voter registration in anticipation of the 1940 presidential election was a part of the year-old branch's program. The branch had fifty-four members, a small fraction of the estimated nineteen thousand blacks who populated the county and outnumbered whites three to one. But any sign of political activity among blacks was startling to the white minority; blacks had not voted in Haywood County since 1884.[3]

The group did not register that day. After the registrar and the city judge both turned them away, they learned that the registration period was not until August. Their determination to register and vote, however, generated a hysterical reaction, and local whites set out to eliminate the young NAACP chapter. Town officials intercepted mail addressed to NAACP officials and banned black newspapers. White employers fired blacks involved with the NAACP, and teachers faced threats of dismissal; merchants and banks refused credit to known members. Tip Hunter, who was also the sheriff-elect, led in targeting local NAACP leadership, ultimately driving Davis, Walker, and at least five others from town, all the while stirring popular fears that "northern Negroes" had infiltrated their community.[4]

Two weeks before Williams's murder, John LeFlore, chairman of the NAACP's southern regional conference, and Milmon Mitchell of the Jackson branch wrote to Walter White reporting on the desperate situation in Brownsville. "I am earnestly asking and pleading with the National Office," Mitchell wrote, "to have this condition thoroughly investigated in order that some solution may be sought for these people. . . . The time is now for the National Office to render some valuable service in this section." White and Thurgood Marshall were traveling when the letters arrived in New York. Roy Wilkins issued a hasty press release calling attention to the troubles and arranged for branch president Walker to report on Brownsville to officials and delegates at the upcoming annual convention meeting in Philadelphia, June 18–23. The fight for voting rights topped the conference's agenda. By the time the conference began, the crisis had peaked. Walker arrived in Philadelphia for the meeting on June 21 with 25¢ in his pocket, having just escaped town in advance of the mob. Three days later, word of Williams's murder reached the assembly, opening the way for the national office to press the Justice Department for a federal investigation.[5]

Elbert Williams was the first known NAACP official killed for his civil rights activities. His murder was particularly glaring at a time when the nation readied itself to aid in the fight against fascism, following the outbreak of World War II in Europe in September 1939. "There is something definitely wrong about a so-called democratic government that froths at the mouth about . . . terrorism abroad, yet has not a mumble of condemnation for the same sort of thing at home," wrote the *Pittsburgh Courier*. President Roosevelt might at least have expressed sympathy to the family of Elbert Williams, the *Courier* noted, but he remained silent. "If Elbert Williams is not avenged, if Elisha Davis, Rev. Buster Walker, and other refugees dare not return home, just because they sought to exercise their right to vote, then democracy . . . is a grim and empty fiction," the *Courier* concluded.[6]

NAACP officials wasted no time in demanding and securing federal action in the case. They had good reason to believe that federal law had been violated, given the apparent role of public officials in violently barring blacks from the ballot box. After Walker's arrival in Philadelphia, Thurgood Marshall phoned assistant attorney general O. John Rogge and arranged for Walker, NAACP legal committee chairman William Hastie, and attorney Leon Ransom to meet with Henry D. Schweinhaut, director of the newly formed Civil Liberties Unit of the Justice Department. The Brownsville case was ready-made for an enterprise dedicated to "vigilant action" in the prosecution of the infringement of "fundamental rights inherent in a free people." After their meeting on June 24, Schweinhaut had an FBI agent dispatched to Brownsville, and assistant attorney general Rogge promised a thorough investigation.[7]

At the close of the Philadelphia convention, White flew to Tennessee to pursue his own investigation and to meet with the U.S. district attorney in Memphis, William McClanahan. White interviewed Elisha Davis, who provided a detailed account of what happened, as well as the names of Tip Hunter and twelve other members of the mob that had abducted him and forced him to leave town. While White had little faith in McClanahan, the swift action and reassurances from the Justice Department elevated his hopes that the guilty parties might ultimately be brought to justice. But time was of the essence, for as long as Tip Hunter and his crowd were unchecked, blacks in Brownsville were completely exposed to mob terror. Irma Newman, a teacher and member of the branch in Brownsville, reported to White that all of the officers were gone and that the whites were trying to drive all NAACP members out as well. She lived in fear that her name would be revealed. "I am on the spot and afraid to stay at my home at night," she confided. "The Brownsville people are anxiously waiting and hoping that the law will take its course."[8]

The Brownsville situation tested the ability of the NAACP to function in the Deep South. Would the association aid those who risked life and limb for it and could it effectively defend its members? Thirty-nine-year-old Elisha Davis owned a service station and was the father of seven children. While he was more fortunate than Elbert Williams, he paid an enormous price for his civic activism. "I gambled everything—my home, my business, my life, my family—in order to prove to those people in Brownsville, Tennessee that the NAACP was alright. I felt that whatever happened I would be safe under the wings of the National Association of the Advancement of Colored People," Davis wrote White after their meeting. Yet, he was in Jackson, Tennessee, separated from his family and fearing for his life as long as he remained in the state. His service station and all of the equipment, he learned, had been taken over by friends of Tip Hunter. In a letter to branch officials, Thurgood Marshall described Davis's fate and urged them to help raise funds to aid Davis and his family. "This is not only a case of mob violence which merits our attention," Marshall wrote, "but it is also a question of our protection to members of this Association." With the aid of the NAACP, Davis finally relocated to Niles, Michigan, and his pregnant wife and their seven children soon joined him. Davis remained closely involved with the case from afar, while struggling to find work and get his life back on track.[9]

Foremost was the question of whether the NAACP could secure federal charges against Tip Hunter and other known members of the mob. "If we are successful in defending the rights of 19,000 . . . in Brownsville," Milmon Mitchell wrote White on July 1, "this will mean that our branch work in West Tennessee will meet with great success in the future. It will be a great victory for the NAACP for our people have been denied the right to vote in Haywood County for fifty years. . . . This is our time to fight the situation to the finish." The Jackson branch president was an agent for the Atlanta Life Insurance Company and made frequent trips to Brownsville, ignoring pleas from his friends who warned that he was risking his life. After a trip in mid-July, he reported: "I could hardly believe my eyes to see known members of the mob . . . walking the streets." But word that the FBI was investigating seemed to have put a halt to the mob violence, at least temporarily. "God only knows what they will do to our people," he noted, if the government does not prosecute them. By October, that seemed highly unlikely. Mitchell reported that Tip Hunter had just taken office as sheriff of the county and "members of the mob that lynched Elbert Williams can be seen in Brownsville each day going about their work as if they had killed only a rabbit." During the recent voter registration period, no blacks dared attempt to register. And why should they? If the Justice Department were not going to prosecute the guilty parties, people knew that no effort would be made to protect them. "The NAACP has successfully pulled the cover off the damnable conditions at Brownsville and we have also exposed the discriminating practices of the Department of Justice," Mitchell declared.[10]

Thurgood Marshall used Mitchell's letter to turn up the pressure on the Justice Department and wrote Assistant Attorney General Rogge urging action. Not willing to rely on FBI agents to do a thorough job, Marshall doggedly gathered evidence in the case. He located Annie Williams, widow of Elbert Williams, who had left Tennessee and moved to New York, and obtained an affidavit from her describing what happened on the night her husband disappeared. He also secured an affidavit from Elisha Davis's wife, Nan. Marshall traveled to Tennessee and interviewed several individuals, including a man who had been in the car the night Williams was abducted, and then went to Chicago to interview one of the former branch officials who had fled from the area. In the course of his investigation, Marshall learned two things of particular consequence. One was that Elbert Williams had been authorized by Elisha Davis to take over his gasoline station business and sell some of the equipment for the benefit of Davis's wife and children. Williams's murder cleared the way for whites to take over the profitable service station. A clue as to why the Justice Department was stalling came to light when Marshall discovered that the FBI agents who had gone to Brownsville took Tip Hunter, the leader of the mob, on their rounds to question witnesses.[11]

In January 1942, a year and a half after the assault on the small group of would-be voters in Brownsville, the Justice Department announced that there was not sufficient evidence to warrant prosecution. In a letter urging that the decision be reconsidered, Marshall charged that the problem was the quantity and not the quality of evidence. The reason there wasn't more evidence, he noted, was due to "the type of investigation made by the Federal Bureau of Investigation." Clearly, black people would not talk in front of the man who had killed one black man and run several others out of town. But Marshall supplied the department with the affidavits and information he had gathered, and it was sufficient to place the matter before a grand jury. "If no action is taken against [Tip Hunter] by the Department," Marshall warned, "the intimidation of other Negroes who want to register and vote will be complete." He pressed on for several months to reactivate the case, to no avail. The decision was final. In his letter to Elisha Davis informing him of the Justice

Department's ruling, a dispirited Marshall closed, saying, "I am more than sorry."[12]

The outcome of the case revealed the political constraints under which the NAACP operated even as it leveraged the growing power of the northern black vote and began cultivating positive relations with sympathetic officials in Washington. In 1942, Francis Biddle, former member of the NAACP legal committee, was attorney general, and for the first time, the Department of Justice was actively pursuing several civil rights cases involving voting and peonage. In a letter to Marshall, almost apologetic in tone, assistant attorney general Wendell Berge reiterated the decision on Brownsville and then provided an update "on current cases which involve the deprivation of civil rights of Negro citizens" in which the department was involved. Nevertheless, its refusal to act in the Brownsville case was a stark reminder of the ability of powerful southern political figures and J. Edgar Hoover's FBI to dictate how far the Justice Department would go in redressing civil rights violations. As Milmon Mitchell observed to Marshall, "I don't think we shall ever have a case more clear-cut than this one"—one involving known public officials engaged in lynching, mob violence, and voter intimidation. Early on, Walter White had begun to suspect that the powerful "McKellar-Crump machine," combining the forces of Senator Kenneth McKellar and Edward Crump, the political boss of Memphis, was holding up action on the Brownsville matter. In the end, those opposed to any federal intervention in Brownsville prevailed, despite the determination and courage of blacks in Tennessee, the exhaustive investigative efforts of Thurgood Marshall, and a chilling assemblage of facts.[13]

Brownsville unfolded against a backdrop of war mobilization, culminating with America's entry into World War II at the end of 1941. It was a time of unprecedented challenges as well as expanding opportunities for the NAACP as the Allies joined under the banner of freedom to fight Nazi tyranny, heralded in President Roosevelt's "Four Freedoms" speech in January 1941. The fate of Elbert Williams magnified the glaring gap between these professed democratic ideals and the reality of life for blacks in the Jim Crow South, and the war heightened the stakes for black Americans throughout the country. The massive defense build-up that began in 1939 fueled the industrial boom that lifted America out of the Depression but left blacks on the periphery. The issue of jobs and economic equality took on even greater urgency. Migration of blacks north and west to centers of industrial production was matched by the influx of black soldiers into the South to train in army camps, multiplying the sites of racial contact and conflict. The experience of black soldiers serving in the segregated armed forces steeled the determination of growing numbers of black Americans to fight at home for the rights that black men and women had enlisted to defend abroad.

The NAACP broadened its efforts along major fronts as its leaders sought to secure the gains of the 1930s and worked to meet the new demands created by the rapid shift to a wartime footing. Increasingly, Walter White's attention stretched between the immediate and varied strivings of black Americans and efforts to institutionalize the NAACP's position in Washington. The wartime expansion of federal power required heightened oversight of federally funded programs and increasing pressure for the full and fair inclusion of black Americans in national defense efforts. In the aftermath of the 1941 threatened March on Washington, the NAACP opened a Washington bureau. A permanent office in the nation's capital allowed White to solidify a relationship with representatives of liberal and labor groups as he worked to influence national policy and the legislative agenda of the New Deal wing of the Democratic Party. White also began cultivating movie moguls in Hollywood as early as 1940 in an ongoing effort to secure positive portrayals of African Americans in a medium that had kept the romance and sentimentality of the Old South alive in popular culture, most recently with the blockbuster *Gone with the Wind*, winner of the Academy Award for best picture in 1939.

The pressures of war amplified the nation's racial divisions and exposed the political challenges facing the NAACP. Southern Democrats, providing critical support for the president's defense program, reasserted their dominance on Capitol Hill and joined with Republicans in dismantling major New Deal programs. Throughout the war, as liberals and labor groups fought to sustain the promise of New Deal reform, race remained a critical fault line. Festering racial tensions in overcrowded urban-industrial areas, outbursts of racial violence throughout the nation, and heightened black protest all illuminated and aggravated the nation's deep racial divide. The NAACP cooperated with a small number of groups active in the hard work of building interracial coalitions around fundamental issues, particularly, equal employment opportunity and voting rights. A shared interest in countering the power of anti–New Deal/antilabor Southern Democrats provided an arena for black-white political alliances that might anchor the New Deal coalition in a politics beyond racial division. The inclusive democratic vision promoted by the NAACP and its allies, however, struggled in the face of the carefully calibrated and racially cautious politics of mainstream and liberal Democrats more inclined to placate the party's southern wing.

Distinctions between the high-profile arena of Washington politics and work in the field became pronounced as civil rights became an issue of national consequence. The cultivation of branches and the boosting of membership remained critical to the financial health of the association. During the war, the rapid growth of membership in major urban centers provided an infusion of funds with relatively little effort on the part of the national office. But equally important, for those who worked primarily in the field, was the investment of time, talent, and energy essential for building a strong movement for racial change, even when it did not bring an immediate monetary return. The spirit motivating black NAACP activists in Brownsville, Tennessee, revealed the potential that was ripe for cultivation in the South, even in remote rural areas. During 1940 and 1941, the field staff doubled, and the legal program made headway in education and voting campaigns. Lawyers and field organizers reinforced each other as they worked to unite communities around a growing challenge to racial barriers and an accelerating fight for full citizenship, while increasing membership rolls and revenue flow to the national office.

As the NAACP expanded its fieldwork during the early 1940s, it sank deeper roots in the South, where organizers found increasing numbers of African Americans determined to exert their civic rights. The murder of Elbert Williams exposed the powerlessness of southern blacks in the face of raw terror. This was a major bulwark of the segregation system and a serious challenge to NAACP efforts in the region. Yet the claim made by Williams and his neighbors to the most fundamental element of citizenship, the vote, would grow more insistent across the South during the war years. Writing from the Black Belt of Alabama in the fall of 1941, field-worker Madison Jones reported, "Negroes here and all the places I stopped in are intent on paying the poll tax, registering, and voting. I find it everywhere I go." Brownsville may have illustrated the limits of the NAACP's ability to protect individuals, but, as Charles Houston had emphasized, the swift response of national officials as well as nearby branches demonstrated that those on the front lines of this fight "would not be left alone." This was a critical element in the kind of role the NAACP was poised to play as the activism of the New Deal era yielded to a more robust demand for citizenship under the burgeoning national defense effort.[14]

In South Carolina, a violent drive to suppress black voting in the textile town of Greenville heightened the sense of purpose that attended the founding of the South Carolina state conference of NAACP branches in November 1939. That fall, the Ku Klux Klan worked with the police to quash a major voter registration campaign led by an interracial coalition of groups, including the local NAACP branch. KKK activists harassed registered black voters, the local newspaper published their names, and the police arrested NAACP branch president James Briar and William Anderson, head of the local NAACP youth council. Briar managed to get to the statewide meeting of branch officers in Columbia to report firsthand on the "terrible happenings" in Greenville. A. W. Wright, newly elected president of the conference, contacted the NAACP's national office, urging them to aid in the Greenville fight and adding, "We are in great need of your presence." Walter White reported the incident to the Justice Department and warned that blacks felt totally unprotected by state and federal authorities and were arming themselves in desperation. While the Justice Department failed to intervene, the Greenville episode only stiffened the resolve of the newly coalesced network of NAACP branches. Over the next two years, a statewide movement to reclaim the franchise emerged in South Carolina, as the NAACP's legal challenge to the all-white primary moved forward in Texas.[15]

Thurgood Marshall announced the renewal of the legal fight against the white primary at the 1940 conference in Philadelphia in a speech just days before learning of the murder of Elbert Williams. He reviewed recent gains, noting the growing power of black voters in northern and western states, which provided a "so called balance of power" and forced "a certain amount of political protection for Negroes nationally as well as locally." But he added, "We do not have any power at all compared to what we need." The main challenge facing the association, he told the delegates, "is to get the Negro the full right to vote in every one of the Southern states." In the South, black political power was essential to securing gains on all other fronts—education, public facilities, employment, and justice in the courts. Furthermore, without black votes in the South, "we cannot shut up the Connollys, the Bilbos," and other southern demagogues who dominated the political process in Washington, dictated national policy on key issues, and jealously guarded against any federal intervention or policy initiative that acknowledged the citizenship rights of blacks.[16]

State Democratic Party rules barring blacks from voting in primary elections were the major barrier to black political participation in most southern states. Marshall reported that black Texans were determined to defeat the all-white primary once and for all. He told about a meeting of the NAACP state conference in Corpus Christi he had attended the previous month. Twelve hundred delegates from all parts of the state had convened and pledged their money and effort to renew the fight against the Democratic white primary. Texans had been waging the fight sporadically since 1923, taking three cases to the U.S. Supreme Court. The 1935 *Grovey* decision practically wiped out the gains made in the earlier cases, but black Texans were undeterred by past losses. "Negroes in Texas do not care whether they lose or not. They are going to fight until they are allowed to vote." With the revival of the white primary fight, Texas emerged as a major arena of NAACP activity and membership growth during the 1940s, illustrating how the mix of local leadership, a responsive national office, and a carefully organized legal challenge could cultivate popular sentiment into a mass movement.[17]

A newly reorganized Houston branch spearheaded the revival of the white primary fight, a role that hardly seemed possible a year earlier. "A hornet's nest . . . the worst I've ever seen," was how national field director Daisy Lampkin described the Houston branch in 1939, plagued as it was by financial mismanagement and political factionalism. But the death of branch president Clifton Richardson elevated Lulu White to the position of acting president. The thirty-nine-year-old White served as adult adviser to the youth council and was an energetic and gifted organizer. She enlisted Lampkin's aid in reviving the branch and electing new officers. White declined pleas that she be a candidate for permanent branch president, but her influence would remain formative. The new branch president, Reverend Albert Lucas, minister of Good Hope Baptist Church, won the support of leading figures in the Houston community and quickly brought in nearly fifteen hundred new members. Lucas moved to further unify the branch behind a new attack on the white primary and called a citywide meeting in March 1940. The group agreed to place the issue on the agenda of the statewide conference of branches in Corpus Christi in May, inviting blacks from around the state as well as representatives of the national office to attend.[18]

The national office welcomed this development. Earlier in the year, Walter White and Houston attorney James Nabrit agreed that it was time to revive the white primary fight. Nabrit had won a major voting rights case for the NAACP before the U.S. Supreme Court in 1939, *Lane v. Wilson*, which by a 6-2 vote overturned a disenfranchisement plan enacted in Oklahoma after the defeat of the grandfather clause in 1915. The Court was now dominated by Roosevelt appointees, including Hugo Black, Felix Frankfurter, William O. Douglas, and Frank Murphy, and its impact had been felt in a number of civil rights–related cases. In February 1940, the NAACP scored a major victory in *Chambers v. Florida*, a case involving four black men who confessed to a murder after a week of brutal treatment. The Court overturned the death sentence of the men on the grounds that they had been forced to confess and were denied due process. In his majority opinion, Justice Black signaled the sensibility of the Court's liberal members, noting that defendants in such cases were most often Southern blacks because "they who have suffered most from secret and dictatorial proceedings have almost always been the poor, the ignorant, the numerically weak, the friendless and the powerless."[19]

In advance of the meeting in Corpus Christi, Thurgood Marshall met with the legal redress committee of the Texas state conference of branches. They sketched out plans for raising an $8,000 defense fund, enlisted William J. Durham to serve as local counsel, and discussed possible plaintiffs. Durham, a World War I veteran, was the most prominent black attorney in the state and long active in civil rights cases. The state conference, held on May 10–12, exceeded all expectations. Mindful of the disastrous *Grovey* case, Marshall emphasized that a united effort under the direction of the national office was essential to mount a successful fight. The conference launched the drive for the defense fund, assigning quotas to each branch, and participants endorsed a ten-year plan. The white primary fight topped the agenda, followed by resolutions to secure educational equality and challenge the entire system of segregation. "Now the Texas group will really go to town," Marshall wrote Walter White. An ebullient Maceo Smith, the guiding force behind the state conference, wrote, "We laid plans that will realize for the Negro of Texas a new era in the fight for civil rights." After a rocky start, they secured a strong plaintiff in Lonnie B. Smith, a dentist from Houston. Over the next several years, as the white primary case made its way to the Supreme Court, NAACP membership in Texas grew to 23,000 members, largely due to the efforts of Maceo Smith, Lulu White, and a small group of leaders working in tandem with the NAACP's legal campaign.[20]

The spirited launching of the white primary fight in Texas coincided with a major gain in the NAACP's educational campaign. In June 1940, the U.S. court of appeals ruled in the case of Melvin Alston, a high school teacher in Norfolk, Virginia, that he suffered discrimination in salary on grounds of race in violation of the due process and equal protection clauses of the Fourteenth Amendment. While the implementation of the *Alston* ruling exposed challenges the NAACP would continue to face in the long road ahead, the ruling set an important precedent that would be used in other communities around Virginia and the South in the equalization fight. *Alston*, however, represented more than a legal victory. Viewed within the fuller context of NAACP activism in Virginia, it was a pivotal moment in the application of Charles Houston's approach to lawyering and organizing, carried forward by Thurgood Marshall. The teacher salary effort had been initiated by Marshall in Maryland, where he had won the first salary equalization case in 1937, sparking equalization efforts throughout that state. With victory in the Maryland case in hand, Marshall shifted his attention to neighboring Virginia, working closely with the coalition of teachers and NAACP branches in developing a suit.[21]

The *Alston* case in Virginia marked the culmination of four years of work— organizing support from teachers and the larger community, raising a defense fund, and finding a plaintiff. The NAACP state conference of branches and the Virginia State Teachers Association established the Joint Committee on Equalization of Teachers' Salaries to coordinate and supervise a statewide campaign. While teachers proved willing to provide funds, most were reluctant to volunteer as plaintiffs and face the likely possibility of losing their jobs. Aline Black, the plaintiff in the first case filed, lost her job when the Norfolk school board declined to renew her contract. Melvin Alston, vice president of the NAACP's Norfolk branch, volunteered to take Black's place, and his case went forward. By this time Richmond attorney Oliver Hill, Marshall's former classmate at Howard Law School, had come on board, serving as lawyer to the Joint Committee. Hill argued *Alston* with Marshall, Leon Ransom, and William Hastie and emerged from the case as the NAACP's main lawyer in the state of Virginia. Marshall turned the Virginia campaign over to Hill, confident that his friend would "bolster the courage of the teachers to realize that they have an attorney in Virginia on hand at all times for whatever problems might come up."[22]

Following the *Alston* victory, Hill stumped the state of Virginia, explaining the meaning of the ruling and emphasizing that it was "up to the Negroes of Virginia to see that this decision is made effective in every city and county of Virginia." The tall, lanky, easy-going Hill, known as "Peanuts" to his Howard classmates, proved to be a tireless organizer. He worked up a memorandum explaining the step-by-step procedure that each community should follow in its effort to secure equal teachers' salaries, emphasizing the importance of consulting with him as they went forward. Within a year after the *Alston* ruling, teacher salary cases were pending in at least eight communities around the state. The fight on the salary front, Hill frequently explained, was "the opening gun in a sustained fight to fully equalize school facilities." He worked with several communities in efforts to gain bus transportation for children and challenge inequalities in high school curricula. Hill spent nearly every weekend traveling around Virginia, explaining the NAACP's program, developing support, urging people to register and vote, and becoming familiar with local concerns and conditions. J.R. Tinsley, head of the Virginia state conference of NAACP branches, frequently accompanied Hill. The two men, working with other NAACP activists and a small but growing corps of black lawyers, helped to organize nine new branches in the year following the *Alston* ruling, in conjunction with the expanding teacher salary fight. With a total of thirty-nine branches in 1941, Virginia claimed the largest number of branches of any state.[23]

In the fall of 1940, Charles Houston resigned from his position as special counsel, officially passing the torch to his protégé, Thurgood Marshall. Marshall had taken on increasing responsibility as co-special counsel after Houston returned to Washington in 1938. By then, Houston's vision had been in large part realized, and the legal campaign had eclipsed the movement for antilynching legislation as a defining element in the NAACP's program. As the ranks of black lawyers engaged in civil rights grew, the courtroom became a primary arena in the battle for equal justice. The organization and litigation of cases in a variety of areas—particularly teacher salaries, voting, and criminal justice—depended upon the involvement of local communities and helped shape and direct rising black demands for justice and full citizenship rights. This was a critical venue in the South, where blacks were barred from effective participation in mainstream politics. Working with NAACP branches, black lawyers like Oliver Hill in Virginia, Arthur Shores in Alabama, A.P. Tureaud in Louisiana, A.T. Walden in Georgia, and S.D. McGill in Florida, along with Marshall and the lawyers affiliated with the national office, served, in Houston's words, as "advisers" and "soldiers" as the movement gained strength and traction during the war years.

While several factors contributed to Houston's departure from his position with the NAACP, the salient one was that his work as architect of the legal program was complete. The groundwork for the campaign was in place and, as legal scholar Mark Tushnet has suggested, "it crystallized in the person of Thurgood Marshall." Energetic, hard-driving, and affable, Marshall was, in Tushnet's words, "an extraordinarily diligent inside man." By contrast, Houston was beginning to feel hemmed in by the routine and the constraints attached to his position on the NAACP staff. "I will grow much faster and be of much more service if I keep free to hit and fight wherever the circumstances call for action," he wrote his father. During the next several years, as a partner in his father's law practice, Houston focused on the issues of jobs and employment, lobbying for federal enforcement of equal rights in defense industries and representing black railway workers in the most important labor case involving black workers to come before the U. S. Supreme Court. He resumed his place on the National Legal Committee and remained closely involved with the work of the NAACP. Significantly, he continued to play a formative role in the follow-up to the 1938 *Gaines* ruling, which stretched to early 1942, a major chapter in the evolving education campaign.[24]

The aftermath of the *Gaines* decision rehearsed many of the difficulties that the NAACP would face over the next several decades as states resisted, stalled, and experimented with ways to subvert the implementation of Court rulings. *Gaines*, the first Supreme Court victory in the campaign for educational equality, held that Missouri was required to provide equal educational opportunities for black citizens within the state. Few believed that Missouri would be able to establish a separate law school equal to the one at the University of Missouri, but that was the path the state legislature started down the following spring, voting to appropriate $200,000 for a law school at Lincoln University, the state-funded college for African Americans. It would be left to the NAACP to prove that this arrangement did not meet the Court's mandate. Further complicating matters, their plaintiff, Lloyd Gaines, had "disappeared." (According to an associate of Houston, Gaines was in Chicago, complaining that the NAACP had done nothing for him.) Meanwhile, immediately following the *Gaines* decision, Lucille Bluford had applied to the top-ranked School of Journalism at the University of Missouri. Having met all of the requirements, she was admitted for the 1939 winter term. When she arrived to enroll, the registrar turned her away, having not realized that she was black. Bluford, managing editor for the *Kansas City Call* and a member of the Kansas City, Missouri, branch of the NAACP, was prepared to press her case, and Houston was eager to take it forward; it was critical to keeping the door open on the *Gaines* ruling. Marshall agreed, telling Houston that the "only way to clearly demonstrate to the country that we mean business is to go after the Bluford case with everything we have."[25]

The twenty-seven-year-old Lucille Bluford, a high-honors graduate from the University of Kansas, was an excellent plaintiff. She was sophisticated, courageous, and prepared to go the distance. Houston thought it especially important that her case "focus[ed] attention on Negro women." In a letter to Bluford and St. Louis attorney Sidney Redmond, Houston analyzed the broader implications of Bluford's challenge. Her application to the Journalism School announced that the state had not "silenced the legitimate and constitutional Negro demands by furnishing a law school for one qualified Negro boy" and emphasized "the utter futility of trying to establish separate schools for every Negro who demands graduate and professional work at the University of Missouri." Indeed, "we want to show the country . . . that more and varied demands for training by Negroes are as inevitable as the tides or the successions of day and night." As Americans became more deeply concerned about developments in Europe, the struggle in Missouri offered an opportunity "to focus ever sharpening attention of the people of the United States on the discriminations and injustices heaped on the Negro citizens in this 'democracy,' and show the country that the danger to democracy in America does not lie so much in Hitler's aggressions as in the repressive and unjust attitudes and practices here in this country; that the 'acid test' of American democracy is not defense against foreign enemies but domestic injustice."[26]

State officials dug in their heels, savoring Missouri's role as the battleground in the fight to maintain racial segregation not only in their schools but the schools of fifteen southern and border states. University lawyers found ways to drag out the legal proceedings, arguing that it was up to Bluford to apply to Lincoln University and, in effect, request that that institution provide her with graduate training in journalism. Houston pressed on, working to expose the state's defiance of the law and compel the state to act affirmatively. "We are in a long fight," he advised, but delays "were not fatal if we make them serve our ends." Houston worked on several fronts, speaking to mass meetings sponsored by NAACP branches in St. Louis, Kansas City, and Columbia, explaining the importance of the case and seeking to raise much-needed funds toward the cost of the litigation. He cultivated sympathetic white opinion, such as that of the Reverend Bradford Abernathy of the First Baptist Church in Columbia, who preached in support of Bluford's constitutional rights from his pulpit, contending that the only legal and Christian thing to do was to admit her to the university. Houston used the courtroom to great effect in drawing out the facts and in educating observers, always seeking to inform and shape the broader public dialogue.[27]

The first trial, held in Columbia in February 1940 was, in Houston's words, "a community event." Young white women from nearby Stephens College sat on the floor and packed the aisles and rear of the courtroom along with students from the University of Missouri Law School and Journalism School. "I tried the case as a social issue as well as a legal issue," Houston reported, "explaining each step so the students could understand. That took us two days." With all of the witnesses he called—Lucille Bluford, Ada Franklin, Dorothy Davis, and Dowdal Davis, all of whom worked for the *Kansas City Call*— Houston questioned them about their academic backgrounds in detail. Each of them, with the exception of Franklin, had graduated from the University of Kansas; Franklin was a graduate of Clark University and had studied in Boston and New York. Houston's line of questioning allowed Bluford to tell about her family, how her father, a graduate of Howard University, had moved from North Carolina to Missouri so that his children would have a better chance in life. Her mother was a graduate of Oberlin, and her brother had earned a master's degree at the University of Michigan. "You could hear the murmur that went over the courtroom as she very quietly and simply recited the facts," Houston wrote. The next day, when Dorothy Davis responded that, yes, she was Phi Beta Kappa, "the court room gasped." Explaining his method, Houston commented that most of the white students in the courtoom "had never seen intelligent Negroes and probably thought that they existed merely as exceptions."[28]

In his cross-examination of the dean of the journalism school, Houston revealed the vagueness of the state's plan to set up a journalism school at Lincoln, observing that the dean was "not trying to set up a school of journalism, he's trying to set up a Negro school of journalism and he knows it's inferior." The case, Houston argued, involved "the Negro's education and the white man's honor" and whether democratic principles would be upheld in Missouri. Lucille Bluford was on the stand for four hours and endured an intensive cross-examination from the university's attorney, W. S. Hogsett. His main line of questioning aimed to prove that Bluford was engaged in a conspiracy with the NAACP "for the ulterior, indirect, and wrongful purpose of attempting to aid said association in a campaign to break down Missouri's policy of separate schools for Negroes." Bluford held her ground so effectively that at one point the students in the courtroom burst into applause following one of her responses, causing the judge to clear the room. During the recesses and when the court was finally adjourned, students crowded around Houston and Bluford. Many of the young white women told her "I hope you get in."[29]

The case dragged on. There were two trials, both ending in the state's favor, based on alleged plans for a School of Journalism at Lincoln, beginning in the winter term of 1942. Confident that a makeshift program could never be equal to the one offered by the state's widely acclaimed Journalism School, Houston was ready to expose the inequities once the program was finally established. The state ducked that prospect. Early in 1942 the University of Missouri announced that the graduate journalism program had been discontinued due to low wartime enrollments, relieving the state of the need to establish a program at Lincoln. Houston learned that graduate courses were offered in the guise of undergraduate courses at the Journalism School; he and Bluford were eager to expose the state's subterfuge. White was reluctant to let the case go, writing, "We have the bear by the tail." But, as he told Houston, there was a limit, given the "demands on us in so many other fields" to how much more the national office could invest in a difficult and drawn-out fight. In the end, the national office declined to pursue the case further. While there were other university cases pending, the fight to implement *Gaines* would not resume until after the war.[30]

The buildup for war extended the reach of racial exclusion and discrimination in industrial centers across the country and magnified the War Department's acceptance "lock, stock, and barrel, of the philosophies and procedures of the South." The integration of black Americans into the national defense effort on an equal basis took on an urgency that quickly eclipsed other areas of activity and thrust jobs and wartime issues to the top of the association's agenda. At the same time, the changes unleashed by the war touched blacks across the nation, fueling expectations, resentments, and demands that the NAACP struggled to give voice and direction to. All of this occurred at a time when the association's annual income had risen to barely more than $70,000 and all felt the pressure to "do a mammoth job on a shoestring."[31]

During a monthlong tour of the West Coast in the fall of 1940, Walter White observed firsthand the widespread discrimination in the aircraft and shipyard industries and found NAACP branches energized around the fight for jobs. Reports from field organizers underscored the urgency of the issue around the country. The Committee for Participation of Negroes in the

National Defense, a group of black World War I officers organized by Rayford Logan and the *Pittsburgh Courier*, had been pressing the federal government since 1938 for full inclusion of blacks in defense work and all branches of the armed services. The NAACP's national office quickly moved to coordinate a targeted effort to meet this problem, instructing branches to forward information on job bias to the national office while each branch continued to organize locally to fight for access to jobs in federally funded defense plants. Protective of the NAACP's role as the leading advocate for civil rights, White ignored the efforts of Logan's group and lobbied allies in the Senate for a full investigation of discrimination in defense industries. He also worked with labor leader A. Philip Randolph and Arnold T. Hill of the National Urban League to secure action by the president and officials involved in war production. Plans for the Senate hearing stalled. The tepid response on the part of the administration, attuned to the interests of industrialists and southern leaders whose support was considered essential to Roosevelt's defense program, compelled White and his allies to consider other tactics.[32]

In January 1941, as White and the NAACP worked to orchestrate mass protest through the branches, Randolph announced that he would lead a march on Washington to protest discrimination in the defense industry and the armed services. The founder and president of the Brotherhood of Sleeping Car Porters, Randolph was the nation's foremost black labor leader and a major voice for civil rights. His idea offered the kind of bold strike that appealed to White's imagination, and the two joined forces in planning the most famous demonstration that never happened. Randolph envisioned bringing ten thousand people to Washington, explaining to White that "something dramatic has got to be done to shake official Washington and the white industrialists and labor forces of America to the realization of the fact that the Negroes mean business about getting their rights as American citizens under national defense." Such a protest, he claimed, would help White's "splendid plan to get the whole question of national defense and the Negro probed by the Senate." White was in complete accord: "I very much agree with you that only a mass demonstration is going to have any effect on the situation in Washington." He lent the full support of the association and its network of branches, determined to ensure that the march would be an "overwhelming success."[33]

They designated July 1 as the date, which came on the heels of the NAACP's annual convention in Houston. On June 3, Randolph sent letters to the president, Eleanor Roosevelt, secretary of war Henry L. Stimson, secretary of the navy Frank Knox, the director and associate director of the Office of Production Management, former president of General Motors William S. Knudsen, and labor leader Sidney Hillman, inviting them to address the many thousands of people who would march against racial discrimination in the nation's capital—a prospect that jolted the Roosevelt administration into action. During the next several weeks there was a flurry of meetings. Eleanor Roosevelt and New York mayor Fiorella LaGuardia, both of whom had earned a level of trust among black Americans, led the effort to persuade Randolph and White to call off the march. The two leaders held firm. The time for talking was done; their demand for "definite, tangible and concrete action" to secure jobs and full participation of blacks in the national defense programs was not negotiable. A high-level meeting with the president, the heads of the armed services, and Knudsen and Hillman followed and included Lester Granger, assistant executive secretary of the National Urban League, and Channing Tobias, secretary of the YMCA's Colored Works Department. Tobias urged White and Randolph to accept Roosevelt's "assurances" that he would remedy the situation. White knew better. His long experience with FDR, White told Tobias, had taught him that the president's promises "are not more than water," forgotten when politically expedient. He and Randolph told Roosevelt that they would call off the July 1 march in exchange for an executive order banning discrimination in defense industries.[34]

At the eleventh hour, the president conceded. White was already in Houston for the NAACP's annual convention when Randolph secured a draft of the proposed presidential order, which was read to White over the phone; he added his approval. The order held that defense industries receiving government contracts would be required to employ workers without regard to race, creed, color, or national origin, and provided for the establishment of a board, the Fair Employment Practices Committee (FEPC), appointed by the president, to receive complaints and grievances from any worker charging discrimination. By the time Executive Order 8802 was issued on the afternoon of June 25, Randolph was already in Houston. That evening he announced the president's order barring discrimination in defense industries in a speech to the NAACP's convention, telling the assembly that the march had been postponed. Emphasizing the significance of their victory, he explained, "There never has been issued in America an executive order affecting Negroes in this country since the Proclamation of Emancipation by Abraham Lincoln." It was a testimony to the power of mass pressure—a pressure, he insisted, that must be sustained to ensure enforcement of this historic mandate.[35]

"Exceedingly limited" was how Walter White described the order. It did not touch on discrimination in the armed forces (a demand neither Randolph nor White expected to be met.). The FEPC, the committee established by the order to receive complaints, served in an advisory capacity to the president. While it was a forum for exposing discrimination and making recommendations, it lacked enforcement power. But it was an opening, and White emphasized that the effectiveness of the order would depend in large part on how they responded. Even the most perfect policy, White told the delegates to the Houston convention, would fail "if it were not policed by organized pressure. We must be on the job constantly or this order will become a dead letter. . . . We urge you to investigate and study every plant in your city which has received an order for the national defense program," document cases of discrimination, and send affidavits to the national office and to the FEPC. "We together will give that Board enough work to keep it busy twenty-four hours a day every day in the year until segregation is completely wiped out."[36]

While the showdown with the Roosevelt administration over jobs in defense industries unfolded, the NAACP brokered a historic breakthrough in black–labor union relations, working through a robust Detroit branch. In the spring of 1941, a major strike by the United Auto Workers (UAW) against Ford Motor Company's River Rouge plant in Detroit pivoted on the position of black workers. By then, the long tradition of black allegiance to Henry Ford had become worn at the edges. Ford's factories had been the source of thousands of jobs for blacks, but they were mostly unskilled and low wage; younger black leaders scornfully referred to the company as an "industrial plantation." Large segments of black Detroit, however, remained deeply skeptical of the UAW's stated commitment to interracial unionism. The union remained a bastion of white privilege and deeply embedded racial attitudes, despite the high-minded ideals and pragmatic goals of some union leaders. But the UAW leadership, as with CIO unions generally, understood that their success depended upon bridging the racial divide, and they found allies among younger black leaders who believed that the future of black workers was with organized labor. In the years leading up to the strike, a younger and aggressive pro-union black leadership in Detroit had emerged, including Charles Diggs, Louis Martin, and the Reverend Horace White, along with Robert Evans and others associated with the Detroit chapter of the National Negro Congress. By 1941, the Detroit NAACP branch, long a bastion of pro-Ford and antiunion sentiment, had become a major arena for the debate that had increasingly divided black Detroit.[37]

Over the previous four years, under the leadership of Dr. James McClendon, the Detroit branch grew from 2,300 members to nearly 6,000, dramatically broadening its base of membership. Strong representation of pro-UAW sentiment countered conservatives who had long dominated the branch. The parallel establishment and growth of the youth council further energized pro-union activity. Gloster Current, who had been recruited by Juanita Jackson to organize Detroit youth for the 1936 NAACP annual convention in that city, played a leading role in building the city's youth council into the most active NAACP youth group in the country. Jobs and labor issues were a major focus of youth council activity, including "Don't Buy Where You Can't Work" campaigns. By 1940, the youth council in Detroit comprised six chapters and an eclectic representation of young black Detroiters, including college and high school students and workers in their early twenties. They functioned under the umbrella of a Central Youth Committee, headed by Current. A part-time college student, Horace Sheffield, who worked in the Ford River Rouge plant, led the West Side Youth Council and emerged as one of the group's most dynamic leaders.[38]

These various elements came together around the UAW's final push to organize the massive Ford River Rouge plant. In advance of the strike, the UAW leadership increased its staff of salaried black organizers and made direct appeals through the black press, pledging to establish equality on the job and to enhance efforts to educate white workers. Ford management hired 2,000 unemployed blacks as strikebreakers. The NAACP charged Ford with injecting race into its struggle with the union and deliberately fueling an explosive situation. After the strike began on April 1, an estimated 1,500 to 2,500 blacks remained in the plant, along with a couple of hundred white service workers. Acting independently of the adult branch, Horace Sheffield and other representatives of the youth council secured a sound car from the UAW and circled the plant appealing to black workers, in the name of the NAACP, to leave the plant. In the tense days that followed, the NAACP senior branch joined the youth council and younger pro-labor leadership in an effort to defuse mounting racial tensions and urge blacks not to participate as strikebreakers, while pro-labor activists such as Louis Martin worked to secure broad support among Detroit's black leadership for the UAW.[39]

After following events closely from New York, Walter White flew to Detroit on April 7 and joined James McClendon to wring full advantage from the moment. In a series of meetings with the UAW leadership, he secured a pledge that the union would protect the status of black workers at Ford and work more aggressively on behalf of black workers in other plants. He then convinced a majority of the executive board of the Detroit branch of the importance of supporting the UAW and at least giving the union a chance. On April 9 White issued a public statement endorsing the union while at the same time prodding its leadership to act on its pledge. Two days later the union claimed victory.

White was justifiably pleased with the outcome. It was apparent to him that the UAW was going to win the strike and that it was in the interest of black workers to be on the side of the union. While the NAACP's position might cost them "support . . . among more conservative folks who are pro-Ford," he was confident the branch would "gain more than enough new members among the rank and file." More importantly, as historians August Meier and Elliot Rudwick observed, the Detroit agreement "set the stage" for the subsequent alliance between the NAACP and the UAW, a foundation stone of the national civil rights coalition. Addressing the annual meeting of the NAACP that summer in Houston, Seattle NAACP official Horace Cayton underscored the significance of this historic shift as well as the challenges and hard work ahead. Pledges and even good intentions on the part of their allies in the CIO would never be sufficient. "Only through constant pressure," Cayton advised, "will any white organization in these United States continue to treat the Negro fairly."[40]

"Militancy" was the first topic White listed in the outline of his annual report for 1941. The struggle that brought the president's executive order and the advances made on the labor front in Detroit revealed the power of protest and sustained, organized action. Echoing the controversial slogan touted by Du Bois during World War I, White promised that there would be no "closed ranks"; the memory of betrayed promises and bitter disillusionment after that war remained fresh. The NAACP would continue to protest segregation and discrimination, confident that it had "the skeleton of the organization that is needed" to unite black Americans in this fight. But he acknowledged that "the machinery is no where near equal to the needs of the grim days ahead." It was time to "put more flesh and bones and sinews on it" for this was a time of great peril and opportunity. The war against fascism had placed the racial practices of America and its Allies on an international stage and linked their efforts to a broader arena of struggle. The war, in the words of newly hired field-worker Ella Baker, was the "proving ground of our political theories and economic and social practices."[41]

The national leadership and the broad dynamic that would guide the NAACP over the next fifteen years coalesced during the war years, with

Walter White, Roy Wilkins, and Thurgood Marshall firmly at the helm. It was hardly inevitable that these three men would continue to link their futures to an organization perpetually perched at the edge of insolvency, and there were signs the team might unravel as late as 1941. According to Walter White, Roosevelt administration officials approached both White and Marshall regarding positions with the newly established FEPC, positions that would have brought a hefty salary increase. It appears that Wilkins alone seriously considered leaving the association in the fall of 1941 for a more secure and financially rewarding position as executive editor of the *New York Amsterdam News*. At the age of 40, the next stretch of years would be critical for his career, and he admitted to White that he had often wondered whether he should depend on the NAACP "in the ripe years of my life and work." He complained that everyone seemed "wedded to the idea that we have always operated on a shoestring and that always some miracle would happen to see that we survive."

In a letter outlining his concerns while also soliciting White's advice, Wilkins argued for a greater effort to bring some financial stability to the NAACP and a complete reorganization of the branch structure. White was sympathetic to Wilkins's desire for greater security but urged him not to discount "the prestige and honor" associated with the work. More importantly, he expressed confidence that the NAACP was "entering a period when its income will permit a larger and better paid staff and a period of even greater service and influence." Wilkins stayed, and he and White, working in tandem with Marshall, charted the future course of the NAACP. The field staff, a more fluid group, lacked a prominent national profile. But they led in expanding the base of the organization and, largely under the direction of Ella Baker, cultivated the militancy and expectations released by the war, helping to shape the fuller contours of a southern movement.[42]

Despite tight budgets, the national office added three new field-workers during 1940 and 1941; they joined the seasoned Daisy Lampkin and E. Frederic Morrow, who had worked as coordinator of branches since 1937. William Pickens, director of branches, had taken extended leave to work in the U.S. Treasury Department and had not been an active presence for several years. Madison Jones, born in 1909, the year the NAACP was founded, was hired late in the fall of 1940 to build up the youth program and youth membership. A New Yorker, Jones was a graduate of Rhodes Prep School, earned a BS at St. John's University, and had been working toward a master's in history at Columbia University, while working full time for an insurance company. Ella Baker joined the staff in February 1941 as a field-worker. The thirty-seven-year-old native of North Carolina and graduate of Shaw University in Raleigh had lived in New York for more than a decade. She had worked on labor and consumer issues; had experience as a teacher, journalist, and public speaker; and had studied at Columbia University and the New School for Social Research. Baker, however, had most impressed Wilkins as someone who "might develop into a money raiser." In June 1941, Walter White recruited Randall Tyus, a graduate of Fisk University and an accomplished salesman, to join the field staff.[43]

Fieldwork remained critical to recruiting the membership essential to the fiscal viability of the organization. The need for funds weighed heavily on the association; adding members and collecting dues became, understandably, a primary goal of the national leadership. White, however, tended to discount the investment of time and talent necessary to build more than a franchise operation capable of meeting the bottom line. White's enthusiasm for Randall Tyus, who had worked as the national sales representative for Rumford Chemical Works, a baking powder concern, was revealing. He initially hoped to hire Tyus as director of branches to replace Pickens, asserting that his experience "in the field of selling" was unmatched by other staff members and offered the kind of fresh approach the organization needed. In his reference for Tyus, A. Philip Randolph agreed that "he seems to have what it takes to put a proposition over." The field staff rebelled at the idea and was supported by Wilkins in their opposition to placing a person who had no experience working with the NAACP in charge of the Department of Branches. Reluctantly, White conceded and brought Tyus on staff as an assistant field-worker, and White himself temporarily assumed the role of director of branches. In contrast to Baker and Jones, Tyus failed to catch fire in the field. After little more than a year he accepted a paid position with the Baltimore NAACP branch.[44]

Differences about the role of fieldwork were illuminated in a report on branch work prepared by Frederic Morrow and Ella Baker late in the summer of 1941 and signed by all members of the field staff. The report was done at the request of the board's Committee on Administration and echoed recommendations made in the 1932 Lonigan report. While not discounting the association's ever-pressing need to increase its annual income, the report advised that the survival and growth of the NAACP and its program depended upon a broader vision. It advocated a reorganization of the branch work along regional lines with the appointment of regional secretaries, fuller attention to the development of strong local leadership, and more frequent visits from national officers to the branches. A tendency to regard branches primarily as revenue-producing agencies eclipsed the opportunity to cultivate them "as permanent centers of information and leadership on vital community and national problems." The relevance of the NAACP to the challenges created by the war depended upon its ability "to catch and hold the imagination of the masses" and help give organizational expression to their desire "for a militant and practical program of action." In short, the strength and power of the association depended upon deliberate and sustained investment at the base, organizing strong branches around the needs and strengths of individual communities, while integrating them into a national program.[45]

Walter White was impatient with this line of thinking. As biographer Kenneth Janken explains, White viewed branches "as expressions of the clout of the national office," in addition to being the primary revenue source for the association. The NAACP's success, as far as he was concerned, depended upon "good public relations and a high national profile." These differing approaches and emphasis were not necessarily incompatible; indeed, all contributed to the unique and growing strength of the NAACP. But White, who frequently clashed with Frederic Morrow, disregarded the report's recommendation. Fieldwork, he believed, should concentrate on areas that promised the greatest returns in terms of membership. Others on the staff, particularly those who spent extended periods in the field, remained sympathetic to the approach advocated by the Morrow-Baker report. Thurgood Marshall and cooperating lawyers in the South were dependent on strong community involvement to develop cases and carry them forward. Ella Baker assumed a critical role during the war years, gaining the confidence of White while working to implement the vision laid out in the Morrow-Baker report.[46]

Ella Baker brought a rare combination of intellect, experience, and talent to the NAACP at a transitional moment in its history. Raised in the small town of Littleton in eastern North Carolina, she had deep southern roots. Her political consciousness and social activism, however, were forged in Depression-era New York. She moved to Harlem after completing college and found a "hotbed of radical thinking." Baker immersed herself in the city's vibrant intellectual and political movements and worked in a variety of activities and organizations, such as the Young Negroes' Cooperative League, the Young People's Forum, and the Workers Education Project of the Works Progress Administration, filling in with freelance journalism and odd jobs to pay the rent. For Baker, as for others of her generation, the Depression had exposed the vulnerability of the individual to broad economic and social forces and elevated the essential role of collective action for securing the welfare of workers, consumers, and other groups. Drawing on traditions of black self-determination, exploring contemporary theories of social change, and engaged in continuing conversation with a broad spectrum of political activists, Baker developed an eclectic approach. As a teacher, organizer, and activist, she sought to cultivate an understanding of the injustices and violence that constrained black lives and of how individuals, acting "in an organized fashion could help to stem [them]." After nearly a decade in New York, Baker sought a position with the NAACP, an organization that afforded a unique opportunity to work on a national scale toward these ends.[47]

Baker applied for a job as youth director in 1938 (it was filled with a part-time worker) and again in 1940. The committee hired Madison Jones, but White and Wilkins were impressed with Baker. She was "an energetic young woman with ideas and initiative, tact and personality," the kind of person, Wilkins noted, who should apprentice under the legendary Daisy Lampkin. Lampkin had surpassed all others in building up huge membership rolls, particularly in major urban and industrial areas. But at the age of fifty-eight, she indicated that the grueling demands of work in the field were taking a toll. Wilkins suggested to Lampkin that Baker might assist her and, in the process, learn from the master. She agreed to have Baker work with her on a membership campaign, in Washington, D.C., but insisted that Baker have a chance to try out "her new ideas in money raising" on her own. She also advised that Baker be assigned to "break in new fields," avoiding places Lampkin had cultivated and where expectations would be high. Conceding nothing to youth, she told White, "I do hope she will like the work and will not find campaigning too strenuous as some of the others have felt."[48]

A petite, attractive woman with a fondness for stylish hats, Baker quickly became known as a tireless and supremely effective organizer. During one of her first membership campaigns in Birmingham she worked closely with the chairman, the Reverend J.W. Goodgame, whom she described as "all preacher, but unlike most of them he knows that it takes work to produce." She and Goodgame visited "barber shops, filling stations, grocery stores and housewives," enlisting people to work. Her efforts helped to broaden the scope of interest in the association; 70 percent of members brought in during the drive came through new campaign workers. An eleven-day campaign in Richmond, Virginia, followed. Richmond branch president and Virginia state conference chair J. R. Tinsley enthused to White that Baker was "one of the most important and wonderful things that has happened to Richmond. . . . Never during her stay . . . did she slacken her pace. She was going from the time of her arrival until the time she left. . . . She has demonstrated to the people of Richmond and over the state of Virginia one characteristic very few people have and that is the . . . outstanding quality of mixing with any group of people and trying to help solve their problems." The places she visited clamored for her to return. Frederic Morrow described her success during these first months with the association as "phenomenal."[49]

Baker believed that community-based organizing was essential to the future growth of the association and the movement it sought to lead. After attending her first annual NAACP convention in Houston in June 1941, she drafted her observations, noting that the cross section of delegates "both geographically and socially" revealed "what a healthy position for growth the Association is in and how imminent is the challenge to gear our organizational machinery to meet the demand for an expanded program." She advised that the annual conference make a greater effort to engage the specific concerns of the delegates and focus on methods for carrying out the NAACP's program on the local level. At the next annual meeting she facilitated a discussion with delegates on the relationship between the branches and the national office. "The work of the National Office is one thing," she explained, "but the work of the branches is in the final analysis the life blood of the Association." In her comments, Baker laid out the importance of organizing around a local issue or problem, "something that can be done in your own community." Take one thing, she advised, "getting a new school building, registering people to vote, getting bus transportation . . . work on it and get it done." She warned of the tendency on the part of branches outside the South to assume that "as long as they help support the National Office and some unfortunate person in Georgia they are doing their job." It was the responsibility of each branch to "take the initiative in developing leadership in all social and economic problems and problems of discrimination, employment and the like which confront the Negro today." A branch has not "done its best" when it has only sent in its annual contribution to the national office. "The Association . . . is dependent on the branches for action."[50]

Although she traveled to all parts of the country, Baker concentrated her efforts in the South, working in large and small communities across the region. During these years she honed the skills and established relationships that were formative in her development as a leading figure in the southern civil rights movement. Baker's "untiring efforts" during a series of membership campaigns in Birmingham helped send their numbers "over the top" to 1,619. Reporting at the end of a day in Pensacola, Florida, she noted: "I have spoken to six student groups (schools) and conferred with several individuals and one teacher group since ten o'clock this morning; and will meet with the executive committee at seven thirty and then address a mass meeting at eight. I go to Mobile tomorrow." Big campaigns in cities and large towns were balanced by work in rural areas. After a long day in Savannah, Baker wrote Walter White, "I must leave now for one of those small church night meetings which are usually more exhausting than the immediate returns seem to warrant; but it's part of the spade work." She took satisfaction when, in those small meetings, "one or more persons" who had been "hard to convince" or even opposed the NAACP's program experienced a "change of heart" and signed up. Baker followed up with letters to the people she worked with, encouraging their efforts. A letter to James Johnson, president of a longshoreman's union in Norfolk, Virginia, was typical: "Only through such capable, sincere and courageous leadership," she told Johnson, "will the workers of America—organized and unorganized—colored and white, be able to achieve full economic security and civic equality for which we all are striving."[51]

Baker engaged all segments of the community. The black church was a bedrock of NAACP organizing efforts. She worked to find a way that would encourage churches to "give more continuous stimulation to civic thinking" by possibly "setting aside a Sunday every month in which some phase of civic life might be discussed." Through access to congregations on Sunday, she added, "the Association can capitalize upon the Southern Brother's penchant for paying on the installment plan." She cultivated the participation of youth, working with teachers, schools, and scout troops, and also reached out to unions and other interracial organizations that shared the democratic vision of the NAACP. "An idea . . . came to me for increasing *Crisis* circulation and bolstering my campaign efforts," she wrote Wilkins. She would "visit some of the pool-rooms, boot black parlors, bars and grills, and tell of the Association, secure individual memberships if possible; but take up a collection on the spot and sell the idea of having *The Crisis* available to regular patrons of the 'business.' . . . This is but another offshoot of my desire to place the NAACP and its program on the lips of all the people . . . the uncouth *masses* included." Baker mused that the fact that she was not "a social elite" placed her at a disadvantage in some quarters. She reported on the great disappointment expressed by the chairwoman of the membership campaign in Jacksonville when Baker begged off an invitation to play a round of golf at the local country club.[52]

"Field hands," as Madison Jones and Baker jokingly referred to their group, played a formative role in shaping the development of the NAACP during the war years and mapping out the challenges that it would face over the next decade. They worked together to reach all parts of the country with notable success, although the South loomed as the front line of the movement. Beyond representing the NAACP, field organizers served as the association's eyes and ears, providing firsthand accounts that personalized the work all were engaged in and affirming a common purpose. Office-bound staff in New York eagerly consumed news sent in from the field. Madison Jones's lengthy typewritten reports during an extensive tour of the South at the end of 1941 were "the talk of the office." Roy Wilkins described reading one of Jones's letters from North Carolina aloud late one Friday afternoon as clerks and secretaries finished up their work; all were especially interested in accounts of "the people who keep the NAACP going."[53]

Thirty-one-year-old Madison Jones headed to the South with a portable typewriter early in November 1941 on a multipurpose assignment that took him from Virginia through South Carolina, Georgia, Alabama, Tennessee, and back to North Carolina. In addition to developing youth councils and college chapters, Jones was expected to survey conditions in various areas, check up on weak branches, and do some advance work in North Carolina for Ella Baker with an eye toward establishing a state conference of branches. As he rode from town to town in the back of a Greyhound bus, this sophisticated New Yorker became a seasoned witness to life under Jim Crow. While rarely mentioning his personal experiences of segregation, there are glimpses of the routine indignities and discomforts. "I am an authority on the back seats of buses," he wrote, "[and] filthy dirty waiting rooms, but like the mail I usually get through." He became absorbed in the lives of the people he met and the challenges they faced—from rural areas in Alabama and North Carolina to centers of defense production, like Memphis, Tennessee, and a major military camp at Fort Bragg in Fayetteville, North Carolina. While circumstances varied greatly from place to place, Jones was consistently struck by a spirit of resistance that was ripe for cultivation. "I am seeing so much and meeting so many people in committees, [at] meetings and personally that I could write a book," he claimed at one point. "There is a gold mine here," he wrote White, "if we want to take the time and money to make an investment of concerted action."[54]

Branch activity along a number of fronts offered a measure of the inroads that the NAACP was making. Jones reported that the association's national defense program had stimulated much support and activity. College chapters in Nashville and Memphis investigated conditions at a nearby defense plant; the Knoxville branch succeeded in getting defense training courses included in the schools; the Paine College chapter in Augusta, Georgia, sponsored a mass meeting on national defense and publicized the lack of USO (United Service Organizations) facilities for black soldiers. Jones profiled a new generation of leadership, like thirty-six-year-old Kelly Alexander who ran his family's funeral business and led in reviving the Charlotte branch in 1940. Alexander and his associates were "drawing the support of the man in the street." In Asheville, North Carolina, Leila B. Michaels, a schoolteacher with many community obligations, "lives and dies NAACP," Jones observed. She revived a dormant branch, which had been mismanaged for years, and built its membership up to nearly five hundred, including 95 percent of the local black schoolteachers. The teachers were reluctant to challenge salary inequities for fear of losing their jobs, Jones reported. But the branch was working to get a bus line for the black section of town and leading a campaign to secure the hiring of black mail carriers and police officers.

Wherever Jones went, he found that blacks were making efforts to vote, and in many cases succeeding. He reported on gains made following the successful suit near Wilkesboro, North Carolina, against the registrar five years earlier. "Every black who has the courage to register votes," and positive results were seen in paved streets, streetlights, and other community improvements. The Talladega, Alabama, branch of the NAACP had launched a citizenship training program, working in conjunction with the churches and clubs. They sponsored classes in Negro history, reading and writing, and a public speaking committee—all dedicated toward getting "people out to vote." In Macon County, Alabama, the heart of the Black Belt, T. Rupert Broady, a twenty-four-year-old Tuskegee Institute professor, refused to give up after the registrar turned him away and the judge of the probate court "stormed out in a rage" when he realized that Broady wanted to vote. After learning that Broady planned to file a suit, the office of the registrar phoned him and requested that he return the next day. Broady did, and he was registered. "That spirit," Jones reported, "is indicative of the trend down through the South."[55]

*   *   *

After America's entry into the war at the end of 1941, NAACP membership numbers skyrocketed. The massive mobilization of troops in the segregated armed forces, the frustrations experienced by blacks in their efforts to obtain defense jobs, and the tightening constraints of segregation in urban areas buckling under the weight of migration further exposed the cruel and unyielding nature of the color line even as the nation enlisted in a global fight to defend freedom and democracy. Reporting on three months of work in Kansas, Minnesota, Indiana, and Ohio in the immediate aftermath of Pearl Harbor, Frederic Morrow wrote that memberships were pouring in. People seeking redress "were signing up with gusto. . . . Former barren spots became oases" while established branches reached numbers beyond the hopes of the "most wishful thinker." When Madison Jones returned south in the summer of 1942 he found that the war "caused the Negro to change almost instantly from a fundamentally defensive attitude to one of offense," and the NAACP was giving organizational expression to this spirit. "The work of the NAACP is jumping and the membership of our branches is trebling," exclaimed Thurgood Marshall, in a letter to a newly revived branch in San Francisco.[56]

In the midst of unprecedented growth, the NAACP struggled to shape the meaning of the war for the broader society. From the start of the defense buildup, the association and the black press worked aggressively to expose how racism jeopardized national defense efforts. The refusal to hire black workers resulted in underutilized manpower in vital defense industries; the segregation and mistreatment of black troops undermined the morale of a large segment of the armed forces; and the system of racial caste, disenfranchisement, and lynch terror that blanketed the southern states compromised America's position as a beacon in the fight against the racial theories of Hitler. But racial attitudes, political constraints, and a failure of leadership all contributed to a functioning consensus within government circles that wartime was no time to "experiment" with any major departures in race relations—which meant letting local customs and Jim Crow practices determine government policy and influence government action.

The War Department's insistence that the American Red Cross establish segregated blood banks in January 1942, after first refusing to even accept any donations from African Americans, was but one example of how easily government agencies yielded to the most irrational and demeaning racial attitudes. Officials acknowledged that there was no scientific justification for such a policy; blood type had no racial markers. Nevertheless, the War Department held that it was "not advisable to indiscriminately mix Caucasian and Negro blood for use in blood transfusions." The guiding consideration, admitted Red Cross chairman Norman H. Davis, was "whether or not the views of the majority of those for whom the blood is being produced . . . are to prevail or whether the views of the minority who wish to donate their blood should prevail." Charles R. Drew, the noted black scientist and surgeon, had made the establishment of the modern blood bank possible when he proved that the separation of blood plasma allowed for long-term storage. He called the policy "indefensible from any point of view." After a short tenure, Drew resigned his position as head of the Red Cross's first blood bank. William Hastie, civilian adviser to the secretary of war, protested a policy made in deference "to those who insist that our country treat the Negro as a loathsome being. . . . Even the saving of lives of soldiers is weighed against the appeasement of the sentiments most alien to our professions."[57]

The federal government's "surrender to Southern racial patterns" was most widely demonstrated in the treatment of black soldiers, serving as a potent spur to the rising tide of black protest and militancy that crested during World War II. There had been some loosening of the barriers that restricted black participation in the armed forces in the First World War, due largely to the efforts of the Committee for Participation of Negroes in the National Defense. All branches of the military were open to black soldiers. An air base was established at Tuskegee to train black pilots. But all was on a strictly segregated basis. Close to 1 million black men and women served in the United States armed forces. The majority of them passed through training camps in the South, where they confronted the raw experience of Jim Crow on and off base. Segregated and crowded into the least desirable areas of military camps, black military personnel were barred from USO facilities, except in those instances when a separate USO club was available, and restricted to segregated recreational facilities, which were scarce and poorly equipped. Off base, black soldiers in uniform faced the humiliating rituals of second-class citizenship and an anxious white populace prepared to enforce the color line. Such a potent brew, combined with the dislocation and overcrowding generated by wartime, fueled rising racial tensions and violent encounters, all formative in the collective war experience of black Americans.[58]

"The people I knew," recalled novelist James Baldwin, "felt a peculiar kind of relief when they knew their boys were being shipped out of the South to do battle overseas. It was perhaps like feeling that the most dangerous part of the journey had been passed." Letters of servicemen and women told about the harsh treatment and violence, stories that were amplified in the black press and that shaped the narrative of a low-intensity race war on the home front. In the spring of 1941, black soldiers found the body of Private Felix Hall hanging from a tree in a wooded area of Fort Benning, Georgia, his hands tied behind his back. At the NAACP's insistence, the War Department conducted an investigation, but the case remained unsolved. In August, a fight between a white military policeman and Ned Turman, a black private on a bus going to Fort Bragg, North Carolina, turned into a shooting match that left both men dead. That night, there were racial clashes on the base, and the NAACP received reports of brutal treatment and intimidation of black soldiers. The NAACP pressed for the prosecution of the M.P. identified by eyewitnesses as the man who killed Turman as well as an investigation of conditions at Fort Bragg and a civilian-military review of the entire military police system's treatment of black soldiers. Secretary of war Henry Stimson reported directly to the NAACP on the results of a special investigation, which concluded that Turman's killer was "unknown" and that the Fort Bragg incident did not have "any semblance" of a racial conflict. The War Department dismissed calls for a review of the military police system.[59]

Areas hosting military camps were cauldrons of racial tension and violence. Alexandria, Louisiana, with three military camps located in close proximity, was "bursting its britches," with some thirty thousand off-duty servicemen crowding in on the weekend. In January 1942, barely two months after Stimson's report on the Fort Bragg case, the arrest of two black soldiers for disorderly conduct led to a dispute between two white and two black M.P.s. The arrival of sixty white M.P.s, local police, and a contingent of state troopers sparked a full-scale riot. Thousands of civilians and soldiers joined in the bedlam; twelve black soldiers and one black woman were shot. In its report on the incident, the War Department conceded that "civilian policemen and one military policeman indulged in indiscriminate and unnecessary shooting." When Madison Jones visited the area at the end of the year, he reported that conditions were "very, very bad as far as the Negro troops are concerned." On the eve of his arrival a white highway patrolman chased down Raymond Carr, a black M.P., and shot him at point-blank range, later bragging that "he had told them he was going to get that 'nigger.'" This case aroused local military authorities, who, when the grand jury refused to indict the officer, joined the NAACP in pressing for the Justice Department to intervene. But the department concluded that the case lacked "those elements promising a successful prosecution."[60]

Jones reported that the bus situation was especially bad. Crowded conditions frequently required the adjustment of the moving line dividing white and black passengers. Drivers requesting that blacks give up their seats to whites often barked orders using "vile and filthy language." In many instances, soldiers were "unmercifully beaten" by bus drivers and police for refusing to move or failing to move swiftly. In one case two black soldiers responded to the driver's crude demands by taking the driver off the bus and beating him for two blocks. Soldiers confided in Jones that they could not "take any more of the treatment." Ammunition was missing from many of the camps, and soldiers implied that it was being stored for future use. They told him that the riot the previous January was "tame" compared to what was coming. At Camp Claiborne, where there were several black tank divisions, "the boys are . . . saying that they expect to drive their tanks down the streets of Alexandria before they drive to the front. This is the situation."[61]

The NAACP kept the pressure on the Justice Department and War Department, submitting reports documenting some of the most egregious cases of attacks on black military personnel. But, as the *New Republic* editorialized, "The field of remedial action [was] always limited . . . by the swollen power of Southern politicians." The NAACP submitted a report fully documenting ten instances of black soldiers assaulted by civilian authorities or military police near bases in Greenville and Leland, Mississippi, during 1942 and 1943, a phenomenon repeated near bases around the South. In Starksville, Mississippi, four white men demanded that Private Rieves Bell strip off his uniform, and beat him when he refused; Bell was subsequently arrested and sentenced to three and a half years in the state penitentiary. In Columbia, South Carolina, a policeman shot Private Larry Stroud in the back of the head. Buses and streetcars were a major site of racial confrontation. Black soldiers were beaten and shot for alleged infractions in cities across the South. Private Charles Reco was forced off a bus in Beaumont, Texas, after taking a seat in the white section, and then shot by two police officers. In Montgomery, Alabama, law enforcement officials brutally beat an army nurse for refusing to move to the black section. A bus driver in Mobile, Alabama, shot and killed Private Henry Williams as he was leaving the bus. The chronic failure of the Justice Department or the War Department to intervene in such instances, the association warned, served "notice to other police officers and the public that Negro soldiers may be attacked with impunity and without any fear of consequences."[62]

William Hastie served as civilian adviser to the secretary of war from late 1940 until January 1943. He reluctantly accepted the post, wary of becoming a cover for racially discriminatory policies. But Thurgood Marshall, Felix Frankfurter, and others persuaded him, insisting that he would be well positioned to expose discrimination against black soldiers and possibly secure some remedies. In the end, his experience revealed how entrenched racial attitudes and political calculations thwarted leadership on this critical issue. Hastie's efforts to secure fair and equitable treatment for black soldiers elicited warnings that attempts to buck accepted "social customs" would jeopardize the war effort, along with complaints that he, like the NAACP, was trying "to advance the colored race at the expense of the army." On the specific issue of civilian and police violence against black soldiers, secretary of war Henry Stimson and others argued that the War Department did not have the legal authority to intervene. Moreover, Stimson clearly did not want such authority. Acknowledging racism in the army, Stimson explained to a white colleague that "this crime of our forefathers had produced a problem which was almost impossible of solution in this country" particularly during a time of war.[63]

Growing black protest and an escalation of racial violence prompted concern within government circles about black morale. Officials viewed black discontent, however, as a problem to be investigated and managed rather than a reflection of conditions requiring remedial action. In June 1942, J. Edgar Hoover launched a massive, yearlong internal investigation to "ascertain the extent of agitation among the American Negro," seeking its causes among alien and subversive forces. He attempted to enlist Walter White in the effort, providing him with the phone numbers of FBI field agents and emphasizing how important it was that "reputable Negro organizations be diligently alert to keep Nazism, Communism, and Fascism from attaching themselves to Negro movements." Other officials were less concerned with the roots of black protest and focused attention on containing it. As Horace Cayton observed, so far as official government policy was concerned "the color line was necessary for the morale of white soldiers, workers, and civilians." The Roosevelt administration employed public-relations efforts, such as a film highlighting the contributions of black troops, and offered token gestures in its attempt to defuse black protest. Jonathan Daniels, race relations adviser to the president, whose father served under Woodrow Wilson, explained it this way: "We thought we had to get a little justice to keep [Negroes] in line. . . . Throw a little meat to the lions."[64]

As soldiers flooded the NAACP with reports of abuses and requests for help, the association turned to the courts in an effort to push back against some of the most egregious injustices suffered by black men and women in the armed services. There was an "overwhelming large number" of cases involving court-martial and dishonorable discharge, often for protesting or resisting discriminatory treatment. In one instance, a seaman was dishonorably discharged for describing discrimination on his base in a letter to his wife. The NAACP participated in the successful defense of four WACs (Women's Army Corps) at Fort Devans, Massachusetts. The women had been court-martialed after refusing to do menial work at the hospital's base when white Wac's were given more "dignified" jobs. Thurgood Marshall intervened in the case of Leroy Clay, a captain in the Ninety-second Infantry, who was convicted of disobeying orders while serving overseas, dishonorably discharged, and sentenced to fifty years in prison. A review of the trial revealed a deliberate effort to discredit Clay and ruin his career. Based on this, the NAACP petitioned on Clay's behalf. His sentence was remitted; he reenlisted in the army and earned an honorable discharge. Marshall and his newly hired assistant, Robert Carter, appealed for clemency for Private Purdie S. Jackson, convicted by court-martial and sentenced to twelve years in prison following a fight with a group of whites who attacked him for entering a "whites only" section of a drugstore in Nashville, Tennessee.[65]

"The wanton branding of Negro soldiers as rapists" was a "stigma" the NAACP devoted "tireless efforts to eradicate." There were many cases involving black soldiers charged with rape on flimsy evidence and convicted under flawed procedures. The most noted case involved three soldiers stationed at Camp Claibourne, Louisiana, outside of Alexandria. Private Richard Adams of Columbus, Ohio, Lawrence Mitchell of Boldurn, Minnesota, and John Bordenave of New Orleans were tried and sentenced to death in the U.S. district court for the alleged rape of Anna Mae Mason, a white woman who had accompanied a white soldier to the base. After consideration of the evidence and further investigation, Marshall, with the strong backing of the Alexandria and New Orleans branches, appealed *Adams v. U.S.* to the U.S.

Supreme Court. He argued the case, his first before that body, in May 1943. The court reversed the conviction on a technicality, holding that the federal court did not have jurisdiction. Marshall then represented the three before a general court-martial at Camp Maxey in Texas, where they were convicted again on July 30, 1943, and sentenced to death. A year later FDR commuted their sentences to life in prison. The men were paroled in 1947.[66]

The worst stateside military disaster to occur during the war generated one of the most widely publicized cases involving the NAACP and black military personnel. In July 1944, 202 black navy seamen were killed in an explosion that rocked Port Chicago, a munitions base on San Francisco Bay. The accident occurred as a direct result of the navy's callous treatment of black enlistees. Only black seamen were assigned to load munitions and explosives onto the transport ships. They had no training, they were poorly equipped, and they were taunted by white officers to speed up, while the officers bet on which division could load faster. The disaster waiting to happen occurred on the evening of July 17, when four thousand tons of munitions exploded, lifting the ship out of the water, killing more than three hundred people, and injuring hundreds more. Three weeks after the deadly explosion, navy officers ordered three hundred black seamen to a loading pier at Mare Island to continue their assignment. A number of the men had been involved in the Port Chicago incident, several had been wounded, and all were now keenly aware of the dangers involved. Nearly all of the men refused the orders, citing lack of training. When their superiors threatened to charge them with mutiny, which was punishable by death in wartime, all but fifty returned to work. The fifty were tried in military court for mutiny. The youngest was seventeen years old; half were under twenty-one, and forty-four of the men had perfect conduct ratings.[67]

At the urging of Joseph James, president of the NAACP's San Francisco branch, Walter White dispatched Thurgood Marshall to the West Coast to observe the proceedings. It was too late for him to participate as a civil defense lawyer. After three days of listening to testimony, Marshall declared that the men "are being tried for mutiny solely because of their race or color." The men had good records, they were respectful, obeyed all other orders, and had not engaged in "collective insubordination." A navy psychiatrist testified that the explosion would have a lasting effect on the minds of all of the men who experienced it. In refusing to handle munitions, they were at worst guilty of disobeying an order. Marshall found that the defense counsel had done "a splendid job . . . within the limitations of Navy rules," but, he wrote later, he had "never run across a prosecutor with a more definite racial bias than that exemplified by Lt. Commander William Coakley."[68]

Upon returning to New York, Marshall wrote secretary of the navy James Forrestal, reporting on the trial and on an investigation he had made regarding the circumstances leading to the court-martial. He outlined a series of questions that emphasized the carelessly dangerous circumstances under which the men were forced to work, the racially charged nature of their assignment and treatment, and noted that none had been given any leave in the aftermath of the explosion. Forrestal sent an evasive response. On October 24, after six weeks of hearings, all of the men were found guilty of mutiny and sentenced to fifteen years in prison. The association joined with the black press and liberal groups in publicizing the case and generating widespread petitions and appeals for a reversal of the convictions. The NAACP obtained permission to represent the men in an appeal before the navy's judge advocate general in Washington. Marshall appeared before the judge advocate general in April 1945, and as of July had not received word on the outcome of the appeal, despite frequent requests. His efforts to make an appeal directly to Secretary Forrestal on behalf of the men were unsuccessful. In January 1946, the men were released from prison under a general amnesty. The felony conviction remained, and they never received veterans' benefits.[69]

Racial struggles in the U. S. military paralleled other hard-fought and often inconclusive gains in American society more generally, notably on the employment front. During a time of wartime industrial expansion, the Fair Employment Practices Committee (FEPC), federal sanction of union rights under the National Labor Relations Act, and pockets of support for interracial unionism broadened the arena for challenging racial barriers to equal employment. While the FEPC was severely limited in terms of funding and enforcement power, it elevated the issue of employment rights to one of national importance, energizing black protest and mobilizing an interracial coalition of supporters. Black complaints to the committee averaged five thousand a year for the duration of the war. Thurgood Marshall and Charles Houston worked closely with the committee and Houston served two terms on the FEPC. A highly motivated staff conducted investigations and staged public hearings throughout the country, exposing discriminatory practices in violation of the president's executive order. In some instances that was sufficient to generate remedial action; in a few cases, presidential directives mandated the hiring of black workers. Compliance was uneven and often collapsed in the face of defiant companies and unions as well as political pressure. Nevertheless, the combination of hearings, appeals to federal agencies, and litigation opened a new front in the struggle for civil rights.[70]

In the West and the Northeast, a major contest around the discriminatory policies of the AFL's International Brotherhood of Boilermakers, Shipbuilders and Helpers of America (IBB) showcased the convergence of black protest, federal mandates, and litigation in what has been described as "one of the most important black protests during the war years." Black shipyard workers in San Francisco, Los Angeles, Portland, Oregon, and Providence, Rhode Island, numbering in the thousands during the peak war years, refused to join auxiliary IBB unions established for black workers. The auxiliary union charged blacks the same dues but provided few of the benefits afforded white unionists. IBB locals pressured the shipbuilding companies to discharge any workers who refused to join auxiliary unions, leading to widespread dismissals. Responding to appeals from black shipyard workers in California and Oregon, the FEPC held a series of public hearings on the West Coast in the fall of 1943. Charles Houston participated in the hearings as assistant counsel to the FEPC. The FEPC found that the auxiliary system was discriminatory and illegal, in effect denying blacks union membership and aggravating manpower shortages in wartime. It ordered the IBB to eliminate discrimination and report on its progress in forty-five days. The IBB ignored the FEPC's "alleged directives" and insisted that shipbuilding companies honor the closed-shop agreement to hire only union members in good standing.[71]

Meanwhile, Marshall teamed up with San Francisco branch president Joseph James, a shipyard worker and head of the San Francisco Committee against Segregation and Discrimination. James was the lead plaintiff in a suit against the Marinship Corporation and IBB Local 6 and won an injunction ordering that men discharged for not joining the auxiliary be rehired pending a hearing. Marshall maintained close contact with James and the two independent attorneys handling the case locally, while he was representing shipyard workers in Providence, Rhode Island. As an indication of the broad support the case had attracted, Marshall told James that he was relying on him to ensure that the NAACP was fully represented, adding, "If we are to have a national fight with the boilermakers, it should be in the name of the NAACP." In December 1944, the California Supreme Court ruled that under a closed-shop agreement the union could not bar blacks from full membership. The ruling compelled the IBB to finally negotiate with the FEPC, although the issue was never satisfactorily resolved. The IBB dissolved the auxiliary unions and chartered "regular subordinate lodges" for black workers, under the same bylaws and with full autonomy—but segregated. Such an arrangement continued to place black workers at a disadvantage, and the FEPC deemed it inadequate. By this time, however, the war was winding down and jobs were drying up.[72]

Racial discrimination in the railroad industry was another highly charged area where some gains were made during the war. The four major railway unions had long barred blacks from union membership and maintained secret agreements with the railroad companies, limiting black workers to low-waged jobs that were least desirable. In 1939, Houston agreed to aid the Association of Colored Railway Trainmen and Locomotive Firemen in their fight for equal access to jobs and fair and impartial representation by the unions. While working on the railway case, he served as an attorney for the FEPC in a series of hearings, including a controversial investigation of the major railways and their unions. FEPC orders that the companies and unions abrogate all racially discriminatory agreements were ignored by most of the parties, compelling President Roosevelt to intervene in an effort to work out an agreement. The FEPC's activity, Houston observed, contributed to a favorable climate for his legal challenge, which reached the U.S. Supreme Court in the fall of 1944 in two cases involving Tom Tunstall and Bester Steele. In *Steele v. Louisville & Nashville Railroad et al.* the Court upheld all of Houston's key arguments, holding that the union, the exclusive bargaining agent as provided for under the Railway Labor Act, had the fiduciary duty to represent all members of the craft "without hostile discrimination, fairly, impartially, and in good faith."[73]

While the *Steele* case set an important precedent, Houston emphasized the limits of litigation in the struggle for equal employment. It had taken five years for the case to make its way to the Supreme Court; all the while the grievances of the workers were not redressed. Appeals to ensure enforcement of the Court's ruling lay ahead. "The judicial process is too hazardous, too cumbersome, too expensive and too slow to furnish adequate relief to workers, either white or black," Houston wrote. He hoped *Steele* would lend support to legislation "with teeth" mandating equal employment opportunity and providing an "administrative tribunal" that can give workers "speedy and inexpensive relief"—in short, a stronger and permanent FEPC.[74]

The FEPC was buffeted from all sides, and went through several administrative shake-ups. It was a lightning rod for southern opposition; key Roosevelt advisers and liberals, anxious to placate the southern bloc in Congress, were lukewarm if not hostile toward the agency. Yet the FEPC created a high-profile public platform for exposing and challenging discriminatory policies, forced employers and unions to at least respond to complaints, and demonstrated that the federal government could act as a catalyst for change. In the process, it galvanized a network of civil rights groups, unions, and religious and progressive organizations around the fight for equal employment policies. Their active support of the FEPC marked the emergence of a loosely defined national coalition dedicated to building support within the Democratic Party and in the legislative arena around the NAACP's civil rights agenda. As historians John Bracey and August Meier noted, the FEPC initiated a political struggle that continued after the agency's demise, one that would ultimately culminate with the enactment of the equal employment section of the 1964 Civil Rights Act.[75]

Beyond hearings, courtrooms, and legislative forums, the "no discrimination" mandate of the president's executive order was fought out on the ground in communities around the country. In Mobile, the Alabama Drydock and Shipbuilding Company stalled for six months before enforcing an FEPC directive requiring that the company upgrade black workers to skilled positions. The major war production facility employed thirty thousand workers; seven thousand were black, and none held skilled positions. The company finally acted in May 1943, with no advance notice or preparation, and promoted twelve blacks to welding jobs on an interracial crew. The next morning, thousands of white workers went on a rampage, assaulting black co-workers with pipes, clubs, bricks, and hammers. More than fifty people were injured by the time federal troops restored order. Management had anticipated trouble, and evidence suggests that they intended to embarrass the Roosevelt administration. In the aftermath, FEPC representatives negotiated arrangements for segregated facilities that allowed for employment of skilled black workers at a time when labor shortages were impeding production. Roughly one thousand black workers, terrorized by the riot, appealed to the War Manpower Commission for a transfer to another site. Their requests were denied.[76]

The combined efforts of black leaders, union officials, and government representatives, aided by growing bonds between the NAACP and individual unions, created a fragile counterpoint to a deepening racial divide. In Detroit, a city festering with racial tension, the UAW leadership was quickly put to the test in the aftermath of its pledge to represent fairly the interests of black workers as part of its agreement with the NAACP in July 1941. The Detroit branch, which reached twenty thousand members by 1943, provided strong

organizational backing for black demands. Yet even sympathetic union leaders walked a fine line as they sought to respond to black grievances without
alienating the majority of union members, steeped in a culture of white privilege and racial segregation. A small group of individuals worked to gain access for blacks to skilled jobs and enforce their seniority rights, in the face of
defiant employers and white workers prone to massive walkouts and wildcat
hate strikes. Among them were Gloster Current, executive secretary of the
NAACP branch, UAW president R.J. Thomas, black newspaper publisher
Louis Martin, and J. Lawrence Duncan, a longtime Detroit resident who
worked as a regional representative for various federal wartime employment
agencies. Determination, negotiating skill, patience, and an ability to bring
federal pressure to bear harvested token gains. In one case, it took six months
of persistent effort, largely by Duncan and Thomas, to secure the promotion
of two black metal polishers at a Packard plant. *Fortune* magazine described
the ordeal as a drawn out "wrestling match" between the company, the union,
and the government "over two American citizens' rights to contribute their
skills to the production of tanks." A year later, 25,000 whites staged a wildcat
strike after a Packard plant upgraded three black workers. At the insistence of
the UAW leadership and the federal government, there was a full investigation of the episode, and the ringleaders of the walkout were fired.[77]

During the war, America became a pressure cooker of black-white confrontations. The stresses of massive wartime dislocation and overcrowding
were compounded by the determination of whites to enforce the color line
while growing numbers of black men and women refused to yield to racist
attitudes and practices. Many fought back. Racial tensions exploded in 1943
in a wave of violence that rocked American cities. During the spring and
summer of that year there were more than two hundred "racial battles," including major outbreaks in Mobile, Beaumont (Texas), Los Angeles, and
Harlem. Detroit was the epicenter. There had been ample warnings, reaching
as high as the Office of War Information, that without aggressive intervention by public officials, the Motor City was a tinderbox waiting to blow. More
than a quarter of a million migrants, mostly southern whites, along with an
estimated forty thousand blacks, had streamed into the already overcrowded
city to fill war production jobs in the fifteen months preceding the riot. When
the fuse was lit on June 20, 1943, officials proved, at best, ill-prepared to cap
the violence.[78]

A fight between blacks and whites at an amusement park in Detroit on a
Sunday afternoon sparked three days of rioting, with blacks and whites wag-

ing pitched battles across the city. In the end, thirty-four people were dead. Blacks comprised twenty-five of the fatalities; seventeen of that number had been killed by police fire, while no whites died at the hands of law enforcement agents. According to an NAACP investigation, the police did little to rein in white mobs while directing "ultimate force" against blacks— "nightsticks, revolvers, riot guns, submachine guns, and deer guns." Blacks engaged in street fighting were not the only targets; investigators found that innocent bystanders were assaulted by the police, including a soldier in uniform and a bank employee on his way to work. A number of black victims were shot in the back. In one case police evacuated the Vernor apartment building using gunfire and tear gas on the grounds that they were looking for an alleged sniper. The likely suspect had already been arrested. Mayor Edward Jeffries initially ignored appeals by black leaders that he declare martial law and call in federal troops; he expressed full confidence in his police force. Finally, the request was made, and federal troops arrived on the scene Monday night, restoring order the next day.[79]

Walter White arrived in Detroit in the midst of the riot and, upon learning of the alleged police bias, promptly arranged for the NAACP to conduct its own investigation. Thurgood Marshall set up an emergency office at the St. Antoine branch of the YWCA on June 24. For the next two weeks he took complaints and sworn affidavits from local citizens, compiling a massive amount of evidence of police abuses. Marshall also oversaw several independent investigations with the assistance of two private detectives from New York—one black and one white. He visited the apartment building targeted by the police and reported that "it resembled part of a battlefield." There were slugs from machine guns, revolvers, and rifles embedded in the walls; locks and apartment doors were broken, and apartments had been ransacked. Having assembled a hefty body of evidence documenting police misconduct, the NAACP joined local black leaders and UAW officials in pressing the governor for a grand jury investigation. Police commissioner John Witherspoon countered by blaming the riot on the black community and charging that the NAACP and the black press were responsible for instigating the trouble. Witherspoon served on the governor's fact-finding committee, and it arrived at a similar conclusion. There was no grand jury investigation. The NAACP's work in the Detroit case netted $15,949 in contributions for the legal defense fund.[80]

In Harlem, six weeks after the Detroit riot, a policeman shot a black soldier in the shoulder during an altercation. It was a minor injury, but rumors that the soldier, Robert Bandy, had been shot and killed by a police officer spread like wildfire. Blacks turned their fury on white-owned businesses, reaping an estimated $5 million in property damage. Five blacks were killed, and more than three hundred people were injured. In a stark contrast to the response of Detroit officials, Walter White and Mayor Fiorello La Guardia joined forces to stem the violence. The two traveled amid the crowds in a sound truck, announcing that Bandy had not been killed and urging people to return home. The mayor made sure black M.P.s were among the federal troops brought in to aid in restoring order. Yet managing riots was not the issue to be attended to, White insisted. The root causes of the riots—"the unchecked brutality against Negro servicemen which has cursed the country" and the "evils of segregation and proscription" that plagued American cities—demanded federal attention and action. Mary McLeod Bethune compared the riots to the Boston Tea Party and the contemporary struggle of colonial people—a strike against oppression and tyranny. They were an expression of a mass consciousness, steeled in the rhetoric of the Four Freedoms, and determined to "break into the free realm of democratic citizenship."[81]

By the summer of 1943, America's racial crisis was inescapable. Vice president Henry Wallace was one of the few members of the administration who conveyed the urgency shared by civil rights leaders. Wallace flew to Detroit in the wake of the riot there and in an address to a crowd of twenty thousand people, identified racial justice and tolerance as major challenges facing America in a postwar world. "Education for tolerance will be just as important as television," Wallace predicted. America's ability to practice democracy at home would determine the nature of its leadership in securing the peace abroad. "We cannot plead for equality of opportunity for people everywhere and overlook the denial of the right to vote for millions of our own people," he explained. He praised organized labor for helping to bridge racial divisions and advance a fuller democracy. At the close of his speech, he appealed to the schools, the churches, and the press to join in helping to educate the American people about "the fundamental decencies and understandings" that were essential if the power of the United States was "to be a blessing and not a curse." FDR privately praised Wallace's speech as "splendid," telling him "you drew blood from the Cave Dwellers!" But the vice president's bold pronouncements on race and civil rights set him on a collision course with the Southern wing of the Democratic Party, ultimately costing him his place on the ticket in 1944.[82]

For the most part, federal officials appeared willfully ignorant of the depths of black frustration, continuing to view it as a problem to be monitored and contained. Black assertiveness and demands, many reasoned, stirred white resistance, thus fueling the racial tensions and violence and undermining the war effort. In the aftermath of the Detroit riot, *PM* published a confidential memo from attorney general Francis Biddle to FDR. Biddle advised that "careful consideration be given to limiting, and in some instances putting an end to, Negro migration into communities that cannot absorb them, either on account of their physical limitations or cultural background." Biddle denied that he had written such a memo. J. Edgar Hoover completed his "Survey of Racial Conditions in the United States" that summer. The massive report targeted "trouble spots" around the country, identifying sources of black agitation and speculating on areas of subversive activities. The best the administration could offer was a public relations initiative emphasizing gains made by African Americans during the war. "I am more disgusted than ever," Thurgood Marshall wrote in August 1943. "Despite all that has been done by the NAACP and others there have only been a few minor changes. The underlying policy of segregation and discrimination is no better and if anything worse. We are still second class citizens as civilians and second class soldiers and officers in the army."[83]

The war reinforced the racial fault lines in American society and further exposed the contradictions and compromises woven deep in the fabric of American life, defying the nation's professed ideals. Gunnar Myrdal called it "an American dilemma" in his timely study for the Carnegie Corporation published early in 1944. Based on five years of fieldwork by the Swedish-born economist and a team of social scientists, the study set "the problem" out in fifteen hundred pages of text, locating its roots in the hearts and minds of white Americans, where prejudice masked the clash between the American creed and a society steeped in structures of racial discrimination and segregation. Much like the founding members of the NAACP, Myrdal's tome implied that since whites were largely responsible for the race problem, they must lead in remedying it. The richly descriptive report exuded a cautious optimism, trusting that by exposing racial conditions in such exhaustive detail, solutions would follow. The experiences of the war years left most black leaders and activists with few illusions about where the impetus for change would come from in postwar America. Black Americans must seize all opportunities to create, in the words of Ralph Ellison, "a democracy in which the Negro is free to define himself for what he is . . . and what he desires to be."[84]

One of the most promising developments of the war years was the emergence of sustained efforts to reclaim the franchise across the South, a movement further stimulated by the NAACP's white primary fight in Texas. On November 12, 1943, Thurgood Marshall, William Hastie, and W.J. Durham argued *Smith v. Allright* before the U.S. Supreme Court. The lower courts had upheld the right of the state Democratic Party to determine its membership and exclude blacks from participating in its primary elections. A 1941 Supreme Court ruling, *United States v. Classic*, provided the underpinning for the argument that Marshall and his colleagues made before the Court in the fourth white primary case heard before that body. In *Classic*, a case that concerned fraudulent practices by election officials in Louisiana, the Court ruled that the primary was an integral part of the election process and therefore the officials were subject to federal sanction. Marshall and his colleagues held that *Smith* raised nearly identical issues. The primary was an integral part of the election machinery in Texas and therefore subject to federal enforcement of the Fifteenth Amendment, barring voter discrimination based on race. Their brief was signed by black attorneys from all parts of the country. The American Civil Liberties Union and the National Lawyers Guild submitted amicus curiae briefs in support of Marshall's argument. Initially, Texas declined to even submit a brief. Speculation that the Court was poised to rule in favor of the NAACP's case may have prompted a belated request by the attorney general of Texas for permission to file a brief. It was granted, and the case was reargued in January 1944.[85]

William Hastie was settling into his seat on an airplane when he opened a newspaper announcing the Court's decision in *Smith v. Allright*. "I just let out one whoop," he recalled, "and if it had not been for the belt I would have gone straight up in the air." On April 3, 1944, the U.S. Supreme Court ruled in an 8-1 decision that the Texas white primary was unconstitutional. The eight justices ruling in favor of Smith were all Roosevelt appointees to the Court; Justice Owen Roberts, author of the *Grovey* ruling, was the sole holdout. The majority held that the *Classic* ruling applied and that the primary was "state action within the meaning of the Fifteenth Amendment." With that, the Court knocked out one of the most effective tools for disenfranchising blacks in Deep South states. The triumph was especially sweet for black Texans, who had raised $11,000 to support the case and exhibited a unity of effort that invigorated the NAACP throughout the state. Plaintiff Lonnie Smith was one in a chorus of voices praising the NAACP, while also acknowledging their white supporters "for the fortitude and perseverance applied to making this a great decision." The two-decade-long struggle, in the words of NAACP attorney J. Alston Atkins, exhibited "the patience, and endurance, and character of the Negro race at its best." But its impact stretched beyond the Lone Star State. "The Texas primary case was the beginning of a complete revolution in our thinking on the right of suffrage," proclaimed Virginia activist Luther P. Jackson.[86]

Democrats in Deep South states promised to blunt the impact of the Court's ruling as Marshall readied the troops for the next stage of the battle. In a memo to all branches in states where the white primary was practiced, Marshall urged them to help get black voters to the polls on primary day and instructed them on how to proceed if they were turned away. South Carolina, where voting-age blacks were in the majority in nearly half of the state's forty-eight counties, led the resistance. Within days of the April 3 ruling, Governor Olin Johnston convened a special session of the state legislature, pledging to do whatever was necessary to ensure that the Democratic Party of the Palmetto State remained a white man's party. The legislators went on to repeal all remaining laws referring to the Democratic Party and primary elections so that the elections would remain completely separate from state regulation. Black Carolinians were prepared to respond. The NAACP leadership in South Carolina had been chomping at the bit to launch their own legal challenge to the white primary, but Marshall had urged them to wait until the Texas case played itself out. Now it was their turn.[87]

In quick response to the governor's action, black newspaper publisher John McCray and Osceola McKaine, a celebrated World War I veteran who led a statewide teacher salary equalization drive, organized the South Carolina Progressive Democratic Party (PDP). While determined to fight in the courts to strike the final blow to the white primary, the PDP wanted to ensure that blacks would be able to participate in all phases of the electoral process in 1944, a presidential election year. The group sent a delegation to the 1944 Democratic convention in Chicago to challenge the seating of the state party's regular delegation, laying South Carolina's defiance in the lap of the national party. John McCray put it bluntly: "[The] national Party is as responsible as the state party for the denial of membership to Negroes in that it tolerates discrimination in the South." Senator Burnett Maybank, a leader of the regular delegation, was equally unequivocal about the implications of the PDP's challenge: "As a Southern Democrat," he proclaimed, "I do not propose to be run out of my Party by either the Negroes, the communists, or Northern agitators . . . it will be my purpose to see that our Party stands where it always has—[for] states rights and white supremacy."[88]

The unprecedented challenge by the all-black delegation was but one sign of a party struggling to hold together a deeply fractured coalition of groups, as the southern bloc pressed to keep the liberal-labor wing of the party in check. Texas also sent two competing delegations to Chicago. After an anti–New Deal faction took over the party machinery, pro-Roosevelt delegates sent their own slate. The credentials committee split the seats between the two Texas groups. Mississippi, Louisiana, and Virginia pledged their delegates to Harry Byrd of Virginia, the standard bearer for anti–New Deal Democrats. Southerners led a fractious fight to unseat Henry Wallace as vice president, and he was replaced on the ticket by compromise candidate Harry Truman. Amid all of this drama, the eighteen-person delegation from South Carolina drew scant attention. The PDP made its case before a special meeting held by the Democratic National Committee. The DNC leaders disqualified the group on a technicality; they had not followed proper procedures for establishing a party and electing delegates. McCray recalled that he and his colleagues took satisfaction in having carried their challenge to Chicago and returned to South Carolina ready to push hard on the voting front.[89]

In South Carolina, the PDP held its own convention, nominated Oseola McKaine for the U.S. Senate, and embarked on a statewide campaign to build their party from the precinct level up. By the end of the summer, the PDP could claim 45,000 members. Working with the state network of NAACP branches, the PDP organized a drive to ensure maximum participation by black voters on election day. McKaine, the first black man to run for statewide office since Reconstruction, challenged Governor Olin Johnston, the Democratic Party's candidate for the U.S. Senate seat vacated by "Cotton Ed" Smith. He campaigned in nearly every county through the fall, linking the developments of the previous decade to the future possibilities within their grasp. The proud history of black Carolinians during Reconstruction was woven through speeches that pointed to the "awakening of progressive forces" stirred by Roosevelt and the New Deal and galvanized during the "Four Freedoms War." The nationalizing influences of the New Deal and the war had penetrated the South, igniting the movement for full citizenship and enlisting white allies. McKaine did not minimize the challenges ahead. The struggle to vote would be "painful, bitter, without glamour . . . a continuing struggle." But if black men and women rejected the idea of being a ruled group, they "must be willing to make every sacrifice necessary to obtain the right to vote."[90]

Fraud, harassment, and the refusal of some polling places to make PDP ballots available on election day diminished the returns for McKaine, who officially tallied 3,214 votes. An irate John McCray wrote Thurgood Marshall: "We have had a hell of a job beating down the fear in these people, in getting their trust and hopes and don't intend to see them come down with their ballot . . . to be robbed, intimidated and frustrated." The PDP and the state NAACP organized the collection of affidavits documenting irregularities and illegal practices during the registration period and general election. Marshall submitted them to the Justice Department along with a brief requesting that criminal action be taken against state election officials in South Carolina. McKaine and McCray challenged the seating of Olin Johnston in the U.S. Senate, charging unfair election practices. The Senate failed to investigate the complaints, and the Justice Department did not bring any charges against South Carolina's election officials. South Carolina would be the primary arena in the NAACP's postwar struggle to secure the full enforcement of *Smith v. Allright* through the courts, as well as a potent spur for boosting South-wide black voter registration and participation.[91]

"Nothing, no nation, will be as it was before when the peace comes. . . . There is no such thing as the status quo," wrote Osceola McKaine.[92] The war had changed American life in ways that could barely be imagined. The service of millions in the armed forces, the uprooting and migration of hundreds of thousands of Americans, and the quickened pace of industrialization and urbanization irrevocably altered the nation's social, economic, and racial map. The massive movement of black southerners to the North and West during the 1940s accelerated a trend that was steadily transforming the nation's racial demographics—one that would continue through the postwar period, marking one of the largest internal migrations in American history. By 1960, half of African Americans would live outside the states that composed the former Confederacy.

The NAACP was well positioned to give shape and voice to black expectations stirred by the war and to lead in the postwar struggle for a democracy that embraced the values and ideals that America trumpeted as a newly dominant world power. By the summer of 1944, the association had topped three hundred thousand members, marking an sixfold increase in just four years.

Beyond providing a critical infusion of funds, the broadening expanse of branches tapped into a new generation of leadership at the base, cultivated by Ella Baker, who became director of branches in 1943. The legal campaign under Thurgood Marshall gave tangible form to the fight against racial discrimination and segregation, with cases in housing, employment, and transportation as well as education rising up from the branches as the war wound down. Marshall's active presence in the field helped reinforce the bonds that connected a national program to the broad and shifting expanse of black life. During 1944 alone, he traveled more than 42,000 miles.[93]

The intersection of race and politics, domestically and globally, held the greatest challenges and opportunities for the NAACP and the movement it had come to represent. Wartime experiences had given rise to "the sharpest cleavage of thinking on the race question in the history of the country." The NAACP's national leadership worked to turn such clarity to its advantage, as liberals and progressives sought to revive the democratic activism of New Deal reform and build a peace anchored in the principles of self-determination and human rights. Following upon the heels of the NAACP's "most active and successful year in the association's history," Walter White cautioned that "heartaches, problems, and hard work" lay ahead. "But," he confidently predicted, "also there lies . . . greater strength out of which will come inevitable greater victories."[94]

8

Justice Now:
Claiming the Postwar Moment

On a Sunday afternoon in July more than thirty thousand people gathered in Chicago's Washington Park for the closing meeting of the NAACP's 1944 annual convention. Fresh from a tour of the battlefields of Europe and North Africa, Walter White addressed the crowd and amplified the militant tone of the wartime gathering. With victory over Germany and Japan in sight, White turned attention to the forces vying to shape the postwar world. He warned of the persistent "racial greed and intransigence" mirrored in the efforts of Britain and France to maintain their colonial empires and of America's unwavering color line—in defiance of the democratic ideals that infused the Allies' cause. As a consequence of the war, black America's struggles had gained international resonance. "Ours is not a lone voice," he assured his listeners. Hundreds of millions in India, Asia, Africa, South America, and the Caribbean were resisting the imposition of the "old order" of imperialism and colonialism, and the "certainty of 'white supremacy,'" and striving to secure and enjoy the "Four Freedoms" trumpeted by the Allied nations. The war revealed that race was "a global question that must be faced and solved."[1]

With the end of the war near and the presidential election just months away, political battles loomed. White blasted the tepid civil rights platform adopted by the Republican National Convention as "weasel worded" and served up a warning to Democrats who would convene in Chicago a week later. Responding to rumors that South Carolinian James Byrnes was favored to replace vice president Henry Wallace on the ticket, White promised that if a southerner was nominated for vice president, the Democrats "can kiss the Negro vote goodbye." The days when northern Democrats could safely cut deals with southern reactionaries while using the Negro vote as "the vanishing pea in a political shell game" were fast receding. By 1944, the wave of wartime migration had pumped up black voting rolls in the North to 2.5 million voters, providing the black electorate with a potential balance of power in seventeen northern states. The challenge and the opportunity lay in leveraging that vote to support candidates who "by words and deeds" demonstrated their commitment to the full citizenship rights of "thirteen million Negroes and to better the lot of all disadvantaged people." Commenting on the oft-repeated threats of revolt coming from the party's southern wing, White declared that "perhaps democracy in America can be saved only by letting the rebels secede until the South is ready to obey the constitution and the laws of human decency."

The massive gathering capped what Thurgood Marshall called "one of the most important conventions we have ever held." Six hundred delegates from forty-two states, including every southern state, attended the NAACP's thirty-fifth annual conference, held at Chicago's Metropolitan Community Church. The yearly meeting had become formative in the development of the NAACP, bringing together men and women from all regions and fusing their disparate efforts into a united movement. For Marshall and other members of the national staff, the annual conference was a prime forum for testing, shaping, and articulating strategies. This concentrated gathering of the faithful magnified the power and meaning of what often felt like isolated struggles. Over a stretch of five days, in plenary sessions, small groups, and informal conversations, conference participants discussed a broad array of issues and concerns relating to employment, labor unions, housing, soldiers and veterans, voting, education, political action, criminal justice, and terrorism, setting the foundation for a crowded postwar agenda. The unifying thread, noted the *Chicago Defender*, was a "militant determination" to carry the fight for full citizenship "to the grass roots of America."[2]

The NAACP emerged from the war primed to lead an assault on the color line and ready to advance its inclusive democratic vision in the dynamic environment of the early postwar years. An explosive growth in membership during the war lifted the association toward the half million mark; for the first time in its history the organization boasted a healthy income. The surge in resources, both human and financial, supported efforts to mobilize blacks and their allies along two major fronts. The ground campaign was the engine of the NAACP movement, organized through the legal program and the branches. As the war wound down, Thurgood Marshall expanded his legal staff and prepared to mount a battle against racial barriers. Ella Baker launched a leadership training program for the branches in 1944, aiming to give form and direction to the growth of the war years while cultivating the "life line" of the NAACP. Complementing the work of Baker and the field staff was Ruby Hurley, who joined the organization in 1943 as the new director of the youth program. Hurley pursued a campaign to enlist young people in the NAACP, an area that had received only sporadic attention in the past.

In the parallel realm of national politics, a growing black electorate aided Walter White in his claim to a place in shaping America's postwar agenda. In a series of legislative battles during the war, White found common ground with labor and liberal groups uninhibited by the racially cautious politics of more tradition-bound Democrats. The NAACP, progressive southerners, labor groups, and New Deal activists joined behind legislation barring the poll tax in federal elections, the first major congressional effort since the 1890s to expand federal protection of voting rights in the South. With strong labor support, the anti–poll tax bill provided a platform for building an interracial coalition committed to an unrestricted vote as a fundamental democratic right. The poll tax disenfranchised more poor and working-class southern whites than blacks, who faced a range of voter restrictions. Southern Democrats led a fierce opposition, raising the shield of states' rights and painting any federal tampering with voting practices as a ploy to enfranchise blacks. Filibusters in the Senate defeated a succession of anti–poll tax bills that passed the House. These same forces went head to head in a battle around the Green-Lucas bill providing for a federally administered program that would enable soldiers overseas to vote in the 1944 presidential election. Mississippi's Senator James Eastland tagged this effort as a grab for Reconstruction-like powers by "power-crazed bureaucrats." He derailed the bill with an alternate one establishing an ineffectual state-run version of the program. The NAACP's defeat of the white primary in the courts in 1944 marked a singular victory in an intensifying struggle to expand voter participation in the South and counter the power of anti-labor, anti–New Deal Southern Democrats.[3]

During the latter years of the war, labor, liberal, and civil rights groups revived the fight for an expanded agenda of New Deal reform. The CIO-Political Action Committee came on the scene in the summer of 1943 and galvanized this effort. Roosevelt's 1944 State of the Union message the following January, calling for an "Economic Bill of Rights," raised the flag of reform and provided a platform. The right to a job, decent housing, a good education, and adequate health care "regardless of station, race or creed," Roosevelt insisted, was fundamental to the rights of citizenship. The CIO-PAC worked to give political heft to these sentiments, taking the fight beyond Capitol Hill, where Southern Democrats could easily paralyze the legislative process, and launching an aggressive program of voter education and registration in the lead-up to the 1944 elections. Relying on a national network of unions and coordinating with liberal, progressive, and civil rights groups, the CIO-PAC's program was backed by "money, brains and an army of willing workers." They developed new techniques of voter education and electioneering, with special tactical approaches to reach women, black voters, and ethnic groups, and coordinated with the NAACP and other groups already working in the South. One of the PAC's unique features, according to the *Chicago Defender*, was "its integration of Negroes" into its organization. The *New York Times* marveled at the upstart movement, unmatched for its "cleverness, effectiveness, and volume." The CIO-PAC helped cohere a loose coalition of forces and energize a full-fledged movement to shape the future course of the Democratic Party in the immediate postwar years.[4]

The 1944 Democratic convention was the site of first major battle over the future direction of the party, and it centered on the vice presidential nomination. Vice president Henry Wallace had kept the spirit and vision of New Deal reform alive during the war and had come to represent its future as much if not more than FDR. Looking toward the postwar world in "The Price of Free World Victory," a 1942 speech, Wallace internationalized the values that shaped his New Deal philosophy and called upon America to lead in advancing economic and human rights on an international scale. He was among a handful of national political figures who demonstrated a genuine concern about racial segregation and discrimination and incorporated the struggle for racial justice as central to the future of American democracy. His challenge to Southern Democrats was on full display at the 1944 convention in a speech seconding the nomination of Roosevelt. He told delegates that the Democratic Party must be a liberal party; Republicans had the best conservative brains and the wealthiest corporate supporters. Liberalism, he explained, was an affirmative philosophy, based on both "political democracy and economic democracy regardless of race, color or religion." Taking direct aim at southern conservatives, Wallace insisted, "The poll tax must go. Equal educational opportunities must come. The future must bring equal wages without regard to sex or race." Several southern delegates walked out during the speech in protest.[5]

In the end, despite Wallace's overwhelming support from core Democratic Party groups, FDR yielded to the pressure of southerners and party bosses and ousted him for compromise candidate Harry Truman, senator from Missouri. The black press and civil rights leaders joined a chorus of protest, with the *Pittsburgh Courier* announcing, "Democrats Sell Race, Wallace to Buy South." Charles Houston protested the way the Democrats "ditched" Wallace, saying that he represented "the progressive position colored people must support." Walter White took small consolation from the fact that James Byrnes did not find a place on the presidential ticket but was disgusted by the way in which Wallace and his supporters were sidelined. Yet the struggle around the Wallace nomination and Wallace's strong showing helped solidify the alliance between the NAACP and the CIO-PAC and other liberal and progressive groups. They would work to develop their strength as an independent force within the Democratic Party while expanding voter registration efforts among their various constituencies, in preparation for future battles.[6]

The NAACP's work with labor and progressive groups to build a strong, racially inclusive political movement overlapped with another major arena of activism that emerged as the war drew to an end, one that was highlighted in White's comments at the mass meeting in Chicago. In linking the struggles of black Americans to anticolonial movements in Africa and Asia, he tapped into an understanding that had gained deep resonance in black popular culture and political thought during the war. The contested meaning of the war was reflected in the Atlantic Charter, the 1941 manifesto of Allied war aims, which proclaimed the right of all people to self-determination. Winston Churchill insisted that it did not apply to colonial subjects while Roosevelt held that it should have universal application—framing a debate that the black press fully engaged during the war. India's demand for immediate independence early in the war and Britain's harsh crackdown on dissidents energized this discussion, focusing attention on Mahatma Gandhi and his uncompromising leadership. The upheavals of the war, the defeat of fascism, and the disruption of European hegemony, poet Langston Hughes observed, exposed "the unmitigated gall of white supremacy around the world." Anticolonial movements on the African continent resonated deeply with black Americans, reinforcing a shared experience of racism rooted in slavery, imperialism, and exploitation. The black press featured prominent coverage and commentary on developments in Africa, helping to forge a common identity with anticolonial movements in a global struggle for freedom. In this fluid terrain, historian Penny von Eschen explains, "Black civil rights activists and anti-colonial activists . . . created a black popular front," one that was "crafted by the left" but embraced "the full range of African American liberals, church leaders, and middle class organizations." The Council on African Affairs and the NAACP both played pivotal roles in giving cohesion and voice to the "new internationalism" that invigorated black thought, politics, and activism in the postwar era.[7]

White wanted to ensure that the NAACP would lead in representing black Americans and the demands of the anticolonial movements in the major forums dedicated to postwar planning—and concluded that W. E. B. Du Bois was essential in achieving this aim. He was willing to overlook a history of personal conflict because, in his estimation, Du Bois knew more than "any other living human being" about the global "problems facing colored peoples." As a result, the seventy-five-year-old Du Bois, recently pushed into retirement by Atlanta University, assumed the position of director of special research in the summer of 1944, setting a pace that "astonished the secretary and the board of directors." Over the several months, he pursued plans for a Pan-African conference in Europe, sponsored a meeting of representatives of anticolonial organizations in New York, prepared for what would be the founding meeting of the United Nations in April 1945, and secured a place for the NAACP as a consultant to the U. S. delegation. Seasoned by a lifetime of struggle and disappointment, Du Bois saw a historical moment of immense urgency and promise. "In this war more than the last," he wrote in *Color and Democracy*, "we face the problem of democracy. How far are we working for a world where the peoples who are ruled are going to have effective voice in their governments?" This question applied as much to the status of blacks in the southern United States as to the colonial subjects of European nations.[8]

The convergence of the labor, progressive, and civil rights activism of the 1930s with the rise of anticolonial movements and the widespread dislocation and political upheaval generated by the war fostered a "politics in the making," in the words of Von Eschen.[9] This loosely coordinated movement, claiming the high rhetoric of the Allied war aims, was dedicated to advancing economic and human rights on a national and global scale. As a participant, the NAACP found a vastly expanded terrain for elevating the challenge to the color line and pressing its demands that the federal government protect and enforce the rights of black citizens. Race was at the nexus of America's burgeoning position as the world's leading democracy, a claim that was diminished by its tolerance of racial discrimination, legally mandated segregation, and widespread political repression in the South. This glaring contradiction provided another window onto the nation's compromise of core democratic values, and a potentially critical lever in the efforts of the NAACP to make civil rights an issue of national and international consequence.[10]

After thirty-five years, the NAACP remained a lean and flexible operation. At the end of the war, it relied on the leadership of a small, eclectic, and talented group of individuals nationally—Walter White, Thurgood Marshall, Ella Baker, Roy Wilkins, and W. E. B. Du Bois—a network of leaders and lawyers in communities across the country, and the activism and support of a growing membership base. Branch work, the legal campaign, and lobbying in Washington continued to structure the work of the association around its defining goals: to end racial discrimination and secure full citizenship for black Americans. The simplicity of these aims and the stark reality of racial segregation and inequality created a unity of purpose that could bridge political and personal differences. There was no clear path through the mire of American racism. With its high profile, broad reach, and improvisational approach, however, the NAACP was positioned to explore the possibilities created by the war while continuing to orchestrate a targeted battle against the racial caste system.

"The main problem we had at the NAACP" after the war, recalled Roy Wilkins, "was coping with success and booming growth." Memberships flooded in from all parts of the country, spurred by worsening racial conditions and rising expectations, often without the intermediary of a field-worker. An expanded legal campaign and program of fieldwork were major avenues for connecting the program of the NAACP with this vast membership base and a racial geography that had been dramatically altered by the war. The war had accelerated trends—migration, urbanization, and industrialization—that steadily nationalized the race problem while enhancing the power of the black vote. Field-workers, along with Thurgood Marshall's team of attorneys, navigated this terrain with an eye toward organizing growing black resistance to the varied manifestations of racial segregation around a broad-based national movement. The struggle for civil rights took on a decidedly southern cast even as racial discrimination became more deeply entrenched beyond the South in the postwar years.[11]

An urgent effort to stem the spread of racial discrimination and violence in the North had led to the founding of the NAACP in 1909. In the intervening decades, the steady growth of black populations in northern cities met with a hardening of segregated patterns in all areas of life and growing racial tensions, conditions that became even more pronounced with the acceleration of black migration during and after World War II. Cities in the Northeast and Midwest saw a significant growth in their black populations during the 1940s, up 50 percent in Philadelphia, 62 percent in New York, 76 percent in Cleveland, 80 percent in Chicago, and 100 percent in Detroit. The West Coast experienced even more dramatic increases, ranging from 168 percent in Los Angeles to 798 percent in the Oakland–San Francisco area. In Las Vegas, the black population grew from 178 to 2,888. In cities across the nation, municipal policies, restrictive covenants, federal mortgage programs, white civic groups, and well-honed "traditions" conspired to reinforce racial divisions, confining blacks to overcrowded neighborhoods and segregated schools. Despite some gains on the employment front, blacks were still largely excluded from skilled jobs, and they were frequently barred from access to restaurants, hotels, and recreational facilities in many cities, often in violation of local and state civil rights statutes. As the numbers of black voters grew, these urban areas became major centers of black politics and activism in the postwar years and sites of the NAACP's largest branches—with Detroit, Cleveland, Baltimore, and Chicago topping the list.[12]

The South remained "way down under the yoke of white supremacy," as one NAACP official put it. But the fight against Jim Crow had quickened during the war years, and NAACP branches and activity provided a venue for advancing demands for voting rights and racial equality. Teacher salary equalization cases bubbled up in cities across the region while the defeat of the white primary stimulated voter registration efforts in all parts of the South. The South experienced the greatest rate of growth in NAACP membership, and a new generation of leaders invigorated local and statewide movements in the face of unyielding white resistance. They included Harry T. Moore in Florida, the Reverend Ralph Mark Gilbert in Georgia, Leila Bell Michael and Kelly Alexander in North Carolina, A.P. Tureaud in Louisiana, and James Hinton and Modjeska Simkins in South Carolina. Seasoned leaders like Lulu White in Texas, J.M. Tinsley in Virginia, and Charles McPherson and E.D. Nixon in Alabama helped channel the militancy of the war years into NAACP branches. Much as they had after World War I, returning soldiers infused the movement with their determination to exercise the freedoms they had fought for. Medgar Evers, Virgil Collier, and Amzie Moore were among the veterans who gave leadership to the NAACP in Mississippi, laying the foundation for a sustained struggle in that state.[13]

Thurgood Marshall and Ella Baker played complementary roles in the NAACP's ground campaign, helping to engage and define the movement that had escalated in the aftermath of the war. Both shared an understanding that, as Marshall bluntly put it, "the NAACP can move no faster than the individuals who have been discriminated against." They worked from different angles to organize and focus the power of black people to challenge the racially-charged practices and barriers that violated and diminished their rights as citizens. Marshall and his small legal team collaborated with local lawyers and individual communities, chipping away at the foundation of racial inequity and building a movement anchored in locally based struggles. As director of branches, Ella Baker concentrated on helping communities to cultivate leadership and develop a program of action around specific needs and issues. Each approach fostered a civic identity based on constitutionally guaranteed rights, rights that would be secured through individual and collective action directed toward local, state, and federal government.

"We must not be delayed by people who say the time is not ripe.... Persons who deny us our civil rights should be brought to justice now," Marshall told a meeting of branch representatives at the 1944 annual conference in Chicago. The thirty-five-year-old attorney-activist sounded like a field general as he mapped out plans for the postwar civil rights campaign. The legal campaign to secure "full enforcement" of citizenship rights had "just begun to scratch the surface." He enumerated the obstacles they faced: southern officials who defied the law, state and federal government officials "reluctant to protect the rights of Negroes," and a Justice Department that had only recently made very tentative steps toward enforcing civil rights statutes "as they apply to Negroes." Marshall applauded the instances where the Justice Department had prosecuted members of lynch mobs and persons guilty of debt peonage but noted its failure to act in cases involving voter intimidation, such as the notorious Brownsville episode, and in the beating and killing of black soldiers by local police. Even after the NAACP had successfully brought numerous cases challenging the exclusion of blacks from juries in violation of federal law, the Department of Justice had failed to prosecute the officials responsible for routinely excluding blacks from jury lists—an action that would have far greater effect in ending the practice. "Civil rights guaranteed by the federal statutes will never become a reality," Marshall advised, "until the U.S. Department of Justice decides that it represents the entire United States and is not required to fear offending any section of the country which believes that it has the God-given right to be above the laws of the U.S. and

the U.S Supreme Court." It was the responsibility of every American to ensure that the law was fairly applied to all regardless of race or color, Marshall
acknowledged, but "the real job has to be done by the Negro population with
whatever friends of the other races . . . [are] willing to join in."[14]

While black voters in the North were beginning to exert some influence in
local and state politics, electoral politics, by and large, continued to reflect the
prejudice of the white majority and the power of Southern Democrats nationally. In such an environment, existing laws, constitutional guarantees, and
the courts provided a platform for black Americans to articulate their citizenship. Marshall emphasized that it was imperative for all to be "thoroughly
familiar with the rights guaranteed by law in order that they may be in a position to insist that all of their fundamental rights as American citizens be
protected." Eighteen states in the North and West had civil rights statutes on
the books, applying in varying degrees to public accommodations, education,
and employment. Where the statutes were weak, Marshall urged efforts to
strengthen them and where strong, in states like Illinois and New York, to
make every effort to enforce them. The "ever-present problem of segregation"
had grown more acute throughout the North during the war, Marshall observed, particularly in the area of housing. He announced that the NAACP
was preparing for "an all-out legal attack on restrictive covenants," reviving
the fight that had stalled nearly two decades earlier. Commenting on the state
of public housing, he reported on a test case in Detroit challenging the federal
policy of segregation and noted the gross inequities that were "the inevitable
result of 'separate but equal' treatment."

In the South, the *Smith v. Allright* ruling invigorated black voting rights
efforts and broadened the opportunity for demanding that the Justice Department enforce the law. Marshall reported that the "threats of many of the
bigots in the South to disregard the ruling of the Supreme Court of the
United States in the recent Texas primary decision has not intimidated a
single person." Blacks in every state in the Deep South had turned out to vote
in the primary elections in 1944. He explained in some detail the two-track
procedures to be followed when election officials turned a prospective black
voter away. The would-be voter and witnesses should record what happened
in sworn affidavits, submit them to the local U.S. district attorney and demand an investigation, while also sending copies to the NAACP's national
office. Marshall would place the matter before the attorney general of the
United States. While he could not guarantee that the attorney general would
pressure reluctant local U.S. district attorneys to prosecute these cases, "we

can assure you that we will give the Attorney General no rest" until he brings pressure to bear on "these reluctant U.S. attorneys throughout the South." There should be "hundreds of cases of this sort" brought every year "until the election officials discover that it is both wiser and safer to follow United States laws than violate them." Yet there were not nearly enough individuals and groups bringing such cases "and demanding action." It was up to them, Marshall emphasized, "to set the machinery" in motion.[15]

Marshall's vision was matched by his singular ability to rally the base and to draw on a range of talent to plan and mount a campaign at the social frontiers of legal practice. With the association on a stronger financial footing, Marshall hired three full-time attorneys and a part-time legal clerk during 1944 and 1945. Robert L. Carter, a twenty-seven-year-old U.S. Army veteran, joined the staff in November 1944. Carter had attended Lincoln University in Pennsylvania, Howard University Law School, and earned a master's in law at Columbia University. As early as his high school days, he had demonstrated a low tolerance for racial constraints. He was the first one to integrate the swimming pool at East Orange (N.J.) High School after a state court ruling barred segregation in public school facilities, even though he could not swim. A harrowing two years as an officer in the quartermaster corps of the army air force taught him that he was "as vulnerable to destruction . . . as the poorest and most unlettered black person." When William Hastie, his former law school teacher, recommended him for a job at the NAACP, he seized the opportunity. An outstanding legal mind, Carter quickly became the "in-house" intellect, responsible for overseeing the preparation of briefs, thus freeing up Marshall to travel the country "encouraging and counseling branches on how to pursue the fight against discrimination." He would serve as Marshall's second in command for more than a decade.[16]

Franklin Williams, a native New Yorker, found his way to a job on the staff in 1945 through a friend who lived in Marshall's apartment building. A graduate of Lincoln University, Williams had just received his law degree from Fordham, where he served as editor of the law review. He initially took responsibility for military cases. Marian Wynn Perry, a young white graduate of Brooklyn College, had helped draft New York state's fair-employment-practices law and worked on the Constitutional Liberties Committee of the National Lawyers Guild. Marshall recruited her in 1945 to work on labor and housing issues. Constance Baker Motley began a twenty-year-long career with the Legal Defense Fund in the summer of 1945, first as a volunteer then as a legal research assistant while still a student at Columbia University Law

School. Although educated at one of the nation's most prestigious law schools, Motley had never heard of *Plessy v. Ferguson* prior to going to work for the NAACP; civil rights law remained the purview of Howard Law School. Upon arriving at Marshall's shop, she found a large, one-room operation, stacked "full of court martial records [from] . . . black servicemen overseas." The work, she recalled, "was my first inkling that I was going to do something I wanted to with my legal education and my life."[17]

Marshall's team was young, smart, and energetic; it had become the force driving much of the NAACP's work by the end of the war. After the association moved late in 1945 to 20 West Fortieth Street, overlooking Bryant Park and the New York Public Library, the legal office gained a little more breathing room—but not much. Four full-time lawyers, two secretaries, and a part-time research assistant were crowded into two rooms. Despite tight quarters and a grinding regimen, Marshall's buoyant personality, informal style, and unassuming manner fostered a congenial work environment. It also raised eyebrows among senior members of the executive staff. White complained to Marshall about the "casualness" and "patterns of behavior" in the "Inc. Fund offices," commenting that the "use of first names . . . between the executives and secretaries does not seem to me good office practice." Du Bois considered Marshall's "unbuttoned office manners to be outlandishly bad," according to biographer David Levering Lewis.[18]

From this small, concentrated nerve center in New York, Marshall and his staff orchestrated campaigns on several fronts in the midst of the "routine" work that made the NAACP a tangible presence in the lives of blacks throughout the country. As Marshall explained in a letter to branch officers, the expanded legal staff was "in a position to better serve our branches and our members" and cooperate in giving "the Negroes of this country the maximum protection of their constitutional rights." While branches were charged with setting up their own machinery for handling legal cases, they were expected to refer all cases to the national office so that it might serve as a clearinghouse and provide the benefit of the expertise of the national legal staff and the national legal committee. Each year, the national staff advised on somewhere between three hundred and four hundred cases that came up from the branches; many were handled by the association's growing network of lawyers affiliated with branches and state conferences around the country.

At the same time Marshall took the legal campaign to a higher level, accelerating the multifront attack on the edifice of the racial caste system—in schools, transportation, housing, and voting—and gearing up for a frontal challenge to the "fiction of separate but equal." Marshall proved exceptionally adept at tapping and pooling the expertise of the nation's leading legal minds and social science experts in an unfolding exploration of the ways in which the law might be used to end publicly structured racial restrictions and inequities. While the legal campaign took on an increasingly southern focus, the postwar fight against housing segregation in northern cities became the pilot for testing new approaches and developing strategies that would be applied in the parallel fight against educational inequalities in the South.[19]

The ambiguously defined terrain of northern-style segregation was hardly less virulent than the South's Jim Crow system, although it offered a very different kind of challenge, one that had long eluded the grasp of the NAACP. The association's defeat of municipal ordinances setting racial boundaries in the 1917 *Buchanan v. Warley* case failed to reverse the trend toward residential segregation. Housing segregation was at the root of all of "the evils of segregation we face today," Marshall wrote in 1944, and a major source of racial friction and tension. The urban racial divide was promoted and maintained by a combination of forces, but restrictive covenants barring the sale or rental of property to African Americans stood as the most immediate and tangible barrier to black residential mobility. With overcrowding and housing shortages reaching crisis levels at the end of the war, growing numbers of blacks sought opportunities to purchase or rent homes in so-called "restricted" areas. In some instances covenants remained idle, but in many places whites sought to enforce these agreements. By 1945 there were more than twenty covenant suits in Los Angeles, affecting a hundred families; sixteen pending in Chicago, involving fifty families; more than a dozen in Washington, D.C.; and others in cities across the country. Marshall reported that lawyers around the country were "clamoring" for guidance on how to best mount an attack on a practice that had been upheld by the courts for nearly two decades.[20]

Residential segregation was a major issue on the NAACP's postwar program, and a legal challenge offered the most direct avenue of attack. But a strong test case of the legality of restrictive covenants required "a carefully worked out plan of procedure." The law was confused, decisions in several states were in conflict, and lawyers had little success in having restrictive covenants declared invalid. Since 1926, the Supreme Court had declined to hear any further cases regarding restrictive covenants, with the exception of *Hansberry v. Lee* in 1940, which yielded a narrow ruling based on a flawed contract. The first order of business was to undertake a complete study of all of the restrictive covenant decisions to date—a huge task for which Marshall recruited twenty-seven-year-old Spottswood W. Robinson III. Marshall also set about coordinating the experience and knowledge of lawyers who had been fighting the cases and tapping leading legal scholars and social science experts to create an innovative approach capable of challenging set legal doctrine.[21]

Spottswood Robinson was "one of the best, if not the best, students produced by Howard University Law School," Marshall noted, and also one who absorbed the principles that Houston had built the law program around. "The turning point of my life," Robinson, a Richmond native, recalled, "was the day I put my foot in there." At Howard it was "drilled into my head . . . [that] the legal education you are getting is not just for you, it's for everybody." Robinson joined the Howard faculty upon graduation in 1939 and worked closely with Charles Houston on a series of restrictive covenant cases in Washington, D.C. In 1943, he joined Oliver Hill and established a law firm in Richmond, which was the legal outpost of the NAACP in Virginia. Dividing his time between the Richmond practice and Howard Law School, Robinson had a full plate, but he did not hesitate to accept Marshall's assignment. Timing, though, was another matter. Marshall wanted a report in hand by the fall of 1944, writing "this is one of the hottest issues we have and we cannot get started on any of these cases without your brief." The thorough and meticulous Robinson would make no promises, telling Marshall that he would "keep at it until I am satisfied that a good job has been done." By December 1944, Marshall's holiday greeting to Robinson exclaimed: "Where the hell is it? Merry Christmas." A growing caseload commanded Robinson's attention, including a challenge to bus segregation. But he steadily researched and hammered out the three-hundred-page study, completing it in the fall of 1945. The report created a common body of knowledge for lawyers around the country and provided the foundation for an ambitious legal challenge.[22]

In July 1945, while still waiting on Robinson's report, Marshall convened a national meeting of thirty-three lawyers and race relations experts in Chicago to begin charting a path to the U.S. Supreme Court. Charles Houston and William Hastie, core members of the NAACP's legal brain trust, were in attendance. Lawyers currently involved in restrictive covenant cases, in addition to Houston, included Loren Miller of Los Angeles, Willis Graves and Francis Dent from Detroit, and sixty-year-old George L. Vaughn of St. Louis, the son of a former slave who had led the fight against the municipal segregation ordinance in that city in 1917. Robinson's detailed grasp of the problem and Houston's engagement of the latest sociological and legal scholarship helped frame the discussions. The group explored strategies and ideas capable of moving beyond a narrow reading of the law as simple enforcement of a private contract to the consideration of the origins of the practice, its impact on community relations, and the consequences of the court's enforcement of restrictive covenants for black citizens. Houston emphasized the vital importance of creating a forum for "educating the public" and challenging the assumptions of whites, particularly regarding their ideas concerning racial definition. What does it mean to be "white"? At what point is a neighborhood no longer "white"? The philosophy of segregation, Houston explained, should be questioned as often as possible. The two-day-long brainstorming session explored a range of questions concerning legal and political strategies, how to exploit public opinion, what issues to raise, how to determine which cases to select for appeal, how to win in the Supreme Court. Participants developed a fuller comprehension of the problem, and a process of collaboration was initiated that would be critical in developing and fine-tuning a Supreme Court challenge. Four of the lawyers in attendance were already conducting attacks in the three cases—Detroit, St. Louis, and Washington, D.C.—that would ultimately be carried to the Supreme Court.[23]

The challenge to restrictive covenants became a laboratory for applying new legal theory and incorporating sociological and economic data in crafting an attack on racial barriers—this would become a trademark of the NAACP's program. By the 1940s, the scientific basis of racial difference and black inferiority that had been used to justify segregation had been discredited, even as it still lingered in the popular mind. Sociological theory and scholarship emphasized environmental factors as formative in limiting black opportunity and in creating the dismal living conditions of the urban "ghetto." During 1945, articles in two major law reviews argued that state court enforcement of restrictive covenants, by promoting racial segregation, violated the equal protection clause of the Fourteenth Amendment. All of this provided grist for the mill of Marshall and his associates. But their task was nonetheless daunting as they worked to develop strong cases capable of "reshaping the judicial mind" and persuading the U.S. Supreme Court to reverse a legal precedent. Over the next several years, Marshall convened an ongoing series of meetings involving lawyers, social scientists, and some of the best legal minds from the academic community, creating a hothouse of ideas and debate as he orchestrated a collaborative effort. Constance Baker Motley attended several of the weekend meetings in New York. "The argument was so sophisticated and new, it required unusually skillful legal thinkers and analysts," she later wrote. "To hear Houston, Marshall . . . and others debate and develop new theory provided me with an amazing legal education."[24]

Schools and education also dominated the NAACP's agenda. While the legal program had begun laying the groundwork for a challenge to educational inequality in the South during the previous decade, the problem of northern school segregation festered. Marshall warned that "the encroachment of segregation in the school system in Ohio and other states is challenging the whole program of the NAACP." School segregation in the North was a product of numerous factors. Increasingly, in large urban areas, residential segregation fostered segregated school patterns, yet policy makers often gerrymandered district lines and used other tactics geared toward ensuring racial separation. In many smaller towns in the North, school districts had established separate schools, regardless of whether or not they violated state civil rights laws. Strategies for eliminating segregation depended upon the local situation and the willingness of black communities to take the lead in exposing the problem, petitioning for redress, and participating in a legal challenge in places where the law had clearly been violated.[25]

The NAACP's national office supported an extensive campaign against northern school segregation; in 1947 Marshall publicly announced that the NAACP would devote significant resources to this effort. Favorable state civil rights laws and black political power provided critical levers. The main challenge was to enlist branches in organizing blacks to demand the right of their children to attend school on a nondiscriminatory basis. Over the next several years, NAACP branches led successful efforts to eliminate formally segregated schools in the North and Midwest—through petitions, boycotts, litigation, and political pressure. In New Jersey and Illinois, the legislatures enacted laws providing for the withholding of funds from schools that excluded blacks, a policy that was effective in helping to eliminate the vestiges of explicitly segregationist school arrangements. Such schools existed primarily in small towns and rural areas. These efforts had little effect in stemming the growth of school segregation in large urban areas, where it appeared to be largely a function of segregated housing patterns and, therefore, beyond legal challenge. School boards in urban areas, however, played an active if more subtle role in promoting racial segregation through the drawing of school district lines, the placement of new schools, and student transfer policies.[26]

The intensity and clarity of the black-white divide in the South offered a bold contrast to the North's more cancerous brand of racial inequity and made it more vulnerable to challenge. By the end of the war, cracks had begun to appear in Jim Crow's armor. Struggles along the color line had escalated during the war as black southerners and soldiers stationed in the region resisted segregation's indignities and sought to exercise their rights—in public spaces, at the voting booth, through the courts. At the same time, scattered biracial efforts to advance labor rights and political participation in the region departed from the old interracial movement that grew up after World War I, centered in the Commission on Interracial Cooperation and its successor organization, the Southern Regional Council. Through the 1940s, the SRC remained dedicated to improving race relations within the confines of segregation. The nationalizing forces of the New Deal, union organizing efforts, and the drive to democratize southern politics created common ground for black and white southerners and loosened the hold of the caste system on a new generation of reformers. In efforts to advance political and economic democracy in the region, organizations like the Southern Conference for Human Welfare, Highlander Folk School, the CIO-Political Action Committee, and various unions worked to undermine the segregation system. They became important allies of the NAACP in the postwar era.[27]

While the struggle for civil rights in the South broadened its base of support, the NAACP played a unique role as a national organization with roots throughout the region. On a fundamental level, the NAACP provided southern blacks with means for seeking redress. After white men murdered the Reverend Isaac Simmons in Amite County, Mississippi, early in 1944 when he refused to give up title to 220 acres of land rumored to have oil, his son appealed to the NAACP. Thurgood Marshall contacted the governor of the state and the Justice Department regarding Simmons's murder, helping to secure the indictment of six men involved in the crime. None were found guilty. Early in 1945, the Memphis branch was energized around a successful fight to obtain the indictment of two police officers charged with raping two black women. The officers were ultimately acquitted, but, as historian Laurie Green writes, African Americans packed the courtroom and made it a public sphere in which "the politics of race could be contested by black Memphians, albeit under circumscribed circumstances." There had been countless cases where local NAACP branches mounted a defense of black men unjustly accused of crimes or were victims of forced police confessions or convicted by juries from which blacks had been systematically barred. The NAACP's prominent role in defending soldiers during the war further enhanced its reputation as a defender of black rights.[28]

During the latter war years, local and statewide NAACP leadership, in concert with Ella Baker and Thurgood Marshall, laid the groundwork for a challenge to the assumptions and practices of the Jim Crow system. The fight for the equalization of teachers' salaries engaged a major segment of the black population in the campaign for fair wages and equal education—by 1943, salary equalization cases were pending in eleven southern states. In July 1944, the arrest of Irene Morgan in Saluda, Virginia, for refusing to give up her seat on a Greyhound bus traveling to Baltimore, Maryland, provided the NAACP with "one of the clearest cases ever presented . . . to test the Jim Crow traveling laws of the southern states" as they applied to interstate transportation. Later that year, the Supreme Court's ruling overturning the all-white primary issued a major blow to Jim Crow and galvanized widespread activism around voting registration and political participation. Within this climate, NAACP branches proliferated, coalescing into statewide organizations in support of a civil rights agenda. Following on the heels of Virginia, Texas, and South Carolina, branches in Florida, Louisiana, Georgia, North Carolina, and Alabama all established state conferences during the war; Mississippi established a state conference in 1946. This loose organizational infrastructure provided the foundation for a south-wide movement, one which went far toward framing civil rights as a national issue in the postwar period.[29]

Harry T. Moore, a Florida schoolteacher, was among the leaders who emerged in the South during the war years. In 1937, while president of the Brevard County NAACP branch, the thirty-two-year-old Moore helped organize a teacher salary equalization suit. A quiet man with a scholarly bearing, he became a dedicated organizer for the NAACP, taking to heart Thurgood Marshall's admonition that "this is not a single battle but a real war." In 1941, the nine branches in Florida joined in establishing a state conference of branches and elected Moore president. Over the next several years, Moore traveled the state, helping to organize branches around a range of issues—employment discrimination in war industries, voting rights, criminal justice cases, racial violence, and teachers' pay. Moore was in frequent correspondence with Ella Baker and reflected her approach to organizing. He invested considerable effort in small towns, where he confronted two major challenges: "an uneducated citizenry" who felt that "this is a white man's country" and "a leadership problem." Many schoolteachers feared that any involvement with the NAACP would cost them their jobs. As for the ministers, some were not well informed, others were "afraid of the NAACP," and there were those who "always put self ahead of the general welfare of the people." But they were "the key to this situation," according to Moore, and he used personal interviews and private conversations "to get our ministers trained to a higher appreciation of the NAACP and its work." Voter registration and voting rights became central to Moore's organizing efforts after the demise of the white primary. In 1946, the Brevard County school board fired Moore and his wife, Harriette, also a teacher. The NAACP placed Moore on salary as a full-time state organizer. That year, the number of branches in Florida reached fifty-two and nearly half of the membership was concentrated in rural areas.[30]

The growth of the NAACP in other southern states during the war and immediate postwar period followed a similar pattern. In neighboring Georgia, the Reverend Ralph Mark Gilbert transformed a flagging organization into a vibrant statewide presence. After arriving in Savannah from Detroit in 1942 to pastor the First African Baptist Church, the dynamic preacher immediately set about reviving the branch in that city. Ella Baker marveled at the membership drive Gilbert coordinated, enlisting five hundred workers to canvass door-to-door. He cultivated the support of other organizations, emphasized mass community involvement, and actively recruited young people; by 1943, Savannah, Georgia, claimed the largest youth council in the nation. Within six months of securing a new charter for Savannah, Gilbert convened representatives from the other five existing branches around the state to organize a statewide conference of branches, with the goal of "making the NAACP articulate on matters affecting the Negroes of the state of Georgia." Gilbert's organizing work was complemented by the expertise of Atlanta's black elite, notably attorney A. T. Walden, who worked closely with Marshall. Reporting on his attendance of a statewide NAACP meeting in Atlanta early in 1945, Marshall exclaimed, "The meeting here was better than good. These people are not kidding—they are doing a job." By 1946, there were fifty-one branches in the state conference, totaling 13,595 members, and Gilbert served as president.[31]

As director of branches since July 1943, Ella Baker was able to implement her vision for the association during its most dynamic period. She was the highest-ranking female on the national staff and oversaw a team of four field organizers. In preparing for a nationwide membership drive in 1944, Baker instructed her associates that the "aim of raising money be properly placed in the background of an all-out mass offensive against discrimination, injustice, and undemocratic practices." Her approach complemented Marshall's own effort to anchor the NAACP in strong, democratic, action-oriented branches which, in her words, should serve as "centers of sustained and dynamic community leadership." Baker promoted organizational structures designed to support local leaders, strengthen their connections within individual states and regions, and integrate them more fully into the national program of the association. She was a catalyst behind the establishment of state conferences, advocated hiring paid executive secretaries for larger branches, and advocated the appointment of regional organizers to work on a continuous basis with local and state leaders. In 1944 she initiated a series of regional leadership training conferences that brought branch leaders in adjoining states together with national staff members, including Thurgood Marshall and Leslie Perry, administrative director of the Washington bureau, to share experiences and strategies and discuss the NAACP's legal and legislative initiatives. Over the next two years, leadership training conferences were held in every part of the nation.[32]

The surge in black political activism in the aftermath of the white primary ruling bolstered the NAACP's organizing efforts in the South, energized efforts by liberal and labor groups to democratize southern politics, and illustrated the interface between litigation and the burgeoning civil rights movement. "Once the Supreme Court opened the door in 1944," noted Palmer Weber of the CIO-Political Action Committee, "the NAACP charged into the whole registration and voting area very hard." The NAACP branch in Birmingham, Alabama, organized a coalition of labor and civic groups in support of a major voter registration drive in that city. In Montgomery, NAACP branch president and union leader E. D. Nixon led 750 citizens to the courthouse to register to vote. The Tuskegee Civic Association in black majority Macon County worked closely with NAACP lawyers in one of the most sustained voting rights campaigns in the South. In North Carolina, the NAACP state conference worked with the CIO-PAC in coordinating a statewide program of citizenship schools to instruct blacks on the mechanics of voting and the "intelligent use of the ballot." Georgia's state conference included workshops on voter registration in rural areas at its annual meetings. Throughout Louisiana, NAACP branches became centers of voter education and organizing activity. State field organizer Daniel Byrd reported that heavy rain and flooding in Hymel, Louisiana, did not deter instructors who had traveled from New Orleans. They "put on hip boots and waded through the water and mud to reach the place set aside for registration classes. More than fifty men and women pulled off their shoes, socks, and stockings . . . and waded in water twelve inches deep in order to learn how to fill out their registration forms." In their efforts to vote, black southerners joined a growing postwar movement to challenge the dominance of the segregationist, anti-labor, antidemocratic Southern Democrats. With the ballot, Harry Moore predicted, "we shall be well on our way to solving some of the most serious problems that have faced us during the past fifty years."[33]

Voting rights gave form, direction, and visibility to the civil rights struggle in the South after 1944. As blacks turned out across the region in record numbers to register and vote, Marshall and a network of NAACP lawyers were prepared to meet efforts by state and local officials to obstruct and deny blacks access to the ballot. South Carolina was joined by Georgia, Alabama, and Florida in efforts to stonewall the implementation of the Supreme Court's white primary ruling, eliciting new legal challenges in each of those states to compel compliance with the law. With the certain demise of the white primary, southern election officials turned their attention to devising schemes for barring blacks from registering. Registrars employed a range of tactics to turn away prospective black voters—arbitrary rules, shortened hours of operation, outright refusals—and states experimented with new laws to maintain a lock on the ballot box, placing the burden on blacks to protest or bring suit. The NAACP inundated the Justice Department with affadavits documenting obstruction by local officials, but the department avoided taking any action that was likely to invite a swift backlash from powerful Southern Democrats. Marshall prepared for the long haul, noting that all signs indicated the NAACP would be involved in legal action against "officers in various localities to ensure Negroes in the South the right to vote" for some years to come. Meanwhile, widespread efforts by black southerners to participate in the political process, backed up by the NAACP and other groups, drove up the number of registered black voters in the year leading up to the 1946 primary elections.[34]

The struggle around voting eclipsed efforts to revive the campaign for equal educational opportunities, which had stalled during the war. Education would be a major item in postwar planning by the individual states, and Marshall warned that unless they moved fast, the policy of discrimination would become more deeply entrenched. In June 1945, he instructed NAACP leaders in the South to survey conditions in their states and map out a program of legal action—in the areas of graduate training, equal school terms, equal schools, and bus transportation for black students. Texas was the only state to demonstrate interest in pushing forward on this front. Exasperated, Marshall exclaimed in a staff meeting that all that was needed was one parent and one child to take a complaint to court. But, unlike voting or even teachers' pay, the uncertain return of school equalization suits, particularly in light of the exposure and risk involved, made recruiting plaintiffs difficult. Over the next year, Marshall refined his thinking on the issue of public education in the South, convened a major meeting of southern NAACP lawyers to coordinate strategies, and began floating plans for a direct attack on segregation, while working to enlist active branch involvement in the education fight.[35]

Franklin Roosevelt's death on April 12, 1945, on the eve of the war's end in Europe, sharpened the divide between the past and the future. On balance, Roosevelt's civil rights record seemed more promise than substance. However, he dramatically altered the direction, reach, and tone of government, promoting it as a tool for advancing the economic security and welfare of all citizens, in ways that implicitly defied racial discrimination. In his notably positive assessment of FDR, Du Bois emphasized that he had created a Supreme Court that embodied his philosophy about government and that he had "given the Negro a kind of recognition in political life which the Negro had never received." The historic crossover of black voters into the Democratic Party in response to FDR's initiatives helped transform a party long identified with the South into a primary arena in the fight for civil rights. Roosevelt's dominating personality and broad appeal barely maintained a veneer of party unity, often at the price of yielding to powerful Southern Democrats. But as he looked beyond the war, he seemed poised to revive and expand the progressive thrust of the New Deal, with the "Economic Bill of Rights" serving as the foundation of his postwar agenda. Moreover, Roosevelt's stated, if ambiguous, commitment to the independence of the European colonies, was embraced by black, labor, and progressive groups working to ensure that human rights and self-determination were central elements in securing the peace.[36]

The founding meeting of the United Nations convened in San Francisco less than two weeks after Harry Truman assumed the presidency. Du Bois and White had secured a place for the NAACP among the forty-two organizations invited by the State Department to attend the meeting as consultants to the U.S. delegation. Mary McLeod Bethune joined them as part of the NAACP group. They met with representatives from African and Asian nations and found delegates from China and the Soviet Union sympathetic to the cause of racial equality and anti-imperialism. In a heady atmosphere of multiracial participants and cross-cultural exchange, the NAACP contingent participated in the crafting of a human rights agenda that prioritized race discrimination and an end to colonialism, an approach that met stiff resistance from the United States.

The U. S. delegation aligned with Britain and France in securing a trusteeship plan that neglected any provision for future colonial independence, a position viewed by Du Bois and his associates as a betrayal of FDR's legacy. The power of southerners in the U. S. Senate reinforced a determined effort on the part of the U. S. delegation to block discussion of America's racial practices and guard against provisions that would compromise the nation's sovereignty in this area. Senator Tom Connolly of Texas, powerful head of the Senate Foreign Relations Committee, was a leading member of the delegation. John Foster Dulles, another member of the delegation, expressed concern that any human rights and nondiscrimination provisions would draw attention "to the Negro problem in the South."[37]

While Du Bois pursued the international aspects of race and colonialism, White concentrated on domestic politics. The NAACP's Washington bureau had institutionalized the association's presence in the nation's capital during the war. The staff expanded to include a director of veterans' affairs in 1945 and a secretary of labor a year later in addition to administrative director Leslie Perry, a Washington attorney. White remained the dominant figure; the bureau was the staging ground for his effort to leverage the power of the black vote and strengthen the association's role as a major participant in the liberal-labor wing of the Democratic Party. The power and dominance of Southern Democrats, bolstered by seniority and Senate rules, reinforced the bonds that united the New Deal coalition and framed the struggle over the future of the Democratic Party in the wake of Roosevelt's death. But many liberal Democrats were uneasy allies in the cause of civil rights and anxious to avoid or contain the explosive and divisive issue of race. This was especially true with regard to the "no discrimination" clause that White and Perry sought to attach to the proliferation of postwar programs, in an effort "to prevent the concept of racial segregation from expanding and strengthening its hold on American life." Toward this end, the NAACP found an important ally in Adam Clayton Powell Jr., the first black congressman from New York, elected in 1944.[38]

The work of lobbying for anti–poll tax bills, antilynching legislation, federal aid to education, and a permanent FEPC provided a means for raising awareness, shaping the debate, and building alliances—even as southern dominance of the legislative process dimmed the possibility of success in the near term. The winding down of the war, however, infused the issue of jobs and the future of the FEPC with an urgency that begged for presidential action. During the summer of 1945, as massive layoffs in war-related industries across the country threatened to eliminate the gains black workers had made during the war, Congress slashed the budget of the FEPC in half, crippling its operations. FEPC director Malcolm Ross reported to Truman that an estimated 450,000 blacks would be displaced in manufacturing alone by the end of 1945 and warned that, without remedial action, discrimination would be frozen as an industrial habit. Truman did little to aid the beleaguered agency but indicated that he would support the continuation of the present committee during the reconversion period and endorse a permanent FEPC. In light of these statements, the FEPC prepared to move forward with several pending cases. The case involving the District of Columbia's Capitol Transit Company led to a major showdown between the Truman administration and Charles Houston, then serving on the FEPC.[39]

The Capitol Transit Company had stonewalled efforts by the FEPC to break its racially discriminatory employment practices for three years, refusing to hire blacks for platform jobs as conductors or motormen. By contrast, transit companies in most major cities had cooperated with the FEPC. In Philadelphia, however, white workers struck after eight black motormen were hired in August 1944, shutting down the transit system. President Roosevelt authorized the army to seize control, breaking the strike. This example of strong presidential action undoubtedly stood as a benchmark as the FEPC sought to bring further pressure to bear on the transit system in the nation's capital. When Capitol Transit workers illegally struck in November 1945, the federal government seized the company and supervised its operation, just as the FEPC was completing the preparation of its findings against the carrier. Committee members voted unanimously to issue a directive calling for the hiring of fourteen black applicants for platform positions, unless the president objected. Acting for his fellow commissioners, Houston informed administration officials of the committee's intentions. An assistant to President Truman phoned Houston and ordered him not to issue the directive. When Houston requested the order in writing, the White House stalled. Houston's request for a meeting with the president was denied, and his letter to Truman went unanswered. On December 3, 1945, Houston resigned from the FEPC in a strongly worded letter to President Truman and publicly announced his departure with a press conference, using the occasion to expose Truman's obstruction of the committee's mandate and to mobilize pressure on the administration.[40]

Clarence Mitchell, who had worked as associate director of field operations for the FEPC, praised Houston's bold action. Without the militant fight waged by Houston and the National Council for a Permanent FEPC, "the agency would have been put to sleep with the issuance of some dry reports." Starved of funds, the FEPC expired six months after Houston resigned. Truman's actions and the half-hearted efforts in Congress demonstrated that there was little intention of establishing a strong, permanent FEPC "if it could possibly be avoided." According to Mitchell, "the lesson to be learned" was that "minorities should never exchange immediate possibilities for real progress . . . for promises of future action." Those professing to have "liberal convictions" must be scrutinized to ensure that "the spoken word will be followed by concrete action." After the FEPC closed its doors, Mitchell joined the NAACP's Washington bureau as head of its new Department of Labor, where he continued the battle to put legislative muscle behind an equal employment agenda.[41]

While the NAACP's efforts bogged down in Washington, an escalating contest over the racial contours of life in the South drove the dynamics of postwar civil rights politics. During 1946, a pivotal election year, black southerners, emboldened by wartime experiences and the fall of the white primary, demonstrated an unwavering determination to exercise their rights in the face of a white South prepared to defend and enforce Jim Crow. The sentiments of U.S. Army veteran William Bailey of Bogalusa, Louisiana, spoke for many black soldiers who returned home at war's end: "I know the price I had paid. Why shouldn't I exercise the rights and privileges of citizenship? If I could go there and make a sacrifice with my life . . . I was willing to do it here, if it meant death. Somebody had to make up their mind, and do something about it, if there was to be changes." Black assertiveness and political organizing in communities around the South fueled a siege mentality among whites, exploding in violent outbreaks and state-sponsored repression, and commanding national attention.[42]

A fragile social fabric and the blunt force of southern justice were dramatically revealed in Columbia, Tennessee, where a fistfight between a black man and a white man, both military veterans, set off a chain of events culminating with a police invasion of the black section of town. On February 25, 1946, a dispute over a radio and harsh words between Gladys Stephenson, a black domestic worker, and twenty-eight-year-old Billy Fleming, son of the radio store proprietor, led to a shoving match between Fleming and Stephenson's nineteen-year-old son, navy veteran James Stephenson. The two men spilled through a plate-glass window onto the street, attracting a crowd of whites. Fleming was left with a gash in his leg; the police arrested James Stephenson and his mother. Local black businessmen Julius Blair, seventy-five-year-old soda fountain proprietor, and James Morton, owner of a funeral home, bailed the Stephensons out of jail later that day. By then, a mob of white men had begun gathering in the town square, and there was talk of lynching; there had been two lynchings in the area over the previous two decades. Blair and Morton took James Stephenson to the nearby black community known as "the Bottom" and made hasty arrangements to get him out of town. They warned the sheriff to keep whites from the area. With tensions high, black veterans led preparations to defend the community. Late that night, four policemen, with groups of armed whites following behind, approached the Bottom and failed to heed the command that they halt. Black men fired shots, wounding all four, none seriously. Whites began firing their weapons but hesitated to enter the Bottom, realizing that blacks were armed and ready to fight back. The sheriff, fearing that the situation was beyond his control, called the governor for help.

State highway patrolmen and National Guardsmen poured into the area throughout the night. Early the next morning, while a contingent of Guardsmen held local whites at bay, several hundred highway police launched a pre-dawn raid on the Bottom. Armed with rifles and machine guns, they shot up locks and kicked down doors, ransacked stores and business establishments, destroyed records and furniture, and looted jewelry and cash. "KKK" was scrawled across one of the coffins in Morton's Funeral Home. No businesses were spared. In what Thurgood Marshall described as "true storm-trooper fashion," the police terrorized the community, spraying gunshots into homes, clubbing and beating residents, and arresting more than one hundred people. James Johnson and William Gordon, two of the men arrested, were shot and killed while in police custody. Local radio and press reports echoed the state's official story about what had happened in Columbia, praising law enforcement agents for suppressing an incipient black insurrection.[43]

The state-led assault on blacks in Columbia drew national attention as well as warnings that it was the beginning of a wave of racial violence rivaling that of 1919. A number of organizations, most notably the Nashville-based

Southern Conference for Human Welfare (SCHW), actively publicized the Columbia events and demanded a federal investigation. The NAACP quickly set its machinery in motion and assumed the dominant role. Working through local contacts, the national office had an attorney on the scene within twenty-four hours to arrange bail for those who had been arrested and to secure the right of the NAACP to represent them in court. Walter White flew to Columbia early in March to investigate conditions firsthand; he met with local leaders and with Tennessee governor James McCord. Upon returning to New York he convened a meeting of representatives of labor, civil liberties, and religious groups. It resulted in the establishment of a national committee, headed by Eleanor Roosevelt and Channing Tobias, to publicize the attack on the Bottom, raise funds for the defense of blacks who had been charged, and press for the indictment of the men who vandalized and shot up the black community. The NAACP hired Oliver "Ollie" Harrington, noted political cartoonist for the *Pittsburgh Courier*, to coordinate a campaign throughout its branches—organizing mass rallies, fund-raising efforts, and letter-writing campaigns to Washington.[44]

Petitions and protests poured into the White House, prompting the attorney general to call for a federal grand jury investigation of the raid and the actions of law enforcement officials. The grand jury proceedings offered an eye-opening display of the workings of Jim Crow justice and the reluctance of the Justice Department to do more than go through the motions. Federal judge Elmer Davis tried to turn attention away from what law enforcement officials had done and make the civil rights community itself responsible for the episode. He advised the all-white jury that they interrogate the activities of the SCHW and other outside organizations as they investigated the role of the police on the night of the raid. The first week of the hearings was devoted to testimony from local police, the heads of the state highway patrol and the National Guard, privileging their account of what happened. The local FBI agent testified that he was unable to identify anyone responsible for the destruction of black businesses and property. It was a week before the first black complainants testified; no official of the Justice Department had interviewed these witnesses or helped to prepare them before they appeared in court. Walter White called the proceedings a flat-out "whitewash."[45]

The grand jury exonerated the law enforcement officials and offered a commendation. "The prompt arrival and deployment of state forces," their report concluded, had "prevented a bloody race war." Here, Marshall exclaimed, is the "best example of what happens" when a corrupt political machine runs the state, and "our federal government" picks an "all white grand jury" and has "only white representatives at the hearing" since the Justice Department has no black employees in responsible positions or any black assistant attorneys in Tennessee. White assailed the grand jury's findings as evidence of the "collapse of the federal machinery for justice in Tennessee." The failure of the federal government to secure indictments of the guilty parties, he warned, sent a signal to state officials and Klan elements throughout the South that they could "terrorize the Negro community during the coming primary election without fear of federal interference."[46]

The federal grand jury's report was issued while the grand jury of the Maury County Circuit Court heard evidence against the blacks arrested during the raids. Thurgood Marshall headed the defense team, which included Nashville attorney Alexander Looby, who served on the NAACP's National Legal Committee; Maurice Weaver, a white lawyer from Chattanooga; and Leon Ransom. Marshall commented that he had never seen a community "so hostile to Negroes" as Columbia. The lawyers commuted ninety miles each day between Nashville and Columbia during the course of the court proceedings. An all-white jury indicted twenty-six black men for attempted murder in the first degree and two for assault with intent to kill. The lawyers fought successfully for a change of venue to Lawrenceburg, Tennessee, where the case dragged on through the summer and into the fall.[47]

While the Columbia events unfolded, the determination of white southerners to dictate the terms of race relations in the postwar South faced new challenges. The surge of black voting across the region in the first major election following the fall of the white primary was the most striking development. After the U. S. Fifth Circuit Court of Appeals struck down Georgia's attempts to bar blacks from voting in the Democratic primary early in 1946, South Carolina was the sole holdout in the ultimately futile effort to defy the Supreme Court's ruling in *Smith v. Allright*. Henry Lee Moon, who served as a southern organizer for the CIO-PAC during 1946, described a "concerted south-wide movement" among blacks "to participate actively in the selection of their local, state, and federal officials." The registration of large numbers of new black voters in Jackson, Mississippi, early in 1946 "alarmed" state Democratic leaders, according to one report, blacks arrived at the county tax collector's office in "groups of a dozen to forty," paid their poll tax and then immediately went to apply for registration. County registrars were not prepared to stop young black men, many of them veterans, who "easily passed the questions fired at them concerning the State and Federal constitution."[48]

As one barrier fell, southern officials hurried to devise new techniques to maintain control of the franchise. During the lead up to the primary elections that summer, Marshall argued two major cases in the Fifth Circuit Court of Appeals involving the efforts of registrars to obstruct black voting in Louisiana and Alabama. In these particular cases, *Hall v. Nagel* and *Mitchell v. Wright*, he aimed to establish a procedural mechanism to bypass state courts and take suits against registrars directly to federal court. Beyond the legal principles involved, the process reflected and reinforced a "new ferment" among black southerners. Marshall marveled at the scene in the New Orleans courtroom in April 1946. "Every available seat and every . . . foot of standing room in the back and around the sides of the courtroom was filled," he reported. "The audience was practically all Negroes with the exception of a few lawyers." Classes from Dillard College and the local high school were joined by "people from Alabama and all sections of Louisiana. It was one of the most representative crowds we have yet seen in these cases." A reporter in the crowd commented on the striking impression that Marshall made, "attired neatly in a dark suit and prominent polka dot tie, his unusual height towering above others and his . . . speeches touched off with a sparkling bit of dry, sarcastic humor that he is so well noted for." Victory made it all the sweeter. The judges unanimously overturned the lower courts' decisions requiring that the cases first be brought in state courts. Since the "registrars were acting under the color of state authority . . . to deprive the Negroes . . . of the right to vote," the opinion concluded that the state court could hardly be expected to redress these grievances. Daniel Byrd, executive secretary of the New Orleans branch, hailed the decision as "the turning point of registration in Louisiana."[49]

Ella Baker was in regular contact with branch leaders, reminding them of deadlines for paying the poll tax and the importance of "backing up the legal victories that have been won striking down the white primaries with vigorous registration and voting campaigns." She advised branches to coordinate their voter registration efforts with labor and progressive groups, making special mention of Osceola McKaine, the South Carolina activist who had helped organize the black-led Progressive Democratic Party and was working as a regional field representative for the SCHW. McKaine had distinguished himself, in the words of Henry Moon, as "the most outstanding and effective mentor in the southwide voter registration drive." During the early part of 1946, Baker led leadership training conferences in Jacksonville, Florida, and Tulsa, Oklahoma, where voter education and registration were primary topics of discussion. Rosa Parks, secretary of the Montgomery, Alabama, branch, attended the Jacksonville meeting with E. D. Nixon. Baker impressed Parks as "smart, funny and strong." The two women became close friends.[50]

While pushing hard on the voter registration front and leading the defense in the Columbia, Tennessee, case, Marshall worked to channel the enhanced activism of the postwar moment into a revived and expanded campaign challenging racial discrimination in public school education. In April 1946, he convened a meeting of lawyers from around the region to report on school conditions in their states, share experiences and knowledge, and agree on a plan that would ensure maximum cooperation in "the prosecution of cases to compel complete equalization of school facilities from the university level through . . . elementary school." The group met in Atlanta, Georgia. Attorneys from nearly every southern state attended; Marshall, Robert Carter, Leon Ransom, and Spottswood Robinson represented the national office. The meeting was Robert Carter's first such conference. Years later he recalled the thrill of "sitting around a table with other black men exchanging views about what should and could be done with our legal talent to better the lot of black children."[51]

Marshall was already planning the move toward an all-out attack on school segregation. But another major chink in Jim Crow's armor came five weeks after the Atlanta meeting. On June 3, ruling in *Morgan v. Virginia*, the Supreme Court overturned a Virginia law requiring segregation in interstate transportation. The case began two years earlier. In July 1944, twenty-seven-year-old Irene Morgan was a passenger on a Greyhound bus from Gloucester County, Virginia, to Baltimore, Maryland. When the bus stopped in Saluda, Virginia, the driver asked her to move to the rear of the bus, and she refused. Police arrested her for violating a state segregation statute; she was tried, convicted of a misdemeanor, and fined $10. The NAACP Virginia state conference of branches and the national office represented Morgan in challenging the law. Spottswood Robinson carried the case through the Supreme Court of Virginia, which upheld Morgan's conviction. Marshall and Hastie argued the case before the U. S. Supreme Court in March 1946. In a 7-1 ruling, the Court held that Virginia's law was unconstitutional because it posed an undue burden on interstate commerce. Commenting from Columbia, Tennessee, Marshall hailed the ruling as "a decisive blow to the evil of segregation and all that it stands for." The decision was limited by the fact that it did not prevent private carriers from requiring and enforcing segregation. Nevertheless, *Morgan* opened the way to future challenges and spurred a direct action protest the following year.[52]

The Court's bus ruling and the school equalization campaign pressed at the edges of the South's racial order while the black vote emerged as an immediate challenge. In 1946, for the first time in fifty years, blacks in towns, cities, and rural areas across the South registered in large numbers, in anticipation of the Democratic primary elections that summer. A network of groups and organizations supported their efforts—including NAACP branches, civic leagues, the CIO Political Action Committee, the SCHW and the Birmingham-based Southern Negro Youth Congress. For progressive white southerners and labor activists, black political mobilization was vital to the democratization of southern politics and the defeat of the antilabor, anti–New Deal bloc in Congress.

But appeals to white supremacy dominated the election season, reaching a peak in Mississippi and Georgia. NAACP branches documented individual episodes of voter harassment and fraud and exposed a wave of political terror and violence dedicated to suppressing the black vote. "Do you want a white man's government, or will you take the risk of being governed by Negroes," asked an editorial in the Jackson, Mississippi, *Daily News*, trumpeting the platform of Senator Theodore Bilbo's reelection campaign. The senator instructed "every red-blooded Anglo-Saxon in Mississippi" to do what was necessary to keep blacks from voting. Stumping across the state, he warned that "if you let a handful go to the polls in July there will be two handfuls in 1947, and from there it will grow into a mighty surge." In the lead-up to the primary elections, there were growing reports of registrars refusing to register blacks. After Etoy Fletcher, a veteran, was turned away by the registrar in Rankin County, a group of whites abducted and beat him, promising to kill him if he attempted to register again. The NAACP national office forwarded Fletcher's affidavit to the Justice Department along with other reports of officials refusing to register blacks and insisted on prompt investigations. In light of Senator Bilbo's widely publicized invitation to whites to block blacks from voting on primary day, Walter White "vigorously urged" that there be an FBI agent at every polling booth "to prevent any violation of [the] right of any qualified voter to cast his ballot on account of race or color and to obtain evidence of actual violation of the right to vote."[53]

On July 2 twenty-one-year-old Medgar Evers led a group of fellow World War II veterans to the county courthouse in Decatur, Mississippi, to vote in the Democratic primary election. They were met by "15 or 20 armed white men," men Evers had grown up with. Evers and his friends left and returned with their guns, which they left concealed in their automobiles, and made a second attempt to enter the polling place and were once again turned back by the mob. In Gulfport, Mississippi, V.R. Collier, the president of the local NAACP branch, and his wife, Ernestine, a schoolteacher, were physically assaulted at the polling place. Collier phoned the FBI office in Jackson from the doctor's office while his injuries were being treated, requesting protection to go back and cast his ballot. Collier reported that the agent said, "It is not our job to give protection, only to investigate." He then called the federal district attorney in Jackson, who advised that he call the FBI. "We Negroes are without any protection at all," Collier concluded. In Pass Christian, the three-man electoral board announced that it was a white primary and told blacks that they could vote if they painted their faces white. The NAACP received many reports of violence and intimidation and the voting tallies reflected their effectiveness. Only half of the 5,000 registered black voters cast a ballot; approximately 350,000 blacks were of voting age in Mississippi.[54]

Events in Georgia paralleled those in Mississippi. Eugene Talmadge described the primary election as the last chance to "save Georgia for the white man."[55] In a tight, three-way race for governor, Talmadge faced an electorate that had grown dramatically in the wake of major electoral reforms. Governor Ellis Arnall, hailed as ushering in "a new political way in the South," had ended the poll tax, reduced the minimum voter age to eighteen, and accepted the Supreme Court's final ruling on the white primary as the law. The number of registered voters in Georgia tripled to nearly one million, and black voter registration in Georgia reached an estimated 135,000, a remarkable increase over the roughly 20,000 registered in 1944. The state constitution limited the governor to one term, so Arnall endorsed businessman James Carmichael. All candidates were committed to maintaining segregation, but Talmadge broke from the pack with an aggressively racist campaign, pledging to restore an all-white Democratic primary and welcoming the endorsement of the Ku Klux Klan. Harkening back to the Reconstruction era, Talmadge warned that if blacks voted in primary elections, "our Jim Crow laws are gone, and our pretty white children will be going to school with Negroes." He told blacks to stay away from the polls, while his supporters around the state orchestrated a widespread purge of blacks from the voting rolls. Pressured by the NAACP, the CIO-PAC, and black civic leaders in Atlanta, federal and state officials tried to counter this bold intervention, but with minimal success. There were massive purges in rural areas and reported instances of cross burnings, night riders, and violence; in Taylor County a sign posted on a local black church warned, "The first Negro to vote will never vote again." On July 17 Talmadge failed to win the majority of the popular vote but claimed victory based on a county unit system that favored rural counties.[56]

While commentators speculated on the meaning of Talmadge's election, the aggressive, race-baiting campaign of the victorious candidate reaped a bloody harvest. Maceo Snipes, a World War II veteran who served in the Pacific, voted in the primary in Taylor County. The next day, a group of white men came to his farmhouse and shot him. Snipes's slaying was quickly overshadowed by the execution-style lynching of two couples in Monroe, Georgia, forty miles from Atlanta. Loy Harrison, a prosperous farmer, had posted bond for Roger Malcolm, who had been arrested for stabbing his employer, and was driving Malcolm and his wife, Dorothy, along with George and May Dorsey, back to his farm to work. George Dorsey had just returned from service overseas in the army; Dorothy and May were sisters. According to Harrison, a mob of twenty men ambushed them on a lonely road, and took the two men from the car. After one of the women called the name of a man in the mob, they took the women as well. The four were lined up and shot in a fusillade of bullets; their faces were "scarcely recognizable from the mass of bullet holes." The "Georgia massacre" stunned national opinion. Walter White described the murders as "the inevitable results of Talmadge's and the Ku Klux Klan's advocacy of violation of the laws of the federal government and human decency." Congressman Adam Clayton Powell Jr. called on President Truman to send troops into Georgia to maintain order. Attorney General Tom Clark promised a complete investigation of the murders by the civil rights section of the Justice Department.[57]

The wave of terror in the South consumed the attention of the national office. In mid-July, the NAACP launched a national campaign around the case of Isaac Woodard, an army veteran beaten so severely by the police that he was left blind. The incident occurred on the day that Woodard was discharged from Fort Gordon, Georgia, after four years in the service, including fifteen months of combat in the Pacific where he earned a battle star. Woodard, still in his uniform, was traveling by bus to Winsboro, South Carolina, when he had a verbal disagreement with the bus driver. The driver called in the police at the next stop in Aiken, South Carolina. When Woodard tried to explain what had happened, the police beat him over the head with a billy club, and bludgeoned his eyes. After spending nearly a month in the veterans' hospital in Columbia, South Carolina, Woodard made his way back to his parents' home in New York and sought the aid of the NAACP. White appealed to the War Department to investigate the case and urged the Justice Department to prosecute the responsible parties. While waiting for federal action, White and Oliver Harrington, the NAACP's new public relations director, launched a massive publicity campaign.

The blinded veteran offered compelling evidence of southern lawlessness and appealed to White's talent as a publicist. He and Harrington enlisted Orson Welles, the famous film and radio personality, in the drive to make the Woodard case a national issue and identify the police officers that beat Woodard. For four weeks in succession, Welles devoted his nationally broadcast radio programs to the case, using material provided by NAACP contacts in South Carolina. The NAACP sponsored several tours by Woodard; branches staged mass meetings to publicize the case, raised money, and sent petitions to the White House demanding an FBI investigation. Half of the funds raised by the branches went to aid Woodard and half to an antimob violence fund. A benefit for Woodard held at Lewisohn Stadium in Harlem on August 18, co-chaired by prizefighter Joe Louis, netted $22,000. Three days later, Leonard Shull, chief of police of Batesburg, South Carolina, was named as the man who had beaten Woodard. The Justice Department filed charges against Shull, and federal district judge Waties Waring presided at Shull's trial later that fall. The police chief admitted to beating Woodard, claiming that Woodard was drunk and disorderly and that he had struck him in self-defense. An all-white jury deliberated for less than thirty minutes and found Shull not guilty.[58]

Heightened demands on the national office and the relentless pressure of work in the field took its toll on the small staff and aggravated organizational weaknesses and tensions. Roy Wilkins, who managed the kinetic flow of activity in the national office, recalled the summer of 1946 as a time of "accumulating anxieties." By early July, Marshall had worked himself to the edge of physical collapse. He toughed it out through three days of preliminary hearings in the Columbia case with a 103-degree temperature before being hospitalized for pneumonia. In an appeal to the board to assist with Marshall's medical bills, White explained that "Mr. Marshall's present condition is in large measure due to the physical and mental strain of the Columbia, Tennessee trials . . . along with the hard work and travel he has been doing without thought to himself." Marshall spent more than a month in Harlem Hospital and was under doctors' orders not to return to work until later in the fall.[59]

Ella Baker left the staff in July after submitting her resignation in May. She had tired of working against the grain of an organizational culture dominated by the personality and authority of Walter White. A democratic ethos defined Baker's approach to her work in the field, yet she found herself part of a structure where there was "almost a complete lack of appreciation for the collective thinking of the staff." Baker offered examples of White's overbearing management style in her letter of resignation, noting that he discounted the opinion of staff members and seemed oblivious to the workloads of the various departments. The branch department had been "without constant, adequate and/or efficient help" for much of the time that Baker had been director. It had gotten to the point where Baker found that too much of her "energy was dedicated to fighting a sense of futility and frustration." In leaving, she made a distinction between the leadership that dominated the national office and the organization itself. "In every possible way," she wrote, "I shall keep the faith with the basic principles of the NAACP and with the faith vested in it by the people."[60]

"To us down here your leaving brings a feeling of deep regret," John LeFlore wrote from Mobile, Alabama. "We have grown to love you." With Baker's departure, branch leaders lost a reliable ally and a steady advocate, one who guarded against an inclination on the part of the New York office to treat the branches primarily as revenue-generating sources. The association lost a talented organizer, who looked beyond the narrow if essential needs of the institution to the larger challenges of how the association could effectively connect with black people around the country and root the movement in their struggles. Baker's approach emphasized the importance of leadership development and local organizing as critical to building on the membership growth of the war years. Neither White nor Wilkins were apparently sorry to see Baker leave. "Walter and Roy liked full control," recalled Robert Carter. "Ella was an independent woman and none of them intimidated her. . . . She was too powerful for them to do anything about." White chose Gloster Current, executive director of the Detroit branch, the NAACP's largest branch, to replace Baker. The Detroit native had impressive administrative experience, minimal exposure to the South, and an approach to branch work that was more in line with White and Wilkins's primary emphasis on membership numbers.[61]

The politically targeted terror that dominated the primary election season announced that there was a long road ahead even as NAACP lawyers scored major courtroom victories. "The legal right is not enough," Thurgood Marshall cautioned. "It will take courage and untiring efforts to enforce [the right to vote] in the South." The Truman administration's record was hardly promising. The president's leadership was erratic—"he wibbled here, wobbled there," said White. While his secretary of state, James Byrnes, insisted on democratic elections in Bulgaria, Byrnes's home state of South Carolina barred blacks from the Democratic primary in defiance of the U.S. Supreme Court—an "indefensible" and "impossible" position, claimed Du Bois. The NAACP continued to pursue a national program, with the challenge to restrictive covenants at the top of its legal agenda and the fight to halt the spread of school segregation in northern cities commanding Marshall's attention. By the end of 1946, however, the "vicious system of second class citizenship" that structured southern life elevated the region and the federal government as the primary battlegrounds in the struggle for civil rights.[62]

The NAACP began a campaign to compel the Truman administration to take responsibility for "making democracy work" in the South. "Pitiless, blatant publicity," advised Du Bois. Speaking to an interracial youth gathering in Columbia, South Carolina, sponsored by the Southern Negro Youth Congress in the fall of 1946, Du Bois instructed: "You have got to make the people of the United States and of the world know what is going on in the South," and make it impossible for anyone living in the South to "not realize the barbarities that prevail here." White concurred, telling the NAACP annual convention that year, "We must pound and pound and pound the conscience of America." In August, White convened a meeting of representatives from labor, civil liberties, and religious organizations, many affiliated with the group founded in response to the Columbia riot. They established the National Emergency Committee against Mob Violence to promote "unified action against the rising tide of mob violence, as evidenced in South Carolina, Georgia, Mississippi and other states." Paralleling the effort to mobilize public opinion was the growing clout of the black vote, a looming challenge to a national Democratic Party dominated by a powerful southern wing. African Americans must serve notice, Marshall insisted, that "it is time to choose up sides." If the current administration, through its actions, sided with "the reactionaries in the South" then "all of us" must remove that group from power. "This," Marshall warned, "we promise to do."[63]

In response to growing pressure, and with mid-term elections on the horizon, President Truman met with a small delegation from the National Emergency Committee against Mob Violence on September 19. Walter White, serving as chief spokesman, reported details of the violent episodes that had occurred in the South and described a pervasive climate of racial terror. White reported that Truman expressed shock, exclaiming, "I had no idea it was so terrible. We must do something!" He told the group that he would establish a committee to investigate the problem and recommend a program of action. White promptly wrote Truman after the meeting, emphasizing that reports and recommendations would not be sufficient. "I hope this will not be considered a substitute for stronger federal legislation against violence," he told Truman, "nor handled in a way as to give Congress an excuse for postponement of action. I mention this because it should be in our thinking." In the following weeks, David Niles, administrative assistant to the president, sought White's advice on individuals who might serve on the committee.[64]

Earlier in September, the board of directors endorsed a proposal by Du Bois to prepare a statement to the General Assembly of the United Nations on the denial of civil and political rights to Americans of Negro descent. White and Wilkins were equally enthusiastic about Du Bois's plan. He intended to expand upon a petition drawn up by the National Negro Congress that Du Bois noted was "well done, but . . . too short and not sufficiently documented." Du Bois recruited leading lawyers and scholars to prepare specific sections of the petition: Earl Dickerson, William Ming, Rayford Logan, Milton Korvitz, and Leslie Perry. The petition would focus on the systematic denial of legally guaranteed rights to African Americans since emancipation, with historical examples and documentation. While the petition sought redress before the United Nations, its greatest potential value would be to focus international attention on racial conditions in the United States as America assumed freedom's mantle in the emerging global contest with the Soviet Union.[65]

While White and Du Bois moved in the arenas of national and international politics, issues of race and justice were on trial in a courtroom in Lawrenceburg, Tennessee, the final chapter of the Columbia riot episode. After a long, drawn out process of jury selection, the trial of the twenty-five black men indicted for attempted murder began in mid-September. The NAACP lawyers, minus Marshall, presented a strong case for self-defense in the face of a menacing white mob, while exposing the state's abuse of power and the lack of evidence linking any of the defendants to the shooting of the police. In his closing argument to the all-white jury, Maurice Weaver, himself a World War II veteran, reminded the twelve jurymen that blacks and whites had fought together against tyranny and oppression in the recent war. Alexander Looby, appealing to a sense of fairness and humanity, asked, "How can we go to the United Nations and demand and insist upon democracy when we don't practice it ourselves?" The state's attorney, Paul Bumpus, appealed to white solidarity as he sketched a scenario where the black defendants were the aggressors, guilty of luring police into the Bottom, while indicting the "pinks and pimps and punks" from outside of Tennessee who used the "tragedy" to spread "grotesque distortions" of the truth. After Leon Ransom called Bumpus on a point of order, the attorney, infuriated at being corrected by Ransom, threatened "to wrap a chair" around his head. In a verdict that stunned the prosecution, the jury acquitted twenty-three of the twenty-five defendants. Ransom immediately appealed the convictions of the two men held guilty; the state ultimately declined to go forward with the prosecution of the two men.[66]

A healthy and rested Marshall returned to Tennessee in November for the trial of the remaining two defendants and faced a harrowing experience. William Pillow and Lloyd Kennedy, charged with assault with intent to kill, went to trial in Columbia on November 18. Pillow was acquitted; Kennedy was convicted and sentenced to up to five years in prison, which Marshall intended to appeal. The night after the verdicts came down, Marshall, Alexander Looby, Maurice Weaver, and Harry Raymond, a reporter for the *Daily Worker*, set out for Nashville in Looby's car with Marshall driving. Just outside of Columbia, eight men, including a deputy sheriff and two highway patrolmen, stopped Marshall, ordered the men out of the car, and searched it for liquor. They found none, and the four continued on their way. The police stopped them a second time and examined Marshall's driver's license. The third time the police stopped them, they arrested Marshall for driving while drunk, and ordered him into their car, advising Looby and the rest to continue on to Nashville. A caravan of three cars carrying Marshall headed down a side road toward Duck River; Marshall recalled that he "feared violence momentarily." But Looby followed close behind, which likely caused the group to make an abrupt turn back toward town. Once there, they took Marshall before J.J. Pogue, the local magistrate. After smelling Marshall's breath, Pogue pronounced that Marshall had not even had a drink and refused to jail him. Marshall and his associates returned to the Bottom and borrowed a car so they might not be easily recognized in their second attempt to drive to Nashville. As soon as they arrived there, Marshall telegraphed attorney general Tom Clark to report what had happened and demand that there be "an immediate investigation and criminal charges against officers participating in this outrage."[67]

Four days later, Marshall was at Dillard University in New Orleans for the eighth annual youth conference of the NAACP. By the end of 1946, the NAACP claimed more than 25,000 members under the age of twenty-five. Marshall observed that there were no young speakers on the program; "this is bad," he told White. Nevertheless, the speakers called on youth to take the lead in pushing against segregation's barriers and claiming full citizenship. Board member Judge Hubert Delaney urged participants to seek "unadulterated equality in every field" and "stop apologizing for being alive." Delaney blasted the silence of "Christian whites" in the face of lynchings, the same people who warn that "the time is not right" to protest oppression. "The time is always right to do the right thing by your fellow man." Young people should not take their cues from a country that talks "of peace and equality" while it cannot "give" equality to its own citizens. *They* must know what they want and take "definite action" to get it. Voting, he emphasized, was essential in the fight for decent housing, good jobs, education, and adequate health care and in the fight against oppression and segregation. Vote "and vote at any cost," he urged.[68]

Marshall's presence at Dillard, just days after his brush with a near-lynching and the final victory in the hard-fought Columbia riot cases, enhanced the aura of one of black America's most celebrated leaders. In addressing the conference's topic, "The Next Twenty Years Toward Freedom for the Negro in America," he placed education at the top of the agenda. He advised the young women and men that they must fight for "everything which is your right from graduate school to kindergarten," making segregation as costly as possible. The color bar in southern professional and graduate schools, he predicted, would soon fall. Marshall criticized the "ghetto psychology" of those northern black educators who supported separate schools. In the area of labor, he urged them to support the trade union movement but not tolerate separate or auxiliary unions. Responding to complaints by northern delegates recounting their first experiences of Jim Crow on buses and trains, Marshall discussed the limitations of the *Morgan* ruling, pledging that the NAACP would contest racial seating on private carriers and that this would "eventually be licked." He briefed the gathering about the ongoing legal challenge to restrictive covenants.[69]

In his discussion, Marshall turned his attention to issues of strategy, talking specifically about "Negroes and white allies" in the North who were applying Gandhian tactics of nonviolent disobedience to challenge racial segregation. Marshall was referring to the interracial Congress on Racial Equality (CORE), founded in 1942, which had engaged in direct action protests targeting public facilities in the North. Now they were planning to ride buses through the South and challenge segregation on interstate transportation in the wake of the *Morgan* ruling. Several individuals had suggested to Marshall that such tactics should be used in the South to awaken the American people to the plight of the Negro in the region. "Don't do it that way," Marshall advised the conference. "In the Deep South any non-violence or disobedience movement . . . would bring violence on the part of the local and State police, result in the imprisonment of hundreds of young people and the death of scores, with nothing achieved except a measure of publicity which we are now getting for our struggles with a minimum of suffering." The wholesale refusal of Negroes to be segregated would lead to a loss of public sympathy "from the cautious and the timid—something we need badly," and would probably be viewed by the press as a provocative invitation to "repression by local authorities." The events of the previous year, including his own experience in Tennessee, made him keenly aware of how completely exposed black southerners were to the unchecked power of local and state police. Protests that pressed beyond the boundaries of established law would be, he believed, counterproductive if not suicidal. As the primary elections that summer had demonstrated, black efforts to simply exercise the right to vote carried significant risks and served as a powerful demonstration of southern obstruction of the law and denial of the most basic right of citizenship.[70]

Two weeks later, black Mississippians drew national attention to the struggle around voting rights. In response to complaints filed with the U.S. Senate regarding the primary election, a special Senate committee went to Mississippi to investigate Senator Bilbo's role in obstructing black access to the polls. Charles Houston, who represented the NAACP at the hearings, reported that the committee did not subpoena witnesses but relied on volunteer testimony. As a consequence, many thought "Mississippi victims might be afraid to testify." But on the morning that the hearings opened, Houston wrote, "two hundred veterans packed the corridors of the courthouse volunteering to testify. . . . Older men, too." They would testify regardless of "possible reprisals against their property, businesses and families." Here, he said, "for the first time in over fifty years, the stinking record of terror and intimidation was exposed in a public statewide hearing."[71]

"Not since Reconstruction days," reported the *Chicago Defender*, had there been so "challenging a manifestation of racial solidarity" in the Deep South. Sixty-eight blacks testified over the course of four days. They included "common laborers and . . . veterans . . . college professors and elderly men," all serving notice that they "intend to make it possible for democracy to survive even in Mississippi." Witnesses told of widespread intimidation and obstruction—there were accounts of beatings, armed men blocking access to polling places, and ballot boxes stuffed with newspapers. The Reverend William A. Bender, the sixty-year-old chaplain of Tougaloo College, told of being turned away from the polling station at gunpoint by a deputy sheriff. A number of witnesses called the names of officers and citizens who had assaulted or intimidated them; many were officials of cities and towns to which the witnesses would return. U. S. Army veterans frequently spoke of "the new law," referring to the 1944 *Smith v. Allright* ruling, which meant that they could vote in the Democratic primary under the protection of constitutionally guaranteed rights. The men spoke with "forcefully moving language," observed a *New York Times* reporter, and collectively "made a picture of a steadily awakening political consciousness."[72]

Senator Allen J. Ellender, Democrat from Louisiana, headed the five-man Senate committee and questioned white witnesses about whether discrimination against would-be black voters was the result of anything Senator Bilbo said. Most stated their belief that blacks had no "moral" right to participate in the Democratic primary, a widely shared sentiment among whites. One sheriff said he advised blacks not to vote in the "white primary" because it was his "job to prevent trouble." Only one witness implied that Bilbo might have influenced him. Bilbo admitted that he had urged whites to use every means possible to keep Negroes from the polls, but added that he had qualified the statement with "lawful," which he said most press accounts neglected to include. Not a single official, Houston observed, "testified to any attempt to protect a citizen in the exercise of his right to vote." He suggested that if justice were to prevail, the hearings "would be followed by criminal trials of Mississippi state officials which would rival . . . German and Japanese war trials."

In the end, the Democratic majority on the committee exonerated Bilbo. The NAACP and other groups continued to lobby the Senate to bar Bilbo from taking his seat due to his efforts to obstruct the electoral process, Bilbo died before the issue could be resolved. As the *New York Times* observed, barring Bilbo from the Senate would not make Mississippi over. Most white Mississippians shared Bilbo's commitment to white supremacy, "a form of government they are determined for the present to maintain." But, the *Times* editorialized, the hearings "gave the rest of the country a liberal education in what white supremacy and one-party rule really mean." They had provided blacks with a platform to "publicly . . . insist on their right to have a voice in the government of Mississippi." Considering the larger significance of the hearings, Houston wrote that now "the eyes of the nation were on Mississippi and the [black] Mississippian could feel he was not standing alone."[73]

The 1946 election season marked a crossroads for black voters, North and South, with important consequences for the civil rights struggle. An estimated six hundred thousand blacks registered in the South during 1946, a threefold increase over the previously recorded two hundred thousand for 1940. This striking development caused some commentators to predict an imminent transformation of southern politics. University of Florida political scientist William Carlton viewed the increase in black voting as "a boon to liberals in their fight within the [Democratic] Party to gain and keep party control." In Alabama, the black vote worked in tandem with liberal and labor groups to help elect James Folsom governor, a pro-labor and racially moderate figure. Moderate candidates, with the energetic support of the CIO-PAC, unseated a handful of incumbents in key congressional races in Georgia, Florida, North Carolina, and Virginia. The CIO-PAC was a major driving force in these races, but its leader, Jack Kroll, acknowledged that the surge in black political participation and the legal victories of the NAACP were critical to these victories and the political realignment essential to ongoing gains. At the end of November, Walter White joined representatives of this burgeoning political alliance—Osceola McKaine, former Georgia governor Ellis Arnall, SCHW president Clark Foreman, CIO-PAC organizer Palmer Weber, and Mary McLeod Bethune—at an SCHW conference in New Orleans to discuss the significance of the South's primary election season. In a rousing speech, Mary McLeod Bethune emphasized the importance of voting to the struggles against mob violence, segregation, and discrimination. "With the franchise," she intoned, "we must get our justice."[74]

While the contours of southern politics might have been shifting ever so slightly, the Republican landslide at the polls on election day was the big story of the mid-term election. Commentators differed on the causes and consequences of the thumping dealt to the Democrats in their worst showing since 1928. Inflation, meat shortages, labor strife, the high cost of living, heightened anti-communism, and Truman's sinking popularity were the litany of factors explaining the Republican sweep. Of all the potential trends evident in the outcome, the defection of black voters from the Democratic Party in major northern urban areas was the cause of deep concern among party leaders. Democrat Adam Clayton Powell Jr., who held on to his congressional seat by a comfortable margin, commented that the Republican landslide was "positive proof of the political maturity of the Negro people" and a "clear warning to the Democratic Party," too long dominated by its southern wing. By taking over the majority in both houses, Republicans knocked out entrenched southern leadership from committee chairmanships. Walter White had no illusions about the Republican Party. But he could not help but take some satisfaction in warning the Democrats that if the Republicans kept some of their promises to black voters, "the present Negro resentment against [the] Bilbo-Talmadge-Rankin-Byrnes domination of the Democratic Party may develop into a force strong enough to decide who will occupy the White House and the Congress in 1948." The Truman administration and the Democratic Party leadership outside the South understood that the concerns of black voters could no longer be safely ignored.[75]

On December 5, with little fanfare, President Truman issued an executive order establishing a committee on civil rights, as promised in the meeting with White and his committee almost three months earlier. The statement accompanying the order emphasized the recent wave of mob violence and the breakdown of law enforcement as the cause for the presidential action. "The constitutional guarantees of individual liberties and of equal protection under the law clearly place on the Federal Government the duty to act when state or local authorities abridge or fail to protect these constitutional rights," the statement soberly announced. The federal government, however, was "hampered by inadequate civil rights statutes. . . . We must provide the Justice

Department with the tools to do the job." Toward this end, the president named fifteen distinguished men and women to the President's Committee on Civil Rights (PCCR), authorizing them to prepare a report with recommendations for "the adoption or establishment by legislation or otherwise of more adequate and effective means and procedures for the protection of the civil rights of the people of the United States."[76]

The president's action was greeted as a "portent of good tidings" in the words of the *Chicago Defender*. But by the end of 1946, the promise of action in the future could not distract from the failure of the federal government to use the power it already had to meet an alarming situation in the South. Co-inciding with the establishment of the PCCR, the NAACP issued a demand for immediate action by the Justice Department in prosecuting the police officers who had harassed Thurgood Marshall and his associates in Columbia, Tennessee, and arrested Marshall under false pretenses. The statement pointed out that the Justice Department had the authority to act under section 20 of the U.S. Criminal Code. "This latest outrage," the statement emphasized, followed a series of failures on the part of the federal government and served to encourage the mob to take the law into its own hands "not only against individual citizens but now upon lawyers while they are engaged in defending victims of mob attack." The actions of the police in Tennessee, if left unchecked, reinforced a belief that southern law enforcement officers could act without any fear of federal intervention.[77]

As the year drew to a close, Marshall identified a pattern of behavior that raised serious questions about the commitment of the Justice Department and its agents to enforcing the law in the South. Following the acquittal of Lynwood Shull, the police chief charged with beating and blinding Isaac Woodard, Marshall wrote to Attorney General Clark objecting to the failure of the special prosecutor and the U.S. district attorney to "vigorously prosecute the case." Marshall cited several points, from the way in which the jury was selected to the final summation arguments. Most egregious was the fact that Claude Sapp, the U.S. attorney in Columbia, South Carolina, did not even ask the jury for a guilty verdict, but made a statement implying that the government would be satisfied with whatever the jury decided. This, Marshall noted, was "an invitation to the jury to bring in a verdict of acquittal." The NAACP's efforts to secure the prosecution of Shull followed careful investigation and were based "on the justifiable belief . . . that the defendant was guilty of a crime against our government and the Negro people in particular."

Had the jury been more carefully chosen and the case properly presented and argued, "we feel certain that a guilty verdict could have been obtained."[78]

Six weeks after the Woodard trial, the federal grand jury investigation of the quadruple murder in Monroe, Georgia, ended with no indictments, prompting Marshall to write a blistering letter to Clark. He protested the consistent failure of the Federal Bureau of Investigation to "identify or bring to trial persons charged with violation of federal statutes when Negroes are the victims." It was incredible that the FBI, with its "incomparable record for ferreting out persons violating our federal laws"—be it spies, saboteurs, or car thieves—came up empty in its investigation of the violent assault on the black community in Columbia, Tennessee, earlier in the year and, most recently, in the "shotgun lynching" of the two couples in Monroe, Georgia. After a three-week investigation in the Georgia case, involving twenty FBI agents and one hundred witnesses, a federal grand jury reported that it was unable "to establish the identity of any persons guilty of violating the civil rights statute." The "uneven administration of federal criminal statutes" when Negroes were the victims, Marshall insisted, was intolerable, and Clark had "the duty and the responsibility" to make a complete investigation of the situation. "There would be very little use to strengthen civil rights statutes," he added, if such conditions persisted.[79]

With a membership of more than four hundred thousand in 1946, the NAACP easily commanded attention as the leading voice for African Americans in the national political arena. Its accomplishments in the wake of the war were quite extraordinary. No other agency, noted the *Chicago Defender*, "could have mobilized public sentiment so adroitly against the wave of violence and recurrent lynchings" that peaked after the war. While known to make exaggerated claims, White was probably correct in describing the President's Committee on Civil Rights as "the creation" of the NAACP. A masterly campaign of public exposure and the growing power of the northern black vote, leveraged through White's well-honed network of contacts inside Washington and among liberal and labor organizations, compelled Truman to create the committee. At the same time, the "brilliant battery" of lawyers working under the direction of Thurgood Marshall pushed the battle forward, nailing down the victory secured by the 1944 white primary ruling, eliminating a major prop of Jim Crow in the *Morgan* ruling, and prevailing in the Columbia, Tennessee, case "against insuperable odds," all the while working with branches around the country to push down racial barriers in housing, education, and employment. The struggle against segregation in the South steadily moved forward. Assessing their achievements, Marshall observed that they had "at best established a beachhead" in "the fight to secure complete and full citizenship for all Americans regardless of their race or color."[80]

9

The Beginning of the End:
Segregation Must Go

Thurgood Marshall arrived in Houston, Texas, on February 23, 1947, in time for a mass meeting sponsored by the local NAACP branch that afternoon. Pleasant Hill Baptist Church, the venue, was a "swell house . . . packed with everyone, including two members of the city council," he wrote Roy Wilkins. When a resolution calling for the end of segregation in public schools was read, "the people tore down the church"—and this, Marshall noted, was before he had spoken. The burst of enthusiasm lifted his spirits. With the NAACP poised to initiate a direct attack on school segregation, the Lone Star State offered fertile ground for what promised to be a long, hard struggle. "There is hardly a Negro in Texas today who is not convinced that segregation is not only bad, but cannot be tolerated," Marshall wrote a few months later. "It is likewise evident that this sentiment does not exist in any other southern state where we are operating."[1]

After a decade of whittling away at state-mandated segregation by attacking the inequities embedded in the system—in teachers' pay, school facilities, bus transportation—Marshall was ready to strike at the heart of Jim Crow. Early in 1946, he and Robert Carter had seized on a ruling in a California case involving the segregation of Mexican American children to sketch out the legal arguments that would buttress the fight. In *Mendez v. Westminster*, a federal district judge held that separate schools based on ancestry and lineage were a violation of the equal protection clause of the Fourteenth Amendment. When the school board appealed the case, Carter prepared an amicus curiae brief for the NAACP, a tightly argued treatise holding that "the equality demanded by the Constitution and under the laws of the United States

cannot be realized under a system of segregation." The brief combined a review of constitutional law with a distillation of sociological studies documenting the harmful effects of school segregation on children as well as on
the nation's civic culture. It also referenced America's international commitments, claiming that the United Nations charter "obligated our government
to promote uniform respect for . . . human rights and fundamental freedoms
for all without distinction as to race." In April 1947 the Ninth Circuit Court
of Appeals issued a narrow ruling prohibiting the segregation of Mexican
children in California without reaching the crucial equal protection issues.
Nevertheless, Carter recalled, the *Mendez* brief served as "a trial run of what
was to come."[2]

It had been twenty years since Du Bois called for "a crusade" against the
wretched state of black education in the South and more than a decade since
Charles Houston offered his stark visual documentation of separate and unequal schools in South Carolina. Conditions through most of the South had
remained unchanged. School spending across the region averaged $18.82 per
black pupil and $58.69 per white student. Marshall believed that nothing
short of a direct attack on segregation could secure equal education, but he
was keenly aware of the difficulties in mounting such a challenge. For many
southern blacks, the idea of school integration was abstract at best, given the
weight of history and the realities of race and power in the South. His account of the reaction to his stump speech in South Carolina, announcing
plans "to fight to the last ditch to remove all segregation" was a measure of the
work that needed to be done. There was "absolutely no applause, but rather a
look of apprehension on the faces of most" of the people present.[3]

As Marshall prepared for the long haul in the South, the NAACP elevated
civil rights to a prominent place on the nation's political agenda. In public
testimony before the President's Committee on Civil Rights, Marshall declared that "the federal government must use its authority to protect all of its
citizens from violence, from the violation of their constitutional and statutory
rights, and to assure to all the equality to which our system is dedicated." This
call echoed the founding principle of the NAACP. Across the years, the
NAACP and its branches waged battles on multiple fronts, securing incremental gains and helping to foster a civic identity and consciousness among
black Americans that defied rigid racial barriers. Beyond relatively modest
and fluctuating membership rolls, the NAACP had come to represent the
strivings of millions of black Americans in the quest for full citizenship rights.
In the process, its "machinery"—the tactical means for realizing federal pro-

tection of those rights—had become more finely tuned. By the late 1940s, the NAACP was positioned to amplify the power of northern black voters in the national arena and also poised to organize the aspirations of black southerners into a full-fledge assault on the foundations of Jim Crow.[4]

The moment was set at the convergence of developments that focused national and international attention on racial discrimination in the United States. A wave of racial violence in the South after the war along with the defection of large numbers of black voters from the Democratic Party during the 1946 midterm elections provided Walter White and his cohort with the leverage needed to persuade President Truman that he must take action. By establishing the President's Committee on Civil Rights, Truman initiated a series of developments that made civil rights a dominant issue in the 1948 presidential campaign. At the same time, the escalation of the cold war and America's emergence as the self-proclaimed force for freedom and democracy in the world exposed the nation's race problem to critical scrutiny, making civil rights an issue with foreign policy implications. Such circumstances appeared to favor the NAACP's appeal to the United Nations as a strategy for compelling the government to take responsibility for securing democratic rights for all citizens, regardless of race. But the domestic politics of the cold war and the unyielding power of Southern Democrats tested the agility of NAACP leaders in their efforts to define and advance a civil rights agenda.

The legal team functioned outside of the high-profile arena of national politics as it mounted a slow, steady insurgency against the edifice of Jim Crow. "We were a small operation," Robert Carter recalled, "trying to use the law to revolutionize race relations by seeking to have the Thirteenth, Fourteenth, and Fifteenth amendments given their intended effect." The lawyers, of course, faced their own set of challenges. The crafting of a litigation strategy capable of unhinging the South's caste system was alone a daunting task, and its application was dependent upon enlisting the support of southern branches and their membership—a steep climb from the vantage point of 1947. But the structure was in place for a movement that married the legal talent and fortitude of a close fraternity of civil rights attorneys with a network of branches and state conferences and a targeted campaign of fieldwork that built on the foundation laid by Ella Baker and others during the war. Marshall was confident of the dividends that a sustained investment in the field would yield. There was an "urgent need for intensive field work from branch to branch and person to person" he told Gloster Current, who had succeeded Baker as director of branches. "We must use additional effort to get our branches sold on the problem [of school segregation], anxious to work on it, and determined to fight the matter out." This was not just essential to the success of the legal campaign, Marshall held, "but necessary to the continued survival of the Association."[5]

Marshall spent roughly two-thirds of his time in the South and had tried cases in every southern state. Clarity of purpose was complemented by a deep connection to southern life built up during a decade of work and travel in the region. He often stayed in private homes, given the scarcity of decent hotels for blacks in the South. Through small and large meetings, consultations with branches, and late-night card games, Marshall became a familiar figure as well as a celebrated leader. He was "of the people," one friend recalled, and could explain cases in ways that all understood: simply put, "We ain't gettin' what we should." A keen observer and a good listener, Marshall became intimately acquainted with the complex realities of black lives under the grip of Jim Crow from the Mississippi Delta to the Low Country of South Carolina and the New South city of Atlanta, and he was prepared to invest the time and effort essential to building from common ground. "It is quite difficult to show many people in the Deep South the evils of segregation when they have . . . lived in segregated areas all of their lives," Marshall wrote Lulu White about divisions among blacks on the issue of segregation. "It is a long drawn out fight . . . but it has to be handled in such a manner as to not split us wide open and not to let us lose the objective that we are all fighting for." His ready access to lawyers and branch leaders in every southern state enabled him to orchestrate a flexible campaign that was attentive to local conditions as they probed for openings to push the legal effort forward. During the 1946 meeting of southern lawyers in Atlanta, Marshall and his associates pooled information on school conditions across the South and reviewed the status of various legal efforts, while sketching out strategies and directions for an expanded effort that combined the push for equalization with a targeted effort taking direct aim at segregation.[6]

While the legal team continued to focus on removing barriers to voting and transportation, the fight against school segregation became the dominant focus of the southern campaign. Up to 1950, the NAACP waged a direct challenge to segregation in the area of graduate and professional education. Three major cases were filed during this period involving plaintiffs suing for admission to state-supported law schools in Oklahoma, South Carolina, and Texas. At the same time, the NAACP supported an accelerated, open-ended challenge to racial discrimination in elementary and secondary schools, working with branches to expose rampant school inequalities and to seek court orders requiring school officials to cease discriminating against blacks. This was in line with the NAACP's approach, chipping away at the legal props of "separate but equal" while testing the willingness of southern towns and cities to equalize educational facilities and opportunities. Such a strategy allowed the lawyers to work with individual communities around issues of schooling, build momentum behind the campaign for educational equality, and expose the inability of southern school boards to satisfy equality under a Jim Crow system of education.

The case of Ada Sipuel was the opening volley in the NAACP's postwar challenge to segregated education, picking up where Charles Houston and Lucille Bluford had left off in 1942. Before that case was aborted due to war-time pressures, Houston was trying to establish that at the level of professional and graduate education, the attempt of states to duplicate opportunities in a racially separate institution was neither economically feasible nor academically possible. Sipuel, a twenty-one-year-old honors graduate from Langston University, Oklahoma's sole black public institution of higher education, applied to the University of Oklahoma Law School in January 1946. She worked closely with Roscoe Dunjee, longtime head of the Oklahoma NAACP state conference of branches, during the application process. When the school rejected Sipuel, citing the state's segregation laws, Dunjee contacted Marshall, advising that Sipuel was prepared to sue for admission to the university, and pledged the resources of the state conference to finance the case. Oklahoma attorney Amos T. Hall was ready to provide local representation.[7]

Like Houston, Marshall believed that "a law suit is an educational process." The response of whites to Sipuel's application revealed diverging points of view that were rarely aired. There was vocal student and faculty support for her admission to the law school, expressed in a large public protest; an editorial in the campus newspaper described separate schools as "impractical, undesirable, and unnecessary." The *Tulsa Tribune* suggested that it was in the state's best interest to admit black students to law and medical school—given the expense of providing separate facilities and also the "serious" as opposed to "social" nature of education at the professional-school level. But the state government put up a solid front. The *Sipuel* case moved slowly through the lower courts. The state trial court dismissed it on the grounds that Sipuel had failed to petition for the establishment of a black law school. After the state supreme court upheld the lower court ruling in April 1947, Marshall and

Hall took the case to the United States Supreme Court. Avoiding the issue of segregation, a unanimous Court relied on *Gaines* in ruling that Oklahoma must provide Ada Sipuel a legal education "in conformity with the equal protection clause of the Fourteenth Amendment and provide it as soon as it does for applicants of any other group."[8]

"I can't see how the regents can give us a school next Monday which is equal in faculty and facilities and the forty year old tradition of the Oklahoma school," remarked an incredulous Dunjee as state education officials hurriedly made separate arrangements for Sipuel in time for the new term. They established a Negro School of Law as a branch of Langston University in a roped-off section of the state capitol, with three law professors and access to the state's law library. Sipuel refused to attend, and Marshall went back to the Supreme Court charging that the state board of regents had defied the Court's mandate. Beyond the glaring inequity of such a makeshift arrangement, Marshall emphasized that equality could not be attained under segregation, whatever the physical arrangements. Marshall emphasized "exclusion of any one group on the basis of race automatically imputes a badge of inferiority to the excluded group."[9]

In a 7-2 ruling, the Court dismissed Marshall's motion because he had not directly challenged in the state court the state's constitutional provision requiring segregation in education. But attention had been directed to the thrust of his argument. Justice Wilcy Rutledge, one of the dissenting votes, contended that Oklahoma was required to end discrimination "at once" and that no decent law school could be created "overnight." The *New York Times* chided the Court for ducking the real issue, which anchored the NAACP's position. "It seems to us that the language of the Fourteenth Amendment must be tortured out of common meaning to make segregated practices in education anything except unconstitutional."[10]

"We can't dodge it any longer," warned former Alabama congressman Joe Starnes. "We must raise the level of our educational and economic opportunities for Negroes." College graduation rates for blacks had doubled to more than eight thousand since 1938, and black colleges bulged with veterans after the war. In preparing to meet postwar demands, southern states had appropriated $86 million for white higher education and a scant $5 million for black colleges. The NAACP's challenge forced states to reckon with the challenge of accommodating increasing numbers of blacks seeking professional and graduate training. The University of Delaware announced that black applicants for graduate and professional courses not offered elsewhere in state-supported black institutions would be admitted to the university without segregation. Arkansas announced that qualified blacks would be admitted to the state university's law school, but that they would be taught in a separate classroom. Shortly thereafter, the University of Arkansas admitted twenty-one-year-old Edith Mae Irby to the university's medical school without restrictions. Immediately following the *Sipuel* ruling, fifteen southern governors entered into a compact seeking congressional approval of a plan to pool their resources and establish regional graduate and professional schools, a proposal that garnered wide support in Congress during the first half of 1948. At the same time, several states facing litigation established separate facilities in an effort to satisfy the *Gaines* ruling.[11]

South Carolina acted quickly when the NAACP filed a suit on behalf of John Wrighten, exposing divisions among blacks over the NAACP's refusal to accept separate facilities. Wrighten, a twenty-seven-year-old veteran, applied to the University of South Carolina Law School during his senior year at South Carolina State College, the state-supported black college in Orangeburg. He sent a copy of his application to James Hinton, director of the South Carolina state conference of branches. Local attorney Harold Boulware and Thurgood Marshall filed a complaint in Wrighten's behalf in January 1947. In February the state legislature appropriated $60,000 for graduate and legal training at South Carolina State College and instructed college officials to use as much as necessary to operate a law program during the coming academic year. The case was tried in June, and Judge Waties Waring held that the state's action appeared to satisfy the *Gaines* requirement that the state provide a legal education "on substantial parity" with what was offered at the university's law school. But Waring warned that if the state failed to follow through, Wrighten would be entitled to enroll at USC Law School.[12]

For Miller Whittaker, president of South Carolina State College, the outcome of the case was welcomed. A law school would enhance the college's prestige, provide an infusion of desperately needed funds, and allow it to fill a chronic need in a state that had only five black practicing attorneys, as compared with eleven hundred white lawyers. When he sought Marshall's assistance in identifying a potential dean and faculty, Marshall stated his opposition to the program, insisting that "the setting up of small law schools can only be labeled as an extension of segregation." Whittaker, however, was more interested in creating educational opportunities and maintaining good relations with the state legislature than in advancing the NAACP's legal agenda, an opinion shared by many blacks in the state, including the leadership of the

NAACP's Charleston branch. Wrighten's primary desire was to study law; he had not bargained for a drawn-out legal procedure and the hostility his suit had generated. He applied to the new program at South Carolina State but then withdrew his application under pressure from NAACP state officials. In light of Wrighten's uncertainty, Marshall was prepared to cut the NAACP's losses and drop the case, but Boulware insisted on going forward. By the time Waring heard the NAACP's appeal the following year, the legislature had appropriated $200,000 for a law building and $30,000 for a library, leaving no doubt about its commitment to abiding by the judge's ruling. Wrighten enrolled at the new law school in the fall of 1949 and graduated in 1952. Ironically, in their effort to dodge desegregation, South Carolina officials established a law school that trained a generation of lawyers who would carry the civil rights struggle forward a decade later.[13]

Texas provided the wedge for moving the challenge to segregation forward. It had one of the strongest NAACP state conferences, energized by the white primary fight and a seasoned group of leaders who had worked closely with Marshall—notably state conference president Maceo Smith, attorney W.J. Durham, and Lulu White, the dynamic executive secretary of the Houston branch. After the white primary win, the Texas group was ready to take the lead in the education fight and set about raising $22,000 to support the effort. They found an ideal plaintiff in Heman Sweatt, a graduate of Wiley College in Marshall, Texas, where he had studied with poet and activist Melvin B. Tolson. The thirty-seven-year-old mail carrier had practically grown up in the NAACP's Houston branch—Lulu White was a close family friend and Lonnie Smith, the plaintiff in *Smith v. Allright*, was his dentist. Sweatt had been active in voter registration efforts and other branch activities, but it was his fight against discrimination at the post office that sparked an interest in attending law school. When he learned from Lulu White that the NAACP was seeking someone to apply to the University of Texas Law School, he volunteered.[14]

Sweatt attempted to enroll at the University of Texas Law School in February 1946, shortly after Sipuel applied to Oklahoma. He was denied on racial grounds and brought suit. In June the trial court in Austin gave the state six months to establish a "substantially equal law school." The following March the legislature established the Texas State University for Negroes in Houston, with a $100,000 appropriation and a promise of up to $3 million. As a short-term measure, the state established a temporary law school in the basement of an office building near the state capitol in Austin, with a "respectable" library and a three-person faculty. Sweatt refused to apply and returned to court. In the interim, two hundred students at the University of Texas established a branch of the NAACP and collected funds to help defray legal expenses. Prior to the start of the trial in May 1947 nearly two thousand white students and faculty held a mass rally in support of Sweatt.[15]

"This is going to be a real showdown fight against Jim Crow education," Marshall told a reporter for the *New York Post* at the start of the trial in Austin's Travis County Courthouse. For the first time in court, Marshall introduced testimony from eminent legal scholars and social scientists to support the claim that separate facilities could never be equal. Earl Harrison, dean of the University of Pennsylvania Law School and Malcolm Sharp of the University of Chicago provided testimony about the intangibles beyond physical facilities that define the law school experience at the University of Texas—such as the student body, prestige, contacts—which could not be duplicated in a new, segregated law school. Calling Robert Redfield, chairman of the anthropology department at the University of Chicago, allowed Marshall to explore the nature of racial classification as lacking any factual or scientific basis and probe the corrosive effect of racial segregation on students, the educational environment, and the practice of citizenship. Nonetheless, few were surprised when the court ruled against Sweatt. But Marshall had constructed a strong record supporting the argument that segregation in itself was unconstitutional, and the *Sweatt* case was on its way to the U.S. Supreme Court.[16]

In the fall of 1947, as *Sweatt* went forward, Marshall announced a pilot "county by county" effort, starting in Virginia, to force the issue of school equalization at the primary and secondary levels, jointly sponsored by the national office and the NAACP's Virginia state conference. Virginia was well prepared for such an undertaking. After nearly a decade of steady growth, the state organization claimed ninety-one branches and 24,843 members, providing a solid funding base along with a strong statewide NAACP presence. The state conference hired Lester B. Banks, World War II veteran and former high school principal, as its first paid executive secretary in 1946 and, with the approval of the national office, established its own legal defense fund. Oliver Hill and Spottswood Robinson, the NAACP's lead attorneys in the state, were the strongest team of civil rights lawyers working in the South. Along with their new law partner, Martin A. Martin, they revived the educational equalization campaign after the war—around teachers' salaries, school facilities, bus transportation, and curriculum. In addition to the Richmond cohort, the state conference had nine more NAACP-affiliated attorneys in locations around the state, ensuring that most branches had ready access to legal counsel.[17]

Spottswood Robinson left his teaching position at Howard and became full-time special counsel to the Virginia NAACP to head up the intensified education campaign. He and Banks worked together, covering an estimated 30,000 miles each year to document conditions, organize community support, and initiate legal action. Banks worked to involve local branches in investigating school conditions and providing potential plaintiffs, while Robinson petitioned school boards to remedy inequities and, when that failed, initiated court action. Both men participated in mass meetings, explaining the educational effort and enlisting support. They became an easily recognizable pair, traveling the back roads of Virginia in Banks's Chevrolet, stuffed with Robinson's books and legal files, with "NAACP" displayed in large letters across the rear window. Commenting on the warm reception they received across the Old Dominion, Banks observed: "The black people just wanted some leadership, someone to lean on." Marshall predicted that the efforts of his colleagues "will make the groundwork for a full-scale legal attack on the segregation laws of the State of Virginia, which have failed to produce even a semblance of equality."[18]

The education campaign took root in the South during 1947, a year of major developments on the civil rights front. The most striking event occurred on April 15 when Jackie Robinson stepped onto Ebbets Field in a Brooklyn Dodgers uniform and cracked the color line in Major League Baseball. While Robinson was making history in New York, a less-heralded development unfolded in the South, one that previewed the direct-action technique that would help ignite massive protests a decade later. Sixteen young men, eight black and eight white, embarked on the first "freedom ride" to test the enforcement of *Morgan v. Virginia*, the recent Supreme Court decision outlawing state-mandated segregation in interstate transportation. They were sponsored by the Fellowship of Reconciliation and its young affiliate, the Congress of Racial Equality, both interracial pacifist organizations. Founded in Chicago in 1942, CORE was dedicated to applying nonviolent direct action to challenge racial discrimination. Its loose federation of local chapters targeted restaurants, recreational centers, and other public places in northern cities that excluded blacks, often in violation of state civil rights laws. With the *Morgan* ruling, CORE organizers recognized an opportunity to go south and lend their efforts toward the implementation of the Court's decision while introducing southerners to the nonviolent movement.[19]

The youthful CORE group and NAACP leaders had an ambivalent relationship. Bayard Rustin and George Hauser, co-organizers of the CORE protest, were impatient with the NAACP's approach. Marshall warned that nonviolent civil disobedience in the South of the late 1940s would bring "wholesale slaughter" and achieve nothing. Others voiced similar concerns, causing the CORE group to revise its original plans to go as far as Louisiana and limit the "Journey of Reconciliation" to the upper South. Despite its reservations, the NAACP provided legal advice and a list of contacts in branches along the planned route. The meticulously planned protest illustrated the value of multiple approaches. The kind of painstaking and laborious campaign waged by NAACP lawyers to change the law was essential; *Morgan* provided the basis for protest. But the enforcement of the law, once changed, raised a new set of challenges.

The young men found that segregation patterns on interstate travel were securely in place; many people had not even heard of the *Morgan* ruling. Traveling in interracial pairs, they visited fifteen cities and conducted twenty-six tests, with whites taking seats in the back of the bus, and blacks in the front. The general response to their intervention was confusion—on the part of the police, the drivers, and the passengers. When drivers or police ordered them to move, the men would refuse and calmly explain the *Morgan* ruling. Near Winston-Salem, North Carolina, a white soldier insisted that the driver force Wallace Nelson to move from the "white" section. The driver said he could not do that and blamed the Supreme Court. In another instance, when the men refused a driver's order to move, he told them that he took his orders from the bus company, not the Supreme Court, and had the pair arrested for creating a disturbance. There were arrests in six places and one incident of violence outside of a bus in Chapel Hill, North Carolina. At a police court trial in Asheville, neither the judge nor the state's attorney knew about the *Morgan* decision and had to borrow the defending attorney's copy of the ruling to read in court. The judge then gave the men the maximum sentence, thirty days. They were released on bond, pending appeal.[20]

The CORE group made plans in advance with NAACP branches, churches, and college groups along their travel route, arranging for more than thirty speaking engagements. In these meetings, the young men explained the *Morgan* decision and reported on what their experiences had been on the buses. They instructed interested groups in the philosophy of nonviolent resistance and its application and urged them to join in helping to break the Jim Crow pattern on interstate travel. Those planning to participate were advised to contact the NAACP lawyer in their area prior to taking any action. NAACP lawyers defended the men who had been arrested over the course of the two-week-long protest and won five of the six cases. Rather than carry the case further, the convicted men, James Peck, Dennis Banks, and Bayard Rustin, went to jail and served a month on the chain gang as another way to dramatize the fight against Jim Crow in the South. North Carolina officials "would have been smart to have refused to jail the men," Charles Houston observed. They failed to see "that great movements of conscience sweep the imagination when men are willing to suffer for what they believe."[21]

As the "freedom riders" made their way from North Carolina to Tennessee, the President's Committee on Civil Rights (PCCR) held the first in a series of public hearings as part of its ten-month-long investigation. The PCCR rightly claimed a place on the "civil rights frontier." Created as a result of the NAACP's protest against mob violence, the committee interpreted its mandate broadly and did not limit its deliberations to the "flagrant outrages" that had caused Truman to appoint it. The committee members pursued an in-depth investigation of racial conditions in the South and "serious civil rights violations in all sections of the country." The fifteen-person body included a cross section of representatives from labor, business, church, social work, and civil rights groups and reflected regional and racial diversity; Walter White had recommended six of the commission members. The two black members were Channing Tobias, director of the Phelps Stokes Foundation and NAACP board member, and Sadie T. Alexander, a prominent Philadelphia attorney and leading civic figure. University of North Carolina president Frank Graham and Dorothy Tilly, an officer with the Women's Society of Christian Service of the Methodist Church in Atlanta, also served. Charles E. Wilson, president of General Electric, was chairman. The committee's staff, headed by Robert Carr, comprised individuals who were strongly in favor of expanded federal intervention to protect civil rights. Carr frequently consulted with White.[22]

The PCCR reviewed a massive array of reports, publications and correspondence and heard testimony from more than forty individuals from government agencies, labor, and civil rights groups. White and NAACP attorney Robert Carter urged the committee to hold hearings in a sampling of northern and southern communities so that they might get "a feel of the corrosive effect of racism on the whole country," as Carter put it. But the PCCR did not venture beyond Washington. It provided a platform, however, for White and Marshall as lead witnesses in the first set of public hearings held in April in the auditorium of the National Archives. Marshall described the national dimensions of racial discrimination and exclusion in striking detail, calling it "the greatest indictment of our American form of democratic government." He emphasized the critical nature of the committee's responsibility. "Practically every Negro in the South," he said, "looks to the National Government for protection of basic civil rights."[23]

Two months later, in a historic speech, President Truman supported improving civil rights protections. On June 29, 1947, he addressed the closing session of the NAACP's annual meeting from the steps of the Lincoln Memorial, the first president to address the thirty-eight-year-old organization. Ten thousand were gathered along the reflecting pool for the occasion; nationwide radio hookups and the State Department's shortwave radio carried Truman's words around the country and across the sea. With Eleanor Roosevelt and Walter White sharing the platform, Truman declared, "We have reached a turning point in the long history of our country's efforts to guarantee freedom and equality to all our citizens." In the place where Martin Luther King Jr. would speak of the dream sixteen years later, the president claimed that if freedom was to be "more than a dream . . . each man must be guaranteed equal opportunity." The immediate task was "to remove the last remnants of the barriers, which stand between millions of our citizens and their birthright," a vaguely phrased reference in a speech that avoided any mention of racial segregation. Truman was most forceful on the issue of racial terror and violence. "Many of our people still suffer . . . the harrowing fear of intimidation . . . the threat of physical injury and mob violence," and, he insisted, "we cannot wait another decade or generation to remove these evils. We must work . . . to cure them now." While local and state government had an important role to play in "providing positive safeguards," Truman warned that "we cannot await the growth of a will to action in the slowest state or the most backward community. Our national government must show the way."[24]

With the presidential election on the horizon, Truman's inaugural speech on civil rights treaded a careful path through the thicket of race, as he sought to do the nearly impossible: court black voters without alienating powerful Southern Democrats. The speech offered no specific program of action and avoided mention of any enabling legislation to give structure to a federal civil rights program, such as an antilynching bill or a permanent FEPC. The one legislative initiative he touted in a speech tinged with the crusading patriotism of the early cold war was a bill to "extend basic civil rights to the people of Guam and American Samoa so that these people can share our ideals of freedom and self government." But this limitation hardly diminished the significance of the occasion. As the *Amsterdam News* noted, "By appearing in person and making a forthright declaration on the burning issue of race prejudice, physical violence and the protection of the citizen by his government, [Truman] made a notable contribution to the fight for democracy and decency in this country."[25]

At the same time, Truman had begun the work of linking "civil rights" to the imperatives of the cold war and improving America's image in the world. "The support of desperate populations of battle-ravaged countries must be won for the free way of life," he announced midway through his talk. "Freedom is not an easy lesson to teach, nor an easy cause to sell." He warned that "peoples beset by every kind of privation . . . may surrender to the false security offered so temptingly by totalitarian regimes unless we can prove the superiority of democracy. Our case for democracy," Truman instructed, "should rest on practical evidence that we have been able to put our house in order. For these compelling reasons we can no longer afford the luxury of a leisurely attack upon prejudice and discrimination."[26]

The cold war emerged full-blown as a dominant force in American life and politics in the months leading up to Truman's NAACP speech. Two major initiatives setting the course of foreign and domestic policy—the Truman Doctrine and the loyalty oath program—challenged assumptions that had informed Walter White's approach to the postwar world and targeted loose political associations that had shaped the struggle for racial justice since the 1930s. The Truman Doctrine, proposed in a speech to Congress late in the winter of 1947, sanctified an alliance with Great Britain dedicated to containing the Soviet Union, drawing stark lines in what Truman described as a worldwide contest between "two ways of life." The crusade had been previewed a year earlier in a speech delivered by Winston Churchill in Fulton, Missouri, with Truman by his side. Churchill's ominous warning that an "iron curtain" had descended across Europe buttressed his call for an Anglo-American military alliance to defend Western democracies against Soviet expansion. In keeping with his strong advocacy for an end to colonialism, White called Churchill's speech "a sleazy method of serving notice on the world that the United States is backing the kind of imperialist program Britain advocates." Churchill, White feared, had exposed the shape of things to come.[27]

On March 12, 1947, in a major speech to a joint session of Congress, Truman requested emergency funding to supplement British aid to the government of Greece in the fight to suppress a Communist-aided insurgency in what he described as a front-line battle essential to securing the "freedoms" of war-damaged nations in the Middle East and Europe. He claimed a broad mandate to thwart the spread of communism, asserting that "it must be the policy of the United States to support free peoples who are resisting attempted subjugation by armed minorities or by outside pressures." Du Bois described the speech as "the most stupid and dangerous proposal ever made by the leader of a great modern nation"—a policy designed to support Britain's faltering empire and advance American corporate interests. Moreover, he observed, it might be premature for the United States to fight freedom's battles overseas, asking, "Can we expect democracy in Greece and not practice it in Mississippi?" While there is no evidence that Walter White was as pointed in his criticism of Truman's speech, he contended that the United States shared at least equal blame with the Soviet Union for fueling a dangerous situation for "want of . . . being sensible enough to sit down and talk honestly with each other."[28]

An executive order establishing a federal loyalty program followed barely a week after the Truman Doctrine was announced, establishing a sweeping program dedicated to purging communists from the federal government. The initiative was partly motivated by a desire to counter plans by the Republican-dominated Eightieth Congress to amplify its campaign to rout communists and their allies from the major institutions of American life. An expanded House Un-American Activities Committee, long a Republican perch for smearing New Deal initiatives, announced a packed schedule of hearings during 1947, focusing on unions, the motion picture industry, educational institutions, and the federal government. With the federal loyalty program, the Truman administration could defuse anti-communism as a Republican issue while helping to unify public opinion behind an expansive foreign policy aimed at containing the spread of communism abroad. The program transformed the issue of domestic communism from one of partisan politics to the realm of national security, with the federal government defining the Communist Party as an agent of a foreign power and implying that anyone associated with it was a security risk. Such associations were liberally

defined to include "membership in, affiliation with, or sympathetic association with any foreign or domestic organization, association, group or combination of persons, designated by the attorney general as totalitarian, fascist,
Communist or subversive." Guilt was no longer just personal or dependent
on overt acts, noted historian Henry Steele Commager, but "an infectious
thing to be achieved by sympathetic association with others presumed to be
guilty or movements presumed to be subversive."[29]

Charles Houston became an outspoken critic of the loyalty program, questioning its purpose and what it revealed about the government's priorities.
Without demonstrating that the country was in imminent threat of attack by
the Soviet Union, the president was willing to sacrifice sacred democratic
rights—the right to dissent and freedom of political association. Infusion of
resources and staff for the FBI to implement the loyalty program drew attention to the FBI's dismal record in investigating subversive activities in the
South. Houston quipped that he might be reassured if the government "would
use 50 per cent of the G-men" it was using to chase communists "as Task
Force No. 2 against the native fascists in Georgia and Mississippi." But he
had little confidence that this would happen and advised that if communists
wanted to seek cover in the South, they "put on white night shirts and wave
the American flag."[30]

The aggressive anti-communism of the cold war and the sticky problem of
"loyalty" challenged political alliances that had grown up since the 1930s—
groups that by their composition, ideals, and activism elevated the fight
against race discrimination. Houston reminded liberals that members of the
Communist Party worked on the front lines of many civil rights struggles,
including "anti-lynching, anti-poll-tax, anti-segregation, integration of Negroes into the labor movement," and participated in efforts to promote "a
broader base of democratic participation" at the grass roots. The NAACP
worked closely with a number of so-called Popular Front groups that origi-
nated in the progressive politics of the New Deal era, interracial groups that
were opened to all who shared their goals, including a consciously antisegre-
gationist policy. These organizations included the National Lawyers Guild,
the National Committee to Abolish the Poll Tax, the Southern Conference
for Human Welfare, and the Progressive Citizens of America (PCA). The
PCA was the coalition of liberal and labor organizations that had developed
around Henry Wallace in the aftermath of the 1944 Democratic convention.
White's critique of postwar foreign policy was closely aligned with the views
of Wallace and the PCA. While attitudes about the Communist Party varied

widely among participants in these loosely defined coalitions, they shared an opposition to the anti-communist orthodoxy that came to dominate postwar America.[31]

Liberals in support of an aggressive anti-communism organized the Union for Democratic Action (UDA) during the war, which was the basis for Americans for Democratic Action (ADA) established in January 1947. Dominated by northern white intellectuals, liberals, and labor leaders, members of the group had little direct association with the eclectic democratic culture that had nurtured the struggle for racial justice. The urgency they applied to exposing and routing out communists as democracy's greatest threat took precedence over struggles being waged along the color line. Historian Arthur Schlesinger, a leading figure in the UDA and ADA, published a lengthy article in *Life* magazine in the summer of 1946 describing communists as cult-like subversives working to advance the aims of Russia and insisting that they be exposed and purged from all liberal and labor organizations. At a time when the NAACP was immersed in the fight to secure voting rights for black southerners and pushing against a wave of terror and violence, Schlesinger ominously warned that the Communist Party was "sinking its tentacles into the NAACP." But he offered no evidence to support this charge. White, whose disdain for the Communist Party stretched back to the Scottsboro case, was not eager to be enlisted in the ranks of the red hunters, or in squabbles dividing liberals and labor groups around this increasingly contentious issue. On the recommendation of the NAACP board, he withdrew from his membership in the PCA and declined offers to join the board of the ADA. Later that year, White wrote in his syndicated column that communism posed less of a threat to the NAACP and American democracy than did professional anti-communists.[32]

While White finessed shifts in national politics, Marshall and his team pushed ahead on the legal front. "The number and type of cases have increased no end," Marshall reported, with major cases involving housing, education, voting, transportation, "and the whole attack on segregation." They were "striking out into new uncharted territory requiring the most careful research as well as the most careful type of planning of legal strategies." But working conditions in the overcrowded national headquarters made this difficult. The six-person legal staff, books, and case files were crammed into two rooms. Marshall shared an office with Constance Baker Motley and Annette Peyser. Robert Carter, Franklin Williams, and Marion Perry shared another.

Describing a typical scene, Marshall wrote: "Yesterday Carter was working with me on the brief in the Texas University case, Marian was working on the Detroit housing case, and Frank was working on the National Guard case . . . and the civil suit for [Isaac] Woodard—all working in the same room and at the same time dictating on these various subjects and answering the phone." He pleaded for more space, warning that under such conditions "it was impossible to do a good job without being seriously handicapped." But there was no relief until the legal offices moved to another building in 1951. Meanwhile, the legal victories mounted.[33]

In July 1947, NAACP lawyers won a ruling from federal district judge Waties Waring outlawing South Carolina's white primary, the last all-white primary still in operation, despite the 1944 Texas ruling. Marshall and Carter worked with South Carolina attorney Harold Boulware on the case, representing Columbia businessman George Elmore, who sued for the right to vote in the primary. With his ruling in this case, Waring emerged as a leading voice for change in the South. A blue blood from Charleston, he was an unlikely ally in the struggle for equal justice. He had presided over all of the cases brought by the NAACP in South Carolina during the 1940s, starting with a teacher salary case in 1943, and exhibited a basic courtesy and fairness that astounded Marshall. Recalling his first case before the judge, he noted that it was "the only case I ever tried with my mouth hanging open half the time." But Waring functioned within the parameters of southern racial practices until the case of Isaac Woodard at the end of 1946 pushed him to question his fundamental assumptions. The plight of the blinded veteran, the racist appeals of the defense counsel, and the failure of the federal government to vigorously pursue the case deeply disturbed Waring. He and his second wife, Elizabeth, a northern transplant, began reading extensively on the history of race relations in the South—books such as W.J. Cash's *The Mind of the South* as well as material Mrs. Waring obtained from Samuel Fleming, a prosperous black shoemaker in Charleston. Waring started making changes in his courtroom. He eliminated the "c" listed after the names of blacks in the jury pool, ended customary segregation in his courtroom, assigned seats in the jury box to ensure integrated seating, and hired Samuel Fleming's son John as his bailiff. With the *Elmore* ruling, the sixty-eight-year-old Waring took direct aim at the customs and beliefs of fellow white South Carolinians.[34]

In his *Elmore* case opinion, Waring dismissed the state's argument that the primary was a private club activity beyond the regulation of the Constitution;

the fact that 290,000 voted in the last primary while only 26,326 voted in the general election was evidence enough of the primary's central role in state politics. In an attempt to emphasize the impact of racially discriminatory voting practices on America's leadership role in the world, Waring quoted from Truman's speech to the NAACP two weeks earlier: "Our case for democracy should be as strong as we can make it. It should rest on practical evidence that we have been able to put our own house in order." The judge closed with his own advice to his fellow citizens. "It is time for South Carolina to rejoin the Union. It is time to adopt the American way of conducting elections." The circuit court of appeals upheld Waring's ruling. Unbowed, the state's Democratic Party worked up another set of party rules and registration requirements aimed at barring blacks, which would culminate with a showdown in Waring's courtroom on the eve of the 1948 primary. In the aftermath of the *Elmore* ruling, whites joined in a determined effort to ruin George Elmore and send a message to other blacks. The Klan burned a cross on his property and threatened Elmore and his family; local banks and merchants cut off Elmore's access to credit and supplies, ultimately destroying his business.[35]

Late in the summer of 1947, Marshall convened a meeting in New York to prepare for what would be one of the NAACP's most important Supreme Court cases. Over the previous five months, lawyers representing plaintiffs from St. Louis, Detroit, and Washington, D.C., had filed petitions with the U.S. Supreme Court challenging restrictive covenants in those cities. The cases represented a range of approaches, from George Vaughn of St. Louis who argued in *Shelley v. Kraemer* that the covenants violated the antislavery provision of the Thirteenth Amendment, to the Washington, D.C., cases, in which Charles Houston and Phineas Indritz drew heavily on sociological material to illuminate "the total effects of racial restrictions." Thurgood Marshall and Loren Miller prepared the brief for the Detroit case *McGhee v. Sipes*, the only case over which the NAACP had direct responsibility. Most significantly, the NAACP had provided a comprehensive review of the current state of the law and actively orchestrated the work of participating attorneys and consultants—steadily working to harness the strength and intelligence of all in crafting the strongest arguments possible.

The attorneys working on each of the cases met in New York on September 6 along with legal scholars, housing experts, social scientists, and representatives from interested organizations—forty-four in all. During the day-long brainstorming session, they pooled their experience and knowledge to explore "all the conceivable arguments that might be presented to the

court." All agreed that material emphasizing the social effects of the covenants would be important in convincing the Court to overturn a legal precedent. The group pursued an exhaustive review of articles and books and
discussed the preparation and publication of relevant sociological material in
reputable journals so that the briefs could be liberally supported with cita-
tions that provided the weight of credentialed professionals and academics. A
team of lawyers and sociologists coordinated this effort, under the direction
of Robert Weaver, the nation's leading expert on housing and race, and University of Chicago sociologist Louis Wirth. Within a few weeks they had
produced a memorandum of several hundred pages and circulated it to the
lawyers working on briefs for each of the cases.[36]

The NAACP-led fight against housing barriers had started as a lonely
battle three decades earlier with the fight against residential zoning laws—by
1947, it had generated a broad front of liberal and labor support for an end to
government-sanctioned housing discrimination. Loren Miller credited this
transformation to a tireless battle that had been "waged in state courts, in
newspapers, in magazines, over the air, and wherever else a hearing could be
had." With a Supreme Court date on the calendar, nineteen organizations
filed amicus curiae briefs on the side of the black plaintiffs, including the
Protestant Council of New York, the American Jewish Congress, the AFL,
the CIO, the Elks, the American Civil Liberties Union, the National Lawyers Guild, the Indian League, and the American Association of the United
Nations. Walter White and others lobbied the Justice Department to join in
as well. But the department remained silent until just a month before the
cases were argued before the Court in January 1948.[37]

In October 1947, major reports released by the NAACP and the Truman
administration brought the plight of black Americans and the costs of race
discrimination to national and international audiences as never before. *An
Appeal to the World: A Statement of the Denial of Human Rights to Minorities in
the Case of Citizens of the United States of America and an Appeal to the United
Nations for Redress* was a collaboration between Du Bois and colleagues in
history, law, and legislative affairs. The book-length document provided a
factually rich and tightly argued indictment of the historic failure of America's social and political institutions to protect "the lives, liberty and property"
of its black citizens. Efforts to get the *Appeal* before the United Nations,
however, ran up against the opposition of the State Department. Meanwhile,

it was quickly overshadowed by *To Secure These Rights*, the report by the President's Committee on Civil Rights, released just a week later.[38]

To Secure These Rights became an instant sensation. The report offered a panoramic view of America's color line at mid-century, and its impact on all phases of life—housing, health care, education, employment, policing, government, voting, military defenses, and international relations. It exposed segregation as a national problem and provided a blueprint for federal action. The committee called for nothing short of a government-led campaign to wipe out racial segregation and secure the enforcement of civil rights. Thurgood Marshall praised it as "one of the most important documents yet produced in this field. . . . The problem of the Negro and other minority groups is now before the public in a manner never equaled before."[39]

Over a million copies of the report were distributed—the government printing office produced 25,000 copies, and Simon and Schuster published and sold 35,000 copies, all at $1 a piece; the progressive newspaper *PM* reproduced the report as a Sunday supplement, offering it for 10¢ a copy; 5¢ for bulk sales of one hundred or more. Black newspapers serialized the report, the American Jewish Committee distributed two hundred thousand summaries, and the *New York Times* printed an abridged version of the committee's recommendations. NAACP branches and civic groups organized workshops to discuss the report, civic and youth groups sponsored discussions, a New York radio station hosted a two-week-long documentary on civil rights, and Dorothy Tilly persuaded the Southern Regional Council to sponsor a meeting devoted to the report in Atlanta. *To Secure These Rights* sparked a national discussion on civil rights, provided ammunition for a more aggressive campaign for civil rights legislation on Capitol Hill, and created a platform for President Truman.[40]

In his State of the Union address, President Truman listed civil rights as a top item on his domestic agenda for 1948. With a very competitive presidential campaign in the offing, the power of the black vote in key northern states would provide political incentive for presidential action on that front. Several battles loomed on Capitol Hill involving the issue of racial segregation, offering a staging ground for testing the muscle of civil rights forces as well as the standing of both parties on this issue. These included legislation for a peacetime draft and a bill supporting the regional university plan cooked up by southern governors. Meanwhile, the legal campaign was functioning at full throttle, with Marshall promising "an all out attack on segregation in all its forms." The campaign to break down race barriers in law and professional schools was well under way. The year began with the NAACP's Supreme Court victory in the case of Ada Sipuel calling for Oklahoma to provide Sipuel with a legal education equal to that available to other citizens in the state.[41]

On January 14, a week after he argued the *Sipuel* case, Marshall returned to Washington for oral arguments in *Shelley v. Kraemer*, the restrictive covenant cases from Detroit, St. Louis, and Washington, D.C. The attorneys from the New York office accompanied Marshall for what many agreed was "our most important case to come before the Supreme Court in this generation." As had been the practice since the 1938 *Gaines* case, Marshall, Houston, and the other attorneys involved in the cases participated in a moot court at Howard Law School the day before their date with the Court, rehearsing their oral arguments and entertaining a tough grilling from professors and students. During their time in Washington, Marshall and his legal staff along with other out-of-town lawyers stayed in a black-owned hotel, which was little more than a rooming house. They took their meals there as well since there were no restaurants nearby that served blacks. The evil they were fighting was an ever-present reality. Nevertheless, spirited evenings of relaxation capped long and grueling days. Constance Baker Motley recalled with amusement that the female proprietor of the hotel "gracefully tolerated Thurgood, Bob Ming, and Ed Dudley who romped around and partied all night like fraternity brothers." On the morning of the Supreme Court hearing, they arranged for a small caravan of black cab drivers to take them to the Court; white cab drivers in Washington rarely picked up black passengers.[42]

Shelley v. Kraemer went "straight to the heart of the protection of the rights of minorities as provided in the constitution," explained civil rights attorney William R. "Bob" Ming, raising the most significant questions that the court had faced since the 1883 civil rights cases. The top brass of the NAACP and attorneys from near and far packed the small hearing room, including William Hastie, James Nabrit Jr., Earl Dickerson, George Hayes, and Judge James Cobb. Cobb had argued *Corrigan v. Buckley* for the NAACP twenty-one years earlier—the restrictive covenant case that set the precedent Marshall and his team aimed to overturn. *Shelley* stood as a measure of the ground that had been gained in the long legal fight against housing discrimination, and was testimony to the NAACP's ability to weld together an increasingly vocal coalition of civil rights advocates. In the immediate aftermath of the civil rights committee's recommendations, the Department of Justice filed an amicus curiae brief, the first time the federal government had weighed in behind an NAACP case. It was a weighty 123-page brief with statements from the State Department, the Housing and Home Finance Agency, the Interior Department, and the Surgeon General.[43]

Marshall, Houston, Miller, Vaughn, and the other participating attorneys—including Philip Perlman, the solicitor general of the United States—reinforced the central argument that restrictive covenants established a pattern of racial discrimination that the state, through court action, could not legally support. In what would be his final appearance before the high court, Houston closed out the two days of debate as an attorney for the petitioners in the Washington, D.C., case, elaborating on points that had already been presented. "By perpetuating covenants," Houston told the Court, "we are perpetuating a second-class citizenship that is embarrassing to our national and international interests." James Crooks, attorney for the white homeowners in the Washington case, countered by arguing that Congress had jurisdiction over Washington and it had no policy against segregation. He added that covenants were not an expression of racial prejudice, but rather of a desire of people to live with those of their own choosing. "We are not dealing with social rights but with civil rights in this case," Houston emphasized in a brief rebuttal to Crooks. "We are not trying to change anyone's prejudice . . . but racism must go." With that the Court adjourned, and the justices began their deliberations.[44]

Two weeks later, on February 2, President Truman delivered a special message to Congress on civil rights, outlining the provisions of an omnibus bill he would send to the body. He requested congressional action on a ten-point program that included antilynching legislation, the establishment of a Fair Employment Practices Commission, better protection of voting rights, a law prohibiting discrimination in interstate transportation, the strengthening of existing civil rights laws, and home rule and suffrage in presidential elections for the District of Columbia. He also requested legislation that would expand and strengthen the capacity of the federal government to enforce civil rights—through the establishment of a permanent Commission on Civil Rights and a Civil Rights Division in the Justice Department. Truman pledged to act in his capacity as president, announcing that he would issue an executive order "containing a comprehensive reestablishment of the federal non-discrimination policy" and that he had instructed the secretary of defense "to take steps to have the remaining instances of discrimination in the Armed Forces eliminated." He concluded his historic address by linking the cause of civil rights to America's interests abroad. "If we wish to inspire the people of the world whose freedom is in jeopardy . . . we must correct the remaining imperfections in our practice of democracy." Hoping the president's message might do the work of illuminating America's commitment to these values, the State Department broadcast it as the lead item on the "Voice of America," which covered the cold war battlefront.[45]

The NAACP leadership supported Truman wholeheartedly while some civil rights advocates criticized Truman for failing to go as far as his civil rights committee in acknowledging the pervasive influence of segregation in American life and taking a forthright stand against Jim Crow. For most, the president's message marked a major step forward and a courageous one in the face of his party's powerful southern bloc. Editorials in the black press hailed Truman's proposals as the strongest civil rights program ever put forward by an American president. Charles Houston, who had had his disagreements with Truman in the past, praised the president and expressed confidence that he would make good on his commitments. Alluding to the high stakes in this presidential election year, Houston said Truman had given the Democratic Party "an unparalleled opportunity to win the confidence . . . of the minorities in the United States." This was no small factor in the calculations driving the potentially explosive issue of civil rights up to the top of the president's agenda. White House counsel Clark Clifford, architect of Truman's campaign, believed the black vote was the key to a Democratic win in November.[46]

For Walter White, who had long preached the potential power of the northern black vote, 1948 was a banner year. A perfect storm of political developments made it highly possible that black voters would determine the outcome of the presidential election. The salience of civil rights as an issue in 1948 was further enhanced by the candidacy of Henry Wallace on a third-party ticket. Wallace ran because of his opposition to a foreign policy driven by an exclusively confrontational and militaristic approach to the Soviet Union. Failure of the Truman administration to at least seek some basis for cooperation with the Soviet Union, Wallace believed, was reckless and dangerous in an age of atomic power—a view Walter White had once shared. In domestic policy, Wallace was distinguished by a long-standing commitment to racial equality and justice—one he actively demonstrated on numerous occasions—in the aftermath of the 1943 Detroit race riot, at the 1944 Democratic convention, and, most recently, in a series of tours through the South during which he refused to address segregated audiences. He was popular among African Americans. With New York governor Thomas Dewey the likely Republican nominee, Clifford predicted a close race in critical battleground states, where a 5 to 10 percent showing for Wallace could tip electoral-rich states in favor or the Republicans. Black voters composed 4 percent or more of all potential voters in New York, New Jersey, Pennsylvania, Ohio, Michigan, and Illinois. It was, Clifford concluded, imperative that the president run on a strong liberal platform and lay claim to the issue of civil rights, advising that the political cost set against the potential gain would be minimal. The South, he predicted, could be counted on as "safely Democratic."

Soon all bets were off. Southern governors dispatched a delegation led by South Carolina's Strom Thurmond to Washington to protest the president's civil rights program. The group had the support of half of the South's representatives in the House of Representatives. Thurmond and his associates met with Rhode Island senator J. Howard McGrath, who served as the head of the Democratic National Committee. Standing in for the president, McGrath defended Truman's message, but emphasized how moderate it was. After all, he did not call for an end to segregation, with the exception of interstate travel, and most of the provisions he put forward were dependent upon congressional action. McGrath implied that something would be done to allay southern concerns, possibly around the platform at the Democratic convention that summer. Thurmond warned that this was not sufficient; they wanted the president to disassociate himself from the sentiments he expressed on February 2. Truman remained publicly committed to his pronouncements, but the administration soon appeared to be in retreat. The president's plans to send an omnibus civil rights bill to Congress fizzled while key legislative battles around segregation in education and the armed services raised questions about the administration's commitment to promoting a civil rights agenda.[47]

The battle over school desegregation shifted to Congress late in February with the introduction of a bill seeking congressional approval of a regional education compact, devised by southern governors in the wake of the *Sipuel* decision. The plan provided for the southern states to take over a fiscally ailing Meherry Medical School, the only black medical school outside of Howard University, and transform it into a state-sponsored regional facility. If this effort succeeded, they believed that the enhanced school would provide an affordable route for offering separate professional and graduate training for black students and fulfill the Court's mandate. The NAACP mounted an intensive lobbying campaign against the bill. Just a week after his meeting with the Thurmond group, Howard McGrath emerged as one of the strongest proponents of the regional school plan, sparking rumors that efforts to heal the breach with Southern Democrats caused by Truman's civil rights plan were well under way. The bill breezed through the Senate Judiciary Committee by a vote of 6-2 and won overwhelming approval in the House, 235-45. Republican senator Wayne Morse, a close ally of the NAACP, led the opposition on the floor of the Senate. Not a single Democrat spoke against the bill, noted the *Chicago Defender*. In a "photo finish," the Senate Republicans led in killing the plan by a 38-37 vote.[48]

While the regional education plan wound its way through Congress the issue of segregation in the armed forces took on added urgency. A February editorial in *The Crisis* on pending legislation to establish a peacetime draft warned that "the vast body of Negro Americans is opposed to this training as long as it is to be on a segregated basis." Promises by the president in his February 2 speech to take steps to eliminate discrimination in the armed forces failed to yield action. On March 22, A. Philip Randolph and the Reverend Grant Reynolds, co-directors of the Committee against Jim Crow in Military Service and Training, led a delegation to the White House to confer with the president. Reporting on conversations with blacks around the country, Randolph told Truman that "Negroes are in no mood to shoulder guns for democracy abroad while they are denied democracy here at home." Truman took offense at such an assertion, but Randolph insisted that the president needed a true picture of what people were thinking as he charted his course.[49]

Over the next week, black leaders amplified their protest. The NAACP convened representatives of twenty black organizations at their New York headquarters on March 27 and issued the "Declaration of Negro Voters." The statement endorsed Truman's civil rights program and advised candidates that support of the complete elimination of "every vestige of segregation and discrimination in the armed forces" was essential to winning black support. Three days later, Randolph dropped a "bombshell" at a hearing before the Senate Armed Services Committee. He told the senators that he would urge black youth to refuse to register or be drafted unless the Selective Service Act included specific provisions barring segregation, testifying: "I personally pledge myself to openly counsel, aid and abet youth, both black and white, to quarantine any Jim Crow conscription system." He promised to enlist black veterans to join in the effort. Randolph talked about a "mass civil disobedience movement along the lines of the magnificent struggles of the people of

India against British imperialism." There was no question that segregation in the armed forces was a major issue for black Americans and a fault line in the 1948 campaign so far as black voters were concerned.[50]

On May 2, civil rights advocates won a major victory when a unanimous Supreme Court struck down judicial enforcement of restrictive covenants based on race. Chief Justice Fred Vinson, writing for the Court, paraphrased the major argument advanced by attorneys for the plaintiffs, ruling that in the cases of *Shelley* and *McGhee* such state action violated the equal protection clause of the Fourteenth Amendment. In the Washington, D.C., case, *Hurd v. Hodge*, the Court held that by enforcing the covenants the district court denied the plaintiffs' rights intended by Congress under the Civil Rights Act of 1866 and in accordance with the public policy of the United States. The significance of the ruling was widely commented upon. Marshall called it "a complete justification of the NAACP's thirty-one-year fight to outlaw discrimination in housing." Observing that the "confinement of Negroes to ever contracting . . . slum sections of American cities . . . has been at the root cause of all the other disadvantages suffered by their race," the *Washington Post* speculated that the Court's ruling was "perhaps the most effective step in the emancipation of American Negroes" since Abraham Lincoln's proclamation in 1863.[51]

Attorney Loren Miller, Marshall's co-counsel on the Detroit case and a veteran in the fight against restrictive covenants in California, cautioned against both underestimating and overestimating the significance of the ruling. In the aftermath of *Shelley*, neighborhood racial boundaries in major cities yielded to some extent as blacks purchased homes in areas that had been shut off by tight enforcement of restrictive covenants. But segregated patterns remained and expanded into rapidly developing suburban areas, as real estate boards, financial institutions, neighborhood groups, and "professional hucksters of prejudice" quickly devised ways to circumvent the ruling and reinforce segregation. The Supreme Court ruling would not have its desired effect on residential segregation, Miller cautioned, without "vigorous effort that is going to take time and that will cost plenty in terms of dollars and cents as well as social action."[52]

The problem with Truman, wrote Nancy Wechsler, former counsel to the PCCR, and *New York Post* columnist James Wechsler, was that he "thought he could carry on the fight for civil rights and still keep almost everybody happy." Early in May, southern state Democratic officials met in Jackson,

Mississippi, for a states' rights conference, united in their opposition to the president's civil rights initiatives. By then, Truman was in full retreat from the agenda he had laid out in February. No action had been taken on the promised executive order ending discrimination in federal employment, and Truman told a press conference in mid-May that no such order was being drafted. He remained quiet on the subject of discrimination in the armed services while his secretary of the army, Kenneth Royall of North Carolina, "publicly and pugnaciously opposed" any change in the Jim Crow army. Attorney general Tom Clark abandoned plans to enlarge the civil rights section of the Justice Department and dropped a proposed campaign to rally public support for the civil rights program. Southern opposition to the administration's proposals had been stronger and more vociferous than either Truman or Clifford had anticipated. As the presidential campaign season heated up, Truman seemed to be working "feverishly" to woo "rebellious Southerners" and prevent a bolt by southern delegates at the Democratic National Convention in mid-July.[53]

Despite the president's stalled program, Truman had gone much further than any of his predecessors in putting the federal government on the side of civil rights. While the NAACP was officially nonpartisan, most of the national executive staff, with the exception of Du Bois, was firmly in Truman's camp. White and Wilkins sought to be of service to Truman by trying to "keep Negroes from wandering off to Henry Wallace," as Wilkins put it. Through *The Crisis*, which Wilkins edited, and in White's columns for the *Chicago Defender* and the *New York Herald Tribune*, both men worked to minimize and diminish Wallace's civil rights record, a clear reversal for White who had been a staunch admirer of Wallace's since at least 1943. Such public displays of loyalty by the association's top leadership were especially meaningful during a closely contested election that could hinge on the black vote, helping to shore up the NAACP's access to the administration and strengthen its hand in pushing a civil rights agenda.[54]

Few believed Wallace had any chance of winning. But his campaign appealed to black Americans tired of the compromises made by Democrats and attracted by Wallace's unwavering support for civil rights. For Du Bois, Truman was completely unacceptable. He believed Wallace's stand on colonialism, his open approach to the Soviet Union, and his racial and labor stands represented positions that black Americans should support. "There is every chance that his positions will win in 2004," Du Bois wryly observed. Charles Houston was sympathetic to Wallace's campaign and saw it as part of the broad struggle against segregation. But he also recognized the value of the Wallace candidacy in pressuring Truman and the Democrats to take action on civil rights. Houston defended the Wallace effort from liberal Democrats who smeared it as a communist-dominated operation. He called such charges "essentially dishonest" and reminded Wallace's critics that they tolerated the worst southern reactionaries. "Certainly there are some Communists in the Wallace movement," Houston countered. "So what? There are fascists in the Democratic Party, such as . . . Eastland and Rankin . . . and I do not see anybody trying to excommunicate them." Even Roy Wilkins advised that tagging Wallace as a "Red" would do little to dissuade supporters who were "accustomed to being mislabeled, misrepresented, and mistreated merely because they want their rights."[55]

The issue was by no means symbolic: Black votes for Wallace in the North and West could tip the presidential election and be decisive in key state and local contests. The South was another country, under the rule of Jim Crow Democrats—a place Truman avoided during the presidential race. The Progressive Party's southern campaign was organized by Louis Burnham, African American executive director of the Southern Negro Youth Congress (SNYC) based in Birmingham since 1939, and Palmer Weber, native white Virginian, former congressional staffer and research director for the CIO-Political Action Committee who served on the national board of the NAACP. They ran the campaign as a "head on attack on the segregation system" and merged their efforts with the SNYC, progressive CIO unions, the Southern Conference for Human Welfare, student groups, and various civic organizations—all dedicated to maximizing black political participation at every level—the registration booth, the Democratic primary, and the election. Burnham and Weber enlisted students as the backbone of the Wallace effort, which focused on voter registration and petitions to get Wallace on the ballot. By working to get the Progressive Party on the ballot in the southern states and running slates of candidates for office in the general election, the party broke through Southern Democrats' domination of the election season. Black candidates were among those running for Congress and the Senate on Progressive Party tickets in the South.[56]

In places like Birmingham, Alabama, the Wallace campaign folded into a loosely coordinated movement that functioned at the edges of a tightly regulated caste system. Charles Houston, who had represented Willie Peterson in Birmingham fifteen years earlier, was encouraged by what he found during a visit to the city late in the spring of 1948. He noted the developments around a planned mass meeting sponsored by the SNYC as part of their annual youth legislature and featuring Glen Taylor, U. S. senator from Idaho and vice presidential candidate on the Progressive Party ticket. Public safety commissioner Eugene "Bull" Connor, who became a national symbol of police repression in 1963, warned that a municipal law requiring segregation and separate entrances for public meetings would be strictly enforced. After the SNYC agreed to observe the ordinance so that their meeting could proceed without being disrupted, Connor pressured the city's large black churches, places where the SNYC had met in the past, to deny the group a meeting space. The Reverend Herbert Oliver, the twenty-three-year-old pastor of Alliance Gospel Tabernacle, offered his church, a small structure that held no more than one hundred people. Organizers set up separate entrances in compliance with city law—blacks through the front door and whites through the back door. Students filled the church, along with a sprinkling of coal miners and local townspeople. When Taylor arrived, he walked up the front steps and attempted to enter through the "colored" entrance. The waiting police threw him on the ground and arrested him. Local NAACP attorney Arthur Shores represented Taylor when he was tried on disorderly conduct charges—"a colored lawyer defending a U. S. Senator is something new," Houston observed. But what most impressed him was that "the meeting was held in spite of police intimidation." The fact "that the challenge to tyranny was made by humble people while the pillars of the community stayed at home shows that we are sound at the core," he wrote. "All over the South the level of resistance of our people in defense of their rights is rising. The new day cannot be so very far away."[57]

There were dramatic signs of change on the voting front throughout the South. Reporting on his travels through the South during the summer of 1948, Palmer Weber wrote Marshall: "I find the Negro leadership everywhere fighting for the ballot as never before. . . . I keep thinking how much the NAACP field staff could accomplish if it were concentrated in the South for the next couple of months." In Richmond, Virginia, an estimated fifty thousand black voters registered in the lead-up to the election season; in June they helped elect Oliver Hill to the city council, the first black to serve in that body since the late nineteenth century. In South Carolina Judge Waring struck down a last attempt by the state Democratic Party to limit black participation, threatening to jail any party officers who failed to abide by his ruling. On the morning of August 10, Marshall was on hand in Charleston to witness the historic sight of black men and women lined up to vote in the Democratic Party primary. An estimated 35,000 African Americans turned out across the state; long lines formed in Columbia before the polls opened at 8 A.M. and continued until the close of polls at 6 P.M. Dr. Robert Mance stayed at the polls in Columbia all day. When a patient tracked him down and complained that he had been waiting for two hours at his office, Mance replied that he was sorry about that, "but I've been waiting 40 years for this thing to happen." That evening Marshall was in Columbia and attended a packed meeting in the auditorium at Allen University. The crowd presented Marshall with a small token of their appreciation: "a Hamilton wrist watch, a portable radio, and two boxes of white shirts."[58]

At the same time, determined efforts to keep blacks from the polls raised new legal challenges for the NAACP and kept black voting numbers down in most parts of the Deep South. In Alabama, the state devised the Boswell Amendment to replace the white primary, authorizing registrars to test whether applicants "understood" the Constitution—used shamelessly to disqualify blacks. The NAACP won a federal court ruling in 1949 ending that practice. In Mississippi, the legislature changed the registration law, requiring a new, statewide registration of all voters. The registration of rural black voters was almost completely wiped out. In 1948 there were seventy-five counties in Mississippi without a single black voter on the registration books. A. P. Tureaud reported that in various parts of Louisiana, registrars refused to appear at the office during designated registration periods and took the registration book to the homes of whites. In Georgia, where Governor Herman Talmadge fueled antiblack activism, county officials purged voting rolls and the Grand Dragon of the Ku Klux Klan warned that "blood will flow in the streets if Negroes vote." The Klan presided over a reign of terror during the primary season in Georgia. There were cross burnings in several parts of the state on the night before the Democratic primary. When Isaiah Nixon turned up at the polling station in Montgomery County on primary day, men at the polling station told him he could vote, but warned him not to. He voted, and that night two white men went to Nixon's home and shot and killed the thirty-one-year-old turpentine worker in front of his wife and six children. Whites beat D. V. Carter, president of the NAACP's Montgomery County branch, for driving blacks to the polls. Fearing for his life, he fled the state.[59]

Beyond the black press, struggles around voting and civil rights in the South were rarely commented on in the mainstream news. The "Solid South" of white supremacy, which dominated popular views of the region, aggressively asserted itself during the 1948 presidential campaign as a fractious

Democratic Party labored in the shadow of anticipated defeat. Nearly four weeks before the Democratic convention met, the Republicans nominated New York governor Thomas Dewey to head their ticket with Governor Earl Warren of California in the vice presidential slot—a formidable team. Dewey had a good civil rights record compared with his contemporaries. As governor, he had supported a strong bill creating a state FEPC program, and he had appointed blacks to professional positions in state government. The Republican Party platform included a civil rights plank distinguished by its stated opposition to segregation in the armed forces. At the same time, the party was weighted down by the Eightieth Congress's dismal record on domestic legislation, including civil rights.[60]

In the weeks leading up to the Democratic convention in Philadelphia, core elements of the party appeared desperate to ward off a thumping in November. There was a general sentiment that the lackluster Truman doomed whatever chances Democrats might have. While Truman sought an accommodation with the party's southern wing, an odd assortment of Democrats launched a drive to draft General Dwight Eisenhower, former army chief of staff, as their party's nominee. ADA liberals, including Minneapolis mayor Hubert H. Humphrey, Chester Bowles, and James Roosevelt made common cause with city bosses and southern malcontents like Governor Strom Thurmond and Georgia senator Richard Russell in this effort. While the liberal wing of the Eisenhower movement pledged to fight for a strong civil rights plank at the convention, they apparently discounted the general's vocal opposition to the integration of the armed forces—a position that made him unacceptable to most black Americans. Walter White charged Eisenhower's liberal supporters with hitching their wagon to an "avowed enemy of liberalism." Eisenhower resolved this problem when he announced that he would not "accept even if nominated."[61]

"The most listless . . . set of delegates ever gathered in the name of democracy," was how one columnist described those who convened in Philadelphia for the Democratic convention in mid-July. In anticipation of the debate over the platform committee's proposed civil rights planks, White and Roy Wilkins placed a full-page ad in the *Philadelphia Bulletin* instructing, "LET 'EM WALK." The majority on the committee had endorsed the administration's proposal, which echoed the 1944 civil rights plank—a vague statement on equal rights which aimed to straddle the issue; White warned that it was completely unacceptable. Southerners introduced a minority plank, seeking an explicit endorsement of states' rights. The liberal minority openly endorsed the Truman civil rights program and called for specific measures including an end to discrimination in the armed forces. It was boosted by Hubert Humphrey's powerful endorsement from the floor of the convention, exhorting that "the time has arrived in America for the Democratic Party to get out of the shadows of states rights and to walk forthrightly in the bright sunshine of human rights." In a major upset, the liberal plank swept up the majority of delegate votes, 651½ to 582½, carried by a consensus of northern and western delegates who agreed that the fate of the party in November would be decided outside the South. The move electrified the convention, with delegates endorsing the party's platform "by a roaring voice vote." One-half of the Alabama delegation walked out (including Eugene "Bull" Connor) joined by the entire delegation from Mississippi. In the final tally for the presidential nomination, Truman received a mere thirteen votes of the southern delegates who remained in the convention hall, but he won the nomination handily. On July 17, the states' rights conference reconvened in Birmingham and selected Strom Thurmond and Governor Fielding Wright of Mississippi to head an independent ticket.[62]

Free of the need to placate southern diehards, Truman moved quickly to embrace his earlier stance on civil rights and rally the forces of Roosevelt's New Deal coalition. In his "fighting" acceptance speech, he announced plans to call Congress back into session to move on housing, education, civil rights, and other domestic issues, pushing the burden for action on these controversial issues into the lap of the Republican-dominated body. On July 26 he issued two executive orders, which fulfilled the pledge he made in his February 2 speech. One established procedures for exposing and eliminating discriminatory employment practices in the federal government. The other, Executive Order 9981, declared that "there shall be equality of treatment in the armed services without regard to race, color, religion or national origin," and stated that this "policy shall be put into effect as rapidly as possible, having due regard to the time required to effectuate any necessary changes without impairing efficiency or morale." The order provided for the establishment of a seven-person committee to oversee a program of desegregation. Satisfied that the program would be implemented, A. Philip Randolph terminated his plans for a civil disobedience campaign, which was scheduled to begin with the implementation of the draft later in August. By standing up to the South and putting himself back in the fight, Truman had "stopped the swing of many toward the Progressives," Charles Houston observed, "because now thousands of colored and liberal white voters can vote the Democratic ticket without apology."[63]

Truman's bold stand for civil rights in the summer of 1948 was matched by Henry Wallace's tour through the South during the first week of September. For a brief moment, the 1948 presidential campaign merged with a direct challenge to racial segregation. For seven days, the former vice president of the United States traveled with an interracial entourage from Virginia to Mississippi, addressing only nonsegregated audiences in speeches that focused on his economic plan to aid the poverty-stricken region and called for an end to Jim Crow. The violent receptions and harassment that greeted Wallace was front-page news nationally. A Wallace supporter was stabbed at a rally in Durham, North Carolina; in the textile town of Hickory, North Carolina, there were shouts of "Kill Wallace." In Birmingham, an angry mob rocked his car, threatening to turn it over before police arrived and cleared a path. *New York Post* columnist James Wechsler was among the press traveling with the Wallace group. In the face of constant physical danger, Wallace preached "the Sermon on the Mount," Wechsler marveled, "and established in at least a dozen southern places that un-segregated meetings could be held without civil war"—meetings in Alabama, Mississippi, Louisiana, Arkansas, and Tennessee. Douglas Hall, reporter for the *Baltimore Afro-American* who covered the trip, wrote that Wallace came closer "to receiving the treatment accorded to colored persons in the South than any other white man I know." He heard Wallace ask the question "that every colored person has asked many times, 'is this America?'"[64]

Large crowds turned out to hear Wallace in towns and cities across the South. They met in churches, college auditoriums, and ballparks, in front of courthouses and on the steps of the state capitol in Jackson, Mississippi. When Bull Connor barred the Wallace group from holding an integrated outdoor meeting in Birmingham, the candidate delivered his message from the local radio station. "Wallace pulled no punches either on the stump or on the radio," Palmer Weber wrote Marshall. "He told folks everywhere that segregation is sin. . . . The various Negro communities were electrified and tremendously heartened to see one white man with guts who was willing to take it standing up." Daisy Bates, who led the school desegregation effort in Little Rock a decade later, was a local organizer for the Progressive Party. Recalling Wallace's visit to her city, she commented, "I had waited all of my life to hear a white man say what he said." Wallace's journey, observed Charles Houston, stirred "thousands of whites and hundreds of thousands of colored people . . . to greater resistance to segregation." The form of that resistance, he wrote, "will vary from time to time and place to place, but the spiritual climate has been formed." The Wallace effort was no longer a "mere political" exercise, but part of "a movement toward freedom which has implications far more significant than the ballot count in the coming election."[65]

Weber advised White to see to it that "Harry S. comes south and slugs," claiming that "he can't lose a thing by so doing and he would enormously help himself and I believe the whole Negro liberation struggle." But Truman stayed away from the South, except for a brief trip to Texas and Oklahoma later in October. In both places, he avoided any mention of civil rights; local Democrats advised it was a "hot issue." During the final days of the campaign, Truman stumped on his civil rights platform before audiences in Philadelphia and Chicago, topped off by the first presidential campaign stop in Harlem, where the president addressed a rally of 65,000 people between 135th Street and Edgecombe Avenue. The showdown at the Democratic convention acknowledged the power of northern black voters and gave ascendance to the issue of civil rights in the 1948 campaign. On election day, Truman lost four southern states to the States Rights Party and carried an estimated 69 percent of black votes in major northern and western cities. Black votes for Truman in California, Illinois, and Ohio made the difference in one of the biggest political upsets in presidential history when Truman beat Dewey. The election also returned Democratic majorities to both houses of Congress.[66]

Political divisions accentuated during the presidential campaign fueled a final rupture between Du Bois and White in the fall of 1948. While Du Bois's efforts to gain a public hearing for the *Appeal* before the U.N. General Assembly stalled in the face of State Department opposition, White became more closely aligned with the Truman administration. That summer he accepted an invitation from the State Department to attend the meeting of the General Assembly in Paris as a consultant to the U.S. delegation. When White instructed Du Bois to prepare a memorandum for him on matters of interest to the NAACP that were likely to be discussed at the meeting, Du Bois refused. He skipped a special meeting called by White on September 7 on the eve of his departure to Paris and instead drafted a memo to

White and the board of directors explaining why he was unable to comply with White's request. The U.S. delegation had clearly expressed its attitude toward matters the NAACP was interested in, Du Bois noted. It had refused "to bring the curtailment of our civil rights to the attention of the General Assembly," and worked to ensure that no other nation would. On the Trusteeship Council, Du Bois charged, the United States had sided with the imperial powers, it sided with Italy in taking most of Eritrea from Ethiopia, and opposed the best interest of India. Without "careful knowledge of the facts" and a clear statement of the NAACP's position on these issues, Du Bois argued that the presence of one of its representatives on the delegation stood as a blanket endorsement of Truman's policies. If they were content "to be loaded on the Truman bandwagon with no chance for opinions and consultations," he warned, "we are headed for a tragic mistake."[67]

Before most board members had a chance to read the memo, it was reported in the *New York Times* by George Streator. The piece claimed that the NAACP was abandoning efforts "to ease the world plight of the Negro people to serve the interests of the Truman administration" and repeated Du Bois's charge that Eleanor Roosevelt had threatened to resign from the Human Rights Commission if the NAACP's petition was introduced at the UN. A number of board members had shared White's desire to cut Du Bois loose, particularly in the wake of his active involvement with the Progressive Party. The leak of his memo to the press was the final straw. Du Bois denied having provided the press with a copy but admitted that he would have been willing to do that. At the board meeting on September 13, William Hastie cited Du Bois's refusal to aid in the preparation for the General Assembly meeting and the leaked memo as grounds for his dismissal, concluding that his continued employment was not in the best interest of the association. While White sailed to Paris, the board voted not to renew Du Bois's contract, which expired at the end December. Du Bois continued to pursue his efforts through the Council on African Affairs, a progressive group that by then was feeling the full brunt of the Red Scare.[68]

The circumstances surrounding Du Bois's departure from the staff of the NAACP reflected personal tensions that had long been simmering between White and him but also pointed to deeper challenges facing a leadership that had been forged in earlier struggles. Charles Houston praised both men in his weekly column, as if bearing witness to the passing of an era. He cautioned against the tendency to take sides in the rift between these two stalwarts and lose sight of the broader history they both helped to shape. White and Du Bois were so "completely different from one another," Houston wrote, yet each had dedicated their remarkable talents to removing the stubborn barriers of racial caste. Du Bois supplied "the vision and intellectual ferment for the beginnings of the NAACP" and was still "a vigorous intellectual rebel" and voice of protest at eighty years of age. While Du Bois worked largely from the center of "the group," White, "a white-washed colored man" had penetrated the white world like no one before him. He was always a "star performer," but he "brought us back everything they were doing and saying" and worked himself into strategic positions that previously would have "been considered absolutely beyond reach." Healthy, honest criticism had its place, but "only fools would attempt to disparage either man." Houston reflected on generational change and pointed out that neither man was indispensable—a fact that did not diminish their importance, but underscored "our own advances." There was an ongoing need for creative and diverse leadership in the grueling battle to break the color barrier and build an inclusive democracy, a reality that spoke to the challenges facing the NAACP as it entered its fortieth year.[69]

After nearly two decades as the executive secretary of the NAACP, White had become a seasoned operator at the highest levels of government—a position he used to good effect, particularly in the years leading up to the 1948 election. Keenly sensitive to political currents, White shelved the NAACP's petition when it met the strong opposition of Eleanor Roosevelt and seized the opportunity to advise the U.S. delegation to the General Assembly. He accused Du Bois of trying to "wreck the association" and claimed credit for practically "waging . . . a one man battle . . . to get something done about human rights and colonies." As he sailed to Paris, mixing with delegates and consultants, White was guardedly hopeful, as he wrote board members, that "our point of view" will have "a fighting chance." But White quickly found that there was no middle ground between Du Bois's confrontational approach and acquiescence to U.S. policy. After he circulated a memo critical of the United States' position on the disposition of Italy's former colonies, he received a stern rebuke for a "serious infringement of confidence" from a leading member of the U.S. delegation who threatened to bar him from future briefings. White muted his public criticism of American foreign policy and soon embraced a narrow approach that linked the domestic struggle for civil rights to the fight against international communism, echoing the dominant government line. He did not abandon his critique of colonialism and at times indicated support for the revolutions sweeping Asia, Africa, and Latin America. But these concerns became sidelined in the NAACP's effort to hold its ground in the domestic political arena and advance the struggle for civil rights within the narrowing confines of the cold war.[70]

By the end of 1948, the cold war dominated American politics and culture, pushing the NAACP to establish its anti-communist credentials. A series of events during the summer and through the fall seemed to give credence to charges that communists had penetrated the major institutions of the nation's life and posed a grave risk to national security. In August, the federal government indicted the top leaders of the American Communist Party on charges of conspiring to overthrow the U.S. government. Later that fall, the indictment of Alger Hiss, former New Dealer and top Roosevelt aide, on charges of perjury appeared to validate Whittaker Chambers's charge that Hiss was one of a number of communist spies who had infiltrated the upper reaches of government. In this climate, groups that openly tolerated communist participation became completely marginalized—a fate that befell the Progressive Party. Liberal and labor groups that failed to openly bar communists attracted scrutiny. In light of the Communist Party's active support of antiracism and civil rights, the NAACP appeared especially vulnerable. The association had occasionally been tagged by groups on the Right as subversive, a tag routinely applied by southern segregationists. It ultimately responded to pressure to ward off charges of communist infiltration, publicly denying such claims, distancing itself from groups on the Left, and finally developing procedures to review charges that particular branches had been "infiltrated" by communists. In 1949, Eleanor Roosevelt commented approvingly, that the NAACP was "one of the best bulwarks we have against communism among our Negro population." At its 1950 convention, the association passed a resolution directing the board to appoint a committee to investigate charges communist infiltration in particular branches and to establish procedures for suspending any branch that came under communist control.[71]

The fight for civil rights legislation in the new Congress dominated the NAACP's national agenda in 1949. While Truman pledged to transform his civil rights program into legislation, he faced many obstacles, including his own limitations as a political maestro. Early in the session southerners joined with Republicans to strengthen the filibuster, the bane of civil rights legislation. Senate Rule 22 had required two-thirds of a Senate quorum, or 32 votes, to enforce cloture and cut off paralyzing debate. The revised measure called for two-thirds of the full majority of the Senate, or 64 votes, to end a filibuster. The new rule passed by a 63-23 vote, with only fifteen Democrats voting against it. Commenting on this turn of events, the *New York Times* observed that Strom Thurmond's States Rights ticket may have garnered a mere 2½ percent of the vote in his presidential bid, but "in the matter of federal action on civil rights we will still be ruled from Birmingham." Southern Democrats who had bolted the party for Thurmond suffered no censure or party discipline. Several "Dixiecrats" held powerful committee positions, including William Colmer of Mississippi, who served on the House Rules Committee, and Senator James Eastland, who became head of the Judiciary Committee's Subcommittee on Civil Rights, where he could hold up all civil rights legislation with the exception of FEPC bills. Despite the pivotal role of black voters in the Democrats' victory, "the heart of Congress," wrote Roy Wilkins, "remained as cold as ever to the cause of civil rights."[72]

The Truman administration introduced a raft of civil rights legislation, including the staples of anti–poll tax and antilynching bills and legislation for a permanent FEPC, as well as New York congressman Emanuel Celler's bill to establish a civil rights division in the Justice Department and strengthen existing civil rights laws. The bills floundered, and the administration agreed that they be postponed until the next session. At the NAACP's 1949 convention in Los Angeles, the association charged Congress with betraying the mandate of the election and implicated Truman as well for failing to pursue a civil rights program with "vigor, persistency and strength." In the face of an emboldened southern bloc and a legislative agenda crowded by competing demands, Marshall advised that White's personal brand of lobbying would not suffice. "If anything is going to be accomplished we must 'go to the country' and bring the country to Washington," he told White. He suggested bringing large numbers of members to the Capitol where they could buttonhole senators personally and demand action. Marshall also advocated staging "terrific mass meetings" in every state where senators were up for reelection in 1950, and make them realize "what the score is"—the kind of mass involvement that succeeded in defeating the nomination of John J. Parker twenty years earlier, the campaign that White had so brilliantly commandeered.[73]

The fight had gone out of Walter White. Personal problems weighed on him, and he had grown weary of the NAACP regimen. The dual battle of

attacking white supremacy and sustaining the fiscal viability of the association showed no signs of slackening. Over the past thirty years, he led the
building up of the association and was responsible for some of its greatest
achievements—going undercover to expose the truth about the massacre in
Elaine, Arkansas, winning the acquittal of Ossian Sweet, enlisting Charles
Houston to initiate the legal campaign, and compelling the Truman administration to confront the issue of civil rights. Along the way, he had gained
access to the highest echelons of power and come to confuse that with power
itself, according to biographer Kenneth Janken. Within the association, he
moved in a tight orbit with Wilkins and Marshall; the unyielding pressure of
the work and the rub of personal ambitions and sensitive egos had frayed
these relationships. White had considered a leave of absence, but in May
1949, he submitted his resignation, to be effective June 1. He had suffered a
heart attack two years earlier and explained to the board that health concerns
prompted his action. He was also interested in pursuing career opportunities
in a more expanded arena. White failed to disclose that he was on the verge
of divorcing Gladys White, his wife of twenty-six years, and marrying Poppy
Cannon, a white woman. Cannon was thrice-divorced, had three children,
and was a successful food writer.[74]

Members of the board worried that White's abrupt departure would leave
the association leaderless at a difficult time. They persuaded him not to resign but to take a year's leave of absence with pay instead. Roy Wilkins would
serve as acting secretary in the interim. Less than two months later, news of
White's marriage to Poppy Cannon exploded on the front pages of the black
press, and, as one insider recalled, "all hell broke loose within the NAACP."
At the time, White and his new wife were on a world tour with *Town Meeting of the Air*, a popular NBC public affairs program. Opinion over the racial
dimensions of White's domestic drama was sharply divided. Many black
women protested White's abandonment of his wife for a white woman. At a
time when interracial marriage was rare (and illegal in twenty-eight states),
critics of White's marriage questioned the racial allegiance of the fair-skinned
civil rights leader and his apparent disregard for how his actions would affect
the NAACP. The episode was a major embarrassment and distraction at a
time when the association was struggling to keep its head above water. Some
board members defended his right to marry whom he pleased; others argued
that White's actions had, in the words of Carl Murphy, "so weakened his
usefulness that the Association will assume a grave risk in attempting to

keep him in office." When he decided to return to the NAACP at the end of his leave, having failed to secure another job, there was strong opposition on the board. Eleanor Roosevelt's active intervention on his behalf was critical to swinging support behind him. The board resolved to allow him to resume his role as executive secretary, but designated Roy Wilkins as chief administrator.[75]

The leadership crisis unfolded at a time of plummeting membership and declining revenue, raising concerns about the future of the association. During 1949, membership dipped to fewer than 250,000—a nearly 50 percent drop over its postwar high. The primary cause, many agreed, was a long overdue hike in membership fees to $2, doubling the annual dues. After branch-related costs were deducted from the 50¢ on each $1 membership the national office received, Walter White estimated that a mere 7¢ was left toward its operating expenses. Two dollars was hardly prohibitive; that this reasonable increase shook so many members loose pointed to deeper weaknesses. With a black population in the United States estimated at 15 million, it seemed astonishing that just a small fraction of black Americans actively supported the work of an organization that "touches and helps every Negro," observed *Pittsburgh Courier* editor P. L. Prattis. Benjamin Mays called it a "tragedy" and a "calamity." Rehearsing the many advances accrued by the "militant but legal battle waged by the NAACP," particularly in the South, he instructed that "if we are going to achieve a larger share of freedom we will have to be willing to pay for it." Such exhortations, which were many, did little to change the fortunes of the NAACP over the next several years. The ebb and flow of membership numbers had been a constant challenge since its founding—and at critical moments it often generated an active engagement of the base. By the late 1940s, with the important exception of the legal campaign, the NAACP's national leadership had become more insulated from the communities it claimed to represent and had invested increasing attention toward securing its hard-won position as a player in the national political arena.[76]

Roy Wilkins represented continuity while offering a dramatic departure from White's style of leadership. In recent years, White had come to serve as the NAACP's ambassador of sorts, hobnobbing in Washington, courting Hollywood moguls, and meeting with foreign dignitaries. While White gallivanted, Wilkins ran the national office, managed the annual conference, edited *The Crisis*, and took care of day-to-day details. On the surface at least, the men appeared to play complementary roles. Wilkins, however, had tired of being second in command and thought that White's departure and his own official elevation to the top post was overdue. The forty-eight-year-old Wilkins was ambitious, dedicated, and hard-working—the ultimate organization man. He was also thin-skinned and could be petty and vindictive. There were rumblings among a minority of board members who questioned whether Wilkins was suited to lead the association. Yet there was no obvious alternative. During his year as acting secretary, he offered a steady hand at the helm and began to put his own stamp on the NAACP with his orchestration of the National Emergency Civil Rights Mobilization (NECRM).[77]

At the NAACP's 1949 convention, delegates endorsed a resolution calling for a coordinated nationwide movement to mobilize support for civil rights legislation along the lines suggested by Marshall. The main event would be a mass lobbying campaign in Washington, D.C., at the start of the Eighty-second Congress in January 1950. Wilkins led in building a broad coalition of support enlisting the major labor, liberal, and religious groups, such as the AFL, the CIO, the UAW, the ADA, the American Jewish Committee, and the Federal Council of Churches of Christ, along with black organizations such as the Negro Elks, fraternities and sororities, and the National Association of Colored Women—more than sixty organizations participated as sponsors.

Days before the start of the mobilization on January 15, Wilkins announced that representatives of "Communist and Communist front organizations" were excluded from the mobilization, and he advised that special registration procedures would be in place "to keep out all undesirables." Such a broad brush approach, a *Pittsburgh Courier* reporter observed, shut out "some . . . innocent rock-ribbed old fashioned Americans too—in the attempt to keep any type of coloring from the mobilization." Virginia Durr, a leader in the anti–poll tax movement, had been active in Henry Wallace's Progressive Party in 1948; she was among those turned away. So were some NAACP members. Wilkins had no apparent qualms about the policy. He had carried a grudge against communists since the days of the Scottsboro case and had no use for so-called fellow travelers. This in part reflected a single-minded determination to protect the NAACP's dominance in the field of civil rights. By 1950, such a public disavowal of "Communists of the whole and half-blooded" was part of the ritual of claiming legitimacy in the realm of Washington politics, if not essential for survival. The CIO had purged its ranks of Communist-affiliated unions and anti-communism was the foundation stone of the ADA. These groups dominated the liberal wing of the Democratic Party and were the NAACP's primary allies in the civil rights coalition of the cold war era. Columnist Marjorie McKenzie pointed to the inherent contradictions of a civil rights group engaged "in acts of exclusion on the grounds of political affiliation." Circumstances, she conceded, made it "inevitable," but, she asked, at what cost "to us and our faith in the democratic process?"[78]

The National Emergency Civil Rights Mobilization drew more than 4,000 delegates from thirty-three states; an estimated 2,891 were NAACP members. A large minority of whites participated, including a 35-person delegation from the University of North Carolina. The three-day-long gathering included meetings with senators and representatives to discuss the current state of civil rights legislation and workshops with legislative representatives on lobbying techniques. Senators Hubert Humphrey, Wayne Morse, and majority leader Scott Lucas addressed the group, as did congressmen Adam Clayton Powell and Jacob Javits. The delegates spent the better part of two days navigating the halls of Congress and meeting with their representatives to press for action on a pending FEPC bill as well as other civil rights legislation. Senator Irving Ives said that the "mobilization has contributed tremendously to the promotion of the civil rights program," and he commented on "the courteous, considerate, and orderly conduct of the delegates." Southern congressmen admitted, noted one reporter, that the "spectacle of a Negro delegation 'from back home'" gave a sense of a rising tide on the civil rights front. Wilkins and a group of labor and civic leaders met with Truman, and the president assured them of his support.[79]

The impact of the civil rights mobilization was difficult to measure. No civil rights legislation passed in that session of Congress, and the filibuster remained an impermeable barrier. Wilkins was satisfied that the effort "created a new consciousness of kind and effort among our own groups" and let Congress know that "Negroes are not apathetic about civil rights." Most importantly, it provided the nucleus for the establishment of the Leadership Conference on Civil Rights later that year, an interracial coalition of civil rights, labor, religious, and civic groups that formed a permanent lobbying presence, under the chairmanship of Roy Wilkins. Arnold Aronson, director of the National Jewish Community Relations Advisory Council, served as secretary. That same year, Clarence Mitchell, who had directed the NAACP's labor bureau, became director of the association's Washington bureau; he would also serve as legislative representative for the LCCR. Mitchell emerged as a supremely effective field general in the prolonged and often unrewarding struggle on Capitol Hill.[80]

While the NAACP and liberal-labor allies found common cause around the staples of the civil rights legislative agenda—antilynching, anti–poll tax, and FEPC legislation—the fight for civil rights across the broad front of domestic legislation revealed sharp differences. One such conflict centered on the Housing Act of 1949, under which the federal government supported a comprehensive program of slum clearance, urban redevelopment, and housing construction, providing a billion dollars in federal loans through state and local agencies and authorizing 810,000 federally funded public housing units. Housing experts such as Robert Weaver and Frank Horne warned that without proper safeguards it was likely that federal funds would be used to crystallize residential segregation patterns, amplify the housing crisis facing blacks, and reinforce and expand the ghetto—warnings that proved prescient. Although the NAACP lobbied hard for an amendment requiring no discrimination or segregation in any programs assisted under the Housing Act, key congressional and liberal allies—including Senators Hubert Humphrey and Wayne Morse, and a vocal segment of the ADA—opposed the NAACP's position on practical grounds. Such a strategy would, they predicted, undermine southern support and ensure the defeat of what liberal Illinois senator Paul Douglas described as a bill that promised to do more for the American people "than virtually any measure I know." Several antisegregation amendments were defeated, and the bill passed without any provisions for federal oversight in the area of racial fairness.[81]

A fight against segregation in Congress in 1949 was a losing proposition. It would find few allies; legislation on major domestic programs would likely be held hostage by Southern Democrats; and it would threaten to completely rupture the Democratic Party. Yet the easy air of resignation on the part of erstwhile liberal allies, who did not shrink from fights in other arenas, troubled NAACP leaders. The problem of racial discrimination, so vividly laid out in *To Secure These Rights* barely two years earlier, was marginalized if not completely overlooked in liberal critiques of the challenges facing democracy in the late forties and 1950s. For example, race was barely mentioned in Arthur Schlesinger's *The Vital Center*, published in 1949, the major statement of cold war liberalism. More than an issue of politics, the paucity of national leadership on the issue of civil rights was itself a reflection of the consequence of racial segregation and the way in which it structured the lives, education, and perceptions of most white Americans. "Racial discrimination was not only operative in all aspects of American life," recalled Robert Carter, "but generally accepted as the norm."[82]

* * *

Reporting on a conference of NAACP lawyers in New York in the summer of 1949, Charles Houston described a scene that measured how far the association had come since his arrival in New York fifteen years earlier to establish the legal program. In 1935, the entire executive staff of the NAACP comprised five people; now there were six full-time lawyers on the legal staff. Houston recited the names of some of the affiliated NAACP lawyers in attendance, demonstrating the strategic reach of the association along the battlefront: "Boulware was up from South Carolina, Hill, Martin and Robinson from Virginia, George Johnson, Nabrit, B.V. Lawson . . . from the District of Columbia, Shores from Birmingham, Lobby from Nashville, Ming from Chicago." All of them were directing various phases in the fight against discrimination in education, employment, transportation, housing, voting, recreation, and abuses of criminal law. A sociologist sat in on their sessions, to help guide their discussion of how to use economic and sociological data in illuminating the effects of segregation and discrimination.[83]

As always, the volume of work far exceeded the capacity of this small and tightly organized team on the cutting edge of the law, with roots in struggles across the country. They labored in the knowledge that, in Houston's words, they could "barely scratch the surface of the needs of our people for legal protection." Many of the plans laid out at the conference would "have to be shelved because the NAACP does not have a large enough legal staff to push all phases of the legal defense at the same time." By the late 1940s, the South was absorbing much of the attention and energy of the legal team and was unquestionably the front line of the struggle. Blacks were completely exposed to the arbitrary will of whites and escalating political violence, raising the basic issue of survival. At the same time, the region's state-mandated segregation system offered a clear target for legal attack in the broader effort to secure an affirmative government commitment to erasing racism from American life. By the end of the decade, the steady work of Marshall and his legal team had merged with the demands of black parents for better school facilities, elevating the fight for equal education as the primary arena in the frontal assault on the legal props of Jim Crow.[84]

While the *Sweatt* case made its way to the U.S. Supreme Court, lawyers in Virginia supported an intensified statewide challenge to educational inequality, and parents in communities in other parts of the South sought out assistance in their efforts to improve the educational opportunities of their children. In Washington, D. C., Gardner Bishop, a barber, led parents of students at Browne Junior High School in a strike to protest grossly overcrowded conditions. In a school built to accommodate 880 students, 1,727 students attended in double shifts. Bishop had no use for the local NAACP branch—an elite group made up of government and professional people; he identified with poor blacks, struggling on the margins of life. After the student walkout and targeted picketing of the school board had gone on for two months with no relief, Bishop approached Charles Houston at a public meeting and simply told him, "I need your help." The two had never met, but Houston had followed news of the protest. He put his arm around Bishop and said, "I know you Bishop, and I'd like to help." They met at Houston's home that night and devised a face-saving scheme for calling off the strike, as author Richard Kluger writes, "on the understanding that Houston would file a whole series of law suits and take other actions aimed at winning equal facilities for the black school children of Washington." This was early in 1948. "Charlie became us, part of the group," Bishop recalled. It was the start of an extraordinary partnership. Over the next two years, the lawyer and "the U Street barber" worked "hand-in-glove," with Houston advising on tactics and strategies, filing suits, and helping to raise money, and Bishop devoting himself to a broad range of protest activities, organizing demands for equalization at all levels of schooling as well as challenging segregation in recreational facilities and in other areas of public life.[85]

In rural Clarendon, South Carolina, efforts by parents to obtain bus transportation from the county for their children in the summer of 1947 got nowhere, but the Reverend Joseph DeLaine and Levi Pearson, the two leaders of the effort, persisted. They established a branch of the NAACP in Clarendon County. In the spring of 1949, DeLaine, Pearson, and a small group of blacks from Clarendon County met with Thurgood Marshall, James Hinton, and Harold Boulware in Columbia. Marshall said it was time to sue for full equalization of educational facilities and told them that the NAACP would support a suit if they could secure twenty plaintiffs—a tall order from which the Clarendon County group did not shrink. DeLaine and his friend the Reverend R. W. Seals organized a series of informational meetings in churches around the county to enlist support. Lester Banks, a leader of the educational drive in Virginia, and South Carolina NAACP executive secretary Eugene Montgomery addressed an overflow crowd at St. Mark's Church in Summerton. County resident Eliza Briggs recalled that it was the first mass civic meeting of its kind ever held in the area, and it generated much talk and excitement. Yet the risks associated with signing up as a plaintiff were evident. Many blacks in the county were tenant farmers and would likely be subject to eviction. Levi Pearson owned his own land but suffered financial ruin at the hands of white merchants and bankers after he sued for bus transportation. Rev. DeLaine and his wife, Mattie, were both fired from their jobs as teachers during this period. It took eight months, but by November 1949, DeLaine had the twenty names Marshall said he needed to bring a suit. Eliza Briggs and her husband, Harry, headed the list. "We figured anything to better the children's condition was worthwhile," Harry Briggs recalled.[86]

From 1947 to 1950, due to the efforts of Banks and Robinson, the NAACP initiated action in seventy-five school districts in Virginia, filed more than twenty cases, and won several victories in lower courts. In a series of cases involving school facilities in the Tidewater area of the state, federal district court judge Sterling Hutcheson issued sweeping decisions calling for school boards to "immediately make plans to equalize the educational facilities and opportunities for Negro children." Oliver Hill and Spottswood Robinson investigated the schools subject to the judge's ruling in Gloucester and King George counties prior to the start of classes in September 1948 and found that a minimum of cosmetic improvements had been made to school facilities. They advised the students not to register for classes and made an attempt to enroll them in the all-white schools to protect the rights of their plaintiffs. Such an affront to the state's segregation laws caused a hysterical reaction from local officials and the governor. The lawyers went on to file contempt charges against school officials in both counties. Under pressure from Judge Hutcheson, school officials in King George County won approval of a $150,000 bond to construct a new school for black students. When officials in Gloucester County failed to take effective action, the judge fined school officials for contempt of court, ultimately forcing them to implement plans for a new school. These cases played out over a two-year period.[87]

The NAACP's project in Virginia helped to organize broad participation in the fight for equal education but also revealed the limitations of the equalization strategy. It was labor intensive, costly, and won only incremental gains. In cases that secured court orders directing school boards to "equalize" facilities, officials found ways to stall, evade, and provide a minimum of improvements. By February 1950, the Virginia state conference was $8,000 in debt. Most significantly, the intensive, statewide equalization campaign had demonstrated that it was not possible to equalize black education within the confines of the segregation system. By stressing physical inequalities, Robinson noted, their approach overlooked the "adverse psychological and other intangible consequences" of segregation. In those instances where suits resulted in construction of "Negro school facilities," Robinson wrote, "we were nailing the lid in our own coffin by the production of newer and costlier monuments to segregation." He predicted that a change in strategy was "inevitable." That change awaited the outcome of Heman Sweatt's suit against the University of Texas Law School, which came before the U.S. Supreme Court in the spring of 1950.[88]

On April 4, 1950, the U.S. Supreme Court heard three cases challenging the doctrine of segregation enshrined in the fifty-four-year-old *Plessy v. Ferguson* ruling. In addition to the *Sweatt* case, the NAACP brought a second case before the Court involving George McLaurin, a sixty-four-year-old student at the University of Oklahoma's Graduate School of Education. McLaurin had gained admission to the university's graduate program, but he was seated at a desk outside the classrom and forced to use other facilities on a segregated basis. The Court also heard *Henderson v. the United States*, which challenged segregated dining facilities on the Southern Railway. Elmer Henderson had been a wartime employee of the FEPC when he brought the suit and was currently director of the American Council on Human Rights. Since the practice of separating black diners behind a curtain was approved by the Interstate Commerce Commission, Belford Lawson, Henderson's attorney, sued the federal government.

The United States Justice Department emerged as a major ally in the NAACP's drive to overturn *Plessy*. U.S. attorney general Howard McGrath represented the federal government in the *Henderson* case. McGrath, who had replaced Tom Clark when Clark was elevated to the Supreme Court, conceded that the government had erred in sanctioning segregation on the railway. The "separate but equal" ruling, McGrath declared, was an "anachronism which a half-century of history and experience has shown to be a departure from the basic constitutional principle that all Americans, regardless of their race or color or religion or national origin, stand equal and alike in the light of the law." Solicitor general Philip Perlman reinforced the NAACP's argument in the amicus curiae briefs he drafted in the *Sweatt* and *McLaurin* cases. "The United States," Perlman wrote, "again urges the court to repudi-ate the 'separate but equal' doctrine as an unwarranted deviation from the principles of equality under law."[89]

In a historic set of unanimous decisions, issued on June 5, 1950, the Su-preme Court struck down racial barriers separating blacks on railroads and in two educational institutions. The justices walked a fine line in each case and stopped short of taking on *Plessy*. But as commentator Arthur Krock ob-served, they left the decades-old precedent "a mass of tatters." The opinions in the *McLaurin* and *Sweatt* cases were tailored to the particular circum-stances and held in both instances that the state had violated the equal pro-tection clause of the Fourteenth Amendment. In outlawing the separation of McLaurin within the University of Oklahoma, the Court set clear limits on state action once blacks had been admitted to a previously all-white public institution, raising the possibility of applying this ruling to other areas of public life. With the *Sweatt* ruling, the justices followed the argument laid out by the NAACP lawyers and conceded that there were "qualities incapable of objective measurement" that had to be taken into account in evaluating whether the equality mandated by law had been satisfied. For the first time, the Court ordered the admission of a black student to an all-white educa-tional institution. In the process, by recognizing "the relevance of intangibles" the justices provided an opening to press ahead with the sociological argu-ment the NAACP legal team had been developing since the end of the war. "Segregation no longer has the stamp of legality," Marshall declared in re-sponse to the Court's decisions.[90]

Three weeks later, forty-three lawyers from around the country and four-teen NAACP branch leaders and state conference presidents from the South met in New York for a two-day conference to map out plans for implement-ing the Court's decision and mounting an all-out attack on segregation. The group realized that the legal staff could move no faster than potential plain-tiffs were willing to move; continuing work in the field dedicated to broaden-ing support behind the revised program was critical. But, Marshall noted, there was "no doubt whatsoever that all phases of segregation in public educa-tion from professional school to kindergarten can be removed through legal action," and he predicted that the breakdown of segregation in recreational facilities and other areas of public life would follow. The conference agreed that, from here on, all education suits would "aim at obtaining education on a non-segregated basis and that no relief other than that will be acceptable."

The annual convention, meeting in Boston immediately thereafter, unanimously adopted a resolution endorsing the new policy.

Charles Houston died in Freedman's Hospital in Washington, D.C., on April 22, 1950. He was fifty-four years old. He had suffered a heart attack the previous October. Friends said he literally worked himself to death. Despite failing health, his pace never slackened. "Trying to urge him to slow down was like talkin' to the wind," said his law partner, Joseph Waddy. During the last year of his life, he was working on railway labor cases, suing for the admission of Esther McCready to the University of Maryland's School of Nursing, meeting with Gardner Bishop upwards of four times a week, and working with the National Lawyers Guild to challenge a Justice Department program to monitor the political beliefs and activities of attorneys. All the while, Houston remained active in the work of the NAACP and in frequent communication with Walter White and Thurgood Marshall. Often he worked through the night to accommodate the demands of his law practice and the needs of the association. He was, as one associate described him, "a philanthropist without money." Shortly before he died, Houston advised Bishop that James Nabrit would work with him in the ongoing struggle for education equality in Washington in what would become one of the five cases that comprised *Brown*.[92]

At a memorial service at Howard University's Rankin Chapel, friends and colleagues tried to capture the spirit of the man and his contribution to the movement that he had done so much to imagine, shape, and lead. William Hastie called him "the Moses of the Negro people in their long journey from second class citizenship." Rare were the "qualities of mind and of spirit and of heart" that Houston embodied, said Clifford Durr, the white Alabamian who then headed the National Lawyers Guild. "No temptation of honor or pressure of hysteria moved him from his course of service" to high principles and broad vision. Marshall claimed that "whatever credit is given him is not enough." Houston himself probably penned his most fitting epitaph in a note he left for his six-year-old son: "Tell Bo I did not run out on him but went down fighting that he might have better and broader opportunities than I had without prejudice or bias operating against him, and in any fight some must fall."[93]

Reflecting on the state of the movement four months before his death, Houston expressed confidence in the gains that had been won and the mounting strength and power of the black struggle for full citizenship rights. "So far as our struggle for civil rights is concerned, I'm not worried about that now. The struggle for civil rights in America is won." Looking ahead, he anticipated the deeper challenges that loomed beyond the necessary and hard-fought struggle to overturn state-enforced discrimination and inequality—that of creating a society "which guarantees justice and freedom for everyone."[94]

10

"On the Threshold of Victory"

"The complete destruction of all enforced segregation is in sight," Thurgood Marshall stated at the end of 1950. For many, such a claim appeared far-fetched if not beyond imagination. Taking stock at the half-century mark, Du Bois observed that in the South, "despite religion, education, and reason, the color line, although perhaps shaken, still stands stark and unbending and to the minds of most good people eternal." Yet after more than a decade of litigation and fieldwork, Marshall was intimately acquainted with the trends and developments that would combine to topple the edifice of Jim Crow. Equal to the string of courtroom victories that had brought them within striking distance of overturning *Plessy v. Ferguson*, Marshall noted the growing determination among black communities to "take the necessary risks and sacrifices to make [full citizenship] a reality with all possible speed." The NAACP's team of lawyers, working in tandem with blacks throughout the South, embodied the confidence born of hard-won battles, the rightness of their cause, and the courage and determination of blacks in places like Clarendon County, South Carolina, and Jackson, Mississippi.[1]

While the attack on state-sponsored segregation moved toward a show-down in the South, racial segregation was becoming more deeply entrenched in cities across the nation. Blacks in the North faced racial barriers caused by both governmental and private discriminatory actions. Housing had become the most pressing issue as the continuing migration of southern blacks northward pressured crowded and deteriorating housing supplies. *Shelley v. Kraemer*, in theory, had removed a major barrier to black mobility, but its impact was minimal in the face of a broad consensus among real estate interests, financial institutions, government agencies, and white civic associations dedicated to maintaining racially homogeneous neighborhoods. Racial bias, market imperatives, and ideas about private property rights all conspired to promote the exclusion and isolation of blacks—despite the success of the NAACP in striking down residential ordinances in 1917 and restrictive covenants in 1948. In the aftermath of World War II, the infusion of government spending for public housing and urban renewal along with other federal policies aiding in the growth of the suburbs not only failed to reverse the pattern of racial separation, but reinforced it.

On the day that the U. S. Supreme Court unanimously struck down segregation in the *Sweatt*, *McLaurin*, and *Henderson* cases, the Court declined to hear the case of *Dorsey v. Stuyvesant Town*, a bellwether in the next phase of the struggle around residential segregation. Stuyvesant Town was the largest urban redevelopment project in the country at the time, an example of the public-private partnership dedicated to slum clearance and urban revitalization that would remake the face of urban America in the postwar era. Under the New York State Redevelopment Corporation Act, the city of New York condemned an area covering eighteen city blocks in lower Manhattan, evicted and relocated ten thousand families, the great majority of whom were black, and sold the land at cost to the Metropolitan Life Insurance Company. Seventy-five percent of the families who were uprooted did not qualify for public housing. Met Life cleared the land and built a development that included thirty-five fourteen-story buildings, with nearly nine thousand moderately priced apartments. In accordance with its agreement with the city, rents were held to a reduced rate and Stuyvesant Town was granted a twenty-five-year-long tax exemption worth $50 million. From the earliest inception of the project, Met Life officials made it clear that blacks would be barred from Stuyvesant Town. As its chairman, Frederick Ecker explained at a city council meeting, "Negroes and whites don't mix."[2]

In response to protests and in an effort to defuse a likely lawsuit, Met Life built Riverton House in Harlem, a middle-income development "for Negroes," seeking cover under the umbrella of "separate but equal." When plans to build Riverton were announced, the NAACP charged that "as long as the Metropolitan maintains a closed-door policy to Negroes in its projects outside the Harlem area, the Riverton project becomes a segregated, Jim Crow housing project." Nonetheless, there were more than fifty thousand applicants for its twelve hundred units. Robert Carter, Constance Baker Motley, and Franklin Williams and their families were among those who obtained apartments in Riverton. Noting the dilemma blacks faced, Carter recalled that "decent affordable housing was a dire immediate need, and that need could only be met within the strictures of segregation—one could reject either the segregation or the housing." Riverton hardly dulled the protest against Met Life's segregationist policies. Civil rights activists urged whites to submit applications to Riverton and a coalition of labor, civil rights, veteran, and civic groups amplified the challenge "to black belt living in New York City."[3]

Michael Dorsey, Monroe Dowling, and Calvin Harper, all veterans, brought a suit against Stuyvesant Town, sponsored by the NAACP, the American Jewish Congress, and the ACLU. They charged that Stuyvesant Town was a product of state action and therefore its exclusion of them solely on grounds of race was a violation of the United States Constitution and the New York State Constitution. Representatives of Stuyvesant Town Corporation countered that as a private entity it was immune from constitutional inhibitions against racial discrimination. The state Supreme Court ruled in favor of Stuyvesant Town, and New York's highest court, the Court of Appeals, voted 4-3 to uphold the right of Stuyvesant Town to bar blacks. The majority opinion held that the silence of state officials in the matter indicated that the public purpose had been fulfilled by the rehabilitation of the area, and the policy of Stuyvesant Town, as a private project, was not subject to the equal protection clause of the Fourteenth Amendment. The opinion also said that the state of New York "consciously and deliberately refrained from imposing any requirement of nondiscrimination . . . as a condition of granting aid in the rehabilitation of substandard areas." Acknowledging "a grave and delicate problem," the majority opinion implied that such a policy was essential to attracting the private investment necessary to achieving the intention of the Redevelopment Act; Robert Moses, the city's construction coordinator, had publicly stated that if such restrictions were applied, "no private venture would go into business." In a strong dissenting opinion, Stanley Fuld cited sixty years of legal precedent up through *Smith v. Allright* and *Shelley v. Kraemer* that established that "state action" meant "exertion of state power in all forms." Stuyvesant Town was a "governmentally conceived, governmentally aided and governmentally regulated program in urban redevelopment" and therefore prohibited from discriminating under the Fourteenth Amendment. Referring to the majority opinion, it contended that "the argument overlooks that the constitutional rights of American citizens are involved and that such rights may not be used as pawns in driving bargains."[4]

In their appeal to the U.S. Supreme Court, attorneys for Michael Dorsey and his associates emphasized that a closely divided Court of Appeals "revealed a sharp division on the interpretation of the line of recent court decisions on the meaning of 'state action.'" The 4-3 decision, they argued, could not be regarded as the final answer in a case that would affect housing constructed under similar redevelopment plans in twenty-five states. The brief cast the policy of excluding blacks from developments like Stuyvesant Town as the third attempt to "corrupt a legitimate device for sound community planning into an instrument for enforcing racial segregation." First, there were municipal zoning ordinances that designated racially defined areas, which were overturned in 1917, followed by racially restrictive covenants, which were finally held to be unenforceable by government. The central role of the state in the Stuyvesant Town project was acknowledged by the admission that government participation was essential to meeting a need that could not be met by the ordinary operation of private enterprise. Underscoring the critical nature of the issue, the plaintiffs noted that the proportion of substandard housing units occupied by nonwhites was almost six times that for whites, and the proportion of overcrowding of nonwhites exceeded whites by four times. Unless equal treatment was assured, "tens of thousands of Negro families, regardless of their economic status may be rendered homeless in the name of urban redevelopment." It was imperative "that the long-debated question of whether there may be racial discrimination in redevelopment projects finally be decided." Only two justices, Hugo Black and William Douglas, voted to hear the case. As four votes were needed to grant certiorari, the Court of Appeals ruling remained the law in New York.[5]

The *Dorsey* case was one battle in a broadening struggle over the shape and direction of the government-assisted development that was recasting American cities and populating burgeoning suburbs in the aftermath of World War II. In addition to the urban redevelopment programs, there was the massive infusion of federal funds for public housing construction under the Housing Act of 1949 and the rapid expansion of private home construction with the assistance of federally insured mortgages under the Federal Housing Administration (FHA). The FHA traditionally followed the lead of real estate concerns and financial institutions in supporting the maintenance of "racially harmonious" neighborhoods. *Dorsey* focused attention on the question that was central across the board—how would these various government-supported programs affect racial patterns during a period of massive building, population movement, and urban restructuring? For civil rights activists and fair housing advocates, the unprecedented role of government in every major area of residential development infused the issue with opportunity and urgency. Housing expert Robert Weaver warned that the combination of slum clearance, "the widespread exclusion of non-whites from new areas and new constructions" and the "continuation of FHA neglect of the Negro market" was creating "new and extremely costly [forms of] discrimination in urban shelter," affecting blacks across the economic spectrum. The deference of federal agencies to local autonomy made it extremely difficult to gain traction in what the NAACP named as a defining challenge in the postwar era. Walter White noted with alarm that housing financed or underwritten in part or wholly by public tax dollars was "forging a new, nationwide and more sinister pattern of segregation than ever before."[6]

As the NAACP's southern movement gained momentum, the spread of racial segregation and discrimination in the North presented a very different set of challenges. In the South, the static nature of a state-enforced caste system, the aggressive defense of segregation by public officials, and the terror, lawlessness, and disenfranchisement employed to maintain white supremacy all worked to provide a clear target for the NAACP's steady, long-term attack on the legal chains of segregation. The amorphous nature of racial segregation in the North offered a striking contrast. Many states boasted civil rights laws; racial segregation had few prominent defenders. As a social reality, segregation in the North was attributed to impersonal forces—a function of property rights, economic interests, and private choices. In the fight against housing discrimination, the NAACP identified the role of government policy in underwriting and even promoting racial segregation but struggled to develop the tools and strategies capable of reversing this trend.[7]

The NAACP sought national standards and enforcement mechanisms for barring racial discrimination—through legislative efforts, pressuring federal housing agencies, and selective lawsuits, including challenges to developers such as William Levitt, who excluded blacks from vast new suburban developments. Chicago was the site of one of the earliest contests over the relationship between slum clearance, urban redevelopment, and the expansion of federally supported public housing. In 1950 the city sought aid under the Housing Act of 1949 for several projects already under way involving the clearance of decaying neighborhoods and redevelopment of land along Lake Michigan by the New York Life Insurance Company and the establishment of up to fifteen thousand units of public housing spread over a dozen sites. An influx of more than a quarter of a million men and women from the South during the previous decade had nearly doubled the city's black population, taxing an already limited and overcrowded housing supply in densely concentrated areas. Nevertheless, the city proposed to locate most of the new public housing units in these areas and only a handful in vacant sections on the outskirts of the city. A federal housing official reported that the proposed projects followed the "lines of least political and neighborhood resistance" and warned that it not only smacked of "Negro clearance," but "at the same time buttresses up existing patterns of segregation."[8]

In what was one of the first major tests over the application of federal funds under the Housing Act, Walter White vigorously protested the proposals and insisted that federal funds and credit "be cut off from those localities which maintained a policy of segregation." Robert Weaver charged that "racial prejudice rather than rational land use" had dictated the selection of public housing sites; he warned that approval by federal housing authorities would give "sanction to Negro containment." The Chicago project sparked a spirited debate within the Housing and Home Finance Agency (HHFA), which included all of the various housing programs, regarding procedures under the new law. The Public Housing Authority (PHA) commissioner pointed out that "both houses of Congress . . . refused to insert such a requirement" in the Housing Act and that "the prohibition on segregation" was "not . . . required" in local contracts. Frank Horne, a special assistant to HHFA chief Raymond Foley, argued that the federal government must exercise responsible oversight, charging that public housing representatives "seemed more concerned with the production of a number of public housing units than with the total effects on the city of Chicago . . . or on the national program." While deliberations over Chicago's proposals continued, other developments in the city focused attention on the racial crisis at the heart of housing development and opportunity.[9]

Moderate and middle-income African Americans faced a different kind of dilemma from poor blacks who were confined to overcrowded public housing units in an expanding ghetto. Employment gains during and after the war had generated increasing demand for better housing opportunities, but as the *Chicago Defender* observed, "It is difficult to build, there is nothing to rent, and [the Negro citizen] takes his life in his hands when he dares to buy." As blacks searching for housing breached informal racial boundaries, white responses fueled what historian Arnold Hirsch described as "chronic urban guerilla warfare." From 1949 to 1951, an estimated twenty thousand black families purchased and occupied property outside of the "established Negro community." During this time, there were over one hundred documented assaults—bombings, arson, mob attacks—on black-owned homes in pre-dominantly white areas of Chicago, a pattern that was repeated in cities around the nation. One of the most publicized incidents involved Percy Julian, the acclaimed chemist who was named Chicago's Man of the Year in 1949. After he purchased a house in the exclusive Oak Park area of Chicago, vandals doused it with kerosene in a failed arson attempt; Julian moved his family into the home, accompanied by armed guards. Several months later, in the spring of 1951, the home was the target of a dynamite blast that fell short of the house.[10]

In the summer of 1951, Harvey Clark Jr. rented an apartment in Cicero, an industrial suburb of seventy thousand on the western boundary of Chicago, home to mostly first- and second-generation Americans. The twenty-nine-year-old Clark, a former air force sergeant and a graduate of Fisk University, had moved to the Chicago area from Nashville in 1949 with his wife, Johnetta, and their two young children. The Clarks were sharing a small two-room apartment with another family of five in a "firetrap" on the South Side of the city when Clark found a five-room modern apartment in a twenty-unit build-ing in Cicero, only a mile and a half from his job as a bus driver with the Chicago Transit Authority. The Clarks apparently were not aware that they would be the first black family to reside in the all-white enclave. Police chief Erwin Konovsky met Clark on the day he attempted to move in and barred him from the building. With the aid of George Leighton, chairman of the legal redress committee of the NAACP's Chicago branch, Clark obtained a restraining order against the police; the judge ordered Konovsky to "exercise the same diligence in seeing that these people move in as you did in trying to keep them out." The Clarks moved into the apartment on July 10. They were away from their apartment that afternoon when a hostile crowd of five hun-dred circled the building. Several members of the mob broke the windows in the family's third floor apartment as the police stood by. Over the next two nights, an estimated five thousand whites rioted outside of the apartment building. Vandals broke into the Clarks' apartment and destroyed their furni-ture and personal belongings—a scene, noted Walter White, that rivaled the action "of many mobs down South." Governor Adlai Stevenson finally sent five hundred National Guardsmen to restore order. By then, the apartment building had been gutted and nearly burned to the ground, four police cars had been overturned, nineteen people were injured, and seventy people were arrested.[11]

Walter White flew to the scene in response to a call from the Chicago NAACP branch. He undoubtedly thought of Ossian Sweet and all that followed in the wake of his fateful move into a white neighborhood in Detroit twenty-five years earlier. White addressed a mass meeting organized by the branch to raise money to aid the Clarks and support a $200,000 damage suit against the city of Cicero, and he took part in a series of meetings with local, state, and federal officials. Still a master of public relations, he arranged for a major press conference at NAACP headquarters in New York early in August, where Henry and Johnetta Clark told their story to radio, television, and newspaper reporters representing national media outlets. White was intent that the sensational aspects of a community gone "berserk" not overwhelm the root of the problem that exploded in Cicero. "The confinement of Negroes to the perilously overcrowded ghetto . . . on the South Side" and the refusal of "real estate associations, mortgage companies, and banks . . . to sell, rent, or grant loans to Negroes outside the ghetto" was the immediate contributing factor, he explained. But ultimate responsibility, he claimed, rested with state and federally funded programs that, through slum clearance and public developments, had displaced ten thousand black families while a growing black population added more pressure on housing. He appealed to federal officials to take the lead in addressing this urgent problem by mandating that "adequate housing . . . be made available to families in accordance with their needs, irrespective of race, national origin or geographic location."[12]

Frank Horne and his associates in the race relations division of the HHFA concurred with White's assessment and seized on the Cicero riot in their campaign against Chicago's redevelopment and public housing proposals. Noting the connections between a history of racial violence in Chicago, a tradition of residential segregation, and the current redevelopment proposals, they "urged rejection of the Chicago plans," noted Arnold Hirsch, "with an eye toward setting a national precedent." Horne cited pending applications from Detroit, St. Louis, Baltimore, Norfolk, Tampa, New Orleans, Dallas, and other cities and observed that the "surrender to the various practices which have created and nurtured racial residential restrictions is reflected in [their] current proposals." He cautioned against federal reinforcement of trends that promised to deepen racial discord. "Surely," Horne implored in a memorandum to Raymond Foley, "the vast powers, funds, and prestige of the

Federal Government are not to be utilized to underwrite official irresponsibility and community immorality." Horne advised that no future redevelopment or public housing projects be approved by HHFA until relocation problems were solved and sites on vacant land beyond established areas of black residence were designated for new public housing units. The HHFA approved the Chicago proposals intact, with a promise of more rigorous oversight in the future—a faint and hardly reassuring nod to the warnings clearly laid out by a small group within the agency.[13]

The Cicero events, most immediately, focused on the response to mob violence targeting African Americans. Initially, the bias of the local authorities was dramatically demonstrated when the Cook County grand jury that investigated the riot failed to indict any of the rioters and instead indicted George Leighton, the NAACP lawyer representing the Clarks, the apartment owner, and the Clarks' realtor for "conspiracy to injure property by . . . causing a depreciation in the real estate market price by renting to Negroes." Thurgood Marshall flew to Chicago immediately to help prepare a legal defense, promising "the fullest use of all of the facilities of the NAACP to assure that this abominable action will not interfere with Mr. Leighton and his work on behalf of the Association." White and Marshall increased pressure on Department of Justice officials for a federal grand jury investigation of the riot as well as the attempted intimidation of Leighton. Perhaps as a result, the Cook County prosecutor ultimately decided not to prosecute Leighton, and the other indictments were thrown out as well. Early in October attorney general Howard McGrath ordered a special federal grand jury to investigate the Cicero "outrage"; U.S. attorney Otto Kerner called nearly two hundred witnesses over a two-week period. Four town officials and three police officers were indicted on charges of violating the Clarks' civil rights; four were ultimately found guilty. The NAACP, the Clarks, and others involved in the case took some satisfaction in at least securing federal prosecution of complicit officials. But Cicero remained all white, housing policies in Chicago were unchanged, and the ghetto expanded. During the 1950s, nearly a half-million blacks migrated to the city, more than doubling its black population.[14]

"Where do we go from here?" asked Walter White at the end of a summary of the NAACP's efforts around the Cicero case. In the long struggle against residential segregation, the ground was continually shifting, and the few court victories, such as *Shelley v. Kraemer*, were pyrrhic in nature. The involvement of federal agencies in postwar housing development was so extensive, explained an NAACP Legal Defense Fund (LDF) report, that it practically

negated the effect of previous court decisions "prohibiting legislative or judicial enforcement of racial restrictions upon the ownership and use of residential property." The objective of a legal strategy to meet the current variations
of the problem was clear—to challenge government sanction of racially discriminatory policies. But the complex and pervasive nature of federal involvement—slum clearance, urban redevelopment, public housing, FHA-insured
mortgages—opened onto a whole new field of legal exploration and legislative strategy in an area that involved entrenched economic and political interests, north and south. Nevertheless, the next stage of the civil rights struggle
was coming into sharp relief. "Racial discrimination in the operation of the
housing market has become the controlling factor in establishing, reinforcing,
and extending patterns of segregated living in American cities," the legal report stated. "The standard practice of *excluding* Negroes from most neighborhoods and restricting them to a few sharply defined areas conditions the
patterns of use of schools, playgrounds, clinics, transportation, and other public facilities." As the legal fight against legally enforced school segregation
moved toward its culmination, the report soberly noted that "unless these
housing restrictions are removed, legislative and judicial restraints against
segregation in public education . . . may be largely neutralized."[15]

At a time when racial segregation remained the norm in American life, the
transformation of the military stood as a testimony to what was possible, although it took nearly five years for President Truman's 1948 executive order
mandating "equality of treatment in the Armed Services" to be fully realized.
The president's interracial Committee on Equality of Treatment and Opportunity in the Armed Services, also known as the Fahy Committee after its
director, Charles Fahy, advised on the implementation of the order. Through
a series of hearings, the committee quickly established that "equality of treatment" required an end to segregation. Secretaries of the navy and the air force
and secretary of defense Louis Johnson advocated a policy of gradual integration. Johnson publicly stated that "segregation in the armed forces is sharply
at variance with our democratic principles . . . reduces the efficiency of our
military strength [and] . . . is damaging to our country's reputation." The
army, however, maintained that the executive order did not require an end to
segregation, that equality could be achieved without abandoning segregation,
and that segregation was necessary both for military and social reasons. The
Fahy Committee, with the strong backing of President Truman, persisted
until the army finally submitted a plan for gradual integration early in 1950,

one that left individual commanders responsible for carrying the policy forward. Strong civilian leadership backed by a firm presidential commitment laid the groundwork for integration of the armed services; the Korean War provided the impetus for implementation.[16]

When North Korea invaded South Korea on June 25, 1950, the United States, in its first major military confrontation of the cold war, determined to fight a ground war under the umbrella of UN forces—a war that U.S. troops stationed in East Asia were not prepared to fight. They were understaffed, ill-equipped, and barely combat ready. Black units operated under even greater disadvantages. During the tumultuous early months of the war, a series of incidents exposed the hold of segregation on the army and its consequences. Few of the black soldiers had engaged in combat during World War II. They were segregated and poorly trained, and many were under the command of white officers who expressed reservations about their ability to fight—undermining the morale critical to building an effective fighting unit. The pressures, dislocation, and confusion of rapid deployment aggravated these problems. In the face of such odds, black troops of the famed Twenty-fourth Infantry captured the town of Yechon, winning the first victory for UN forces in the Korean conflict. But this achievement was soon overshadowed by reports of mass arrests and courts-martial of black soldiers, filtered out in stories by James Hicks, reporting in Korea for the *Baltimore Afro-American* and Frank Whisonant of the *Pittsburgh Courier*. In response to the alarming news, Thurgood Marshall publicly promised that "the NAACP is ready to defend with all of its resources any of these servicemen upon determining that they are victims of racial discrimination." The convicted soldiers quickly contacted the NAACP asking for aid, and Marshall was soon on his way to Japan and Korea.[17]

Marshall spent nearly six weeks in East Asia early in 1951, reviewing military records, meeting with the men who were imprisoned, and visiting with troops of the Twenty-fourth Infantry serving on the front lines. The glaring inequities and abuses endured by black troops were "more terrible than you can imagine," Marshall reported. Some of the consequences were revealed in what unfolded around the courts-martial. Thirty-two black and two white soldiers were tried and convicted for violating the seventy-fifth article of war—fleeing or failing to obey orders in the face of the enemy. Marshall's investigation revealed that there had been many instances of American troops—white and black—retreating before the onslaught of superior North

Korean forces during the early months of the war, even cases of white commanders abandoning their troops. But black troops had clearly been singled out and charged with the ultimate war crime. Marshall's review of each case showed a reckless disregard for the facts. For example, one soldier charged and convicted for not being at his post was in the hospital, under military orders; another was in bed under medication for serious head injuries when he failed to respond to an order. Both were sentenced to life in prison, as were thirteen other convicted soldiers; one was given a death sentence. By contrast, the two white soldiers received one- and three-year sentences. The entire process reeked of Jim Crow justice—the men were denied free choice of counsel, and they were hastily tried in a procedure dominated by white officers. Marshall won a reduction of sentences in twenty-two of the cases, and attorneys on the NAACP's legal staff pursued the cases further. Beyond securing some semblance of justice for these men, Marshall insisted that attention stay focused on the root of the problem—the persistence of rigid racial segregation in the Far Eastern command under General Douglas MacArthur, in violation of the president's order.[18]

Less than two months after Marshall returned from Japan, Truman relieved MacArthur of his post following a public confrontation between the president and the general over the prosecution of the war in Korea. Alabama attorney Arthur Shores teased Marshall, "I am sure you are well satisfied with your trip, since you succeeded in getting MacArthur fired." Although the two events were not related, the removal of MacArthur hastened the change that Marshall claimed was essential. General Matthew Ridgeway, the new Far Eastern commander, promptly initiated the integration of all blacks under his jurisdiction. By this time, the successful integration of the air force, navy, and several army units under combat conditions had demonstrated that integration worked and made for a stronger, more efficient military. On July 26, 1951, the army set a six-month deadline for the integration of all troops in East Asia. Forces in Europe followed along at a slower pace. In October 1953, the army announced that integration of its forces was virtually complete. Throughout this process, southern congressmen were carried along by the convergence of events in the field, well-placed leadership, and the growing realization among key civilian and military leaders that desegregation was in the national interest.[19]

While the successful integration of the armed services was the product of numerous factors, strong presidential leadership stood out as the primary one.

The steady fall of the color bar in the military arena during the early 1950s, however, came at a time when President Truman seemed inclined to "surrender to the Dixiecrats." A series of presidential appointments early in 1951 generated much discussion among NAACP board members. Truman selected former Florida governor Millard Caldwell to serve as head of civilian defense; Caldwell had been a leader in the effort to secure congressional approval of the regional school plan to maintain segregated professional education. Michael Ramspeck, former Georgia congressman and ardent foe of all civil rights legislation, was chosen by Truman to head the Civil Service Commission. White and a small delegation met with Truman to register their disapproval; the meeting was brief and the president made no commitments. Even more troubling than Truman's high-profile appointments of segregationists was his administration's "conspicuous failure" to appoint qualified blacks to numerous federal judiciary posts. While pleased with the elevation of William Hastie to the U.S. Court of Appeals in 1949, the association noted that out of sixty-four persons nominated and confirmed as United States district judges, not one was black. Earl Dickerson pointed out that of the seven thousand lawyers in a wide variety of federal positions there were twenty-four blacks—one-half of one percent.[20]

Clarence Mitchell, the NAACP's Washington bureau director, dug in for the long haul on Capitol Hill, where the prospects for congressional action became even bleaker. The defeat of northern Democrats in the 1950 midterm elections reduced the party to a thinner edge of control in Congress and left southerners holding the majority of Democratic seats in the House and just one seat shy of a majority of Democratic seats in the Senate. The new Senate leaders of the Eighty-second Congress, majority leader Ernest McFarland of Arizona and majority whip Lyndon Johnson of Texas, were opposed to FEPC legislation and any liberalization of the rule governing filibusters. Mitchell was, by virtue of his experience and temperament, ideally suited to keeping a civil rights agenda alive. He maintained a close watch over legislative developments, shored up and expanded the coalition of interests committed to civil rights, and worked tirelessly to educate and persuade lawmakers that civil rights legislation was both possible and necessary. Walter White marveled at his protégé's rare ability to talk "with all types of people and gain their confidence"—a quality that served him well in Washington during the barren years of the 1950s, as he cultivated and shaped future opportunities.[21]

*   *   *

"In no recent year," wrote Walter White in his 1951 report, "have Negroes had to fight so hard to hold onto faith in democracy." Those committed to the work of the association were sustained in part by a confidence in its vision, a belief that right would ultimately triumph, and a dogged determination—in the face of what often appeared to be insurmountable odds. In the gloomy days of the early fifties, White insisted that "democracy can no more continue to deny us our right to freedom than it can stop the social revolution which is sweeping through Asia today and is beginning to sweep through Africa and Latin America." He reminded the 1952 annual convention that "by resolute and adamant opposition to the foes of democracy, we have measurably altered the pattern of American racial opinion and actions. We are going to continue fighting for [equality] with every democratic weapon at our command—better to die on our feet." In the South, where lawlessness, violence, and oppression continued unabated, the NAACP's struggle reached its most potent expression, ultimately bringing the association its greatest victory and elevating the fight against racial segregation to a new level of intensity.[22]

Fierce resistance to any loosening of racial restrictions heightened in the late forties and early fifties. In Georgia, arch-segregationist Governor Herman Talmadge worked in tandem with a resurgent Ku Klux Klan to dismantle "the nascent civil rights movement" that had emerged during and after the war. Talmadge pushed through new voting laws that enhanced the power of local officials to disqualify potential black voters; those who persisted in their claim to citizenship rights risked severe economic and physical reprisals. Black voter registration declined in most parts of Georgia along with NAACP membership. When voting rights activist Alvin Jones accompanied five blacks to register in Lebeau, Louisiana, in 1950, whites inside the registrar's office assaulted the group and beat Jones so badly that they left a hole in his head—all while the sheriff looked on. Police commissioner Eugene "Bull" Connor stirred racial passions to a fever pitch in Birmingham. After NAACP lawyers defeated a racial zoning ordinance aggressively promoted by Connor, the home of plaintiff Mary Means Monk was dynamited; bombing and arson continued in the contested area, which became known as "Dynamite Hill." Police brutality was "a contagion" in the South, in the words of one Mississippi activist—notoriously so in Birmingham. During 1951, police in that city gunned down twenty-eight black men, none of whom had been accused of a capital crime. Such complete "lack of protection from law enforcement officials" in Birmingham was repeatedly called to the attention of the Justice Department. The "complete failure of the Department to take affirmative action" in these cases, Marshall charged, was "a contributing factor to the increasing temper of lawlessness."[23]

Criminal justice cases involving the violations of blacks' rights during this period were "probably more shocking than at any time in the history of the Association," Marshall declared. One of the most notorious episodes unfolded in Groveland, Florida, located in Lake County, the center of the state's citrus-producing industry. A seventeen-year-old white woman accused four black men of rape; no physical evidence that the woman had been sexually assaulted was ever produced. Sheriff Willis McCall quickly had the suspects rounded up. A posse led by McCall shot and killed Ernest Thomas, one of the four men accused. After confessions were beaten out of the three remaining defendants—sixteen-year-old Charlie Greenlee, and Walter Irvin and Sam Shepherd, both twenty-two years of age—McCall publicly announced that all had confessed, fueling a media frenzy around the case. When efforts of a white mob to storm the jail were turned back, hundreds rampaged through the black section of town, burning down three homes and causing four hundred blacks to flee the area. The NAACP, led by Franklin Williams, represented the men; McCall referred to Williams as "that nigger lawyer." An all-white jury found the three men guilty; Judge Truman Futch sentenced Shepherd and Irvin to death in the electric chair. The NAACP appealed the case to the U.S. Supreme Court, which, in April 1951, unanimously reversed the convictions, ruling that Lake County's method of jury selection had "discriminated against the Negro race." In a scorching opinion, Justice Robert Jackson declared that the trial and the events surrounding it did not meet "any civilized concept of due process."[24]

Major cases in Virginia and North Carolina illuminated the ongoing efforts to secure elemental justice. In February 1951, seven black men were executed in Martinsville, Virginia, for the rape of a white woman, following two years of appeals and fifteen judicial actions tirelessly pursued by Martin A. Martin for the NAACP Virginia state conference of branches. The men were tried by all-white juries in six separate cases. In a direct challenge to the discriminatory application of the death penalty, Martin entered evidence that since 1908, when the state had taken over executions, forty-five black men had been executed for rape while no white men had. Later in 1951, in Yanceyville, North Carolina, Mack Ingram, a forty-four-year-old farmer, was tried and convicted of attempted assault of a white woman from a distance of at least sixty feet, and sentenced to two years of hard labor. Robert Carter joined with local NAACP lawyers in appealing the conviction in the infamous "assault by leering" case and after two years of appeals won a reversal of Ingram's conviction.[25]

This was the atmosphere in the South as the NAACP concentrated its attention and resources on the region. "While fighting segregation in the South," Marshall emphasized at the 1951 annual meeting, "we do not intend to lose the battle in other sections of the country." But the power for racial change nationally had become bound up in the southern struggle, particularly as efforts to influence legislation and presidential action stalled and the promise of Truman's civil rights report faded. The escalating fight against segregated education in the South would establish a blueprint for legal action to eliminate all enforced segregation. At the same time, the removal of the color line at the ballot box was not only essential to redressing local injustices, but offered a critical route to "altering the temper and actions" of a Congress dominated by hard-line southern segregationists. The NAACP claimed a broad foundation in the region. Even though membership rolls had flagged in recent years, sixty percent of the association's branches were located in the South, and it was there that prospects for future growth were deemed most promising. At a time of fiscal austerity, the NAACP invested in an expanded program of fieldwork to shore up and enlarge its southern base while the legal challenge to school segregation entered its most ambitious phase.[26]

In April 1951, the national office sent Ruby Hurley to Birmingham on a temporary assignment as "regional coordinator" to help with membership campaigns in Alabama, Georgia, Mississippi, Tennessee, and Florida, and to drum up attendance for the annual convention to be held in Atlanta that summer. The forty-one-year-old Hurley had been with the association for more than a decade. In 1939, while working at the Industrial Bank in her hometown of Washington, D.C., and attending law school at night, she joined the citizens committee organized to secure a concert venue for Marian Anderson, leading to her involvement with the local branch of the NAACP. She moved to New York in 1943 to direct the association's youth division. Her work as youth secretary involved extensive travel around the country, but little had prepared her for living and working in the Deep South. Like most people in the North, Hurley later recalled, her ideas about living in the South had been shaped by what she had read "in the *Afro*, and the *Courier* and the Chicago *Defender* . . . and I wondered how in the world I was going to make it." She arrived in Birmingham at the height of the bombing crisis and wrote that "apathy and fear . . . and tension are thick." There were twelve people at the first meeting of the local branch she attended. Hurley took a room for $20 a week, "a good distance" from the cramped office she shared with the NAACP's Birmingham branch at the Masonic Temple Building downtown. "I haven't been able to stomach these Birmingham busses yet" she told a co-worker in New York, and even while pinching pennies, she taxied to the office during the first few weeks."[27]

Hurley helped to revive the Birmingham branch and traveled throughout the five-state region from her base there. She met with small and large groups and held statewide and regional workshops that combined discussions on local issues, political action, current legal cases, and strategies for conducting membership campaigns. It was an eye-opening experience. "Negroes, particularly in smaller communities in Mississippi and Alabama were very anxious to do something about their problems," she later recalled. "They knew things weren't right, but they didn't quite know how to go about effecting change." The NAACP offered the tools and, as she saw it, an "umbrella" for connecting individual and community efforts around a program of action. In Tennessee, where statewide membership had dropped to barely four thousand from a high of eleven thousand in 1948, Hurley talked about reviving branches and building up membership and emphasized the importance of taking the NAACP "to the people" by making contact through groups in the community—labor, church, school, youth, barbers, beauticians, fraternity, sorority, doctors, dentists and others. In Cordele, Georgia, where Hurley met with branch representatives from the southern part of the state, the group took her on a tour of black and white schools in the area. Of primary concern was the problem of effective leadership. Hurley agreed that the branch representatives should work "to stimulate the interest of *all* persons in the community" and "not wait for leadership to come from . . . professional persons."[28]

In Jackson, Mississippi, Hurley participated in a conference attended by forty NAACP delegates from around the state and found a strong ally in the Reverend William Bender, recently hired as a field-worker for Mississippi. At sixty-four, the former chaplain of Tougaloo College was a fearless and effective organizer who had stood down armed whites during the 1946 Democratic primary. In one year, Bender helped boost the state membership from 849 to 1,303 and added seven new branches, to make a total of twenty-one statewide. Reporting on the conference, Hurley identified the major problems on the state NAACP's agenda: voting, education, and membership "in that order." The greatest problem, however, was fear. Hurley joined with Bender in urging the national office to send in well-known figures such as

A. Philip Randolph to speak at mass meetings in various parts of the state as a way to counteract the pervasive terror. "I cannot over-emphasize the importance of our recognizing the needs of Mississippi," she told her New York associates.[29]

As the end of Hurley's assignment approached, Bender and Georgia state conference director William Boyd met with Walter White at the annual convention. They urged that Hurley remain in the South. She provided what had been missing since Ella Baker's departure five years earlier—a strong and active national presence, attentive to the conditions and desires of people living under the heel of Jim Crow. Thurgood Marshall praised Hurley for "doing an excellent job of demonstrating the necessity for our people in those areas to take advantage of what the law says they are entitled to." White and branch director Gloster Current needed little convincing. The board had long considered establishing a southeastern regional office as soon as funds were available. Hurley had demonstrated what such a presence could achieve. After the Atlanta convention she returned to New York, packed up her apartment, and relocated to Birmingham. Reflecting two decades later on this dramatic change in her life, Hurley explained, "I never really had much time to think about me. . . . We had nobody living in the South working with people on their immediate needs. . . . There was so much work to be done."[30]

While branches in the South worked on a variety of issues, the fight against segregation became the connecting tissue of a South-wide NAACP movement, with schools targeted as the first line of offense. Roy Wilkins emphasized the primacy of the education fight in his speech to the 1951 convention: "More damage . . . has been done [to our children and young people] by the denial of equal opportunity in education than by all the lynching mobs in our history." By then, a general consensus had emerged around the claim that there could be no equality under segregation, representing a sea change in sentiment reaching into the Deep South. At the Cordele conference Hurley had attended in south Georgia a month earlier, the delegates had agreed that "equalization of educational opportunities can only become an accomplishment when Negro and white students attend the same schools." In November 1951, the Mississippi state conference passed a resolution declaring, "We reject the 'separate but equal' theory" and called "upon our Branches in the State of Mississippi to take any and all necessary legal steps to end segregation in public education from elementary and secondary levels to graduate and professional levels."[31]

The contours of the looming battle in the South emerged in the year following the rulings in the *Sweatt* and *McLaurin* cases. During this period, the NAACP launched its attack on segregation in primary and secondary schools while implementing the gains achieved in the 1950 decision. Only one public university, the University of Louisville, admitted blacks to its graduate and professional schools in compliance with the Supreme Court's rulings; West Virginia, Arkansas, and Delaware had already lowered the color bar. It took NAACP-sponsored suits to open the doors at universities in Virginia, Maryland, North Carolina, and Louisiana. By 1951, nearly one thousand black men and women had enrolled in schools where they had previously been barred without any major incidents. Resistance remained pervasive in several states. While cases went forward in Florida and Tennessee, Governors James Byrnes of South Carolina and Herman Talmadge of Georgia pledged to maintain segregation at all costs. Shortly after her arrival in Birmingham, Hurley announced that suits would be filed in Alabama and Mississippi as soon as cases could be developed, sparking a tirade from Governor Fielding Wright of Mississippi. Wright joined Byrnes and Talmadge and declared that "the state of Mississippi must resist these efforts of the NAACP to the fullest extent of its resources." He pledged that "we shall insist upon segregation regardless of the costs and consequences" and announced plans to introduce legislation aimed at equalizing educational opportunities within the state.[32]

The opening phase of the school campaign to desegregate primary and secondary schools pivoted on the case from Clarendon County, which grew from the failed efforts of black parents to obtain county support for a school bus in 1947. After the NAACP lawyers and southern representatives decided to go forward with a direct challenge to segregation, South Carolina leader James Hinton obtained the agreement of the parents who had signed the petition to sue for school equalization. But Robert Carter, who was in charge of preparing the case, wanted to be sure that the parents were fully aware of the pressures they would face, so he traveled down to the rural county in the old plantation section of South Carolina to meet with the men and women who would be involved. "*Plessy* was still deeply entrenched, legally and morally," Carter later recalled. "It seemed like an impregnable wall."

The parents who would be plaintiffs in the suit met with Carter at St. Mark's Church in Summerton. He went over each paragraph of the legal complaint, explaining it in layman's language, and emphasized that the suit's purpose was to have their children go to school with white children. All those named in the lawsuit who were employed locally should expect to lose their jobs; they and their families would be exposed to threats, violence, and possibly loss of life. Understanding that, Carter advised that anyone who wanted to withdraw from the case should do so, without any shame or embarrassment. To his surprise, only two parents decided not to continue with the litigation. He ended the meeting by saying that while he realized the dangers they faced, the NAACP felt that it was time to fight segregation head on. Carter recalled, "a gray-headed sage sitting in the corner of the church said [in response], 'We wondered how long it would take you lawyers to reach that conclusion,' a remark greeted by laughter and applause." Several men and women who had signed the equalization petition the previous November, including Harry and Eliza Briggs, had already lost jobs and suffered other economic reprisals. "Our determination was hardened by this point," Joseph DeLaine recalled, and they were ready "to go for broke." Carter returned to New York tremendously encouraged and energized.[33]

Carter took on the task of devising a strategy to establish the inherent inequality of separate schools at the primary and secondary level. The challenge was different from what the legal staff had confronted in the law and graduate school cases—where intellectual exchange and professional contacts were formative factors. While the negative effects of segregation were obvious at the graduate level, Carter recalled, "no one had figured out how to isolate the school segregation factor" at the grade school and high school level. He immersed himself in social science literature, focusing on evidence of the psychic damage inflicted by segregation. That led him to the work of Kenneth Clark, then a thirty-seven-year-old assistant professor of psychology at the City University of New York.[34]

Clark had presented a paper at the White House Midcentury Conference on Youth based on a test he and his wife, Mamie Clark, had developed using dolls to illustrate the effects of racism on children. In this exercise, when African American children were presented with a white and a brown doll, "they showed an unmistakable preference for the white doll and a rejection of the brown doll." After reading the study, Carter met with Clark and promptly enlisted him as an expert witness and adviser to the legal team. Clark later admitted that he "had some doubts about the effectiveness of the legal approach . . . but I guess I was envious that they were doing something specific to improve things and I was off in the scholarly area." Convincing the NAACP's national legal committee was not as easy as signing Clark on. In a highly charged meeting to review Carter's plans, several committee members derided the "doll test" and questioned his reliance on a social science approach. Carter held his ground, convinced that social science evidence would work and pressing his critics to offer an alternative approach. They had none. Marshall was persuaded and later recalled, "I thought the doll test was a way of showing injury to these youngsters. . . . I wanted this kind of evidence on the record."[35]

Briggs v. Elliot, the Clarendon County case, was one of five cases that ultimately composed *Brown v. Board of Education*. Marshall and his team were intent on presenting the question of school segregation to the Court in a variety of communities, reaching from the border state of Kansas to the states of Deep South. The fast-paced process unfolded over the course of barely three years, building upon decades of work and drawing upon the talent, vision, and courage of countless individuals. The circumstances surrounding the *Briggs* trial in May 1951, however, revealed the fusion of elements that brought the NAACP, the South, and the nation to the edge of momentous change.

Marshall, Carter, Clark, and Spottswood Robinson traveled together by train to Charleston, arriving a week before the start of the trial. When they arrived in Charleston they set up shop at the home of local NAACP supporters Reginald and Eva Boone. The place was abuzz with activity as the lawyers prepared for the case. Clark spent two days over in Clarendon County, interviewing the children at Scott's Branch School—his first exposure to the oppressive and terror-laden climate of the Deep South. "The fact that our side was playing for keeps really sank through to me," he later recalled. Back at the Boone house, though, a festive atmosphere prevailed. Working sessions and meals took place around a large table in the attached garage, where a cool breeze gave some respite from the heat and humidity. Eva Boone hired a cook to feed "the overflow of lawyers, reporters, expert witnesses, stenographers, [and] NAACP hands" and the well-wishers who dropped in. *New York Post* reporter Ted Posten, a longtime associate of the NAACP lawyers, was there. He remembered "an inner joyousness affecting everyone in the place." For Kenneth Clark, the entire Charleston experience "really opened my eyes. I saw the tremendous psychological investment these men had in this case . . . and of course my life hasn't been the same since."[36]

Before dawn on the morning of May 28, 1951, the first day of the trial, Eliza Briggs met her neighbors at St. Mark's Church in Summerton and joined a caravan of cars headed for Charleston. Black men and women began lining up outside the federal courthouse at sunrise and continued coming all morning. By the time the lawyers arrived, the line stretched from the second-story courtroom down the hall and stairway, through the lobby, down the front steps, and along the sidewalk. The courtroom seated 150; more than 500 people waited, and more came. Eliza Briggs was guaranteed a seat given that the case bore her family's name. James Gibson, a farmer who rode over from Clarendon County, was among the hundreds who lined up outside. "I never got tired of standing that day," he said. "The fact that Judge Waring was up there meant that we were going to get a hearing." During the course of the trial, news found its way to Gibson and the others gathered along the hallways and on the street. "Whenever the NAACP lawyer made a point," Posten recalled, "someone got up and whispered it to the line, and it would travel right down the corridor and down the steps to the throng outside."[37]

The court was called to order at 10 A.M. by John Fleming, the black bailiff. Judge John J. Parker presided over the special three-judge session of the U.S. District Court for the Eastern District of South Carolina, which was required because the case attacked the constitutionality of a state statute. Parker was joined by George Bell Timmerman and Waties Waring. Charleston attorney Robert McCormack Figg, who represented the Clarendon County School Board, promptly dropped a bombshell. He acknowledged that inequalities existed in the county's educational facilities and pointed to recent action by the state legislature approving Governor Byrnes's proposal for a new sales tax to fund a multimillion-dollar school equalization program. Figg's blanket concession clearly aimed to defuse a major component of the NAACP's case, organized around presenting evidence of the inequities while also demonstrating that the state's segregation statutes were unconstitutional. Undeterred, Marshall and his team proceeded as planned, with several expert witnesses laying out the crude conditions of black schooling in Clarendon County—where, for example, four outdoor "earth toilets" with no running water were provided for the 694 students at Scott's Branch School.[38]

With Kenneth Clark's testimony, Robert Carter steered the NAACP toward a final showdown, attacking the legal facade of separate but equal. In response to Carter's questioning, Clark reported on the results of his interviews with sixteen children in Clarendon County, placing them within the context of his previous work as well as a large body of literature in psychology, anthropology, and sociology—all of which led him to conclude that segregation had "definitely detrimental effects on the personality development of the Negro child." Figg exerted little effort to undercut Clark in his cross-examination of Clark. He trivialized Clark's methods and assumed his testimony would not adversely impact his case. Carter brought on a number of other expert witnesses he had identified and enlisted over the previous ten months to buttress the argument that segregation had harmful emotional, psychological, and even physical effects on black children. These witnesses included James L. Hupp, dean and professor of education and psychology at West Virginia Wesleyan College; Helen Trager, a lecturer at Vassar who had conducted racial attitude tests similar to the Clarks'; and David Kreich, visiting associate professor of psychology at Harvard and author of a widely respected textbook, *Theory and Problems of Social Psychology*.[39]

The high point of the trial came when Thurgood Marshall cross-examined one of the defense's few witnesses, ironically named E. R. Crow. Crow was the director of the three-week-old South Carolina Educational Finance Commission, hurriedly established to oversee the state's massive school spending plan. Marshall peppered Crow with questions. What guarantees were there to ensure that sufficient funds would be spent on black schools? How many blacks served on the new state commission? Were there plans to hire any? It was a "withering cross examination," Carter recalled, compelling the witness to admit widespread disparity. At the end of each question, Marshall would pronounce "Mr. Crow's name, allowing the blacks in the audience to supply the nuance of 'Jim' to Mr. Crow" to their delight. It was a masterly performance.[40]

In his closing argument, Marshall observed: "In South Carolina, you have admitted to the inferiority of Negro schools. All your state officials are white. All your school officials are white. It is admitted. That's not just segregation. It's exclusion from the group that runs everything." The defense had made no attempt to counter the evidence of the harm caused by segregation. Rather, the state appealed to the court for time to eliminate the inequalities which, the defense admitted, violated the law. "I know of no statute that permits anyone to come into court and ask time to stop doing something which is unlawful," Marshall argued, and he concluded that "there is no relief for the Negro children of Clarendon County except to be permitted to attend existing and superior white schools." Figg countered that separate schools were legal, conceded that they must be equal, and emphasized that the state had pledged $40 million to correct rampant inequality. Marshall had the last word. "Negroes must be offered the exact [same] thing. If the white child is permitted to obtain an education without mental roadblocks, the Negro child must be permitted."[41]

The significance of the case reached beyond whatever the trial court decided. Longtime board member John Hammond, the musical impresario, attended the hearing and reported at the June board meeting a week later that the NAACP had finally struck "pay dirt" so far as the masses of blacks in the South were concerned. The case affected every black family, as demonstrated by the hundreds who turned out for the trial. For the first time, he said, he felt "the NAACP was able to get the whole story of the futility of segregation before the white southerners as well as the Negroes." James Hinton wrote that "the very sight of the trial lifted them to a deeper appreciation of the NAACP and its aims and purposes." For Marshall, Charleston was a measure of how far they had traveled in four short years, when he first began laying the groundwork for a frontal attack on Jim Crow. "The Negroes from Clarendon County and from all over the South jammed the courthouse standing shoulder to shoulder, hot and uncomfortable, for a single purpose—to demonstrate to all the world that Negroes in the South are determined to eliminate segregation from American life."[42]

On June 21, in a 2-1 decision, the court upheld segregation in the Clarendon County schools. Judge Parker's opinion cited tradition, history, and precedence. He wrote that "when seventeen states and the Congress of the United States have for more than three quarters of a century required segregation of the races in the public schools, and when this has received the approval of the leading appellate courts of the country . . . it is a late day to say that such segregation is violative of fundamental constitutional rights. . . . If conditions have changed so that segregation is no longer wise, this is a matter for the legislatures and not the courts." The opinion instructed the state to "promptly" furnish equal educational facilities for the black students in their districts and to report back to the court on their progress within six months.[43]

Judge Waring filed a twenty-one-page dissent. If segregation was wrong, as the Court had ruled in *Sweatt* and *McLaurin*, "then," he insisted, "the place to stop it is in the first grade." Undeniably founded on racial prejudice, "segregation can never produce equality," Waring wrote, "and is an evil that must be eradicated. This case presents the matter clearly for adjudication, and I am of the opinion that all of the legal guideposts, expert testimony, common sense and reason point unerringly to the conclusion that the system of segregation in education adopted and practiced in the state of South Carolina must go and must go now. Segregation is per se inequality." Not long after writing this opinion, Waring retired from the court, and he and his wife moved to New York. There was nothing further Waring could do as a jurist to advance desegregation, and he had wearied of the insults, threats, and social isolation that resulted from his forthright stand on racial issues. "You hate to be in a foreign land where you're hated all the time," he wrote to his friend John Hammond.[44]

Barely a week after the South Carolina ruling, Robert Carter and twenty-six-year-old Jack Greenburg, the newest addition to the legal team, were in Topeka, Kansas, to try the next school case. A graduate of Columbia University Law School, Greenburg had joined the NAACP's legal staff in the fall of 1949. In his first major case, Greenburg worked with Delaware attorney Louis Redding representing thirty black college students in their suit to obtain admission to the University of Delaware. The pair won the first court ruling that required a state university to admit black students at the undergraduate level, based on findings that the facilities at the state-supported black college were "grossly inferior." Carter assigned Greenburg the task of lining up social science experts in the Midwest for the Topeka case. The trial provided a major platform for broadening the claim that segregation was inherently unequal and harmful to black school children.[45]

Elementary schools had long been segregated in Topeka under the mandate of the school board, not by state law. In Kansas, a state statute allowed cities larger than fifteen thousand to segregate their schools. The arrangement lacked the state pressure common in the South, and, Carter reasoned, might yield a favorable ruling or at least "a different kind of analysis of the problem." Nevertheless, Topeka, the state's capital city, was a segregated town and the school board was determined to maintain separate schools for grades one through six. The black community was divided over the issue; black teachers, in particular, were committed to maintaining black schools. The groundwork for the court challenge had been laid by longtime black civil rights lawyer Elisha Scott; Esther Brown, a young white mother who embraced the cause of school desegregation; and Burnett McKinley, the fifty-two-year-old son of a former slave, who led Topeka's fledgling NAACP branch. McKinley began petitioning the school board in 1948 to end school segregation and got nowhere. In the summer of 1950, McKinley wrote Walter White that the branch was ready to bring a lawsuit to end school segregation in Topeka. From then on, Carter, "the battlefront commander" of the new legal strategy, was in frequent contact with McKinley and his legal committee in preparation for legal action as the branch began enlisting plaintiffs for what became *Brown v. Board of Education of Topeka*.[46]

Oliver Brown, the father of nine-year-old Linda Brown, led the list of the thirteen plaintiffs filing suit on behalf of their children. The case was heard

before a three-judge panel during the last week of June 1951. In a striking contrast to the Charleston hearing, the courtroom was barely half full.
Greenburg, with the aid of Esther Brown, had enlisted an impressive group
of expert witnesses, mostly from universities in Kansas. Two witnesses documented the physical disparities between black and white schools, though the
gap was nowhere near as stark as in Clarendon County. In Topeka, however,
the cumulative impact of testimony from nearly a dozen witnesses, including
psychologists, sociologists, and educators, illuminated the effects of legally
mandated segregation on the personality development and social adjustment
of black children in a white majority society. Louisa Holt's brief testimony
was a high point. Holt, an assistant professor of psychology at the University
of Kansas, had been affiliated with the world-famous Menninger Clinic and
was the mother of two children who attended the local public schools. In
response to questioning from Robert Carter, she explained, quite simply, that
"enforced segregation" created "a sense of inferiority [that] must always affect
one's motivation for learning since it affects the feelings one has of oneself as
a person."[47]

Judge Walter Huxman, writing for a unanimous court, observed that if
"segregation within a school" or the "denial of the right to commingle with
the majority group" violated due process in the case of law and professional
schools, it was difficult to see "why such a denial would not result in the same
lack of due process in the lower grades." The court held, however, that since
the Supreme Court had clearly confined its rulings to graduate schools only,
Plessy was "still presently" controlling with regard to segregation in the lower
grades. But the opinion included nine "findings of facts" that affirmed many
of the claims advanced by the social scientists. Finding VIII stated that:

> Segregation of white and colored children in pubic schools has a detri-
> mental effect upon the colored children. The impact is greater when it
> has the sanction of law; for the policy of separating the races is usually
> interpreted as denoting the inferiority of the Negro group. A sense of
> inferiority affects the motivation of the child to learn. Segregation with
> the sanction of law, therefore, has a tendency to retard the education and
> mental development of Negro children and deprive them of the benefits
> they would receive in a racially integrated school system.[48]

The Kansas court went much further "than we had any reason to expect or
hope," Carter later recalled. By acknowledging psychological damage in the

"finding of fact," the decision appeared to challenge the Supreme Court "to take a fresh look" at *Plessy*.[49]

The power of the legal campaign rested at the nexus of a strategic litigation program and a rising surge in black intolerance for segregation's humiliations and inequities—a convergence Marshall highlighted in his speech to the NAACP's 1951 annual convention in Atlanta, just after the Clarendon County ruling. Observing that the time for "fortitude and patience" had passed, he took special note of black youth who wanted "their American birthright NOW!" Marshall was probably thinking of sixteen-year-old Barbara Johns when he advised that young people were "determined . . . to fight alone . . . should we hesitate or falter." In April, Johns had led more than 450 students in a mass walkout from R. R. Moton High School in Prince Edward County, Virginia, to protest the abysmal conditions of the county's only black high school, initiating developments that culminated in a third school desegregation case.[50]

Barbara Johns's family had deep roots in Prince Edward County, situated at the center of the state in the tobacco country known as Southside Virginia. With a population of more than fifteen thousand, the racial balance of the county slightly favored whites by 55 percent to 45 percent. Moton High School, located in the town of Farmville, was the first black high school in the county when it opened in 1927. In 1939 the county constructed a new building to accommodate 180 students; by the late 1940s close to 400 students attended the school. In 1948, the school board authorized three tar paper barrack-like structures to temporarily meet the needs of the growing school population. Heated by stoves, they were cold and drafty, leaked when it rained, and the peculiar odor of tar paper mixed with stove fumes hung in the air. The "tar paper shacks" gave the school grounds the look of a chicken farm. The county school board had been promising to build a new high school since 1948. By the time Barbara Johns was a sophomore in 1950–51, no plans had materialized. She resolved that something must be done.[51]

A quiet, attractive young woman, Johns was a good student and active in school affairs. She had traveled around the state and seen other high schools and was aware of the modern facilities at the all-white Farmville High School. In the fall of 1950, she sought out John Stokes, president of the senior class. They talked about the failed efforts on the part of their parents and the PTA to get a new school. Johns told him of her plan for a student strike to pressure the county to build a new school. The idea appealed to Stokes, who was struck by Johns's commitment and her personal qualities: "I knew if anyone could pull this off, she could," he later recalled. The two enlisted a group of twenty students, selected for their "character and leadership skills" and representing different sections of the county. Naming their effort the Manhattan Project, after the top-secret nuclear program during World War II, the group worked quietly over several months.

On Monday morning April 23, 1951, Johns and her associates flawlessly executed their plan. They arranged for the principal, Boyd Jones, to be called away from school to investigate a reported "disturbance" involving students at the bus station and then dispatched message slips to all classes summoning them to the auditorium for an assembly. The strike committee appeared on the stage. Johns announced that the meeting was for students only and asked the teachers to leave. Most left voluntarily; two football players removed one resistant teacher from the assembly. Johns spoke to the students about the conditions they faced every day and said nothing would change until they did something. She explained the plan for students to walk out and not to return to school until the school board began construction of a new building. If they stuck together, she assured them, none of them would be punished; Farmville's jail was too small to hold all of them. At the end of the meeting, all 456 students marched out.[52]

After leaving school, members of the strike committee met with the Reverend L. Francis Griffin, minister of the First Baptist Church and head of the local NAACP branch. He was in complete sympathy with the students. On his advice, they contacted Oliver Hill and Spottswood Robinson. The Richmond lawyers were working on a school desegregation case in Pulaski County that they hoped to carry to the Supreme Court. But they agreed to stop and meet with the student leaders on their way to Pulaski two days later. The high morale and determination of the students surprised and impressed the attorneys. When Robinson explained that the NAACP could only aid the group if they sued for desegregation, the students were prepared to go forward. Oliver Hill recalled, "We didn't have the heart to say no. We said if their parents would support them, we would back them up." The next night students and parents, numbering close to one thousand, packed a mass meeting in the high school auditorium with NAACP state secretary Lester Banks. They voted overwhelmingly to support school desegregation. On May 3, the firm of Hill, Robinson, and Martin petitioned the school board to end school segregation in the county schools, and the students returned to school the following Monday, ending the two-week-long strike. As expected, the school board refused to grant their petition. On May 23, before boarding the train to

Charleston for the Clarendon County case, Spottswood Robinson filed suit in the federal courthouse in Richmond on behalf of 117 Moton students challenging the state laws requiring school segregation in Virginia.[53]

By the fall of 1951, in the words of Walter White, an "anti–civil rights movement" was on the rise in the South. While states pumped funds into upgrading black public schools, governors in South Carolina, Georgia, and Mississippi floated plans to end public education in the event the U.S. Supreme Court overturned school segregation. South Carolinians voted two to one in support of Governor Byrnes's proposal. There was a cross burning at Moton High School. Prince Edward's black community went into "cover mode," armed and prepared to defend their families. Fearing for her safety, Barbara Johns's parents sent her to Montgomery, Alabama, to finish high school. She lived with her uncle, Vernon Johns, pastor of Dexter Avenue Baptist Church. In October 1951, the Reverend Joseph DeLaine's home in Summerton, South Carolina went up in flames. The fire department came but did nothing; they said DeLaine's home was outside the city limits. Violence and terror remained the primary weapons in the battle to protect the "southern way of life," and increasingly the NAACP and its work became a target.[54]

Florida emerged as a center of racial terror during the last half of 1951. Conflicts around housing and jobs along with modest but steady civil rights gains contributed to a spike in Klan activity. There were several unsolved murders of black men attributed to the Klan, and a series of bombings in the summer and fall destroyed black-occupied apartment buildings in Orlando and Miami. Early in November, preparations for new trials in the infamous Groveland case were under way, reopening one of the most highly charged episodes in the state's recent history. The Supreme Court's reversal of the convictions of Samuel Shepherd and Walter Irwin a year earlier had been an important victory for the NAACP and its state leader Harry Moore. On November 6, the day before pretrial hearing was scheduled to begin, Sheriff Willis McCall shot defendants Shepherd and Irwin while transporting them between jails, killing Shepherd and seriously wounding Irwin. The men were handcuffed together and each one was shot three times. McCall said that the men had jumped him while he was changing a tire, and he pleaded self-defense.[55]

Thurgood Marshall flew to Orlando, interviewed Irwin in his hospital bed and demanded state and federal investigations. A coroner's jury held that the sheriff acted in self-defense, and Judge Truman Futch, who had presided over

Shepherd's and Irwin's first trial, chose not to impanel a grand jury to investigate the shootings. Marshall charged that the unpunished murder of Shepherd and attempted murder of Irwin had replaced "the old type of lynching" and was the state's way of defying the U.S. Supreme Court after it had overturned the original conviction of the men. At the start of Irwin's hearing in mid-December, Judge Futch barred Marshall and Jack Greenburg from participating because, he said, the NAACP had stirred up trouble in the community. Two local lawyers working for the association handled Irwin's defense. Marshall remained actively involved, focusing public attention on developments around the Groveland case. A bomb threat did not keep him from addressing a packed meeting at Mt. Zion Baptist Church in Miami on December 17. Local authorities surrounded the church with armed guards.[56]

Harry Moore attended the meeting in Miami. A week later, on Christmas night, a bomb exploded under his home in Mims, Florida, blasting Moore and his wife, Harriette, out of their bed. Moore died en route to the hospital; his wife succumbed to her injuries a week later. The former schoolteacher had been the leading civil rights figure in Florida for more than a decade, heading the state NAACP and the Progressive Voters League. His murder was national news and generated a storm of protest. Florida governor Fuller Warren along with the NAACP and other organizations offered rewards totaling nearly $20,000 for the capture of the Moores' killers. Local, county, and state officials mounted separate investigations, in addition to the FBI and a federal grand jury investigation. None of these efforts succeeded in identifying the murderers of Harry and Harriette Moore. The murder of a prominent civil rights leader, even in the racially violent climate of the South, marked a chilling turn, wrote *Pittsburgh Courier* columnist Marjorie McKenzie, ending the time when it could be assumed that "our leaders, though bold," were safe. "There is no security for any of us," said Atlanta branch president C. L. Harper. Commenting on Moore's murder in light of the Groveland shootings, the *Washington Post* editorialized, "When state officers flout the law, it can be scarcely surprising that the lynch spirit should spread."[57]

Less than a month after the Moores' murder, more than one hundred NAACP leaders representing fifteen southern states gathered for a two-day emergency meeting in Jacksonville, Florida, joined by Marshall, Ruby Hurley, and Roy Wilkins. In a public display of unity and fighting spirit, the group paid tribute to Moore and pledged that his work to advance "freedom, justice, equality and security for all citizens" would continue throughout the South.

Illness prevented White from attending the meeting. In his message to the conference, he said that Talmadge, Byrnes, and others like them who "deliberately stir up hatred" to advance personal and sectional interests bore responsibility for "this new era of hate and violence." During the two-day meeting, held at the local YWCA, delegates established a committee of representatives from each state to coordinate a program of political education and action and expand the "fight for the right of every Negro in the South to register and vote." On the final evening of the meeting, African Americans packed Bethel Baptist Institutional Church for a mass meeting, lining the walls and spilling into the street. In the intense climate of fear, Bethel was the only large church that would provide the NAACP with meeting space.[58]

Voter education and registration was a unifying goal that southern branches organized around. Three months after the Jacksonville meeting, southern NAACP leaders gathered in Atlanta for a political action institute, to share experiences and strategies for boosting black voter turnout in the face of voter restrictions, purging of voting rolls, hostile registrars, and intimidation. There were notable successes. For example, Ruby Hurley reported that efforts of the branch president in Henry County in southeast Alabama succeeded in registering the first blacks to vote in that county since Reconstruction. But the dramatic gains that followed in the wake of the white primary decision had leveled off by the early 1950s. Between 1947 and 1952, the number of registered black voters in the South had barely doubled to slightly more than 1 million voters, far short of the NAACP's goal of 2 million registered voters by 1952. In twenty-four Black Belt counties from South Carolina to Mississippi, not a single black voter was registered at the end of 1952.[59]

Against the weight of law, custom, and repression, the fight against school segregation had emerged as a force capable of disrupting the South's rigid racial structure. Early in the spring of 1952, there were back-to-back rulings as the legal challenge moved toward the U.S. Supreme Court. In Richmond, a three-judge federal court, in *Davis v. County School Board of Prince Edward County*, held that racial separation had "for generations been part of the mores of her people." The court found that separate systems caused "no hurt or harm to either race." It ordered the Prince Edward school board to pursue the equalization of school facilities with "dispatch." Two weeks later, Chancellor Collin Seitz gave his ruling in two Delaware school cases. Seitz, who personally visited the schools, found the facilities for white students "vastly superior" to those provided for black students. While remaining within the confines of *Plessy*, he held that the plaintiffs were entitled to immediate relief under the "separate but equal" doctrine and ordered them admitted to the white schools. This, Marshall announced, was "the first real victory in our campaign to destroy segregation of American pupils in elementary and secondary schools."[60]

In mid-April, as the NAACP prepared to challenge segregation in the U.S. Supreme Court, Howard University convened a conference on the "Courts and Racial Integration in Education." The meeting, organized by Charles Thompson and bearing Marshall's stamp, was designed in part to address the concerns raised by some, particularly Marjorie McKenzie, the lawyer and newspaper columnist, who argued that the NAACP was moving too fast. More broadly, it provided a forum for reviewing the legal campaign and its relationship to what had been a defining purpose of the association: the elimination of all racial barriers from American life and securing full constitutional rights. Organizers of the conference were confident that victory over *Plessy* was within reach. But what would it mean? How should they prepare for a Court ruling striking down the fifty-year-old precedent? These questions remained uppermost during the forum. For the lawyers and others who had worked for years toward this moment, there was a palpable sense that they were poised on the brink of a new era. Tellingly, this remarkable public gathering escaped the attention of the *Washington Post* and the *New York Times*; it was fully covered by leading black newspapers.[61]

More than three hundred men and women attended the Howard conference. They represented twenty-seven states and forty-eight organizations. Thompson invited representatives of school boards in every southern state. It is not clear whether any attended. But this reflected the spirit of the conference, designed to facilitate an honest and open discussion about school segregation, the campaign to dismantle it, and how to plan for the future. There was a full airing of questions regarding the wisdom of an all-out attack on segregation and its potential consequences. Harry Ashmore, editor of the *Arkansas Gazette*, cautioned that any Court mandate for school desegregation would be opposed by the majority of white southerners. He predicted violent resistance and the closing of schools, especially in counties with black majorities, and suggested that equalization efforts by southern states be given a chance to work. Several others who supported the goals of the NAACP's campaign warned that the Court was sensitive to political currents and should not be expected to issue a ruling that could not be enforced. John Frank of Yale Law School noted the growth in "moral opposition to racial discrimination" over the previous two decades, paralleled by judicial decisions broadening the application of the Fourteenth Amendment. He cautioned against relying too heavily on the courts and specifically advised that the NAACP not press at this time for the "ultimate" decision in the grade school cases, but allow the Court room to maneuver. Echoing McKenzie, he feared that a negative decision would be "an incalculable loss" and setback for the antisegregation forces.[62]

Black lawyers, educators, and others who had long been involved with the NAACP's campaign contended that conditions had never been more favorable for bringing such a challenge before the Court. "Recent cases," Marshall explained, "have been closing the doors of escape from a clear-cut determination of the validity or invalidity of this [separate-but-equal] doctrine." Broader political currents, they argued, further enhanced the likelihood of a favorable ruling. "It is inconceivable to me," Frank Horne said, "that the U.S. Supreme Court, in view of the present climate of international opinion . . . will be able or willing to say . . . that legally enforced segregation based on color or race is consonant with our precepts of democracy." The United States was engaged in a "destiny-making struggle" with the Soviet Union to win the confidence of black and brown people in Africa and Asia, noted Howard University president Mordecai Johnson. A decision "to confirm segregation as a permanent part of American life, acceptable under the Constitution" would precipitate disaster. In the white South's attempt "to cling to *Dred Scott* and *Plessy*," claimed James Nabrit, "the twentieth century is against them; world politics is against them; the self interest of the United States is against them; and, the Constitution of the United States is against them."[63]

The probability that the Court would rule in their favor raised the question, what next? It was widely acknowledged within NAACP circles that a Court decision striking down school segregation would be the first step on the road to ending all state-enforced segregation. Yet Marshall attempted to prepare everyone for the long haul. He explained the limited reach of such a school ruling, predicting that they would need to go county by county and state by state to enforce it for schools beyond the specific cases the Court ruled on. Legally enforced segregation in other areas, such as transportation and public accommodations, would not be directly affected. Discussions focused attention on the process of implementing a desegregation mandate while keeping an eye on the ultimate goal, the full integration of American society, North and South. What would integration look and feel like? It must mean more than "mere physical occupancy," noted Lincoln University president Horace Mann Bond. "We need to plan for genuine integration on our terms and fight for it."

In considering the immediate future, several speakers speculated on likely white southern reactions to a Court order ending school segregation. Virginia attorney Oliver Hill discounted predictions. He emphasized the need for working to "get on closer terms with white people in order to convince them that there is something here desirable—integration." Mordecai Johnson imagined the type of leadership that could summon the will to break through the racial structures, attitudes, and fears that permeated the white southern experience, a leadership that possessed "the deepest convictions about the possibilities of human nature and about the nature of democracy." There was a full engagement of the broad forces at play, revealing a shared sense that they were entering uncharted waters. A favorable decision would, at the least, noted Nabrit, "remove the barrier of illegality from the pathway to integration." But he advised that they not get too distracted by the looming challenges down the road. "Let the Supreme Court worry over community attitudes," he told them. "Let us worry over the problem of pressing for our civil rights."[64]

The uncertainty attached to the broad process of desegregation contrasted with the confidence displayed by the attorneys and others familiar with the NAACP's litigation campaign when they considered one of its most important achievements. The program crafted by Charles Houston at Howard Law School nearly two decades earlier and implemented through the NAACP provided a structure and focus for organizing and articulating the rising expectations, hopes, and demands of black Americans. While barred from meaningful participation in the electoral process in the South, blacks had discovered that "the Constitution" could be "a revolutionary document," used through application in the courts to advance "their basic civil rights," observed Mordecai Johnson. Marshall and the attorneys working in the field helped facilitate this transformation and experienced it firsthand. Cases grew from the ground up as branches and civil rights lawyers pursued elemental justice while chipping away at the foundations of the segregation system. In the aftermath of legal victories, notably the white primary ruling, blacks took full advantage of broadening opportunities to exert their rights as citizens. By 1950, Spottswood Robinson felt pressure to keep up with rising black demands. The protest mounted by the students in Farmville, he said, was "the most perfect organization of a movement of that type I have ever . . . been associated with." Marshall described "the courage of Negroes in Clarendon County, South Carolina . . . and in Farmville, Virginia," as "a landmark in the struggle for citizenship," demonstrating the kind of determination and action that would be critical in the years ahead. If the Court overturned segregation in the public schools, Nabrit predicted, this spirit would grow, stirring "to action that at times dormant will to first class citizenship within the Negro community."[65]

The NAACP's long struggle for racial equality would center on the U.S. Supreme Court for the next two years. In the months following the Howard conference, the justices consolidated the cases on appeal from South Carolina, Kansas, Virginia, and Delaware under the rubric of *Brown v. Board of Education of Topeka*. They were joined by *Bolling v. Sharpe* from Washington, D.C., the case organized by Gardiner Bishop, Charles Houston's former client, now represented by James Nabrit. The Court scheduled arguments for the second week in December 1952. [66]

In the final days of the Truman administration, the U.S. Supreme Court began considering a group of cases that, as one journalist observed, were "perhaps the most fateful in Negro history since the *Dred Scott* decision on slavery." The question before the Court was straightforward: Did school segregation violate the equal protection clause of the Fourteenth Amendment? In light of history and racial custom, the pressures surrounding the cases combined with the well-matched legal talent contributed to a high-stakes drama unlike any major Court case in recent memory. The lead attorney among the battery of lawyers defending segregation was John W. Davis, the 1924 presidential candidate who was widely considered to be among the best constitutional lawyers in the country. At forty-four, Thurgood Marshall was nearly half Davis's age. Marshall had honed his brilliance and tactical skill during nearly two decades of intense work on the cutting edge of constitutional law, collaborating with a broad range of legal practitioners and scholars, and winning every case he had brought before the nation's highest court. The *Pittsburgh Courier* found irony in the fact "that no one ... thought for a minute that these barristers were not equal according to the most exacting standards . . . although the issue was equality versus inequality of so-called races."[67]

Across three days of hearings, Marshall and the NAACP's legal team laid out the arguments that had been developed around the five cases; namely, that segregation in education was inherently unequal and in violation of the Constitution. The attorneys for the states held close to the argument that classification of students according to race was in the purview of state power and did not offend the Fourteenth Amendment. They advanced a parallel claim, emphasizing the perils of a Court order to end segregation. Davis predicted such a ruling would create a condition "that one cannot contemplate with equanimity." The justices sought greater clarity and more time. In June 1953, they ordered the five cases reargued, instructing the lawyers for both sides to consider a series of questions that addressed the following concerns: What evidence was there, if any, that the Congress that submitted the Fourteenth Amendment, and the ratifying states, contemplated the abolition of segregation in public schools? If the answers did not resolve this issue, was it within the Court's power to end segregation in public schools? Finally, if the Court decided that school segregation violated the Fourteenth Amendment, what procedure could the Court follow to provide for implementation of the ruling?[68]

Marshall and his associates orchestrated a summer-long research project that spilled into the fall and culminated with a three-day seminar-style conference. They enlisted more than two hundred lawyers and historians from across the nation, including the most talented scholars of that generation, such as John Hope Franklin and C. Vann Woodward. It was undoubtedly the most intensive exploration of the history of the Fourteenth Amendment and the broader social, historical, and political forces that shaped the transition from slavery to freedom and citizenship ever undertaken. Those who came to New York fell in step with Marshall, working practically around the clock. At midnight, Franklin recalled, Marshall would suggest, "Why don't we take a fifteen minute break." The final results of this massive effort were distilled and incorporated into a 235-page legal brief written by Spottswood Robinson. The brief consolidated the NAACP's position in the four state cases and argued that evidence showed the Fourteenth Amendment intended to prohibit state-imposed racial discrimination. Furthermore, it held that state segregation laws violated all conventional tests for a reasonable basis to state classification of citizens.[69]

After all parties filed briefs in response to the Supreme Court's order, the final arguments were heard December 7–9, 1953. Earl Warren, appointed as chief justice following the death of Fred Vinson two months earlier, presided. The history surrounding the Fourteenth Amendment proved to be inconclusive in terms of the questions raised by the Court, inviting each side to provide its own interpretive framework. Representing South Carolina, the eighty-one-year-old Davis grounded his defense of the state's school segregation laws in history, custom, and legal precedent and claimed that nothing in the legislative history made segregation illegal. Davis pledged the "good faith and intention" of South Carolina "to produce equality for all of its children," in line with the mandate established by *Plessy*. He addressed the Court's evident concern about the implementation of a desegregation order by spotlighting the fact that there were 2,800 black children and 300 white children in Clarendon County. "Who is going to disturb that situation," he asked, suggesting that it offered further justification for the state's action in classifying the school children by race. During his presentation to the Court, Marshall compared segregation laws to the Black Codes instituted after slavery. The only way for the Court to uphold school segregation laws was to "find for some reason Negroes are inferior to all other human beings." The South's caste system represented "an inherent determination that the people who were formerly in slavery, regardless of anything else, shall be kept as near that stage as is possible. Now is the time, we submit, that the Court should make it clear that that is not what our Constitution stands for."[70]

On May 17, 1954, the Supreme Court voted 9-0 to overturn school segregation. The unanimous opinion, written by Warren, struck directly at the heart of *Plessy*. Tangible and physical factors were not a sufficient measure "in considering the effect of segregation on public education." Stepping up to the question that was at the core of the NAACP's case, the justices asked, "Does segregation of children in public schools solely on the basis of race . . . deprive the children of the minority group equal educational opportunity? We believe it does." Citing the social science evidence presented as an addendum to the brief and quoting from the Kansas ruling, the opinion stated that "to separate [children] from others of similar age and qualification solely because of their race generates a feeling of inferiority as to their status in the community that may affect their hearts and minds in ways unlikely ever to be undone." It continued, "We conclude that in the field of public education the doctrine of 'separate but equal' has no place. Separate facilities are inherently unequal." The Court instructed the parties to prepare arguments to aid in the formulation of decrees to determine the method of relief.[71]

Brown hit like a thunderclap. While the Court left the thorny issue of implementation to a later resolution, the clear, simple, unambiguous language of the decision announced a seismic shift away from the nation's long accommodation of the South's racial caste system. The fact that it was unanimous and "the language it used" made the Court's ruling "most gratifying," said a euphoric Marshall. "Once and for all it's decided, completely decided." Many compared the Court's ruling to the Emancipation Proclamation. "The greatest step forward . . . since the Civil War," said a man in Pittsburgh. S.H. Giles of Atlanta described it as "the dawn of a new day." In a letter to a friend on May 18, native North Carolinian Pauli Murray strained to find words to convey her emotions in the presence of "one of the biggest moments in American history." She described mostly "a feeling of relief that we are now on the right track . . . and the principles are clear and in harmony with our most time honored traditions." In Jacksonville, Florida, seventeen-year-old Avon Kirkland showed the *Florida Union* headlines announcing the Court's ruling to his mother and asked her what it meant. Fighting back tears, Lula Mae Kirkland looked at her son and said, "Boy, this means that you and your sister have a chance."[72]

"Shock," "disappointment," "anger," and "caution" described the responses of the South's political leaders to the Court's unanimous decision. While Governor Herman Talmadge promised "continued and permanent segregation of Georgia's schools," Tennessee's governor, Frank Clement, warned against "snap judgments," and a top education official in Florida advised that the state "begin preparing for integration." The South would have a year to absorb the impact of the ruling before the Court set down instructions for implementation. There was no conceivable way, Marshall said, for extremists like Talmadge and South Carolina governor James Byrnes to "get around this clear-cut interpretation of the Constitution." No state legislature, he said, was going to buck "the Supreme Court or any federal agency." He expected that in light of the Court's decision, "in the South ... as well as the North, the people will get together for the first time and work this thing out."[73]

"For roughly a year after the decision," Robert Carter recalled, "it did look as if *Brown* would be accepted by white communities in the South." The attorneys and national staff worked closely with branches, advising them to petition school boards to initiate desegregation, work with other community groups, and monitor local sentiments. In May of 1955, *The Crisis* estimated that more than five hundred school districts had peacefully and voluntarily desegregated. Among them were four of the six communities included in the *Brown* case—Washington, D.C., Topeka, and two school districts in Delaware. The school districts were almost all in the border states of Missouri, Kansas, West Virginia, and Maryland, although two districts in Arkansas— Fayetteville and Hoxey—desegregated. There were a handful of disturbances, stirred up by pro-segregation agitators, that underscored the need for strong, decisive leadership on the part of public officials. While South Carolina,

Mississippi, and Georgia promised to close their schools rather than integrate them, the NAACP's leadership expressed confidence that most white southerners would not accept such extreme measures.[74]

In April 1955, the Supreme Court heard arguments concerning the decree that would guide the desegregation process. The Court had invited all of the affected states to file briefs, and an additional six southern states did as well. The southern attorneys general joined in calling for a plan that allowed for gradual, open-ended implementation of the school desegregation ruling, a position supported by President Dwight Eisenhower's Justice Department. The southerners warned that a strict timetable risked disastrous consequences and would jeopardize the public school system. The government's brief emphasized a common theme put forward by the southern states, advising the Court to consider the "psychological and emotional factors" affecting white communities in the face of such a dramatic transformation. The NAACP attorneys urged the Court to set a firm deadline for compliance. If the rights of the children of Prince Edward County were going to be satisfied, "they must be satisfied while they are still children," Spottswood Robinson told the Court. Marshall observed that the argument to postpone the granting of constitutional rights was never made "until Negroes are involved." While the NAACP attorneys acknowledged that some time might be required for administrative adjustments in the changeover to a nonsegregated system, anything less than a fixed date for compliance would invite delay and defiance of the Court's ruling.[75]

The Court's decree, issued on May 31, 1955, observed that varied local circumstances should be taken into account and designated federal district courts to oversee the implementation of the desegregation process. No deadline was set. The ruling held that "the courts will require that the defendants make a prompt and reasonable start toward full compliance with the May 17, 1954 ruling." The NAACP and its attorneys were prepared to work with communities around the South and through the courts, when necessary, to ensure that school desegregation was implemented without delay, and they expressed confidence that they had the necessary "legal weapons" to do so. A week after the Court's ruling, NAACP officials from across the South met with NAACP attorneys in Atlanta to map out a program of action. They acknowledged that the Court's implementation decree placed "a challenge on the good faith of public officials, on the militancy of Negroes, and on the integrity of the federal courts." The South-wide NAACP conference instructed branches to immediately file a petition with their local school boards, calling attention to the May 31 ruling and requesting that steps be taken to reorganize schools on a nondiscriminatory basis.[76]

Events on the ground in Orangeburg, South Carolina, previewed what was to come. In July, fifty-seven black men and women submitted a petition to the Orangeburg school board calling on the board to "take immediate concrete steps to reorganize the public schools on a nondiscrimination basis." A week earlier, South Carolina governor George Bell Timmerman had publicly declared that the Court's desegregation order was unconstitutional. The *Orangeburg Times and Democrat* published the petition to the school board along with the names and addresses of the signers, initiating a campaign of harassment dedicated to forcing petitioners to remove their names. People who refused lost their jobs, had their credit cut off and their home loans foreclosed, and renters were evicted. Blacks in Orangeburg responded by organizing a selective buying campaign, targeting the merchants and business owners behind the campaign of economic reprisals, which had been led by the White Citizens Council. When students returned to South Carolina State College that fall they joined in the boycott, which escalated into a major confrontation with local and state officials. The experience of blacks seeking school integration in Orangeburg was repeated in many of the sixty communities where blacks petitioned local school boards that summer.[77]

In the aftermath of the May 1955 ruling, southern white resistance to school desegregation mounted into a wave of defiance that engulfed the region. The White Citizens Council, formed in Sunflower County, Mississippi, in July 1954, organized white opposition to desegregation into a South-wide movement and worked in tandem with local and state officials to block implementation of the Court's ruling and crush individuals and groups promoting desegregation—combining economic pressure, state power, and violence. At its peak in 1956, the council's membership topped 250,000. In the spring of 1956, nineteen U.S. senators and eighty-two congressional representatives from the South signed a "Declaration of Constitutional Principles," popularly known as the "Southern Manifesto." The statement charged that the Court's ruling had no legal basis and supported resistance to "forced integration by any lawful means." Southern state legislatures enacted a battery of laws designed to forestall school desegregation and cripple the NAACP.[78]

National political leadership collapsed in the face of southern defiance. President Eisenhower never publicly endorsed *Brown,* and he privately opposed it. "I don't believe you can change the hearts of men with law or decisions," he commented. The Democratic Party stretched to placate a united and rebellious southern wing. Adlai Stevenson, the party's presidential candidate in 1952 and 1956 was, according to one historian, "uncomfortable with liberals who were intransigent on the civil rights issue." The legal and constitutional issues were submerged as Democrats, many of whom had been sympathetic to the cause of civil rights, attempted to carve out a middle ground between the "segregationists" and the "antisegregationists." Eleanor Roosevelt, a close friend and supporter of Stevenson's, commented: "I think understanding and sympathy for the white people in the South is as important as understanding and sympathy for the colored people." Hubert Humphrey, angling for a possible vice presidential slot on the Democratic ticket, said that he thought more in terms of "observance" than "enforcement." As for the platform in 1956, Humphrey promised the impossible: "We're going to have a strong plank on civil rights" but one that would be acceptable to the South. The party's platform that year briefly referred to "recent decisions of the Supreme Court relating to segregation in publicly supported schools" and passively "rejected all proposals for the use of force to interfere with the orderly determination of these matters by the courts."[79]

The struggle against segregation in the South pushed up against the full force of white resistance, holding ground in some places, inching forward in others, and occasionally securing a major breakthrough. In July 1955 the U.S. Court of Appeals for the Fourth Circuit, ruling on Sarah Mae Flemming's challenge to bus segregation in Columbia, South Carolina, held that "separate but equal" could no longer be regarded "as a correct statement of the law," a ruling that applied to the states within the court's jurisdiction. Five months later, Rosa Parks refused to give up her seat on a Montgomery bus. Remembering that moment, Parks later recalled: "I had decided that I would have to find out once and for all what rights I had as a human being and a citizen even here in Montgomery, Alabama." Parks had worked with E. D. Nixon in the local NAACP branch for more than a decade. Following Parks's arrest for violating the segregation laws, Nixon joined with Joanne Robinson, a leader of the Women's Political Council, to enlist local ministers to organize a boycott of the buses. It lasted for 381 days and propelled the twenty-six-year-old Reverend Martin Luther King Jr. into a prominent leadership role. While Montgomery blacks boycotted, local attorney Fred Gray worked with Robert Carter and the NAACP's national office in bringing a legal challenge to bus segregation. On November 13, 1956, the U.S. Supreme Court held that the law mandating segregation on buses was unconstitutional, leading to the integration of the buses and the end of the boycott.[80]

While the Montgomery bus boycott rolled on, the school petition and the economic boycott of white merchants in Orangeburg triggered a state effort to crush the antisegregation movement. In March 1956, the state legislature announced plans for an investigation of NAACP activity at South Carolina State College, and the governor ordered police surveillance of the campus. When students went on strike to protest the state's action, school authorities expelled Fred Moore, the student body president and twenty-five other student leaders. At the same time, the legislature passed a law decreeing that members of the NAACP were not eligible for state employment, holding that membership in the NAACP was "wholly incompatible with the peace, tranquility and progress that all citizens have the right to enjoy." In Orangeburg County, twenty-four teachers refused to take an oath that they were not members of the NAACP; the county refused to renew their contracts for the next school year. Seventeen of the teachers, represented by the NAACP, challenged the law as a violation of the Fourteenth Amendment. After the plaintiffs appealed the case to the U.S. Supreme Court, the state legislature repealed the law and substituted a new law requiring all state employees to provide complete information regarding memberships in any organizations, leaving NAACP members open for reprisal.[81]

By 1956, southern states had mounted an all-out war on the NAACP. Five states required the NAACP to register and provide membership lists. The refusal of the NAACP to abide by a court order to turn over membership lists in Alabama led to the banning of the association from Alabama for nearly a decade. Ruby Hurley moved the NAACP's southeast regional office to Atlanta. The NAACP was also banned from Arkansas and Texas for a period of time. Southern states enlisted the Internal Revenue Service to investigate the NAACP's tax status. Six states curtailed the NAACP's access to the courts and provided criminal penalties for "stirring up litigation." In 1957, Oliver Hill, Spottswood Robinson, and Thurgood Marshall were in federal district court in Richmond defending their activities in school cases prior to 1954 in an effort to defeat a battery of state laws aimed at crippling the association. Most states established investigating committees designed to expose the NAACP's activities and publicly identify and harass its membership. In the immediate post-*Brown* years, such a massive assault diverted resources and energy to defending the association's right to function in the South, while having a chilling effect on membership and undermining the school desegregation effort. In South Carolina alone, membership fell from 8,266 to 2,202 between 1955 and 1957. In many places, branches disbanded and people created other organizations, such as the Alabama Christian Movement for Human Rights in Birmingham and the Orangeburg Movement for Civic Improvement in South Carolina.[82]

The NAACP held on in the South, and the movement it had cultivated found outlets in other groups and organizations. The association maintained a beachhead in Mississippi under the leadership of Medgar Evers, a World War II veteran and graduate of Alcorn College who became the state's field secretary in the immediate aftermath of the *Brown* ruling. Evers worked with a small network of leaders, including Amzie Moore and Aaron Henry, to keep the NAACP alive and active. In August 1955, the brutal murder of fifteen-year-old Emmett Till drew national attention to the violence and lawlessness that reigned in the Magnolia State. Just two months before, the Reverend George Lee, a leader of the NAACP's Belzoni branch who was active in voter registration efforts, was ambushed and murdered. The same month that Till was killed, a state representative shot and killed voting rights activist Lamar Smith on the courthouse lawn in Brookhaven in broad daylight. Evers, who would be assassinated in 1963, pushed ahead in the face of great personal risk and was encouraged by the Montgomery bus boycott and the fresh leadership of Martin Luther King Jr. He traveled 78,000 miles around the state from 1956 to 1958. Voting remained a major focus of NAACP activity. In 1958 Evers reported that "there has been no desegregation in any phase of community life anywhere in Mississippi, particularly in education and transportation."[83]

The widely publicized violence in Mississippi, Attorney General Herbert Brownell's determination to remedy the Justice Department's inability to respond to egregious civil rights violations, and a desire among Republicans to cultivate the support of northern black voters combined to create an opening for Clarence Mitchell to organize bipartisan support for what became the Civil Rights Act of 1957. By the time the legislation made its way through the gauntlet of the U.S. Senate under the leadership of Lyndon Johnson, it had been shorn of its most potent provisions and steered clear of the desegregation issue. The Civil Rights Act, the first civil rights legislation in more than eighty years, created the Civil Rights Commission, which was authorized to hold public hearings and take testimony under oath. It established a full-fledged Civil Rights Division headed by an assistant attorney general; and empowered the attorney general to bring an injunction against any individual who interfered with a citizen's right to vote, though an amendment providing for a jury trial made it highly unlikely that violators would be successfully prosecuted. In the short term, the legislation did little to redress the balance of power in the South, but it initiated the type of federal engagement that, in the words of civil rights activist Bob Moses, provided "crawl space" for blacks striving to exercise the right to vote.[84]

In September 1957, the showdown over the desegregation of Little Rock High School played out on a national stage when Governor Orval Faubus's defiance of a federal court order forced President Eisenhower to respond. Faubus called out the National Guard to bar the court-ordered entry of nine black students into Central High School, fueling an explosive mob scene around the school, endangering the lives of the students, and creating a constitutional crisis. After several weeks of stalemate, Eisenhower sent the 101st Airborne and federalized the Arkansas National Guard to enforce the desegregation order. The nine students entered the school, escorted by federal troops. A military presence remained there through the school year. Local NAACP leader Daisy Bates mentored and supported the students, young men and women whose bravery and dignity inspired a generation of young people. Faubus closed the four public high schools in Little Rock for the 1958–1959 school year rather than have them integrate.[85]

In 1959, Prince Edward County closed its schools; they remained closed until 1964. Clarendon County schools remained segregated. At the start of 1960, schools in Alabama, Georgia, Louisiana, Mississippi, and South Carolina were still completely segregated. The *Southern School News* estimated that 6 percent of the region's 3 million black schoolchildren attended school with white children. In November 1960, court-ordered school desegregation began in Louisiana when four first-grade girls entered previously all-white elementary schools in New Orleans. Mobs taunted and threatened the children as they made their way to school.[86]

The atmosphere was "almost as bad as South Africa," wrote Alabama civil rights activist Virginia Durr early in 1960. "The police and the political powers are not going to give an inch and the Negroes are not going to back down." As an organization, the NAACP bore the full brunt of the South's effort to maintain segregation and crush any challenges to the racial order. While desegregation efforts stalled in the face of a broadly orchestrated campaign of massive resistance, the efforts of the Justice Department to prosecute voting rights cases proved to be almost completely ineffectual. By early 1960, the department had brought only four cases and won favorable rulings in just two, resulting in no significant changes in voting practices.[87]

The mandate of *Brown* and the crisis it generated would not be contained. In Haywood County, Tennessee, where voting rights activist Elbert Williams had been murdered two decades earlier, blacks organized the Haywood County Civic and Welfare League in 1959 to promote voter registration. Registrars turned potential black voters away, and white landowners and businessmen initiated a campaign of mass evictions, intimidation and economic reprisals against blacks who attempted to vote—all in violation of the 1957 Civil Rights Act. The civic league appealed to the Civil Rights Division of the Justice Department and the department filed a suit late in the summer of 1960. John Doar, a young lawyer from Wisconsin who had joined the division in July, found the FBI's reports from Haywood County "incomplete." He went to Brownsville, the county seat, to investigate—an eye-opening experience. Doar collected affidavits from blacks who had been evicted, took photographs, and developed a strong and ultimately successful case against Haywood County business leaders and officials. In the aftermath of Doar's visit to Tennessee, he and the small cohort of lawyers in the civil rights division went into the Deep South regularly to investigate complaints, gather evidence, and bring suits against those who violated the Civil Rights Act. "We worked as hard as we could to enforce the law," in the face of determined resistance, Doar later recalled. He and his colleagues quickly learned that the effort to secure voting rights could not effectively be pursued in isolation from a challenge to the caste system.[88]

There were countless instances of individuals pushing against racial boundaries. In 1958 NAACP youth chapters in Wichita, Kansas, and Oklahoma City organized student sit-ins at segregated lunch counters in the their towns, and succeeded in integrating them. That same year, Medgar Evers staged a one-man protest when he rode at the front of the bus on a trip from North Carolina back to Jackson, Mississippi, refusing to move after being attacked by a white passenger and threatened by police in Meridian, Mississippi. On February 1, 1960, four students from North Carolina A&T College sat in at a segregated lunch counter in Woolworth's in Greensboro, North Carolina. Within a week the sit-ins had spread to other cities and towns in the state. By the end of February, there were sit-in protests in thirty-one southern cities across eight states. In April, young people form the sit-in movement organized the Student Nonviolent Coordinating Committee. The following May, just months after John F. Kennedy's inauguration, a second band of "freedom riders" traveled on busses into the South, refusing to be segregated.[89]

The final assault on Jim Crow was underway.

Epilogue: Mirror of America

We put up to the American people the raw, naked, ugly, brutal facts.
We attempted to hold the mirror of America as it was before the nation.
—*James Weldon Johnson, 1923*[1]

In the early 1960s, the South commanded attention as the most glaring reflection of the "brutal facts" of America's struggle over race. The region became a testing ground for the nation's commitment to the rule of law, to fundamental constitutional guarantees, and to the possibility of a society beyond racial segregation and inequality—a crossroads of the movement that began more than a half-century earlier with the founding of the NAACP. The final attack on state-enforced segregation was carried forward by thousands of men and women, young and old, black and white. They sat in, marched, and attempted to register to vote. They were clubbed, beaten, jailed, and murdered in an epic struggle between freedom and repression, captured by photographs and film, broadcast on the nightly news, and carried around the world. This moment, which seemed to stand apart from history, rested on a community of effort stretching across several generations, cultivated by an association of women and men dedicated to removing racial barriers from American life and securing equal justice under law.

Other organizations moved to the fore in the 1960s, amplifying claims to the constitutional guarantees of the Reconstruction amendments, reinvigorated by the U.S. Supreme Court with the 1954 *Brown* ruling. But the ground had already been tilled. Ella Baker built on her work with the NAACP during the 1940s when she convened the meeting that led to the founding of the

Student Nonviolent Coordinating Committee. She sent Bob Moses into Mississippi armed with the names of the people she had met fifteen years earlier. The "NAACP people" who had survived in Mississippi, Moses later recalled—Amzie Moore, E.W. Steptoe, C.C. Bryant, Medgar Evers, and others—made the Mississippi movement of the sixties possible. "It is inconceivable that we could have taken root without them," he said. The imprint of earlier struggles was everywhere.[2]

In the wake of massive protests and a growing national intolerance for the extremes of southern racism, the legislative fight that the NAACP had initiated during Woodrow Wilson's administration reaped its greatest reward. Over the decades, James Weldon Johnson, Walter White, Roy Wilkins, and Clarence Mitchell led the building of a coalition of support in Washington around the NAACP's civil rights agenda. The coalition found its fullest expression in the civil rights legislation of the mid-1960s, which incorporated many of the recommendations of the seventeen-year-old report, *To Secure These Rights*. The 1964 Civil Rights Act outlawed segregation in public accommodations, authorized the U.S. Attorney General to file suits to enforce school desegregation, and prohibited employment discrimination based on race and sex. In 1965, President Lyndon Johnson signed the Voting Rights Act outlawing discriminatory voting practices and providing for federal oversight of election procedures in states with a history of voter discrimination.

While overt barriers fell, deeper structures of racial segregation and injustice remained. Urban rebellions rocked American cites from 1964 to 1968 and forced attention on the racial inequalities that plagued northern communities. The Kerner Commission, established by President Johnson to investigate the "racial disorders," famously concluded that "our nation is moving toward two societies, one black, one white—separate and unequal." The report described the consequences of a trend that founders of the NAACP had identified sixty years earlier. In the very first editorial published in *The Crisis* in 1910, W.E.B. Du Bois had warned of the corrosive social effects of a movement toward school segregation in northern cities. The NAACP and its branches exposed, resisted and protested the spread of segregation and discrimination beyond the South. Violent racial confrontations across the decades—in Springfield, East St. Louis, Harlem, Detroit, Cicero and many other urban areas—laid bare the racial divide, at times generating official reports but little more. The NAACP's long and persistent fight against residential segregation exposed the array of forces that promoted and reinforced the racial divide in the North.[3]

The NAACP's very existence—an interracial organization founded just after segregation triumphed in the South and as the color line extended its grip in the North—offered a singular counterforce to the racial beliefs and practices that structured American life deep into the twentieth century. Open to all, it attracted a largely black membership and was the leading voice for the full integration of American society. Its power lay in the synergy it created between a national program dedicated to securing federal protection of constitutionally guaranteed rights and a grassroots movement of local people organized in membership branches across the country, knitted together by field-workers and civil rights attorneys, annual meetings and statewide organizations. While African American protest embraced a variety of goals and tactics, the NAACP distinguished itself, in the words of Charles Houston, as "the crystallizing force of Negro citizenship." It encompassed a movement that reached into all parts of the nation and engaged developments that were continually reshaping the nation's social and political landscape.

At a time when dominant racial attitudes and widespread disenfranchisement of black Americans limited effective action through traditional modes of political redress, the NAACP used the courts as a primary venue for claiming constitutionally guaranteed rights. Moorfield Storey, Arthur Spingarn and Clarence Darrow were among the first generation of lawyers who laid the foundation for what would become a distinguishing feature of the NAACP's program. Charles Houston realized the full potential of litigation as a movement-building strategy, targeting the roots of American apartheid. In the South of the Scottsboro era, Houston identified a critical problem: how to cultivate the political will to struggle in a brutally repressive society dedicated to maintaining white supremacy. The black lawyer, Houston believed, must be a "social engineer," working through the courts and in the larger society to secure elemental justice. This, he believed, was essential to cultivating a faith in the system and was a prelude to mounting the fight for basic citizenship rights. As they steadily knocked the legal props out from under the caste system, Houston and his team created an arena for educating public opinion and supporting the growth of active and politically engaged NAACP branches. The attorneys identified violations of federal law and placed them before the Justice Department, rarely securing federal action but forcing the government to respond.

While the NAACP pushed forward on multiple fronts, the courts emerged as the staging ground for its ambitious campaign to end segregation, remove barriers to voting, and secure the equal protection of the law. The NAACP's chief lawyers, national officials, and field-workers well understood that the object of its litigation program was as much to build up the institutional capacities of local chapters and foster a self-sustaining movement as it was to gain Supreme Court victories. During the 1940s and 1950s, the NAACP organized a legal insurgency that linked the talents and dedication of a generation of lawyers with the growing aspirations and demands of black southerners for the full rights of citizenship. On the way to legal victories, the courtroom became a "theater," Robert Carter recalled, where black men and women watched black lawyers assert their professional authority in white-dominated settings, a rare scene in the South. Houston's prediction in 1935 that the black lawyer could transform the South in twenty-five years revealed a patience, fortitude, and confidence that sustained a long legal struggle. And his prediction was borne out. When Thurgood Marshall saw hundreds of men and women lined up outside the federal courthouse in Charleston, South Carolina, for the hearing in the Clarendon County school case, he knew Jim Crow's days were numbered.

The *Brown* decision, the fall of segregation in the South, and the sweeping civil rights legislation of 1964 and 1965 vastly altered the terrain of race relations and civil rights in the United States. It was an end and a beginning. The eradication of legally enforced segregation and the expansion of federal protection of citizenship rights achieved the goals that inspired the founding of the NAACP and affected all segments of society. The dramatic culmination of the struggle against Jim Crow fostered an era of protest and civic activism reflected in an array of social movements during the 1960s and beyond. Equally significant, the legislative gains of the civil rights movement transformed the role of government in American life and supported the demands of other groups, most notably women, in the quest for the equality of opportunity and treatment all Americans now claim as a birthright.

There were major changes in the NAACP in the years following the *Brown* ruling. Walter White died in 1955 and was succeeded by Roy Wilkins, who served as executive director until 1977. Thurgood Marshall separated the Legal Defense Fund from the NAACP, removing a major element in the machinery that had shaped the NAACP movement. Jack Greenburg succeeded Marshall as head of the LDF in 1961. Robert Carter became general counsel of the NAACP and rebuilt the legal arm of the association. Under his leadership, the organization launched an ambitious challenge to school segregation in the North in 1961, expanding the application of *Brown's* mandate through community action and, when necessary, litigation in an effort to dismantle segregation in schools across the country. While civil rights legislation and federal protection of voting rights opened up new venues for racial advancement, the struggle for equal opportunity and racial justice remained centered in NAACP branches in many communities across the country. [4]

In 1965, at the high point of presidential and legislative action, Lyndon Johnson turned attention to "the next and most profound stage of the battle for civil rights." In a commencement speech at Howard University he declared: "You do not wipe away the scars of centuries by saying 'now you are free.'" Johnson committed the nation to seeking "not just equality as a right and a theory but equality as a fact and as a result." Yet more than forty years later, wide racial gaps persist in nearly every measure of social well being— education, employment, income, housing , health, and criminal justice. Since the late 1980s, after several decades of school desegregation, the segregation of public schools has steadily increased. The racial demographics of America's prison population are stark: an estimated one in nine black men between the ages of twenty and thirty four are incarcerated. Reflecting on the stubborn hold of the "color line" at the end of the twentieth century, historian John Hope Franklin advised that "perhaps the very first thing we need to do as a nation and as individual members of society is to confront our past and see it for what it is . . . and not explain it away, excuse it, or justify it." [5]

The story of the National Association for the Advancement of Colored People sets America's racial past in sharp relief. Its history prior to the 1960s reveals that there was no set of tools or single strategy capable of resolving America's "original sin," only endless opportunities to move the nation closer to its professed ideals. The NAACP's formative role in the struggle for civil rights is not measured by any one achievement. It rests in the lives of men and women who, in the face of seemingly insurmountable odds, fought racial discrimination in its many guises and worked toward realizing an inclusive democracy. While holding up "the mirror of America as it was" they built a movement around a vision of what America could be.

The inauguration of Barack Obama as president of the United States coincided with the NAACP's centennial year. The historic moment was anticipated by Charles Houston sixty years earlier, as he stood on Pennsylvania Avenue with his five-year-old son during Harry S. Truman's inaugural parade. Looking at the crowd that had gathered he kept wondering whether "the first [black] president of the United States was among the children" watching the parade "in person or by television or listening to it over the radio or whether he has been born." He told the readers of his column in the *Bal-timore Afro-American* that "if we can speed our rate of progress and self disci-pline some of us may live to see him inaugurated." By then, though, "it will not make any difference . . . what blood he has. The sole question is likely to be simply whether he is the best man (or woman—why not?) for the job."[6]

Notes

Key to Abbreviations

BL/Yale: Beinecke Rare Book and Manuscript Library, Yale University
CHH: Charles Hamilton Houston
EJB: Ella J. Baker
JWJ: James Weldon Johnson
MSRC: Moorland Spingarn Research Center, Howard University
NAACP/mf: Papers of the National Association for the Advancement of Colored People on microfilm (followed by part, reel, and where helpful frame numbers)
OGV: Oswald Garrison Villard
TM: Thurgood Marshall
WFW: Walter F. White

Chapter 1: Call to Action

1. W.E.B. Du Bois, *Dusk of Dawn: An Essay Toward an Autobiography of a Race Concept* (New York: Harcourt, Brace, 1940), 225.

2. 1898 Wilmington Race Riot Commission Final Report, May 31, 2006 (Raleigh: North Carolina Office of Archives and History, 2006), 121–54, 177–80; *The Crisis*, February 1913, 194.

3. *New York Times*, June 23, 1915, 10.

4. W.E.B. Du Bois, "Of Booker T. Washington and Others," *The Souls of Black Folk* (New York: Norton, 1999), 34–45.

5. David Levering Lewis, *W.E.B. Du Bois: Biography of a Race, 1868–1919* (New York: Henry Holt, 1993), 295–96; James McPherson, *The Abolitionist Legacy: From Reconstruction to the NAACP* (Princeton, NJ: Princeton Univ. Press, 1995), 368–71.

6. Lewis, *W.E.B. Du Bois: Biography of a Race*, 217–24, 348–52.

7. Ibid., 316–22; W.E.B. Du Bois, *The Autobiography of W.E.B. Du Bois* (New York: International, 1968), 248–51.

8. Lewis, *W.E.B. Du Bois: Biography of a Race*, 328–29, 333–34; Oswald Garrison Villard to Hugh Gordon, September 19, 1906, Oswald Garrison Villard Papers, Houghton Library, Harvard University, Box 1460 (hereafter cited as OGV Papers); McPherson, *Abolitionist Legacy*, 370–74.

9. McPherson, *Abolitionist Legacy*, 370–74.

10. John L. Crouthamel, "The Springfield Race Riot of 1908," *Journal of Negro History* 45 (July 1960): 164–81.

11. William English Walling, "The Race War in the North," *Independent*, September 3, 1908, 529–34.

12. Charles Flint Kellogg, *NAACP: A History of the National Association for the Advancement of Colored People, 1909–1920* (Baltimore: Johns Hopkins Univ. Press, 1967), 11–12; Mary White Ovington, *The Walls Came Tumbling Down* (New York: Harcourt, Brace, 1947), 102–3; Oswald Garrison Villard, *Fighting Years: Memoirs of a Liberal Editor* (New York: Harcourt, Brace, 1939), 192.

13. "The Call: A Lincoln Emancipation Conference," appendix A in Kellogg, *NAACP*, 297–99.

14. Kellogg, *NAACP*, 15–17; OGV to Francis Garrison, May 4, 1909, OGV Papers, Box 1460; Du Bois, *Dusk of Dawn*, 224.

15. OGV to William Lloyd Garrison, February 24, 1909, OGV Papers, Box 1267; OGV to Francis Garrison, April 15, 1909, OGV to Francis Villard, May 26, 1909, OGV Papers, Box 1460; OGV to Booker T. Washington, May 26, 1909, OGV Papers, Box 4099.

16. Booker T. Washington to OGV, May 28, 1909, OGV Papers, Box 4099; Louis R. Harlan, *Booker T. Washington: The Wizard of Tuskegee, 1901–1915* (New York: Oxford Univ. Press, 1983), 29.

17. W.E.B. Du Bois, "National Negro Conference," *Survey*, June 12, 1909, reprinted in Herbert Aptheker, ed., *Documentary History of the Negro People in the United States*, vol. 2 (New York: Citadel Press, 1969), 924; *New York Times*, June 2, 1909, 9.

18. Stephen J. Gould, *The Mismeasure of Man* (New York: Norton, 1996), 23, 62–70, 368; Frederick L. Hoffman, *Race Traits and Tendencies of the America Negro*, with introduction by Paul Finkelman (Clark, NJ: Lawbook Exchange, 2004), i–vii. Metropolitan Life Insurance Company was a major exception, and continued to insure blacks.

19. *Proceedings of the National Negro Conference, 1909* (New York: Arno Press, 1969), 14–26; Edward J. Beardsley, "The American Social Scientist as Activist: Franz Boas, Burt G. Wilder, and the Cause of Racial Justice, 1900–1915," *Isis* (March 1973): 53, 57–58, 63.

20. *Proceedings of the National Negro Conference*, 71–73, 149–52.

21. Ibid., 110–20, 121–26.

22. Ibid., 180–206.

23. Ibid., 174–79.

24. Du Bois, "National Negro Conference," 926; Alfreda M. Duster, ed., *Crusade for Justice: The Autobiography of Ida B. Wells* (Chicago: Univ. of Chicago Press, 1970), 323; *New York Times*, June 2, 1909, 9.

25. OGV to Francis Garrison, June 4, 1909, OGV Papers, Box 1460; Ovington, *Walls Came Tumbling Down*, 106.

26. "Resolutions," *Proceedings of the National Negro Conference*, 222–25; Du Bois, "Negro National Conference," 926.

27. Ovington, *Walls Came Tumbling Down*, 106; Duster, *Crusade for Justice*, 323–26.

28. William English Walling, "The Founding of the NAACP," *The Crisis*, July 1929, 226; Mary White Ovington, "Beginnings of the NAACP," *The Crisis*, June 1926, 77; W.E.B. Du Bois to Joel Spingarn, October 28, 1914, Joel E. Spingarn Papers, BL/Yale, Box 1; Kellogg, *NAACP*, 53–54.

29. "National Negro Conference," *Horizon: A Journal of the Color Line* 5 (November 1909), reprinted in Herbert Aptheker, ed., *Writings in Periodicals Edited by W.E.B. Du Bois: Selections from* Horizon (White Plains, NY: Kraus-Thomson Organization, 1985), 80–81; Du Bois, "National Negro Conference," 924–27.

30. Ovington, *Walls Came Tumbling Down*, 105; OGV to Francis Garrison, June 7, 1909, OGV Papers, Box 1460.

31. Minutes, National Negro Committee, November 8, 1909, April 18, 1910, NAACP/mf p1 r1; OGV to Francis Garrison, December 7, 1909, OGV Papers, Box 1460; Kellogg, *NAACP*, 37–42; Lewis, *W.E.B. Du Bois: Biography of a Race*, 401.

32. "Mr. Washington in Politics," *New York Evening Post*, April 1, 1910; OGV to Booker T. Washington, June 4, 1909, OGV Papers, Box 4099; OGV to Francis Villard, November 15, 1909, OGV to Francis Villard, April 22, 1910, OGV Papers, Box 1460; Kellogg, *NAACP*, 39–40.

33. Proceedings of the National Negro Conference, May 1910, NAACP/mf p1 r8; OGV to Francis Villard, May 17, 1910, OGV Papers, Box 1460. Franz Boas's address to the 1910 meeting, "The Real Race Problem," was reprinted in the second issue of *The Crisis*, December 1910, 22–25.

34. Proceedings of the National Negro Conference, May 1910, NAACP/mf p1 r8; W.E.B. Du Bois, "The National Association for the Advancement of Colored People," *Horizon*, July 1910, reprinted in Aptheker, *Selections from* Horizon, 119–21; Kellogg, *NAACP*, 43–45; Lewis, *W.E.B. Du Bois: Biography of a Race*, 405. Most of the members of the national committee were from New York. Only two were from the South—John Hope, president of Atlanta University, and Leslie Pinckney Hill, Manassas, Virginia.

35. Proceedings of the National Negro Conference, May 1910, NAACP/mf p1 r8; Kellogg, *NAACP*, 43–45; Mary White Ovington, "Beginnings of the NAACP," *The Crisis*, June, 1926, 77; William English Walling, "The Founding of the NAACP," *The Crisis*, July 1929, 226; OGV to Francis Garrison, February 7, 1913, OGV Papers, Box 1464.

36. Walling to Du Bois, June 8, 1910, in Herbert Aptheker, ed., *The Correspondence*

of W.E.B. Du Bois, Selections, 1877–1934 (Amherst: Univ. of Massachusetts Press, 1973), 170; Du Bois, "The National Association for the Advancement of Colored People," *Horizon*, July 1910, 121.

37. Du Bois, *Autobiography*, 257.

38. *New York Evening Post*, May 31, 1910, 1; OGV to Francis Villard, June 1, 1910, OGV Papers, Box 1461; minutes of the executive committee, November 29, 1910, NAACP/mf p1 r1; *The Crisis*, December 1910, 26, February 1911, 17, March 1919, 231; Kellogg, *NAACP*, 58–60.

39. Kellogg, *NAACP*, 62–64, 212–14; OGV to Francis Garrison, January 19, 1912, OGV Papers, Box 1463; *The Crisis*, February 1912, 157; minutes, board of directors, February 4, 1913, April 1, 1913, Papers of the National Association for the Advancement of Colored People, Manuscript Division, Library of Congress, Box I:A1 (hereafter cited as NAACP Papers).

40. OGV to Francis Garrison, January 6, 1911, OGV Papers, Box 1462; minutes of executive committee, February 7, 1911, March 3, 1911, April 11, 1911, NAACP/mf p1 r1; "Report on the Third Annual Conference," *The Crisis*, May 1911, 24–25.

41. Reprint of editorial from *New York Evening Post* in *The Crisis*, December 1911, 60; minutes of executive committee, March 7, 1911, NAACP/mf p1 r1; *The Crisis*, February 1912, 158–59.

42. B. Joyce Ross, *J.E. Spingarn and the Rise of the NAACP* (New York: Atheneum, 1972), 4–11.

43. J.E. Spingarn, address before the Twentieth Annual Mass Meeting of the National Association for the Advancement of Colored People, January 4, 1931, NAACP Papers, I:A24; OGV to Joel Spingarn, October 17, 1910, October 19, 1910, Joel Spingarn Papers, MSRC, Box 95–11.

44. Ross, *J.E. Spingarn*, 13–14; *New York Times*, April 10, 1911; *The Crisis*, February 1912, 158–59; Memorandum re testing the right of colored people to sit in orchestra in theaters in New York, March 11, 1912, Joel Spingarn Papers, MSRC, Box 95–14.

45. Morton's grandfather was the Reverend Samuel Francis Smith; "Dangers of Race Prejudice," *New York Times*, January 22, 1906; *New York Times*, October 8, 1941, 23; minutes, board of directors, May 2, 1911, minutes, executive committee, January 3, 1910; minutes, board of directors, June 6, 1911; minutes, board of directors, July 2, 1912, NAACP/mf p1 r1; Kellogg, *NAACP*, 146; May Childs Nerney to James F. Morton, October 31, 1912, NAACP Papers, I:C1; McPherson, *The Abolitionist Legacy*, 128–30; OGV to Francis Garrison, January 19, 1912, OGV Papers, Box 1463.

46. Minutes, executive committee, November 29, 1910, minutes, board of directors, July 2, 1912, NAACP/mf p1 r1; William E. Walling to OGV, [1910], NAACP Papers, I:C1; OGV to Francis Garrison, January 6, 1911, June 4, 1911, OGV Papers, Box 1462; M.C. Nerney to Dr. V. Morton Jones, October 31, 1912, W.E.B. Du Bois and M.C. Nerney to "Dear Friend," November 4, 1912, OGV to Mary Church Terrell, September 18, 1913, NAACP Papers, I:C1.

47. W.E.B. Du Bois and M.C. Nerney to "Dear Friend," November 4, 1912, OGV

to Mary Church Terrell, September 18, 1913, NAACP Papers, I:C1; *The Crisis*, February 1912, 157.

48. Fifth session, sixth annual meeting of the NAACP, Baltimore, May 5, 1914, 9, NAACP Papers I:B1.

49. "The Second Birthday," *The Crisis*, November 1912, 27–28.

50. *The Crisis*, November 1910, 10, April 1911 (Stockton), 5, January 1911 (Mobile).

51. *The Crisis*, November 1911, 20, February 1912, 157. NAACP, Fourth Annual Report, 1913, NAACP Papers, I:A25.

Chapter 2: Welding the Hammers

1. *The Crisis*, April 1912, 236–37, August 1912, 178–79, October 1912; "An Open Letter to Woodrow Wilson," *The Crisis*, March 1913, 237.

2. Richard B. Sherman, *The Republican Party and Black America: From McKinley to Hoover, 1896–1932* (Charlottesville: Univ. Press of Virginia, 1973), 100–111; W.E.B. Du Bois, "Mr. Taft," *The Crisis*, October 1911, 243; Du Bois, "Mr. Roosevelt," *The Crisis*, September 1912, 235–36. On April 9, 1912, in the heat of the presidential election campaign, Taft publicly condemned lynching for the first time in a speech at a black church in Washington, D.C. Eugene V. Debs also ran for the presidency in 1912 on the Socialist Party ticket; he did not address the issue of race.

3. August Meier, "The Negro and the Democratic Party, 1875–1915," *Phylon* 17 (1956): 181–89.

4. Ibid., 189; Lewis, *W.E.B. Du Bois: Biography of a Race*, 423–24; Du Bois, "The Election," *The Crisis*, December 1912, 65; Woodrow Wilson to Bishop Alexander Walters, October 16, 1912, NAACP Papers, I:C1; *The Crisis*, November 1912, 29; OGV to Francis Garrison, May 13, 1913, April 14, 1914, OGV Papers, Box 1463.

5. Du Bois, "The Election;" Kathleen L. Wolgemuth, "Woodrow Wilson and Federal Segregation," *Journal of Negro History* (April 1959), 158; Meier, "The Negro and the Democratic Party," 190.

6. Sherman, *Republican Party and Black American*, 113.

7. George C. Osborn, "The Problem of the Negro in Government, 1913," *Historian* 23 (1961): 330–32.

8. Ibid., 337–38; *The Crisis*, November 1913, 333–34; May Childs Nerney, "Segregation in the Government Departments at Washington," September 30, 1913, NAACP Papers, I:C70; C. Vann Woodward, *The Strange Career of Jim Crow* (New York: Oxford Univ. Press, 1955), 77.

9. OGV to Francis Garrison, July 13, 1913, OGV Papers, Box 1463; Osborn, "Negro in Government," 339.

10. *The Crisis*, October 1913, 298–99; NAACP, Fourth Annual Report, 1913 (New York, 1914), 12–14; William Monroe Trotter to NAACP, August 19, 1913, NAACP Papers, I:C1.

11. *The Crisis*, July 1912; May Childs Nerney obituary, *New York Times*, December

19, 1959, 27. Nerney, a graduate of Cornell University (1902) and New York State Library School (1907), had served as secretary to the state librarian in Albany, N.Y., worked with the League of Women Voters in New York, and served on the national board of the YWCA, Consumer's Cooperative Service. Elliot Rudwick and August Meier, "The Rise of the Black Secretariat in the NAACP, 1909–1935," in August Meier and Elliott Rudwick, *Along the Color Line: Explorations in the Black Experience* (Urbana: Univ. of Illinois Press, 1976), 96–97; Nerney, "Segregation in the Government Departments."

12. *The Crisis*, November 1913, 342–43; OGV to Francis Garrison, October 10, 1913, OGV Papers, Box 1463.

13. OGV to Francis Garrison, October 28, 1913, OGV Papers, Box 1463; *The Crisis*, December 1913, 89–90; Neval H. Thomas report, sixth annual meeting, Baltimore, May 4, 1914, NAACP Papers, I:B1.

14. "How One Branch Reaches the People," *The Crisis*, May 1914, 32; Neval H. Thomas report; NAACP, Fourth Annual Report, 1913, 36–37.

15. Report of the secretary, executive session, sixth annual conference, Baltimore, May 5, 1914, NAACP Papers, I:B1; NAACP, Fifth Annual Report, 1914, reprinted in *The Crisis*, April 1915, 290–93; *The Crisis*, March 1915, 246; Dickson D. Bruce Jr., *Archibald Grimké: Portrait of a Black Independent* (Baton Rouge: Louisiana State Univ. Press, 1993), 194–95.

16. NAACP, Fourth Annual Report; *The Crisis*, February 1915, 190; *The Crisis*, March 1916, 248; Bruce, *Grimké*, 202–3.

17. Bruce, *Grimké*; Rudwick and Meier, "Rise of the Black Secretariat in the NAACP," 97.

18. Report of the secretary, executive session, sixth annual meeting, Baltimore, May 5, 1914; *The Crisis*, April 1914, 290; Bruce, *Grimké*, 194–95, 211–12.

19. *The Crisis*, March 1914, 247–48, April 1914, 291–92, July 1914, 124, February 1915, 189, April 1915, 290–93; Fifth Annual Report, *The Crisis*, April 1915, 290–91.

20. OGV to Francis Garrison, October 23, 1913, January 23, 1914, OGV Papers, Box 1463; NAACP, Fourth Annual Report, 1913, 36–38; *The Crisis*, December 1913, 90–91.

21. OGV to Francis Garrison, February 7, 1913, OGV Papers, Box 1463; OGV to Francis Garrison, March 14, 1913, OGV Papers, Box 1463; Du Bois to OGV, March 18, 1913, OGV Papers, Box 946; minutes, board of directors, March 11, 1913, NAACP/mf p1 r1; On tensions between Du Bois and Villard, see Du Bois to Mary White Ovington, April 9, 1914, in Aptheker, ed., *The Correspondence of W.E.B. Du Bois*, 188–91; Du Bois to Joel Spingarn, October 28, 1914, Joel Spingarn Papers, BL/Yale, Box 1.

22. Du Bois to OGV, March 18, 1913, OGV Papers, Box 946; OGV to Joel Spingarn, March 20, 1913, OGV Papers, Box 946; Ross, *Spingarn*, 67–68; Kellogg, *NAACP*, 96; *The Crisis*, February 1914, 188.

23. *The Crisis*, January 1914, 133–34; *The Crisis*, September 1913, 235 ("hog" quote); Kellogg, *NAACP*, 98–99.

24. Memorandum from Walter White, May 18, 1934, based on conversation he had with Joel Spingarn, NAACP Papers, I:C287.

25. Spingarn to Du Bois, October 24, 1914, Joel Spingarn Papers, BL/Yale, Box 1; Rudwick and Meier, "Rise of the Black Secretariat in the NAACP," 100–101.

26. Du Bois to Spingarn, October 28, 1914; Du Bois to Mary White Ovington, April 9, 1914.

27. Ibid.

28. *The Crisis*, March 1916, 38.

29. Du Bois to Spingarn, October 28, 1914.

30. Kellogg, *NAACP*, 98–112.

31. Lewis, *W.E.B. Du Bois: Biography of a Race*, 495–96; Kellogg, *NAACP*, 101–15.

32. "The Northward Migration," *The Crisis*, June 1911, 56; NAACP, Fourth Annual Report, 1913, 8–10; *The Crisis*, June 1913, 91.

33. W.E.B. Du Bois, "The Vigilance Committees: A Call to Arms," *The Crisis*, May 1913, 26–27; *The Crisis*, April 1914, 285.

34. W.E.B. Du Bois, *The Crisis*, July 1913, 130–32; Du Bois, "Colored California," *The Crisis*, August 1913, 192–95; Du Bois, "The Great Northwest," *The Crisis*, September 1913, 237–39; Lonnie Bunch, "A Past Not Necessarily Prologue: African Americans in Los Angeles," in Norman M. Klein and Martin J. Schiesl, eds., *20th Century Los Angeles: Power, Promotion, and Social Conflict* (Claremont, CA: Regina Books, 1991), 103–8.

35. E. Burton Ceruti to W.E.B. Du Bois, September 23, 1913, NAACP Papers, I:G15; Quintard Taylor, *The Forging of a Black Community: Seattle's Central District from 1870 through the Civil Rights Era* (Seattle: Univ. of Washington Press, 1994), 88–89.

36. *The Crisis*, March 1914, 227, July 1914, 140–41, February 1915, 188, March 1915, 249; Ross, *J.E. Spingarn*, 28–33; OGV to Francis Garrison, October 23, 1914, OGV Papers, Box 1464; J.E. Spingarn, "The Second Quarter Century of the NAACP," delivered at the twenty-sixth annual conference of the NAACP, St. Louis, Missouri, June 25, 1935, NAACP Papers, I:B11.

37. Ross, *J.E. Spingarn*, 33–34; NAACP, report of branches, executive session, sixth annual meeting, Baltimore, May 1914, 8, 14, NAACP Papers, I:B1; Kenneth L. Kusmer, *A Ghetto Takes Shape: Black Cleveland, 1870–1930* (Urbana: Univ. of Illinois Press, 1976), 260.

38. *New York Evening Post*, May 13, 1914, 9; Fifth Annual Report, *The Crisis*, April 1915; *The Crisis*, June 1914, 87, July 1914, 121; Joel Spingarn, "The Second Quarter Century."

39. *The Crisis*, December 1913, 90–91, January 1914, 139–40; Charles Brinsmade, "Our Legal Bureau," *The Crisis*, April 1914, 291–92, May 1914, 36.

40. *The Crisis*, January 1914, 139; Fourth Annual Report, 1913, 29.

41. Fourth Annual Report, 1913, 20–30, 49; "The New Legal Bureau," *The Crisis*, January 1914, 139–40.

42. *The Crisis*, March 1912, 204, July 1912, 125, June 1913, 90–91, July 1914, 140–41; business meeting, report of branches, 2nd session, sixth annual conference, May 4, 1914, NAACP Papers, I:B1; "Legal Work," Fifth Annual Report, *The Crisis*, April 1915, 288. *The Crisis* reported that suits to enforce civil rights laws in restaurants were won in Los Angeles, New York, and Cleveland, April 1915, 272.

43. Allen H. Spears, *Black Chicago: The Making of a Negro Ghetto, 1890–1920* (Chicago: Univ. of Chicago Press, 1967), 20–25; Gilbert Osofksy, *Harlem: The Making of a Ghetto; Negro New York, 1890–1930* (New York: Harper Torchbooks, 1966), 12–21, 105–9, 127; *The Crisis*, January 1912, 99, March 1912, 201, February 1913, 169; "The Negro Invasion," *New York Times*, December 17, 1911, 14.

44. *The Crisis*, November 1911, 7–8, January 1912, 255, June 1912, 64; minutes, board of directors, December 11, 1911, NAACP/mf p1 r1; "Dynamite in Kansas City," *The Crisis*, February 1912, 160–62; Fourth Annual Report, 1913, 23; OGV to Francis Garrison, October 23, 1913, OGV Papers, Box 1463; Philadelphia branch report, minutes, board of directors, October 6, 1914, NAACP Papers, I:A1.

45. *The Crisis*, November 1910, 6, 8, 11; W. Ashby Hawkins, "A Year of Segregation in Baltimore," *The Crisis*, November 1911, 27; G.R. Walker, "The Color Problem of Baltimore," May 4, 1914, NAACP, sixth annual meeting, Baltimore, NAACP Papers, I:B1; OGV to Francis Garrison, September 25, 1913, OGV Papers, Box 1463.

46. "Legal Work," Fifth Annual Report, 1914, *The Crisis*, April 1915, 289–90; "Legal Work," Fourth Annual Report, 1913, 22–23; minutes, board of directors, July 7, 1914, NAACP/mf p1 r1.

47. Patrick Shaheen McElhone, "The Civil Rights Activities of the Louisville Branch of the National Association for the Advancement of Colored People: 1914–1960" (master's thesis, University of Louisville, 1976), 17–18; Charles Brinsmade, legal report, Fourth Annual Report, 1913, 22–23; minutes, board of directors, July 14, 1914, NAACP Papers, I:A1; *The Crisis*, August 1914, 168, September 1914, 236.

48. McElhone, 19–20; George C. Wright, *Life Behind the Veil: Blacks in Louisville, Kentucky, 1865–1930* (Baton Rouge: Louisiana State Univ. Press, 1985) 233–34; *The Crisis*, August 1915, 198–99, September 1915, 243–44.

49. Minutes, board of directors, October 6, 1914, NAACP/mf p1 r1; minutes, board of directors, January 5, 1915, NAACP/mf p1 r1; *The Crisis*, March 1916, 251; report of the chairman, Legal Bureau, sixth annual meeting, January 3, 1916, 12–13, NAACP Papers, I:A8.

50. *Washington Post*, September 29, 1914, 6, October 5, 1913, 16, October 15, 1913, 6; *Chicago Defender*, June 26, 1915, 1, July 10, 1915, 1; *New York Times*, November 9, 1910, 6, June 22, 1915, 8.

51. Report of the chairman, sixth annual meeting, January 3, 1916, NAACP Papers, I:A8; *The Crisis*, August 1915, 197; Kellogg, *NAACP*, 205–6; *Chicago Defender*, June 26, 1915, 1, July 10, 1915, 1, 8.

52. Thomas E. Cripps, *Slow Fade to Black: The Negro in American Film, 1900–1942* (New York: Oxford Univ. Press, 1977), 41–53; W.E.B. Du Bois, "Fighting a Race Calumny," *The Crisis*, May 1915, 40; May Childs Nerney to OGV, March 9, 1915, Nerney, memorandum to Joel Spingarn, March 13, 1915, NAACP Papers, I:C299.

53. Du Bois, "Fighting a Race Calumny," 40–42; *Chicago Defender*, March 13, 1915, March 27, 1915; Cripps, *Slow Fade*, 55–58.

54. Du Bois, "Fighting a Race Calumny, Part II," *The Crisis*, June 1915, 87–88; *The Crisis*, July 1915, 147–48, October 1915, 295, December 1915, 85, January 1916, 139–40; Sixth Annual Report, 1915, reprinted in *The Crisis*, March 1916, 251, 255–62; Cripps, *Slow Fade*, 56, 63. *Chicago Defender*, April 24, 1915, 1, May 29, 1915, 1, June 5, 1915, 8, July 31, 1915, 4, September 11, 1915, 8, October 2, 1915, 1, October 23, 1915, 1, December 4, 1915, 1, March 18, 1916, 1; report of the chairman to the board of directors, January 3, 1916, NAACP Papers, I:A1.

55. Minutes, board of directors, February 4, 1913, NAACP Papers, I:A1; report of the national secretary, executive session, sixth annual meeting, Baltimore, May 5, 1914, I:B1.

56. Report of the chairman of the board of directors, Fifth Annual Report, *The Crisis*, April 1915, 293; report of the national secretary, executive session, sixth annual meeting, Baltimore, May 5, 1914, NAACP Papers, I:B1

57. Report of the chairman of the board of directors, Fifth Annual Report, *The Crisis*, April 1915, 293; Mark Schneider, *Boston Confronts Jim Crow, 1890–1920* (Boston: Northeastern Univ. Press, 1997), 136–37.

58. Kathryn Johnson to Roy Nash, August 6, 1916, August 17, 1916, August 19, 1916, NAACP Papers, I:C67.

59. Johnson to Nash, August 10, 1916, NAACP Papers, I:C67; Kathryn Johnson report, sixth annual meeting, Baltimore, May 4, 1914, NAACP Papers, I:B1; Johnson to Nash, April 20, 1916.

60. Johnson report, sixth annual meeting, Baltimore, May 4, 1914, NAACP Papers, I:B1.

61. Ibid.

62. Minutes, board of directors, September 1, 1914, NAACP Papers, I:A1; Johnson to May Childs Nerney, March 10, 1916, Johnson to Nash, July 11, 1916, NAACP Papers, I:C67.

63. Johnson to Nerney, September 17, 1915, NAACP Papers, I:C67.

64. Ibid.

65. Johnson to Nerney, September 16, 1915, September 23, 1915, NAACP Papers, I:C67.

66. Johnson to Nerney, November 29, 1915, December 31, 1915, NAACP Papers, I:C67.

67. Johnson to Nerney, January 10, 1916, January 14, 1916; Johnson to Mary White Ovington, January 20, 1916; Johnson to Nash, February 22, 1916, NAACP Papers, I:C67; *The Crisis*, April 1916, 307–8.

68. Johnson to Nash, March 10, 1916, NAACP Papers, I:C67.

69. Ibid.

70. Johnson to Nash, April 20, 1916, NAACP Papers, I:C67.

71. Ibid.

72. Johnson to Nash, April 26, 1916, NAACP Papers, I:C67.

73. Ibid.

74. Francis N. Cardoza to Joel Spingarn, August 8, 1916; Johnson to Nash, July 11, 1916; Johnson to Nash, July 22, 1916; Nash to Johnson, August 16, 1916; Johnson to Nash, August 17, 1916, NAACP Papers, I:C67; Thea Arnold, "Kathryn Magnolia Johnson," in Darlene Clark Hine et al., eds., *Black Women in America: An Historical Encyclopedia* (Brooklyn, NY: Carlson, 1993), 645.

75. Minutes of sixth annual meeting, January 3, 1916, NAACP Papers, I:A8. Washington, D.C., was the largest branch, with more than 1,100 members (see Sixth Annual Report, published in *The Crisis*, March 1916, 255–62 for highlights of branch activity).

76. Minutes of sixth annual meeting, January 3, 1916, 35–36, NAACP Papers, I:A8.

77. Ibid., 33–36.

78. W.E.B. Du Bois, "Notes on Amenia Conference," W.E.B. Du Bois Papers, microfilm, reel 5, frame 312.

79. Program, Amenia Conference, August 24–26, 1916, Joel Spingarn Papers, MSRC; W.E.B. Du Bois, "The Amenia Conference: An Historic Negro Gathering," Troutbeck Leaflet No. 8, Troutbeck Press, 1925, 8–12.

80. Du Bois, "The Amenia Conference," 12–13; Lewis, *W.E.B. Du Bois: Biography of a Race*, 519–21.

81. Lewis, *W.E.B. Du Bois: Biography of a Race*, 524; Du Bois to Johnson, November 1, 1916, W.E.B. Du Bois Papers, microfilm, reel 5, frame 451; James Weldon Johnson, *Along This Way: The Autobiography of James Weldon Johnson* (New York: Viking, 1933), 308–9.

82. Johnson, *Along This Way*, 209.

Chapter 3: Going South: The NAACP in the World War I Era

1. *Savannah Tribune*, March 10, 1917, NAACP Papers, I:G46.

2. "Freeing America," Sixth Annual Report, 1917, NAACP Papers, I:A25; Wilson Jefferson, "National Association Meeting," *Georgia Baptist* (Augusta), March 8, 1917, NAACP Papers, I:G46.

3. "Freeing America;" Wilson Jefferson, "The National Association for the Advancement of Colored People," *Georgia Baptist* (Augusta), February 15, 1917, NAACP Papers, I:G46.

4. For biographical information, see Johnson, *Along This Way*, quote, 205–6.

5. Minutes, board of directors, April 9, 1917, NAACP Papers, I:A1; Johnson, *Along This Way*, 314–15; W.E.B. Du Bois, "The Heart of the South," *The Crisis*, May 1917, 18.

6. Minutes, board of directors, April 9, 1917, NAACP Papers, I:A1.

7. Ross, *J.E. Spingarn*, 85–97; Genna Rae McNeil, *Groundwork: Charles Hamilton Houston and the Struggle for Civil Rights* (Philadelphia: Univ. of Pennsylvania Press, 1983), 36–38; minutes, board of directors, May 14, 1917, NAACP Papers, I:A1.

8. Johnson, *Along This Way*, 316.

9. James Weldon Johnson, report on tour of branches in the Middle West, minutes, board of directors, July 9, 1917, NAACP Papers, I:A1; Spears, *Black Chicago*, 89.

10. Investigation of the burning of Ell Persons at Memphis by James Weldon Johnson, NAACP Papers, I:C367; "Memphis May 22, A.D. 1917," supplement to *The Crisis*, July 1917, 1–4.

11. Minutes, board of directors, July 9, 1917, NAACP Papers, I:A1; B.M. Rody to May Nerney, May 29, 1914; B.M. Rody to W.E.B. Du Bois, May 27, 1915; JWJ to Robert Church, June, 19, 1917; JWJ to B.M. Rody, June 26, 1917; JWJ to Robert Church, June 26, 1917; JWJ to Robert Church, October 8, 1918; *Washington Bee*, July 7, 1917 (clipping); application for charter for Memphis branch, June 1917, NAACP Papers, I:G199.

12. "The Migration of Negroes," *The Crisis*, June 1917, 63–69; minutes, board of directors, April 9, 1917, NAACP Papers, I:A1; Lewis, *W.E.B. Du Bois: Biography of a Race*, 527.

13. Elliott Rudwick, *Race Riot at East St. Louis, July 2, 1917* (Urbana: Univ. of Illinois Press, 1964), 7–40, 165; Lewis, *W.E.B. Du Bois: Biography of a Race*, 536–37.

14. W.E.B. Du Bois, "The Massacre at East St. Louis," *The Crisis*, September 1917, 219–38; Lewis, *W.E.B. Du Bois: Biography of a Race*, 538.

15. Rudwick, *Race Riot*, 50–51; Du Bois, "Massacre of East St. Louis," 219; Lewis, *W.E.B. Du Bois: Biography of a Race*, 538; Du Bois, "Massacre of East St. Louis," 215–16.

16. Minutes, board of directors, September 17, 1917, NAACP Papers, I:A1; press release, November 17, 1917, NAACP Papers, I:G76.

17. In response to Florence Kelley's inquiry about whether she could march, James Weldon Johnson replied that "the committee in charge of the parade have not made any special effort to have white people march, but they would be glad to have those who wish to participate to do so." He went on to instruct her that the women would assemble at 56th Street and would dress in white. JWJ to Florence Kelley, July 27, 1917, NAACP Papers, I:C1; Johnson, *Along This Way*, 320–21; *New York Call*, July 29, 1917; memorandum of the NAACP: reproduction of comments from the New York daily presses on the Negro Silent Protest Parade, NAACP Papers, I:C432.

18. *New York Call*, July 29, 1917; *New York Age*, August 2, 1917; *Washington Bee*, August 11, 1917, NAACP Papers, I:C334.

19. Robert Haynes, *A Night of Violence: The Houston Riot of 1917* (Baton Rouge: Louisiana State Univ. Press, 1976), 1, 35–36, 60–88.

20. Martha Gruening, "Houston: An Investigation," *The Crisis*, November 1917, 14–19; Haynes, *A Night of Violence*, 90–166.

21. *New York Times*, August 24, 1917, 1; Gruening, "Houston" 14–19; Memorandum of the Activities of the N.A.A.C.P. in the Houston, Texas Riot Cases since Their Inception, n.d., NAACP Papers, I:C1; Haynes, *A Night of Violence*, 254–73; *Chicago Defender*, November 10, 1917, 1.

22. Haynes, *A Night of Violence*, 1–7; *Washington Post*, December 12, 1917, 4.

23. W.E.B. Du Bois, "Thirteen," *The Crisis*, January 1918, 114; Memorandum of the Activities of the N.A.A.C.P. in the Houston, Texas Riot Cases.

24. Memorandum of Activities of the N.A.A.C.P. in the Houston, Texas Riot Cases; Haynes, *A Night of Violence*, 279–80; Johnson, *Along This Way*, 323–24.

25. *Charles H. Buchanan v. William Warley*, Supreme Court of the United States, November 5, 1917, NAACP Papers, I:G76; Wright, *Life Behind the Veil*, 235–38; *Chicago Defender*, November 10, 1917, 1.

26. Wright, *Life Behind the Veil*, 238.

27. Ovington, *Walls Came Tumbling Down*, 147–48; Meier and Rudwick, "Rise of the Black Secretariat in the NAACP," 106–7.

28. Walter F. White, *A Man Called White* (Athens: Univ. of Georgia Press, 1995), 35–37.

29. Kenneth Janken, *White: The Biography of Walter White, Mr. NAACP* (New York: New Press, 2003), 29–31; Walter F. White, "The Burning of Jim Ilherron: An NAACP Investigation," *The Crisis*, May 1918, 16–20.

30. Walter F. White, "The Work of a Mob," *The Crisis*, September 1918, 221–24; Janken, *White*, 31–33; John Shillady to Mary White Ovington, July 16, 1918, NAACP Papers, I:C74.

31. "Brief Summary of Anti-lynching Work," *The Crisis*, February 1919, 182–84; Janken, *White*, 33–34.

32. Patricia Bernstein, *The First Waco Horror: The Lynching of Jesse Washington and the Rise of the NAACP* (College Station: Texas A&M Univ. Press, 2005), 161–62; "Brief Summary of Anti-lynching Work," 182–84; Robert L. Zangrando, *The NAACP Crusade Against Lynching, 1909–1950* (Philadelphia: Temple Univ. Press, 1980), 41–42.

33. Zangrando, *NAACP Crusade Against Lynching*, 42–44.

34. John Shillady to William English Walling, July 19, 1918, NAACP Papers, I:C74; Kellogg, *NAACP*, 230–31.

35. Minutes, board of directors, May 13, 1918, July 8, 1918, April 12, 1920, NAACP Papers I:A1; Johnson, *Along This Way*, 330.

36. Based on a review of a selection of branch files from California, Michigan, Ohio, Colorado, Connecticut, Kansas, Illinois, Indiana, Maine, NAACP Papers; *New York Times*, July 13, 1913, 4; L.H. Lightner (Denver branch) to May Childs Nerney, August 8, 1918, NAACP Papers, I:G27; *Branch Bulletin*, January 1920, NAACP Papers, I:C433.

37. *The Crisis*, May 1917, 19; WFW to C. Stewart Dupree, March 21, 1981, NAACP Papers, I:G13.

38. Johnson, *Along This Way*, 315–16.

39. Atlanta branch files, 1917–1919, NAACP Papers, I:G43.

40. Richard Mickey to Roy Nash, May 10, 1917; Sen. Knute Nelson to R.A. Skinner, June 26, 1917; Rep. C.B. Miller to R.A. Skinner, June 25, July 9, 1917; Edwin Harleston to John Shillady, November 2, 1918; Richard Mickey to NAACP, December 21, 1917, NAACP Papers, I:G215; Peter Lau, *Democracy Rising: South Carolina and the Fight for Black Equality Since 1865* (Lexington: Univ. of Kentucky Press, 2006), 41–46.

41. JWJ to J.C. Lindsay, June 30, 1917; J.G. Lemon to JWJ, July 30, 1917, NAACP Papers, I:G46; Wilson Jefferson to JWJ, May 7, 1917, NAACP Papers, I:G45; Margaret Down McCleary to JWJ, June 18, August 9, August 15, August 27, 1917, NAACP Papers, I:G41; Butler Nance correspondence from Columbia, S.C., branch, 1917–1920, NAACP Papers, I:G196.

42. JWJ to McCleary, August 20, 1917, NAACP Papers, I:G41; JWJ to Towns, February 25, 1919, Towns to JWJ, February 26, 1919, NAACP Papers, I:C3; minutes, board of directors, October 14, 1918, NAACP Papers, I:A1.

43. Minutes, board of directors, October 14, 1918, NAACP Papers, I:A1; Mary Talbert to John R. Shillady, May 16, 1919, NAACP Papers, I:C76; Lillian Williams, "And I Still Rise: Black Women and Reform Buffalo, New York, 1900–1940," *Afro Americans in New York Life and History* 14 (July 1990), 10–11.

44. Talbert to Shillady, May 16, 1919, NAACP Papers, I:C76; Williams, "And I Still Rise," 10–11; Talbert to JWJ, December 23, 1918; Talbert to JWJ, February 24, 1919; C.B. Charlton to Shillady, November 27, 1918, NAACP Papers, I:G202, Talbert to Mary White Ovington, March 3, 1919, NAACP Papers, I:C76; JWJ to Talbert, March 3, 1919, NAACP Papers, I:C2; Steven A. Reich, "Soldiers of Democracy: Black Texans and the Fight for Citizenship, 1917–1921," *Journal of American History* (March 1996), 1490–91; NAACP, press release, August 23, 1919, NAACP Papers, I:C4.

45. Gerald E. Shank, "Race, Manhood and Manpower: Mobilizing Rural Georgia for World War I, *Georgia Historical Quarterly* (Fall 1997), 653–55; Tera Hunter, *To Joy My Freedom': Southern Black Women's Lives and Labor after the Civil War* (Cambridge, MA: Harvard Univ. Press, 1997), 230.

46. James Jordan to NAACP, August 14, 1918, NAACP Papers, I:C417; Hunter, *To Joy My Freedom'*, 227–32.

47. Minutes, board of directors, October 14, 1918, NAACP Papers, I:A1; R.E. Watson and Rev. A.W.D. Reddick, Open Letter to the Chamber of Commerce, Pine Bluff, Ark., and to the Public [1918]; John Hurst to Shillady, October 26, 1918, NAACP Papers, I:C417.

48. WFW to Shillady, October 26, 1918, NAACP Papers, I:C417; "Ferguson Appeals to Sec. McAdoo," *Birmingham Reporter*, October 5, 1918; WFW, "'Work or Fight' in the South," *New Republic*, March 1, 1919, provides a summary of White's investigation. Brief reports on his findings in Alabama, Arkansas, Georgia, Florida, Louisiana, Mississippi, and Tennessee can be found in NAACP Papers, I:C417.

49. WFW to Shillady, November 14, 1918; G.R. Hutto to WFW, October 21, 1918, NAACP Papers, I:C417.

50. WFW to Shillady, November 16, 1918, NAACP Papers, I:C417.

51. R.R. Williams to OGV, December 24, 1918; R.R. Williams to Shillady, January 10, 1919; Shillady to R.R. Williams, December 27, 1918; Rev. James Brown et al. to Shillady, July 12, 1919, NAACP Papers, I:D49.

52. Application for charter, Anniston–Hobson City, Alabama, April 14, 1919, approved June 3, 1919, NAACP Papers, I:G1. Correspondence re Caldwell case included in several files, NAACP Papers, I:D49; see, esp., Morton to White, memorandum re Caldwell case, June 6, 1919, James Cobb to Newton Baker, secretary of war, November 12, 1919; James Cobb to JWJ, July 21, 1919, James Cobb to Shillady, February 14, 1920, March 6, 1920, April 24, 1920; R.R. Williams to Shillady, July 26, 1919; Caldwell case: receipts and expenditures by the Anniston branch [1920]. More than two hundred blacks from around the country responded to a March 1920 *Crisis* appeal that "Negroes who believe in Negro manhood immediately send one dollar each to J.E. Spingarn, Treasurer . . . for Caldwell's defense," March 1920, 233.

53. McNeil, *Groundwork*, 42; National Office of the League for Democracy pamphlet, League for Democracy file, Federal Surveillance of Afro-Americans, microfilm; W.E.B. Du Bois, "Returning Soldiers," *The Crisis*, May 1919, 14; P.A. Austin to Shillady, July 15, 1919, NAACP Papers, I:G200; Reich, "Soldiers of Democracy," 1493–94.

54. Addresses and proceedings of NAACP annual conference in Cleveland, 1919, NAACP Papers, I:B2.

55. Mark Robert Schneider, *"We Return Fighting": The Civil Rights Movement in the Jazz Age* (Boston: Northeastern Univ. Press, 2002), 29–30; Constance McLaughlin Green, *The Secret City: A History of Race Relations in the Nation's Capital* (Princeton, NJ: Princeton Univ. Press, 1967), 190–93; James Weldon Johnson, "The Riots," *The Crisis*, September 1919, 241–42; "For Action on Race Peril," *New York Times*, October 5, 1919, 112; NAACP, "An Appeal to the Conscience of the Civilized World," February 1920, NAACP Papers, I:C438.

56. *The Daily Herald*, October 16, 1919, Tuskegee Institute clipping file, reel 10.

57. Shillady to T.E. Pinson, May 19, 1920; D.D. Foote to JWJ, written on JWJ to Foote, January 30, 1919; Rev. A.J. Browne to Shillady, July 17, 1919, NAACP Papers, I:106; Oswald Braithwaite to Shillady, September 20, 1919, NAACP Papers, I:G199.

58. P.A. Williams to WFW, July 26, 1919, NAACP Papers, I:G200; NAACP press release, August 23, 1919; Reich, "Soldiers of Democracy," 1499; JWJ to Mary White Ovington, August 20, 1919, NAACP Papers, I:C4.

59. NAACP, "Mobbing of John R. Shillady," September 1919, NAACP Papers, I:C438; Ovington, *Walls Came Tumbling Down*, 173–75.

60. "Mobbing of John Shillady"; *New York Times*, August 23, 1919, 10; August 24, 1919, 15.

61. Nan Woodruff, *American Congo: The African American Freedom Struggle in the Delta* (Cambridge, MA: Harvard Univ. Press, 2003), 74–85.

62. Ibid., 85–99.

63. Walter White, "Massacring Whites in Arkansas," *Nation*, December 6, 1919; Woodruff, *American Congo*, 97–105; Janken, *White*, 51–55; Robert Cortner, *A Mob Intent on Death: The NAACP and the Arkansas Riot Case* (Middletown, CT: Wesleyan Univ. Press, 1988), 1–38.

64. Robert K. Murray, *Red Scare: A Study in National Hysteria, 1919–1920* (Minneapolis: Univ. of Minnesota Press, 1955), 78–79, 190–238; William Preston, *Aliens and Dissenters: Federal Suppression of Radicals, 1903–1933* (Cambridge, MA: Harvard Univ. Press, 1963).

65. Reich, "Soldiers of Democracy," 1499–1500; "For Action on Race Peril," *New York Times*, October 5, 1919, 112; memorandum by Ethel Stowe re visit of Department of Justice agent, October 16, 1919, NAACP Papers; Lewis, *W.E.B. Du Bois: Biography of a Race*, 571.

66. Mary White Ovington to branch presidents, November 21, 1919, NAACP Papers, I:B2. Branch responses.

67. Morton Sosna, *In Search of the Silent South: Southern Liberals and the Race Issue* (New York: Columbia Univ. Press, 1977), 20–24; Harry Pace to Mary White Ovington, December 30, 1919, NAACP Papers, I:B2; *New York Globe*, June 3, 1920.

68. NAACP, meeting of the Atlanta conference committee, March 18, 1920; Shillady to Ovington, memo, March 5, 1920; Truman Gibson to Shillady, March 30, 1920, NAACP Papers, I:B2; *Branch Bulletin*, April 1920, NAACP Papers, I:B3.

69. WFW to the Colored Press, May 22, 1920, NAACP Papers, I:B3; *Atlanta Constitution*, May 30, 1920, 7c; NAACP, press release, June 12, 1920, NAACP Papers, I:B3.

70. *New York Times*, May 31, 1920, 7; *Christian Science Monitor*, May 31, 1920, 4.

71. *New York Globe*, June 2, 1920; *Atlanta Constitution*, June 2, 1920, 4.

72. *New York Times*, May 31, 1920, 7, June 2, 1920, 3; *Atlanta Constitution*, June 1, 1920, 11.

73. *Atlanta Constitution*, June 2, 1920, 4. Previous recipients of the Spingarn Medal were Ernest Just (1915), Col. Charles Young (1916), Harry T. Burleigh (1917), William Stanley Braithwaite (1918), and Archibald Grimké (1919).

74. "Du Bois Asks Ballot for Negro in South," *New York Times*, June 3, 1920, 7; *New York Globe*, June 3, 1920; *Atlanta Constitution;* June 3, 1920, 9.

75. *Greenwood (MS) Daily Commonwealth*, reprinted in *New York Age*, February 15, 1919.

76. Thomas Henry to WFW, August 7, 1920; Addie Hunton to Mary White Ovington, October 25, 1920, NAACP/mf p4 r2.

77. W.E.B. Du Bois, "The Republicans and the Black Voter," *Nation*, June 5, 1920, 757–58.

78. Charles McPherson to NAACP, November 18, 1920; Clara Mann, affidavit, November 6, 1920; W.E. Morton to NAACP, October 14, 1920; Mrs. S.S. Humbert

to NAACP, November 9, 1920; Butler Nance to JWJ, November 17, 1920, NAACP/mf p4 r2.

79. Clara Mann to WFW, October 30, 1920; Channing Tobias to JWJ, October 21, 1920; H.W. McNamee to NAACP, June 6, 1920; WFW to Oklahoma branches, June 28, 1920; Caesar Simmons to JWJ, July 14, 1920, NAACP/mf p4 r1.

80. *New York Times*, November 4, 1920, 1; Walter F. White, "Apportionment of Representatives," testimony before the Committee on the Census, U.S. House of Representatives, 66th Cong., 3rd sess., December 29, 1920, 49; WFW, "Election Terror in Florida," *New Republic*, January 12, 1921, 195–97.

81. Hearings before the Committee on the Census, January 4–6, 1921, 42–61; *Washington Post*, December 31, 1920, 8; *New York Times*, December 31, 1920, 2.

82. Hearings before the Committee on the Census, 35–38, 68–79.

83. Ibid., 76–77; *New York Times*, December 31, 1920. (Southern representatives inserted the term "nigger" into the record of the testimony, a term they did not use in the hearings. JWJ brought this "cowardly tactic . . . pretending to their folks at home that they dared use this insulting word to the colored witnesses to Congressman Siegel's attention." He asked Siegel to correct the record to conform with the facts. JWJ to Isaac Siegel, January 24, 1921, NAACP Papers, I:C399.

84. Minutes, board of directors, January 10, 1921, report of the secretary, February 1920, NAACP/mf p1 r4; WFW to Butler Nance, January 20, 1921, NAACP Papers, I:G196.

85. *Washington Bee*, January 29, 1921; *Houston Observer*, January 15, 1921.

86. *New York Times*, May 7, 1921, 8.

87. Caesar Simmons to NAACP, August 5, 1920; Janie Lowder to NAACP, October 10, 1920; Butler Nance to William Pickens, November 14, 1920, NAACP/mf p4 r1.

88. Jim Colman to the NAACP, January 6, 1921; A.L. Henderson, Walter Nelms, L.H. Batie, et al. to Joel Spingarn, April 16, 1921, charter application Democrat, Arkansas, approved, June 21, 1921; Joe M.C. Henry to NAACP, May 6, 1921; A.L. Henderson to Mary White Ovington, November 28, 1921; William J. Burns to WFW, September 12, 1922, NAACP Papers, I:G11; Woodruff, *American Congo*, 112–22.

89. Membership Growth, 1912–1957, NAACP Papers, III:A37.

Chapter 4: Making a Way: The "New Negro" in Postwar America

1. Alfred L. Brophy, *Reconstructing the Dreamland: The Tulsa Riot of 1921; Race, Reparations and Reconciliation* (New York: Oxford Univ. Press, 2002), 23; Alain Locke, "The New Negro," in Alain Locke, ed., *The New Negro* (New York: Atheneum, 1968), 10.

2. Brophy, *Reconstructing the Dreamland*, 24–62; WFW, quoted in Schneider, *We Return Fighting*, 159.

3. Mary White Ovington to JWJ, March 11, 1921, NAACP Papers, I:B4.

4. William W. Giffin, *African Americans and the Color Line in Ohio, 1915–1930* (Columbus: Ohio State Univ. Press, 2005), 89–138; Quintard Taylor, *In Search of the Racial Frontier: African Americans in the West, 1528–1990* (New York: Norton, 1998), 222–37; Spears, *Black Chicago*, 203–22; Osofsky, *Harlem*, 127–49.

5. Winston James, *Holding Up the Banner of Ethiopia: Caribbean Radicalism in Early Twentieth-Century America* (New York: Verso, 2000), 122–84; David Levering Lewis, *When Harlem Was in Vogue* (New York: Oxford Univ. Press, 1989), 45–49, 125–26; Robert A. Hill, ed., *The Marcus Garvey and Universal Negro Improvement Association Papers*, vol. 1 (Berkeley: Univ. of California Press, 1983), xxx–lx; William Pickens, "Africa for the Africans," *Negro World*, December 17, 1921.

6. On Garvey and the NAACP: "Herbert Seligmann Interviews Marcus Garvey and Writes His Impressions," *New York Age*, December 10, 1921, 1; Alice Woody McKane to Herbert Seligmann, December 21, 1921, NAACP/mf p13 r35 f689, 641; This communication notes she is member of UNIA, NAACP, and the National Equal Rights League. James Weldon Johnson, address delivered at NAACP thirteenth annual conference, June 19, 1922, Newark, NJ, NAACP Papers, I:B5.

7. Rudwick and Meier, "Rise of the Black Secretariat in the NAACP," 112–13.

8. JWJ to Julian St. George White, April 1, 1921, NAACP Papers, I:C7.

9. James Weldon Johnson, address delivered at NAACP thirteenth annual conference, June 19, 1922, Newark, NJ, NAACP Papers, I:B5; Rudwick and Meier, "Rise of the Black Secretariat in the NAACP," 111; JWJ to Moorfield Storey, December 19, 1925, NAACP/mf p1 r17 f606. Johnson notes that for the past two to three years the records showed that 85 percent of the NAACP's support came from black people.

10. Richard B. Sherman, "The Harding Administration and the Negro: An Opportunity Lost," *Journal of Negro History* 49 (July 1964): 152; report of the secretary, board of directors meeting, May 1921, NAACP Papers I:A15. In 1890–91 Congress considered and ultimately defeated a bill that would have provided for federal supervision of federal elections.

11. William B. Hixon, "Moorfield Storey and the Defense of the Dyer Anti-lynching Bill," *New England Quarterly* 42 (March 1969): 69–73; Ernest Havier, "Political Effect of the Dyer Bill," *New York Times*, July 9, 1922, 33; "Antilynching Bill," editorial, *Washington Post*, January 28, 1922, 6; "The Equal Protection of the Laws," editorial, *Chicago Defender*, January 21, 1922, 20; *Washington Post*, January 1, 1922, 3; Sherman, "Harding Administration," 161.

12. Johnson, *Along This Way*, 362–65.

13. Ibid., 365–66; report of the secretary, February 1922, NAACP Papers, I:A15; *Washington Post*, January 26, 1922, 3, January 28, 1922, 6; *New York Times*, July 9, 1922, 33.

14. *New York Times*, June 12, 1922, 4, July 1, 1922, 12; Johnson, *Along This Way*, 366–68; "Mob Burns Three Negroes at the Stake," *New York Times*, May 7, 1922, 1; "Negro Boy Tortured and Burned in Georgia after Killing a White Woman," *New York Times*, May 19, 1922, 1; "Boy 15 Is Tortured over Slow Fire," *Washington Post*, May 19, 1922, 1.

15. Mary B. Talbert, minutes of the executive committee of the Anti–lynching Crusaders [1922], NAACP, Mary B. Talbert to State Director, July 25, 1922, Mary B. Talbert to Mary White Ovington, October 21, 1922, NAACP/mf p7B r3; *Washington Post*, June, 4, 1922, 22, June 15, 1922, 2, June 19, 1922, 3; *New York Times*, June 4, 1922, 22, June 15, 3.

16. *New York Times*, July 1, 1922, 1, September 22, 1922, 14.

17. WFW to Emily Osgood, October 25, 1922, NAACP/mf p7B r1; "The Shame of America," *New York Times*, November 23, 1922, 19.

18. *Washington Post*, November 29, 1922, 2, November 30, 1922, 5, December 1, 1922, 10, December 3, 1922, 30, December 5, 1922, 4; *New York Times*, December 3, 1922, 1, editorial, December 4, 1922, 16; *Chicago Defender*, December 9, 1922, 8; *Pittsburgh Dispatch*, editorial, reprinted in *Washington Post*, December 6, 1922, 6; editorial, *Indianapolis News*, reprinted in *Washington Post*, December 7, 1922, 6.

19. Report of secretary for November meeting of the board, 1922, NAACP Papers, I:A15; JWJ address to annual meeting of the NAACP, January 3, 1923, NAACP/mf p1 r13 f391.

20. Johnson, *Along This Way*, 371–73; Woodruff, *American Congo*, 116; Schneider, *We Return Fighting*, 116.

21. Schneider, *We Return Fighting*, 209–11.

22. Cortner, *Mob Intent on Death*, 1–2, 106–30, 136–37, 154–58, 192–95. The six men were ultimately freed, as were six other defendants who had been sentenced to death.

23. Schneider, *We Return Fighting*, 54–60; Addie W. Hunton and Kathryn M. Johnson, *Two Colored Women with the American Expeditionary Forces in France* (Brooklyn, NY: Brooklyn Eagle Press, 1920).

24. Addie Hunton, report of Department of Branches, June 1923, NAACP Ppaers, I:A15; Addie Hunton to Mary White Ovington, March 21, 1921, reports: May 4–6, 1921, August 1922, January 3–February 7, 1923, February 7–March 7, 1923, NAACP Papers, I:C177.

25. C. Frederick Douglass to JWJ, February 23, 1921, NAACP Papers, I:G41; "Negro Minister Told to Leave: Speech by Columbian Angers Hampton Folk" [1921], NAACP Papers, I:G196; Charles McPherson, June 19, 1922, NAACP Papers, I:G1; Hunton, report, January 3–February 7, 1923.

26. Eugene Levy, *James Weldon Johnson, Black Leader, Black Voice* (Chicago: Univ. of Chicago Press, 1973), 228–29; report of the director of branches, November 1923, February 1924, April, 1924, June 1924, NAACP Papers, I:A15.

27. Gloria Garrett Samson, "Toward a New Social Order: The American Fund for Public Service: Clearinghouse for Radicalism in the 1920s" (doctoral dissertation, University of Rochester, 1987), 237–38.

28. WFW, "Forward to Legal Work," annual report for 1924, NAACP Papers, I:A25; Mark V. Tushnet, *The NAACP's Legal Strategy Against Segregated Education, 1925–1950* (Chapel Hill: Univ. of North Carolina Press, 1987), 1–2.

29. WFW, "Forward to Legal Work"; report of the secretary, July 1925, report of the

secretary, December 1926, NAACP Papers, I:A16. On extradition cases: see James Weldon Johnson and Herbert Seligmann, "Legal Aspects of the Negro Problem [1928], NAACP Papers, I:C420; annual report of the NAACP, 1927, 7–11, NAACP Papers, I:A25.

30. Darlene Clark Hine, *Black Victory: The Rise and Fall of the White Primary in Texas* (Columbia: Univ. of Missouri Press), 113–19.

31. Press release: "Indianapolis Citizens Determined to Fight Segregation Ordinance to the Finish," March 19, 1926; WFW to Olivia Taylor, March 25, 1926; R.L. Brokenburr to WFW, November 23, 1926, NAACP/mf p5 r2, f540, 545, 549; report of Department of Branches, October 1924, report of Department of Branches, December 1924, NAACP Papers, I:A15. NAACP branches defeated segregation ordinances in Winston-Salem, Baltimore, Norfolk, and Dallas through local courts; the U.S. Supreme Court overturned ordinances enacted in New Orleans (*Harmon v. Tyler*) and Richmond (1929). Clement E. Vose, *Caucasians Only: The Supreme Court, the NAACP, and the Restrictive Covenant Cases* (Berkeley: Univ. of California Press, 1959), 52; Davison M. Douglas, *Jim Crow Moves North: The Battle over Northern School Segregation, 1865–1954* (New York: Cambridge Univ. Press, 2005), 132; "Residential Segregation in America Depends on NAACP Case in Supreme Court," press release, September 12, 1924, NAACP/mf p11 r28 f936–37.

32. Minutes, board of directors, July 9, 1923; report of the secretary, February 1924; report of the secretary, October 1924, report of secretary, December 1924, NAACP Papers, I:A15.

33. Report of the secretary, October 1925, NAACP Papers, I:A15; report of the secretary, October 1924, August 1925, NAACP Papers, I:A15; minutes, board of directors, September 13, 1926, report of the secretary, December 1927, NAACP Papers, I:A16.

34. Kevin Boyle, *Arc of Justice: A Saga of Race, Civil Rights, and Murder in the Jazz Age* (New York: Henry Holt, 2005), 102–115, 141–43.

35. Ibid., 144–45; Walter F. White, "Segregation Comes North," typed manuscript [1925], NAACP/mf p11B r28 f1047–54;

36. White, "Segregation Comes North"; Walter F. White, "The Sweet Trial," *The Crisis*, January 1926, 126; Boyle, *Arc of Justice*, 140–41, 150–56.

37. JWJ, letter to the editor, *New York Herald Tribune*, August 4, 1925; Boyle, *Arc of Justice*, 205–6; JWJ to Moorfield Storey, September 12, 1925, October 20, 1925, NAACP/mf p1 r17 f586–89; press release, September 18, 1925, NAACP/mf p11B r28 f998–99.

38. JWJ to Rev. R.L. Bradby, September 11, 1925; M.W. Hayes McKinney to JWJ, September 12, 1925; WFW to Judge Ira Jayne, September 14, 1925, NAACP/mf p5 r2 f929, 931–32, 937.

39. Boyle, *Arc of Justice*, 156–69.

40. WFW to JWJ, September 16, 1925; WFW to JWJ, September 17, 1925, NAACP/mf p5 r2 f943–44, 1031–32; Janken, *White*, 71–75; William E. Davis et al. to W. Hayes McKinney, September 29, 1925, NAACP/mf p5 r2 f1086.

41. JWJ to Clarence Darrow, October 7, 1925; press release: "Clarence Darrow to Defend Negroes Who Fired into Detroit Mob," October 15, 1925; NAACP/mf p5 r2 f1037, 1089; Boyle, *Arc of Justice*, 230–46.

42. "NAACP Starts $50,000 Defense Fund as Sweet Trial Opens in Detroit," press release, October 20, 1925, NAACP/mf p5 r3 f37; *Detroit Independent*, October 23, 1925; Floyd Calvin, *Pittsburgh Courier*, October 1924, NAACP/mf p5 r2 f1010; *Philadelphia Public Journal*, editorial, October 10, 1925.

43. Boyle, *Arc of Justice*, 256–301; Walter White, "The Sweet Trial," 128.

44. Boyle, *Arc of Justice*, 300–301; JWJ to Moorfield Storey, December 19, 1925, December 22, 1925, NAACP/mf p1 r17 f606, 607.

45. James Weldon Johnson, "Detroit," *The Crisis*, 118–20; Boyle, *Arc of Justice*, 331–34.

46. W.E.B. Du Bois, "The Sweet Trial," *The Crisis*, July 1926, 114; Vose, *Causasians Only*, 51.

47. Vose, *Caucasians Only*, 17–19; Schneider, *We Return Fighting*, 287–90.

48. Hine, *Black Victory*, 111–41.

49. W.E.B. Du Bois, "Education," *The Crisis*, October 1931, 350; W.E.B. Du Bois, "Education," *The Crisis*, February 1930, 65.

50. W.E.B. Du Bois, "Segregation," *The Crisis*, November 1910, 10.

51. Douglas, *Jim Crow Moves North*, 79, 140–63; V.P. Franklin, *The Education of Black Philadelphia: The Social and Educational History of a Minority Community, 1900–1950* (Philadelphia: Univ. of Pennsylvania Press, 1979), 74–77; W.E.B. Du Bois, "The Tragedy of Jim Crow," *The Crisis*, August 1923, 170; Robert L. Carter, *A Matter of Law: A Memoir of Struggle in the Cause of Equal Rights* (New York: New Press, 2005), 14.

52. Douglas, *Jim Crow Moves North*, 172–86.

53. W.E.B. Du Bois, "The Negro and Northern Public Schools," *The Crisis*, March 1923, 205; Du Bois, "The Tragedy of Jim Crow," 172.

54. Douglas, *Jim Crow Moves North*, 188–89, 209.

55. August Meier and Elliott Rudwick, "Early Boycotts of Segregated Schools: The Case of Springfield, Ohio, 1922–1923," in Meier and Rudwick, *Along the Color Line*, 289–306; report of the secretary, board of directors, March 9, 1923, NAACP Papers, I:A15.

56. "Colored Folk Make National Issue of Educational Segregation," *New York Daily News*, March 12, 1927; "Jim Crow Law Is Enforced in Jersey Schools," *New York World*, March 11, 1927; "Jersey Negroes Fight School Segregation," *New York Times*, March 11, 1927; Eugene R. Hayne to commissioner of education, March 11, 1927, NAACP/mf p3A r12 f933–34.

57. JWJ to Eugene R. Hayne, March 11, 1923, JWJ to New Jersey branches, March 11, 1927, NAACP/mf p3A r12 f942, 939; JWJ to Hayne, April 2, 1927, NAACP/mf p3A r13 f004–05; *Pittsburgh Courier*, April 2, 1927, 1; *New York Times*, March 24, 1927, 52, June 30, 1927, 35; "Toms River's Colored Citizens," *Philadelphia Tribune*, July 14, 1927.

58. Douglas, *Jim Crow Moves North*, 205–13; Franklin, *Education of Black Philadelphia*, 84; NAACP annual report, 1927, 6–7, NAACP Papers, I:A25; report of the secretary, February 1928, NAACP Papers, I:A26; Kelly Miller, "Is the Color Line Crumbling?" *Opportunity*, September 1929, 284.

59. Du Bois, "The Tragedy of Jim Crow," 170–71.

60. Louis L. Athey, "Florence Kelley and the Quest for Negro Equality," *Journal of Negro History* 56 (October 1971): 252; Florence Kelley, "The Sterling Discrimination Bill," *The Crisis*, 251–55; minutes, board of directors, January 3, 1922, NAACP Papers, I:A2.

61. W.E.B. Du Bois, "Florence Kelley" [1923], W.E.B. Du Bois Papers, Department of Special Collections and University Archives, W.E.B. Du Bois Library, University of Massachusetts, Amherst; minutes, board of directors, February 14, 1923, NAACP Papers, I:A2; Mary White Ovington to J.W. Lane, March 3, 1923, Mary White Ovington to Joseph P. Loud, March 20, 1923, NAACP/mf p3A r19 f736; report of the Committee on Southern Education, June 19, 1923, NAACP/mf p3A, r19 f817.

62. "Southern States' Denial of Education Cause of Negro Migration, Is Charged," press release, June 29, 1923, NAACP/mf p3A, r19 f880.

63. W.E.B. Du Bois to the Trustees of the Garland Fund, November 9, 1924; W.E.B. Du Bois, memorandum to James Weldon Johnson, January 15, 1925; W.E.B. Du Bois, report to the directors of the American Fund for Social [sic] Service on a Study of Public Common School Education in the South for Negroes, October 1926, American Fund for Public Service records, microfilm, reel 7.

64. "The Negro Common School in Georgia," *The Crisis*, September 1926, 249–64; "The Negro Common School, Mississippi," *The Crisis*, December 1926, 90–102; "The Negro Common School in North Carolina," *The Crisis*, May 1927, 79–80, 96–97; "The Negro Common School in North Carolina," June 1927, 117–18, 133–34; "South Carolina Negro Common Schools," *The Crisis*, December 1927, 330–32; Horace Mann Bond, "The Negro Common School in Oklahoma," *The Crisis*, April 1928, 113–16, 136–38, July 1928, 228, 243–46; W.E.B. Du Bois, "Education," *The Crisis*, April 1929, 132.

65. JWJ to WFW, April 13, 1923, NAACP/mf p2 r7 f365.

66. David Levering Lewis, *W.E.B. Du Bois: The Fight for Equality and the American Century, 1919–1963* (New York: Henry Holt, 2000), 153; James Weldon Johnson, ed., *The Book of American Negro Poetry* (New York: Harcourt, Brace, 1931), 21.

67. James Weldon Johnson, "Race Prejudice and the Negro Artist" (originally published in *Harper's*, November 1928), in Herbert Aptheker, ed., *A Documentary History of the Negro People in the United States* (New York: Carol, 1993), 588; Lewis, *When Harlem Was in Vogue*, 89–96, 179 ; Lewis, *W.E.B. Du Bois: The Fight for Equality and the American Century*, 155–60; Johnson, *Along This Way*, 380.

68. Lewis, *When Harlem Was in Vogue*, 156–57, 215–16; Locke, "The New Negro," 3–16.

69. Tess Chakkalakal, "'Making a Collection': James Weldon Johnson and the Mis-

sion of African American Literature," *South Atlantic Quarterly* (Summer 2005): 522–41; Janken, *White*, 95–119; Johnson, *Along This Way*, 374–75; Lewis, *W.E.B. Du Bois: The Fight for Equality and the American Century*, 171.

70. W.E.B. Du Bois, "Criteria of Negro Art," *The Crisis*, October 1926, 290–97.

71. Ibid., 290, 294; Lewis, *W.E.B. Du Bois: The Fight for Equality and the American Century*, 171.

72. Janken, *White*, 129–34.

73. Janken, *White*, 127–35; Donald Lisio, *Hoover, Blacks, and Lily-Whites: A Study of Southern Strategy* (Chapel Hill: Univ. of North Carolina Press, 1985), 82–92; "An Appeal to America," *The Crisis*, December 1928, 416.

74. W.E.B. Du Bois, "The Negro Citizen," *The Crisis*, May 1929, 154–56, 171–73.

75. Ibid., 155; W.E.B. Du Bois, "The Campaign of 1928," *The Crisis*, December 1928, 418; Janken, *White*, 135.

76. The year was 1925: report of the director of branches, January 1926, NAACP Papers, I:A26. Robert Bagnall emphasized the importance of arousing an awareness of the consequences of segregation in the branches and, through them, the larger black community, NAACP/mf p1 r15; Bagnall, report on Midwest trip, October 27, 1924; Bagnall to JWJ [1926], f360; Bagnall to WFW [1926], f362, NAACP/mf p1 r15 f298, 360, 362; report of the Department of Branches, July 1925, October 1927, December 1927, NAACP/mf p1A r15. Bagnall submitted a monthly report to the board, which provides details of fieldwork conducted by him and Pickens. Minutes, board of directors, April 8, 1929, NAACP Papers, I:A2.

77. Figure on branches: Committee on Negro Work, memoradum to the directors of the American Fund for Public Service, May 28, 1930, 3, NAACP/mf p3A r11 f362. On fieldwork, see especially Robert Bagnall's reports and correspondence, NAACP/mf p1 r15, e.g., report of Midwest trip, October 27, 1924, f298–303, Bagnall to JWJ [1926], f360, Bagnall to WFW [1926] on plans for conference on "How to Combat Segregation, Our Greatest Menace in the North," f362. Giffin, *African Americans and the Color Line in Ohio*, 159–67; on state conferences: report of the Department of Branches, October 1929, December 1929, NAACP Papers, I:A26; Bagnall to Daisy Lampkin, March 4, 1930, NAACP/mf p1 r15 f478.

78. Report of the Department of Branches, January 1927, June 1927, December 1927, May 1928, June 1929, NAACP Papers, I:A15; Bagnall to William Pickens, May 31, 1927, NAACP/mf p1 r15 f378.

79. Report of the Department of Branches, September 9, 1929, NAACP Papers I:A16; Bagnall, memorandum to the board of directors, October 14, 1929, NAACP/mf p1 r18 f189; "Daisy Elizabeth Adams Lampkin," in Hine, *Black Women in America*, 690–93; Daisy Lampkin to WFW, October 25, 1929, NAACP/mf p1 r18 f190.

80. Bagnall to Lampkin, February 5, 1930, Bagnall to Lampkin, March 4, 1930, NAACP/mf p1 r15 f471, 478.

81. Lampkin to Bagnall, February 14, 1930, Lampkin to WFW, October 20, 1930,

Lampkin to Bagnall, October 20, 1930, Lampkin to Bagnall, October 29, 1930, Lampkin to Bagnall, November 28, 1930, NAACP/mf p1 r18 f478, 300, 297, 305, 316.

82. W.E.B. Du Bois, "What the NAACP Has Meant in American Life," twentieth annual convention, Cleveland, Ohio, June 26, 1929, NAACP/mf p1 r8 f1301.

83. Report of the acting secretary, April 1930, NAACP/mf p1 r6 f176; A.M. Rivera to WFW, March 25, 1930, WFW to A.M. Rivera, March 29, 1930, WFW to Hon. Roscoe C. McCullough, April 2, 1930, NAACP/mf p11B r26 f312–14, 369; Roy Wilkins, *Standing Fast: The Autobiography of Roy Wilkins* (New York: Da Capo Press, 1994), 19; Kenneth W. Goings, *"The NAACP Comes of Age": The Defeat of John J. Parker* (Bloomington: Indiana Univ. Press, 1990), 23–24

84. Statement to the Sub-committee of the Senate Judiciary Committee on Behalf of the National Association for the Advancement of Colored People, April 5, 1930, by Walter White," NAACP/mf p2B r26 f402.

85. WFW to A.M. Rivera, April 7, 1930, NAACP/mf p11B r26 f390; Goings, *"NAACP Comes of Age,"* 25–27.

86. Walter White, "The Negro and the Supreme Court," *Harper's Monthly Magazine*, January 1931, 238–246; Lampkin to Bagnall, April 17, 1930, NAACP/mf p1 r18 f238.

87. WFW, memorandum re Parker confirmation . . . long distance conversation with Ludwell Denny, April 18, 1930, NAACP/mf p11B r26 f778; White, "The Negro and the Supreme Court," 240; Lisio, *Hoover, Blacks, and Lily-Whites*, 216–18.

88. "Radicalism's Brief Triumph," editorial, *Washington Post*, May 8, 1930, 1, 6; *New York Times*, April 27, 1930, 55; "The Senate and the Supreme Court: A New Test," *New York Times*, May 11, 1930, 53; White, "The Negro and the Supreme Court," 240, 242; W.E.B. Du Bois, "The Defeat of Judge Parker," *The Crisis*, July 1930, 225–27, 248; Lisio, *Hoover, Blacks, and Lily-Whites*, 229.

89. Janken, *White*, 145–48; Du Bois, "The Defeat of Judge Parker," 225.

90. Minutes, board of directors, May 12, 1930, NAACP Papers, I:A2.

91. Digest of the report of Committee on Negro Work to the directors of the American Fund for Public Service, July 8, 1930, AFPS Papers, 3A, 1, 451; Tushnet, *NAACP's Legal Strategy*, 8, 13–15.

92. Memorandum to the directors of the American Fund for Public Service, May 28, 1930, 2, 12, AFPS Papers, 3A, 1, 360.

93. Ibid., 3–10.

94. W.E.B. Du Bois, "What the NAACP Has Meant to American Life," twentieth annual convention, Cleveland, June 26, 1929, NAACP/mf p1 r8 f1292; "Address of James Weldon Johnson before the twentieth annual meeting of the National Association for the Advancement of Colored People," January 4, 1931, NAACP/mf p1 r13 f1216.

95. "Address of James Weldon Johnson before the twentieth annual meeting of the NAACP."

Chapter 5: Radical Visions: The Depression Years

1. Hollace Ransdell, "Report on the Scottsboro, Ala. Case," for the American Civil Liberties Union, May 27, 1931, 4–5, NAACP Papers, I:D69; Dan T. Carter, *Scottsboro: A Tragedy of the American South* (Baton Rouge: Louisiana State Univ. Press, 1969), 22.

2. Carter, *Scottsboro*, 16–23; Dr. P.A. Stephens to Walter White, April 2, 1941, NAACP Papers, I:D68.

3. Carter, *Scottsboro*, 23–43, 186–87, 232–34.

4. W.E.B. Du Bois, "Is the NAACP Lying Down on Its Job?" *The Crisis*, October 1931, 343–345. Mary White Ovington to OGV, July 22, 1934, OGV Papers, Box 2921.

5. W.G. Porter to NAACP, March 29, 1931, P.A. Stephens to WFW, April 2, 1931, WFW to William Andrews, April 6, 1931, Andrews to Stephens, April 9, 1931, April 10, 1931, G.H. Thornhill to NAACP, April 14, 1931, WFW to Thornhill, April, 15, 1931, William Pickens to Miss Massie, April 13, 1931, NAACP Papers, I:D68.

6. Ovington to OGV, July 22, 1934.

7. Robin D.G. Kelley, *Hammer and Hoe: Alabama Communists During the Great Depression* (Chapel Hill: Univ. of North Carolina Press, 1990), 13–33.

8. James Goodman, *Stories of Scottsboro* (New York: Vintage Books, 1994), 24–25; Carter, *Scottsboro*, 49–53.

9. WFW to Clarence Darrow, April, 10, 1931, NAACP Papers, I:D69; William Pickens to editor of *Daily Worker*, April 19, 1931.

10. "NAACP Preparing for Defense of 8 Convicted Alabama Boys," April 24, 1931, NAACP Papers, I:D69; Mary White Ovington to William Pickens, April 30, 1931, in minutes, board of directors, May 11, 1931, NAACP Papers, I:A3.

11. Carter, *Scottsboro*, 54–62.

12. WFW to Robert Bagnall and Herbert Seligmann, May 3, 1931, NAACP Papers, I:D68.

13. Ibid.; WFW to Bagnall and Seligmann, May 5, 1931; WFW to William Pickens, May 12, 1931, NAACP Papers, I:D68.

14. WFW to the editors of the colored press, May 11, 1931, NAACP Papers, I:D68.

15. *Washington World*, May 29, 1931, July 24, 1931; *Chicago Tribune*, May 30, 1931; *Oklahoma Black Dispatch*, May 14, 1931; *Chicago Whip*, May 30, 1931; *Atlanta Daily World*, May 15, 1931.

16. W.E.B. Du Bois, "The Scottsboro Cases," *The Crisis*, September 1931, 313–14; Robert Weaver, interview, April 16, 1992; Charles Houston to editor of *Amsterdam News*, May 25, 1933. For a discussion of the broad impact of leftist politics on the thought and legal strategies of black civil rights lawyers during this period, see Kenneth W. Mack, "Law and Mass Politics in the Making of Civil Rights Lawyers," *Journal of American History* 93 (2006): 37–62.

17. Lewis, *W.E.B. Du Bois: The Fight for Equality and the American Century*, 285; Raymond Wolters, *Negroes and the Great Depression: The Problem of Economic Recovery* (Westport, CT: Greenwood, 1970), 90–92; Charles Edward Russell to Mary White Ovington, November 25, December 1, December 6, 1931, NAACP Papers, I:A25; Nancy J. Weiss, "Long Distance Runners of the Civil Rights Movement: The Contributions of Jews to the NAACP and the National Urban League in the Early Twentieth Century," in Jack Salzman and Cornel West, eds., *Struggles in the Promised Land: Toward a History of Black-Jewish Relations in the United States* (New York: Oxford Univ. Press, 1997), 136–37.

18. John Britton, interview with Arthur Spingarn, March 6, 1968, Ralph Bunche Oral History Collection, MSRC; Daisy Lampkin to Robert Bagnall, November 11, 1931; Lampkin to WFW, February 21, 1931, NAACP Papers, I:C67; Richetta Randolph to JWJ, October 10, 1930; Richards memorandum to Mary White Ovington, January 19, 1931, JWJ, BL/Yale, Box 16; Lewis, *W.E.B. Du Bois: The Fight for Equality and the American Century*, 278–79; Janken, *White*, 163–64.

19. Report on *The Crisis*, April 1931, NAACP Papers, I:A17; Lewis, *W.E.B. Du Bois: The Fight for Equality and the American Century*, 276, 282–83, 292.

20. Lewis, *W.E.B. Du Bois: The Fight for Equality and the American Century*, 283–85; Janken, *White*, 166–67, 183.

21. Janken, *White*, 165–67; Lewis, *W.E.B. Du Bois: The Fight for Equality and the American Century*, 281, 293–94.

22. Janken, *White*, 172–73.

23. Minutes, board of directors, April 11, 1932, NAACP Papers, I:A3; Janken, *White*, 173–75.

24. "The Negro Editors on Communism: A Symposium on the American Negro Press," *The Crisis*, April 1932, 117–19, May 1932, 154–56, 177; W.E.B. Du Bois, "Colored Editors on Communism," *The Crisis*, June 1932, 190–91.

25. Advance material for address by Walter White at Washington Auditorium on May 22, May 13, 1932; "What Is Wrong with the NAACP?" address delivered by W.E.B. Du Bois before the twenty-third annual conference of the NAACP, Washington, D.C., May 18, 1932, NAACP Papers, I:B8.

26. "The NAACP in Washington," *The Crisis*, May 1932, 159; "The 23d Conference of the NAACP," *The Crisis*, July 1932, 218–19.

27. Hon. Robert M. LaFollette Jr., speech to the twenty-third annual conference of the NAACP, May 22, 1932, Hon. Robert Bulkley, speech to the twenty-third annual conference of the NAACP, May 18, 1932, advance material for address by Walter White, NAACP Papers, I:B8.

28. Nathan Margold, preliminary report to the Joint Committee Supervising the Expenditure of the 1930 Appropriation by the American Fund for Public Service to the NAACP, n.d., NAACP Papers, I:C199; Margold to WFW, May 2, 1932, NAACP Papers, I:C196; "A Program of Legal Defense for Negroes," address delivered by Nathan R. Margold before the twenty-third annual conference of the NAACP, Washington, D.C., May 20, 1932, NAACP Papers, I:B8.

29. "Cooperation between the National Bar Association and the N.A.A.C.P.," discussion by Charles H. Houston before the twenty–third annual conference of the NAACP, May 20, 1932, NAACP Papers, I:B8. The results of Houston's survey and his ideas on this subject are developed more fully in Charles Hamilton Houston, "The Need for Negro Lawyers," *Journal of Negro Education* 4 (January 1935): 49–52. Raymond Pace Alexander, president of the NBA, 1930–31, addresses the issue in "The Negro Lawyer," *Opportunity*, September 1931, 268–71.

30. W.E.B. Du Bois, address delivered during the twenty-third annual conference of the NAACP, Harper's Ferry, WV, May 21, 1932, NAACP Papers, I:B8; WFW to JWJ, May 27, 1932, JWJ Papers, BL/Yale, Box 24.

31. WFW to JWJ, May 27, 1932; Lewis, *W.E.B. Du Bois: The Fight for Equality and the American Century*, 300–301.

32. Hine, *Black Victory*, 160–72; report of the secretary, July 1932, NAACP Papers, I:A17.

33. McNeil, *Groundwork*, 24–42.

34. McNeil, *Groundwork*, 49–53; "The Harvard Nile Club," November 20, 1922; to the president and members of the Harvard Nile Club, February 23, 1923, correspondence with Charles Houston file, William L. Houston Papers, Manuscript Division, Library of Congress.

35. McNeil, *Groundwork*, 56, 67–70.

36. "Howard University School of Law," a report prepared for the Association of American Law Schools by M.T. Van Hecke, November 18, 20, 1933, NAACP Papers, I:A27; McNeil, *Groundwork*, 79; Gilbert Ware, *William Hastie: Grace Under Pressure* (New York: Oxford Univ. Press, 1984), 31.

37. McNeil, *Groundwork*, 68, 71, 84–85; Tushnet, *NAACP's Legal Strategy*, 30; Thurgood Marshall, interviewed by Richard Kluger, December 28, 1973, *Brown v. Board* Collection, Manuscripts, and Archives, Yale University Library.

38. CHH, "An Approach to Better Race Relations," address delivered to the thirteenth national YWCA convention, May 5, 1934, YWCA of the USA Collection, Sophia Smith Collection, Smith College Libraries, microfilm reel 32.

39. Correspondence between CHH and William Patterson, CHH Papers, MSRC, Box 26; CHH to Carol King, May 31, 1934; Statement of Charles Houston in Debate with Bernard Ades before the Liberal Club of Howard University, March 28, 35, CHH Papers, MSRC, Box 26; McNeil, *Groundwork*, 207.

40. Statement of Charles Houston in Debate with Bernard Ades; CHH to William Patterson, June 22, 1933; CHH, Cooperation between the NBA and the NAACP, May 20, 1932; CHH to William Patterson, June 22, 1933, CHH Papers, MSRC, Box 26; CHH to WFW, October 17, 1933, NAACP Papers, I:D52.

41. WFW to Roger Baldwin, November 11, 1932, NAACP Papers, I:C196; Carter, *Scottsboro*, 160, 334; *Black Victory*, 124–27.

42. Jobs and Justice Feature, 1932 annual report, NAACP Papers, I:A25; "The Campaign at Boulder Dam," address by Jesse S. Heslip before the twenty-fourth an-

nual convention of the NAACP, June 30, 1932, NAACP Papers, I:B9; report of the secretary, May, July, August, 1932, NAACP Papers, I:A27.

43. Jobs and Justice Feature, 1932 annual report; reports of the secretary, September 1932, October 1932, November 1932, December 1932, February 1933, March 1933, NAACP Papers I:A17; Roy Wilkins, "Mississippi Slavery in 1933," *The Crisis*, April 1933, 81–82.

44. WFW to CHH, March 6, 1933; WFW to Butler Wilson, January 18, 1933, Butler Wilson to WFW, January 19, 1933; Memorandum re long-distance telephone conversation with Butler R. Wilson re the Crawford case, January 26, 1933; Butler Wilson to WFW, February 11, 1933; WFW to Butler Wilson, February 17, 1933, NAACP Papers, I:D51; Helen Broadman, "The South Goes Legal" (based on her investigation for the NAACP), *Nation*, March 8, 1933, 258–60; *New York Times*, January 18, 1933, 1.

45. WFW to CHH, March 6, 1933, CHH to WFW, March 8, 1933, March 9 and 10 1933; CHH and Edward P. Lovett, confidential memorandum on trip to Leesburg, Virginia, March 9, 1933, NAACP Papers, I:D51.

46. CHH to WFW, March 10, 1933, March 12, 1933, April 15, 1933; WFW to J. Weston Allen, April 17, 1933, NAACP Papers, I:D51.

47. CHH to WFW, March 10, 1933; WFW to Arthur Spingarn, March 11, 1933, CHH to WFW, March 17, 1933, NAACP Papers, I:D51.

48. CHH to Butler Wilson, March 11, 1933; CHH to WFW, April 2, 1933, April 21, 1933; CHH to J. Weston Allen and Butler Wilson, April 3, 1933; WFW to CHH, April 1933, NAACP Papers I:D51.

49. *New York Times*, April 24, 1933, 19; NAACP press release, April 24, 1933; memorandum to Wilkins from WFW, April 26, 1933; NAACP press release, April 26, 1933, NAACP Papers, I:D51.

50. WFW to editors of *Weekly Press*, April 28, 1933; CHH to William Patterson, June 22, 1933, WFW to CHH, June 20, 1933, NAACP Papers, I:D51; report of the secretary, board of directors, July 1933, NAACP Papers, I:A3.

51. Conrad O. Pearson and Cecil McCoy to WFW, February 6, 1933, NAACP Papers, I:D96; Richard Kluger, *Simple Justice* (New York: Vintage Books, 2004), 155.

52. Pearson and McCoy to WFW, February 6, 1933, WFW to Pearson and McCoy, February 8, 1933, March 6, 1933, Pearson and McCoy to WFW, March 19, 1933, WFW to Pearson, March 20, 1933, McCoy to WFW, March 21, 1933, WFW, memorandum re call from Houston, March 22, 1933, William Hastie to WFW, March 22, 1933, NAACP Papers I:D96.

53. Hastie to WFW, March 25, 1933; WFW to McCoy, March 22, 1933; Pearson to WFW, March 31, 1933, NAACP Papers, I:D96.

54. WFW to Arthur Spingarn, April 6, 1933, *Durham (NC) Sun*, editorial, April 7, 1933; Frank Graham to WFW, April 10, 1933, NAACP Papers, I:D96; Ware, *William Hastie*, 31.

55. WFW to McCoy, June 12, 1933, NAACP Papers, I:D96; report of the secretary, June 1933, NAACP Papers, I:A17; WFW to JWJ, June 7, 1933, NAACP Papers, I:C78.

56. William H. Hastie, address at convocation, Virginia Union University, November 13, 1957, William H. Hastie Papers, Harvard Law School.

57. Charles McPherson to WFW, July 12, 1933, NAACP Papers, I:D65; *Birmingham News*, June 29, 1933.

58. CHH to WFW, July 20, 1933, WFW to CHH, July 22, 1933, WFW to Edward Lovett, July 28, 1933, CHH to Robert Moton, July 29, 1933, NAACP Papers, I:D65.

59. Confidential memorandum re *State v. Peterson*, Birmingham, Alabama, September 2, 1933, CHH to WFW, August 8, 1933, CHH to WFW, September 4, 1933, WFW to CHH, September 6, 1933, NAACP Papers, I:D65.

60. Charles Houston et al., memorandum brief for the Attorney General of The United States, "III: The Deprivation of the Rights, Privileges or Immunities Secured to or Protected for the Aforesaid Dan Pippen, Jr. and A.T. Harden by the Constitution and Laws of the United States, was made by Reason of Their Color and Race," October 1933, CHH Papers, MSRC, Box 25.

61. CHH to Stephen T. Early, August 16, 1933, CHH Papers, MSRC, Howard University, Box 25; *Washington Afro-American*, September 2, 1933.

62. CHH to Stephen Early, August 23, 1933, published in *Washington Afro-American*, September 2, 1933; *Washington Afro-American*, August 26, 1933. Houston ended his August 23 letter to Early, noting, "Incidentally, official courtesy would seem to demand that the White House staff omit such language as 'What do you boys want?' when addressing grown men, albeit Negroes. Such discourtesy should be beneath the dignity of the central administration for its own sake."

63. W.E.B. Du Bois et al., "Second Amenia Conference," NAACP Papers I:C229; W.E.B. Du Bois, "Youth and Age at Amenia," *The Crisis*, October 1933, 226.

64. Du Bois, "Youth and Age at Amenia," 226–27; Louis Redding to Roy Wilkins, September 2, 1933; Frances Williams to WFW, August 23, 1933, NAACP Papers, I:C229; CHH, "An Approach to Better Race Relations."

65. Redding to Wilkins, September 2, 1933; Janken, *White*, 177.

66. Information taken from monthly reports of the secretary, 1931–33, NAACP Papers, I:A17; On Flossie Bailey, see James H. Madison, *A Lynching in the Heartland: Race and Memory in America* (New York: Palgrave, 2001), 63–67, 95–96.

67. O.B. Cobb, "The Berwyn School Case," before the twenty-fifth annual conference of the National Association for the Advancement of Colored People, Oklahoma City, OK, June 28, 1934; Mack, "Law and Mass Politics," 53; report of the secretary, May 1934, NAACP Papers, I:A17.

68. Reports of the secretary, May, June, July, October 1932, NAACP Papers, I:A17.

69. Report of the secretary, October 1932.

70. Report of the secretary, July 1932; Hine, *Black Victory*, 144–61.

71. Report of the secretary, March, April, October 1932, September 1934, NAACP Papers, I:A17.

72. Ibid.

73. Report of the secretary, October 1931, March 1932, May 1932, NAACP Papers, I:A17.

74. Roscoe Dunjee, "In Oklahoma," *The Crisis*, September 21, 1933; Roscoe Dunjee, twenty-fifth annual convention of the NAACP, Oklahoma City, 1934, NAACP Papers, I:B10; "U.S. Supreme Court Agrees to Hear Jess Hollins Case," press release, n.d.; Dunjee to WFW, December 19, 1933, NAACP Papers, I:D59.

75. Report of the secretary, June 1933; report of the Department of Branches, December 1933, NAACP Papers, I:A17; Wilkins to Dunjee, March 13, 1933, NAACP Papers, I:D59; NAACP annual convention, Chicago, June 20–July 2, 1933; WFW, "The Chicago Conference," July 6, 1933, NAACP Papers, I:B9.

76. WFW, "The Chicago Conference;" Earl Dickerson, welcome address, June 29, 1933, NAACP, twenty-fourth annual convention, address delivered by CHH before the twenty-fourth annual convention, July 2, 1933, NAACP Papers, I:B9.

77. Patricia Sullivan, *Days of Hope: Race and Democracy in the New Deal Era* (Chapel Hill: Univ. of North Carolina Press, 1996), 88; CHH to WFW, October 17, 1933, NAACP Papers, I:D52.

78. *Pittsburgh Courier*, September 9, 1933; CHH, "Justice for All," December 19, 1934, NAACP Papers, I:D52; *Memorandum Brief for the Attorney General of the U.S. re Prosecution of R.L. Shamlin, Sheriff of Tuscaloosa Co. Alabama under section 52, chapter 3, title 18, U.S. Code*, October 13, 1933, CHH Papers, MSCR, Box 25.

79. *Memorandum Brief for the Attorney General re Prosecution of R.L. Shamlin*, NAACP pamphlet, 46–47; Memorandum Report to the ILD, ACLU, and the NAACP, October 13, 1933, CHH Papers, MSRC, Box 25; CHH to WFW, October 30, 1933, NAACP Papers, I:C64.

80. CHH to WFW, October 16, 1933, WFW to CHH, October 17, 1933, CHH to WFW, October 17, 1933, NAACP Papers, I:D52; memorandum on conference held Sunday, October 22, 1933, at residence of Arthur B. Spingarn, October 23, 1933, NAACP Papers, I:A27; memorandum from Mr. White re long distance telephone conversation with Mr. Charles H. Houston, November 1, 1933, NAACP Papers, I:C64.

81. CHH to Charles McPherson, January 28, 1934, NAACP Papers, I:D52.

82. Charles McPherson to WFW, October 18, 1933; CHH to WFW, January 24, 1934; CHH to John Altman, January 28, 1934; McPherson to WFW, November 3, 1933; CHH to John Altman, November 9, 1933; Altman to WFW, November 14, 1933, CHH to McPherson, January 28, 1934; CHH to WFW, October 30, 1933; memorandum from Mr. White re long distance telephone call with CHH, NAACP Papers, I:D52; *Birmingham Age-Herald*, August 24, 1933.

83. "Richmond Grand Jury Will Include Negroes," *New York Times*, August 10,

1933, 18; Charles H. Houston and Leon A. Ransom, "The Crawford Case: An Experiment in Social Statesmanship," *Nation*, July 4, 1934, 19; McNeil, *Groundwork*, 91.

84. Houston and Ransom, "Crawford Case," 18; McNeil, *Groundwork*, 91–92.

85. Frank Getty, "The Dramatic Leesburg Murder Trial," *Washington Post Magazine*, December 31, 1933, 3, 15; WFW, "George Crawford—Symbol," December 20, 1933, NAACP Papers, I:D52.

86. Getty, "Dramatic Leesburg Murder Trial," 15; Houston and Ransom, "Crawford Case," 18.

87. WFW to the branches, re Crawford case, October 20, 1933, NAACP Papers, I:D52; Helen Broadman and Martha Gruening, "Is the NAACP Retreating?" *Nation*, June 27, 1934; Thomas Young to WFW, February 15, 1934; WFW to Thomas Young, February 20, 1934; Percival Prattis to WFW, September 12, 1934, NAACP Papers, I:D52; "The Crawford Case," *The Crisis*, May 1934; Houston and Ransom, "Crawford Case," 18.

88. Houston and Ransom, "Crawford Case," 18–19.

89. WFW to CHH, December 18, 1933, NAACP Papers I:D52; WFW to Arthur Spingarn, July 8, 1933, NAACP Papers I:C78; WFW to Nathan Margold, May 22, 1934, NAACP Papers I:C196; memorandum from the secretary to the board of directors, October 6, 1934, JWJ Papers, BL/Yale, Box 24.

90. WFW to McPherson, January 9, 1934, John Altman to CHH, April 9, 1934, NAACP Papers I:D65, CHH to WFW, January 24, 1934, NAACP Papers, I:D66; *Memorandum Brief for the Attorney General re Prosecution of R.L. Shamlin*, 47.

91. Robert C. Weaver, interview, April 16, 1992; CHH to WFW, September 13, 1934, November 2, 1934, NAACP Papers, I:C64; CHH to William Patterson, June 22, 1933, CHH Papers, MSRC, Box 26; CHH to J. Alston Atkins, May 15, 1935, NAACP Papers, I:D92.

92. McNeil, *Groundwork*, 84–85; CHH to J. Reuben Sheeler, October 14, 1935, NAACP Papers, I:D96; William H. Hastie, "Toward an Egalitarian Legal Order, 1930–1950," *Annals of the American Academy of Political and Social Science* 407 (May 1973): 26.

93. CHH, "The Need for Negro Lawyers," 51–52; CHH to Sheeler.

Chapter 6: Crossroads: Protest and Politics in the New Deal Era

1. Interview with Robert Weaver, January 13, 1992.

2. WFW to Mother Katherine Drexel, June 3, 1933, NAACP Papers, I:C382; Roy Wilkins to Robert Church, October 4, 1933. When White toured the levee camps in the summer of 1934 with Charles Houston and John P. Davis, they found working conditions, although still deplorable, had improved significantly.

3. Sullivan, *Days of Hope*, 45.

4. Ibid., 46; Interview with Robert Weaver, January 13, 1992; Wilkins to WFW, August 14, 1933, NAACP Papers, I:C78.

5. Wilkins to WFW, August 14, 1933; Wolters, *Negroes and the Great Depression*, 110–13, 124–35; Sullivan, *Days of Hope*, 51–56.

6. Sullivan, *Days of Hope*, 24–25, 44–46.

7. Zangrando, *The NAACP Crusade*, 99, 103–4; *New York Times*, October 19, 1933, 1, December 1, 1933, 4.

8. JWJ to WFW, October 30, 1933, JWJ Papers, BL/Yale, Box 24.

9. Memorandum on conference held at residence of Arthur B. Spingarn, October 23, 1933, NAACP Papers, I:A27; report of the secretary for February 1934 board meeting, NAACP Papers, I:A17; *New York Times*, December 7, 1933, 1, 2; Zangrando, *NAACP Crusade*, 111–12. Du Bois found hope in Roosevelt's forthright statement, commenting, "Roosevelt, with his great radio audience, has declared frankly that lynching is murder. We all knew it, but it is unusual to have a president of the United States admit it," *The Crisis*, January 1934, 20.

10. Janken, *White*, 202–9; Zangrando, *NAACP Crusade*, 110–17; Marion Elizabeth Rodgers, "H.L. Mencken: Courage in a Time of Lynching," *Neiman Reports*, Summer 2006.

11. WFW to JWJ, February 28, 1934, JWJ Papers, BL/Yale, Box 24; Janken, *White*, 203–4; Zangrando, *NAACP Crusade*, 117–18; *Washington Afro-American*, February 24, 1934, 1, 2, 6, 9, March 3, 1934, 9.

12. *Washington Afro-American*, February 24, 1934, 1; *New York Times*, February 21, 1934, 16; NAACP, 1934 annual report, chap. 4, 5; Interview with Robert Weaver, January 19, 1992.

13. Zangrando, *NAACP Crusade*, 118–21; Janken, *White*, 210–12.

14. WFW to Homer Cummings, October 9, 1934; CHH to Homer Cummings, December 10, 1934, CHH telegram to NAACP, December 14, 1934; "Police Arrest NAACP Pickets at National Crime Conference," press release, December 14, 1934; WFW to John Henry Hammond, December 15, 1934; Wilkins to CHH, December 19, 1934; Ralph Bunche to WFW, January 4, 1935, NAACP Papers, I:C230; *Washington Afro-American*, December 22, 1934, 1–2, 10.

15. Lewis, *W.E.B. Du Bois: The Fight for Equality and the American Century*, 316–17.

16. Ibid.; memorandum from the secretary re the NAACP and *The Crisis*, March 12, 1934, NAACP Papers, I:C287.

17. *New York Times*, May 14, 1933, 35; W.E.B. Du Bois, "On Being Ashamed of Oneself: An Essay in Race Pride," *The Crisis*, September 1933, 199–200; Lewis, *W.E.B. Du Bois: The Fight for Equality and the American Century*, 330–31.

18. A.C. MacNeal to WFW, October 20, 1933, NAACP Papers, I:G51; Lewis, *W.E.B. Du Bois: The Fight for Equality and the American Century*, 335; Du Bois, "Segregation," *The Crisis*, January 1934, 20.

19. WFW to Du Bois, January 15, 1934, NAACP Papers, I:C287; Du Bois, "Subsistence Homestead Colonies," *The Crisis*, March 1934, 85.

20. Du Bois, "A Free Forum," *The Crisis*, February 1934, 52; "Segregation in the

North," *The Crisis*, April 1934, 115–16; "Segregation and Self-Respect," *The Crisis*, March 1934, 85.

21. Du Bois, "William Monroe Trotter," *The Crisis*, May 1934, 134; *Washington Afro-American*, April 14, 1934; Du Bois, "Integration," *The Crisis*, April 1934, 117.

22. WFW, "Segregation—a Symposium," *The Crisis*, March 1934, 80–81; Du Bois to WFW, January 17, 1934, NAACP Papers I:C287; Du Bois, "Segregation in the North," *The Crisis*, April 1934, 115.

23. G.A. Steward to WFW, February 23, 1934; William Lloyd Imes to board of directors, June 11, 1934; Harry E. Davis to board of directors, June 9, 1934, Carl Murphy to board of directors, May 17, 1934; William H. Hastie, *New Negro Opinion* (Washington, D.C.), January 25, 1934; "Some [press] opinions regarding D.B.'s position," n.d., NAACP Papers, I:C287.

24. Harry Smith to Du Bois, July 2, 1934; WFW to James McClendon, May 7, 1934, I:C287; Du Bois, "The Board of Directors on Segregation," *The Crisis*, May 1934, 195; Du Bois to the board of directors, June 1, 1934, NAACP Papers, I:C287.

25. Resolution, board of directors, June 11, 1934, WFW to Joel Spingarn, June 12, 1934, Du Bois to the board of directors, June 26, 1934, resolution, board meeting, July 9, 1934, NAACP Papers, I:C287; *Washington Afro-American*, June 23, 1934, 1; Wolters, *Negroes and the Great Depression*, 291–92.

26. Janken, *White*, 191–93; WFW, address to annual convention, Baltimore, July 1936, NAACP Papers, I:B13.

27. "Future Plan and Program of the NAACP" [1935], NAACP Papers I:B11; Harry E. Davis to WFW, March 20, 1934, WFW to Davis, March 23, 1934, WFW to Sen. James Couzens, April 11, 1934, NAACP Papers, I:C287; report of the secretary to the board of directors, July 1935, 2, NAACP Papers, I:A18; Wolters, *Negroes and the Great Depression*, 183–87, 310–16. Other members of the Committee on Future Planning included Mary White Ovington and James Weldon Johnson.

28. *New York Times*, April 17, 1935, 1, April 22, 1935,1, May 2, 1935, 1; report of the secretary to the board of directors on the Costigan-Wagner antilynching bill, NAACP Papers, I:A18.

29. Nancy Weiss, *Farewell to the Party of Lincoln: Black Politics in the Age of FDR* (Princeton, NJ: Princeton Univ. Press, 1983), 157–68.

30. CHH, memorandum for the Joint Committee of the NAACP and the American Fund for Public Service, October 26, 1934; CHH, memorandum for the Joint Committee, November 14, 1935, NAACP Papers I:C199, CHH, memorandum to Ransom, Leeky, Cowan, Redmond, and Marshall, September 17, 1936, NAACP/mf p2 r3 f592.

31. CHH, memorandum for Joint Committee, October 26, 1934; CHH, memorandum for Joint Committee, November 14, 1935; CHH to Thurgood Marshall, September 17, 1935, NAACP/mf, p2 r3.

32. Minutes, board of directors, November 13, 1934, NAACP Papers, I:A3; CHH to WFW, November 1, 2, 4, and 7, 1934; Itinerary of Charles H. Houston and Edward P. Lovett, November 13–December 10, 1934, NAACP Papers, I:C64.

33. CHH to WFW, September 14, 1933, NAACP Papers I:D66; report of meeting of Joint Committee . . . held at residence of Arthur B. Spingarn, March 21, 1935, NAACP Papers, I:C199; CHH to WFW, May 12, 1935, NAACP Papers, I:D93; WFW to CHH, December 11, 1934, NAACP Papers, I:C230; *Educational Inequalities in South Carolina*, film, by Charles Houston and Edward Lovett (1935).

34. WFW to Daisy Lampkin, January 1, 1933, NAACP Papers, I:C78; Juanita Jackson to WFW, December 7, 1933, NAACP Papers, I:G85; J.W. Haywood Jr. to CHH, October 6, 1934, NAACP Papers, I:D93; CHH to TM, December 23, 1935 NAACP/mf p2 r3.

35. WFW to Juanita Jackson, November 29, 1933, Juanita Jackson to WFW, December 7, 1933, WFW to Juanita Jackson, December 13, 1933, WFW to Charles Trigg, January 26, 1934, Juanita Jackson to WFW, February 7, 1934, WFW to Juanita Jackson, February 8, 1934, Juanita Jackson to WFW, May 29, 1934, Wilkins to Juanita Jackson, June 5, 1934, NAACP Papers, I:G35; Thurgood Marshall to CHH, September 21, 1934, I:D93; TM to CHH, December 18, 1934, NAACP Papers, I:C196.

36. Thurgood Marshall, memorandum re University of Maryland mandamus case, March 18, 1935, NAACP "University of Maryland Sued by Student Who Would Enter Law School," press release, April 20, 1935; conference notes, Thurgood Marshall, Edward P. Lovett, Charles H. Houston, Baltimore, May 10, 1935; CHH, memorandum for Joint Committee, May 11, 1935; TM, memo, May 25, 1935; NAACP, "Maryland U Color Bar Smashed by NAACP Lawyers," press release, June 21, 1935; CHH to Isadore Polier, July 3, 1935, NAACP Papers, I:D93.

37. Alain Locke to CHH, June 21, 1935, Roger Baldwin to CHH, June 20, 1935, CHH to Roy Wilkins, June 20, 1935, CHH to Carl Murphy, June 2, 1935, CHH to P.B. Young Jr., May 15, 1935, CHH to Theodore Berry, May 3, 1935, NAACP Papers, I:D93; CHH, memorandum for Joint Committee, July 29, 1935, 4, NAACP Papers, I:D199.

38. Photo of Murray and Marshall reprinted in *The Crisis*, December 1935, 364; CHH to TM, September 21, 1935, September 30, 1935, January 3, 1936; CHH to Donald G. Murray, March 5, 1936, NAACP/mf p2 r3; CHH memorandum to Juanita Jackson, Thurgood Marshall, Leon Ransom, William Hastie, Roy Wilkins, December 24, 1935, CHH, memorandum for Joint Committee, January 11, 1936, NAACP Papers, I:C199.

39. CHH to TM, September 21, 1935; TM to CHH, September 19, 1935, NAACP Papers, I:D93. On Marshall's work in Maryland, see TM to CHH, May 7, 1935, May 14, 1935, May 29, 1935, NAACP Papers, I:D93; Tushnet, *NAACP Legal Strategy*, 59–69.

40. CHH, memorandum for Joint Committee, November 14, 1935, NAACP Papers, I:C199; CHH, memorandum to Joint Committee, January 11, 1936, CHH, memorandum for Joint Committee, July 24, 1936, NAACP Papers, I:C200; Tushnet, *NAACP's Legal Strategy*, 54.

41. *New York Times*, September 1, 1935, E6; CHH, memorandum for Joint Com-

mittee, November 14, 1935; CHH, memorandum for Joint Committee, November 14, 1935, NAACP Papers, I:C199; statement re interview with Charles H. Houston, July 19, 1935, NAACP Papers, I:C196.

42. CHH to TM, September 17, 1935; CHH, memorandum for Joint Committee, November 14, 1935; CHH, memorandum for Joint Committee, July 24, 1936; CHH, memorandum for Joint Committee, January 11, 1936; CHH, memorandum to the Negro press, January 17, 1936; Author interview with John Hope Franklin, February 22, 2005.

43. CHH, memorandum for Joint Committee, July 24, 1936, NAACP Papers, I:C200.

44. CHH to Robert W. Dunn, May 27, 1935, NAACP Papers, I:D93; CHH, memorandum for Joint Committee, January 11, 1936, NAACP Papers, I:C200; Thomas Dabney to WFW, December 20, 1933, NAACP Papers, I:C293; Larissa M. Smith, "Civil Rights Vanguard: Black Attorneys and the NAACP in Virginia," in Peter F. Lau, ed., *From the Grassroots to the Supreme Court:* Brown v. Board of Education *and American Democracy* (Durham, NC: Duke Univ. Press, 2004), 132–35.

45. CHH to Budget Committee, November 3, 1935, NAACP Papers; CHH to Eugene West, October 4, 1935, CHH to W.P. Milner, October 4, 1935, October 14, 1935, October 15, 1935, Milner to CHH, October 14, 1935, November 8, 1935, NAACP Papers, I:G208.

46. CHH, memorandum to the Negro press, January 17, 1936; W.E.B. Du Bois, "Federal Action Programs and Community Action in the South," *Social Forces, 1940–41*, 377; CHH, "Don't Shout Too Soon," *The Crisis*, March 1936, 91.

47. Weiss, *Farewell to the Party of Lincoln*, 64; CHH, "An Approach to Better Race Relations"; report of the secretary, December 1935, NAACP Papers, I:A18.

48. CHH to WFW, May 23, 1935, NAACP Papers, I:C64; report of the secretary, October 1935, December 1935, NAACP Papers, IA:18; minutes, board of directors, December 9, 1935, NAACP Papers, I:A3.

49. Hine, *Black Victory*, 193–209; Jack Atkins to CHH, May 12, 1935, CHH to Atkins, May 15, 1935, NAACP Papers, I:D92; Michael Gillette, "The NAACP in Texas, 1937–1957" (PhD diss., University of Texas, 1984), 5–8.

50. CHH, "Educational Inequalities Must Go!" *The Crisis*, October 1935, 300.

51. Cheryl Lynn Greenburg, *"Or Does It Explode?" Black Harlem in the Great Depression* (New York: Oxford Univ. Press, 1991), 66.

52. Ibid., 3–6; Hubert Delany, "Unemployment and Relief," speech to the twenty-sixth annual convention of the NAACP, St. Louis, MO., June 26, 1935, NAACP Papers, I:B11.

53. August Meier and Elliott Rudwick, "The Origins of Nonviolent Direct Action in Afro-American Protest: A Note on Historical Discontinuities," in Meier and Rudwick, *Along the Color Line*, 314–39; Kimberly Phillips, *Alabama North: African American Migrants, Community, and Working Class Activism in Cleveland, 1915–1945* (Urbana: Univ. of Illinois Press, 1999), 190–225.

54. Meier and Rudwick, "Origins of Nonviolent Direct Action," 331–32; William

Pickens to WFW, May 20, 1935, L.C. Blount to WFW, March 22, 1935, NAACP Papers, I:G97; August Meier and Elliott Rudwick, *Black Detroit and the Rise of the UAW* (New York: Oxford Univ. Press, 1979), 16–21; Beth Bates, "A Tale of Two Cities: Revitalizing the NAACP in Chicago and Detroit during the 1930s," paper presented at the annual meeting of the Organization of American Historians, St. Louis, MO., April 1, 2000, 6–11; Christopher Reed, *The Chicago NAACP and the Rise of Black Professional Leadership* (Bloomington: Indiana Univ. Press, 1997), 96–108; Phillips, *Alabama North*, 218–29; John Hope Franklin, *Mirror to America: The Autobiography of John Hope Franklin* (New York: Farrar, Straus & Giroux, 2005), 66; minutes, board of directors, June 1937, NAACP Papers, I:A3.

55. CHH to Roy Wilkins, May 22, 1935, NAACP Papers, I:C64; from the program of the national conference held under the auspices of the Joint Committee on National Recovery, Social Science Division, Howard University, May 18–20, 1935 (Houston's comments written on cover), NAACP Papers, I:C64; main papers read at conference were published in the *Journal of Negro Education*, January 1936; Wolters, *Negroes and the Great Depression*, 353–58.

56. John P. Davis to WFW, December 23, 1935; WFW to Carl Murphy, December 28, 1935; Wilkins to John P. Davis, January 21, 1936; Roy Wilkins to CHH, February 15, 1936; Wilkins, memorandum to the board of directors on the NNC, March 9, 1936, NAACP Papers, I:C383; CHH memorandum to WFW, February 25, 1936; Wolters, *Negroes and the Great Depression*, 333–35, 359–66; Beth Tompkins Bates, "A New Crowd Challenges to the Agenda of the Old Guard in the NAACP," *American Historical Review* 102 (April 1997): 360–70.

57. CHH to WFW, May 23, 1935; CHH to WFW, November 5, 1934, NAACP Papers, I:C64; CHH to WFW, February 9, February 23, 1935, Wolters, *Negroes and the Great Depression*, 340.

58. CHH to Roy Wilkins, May 22, 1935, NAACP Papers, I:C64.

59. Roy Wilkins to Joel Spingarn, May 23, 1935; Wilkins to WFW, July 17, 1935, NAACP Papers, I:B11.

60. "Speakers who's who" at the twenty-sixth annual conference of the NAACP, St. Louis, MO, June 25–30, 1935, notes for press release on conference, n.d., CHH to officers and delegates of twenty-sixth annual conference, June 24, 1935, NAACP Papers I:B11; report of the secretary for July 1935, NAACP Papers, I:A10.

61. CHH, Statement of the Legal Activities of the NAACP, 1935 annual conference, St. Louis, MO, NAACP Papers, I:B11; McNeil, *Groundwork*, 121–22;

62. CHH to officers and delegates of twenty-sixth annual conference, St. Louis, MO, June 24, 1935, NAACP Papers, I:B11.

63. Notes for press release, June 25, 1935; notes for press release, n.d.; J.L. LeFlore, "Suggestions Regarding Matters Which We Think Should Be Included in the Resolutions of the St. Louis Conference," NAACP Papers, I:B11; NAACP conference notes, Baltimore, n.d., NAACP Papers, I:B13.

64. *Washington Tribune*, July 7, 1936; WFW, address before the twenty-seventh annual convention of the NAACP, Baltimore, MD, July 5, 1936; *Amsterdam News*, July

4, 1936, NAACP Papers, I:B13; Weiss, *Farewell to the Party of Lincoln*, 184–86.

65. *Baltimore Evening Sun*, June 30, 1936.

66. WFW, address before the twenty-seventh annual convention; report of resolutions committee of twenty-seventh annual convention; *Chicago Defender*, July 1, 1936.

67. Weiss, *Farewell to the Party of Lincoln*, 181–90.

68. Ibid., 192–203, 212; Sullivan, *Days of Hope*, 92–93.

69. Weiss, *Farewell to the Party of Lincoln*, 205–8.

70. Ibid., 209–14; Sullivan, *Days of Hope*, 144.

71. Robert C. Weaver, "The Negro and the Federal Government," address at the twenty-eighth NAACP annual convention, Detroit, MI, June 30, 1937, NAACP Papers, I:B14.

72. Sullivan, *Days of Hope*, 61–67

73. CHH to officers and delegates of the twenty-sixth annual convention, St. Louis, MO, June 24, 1935, 5.

74. Weiss, *Farewell to the Party of Lincoln*, 241–49; *Baltimore Afro-American*, July 4, 1936; CHH, memorandum to the executive staff, March 2, 1938, NAACP Papers.

75. CHH to TM, September 17, 1936; TM to CHH, September 19, 1936; CHH to Joint Committee of the NAACP and the American Fund for Public Service, September 28, 1936; TM to WFW, October 6, 1936, NAACP/mf p2 r3 f591–608.

76. CHH to WFW, March 9, 1936, NAACP Papers, I:C197; CHH to Arthur Spingarn, November 5, 1937; CHH to Z. Alexander Looby, June 10, 1937, NAACP Legal Committee, December 3, 1937, NAACP Papers, I:A27; minutes, board of directors, November 14, 1938, January 3, 1939, June 12, 1939, NAACP Papers, I:A3.

77. Thurgood Marshall, interviewed by Richard Kluger, December 12, 1973, *Brown v. Board* Collection, Yale University Libraries; J.L. LeFlore, report to twenty-seventh annual convention, Baltimore, MD, July 1936, NAACP Papers, I:B13; CHH, "A Call to Conference" to NAACP branches in Alabama, Florida, Louisiana, and Mississippi, April 13, 1936; presidents and secretaries of branches in Southern Regional Conference, February 1937, NAACP Papers, I:G1.

78. Report on National Education Program to twenty-eight NAACP annual convention, June 24, 1937, Detroit, NAACP Papers, I:B13.

79. CHH to TM, September 19, 1936; report of the budget committee, December 3, 1937, NAACP Papers, I:A27; finance committee, plan of campaign (1938), minutes of finance committee meeting, October 25, 1938, NAACP Papers, I:A27.

80. CHH to WFW, October 15, 1938; CHH to Roger Baldwin, October 16, 1938; CHH to Osmond Fraenkel, October 16, 1938; WFW to CHH, October 17, 1938; WFW to Roger Baldwin, October 17, 1938; Roger Baldwin to WFW, October 28, 1937; WFW to Roger Baldwin, October 29, 1938, NAACP Papers, II:L1.

81. Minutes, board of directors, December 1938, NAACP Papers, I:A3; *Baltimore Afro-American*, November 12, 1938, 1; Carter, *A Matter of Law*, 26.

82. *New York Times*, December 13, 1938, 1; Morris Ernst to WFW, December 16,

1938, NAACP Papers, II:L1; Pauli Murray, *Song in a Weary Throat: An American Pilgrimage* (New York: Harper & Row, 1987), 115.

83. *New York Times*, December 13, 1938, 10; Virginius Dabney, "South Put in a Quandary," *New York Times*, December 18, 1938, 84; Tushnet, *NAACP Legal Strategy*, 74–77.

84. Minutes, board of directors, October 9, 1939, NAACP/mf p1 r2; McNeil, *Groundwork*, 149–52; Mark Tushnet, *Making Civil Rights Law: Thurgood Marshall and the Supreme Court* (New York: Oxford Univ. Press, 1994), 27.

85. Janken, *White*, 246–47; *Montgomery Advertiser*, February 28, 1939; CHH to WFW and Hubert Delaney, March 4, 1939; CHH to Sen. Robert LaFollette, March 5, 1939, NAACP Papers, II:L1; *Times Herald*, March 7, 1939.

86. WFW to Godfrey L. Cabot, March 31, 1939, NAACP/mf p2A r13 f425; WFW to Marian Anderson, April 4, 1939, NAACP Papers, II:L1; Janken, *White*, 247–48; Ernest Lindley, "Voice from the Temple," *Washington Post*, April 12, 1939.

87. *Baltimore Afro-American*, April 15, 1939, 1, 9; Ralph Matthews, "National Anthem Rings True for Easter Throng," *Baltimore Afro-American*, April 15, 1939, 1; Lindley, "Voice from the Temple;" Interview with Robert L. Carter, September 27, 2007.

88. Matthews, "National Anthem."

Chapter 7: In the Shadow of War: Battlefields for Freedom

1. WFW to William Callahan, July 1, 1940, NAACP Papers, II:A406.

2. Annie Williams, deposition, September 11, 1940, NAACP Papers, II:A406; "Lynch Victim Widow Leaves for New York," *Memphis Press-Scimitar*, July 3, 1940, NAACP Papers, II:B101; handwritten notes [1940] on cases of Everett [sic] Williams and Elisha Davis, NAACP Papers, II:B101.

3. Application for charter of Brownsville branch, submitted March 12, 1939; approved June 12, 1939, NAACP Papers, I:G198; Elisha Davis to John LeFlore, June 5, 1940; J. Emmet Ballard to John LeFlore, June 11, 1940, O.B. Taylor to secretary, NAACP, June 29, 1940, Milmon Mitchell to WFW, June 16, 1940, NAACP Papers, II:B101.

4. O.B. Taylor to secretary, NAACP, June 29, 1940; "More Negroes Disappear and Feeling Grows," *Memphis Press-Scimitar*, June 28, 1940, 10; Mitchell to WFW, June 16, 1940; Brownsville, Tennessee, Investigation, June 27, 1940, NAACP Papers, II:B101; Statement of Facts in the Brownsville, Tennessee, case, NAACP Papers, II:A406.

5. John LeFlore to WFW, June 7, 1940; LeFlore to William Pickens, June 13, 1940; Mitchell to WFW, June 16, 1940; Cassandra Maxwell to Mitchell, June 16, 1940; remarks by Rev. Buster Walker, thirty-first annual conference of the NAACP, Phildelphia, June 21, 1940; Thurgood Marshall telegram to Gov. Prentice Cooper, June 24, 1940, NAACP Papers, II:B101; excerpts from NAACP annual report for 1940, chap. 2, Anti-lynching bill, NAACP Papers, II:A406.

6. *Pittsburgh Courier*, editorial, August 10, 1940.

7. TM to Robert Davis, June 27, 1940, NAACP Papers, II:B101; O. John Rogge to WFW, July 10, 1940, NAACP Papers, II:A406; Robert K. Carr, *Federal Protection of Civil Rights: Quest for a Sword* (Ithaca, NY: Cornell Univ. Press, 1947), 1.

8. WFW to Wilkins, telegram, June 28, 1940; WFW to William Hastie, July 1, 1940, I.L. Newman to WFW, July 9, 1940, NAACP Papers, II:B101; WFW to William McClanahan, July 1, 1940; WFW to Rogge, July 1, 1940; Wilkins to FDR, July 19, 1940, NAACP Papers, II:A406.

9. Elisha Davis to WFW, June 29, 1940, August 19, 1940, NAACP Papers, II:A406; TM to branch officers, July 31, 1940, NAACP Papers, II:B101.

10. Mitchell to WFW, July 1, 1940, July 17, 1940; Mitchell to TM, August 16, 1940; Mitchell to WFW, October 9, 1940, NAACP Papers, II:B101.

11. TM to Wilkins, August 27, 1940; TM to Rogge, October 9, 1940, NAACP Papers, II:B101; TM to Annie Williams, September 3, 1940; Annie Williams, affidavit, September 11, 1940; TM to Rogge, October 29, 1940, TM to Annie Williams, December 1, 1941; TM, memorandum re interview with Annie Williams Boone . . . concerning . . . "property deal," December 12, 1941; TM, memoranda re Brownsville, Tennessee, December 9, 1941, December 11, 1941, Frank Reeves to Elisha Davis, December 11, 1941, NAACP Papers, II:A406.

12. TM to Wendell Berge, January 30, 1942, TM to Francis Biddle, January 30, 1942; TM to Mitchell, January 31, 1942; Mitchell to Francis Biddle, February 16, 1942; Mitchell to TM, February 17, 1942, TM to Mitchell, March 17, 1942, TM To Elisha Davis, September 4, 1942, NAACP Papers, II:A406.

13. Wendell Berge to TM, February 11, 1942, Mitchell to TM, February 17, 1942, NAACP Papers, II:A406; WFW to Frank Smith, September 19, 1940, NAACP Papers, II:B101.

14. Madison Jones to WFW, November 14, 1941, NAACP Papers, II:A588.

15. Sullivan, *Days of Hope*, 144–45.

16. Thurgood Marshall, "Attacking the White Primary," June 20, 1940, NAACP thirty-first annual conference, NAACP Papers, II:A28.

17. Ibid. State party rule barred blacks from voting in the Democratic primary in all southern states with the exception of North Carolina, Tennessee, and Florida; in Virginia the state party rule remained on the books, but had been nullified by a lower federal court ruling. Nevertheless, some counties in each of these states barred blacks from voting in the Democratic primary. V.O. Key, *Southern Politics in State and Nation* (New York: Knopf, 1949), 620.

18. Gillette, "The Rise of the NAACP in Texas," 8–10; Merline Pitre, *In Struggle Against Jim Crow: Lulu White and the NAACP, 1900–1957* (College Station: Texas A&M Univ. Press, 1999), 32–34.

19. Gillette, "The Rise of the NAACP in Texas," 16–17; Kluger, *Simple Justice*, 220–21; Caroline Emmons, "Flame of Resistance: The NAACP in Florida, 1910–1960" (PhD diss. Florida State University, 1998), 64–65.

20. Gillette, "The Rise of the NAACP in Texas," 16–26; Marshall, "Attacking the White Primary."

21. Tushnet, *NAACP Legal Strategy*, 59–61, 77–81.

22. Larissa Smith, "A Civil Rights Vanguard: Black Attorneys and the NAACP in Virginia," 135–40.

23. Ibid., 140–42.

24. McNeil, *Groundwork*, 148–71; Tushnet, *NAACP Legal Strategy*, 47–48.

25. Wilkins to WFW, April 2, 1939, Henry Espy telegram to WFW, April 19, 1939, NAACP Papers, I:D95; CHH to Sidney Redmond, re Wm. Patterson's account of seeing Gaines in Chicago, October 23, 1939, S.W. Canada to Lucille Bluford, January 19, 1939, CHH to Bluford, January 27, 1939; TM to CHH, September 26, 1941, NAACP Papers, II:L41.

26. CHH to Bluford and Redmond, September 12, 1939, NAACP Papers, II:L41.

27. CHH, memorandum to NAACP re Bluford case, June 4, 1940, NAACP Papers, II:B201.

28. CHH, memorandum to Walter White, Roy Wilkins, and Thurgood Marshall, February 12, 1940, NAACP Papers, II:B201.

29. Dorothy Davis to Roy Wilkins, February 11, 1939 (*sic*; trial was February 1940); letter includes draft of her story for the *Kansas City Call*; "Missouri Now Battleground on Negro Issue," *Norfolk Virginia Pilot*, April 19, 1942, IV, 1.

30. "Missouri U. Cancels Journalism Course to Bar Race Students," NAACP press release, March 27, 1942; Bluford to CHH, March 31, 1942; CHH to Bluford, April 26, 1942; Harold Wilkie to Bluford, May 1, 1942; CHH, memorandum for the office: Walter, Roy, Thurgood, May 6, 1942; WFW to TM, April 17, 1942, WFW to TM, April 17, 1942; memorandum to Mr. White from Robert L. Carter, August 1, 1946, NAACP Papers, II:B202.

31. Janken, *White*, 261; E. Frederic Morrow to William Carr, December 4, 1940, NAACP Papers, II:A592; "The Armed Forces," 1941 annual report, NAACP Papers, II:A59.

32. Janken, *White*, 250–54; John H. Bracey and August Meier, "Allies or Adversaries? The NAACP, A. Philip Randolph and the 1941 March on Washington," *Georgia Historical Quarterly* 125 (Spring 1991): 3–7.

33. Bracey and Meier, "Allies or Adversaries?" 7–8.

34. Ibid., 8–15; Janken, *White*, 256–57.

35. Bracey and Meier, "Allies or Adversaries?" 15–16; A. Philip Randolph, "Employment in Defense Industries," address delivered before the thirty-second annual convention of the NAACP, Houston, TX, June 25, 1941, NAACP/mf p1 r10 f1201.

36. WFW, address delivered before the thirty-second annual convention of the NAACP, Houston, TX, June 27, 1941, NAACP/mf p1 r10, f1260; Janken, *White*, 261.

37. Meier and Rudwick, *Black Detroit and the Rise of the UAW*, 3–33.

38. Ibid., 34–78.

39. Ibid., 78–98.

40. Ibid., 98–107; WFW to Daisy Lampkin, April 12, 1941, Detroit youth files, NAACP Papers; Horace Cayton, "A Strategy for Negro Labor," speech to the 1941 NAACP annual convention, Houston, TX, June 24, 1941, NAACP/mf p1 r10 f1190–1204.

41. Secretary's report for annual meeting, January 5, 1942, NAACP Papers, II:A59; Ella J. Baker, script used on NAACP radio hour, February 8, 1943, NAACP Papers, II:A573.

42. Wilkins to WFW, September 25, 1941; WFW to Wilkins, September 27, 1941, NAACP/mf p 17 r29 f186–92. White notes that he had offers from Fiorello La Guardia and that Mark Ethridge asked whether he would consider a job with the FEPC for an annual salary of $9,000; White was then earning $5,000. White also writes that Thurgood Marshall had been recommended by William Hastie for a position with the FEPC, paying $5,600; he was then earning $3,240 with the NAACP.

43. Madison Jones to WFW, May 18, 1940; press release, October 18, 1940, NAACP Papers, II:A588; EJB to WFW, September 24, 1938, NAACP Papers, II:A572; Wilkins to Daisy Lampkin, November 2, 1940, NAACP/mf p17 r9 f77; Randall Tyus to WFW, June 9, 1941, NAACP Papers, II:A590.

44. Coordinator of branches (E. Frederic Morrow) memorandum to the Committee on Administration, August 18, 1941: Forwards report signed by Daisy E. Lampkin, Ella J. Baker, Madison S. Jones, E. Frederic Morrow, NAACP Papers, II:A592; WFW to Madison Jones, February 4, 1941, NAACP Papers, II:A588; Randall Tyus to WFW, June 9, 1941; WFW to E. Frederic Morrow, July 17, 1941, A. Philip Randolph to WFW, July 24, 1941, Wilkins to WFW, July 25, 1941, NAACP Papers, II:A599. Wilkins's correspondence with Morrow emphasizes that money raised is the measure of success in the field.

45. E. Frederic Morrow to WFW, July 30, 1941: notes he and Ella Baker are working on the report; report on branch work, signed by Daisy Lampkin, Ella J. Baker, Madison S. Jones, and E. Frederic Morrow, submitted by Morrow to the Committee on Administration, August 18, 1941, NAACP Papers, II:A592.

46. Janken, *White*, 265; E. Frederic Morrow to WFW, memorandum, August 21, 1941; report of the coordinator of branches, September 1941 board meeting, August 25, 1941, NAACP Papers, II:A592; WFW, memorandum to the board of directors, January 26, 1942, NAACP Papers, II:A127.

47. Barbara Ransby, *Ella Baker and the Black Freedom Movement* (Chapel Hill: Univ. of North Carolina Press, 2003), 103–13; EJB, "Experience Sheet," NAACP Papers, II:A572; EJB, "Developing Community Leadership," in Gerda Lerner, ed., *Black Women in America* (New York: Vintage Books, 1973), 347.

48. EJB to WFW, September 24, 1938, NAACP Papers, II:A572; Wilkins to Daisy Lampkin, November 2, 1940; Daisy Lampkin to WFW, December 30, 1940, February 1, 1940, NAACP/mf p17 r9 f74, 100, 126.

49. EJB to Wilkins, March 20, 1941, April 10, 1941, NAACP Papers, II:A572; E. Frederic Morrow to Jerry Gilliam, September 22, 1941, NAACP Papers, II:C307;

Ransby, *Ella Baker*, 115.

50. EJB, notes on Houston convention, July 15, 1941, NAACP Papers, II:A572; EJB, conducting membership campaigns, thirty-third annual convention, Los Angeles, 1942, NAACP/mf p1 r11 f201–3.

51. EJB to Lucille Black, received March 28, 1942; EJB to WFW, December 3, 1942, NAACP Papers, II:A572.

52. EJB to Lucille Black, November 20, 1942, NAACP Papers, II:C307; EJB to Roy Wilkins, March 11, 1942, EJB to Lucille Black, March 11, 1942, NAACP Papers, II:A572.

53. Madison Jones to EJB, April 10, 1942; EJB to Madison Jones, April 20, 1942; Wilkins to Madison Jones, November 11, 1941, December 1, 1941, NAACP Papers, II:A588.

54. Frank Turner, inventory of Madison Jones's furniture, July 9, 1941; WFW to Jones, February 4, 1941; Madison Jones to WFW, May 8, 1941, Madison Jones to Wilkins, November 25, 1941, NAACP Papers, II:A588.

55. Madison Jones to Wilkins, November 14, 1941, November 19, 1941, November 27, 1941, December 4, 1941, December 10, 1941; Madison Jones to WFW, November 29, 1941, December 2, 1941, NAACP Papers, II:A588; Robert J. Norrell, *Reaping the Whirlwind: The Civil Rights Movement in Tuskegee* (New York: Knopf, 1985) 44–45.

56. E. Frederic Morrow, "Westward Look—the Land Is Bright!" (1942), typed manuscript, NAACP Papers, II:A593; Madison Jones to WFW, July 21, 1942, NAACP Papers, I:A77; TM to Berlinda Davison, February 18, 1944, NAACP/mf p13C r1 f90.

57. Ware, *William Hastie*, 107–9.

58. "Negroes in the Armed Forces," *New Republic*, October 18, 1943, 541–44; NAACP, "The Armed Forces," annual report, 1941, NAACP Papers, II:A59; Merl E. Reed, *Seedtime for the Modern Civil Rights Movement: The President's Fair Employment Practices Committee, 1941–46* (Baton Rouge: Louisiana State Univ. Press, 1991), 11; John Hope Franklin and Alfred A. Moss Jr., *From Slavery to Freedom* (New York: McGraw Hill, 1994), 438.

59. James Baldwin, *Notes of a Native Son* (Boston: Beacon, 1955), 101; NAACP, "The Armed Forces," annual report, 1941, NAACP Papers, II:A59.

60. Adam Fairclough, *Race and Democracy: The Civil Rights Struggle in Louisiana, 1915–1972* (Athens: Univ. of Georgia Press, 1995), 75–76, 78; Robert A. Hill, ed., *FBI's RACON: Racial Conditions in the United States During World War II* (Boston: Northeastern Univ. Press, 1995), 326; Madison Jones to Walter White, memorandum, December 21, 1942, II:A588; NAACP "The Armed Forces," annual report, 1944, NAACP Papers, II:A59.

61. Madison Jones to Walter White, memorandum, December 21, 1942.

62. "Negroes in the Armed Forces," *New Republic*, October 15, 1943, 543; Harvard Sitkoff, "Racial Militancy and Interracial Violence in the Second World War, *Journal of American History* 58 (December 1971): 668–70; Ware, *William Hastie*, 116; Bruce

Nelson, "Organized Labor and the Struggle for Black Equality in Mobile During World War II," *Journal of American History* 80 (December 1993): 967.

63. Ware, *William Hastie*, 97–130; Elting E. Morison, *Turmoil and Tradition: A Study in the Life and Times of Henry L. Stimson* (Boston: Houghton Mifflin, 1960), 554–55.

64. J. Edgar Hoover to Special Agents in Charge, June 22, 1942, reprinted in Hill, ed., *The FBI's RACON*, 622–24; Sitkoff, "Racial Militancy," 669–71; Sullivan, *Days of Hope*, 162–63, 166–67.

65. Legal Department reports, 1941–45, NAACP Papers, II:B97.

66. A.P. Tureaud to William Hastie, August 12, 1942, "3 Soldiers Convicted on 'Rape' Charge in Louisiana Court," press release, August 14, 1942, TM to William Hastie, September 9, 1942, TM to Truman Gibson, August 3, 1943, TM to James V. Bennett, August 1, 1944, NAACP/mf p9B r16 f248, 257, 328, 715, 806; Fairclough, *Race and Democracy*, 78.

67. Robert L. Allen, *The Port Chicago Mutiny* (New York: Warner Books, 1989), 56–66; *Chicago Defender*, September 23, 1944, 1.

68. Walter White to Mr. Marshall, memorandum, October 3, 1944; "Race, Not Mutiny Is Issue in Trial of 50 Negro Seamen," press release, October 13, 1944, TM to James V. Forrestal, October 19, 1944, Forrestal to TM, November 17, 1944, TM to Forrestal, July 13, 1944, NAACP Papers, II:A637.

69. TM to Forrestal, July 13, 1944; Allen, *Port Chicago Mutiny*, 132–35; TM to Forrestal (rough draft), November 14, 1945, NAACP Papers, II:A637; outline of report of the secretary, 1945, NAACP Papers, II:A60; annual legal report, 1945, 15–16, NAACP Papers, I:B97.

70. Reed, *Seedtime for the Modern Civil Rights Movement*, 1–17, 148–49, 345–57.

71. Ibid., 267–84, 304–6, 353.

72. Joseph James, Report on Aux. Situation with Reference to Int. Brotherhood of Boilermakers, Local #6 and Negro Workers of Marinship Corp, Bethlehem, Western Pipe & Steel (July 1942–January 1944), NAACP/mf p 13C r1 f121; TM to Berlinda Davison, February 18, 1944; TM to Joseph James, February 29, 1944; James to TM, March 13, 1944, TM to James, March 22, 1944, James to TM, May 5, 1944; TM to James, May 15, 1944, TM to WFW, July 5, 1944; [George] Anderson and [Herbert] Resner to TM, telegram, January 2, 1945, NAACP/mf p13C r1 f190–217; Reed, *Seedtime for the Modern Civil Rights Movement*, 285–91.

73. McNeil, *Groundwork*, 158–70.

74. CHH, letter to the editor, *New York Herald Tribune*, April 13, 1945.

75. McNeil, *Groundwork*, 170; Bracey and Meier, "Allies or Adversaries?" 3; J.A. Wechsler, "Pigeonhole for Negro Equality," *Nation*, January 23, 1943, 121–22; Reed, *Seedtime for the Modern Civil Rights Movement*, 27, 90–105.

76. Reed, *Seedtime for the Modern Civil Rights Movement*, 66–76, 117–21; Sullivan, *Days of Hope*, 157–58; Nelson, "Organized Labor and the Struggle for Black Equality," 952, 978–82.

77. Meier and Rudwick, *Black Detroit*, 109–73.

78. Ibid., 192–206; NAACP, *What Caused the Detroit Race Riot*, preface, July 1943, NAACP Papers, II:A505.

79. Thurgood Marshall, "Activities of Police During the Riots June 21 and 22, 1943," in *What Caused the Detroit Race Riot*, 29–35.

80. Ibid., 33; Meier and Rudwick, *Black Detroit*, 195–97; Wilkins to TM, August 27, 1943, NAACP Papers, II:A593.

81. Walter White, "Behind the Harlem Riot," *New Republic*, August 16, 1943, 220–22; Sitkoff, "Black Militancy," 675; Mary McLeod Bethune, "Certain Inalienable Rights," in Rayford Logan, *What the Negro Wants* (New York: Agathon Press, 1969), 249, 251.

82. Sullivan, *Days of Hope*, 180–81.

83. Francis Biddle, quoted in Earl Brown, "The Story Behind the Riot," Public Affairs Committee, New York, October 1943, NAACP Papers, II:A593. Also cited in NAACP annual report, June 26, 1944, NAACP Papers, II:A593; TM to E. Frederic Morrow, August 28, 1943, NAACP Papers, II:A593.

84. Ralph Ellison, "*An American Dilemma*: A Review," (1944).

85. Hine, *Black Victory*, 202, 217–18.

86. Ibid., 218–23; Sullivan, *Days of Hope*, 149.

87. Sullivan, *Days of Hope*, 147, 169–70.

88. Ibid., 170–71.

89. Ibid., 171–72, 189–90.

90. Ibid., 189–91.

91. John McCray to Thurgood Marshall, November 9, 1944, Marshall to McCray, November 13, 1944, NAACP Papers, II:B205.

92. Quoted in Sullivan, *Days of Hope*, 141.

93. Walter White, addressa at closing meeting of Wartime Conference, July 16, 1944, Chicago, NAACP/mf p1 r11 summary of mileage and meetings, Annual Report file, 1944, NAACP Papers, II:A59.

94. Highlights of the report to the thirty-forth annual meeting of the NAACP, New York, January 4, 1943, NAACP Papers, II:A59; Walter White, address at closing meeting of Wartime Conference, July 16, 1944, Chicago.

Chapter 8: Justice Now: Claiming the Postwar Moment

1. Walter White, address at closing meeting of Wartime Conference, July 16, 1944; *Chicago Defender*, July 22, 1944, 1.

2. TM to Herbert Resner, July 18, 1944, NAACP/mf p13C r1; *Chicago Defender*, July 22, 1944, 1.

3. Sullivan, *Days of Hope*, 106–8, 114–21, 130–31.

4. Ibid., 172–73.

5. Henry A. Wallace, "The Price of Free World Victory," in *Democracy Reborn* (New York: DaCapo Press, 1993), 190–96; Sullivan, *Days of Hope*, 179–84.

6. Sullivan, *Days of Hope*, 184–86.

7. Penny Von Eschen, *Race Against Empire: Black Americans and Anti-colonialism, 1937–1957* (Ithaca, NY: Cornell Univ. Press, 1997), 1–43, 70–78.

8. Carol Anderson, *Eyes Off the Prize: The United Nations and African American Struggles for Human Rights, 1944–1955* (New York: Cambridge Univ. Press, 2003), 33–34; Lewis, *W.E.B. Du Bois: The Fight for Equality and the American Century*, 497–502.

9. Von Eschen, *Race Against Empire*, 3.

10. Ibid.

11. Roy Wilkins, *Standing Fast: The Autobiography of Roy Wilkins* (New York: Da-Capo Press, 1994), 189.

12. Martha Biondi, *To Stand and Fight: The Struggle for Civil Rights in Postwar New York City* (Cambridge, MA: Harvard Univ. Press, 2003), 1–20; Quintard Taylor, *In Search of the Racial Frontier*, 250–71; Matthew J. Countryman, *Up South: Civil Rights and Black Power in Philadelphia* (Philadelphia: Univ. of Pennsylvania Press, 2006), 28–40; Andrew Fearnley, "'Your Work Is the Most Important, but Without Branches There Can Be No National Work': Cleveland's Branch of the NAACP, c.1929–c.1968," unpublished article, 4, copy in author's possession.

13. Hubert Delany, keynote address, eighth annual youth conference, New Orleans, LA, November 21–24, 1946, NAACP Papers, I:E8; John Dittmer, *Local People: The Struggle for Civil Rights in Mississippi* (Urbana: Univ. of Illinois Press, 1994), 1–18.

14. Thurgood Marshall, "Legal Attack to Secure Civil Rights," NAACP annual meeting, Chicago, 1944, NAACP/mf p1 r17.

15. Ibid.

16. TM to branches (draft), November 11, 1945; TM to WFW, November 14, 1945, NAACP Papers, II:B99; Carter, *A Matter of Law*, 14–15, 37–53; William Hastie to TM, June 3, 1944, NAACP Papers, II:B135.

17. Carter, *A Matter of Law*, 56–59; Kluger, *Simple Justice*, 271–73; Constance Baker Motley, *Equal Justice Under Law: An Autobiography* (New York: Farrar, Straus & Giroux, 1999), 58–59, 95.

18. Carter, *A Matter of Law*, 59; Mark Tushnet, *Making Civil Rights Law: Thurgood Marshall and the Supreme Court, 1936–1961*, 37; WFW to TM, July 17, 1945, NAACP Papers, II:B99; Lewis, *W.E.B. Du Bois: The Fight for Equality and the American Century*, 498.

19. TM, draft of letter to branches, November 14, 1945, NAACP Papers, II:B99; Thurgood Marshall, acceptance speech as Spingarn medalist, NAACP conference, Cincinnati, OH, June 28, 1946, NAACP Papers, II:A31.

20. TM to Spottswood Robinson III, May 2, 1944; TM to Roger Baldwin, June 9, 1944; TM to Simon Gross, July 27, 1944, NAACP Papers, II:B135; Vose, *Caucasians Only*, 56–57.

21. TM to Roger Baldwin, June 9, 1944; TM to Spottswood Robinson III, May 2, 1944. In *Hansberry v. Lee* the Court ruled in favor of Carl Hansberry in a case supported by the Chicago's NAACP branch, holding that the particular covenant in question did not have the required number of signatures and was therefore improp-

erly enforced. As a result of this ruling, a twenty-seven-block area in Chicago was open for black families to rent or purchase homes. Vose, *Caucasians Only*, 55–56.

22. TM to Roger Baldwin, June 9, 1944; "In Memoriam: Spottswood Robinson, 1916–1998," *Journal of Blacks in Higher Education*, Winter 1998–1999, 39; Spottswood Robinson to TM, May 19, 1944; TM to Spottswood Robinson, December 16, 1944, NAACP Papers, II:B135; McNeil, *Groundwork*, 177.

23. Vose, *Caucasians Only*, 57–64.

24. Ibid., 64–71; Motley, *Equal Justice Under Law*, 67–68.

25. TM to Charles P. Lucas, December 13, 1945, NAACP Papers, II:B145; annual report, Branch Department, 1946, 3–6, NAACP Papers, II:A60.

26. Douglas, *Jim Crow Moves North*, 237–65.

27. Sullivan, *Days of Hope*, 163–67, 194–95, 202–03.

28. Report of Legal Department, July/August 1944, October 1944, NAACP Papers, II:B97; Dittmer, *Local People*, 15; Laurie B. Green, *Battling the Plantation Mentality: Memphis and the Black Freedom Struggle* (Chapel Hill: Univ. of North Carolina Press, 2007), 81–101; "Criminal Cases," (1945), report draft, NAACP Papers, II:B99; Alexander Looby to TM, February 18, 1947, NAACP Papers, II:B99.

29. Report of the Legal Department, July 1943, NAACP Papers, II:B97; "The Right to Public Accommodations" (1945), NAACP Papers, II:B99; Emmons, "Flame of Resistance," 112; Fairclough, *Race and Democracy*, 78; Stephen G.N. Tuck, *Beyond Atlanta: The Struggle for Racial Equality in Georgia, 1940–1980* (Athens: Univ. of Georgia Press, 2001), 50; Raymond Gavins, "The NAACP in North Carolina During the Age of Segregation," in Armstead Robinson and Patricia Sullivan, eds., *New Directions in Civil Rights Studies* (Charlottesville: Univ. Press of Virginia, 1991), 109; Dorothy A. Autrey, "The National Association for the Advancement of Colored People in Alabama, 1913–1952" (PhD diss., University of Notre Dame, 1985), 191; Dittmer, *Local People*, 31.

30. Emmons, "Flame of Resistance," chaps. 4–5, Thurgood Marshall quote, p. 95; Harry T. Moore, "The Work of the NAACP in Florida" (1947), NAACP Papers, II:C35; Ransby, *Ella Baker*, 129.

31. Tuck, *Beyond Atlanta*, 51–65; TM to Wilkins, March 12, 1945, NAACP Papers, II:B99.

32. Ransby, *Ella Baker*, 137–38, 142; EJB to the Executive Staff, memorandum in re A Nation-wide Membership Campaign in 1944; EJB, "Program for Development of Branches," memorandum, July 6, 1943, NAACP Papers, II:A573; EJB to Conference Delegate, November 14, 1944; Agenda, Leadership Training Conference, Atlanta, March 10–11, 1945; Regional Leadership Training Conferences, 1945, NAACP Papers, II:C376; TM to EJB, March 8, 1946, NAACP Papers, II:B99.

33. Sullivan, *Days of Hope*, 195; Autrey, "The National Association for the Advancement of Colored People in Alabama," 211–16, 242–45; Gavins, "North Carolina in the Age of Jim Crow," 118; Tuck, *Beyond Atlanta*, 54; Daniel Byrd, address to thirty-seventh annual convention (1946), NAACP Papers, II:A31.

34. TM, "The Right to Vote" (1945), NAACP Papers, II:B99; TM, article for the

New York Age, December 24, 1945, NAACP Papers, II:B99; Thurgood Marshall, acceptance speech as Spingarn medalist, NAACP conference, June 28, 1946.

35. TM, memorandum to state conference of branches, June 29, 1945, NAACP Papers, II:B67; minutes of staff conference, November 7, 1945, NAACP/mf p7 r4 f106–8; TM, article for the *New York Age*, December 14, 1945.

36. W.E.B. Du Bois, "An Estimate of FDR," *Chicago Defender*, May 5, 1945, published in David Levering Lewis, ed., *W.E.B. Du Bois: A Reader* (New York: Henry Holt, 1995), 480–81; William C. Berman, *The Politics of Civil Rights in the Truman Administration* (Columbus: Ohio State Univ. Press, 1970), 8–24; Von Eshen, *Race Against Empire*, 70, 100–101.

37. Anderson, *Eyes Off the Prize*, 41–55; Von Eschen, *Race Against Empire*, 82; Lewis, *W.E.B. Du Bois: The Fight for Equality and the American Century*, 504–9.

38. David William Hazel, "The National Association for the Advancement of Colored People and the National Legislative Process, 1940–1954" (PhD diss., University of Michigan, 1957), 92–109, quote on p. 92.

39. Reed, *Seedtime for Modern Civil Rights Movement*, 321–35.

40. Ibid., 332–35; Countryman, *Up South*, 30–31.

41. Denton Watson, *Lion in the Lobby: Clarence Mitchel, Jr.'s Struggle for the Passage of Civil Rights Laws* (New York: Morrow, 1990), 149–51.

42. Adam Fairclough, *Race and Democracy*, 105.

43. Gail Williams O'Brien, *The Color of Law: Race, Violence and Justice in the Postwar South* (Chapel Hill: Univ. of North Carolina Press, 1999), 7–33; TM, acceptance speech as Spingarn medalist, June 28, 1946.

44. O'Brien, *Color of Law*, 34–36; *Atlanta Daily World*, March 22, 1946, 1, March 28, 1946, 1, April 25, 1946, 1.

45. O'Brien, *Color of Law*, 37–39; TM to Tom Clark, December 27, 1946, NAACP Papers, II:A410; *Atlanta Daily World*, June 18, 1946, 1; Walter White, "Columbia Whitewash," *Chicago Defender*, June 22, 1946, 15.

46. O'Brien, *Color of Law*, 38–39; Thurgood Marshall, acceptance speech as Spingarn medalist, June 28, 1946; White, "Columbia Whitewash," 15.

47. O'Brien, *Color of Law*, 39–40; *Atlanta Daily World*, June 22, 1946, 1.

48. Henry Lee Moon, *The Balance of Power: The Negro Vote* (Garden City, NY: Doubleday, 1948), 178–79.

49. TM, memorandum to the office, April 8, 1946, NAACP Papers, II:B137; Adam Fairclough, "Thurgood Marshall's Pursuit of Equality Through Law," in Preston King and Walter Earl Fluker, *Black Leaders and Ideologies in the South: Resistance and Nonviolence* (New York: Routledge, 2005), 188–89. Fairclough, *Race and Democracy*, 105.

50. EJB to branch president, January 11, 1946, NAACP Papers, II:A573; Moon, *Balance of Power*, 194; schedule, 1946 Leadership Training Conferences, NAACP Papers, II:C307; Douglas Brinkley, *Rosa Parks: A Life* (New York: Penguin, 2000), 68–69.

51. TM to officers of state conferences and branches interested in cases to equalize

educational opportunities in the South, April 1, 1946; TM, memorandum to the office, April 8, 1946; Digest of Proceedings of Atlanta Conference; "NAACP Lawyers Survey Jim Crow in Education," press release, April 27, 1946, NAACP Papers, II:B137; Carter, *A Matter of Law*, 62–65.

52. TM to Richard Westbrooks, June 20, 1945; TM to Wilkins, November 28, 1945; TM to J.M. Tinsley, December 11, 1945; "U.S. Supreme Court Strikes Blow at Segregation," June 3, 1946; Robert L. Carter, "The Implications of the Morgan Case," NAACP Papers, II:B190.

53. "White Supremacy Is in Peril," *Jackson (MS) Daily News*, May 27, 1946; Dittmer, *Local People*, 2; T.B. Wilson to WFW, May 27, 1946, NAACP/mf p4 r9; Etoy Fletcher, affidavit, June 15, 1946, NAACP/mf p4 r8; Daniel Byrd to TM, June 4, 1946; Robert L. Carter to Tom Clark, June 22, 1946; *Sunday Washington (DC) Star*, June 23, 1946, A2; World War II veterans, signed statement, Greenville, MS, June 25, 1946; WFW to Tom Clark, July 1, 1946, NAACP/mf p4 r9.

54. Dittmer, *Local People*, 1–3; "On the 2d of July, 1946; Gulfport, MS, . . ." statements by V.R. Collier et al.; Rev. George Strype to Hon. Lamar Caudley, July 2, 1946; Daniel Byrd to TM, July 6, 1946; Theron Caudle to WFW, July 9, 1946, NAACP/mf p4 r9.

55. George Hatcher, "Rural Vote Gave Talmadge Victory in Georgia Test," *New York Times*, July 21, 1946, E10.

56. Tuck, *Beyond Atlanta*, 62–69; Sullivan, *Days of Hope*, 211–13.

57. *New York Times*, March 18, 2007, 16; Sullivan, *Days of Hope*, 213–14; *New York Times*, July 27, 1946, 1, 32; John Mebane, "Georgia Weighs Monroe Murders," *New York Times*, August 4, 1946, 77.

58. Isaac Woodard, affidavit, April 23, 1946; WFW to Robert Patterson, May 6, 1946, Patterson to WFW, June 17, 1946; WFW to Tom Clark, July 17, 1946; WFW to Orson Welles, July 24, 1946; WFW to NAACP branches, July 25, 1946; memorandum: Batesburg, S.C., police system, August 22, 1946; "U.S. to Try Cop Who Blinded Wounded Veteran," *PM*, n.d.; Franklin Williams to TM, memorandum re acquittal of Lynwood Shull, November 12, 1946, NAACP/mf p8B r28; *New York Times*, August 19, 1946, 20. For discussion of Welles's involvement in the case see Simon Callow, *Orson Welles: Hello Americans* (New York: Penguin, 2006), 323–42.

59. WFW to Gloster Current, August 19, 1946, NAACP/mf p26A r4, f999; Wilkins, *Standing Fast*, 190–92; WFW to the Committee on Administration, July 12, 1946, WFW to board of directors, September 9, 1946; WFW to TM, October 3, 1946; TM to Committee on Administration, December 4, 1946, NAACP Papers, II:B99.

60. EJB to WFW, May 15, 1946, NAACP Papers, II:A573.

61. J.L. LeFlore to EJB, June 19, 1946, NAACP Papers, II:A573; Robert L. Carter, telephone interview, May 9, 2008.

62. Walter White, address at closing session of the thirty-seventh annual convention of the NAACP, Cincinnati, OH, June 30, 1946; Thurgood Marshall, acceptance speech as Spingarn medalist, June 28, 1946; W.E.B. Du Bois, "Behold the Land," in

Esther Cooper Jackson, ed., *Freedomways Reader: Prophets in Their Own Country* (Boulder, CO: Westview, 2000), 8.

63. Du Bois, "Behold the Land," 9; WFW, closing address, June 30, 1946; Thurgood Marshall, acceptance speech as Spingarn medalist, June 28, 1946; National Organizations Meet to Plan Joint Action on Wave of Terror in the South, August 8, 1946, NAACP/mf p8B r28.

64. Berman, *Politics of Civil Rights in the Truman Administration*, 50–52.

65. Du Bois to WFW, August 1, 1946; Du Bois to WFW, August 26, 1948, WFW, memorandum to the Committee on Administration, August 28, 1946; Roy Wilkins to WFW, September 3, 1946; NAACP petition to the United Nations, chronology, NAACP Papers, II:A637.

66. O'Brien, *Color of Law*, 44–52; *Atlanta Daily World*, September 22, 1946, 1.

67. O'Brien, *Color of Law*, 52–54; Gloster Current to branch officer, November 25, 1946, NAACP Papers, II:B99; *Atlanta Daily World*, November 24, 1946, 1; *New York Times*, November 24, 1946, 56. Tushnet, *Making Civil Rights Law*, 54–55.

68. TM to WFW, December 25, 1946, NAACP Papers, II:B99; Hubert Delaney, keynote address, eighth annual youth conference, New Orleans, November 21–24, 1946, NAACP Papers, II:E8; George Streator, "Bids Negroes Seek Complete Equality," *New York Times*, November 22, 1946, 24.

69. George Streator, "Negroes Cautioned on Resistance Idea," *New York Times*, November 23, 1946, 14.

70. Ibid.

71. Charles H. Houston, "Spotlight on Mississippi," *Baltimore Afro-American*, December 14, 1946, 1.

72. Ibid; *New York Times*, December 2, 3, 1946; "A New Day for the South," *Chicago Defender*, December 14, 1946, 14; *Chicago Defender*, December 14, 1946, 1; "Education by Bilbo," *New York Times*, December 10, 1946; Harold B. Hinton, "Bilbo Hearings Turn on Rights of Negroes," *New York Times*, December 8, 1946, 126; Dittmer, *Local People*, 3–9.

73. Hinton, *New York Times*, December 8, 1946; *New York Times*, December 4, 1946; "Education by Bilbo," *New York Times*, December 10, 1946; Houston, "Spotlight on Mississippi," 1.

74. NAACP, "Negro Vote in the South: 1946," NAACP/mf p4 r8; Sullivan, *Days of Hope*, 215–20.

75. Berman, *Politics of Civil Rights*, 53–55; *Chicago Defender*, November 16, 1946, 3; Sullivan, *Days of Hope*, 233–35.

76. President's Committee on Civil Rights, *To Secure These Rights: The Report of the President's Committee on Civil Rights* (New York: Simon and Schuster, 1947), vii–ix.

77. *Chicago Defender*, December 21, 1946; "NAACP Demands Justice Department Action," *Atlanta Daily World*, December 6, 1946, 1.

78. TM to Tom Clark, November 14, 1946, NAACP/mf p8B r28. Marshall's letter is probably based on a report written by Franklin Williams, who accompanied Isaac Woodard to the trial. Franklin Williams to Thurgood Marshall, "Acquittal of Lyn-

wood L. Shull in the case of Isaac Woodard, Jr.," memorandum, November 12, 1946, NAACP/mf p8B r28.

79. TM to Tom Clark, December 27, 1946; TM to WFW, memorandum, January 23, 1947, NAACP Papers, II:A410.

80. Branch membership–1946, NAACP Papers, II:A60; *Chicago Defender*, November 2, 1946, 14; TM, acceptance speech as Spingarn medalist, June 28, 1946.

Chapter 9: The Beginning of the End: Segregation Must Go

1. TM to Roy Wilkins, February 24, 1947; TM to Gloster Current, memorandum, July 8, 1947, NAACP Papers, II:B99.

2. Brief for the National Association for the Advancement of Colored People as Amicus Curiae, in *Westminster School District of Orange County et al. v. Gonzalo Mendez et al.*, United States Court of Appeals for the Ninth Circuit, 8, 10; Neil Foley, "'God Bless the Law, He is White': Legal, Local, and International Politics of Latina/o and Black Desegregation Cases in Post World War II California and Texas," in Juan Flores and Renato Rosaldo, eds., *A Companion to Latino Studies* (New York: Wiley-Blackwell, 2007) 302–3; Carter, *A Matter of Law*, 65–66.

3. Amicus curiae brief, *Mendez et al.*, 14; TM to Gloster Current, memorandum, July 8, 1947, NAACP Papers, II:B99; TM to Lulu White, August 21, 1945, II:C194.

4. Thurgood Marshall, statement before the President's Committee on Civil Rights, April 17, 1947, NAACP/mf p18C r28.

5. Carter, *A Matter of Law*, 176; TM to Current, July 8, 1947.

6. TM, statement before the President's Committee on Civil Rights, April 17, 1947; Charles Thompson, interview by Richard Kluger, March 16, 1971, *Brown v. Board* Collection; TM to Lulu White, August 21, 1945, NAACP Papers, II:C194; Digest of Proceedings of Atlanta Conference.

7. *Chicago Defender*, January 26, 1946, 3.

8. James Poling, "Thurgood Marshall and the 14th Amendment," *Colliers*, February 23, 1952, reprinted in *Reporting Civil Rights*, Part I (New York: Library of America, 2003), 146; Tushnet, *NAACP Legal Strategy*, 120–21; Kluger, *Simple Justice*, 259–60; *Chicago Defender*, August 3, 1946, 13.

9. *Washington Post*, January 20, 1948, 1; Kluger, *Simple Justice*, 528.

10. *Washington Post*, January 20, 1948, 1; Kluger, *Simple Justice*, 260–61; Tushnet, *Making Civil Rights Law*, 129–30; *New York Times*, January 15, 1948, 22; *The Crisis*, April 1948, 123; Williams, *Thurgood Marshall*, 177–79.

11. *The Crisis*, March 1948, 73; minutes, board of directors, March 8, 1948, May 1948; Scott Baker, *Paradoxes of Desegregation: African American Struggles for Educational Equity in Charleston, South Carolina, 1926–1972* (Columbia: Univ. of South Carolina Press, 2006), 77; *Chicago Defender*, September 4, 1948, 1.

12. *New York Times*, January 19, 1948, 21; *Chicago Defender*, March 20, 1948, 1; Baker, *Paradoxes of Desegregation*, 76–82.

13. Baker, *Paradoxes of Desegregation*, 79–81; TM to John Wrighten, September 29, 1947, NAACP Papers, II:C181.

14. Michael L. Gillette, "Heman Marion Sweatt: Civil Rights Plaintiff," in Alwyn Barr and Robert A. Calvert, *Black Leaders: Texans for Their Times* (Austin: Texas State Historical Society, 1981), 162–65; minutes, board of directors, September 8, 1947, NAACP Papers, I:A5.

15. Gillette, "Heman Marion Sweatt," 167–73, 261–62; Kluger, *Simple Justice*, 261–62; Poling, "Thurgood Marshall," 145–46.

16. Tushnet, *Making Civil Rights Law*, 132; Kluger, *Simple Justice*, 262–66. In an editorial in the *Houston Informer*, newspaper publisher Carter Wesley challenged Marshall's singular emphasis on desegregation. While Wesley supported the *Sweatt* case, he also supported the establishment of what became Texas Southern University for Negroes, arguing that it would expand educational opportunities "more effectively and immediately." Marshall responded to Wesley in a speech to a statewide NAACP meeting in Denison late in the summer of 1947. "There is no easy answer to segregation and discrimination," Marshall acknowledged. What "we have to decide," he explained, was "whether we want separate schools or an end of segregation." For him, the answer was clear. "We are convinced that it is impossible to have equality in a segregated system, no matter how elaborately we build the Jim Crow citadel and no matter [what] we label it." Nevertheless, he did not minimize what they were up against. "The fight is . . . going to be just as difficult as you can imagine," he told them—and long, maybe even taking "more years than the fight against the white primary." TM, preliminary statement, Texas State Conference of Branches, Denison, TX, September 5, 1947, NAACP/mf p18Λ 59; Pitre, *In Struggle Against Jim Crow*, 92–104.

17. Smith, "A Civil Rights Vanguard: Black Attorneys and the NAACP in Virginia," 144–46.

18. Ibid.; Thomas Dabney, October 2, 1947, NAACP Papers, II:B99; special release, October 31, 1947, NAACP Papers, II:B67; Kluger, *Simple Justice*, 472–73.

19. August Meier and Elliott Rudwick, *CORE: A Study in the Civil Rights Movement, 1942–1968* (Urbana: Univ. of Illinois Press, 1975), 4–35.

20. Ibid., 34–35; George M. Houser and Bayard Rustin, "Journey of Reconciliation: A Report," NAACP Papers, II:B190; Ray Arsenault, *Freedom Riders: 1961 and the Struggle for Racial Justice* (New York: Oxford Univ. Press, 2006), 33–38.

21. James Peck, "Not So Deep Are the Roots," *The Crisis*, September 1947, in *Reporting Civil Rights*, 92–97; Charles H. Houston, "Our Civil Rights," *Baltimore Afro-American*, April 30, 1949.

22. Minutes, board of directors, February 10, 1947, NAACP Papers, I:A5.

23. Robert L. Carter to Mr. Jones, February 27, 1947; Leslie Perry to Walter White, April 14, 1947, Walter White notes from testimony before the President's Committee on Civil Rights; WFW to Mr. Harrington, April 21, 1947, Thurgood Marshall, statement before the President's Committee on Civil Rights, April 17, 1947, NAACP/mf p18C r28.

24. Harry S. Truman, speech to NAACP, June 29, 1947, reprinted in *Washington Post*, June 30, 1947, 4.

25. Ibid.; "Mr. Truman and Human Rights," *New York Amsterdam News*, July 5, 1947, 8.

26. Truman, speech to NAACP, June 29, 1947.

27. President Harry S. Truman, address before a joint session of Congress, March 12, 1947; Winston Churchill, "Sinews of Peace," speech at Westminster College, Fulton, MO, March 5, 1946; WFW, "U.S. Hides Behind Imperialist Skirts," *Chicago Defender*, March 16, 1946, 16; Janken, *White*, 300–301.

28. Truman, address before a joint session of Congress, March 12, 1947; *Chicago Defender*, April 19, 1947, 4; Walter White, "People, Politics, and Places," *Chicago Defender*, January 10, 1948, 15.

29. Sullivan, *Days of Hope*, 237–40.

30. Charles H. Houston, Along This Way (column), *Baltimore Afro-American*, April 12, 1947, May 3 1947.

31. Sullivan, *Days of Hope*, 225–30, 235–37, 240; Carter, *A Matter of Law*, 76.

32. Sullivan, *Days of Hope*, 230–37; Arthur Schlesinger, "The U.S. Communist Party," *Life*, July 29, 1946; Janken, *White*, 307.

33. TM to WFW, January 31, 1947, TM to WFW, October 13, 1947, TM to Committee on Administration, October 27, 1947, NAACP Papers, II:B99.

34. Tinsley E. Yarbrough, *A Passion for Justice: J. Waties Waring and Civil Rights* (New York: Oxford Univ. Press, 1987), 43–54.

35. Ibid., 60–65; Carolyn Click, "A Man Lost to History," *Columbia (SC) State*, March 3, 2003.

36. Vose, *Caucasians Only*, 151–63; Kluger, *Simple Justice*, 254.

37. Loren Miller, "Supreme Court Decision—an Analysis," *The Crisis*, September 1948, 266; *Baltimore Afro-American*, January 24, 1948, 1; *New York Times*, December 5, 1947, 1; Vose, *Caucasians Only*, 163–64.

38. Essays include: W.E. Burghardt Du Bois, introduction to *Statement of the Denial of Human Rights to Citizens of Negro Descent*; William Ming Jr., "The Present Legal and Social Status of the Negro; Milton Konvitz, "The Negro and American Law"; Earl Dickerson, "The Denial of Legal Rights of American Negroes"; Rayford Logan, "The United Nations and the Rights of Minorities"; Leslie Perry, "Patterns of Discrimination in Fundamental Human Rights," NAACP Papers, II:A637.

39. "NAACP Counsel Declares Civil Rights Report Basis for Action Now," press release, October 31, 1947, II:A637.

40. Ibid.; WFW, *Chicago Defender*, November 22, 1947, 15; *New York Times*, October 30, 1947, 14; President's Committee on Civil Rights, *To Secure These Rights: The Report of President Harry S. Truman's Committee on Civil Rights*, edited with an introduction by Steven F. Lawson (Boston: Bedford/St. Martin's, 2004), 31.

41. *Baltimore Afro-American*, January 3, 1948; *Pittsburgh Courier*, January 17, 1948, 20; Berman, *Politics of Civil Rights*, 81–82.

42. Vose, *Caucasians Only*, 199–200; Motley, *Equal Justice Under Law*, 68.

43. *Baltimore Afro-American*, January 24, 1948, 1; William Ming, "Minority Group Property Rights Hang in Balance," *Pittsburgh Courier*, January 24. 1948, 1; *Chicago Defender*, January 24, 1948, 3; *Pittsburgh Courier*, December 13, 1947, 5, January 17, 1948, 1; Lem Graves, "Washington Notebook," *Pittsburgh Courier*, January 17, 1948, 3; Vose, *Caucasians Only*, 171–74.

44. *Baltimore Afro-American*, January 24, 1948, 1, 12; *Pittsburgh Courier*, January 24, 1948, 1; Vose, *Caucasians Only*, 199–205. Arguing the Detroit case, Marshall drew attention to the wealth of statistical information and sociological data accompanying the briefs, documenting the poverty, disease, and increased crime resulting from the overcrowded conditions created by covenants. Felix Frankfurter questioned Marshall regarding the relevance of this material to the specific legal argument he was advancing. Following a brief discussion, Frankfurter agreed that it may have merit in terms of public policy and particularly with regard to the District of Columbia, which was under federal jurisdiction.

45. "Text of President Truman's Message on Civil Rights," *New York Times*, February 3, 1948, 22; Berman, *Politics of Civil Rights*, 85.

46. James and Nancy Wechsler, "The Road Ahead for Civil Rights: The President's Report: One Year Later," *Commentary*, October 1948, 298–99; Berman, *Politics of Civil Rights*, 85, 90, 91, 94; Charles H. Houston, *Baltimore Afro-American*, February 14, 1948.

47. Berman, *Politics of Civil Rights*, 1–83; Sullivan, *Days of Hope*, 224–28, 247.

48. Minutes, NAACP board of directors, March 8, 1948; Hugh M. Gloster, "The Regional School Plan," *Crisis*, August 1948, 233–36; *Chicago Defender*, March 20, 1948, 1.

49. *The Crisis*, February 1948, 41; Berman, *Politics of Civil Rights*, 97–98; Charles H. Houston, Along This Way (column), *Baltimore Afro-American*, April 3, April 10, 1948.

50. Richard M. Dalfiume, *Desegregation of the Armed Forces: Fighting on Two Fronts, 1939–1953* (Columbia: Univ. of Missouri Press, 1976), 163–65; Berman, *Politics of Civil Rights*, 98–99; *Baltimore Afro-American*, April 10, 1948, 1; "The Negroes and the Draft," *The Crisis*, May 1948, 140; *The Crisis*, editorial, April 10, 1948, 136.

51. Vose, *Caucasians Only*, 205–10; *New York Times*, May 4, 1948, 1, 2; *Baltimore Afro-American*, May 15, 1948, 15; editorial, *Washington Post*, editorial, May 6, 1948, 16; "Let Freedom Ring," *Chicago Defender*, May 15, 1948, 14.

52. Miller, "Supreme Court Decision," 265–66; Vose, *Caucasians Only*, 213.

53. Wechsler and Wechsler, "The Road Ahead for Civil Rights," 298–99; Berman, *Politics of Civil Rights*, 100–102.

54. Wilkins, *Standing Fast*, 200; Janken, *White*, 315–16; Clarence Mitchell to WFW, May 20, 1948, NAACP Papers, II:A633.

55. CHH, Along the Highway (column), *Baltimore Afro-American*, February 7, 1948; "Candidate Wallace," *The Crisis*, February 1948, 41.

56. Sullivan, *Days of Hope*, 251–57; Green, *Battling the Plantation Mentality*, 100.

57. CHH, Along the Highway (column), *Baltimore Afro-American*, July 10, 1948;

Louis E. Burnham, "The Birmingham Story," unpublished article, private files of Dorothy Burnham; author's telephone interview with the Reverend Herbert Oliver, November 17, 2008.

58. *New York Times*, January 6, 1948, 21; "New Richmond Councilman," *The Crisis*, July 1948, 201; Palmer Weber to TM, September 13, 1948, NAACP Papers, II:A142; *Baltimore Afro-American*, August 21, 1948.

59. Résumé of NAACP legal conference, June 21, 1948, NAACP Papers, II:A41; Norrell, *Reaping the Whirlwind*, 56, 66, 76; Charles H. Houston, Along the Highway (column), *Baltimore Afro-American*, December 11, 1948; *Atlanta Daily World*, September 15, 1948, 1; Tuck, *Beyond Atlanta*, 54, 77–79; Dittmer, *Local People*, 28.

60. Berman, *Politics of Civil Rights*, 103–4; "The GOP's Broken Promises," editorial, *Baltimore Afro-American*, June 19, 1948.

61. Berman, *Politics of Civil Rights*, 104–8; Dalfiume, *Desegregation*, 167; *Baltimore Afro-American*, editorial, July 17, 1948; Manfred Berg, *Ticket to Freedom: The NAACP and the Struggle for Black Political Freedom* (Gainesville: Univ. Press of Florida, 2005), 130.

62. Anne O'Hare McCormick, "The Vacuum of Leadership Roosevelt Left Behind," *New York Times*, July 14, 1948, 22; James Reston, "Figures of New Deal Era Missing from Convention," *New York Times*, July 13, 1948, 7; *New York Times*, July 15, 1948, 1; Berman, *Politics of Civil Rights*, 107–18.

63. James Reston, "In a Fighting Mood," *New York Times*, July 15, 1948, 1; Berman, *Politics of Civil Rights*, 116–24; CHH, Along the Highway (column), *Baltimore Afro-American*, July 31, 1948.

64. James Wechsler, "My Ten Months with Wallace," *Progressive*, November 1948, 5; Douglas Hall, "Writer Says Wallace Gave South New Baptism of Freedom," *Baltimore Afro-American*, September 18, 1948; for an account of the Wallace tour, see Sullivan, *Days of Hope*, 249–73.

65. Palmer Weber to TM, September 11, 1948, NAACP Papers, II:A142; Author interview with Daisy Bates, January 21, 1982; CHH, Along the Highway (column), *Baltimore Afro-American*, September 11, 1948.

66. Weber to TM, September 11, 1948; Berman, *Politics of Civil Rights*, 124–28; Biondi, *To Stand and Fight*, 143–44.

67. Du Bois, memorandum to the secretary and the board of directors, September 7, 1948, NAACP Papers, II:A639; Janken, *White*, 117–18.

68. George Streator, "Racial Unit Scored as Aiding Truman," *New York Times*, September 9, 1948; minutes, board of directors, September 13, 1948, NAACP/mf p1 r3 f838.

69. CHH, *Baltimore Afro-American*, October 10, 1948.

70. Janken, *White*, 310–13.

71. *New York Times*, July 21, 1948, 1; *New York Times*, December 19, 1948, E7; Berg, *Ticket to Freedom*, 131–39; Eleanor Roosevelt, My Day (syndicated column), July 11, 1949.

72. Berman, *Politics of Civil Rights*, 138–63; Wilkins, *Standing Fast*, 203.

73. Berman, *Politics of Civil Rights*, 157–63; TM to WFW, February 16, 1949, NAACP Papers, II:A195.

74. Janken, *White*, 334–36, 346.

75. Ted Posten, interviewed by Richard Kluger, July 22, 1971, *Brown v. Board* Collection; minutes, board of directors, May 9, 1949, NAACP/mf p1 r3 f929; Janken, *White*, 338–49.

76. WFW, memorandum to the Committee on Administration, January 26, 1948, NAACP/mf p17 r21; minutes, board of directors, July 14, 1949, NAACP/mf p1 r3 f953; "Civil Rights Gains for 1949 Reviewed," *New York Times*, July 9, 1950, 70; Hubert Delaney to Roy Wilkins, November 18, 1949, Arthur Spingarn Papers, Manuscript Division, Library of Congress (microfilm) reel 17; P.L. Prattis, "The Horizon," editorial, *Pittsburgh Courier*, October 14, 1950; Marjorie McKenzie, "The NAACP Needs Your Help Right Now," *Pittsburgh Courier*, November 25, 1950, 14; Benjamin Mays, "Negroes Fail to Appreciate the Fine Work of the NAACP," *Pittsburgh Courier*, June 23, 1951; Jane Bolin to Arthur Spingarn, March 9, 1950, NAACP Papers II:A124.

77. Judge Jane Bolin and Hubert Delaney were among those who did not support Wilkins's appointment as acting secretary: minutes, board of directors, June 13, 1949; Hubert Delaney to Roy Wilkins, November 22, 1949, Spingarn Papers.

78. Wilkins, *Standing Fast*, 209–11; *Washington Post*, January 15, 1950, M9; *Pittsburgh Courier*, January 28, 1950, 32; Louis Lautier, The Capitol Spotlight (column), *Baltimore Afro-American*, January 28, 1950; Marjorie McKenzie, "Pursuit of Democracy," *Pittsburgh Courier*, January 28, 1950.

79. David William Hazel, "The NAACP and the Legislative Process, 1940–1955" (PhD diss., University of Michigan, 1957), 203–6.

80. *Pittsburgh Courier*, January 21, 1950, 1; January 28, 1950; Marjorie McKenzie, "Pursuit of Democracy," *Pittsburgh Courier*, January 28, 1950; *Washington Post*, January 15, 1950, 1; Watson, *Lion in the Lobby*, 181–82.

81. Arnold Hirsch, "Choosing Segregation: Federal Housing Policy Between *Shelley* and *Brown*," in John F. Bauman et al., eds., *From Tenements to the Taylor Homes* (University Park: Pennsylvania State Univ. Press, 2000), 214–16; minutes, board of directors, May 9, 1949, NAACP/mf p1 r3 f929; National Public Housing Conference, "Short Summary of S. 1070, the Housing Bill Sponsored by 22 Senators," March 7, 1949, Leslie Perry to NAACP branches, November 4, 1949; statement by Leslie Perry, NAACP, before the Senate Banking and Currency Subcommittee on S. 138 and S. 712, bills to provide a comprehensive housing program, February 16–17, 1949; "Ban Housing Jim Crow, NAACP Urges Congress," press release, February 17, 1949; Marian Wynn Perry to Roy Wilkins, April 19, 1949; NAACP Washington bureau press release, April 28, 1949; Leslie Perry to Roy Wilkins, June 20, 1949; Thurgood Marshall to Senator Irving Ives, July 6, 1949; Paul Douglas, address on slum clearance and the housing bill (S. 1070) before the Senate, April 19, 1949, NAACP Papers II:A308; William E. Leuchtenburg, "The Politics of Segregation," *New Leader*, January 14, 1950, 27–30. Explaining his opposition to an antisegregation

rider to the Education Bill of 1949, Senator Humphrey declared, "As much as I detest segregation, I love education more. I believe education is the fundamental answer, in the long run, to the problem of segregation." Quoted in Hazel, "NAACP and the Legislative Process," 211–12.

82. Henry Lee Moon, "The Politics of Inertia," *New Leader*, February 4, 1950, 5; Moon to Roy Wilkins, December 22, 1949, NAACP Papers; Arthur Schlesinger, *The Vital Center: The Politics of Liberalism* (Boston: Houghton Mifflin, 1949), 190, 252; Walter A. Jackson, "White Liberal Intellectuals, Civil Rights, and Gradualism, 1954–60," in Brian Ward and Tony Badger, eds., *The Making of Martin Luther King, Jr.* (New York: New York Univ. Press, 1996), 97; Carter, *A Matter of Law*, 96.

83. CHH, Our Civil Rights (column), *Baltimore Afro-American*, February 12, 1949, July 2, 1949.

84. CHH, Our Civil Rights, July 2, 1949.

85. *Washington Post*, March 9, 1947, M1; Kluger, *Simple Justice*, 513–36; Gardiner L. Bishop, interviewed by Richard Kluger, August 22, 1974, *Brown v. Board* Collection.

86. Kluger, *Simple Justice*, 18–23; Harry and Eliza Briggs, interviewed by Richard Kluger, November 29, 1971, *Brown v. Board* Collection.

87. Smith, "A Civil Rights Vanguard: Black Attorneys and the NAACP in Virginia," 145–47; Larissa M. Smith, "Securing the 'Equal' in Equal Opportunities: The Virginia NAACP's Campaign Against Segregated Education, 1947–1951," paper presented at the Virginia Forum, Winchester, Virginia, April 2006.

88. Ibid.

89. Kluger, *Simple Justice*, 276–78; *New York Times*, April 9, 1950, 19; *Baltimore Afro-American*, February 18, 1950; *Chicago Defender*, June 17, 1950.

90. Arthur Krock, "A Historic Day in the Supreme Court," *New York Times*, June 6, 1950, 8; Kluger, *Simple Justice*, 280–83; Tushnet, *The NAACP Legal Strategy*, 132.

91. *Pittsburgh Courier*, July 8, 1950; Resolutions adopted, NAACP annual convention, June 20–25, 1950, Boston, MA., NAACP Papers, II:A47.

92. *Baltimore Afro-American*, April 29, 1950, 1; McNeil, *Groundwork*, 206–11; Joseph Waddy, interviewed by Richard Kluger, September 30, 1971, *Brown v. Board* Collection; Gardiner Bishop, interviewed by Richard Kluger.

93. *Chicago Defender*, May 6, 1950, 1, May 20, 1950, 6; *Baltimore Afro-American*, May 6, 1950; *New York Amsterdam News*, May 27, 1950, 8; McNeil, *Groundwork*, 212.

94. CHH, personal recording (transcript), December 1949, Washington D.C., printed in Catherine Ellis and Stephen Drury Smith, *Say It Plain: A Century of Great African American Speeches* (New York: New Press, 2005).

Chapter 10: "On the Threshold of Victory"

1. From address by Thurgood Marshall at the forty-second annual convention of the NAACP, Atlanta, Georgia, Municipal Auditorium, June 28, 1951, 14, NAACP

Papers II:A45; First quote from "Civil Rights at Mid-Century," NAACP Forty-second Annual Report, 1950, 7–8, NAACP Papers, II:A60; W.E.B. Du Bois, "Twentieth Century: 'The Century of the Color Line,'" "The American Negro in 1950," *Pittsburgh Courier*, January 14, 1950, 8; Summary of Legal Department's Annual Report for 1951, NAACP Papers.

2. *Dorsey et al. v. Stuyvesant Town Corporation and Metropolitan Life Insurance Company*, Supreme Court, State of New York, plaintiffs reply brief, July 11, 1947, NAACP Papers, II:B131; Biondi, *To Stand and Fight*, 124–25. Cities could only condemn or take land if it was for a public purpose. Charles H. Houston, Along This Way, *Baltimore Afro-American*, October 23, 1948.

3. *New York Amsterdam News*, November 25, 1944, 1a, April 14, 1945, 1a, December 14, 1946, 28; Biondi, *To Stand and Fight*, 123–24; Carter, *A Matter of Law*, 69–70.

4. *New York Amsterdam News*, August 2, 1947, 1; Biondi, *To Stand and Fight*, 125; Reprint of opinions, court of appeals, *Dorsey et al. v. Stuyvesant Town Corporation*, Commission on Law and Social Action, American Jewish Congress, NAACP Papers, II:131.

5. Petition for a writ of certiorari, Supreme Court of the United States, *Dorsey et al. v. Stuyvesant*, October 1949, NAACP Papers, II:B131; *Chicago Defender*, June 17, 1950, 5.

6. Walter F. White, speech before annual convention, Oklahoma City, June 29, 1952; Robert C. Weaver, remarks at forty-third annual convention of the NAACP, Oklahoma City, June 27, 1952, NAACP Papers, II:A48; Arnold R. Hirsch, "'Containment' on the Home Front: Race and Federal Housing from the New Deal to the Cold War," *Journal of Urban History* 26 (January 2000): 162–63.

7. Thurgood Marshall, address at forty-second annual convention of the NAACP, June 28, 1951.

8. "Levitt Hailed [*sic*] into Federal Court," *The Crisis*, March 1955, 158–59, 190; Robert C. Weaver, *The Negro Ghetto* (New York: Russell & Russell, 1948), i; Charles Abram, "The Time Bomb That Exploded in Cicero: Segregated Housing's Inevitable Dividend," *Commentary*, November 1951, 408–14; Arnold Hirsch, *Making the Second Ghetto: Race and Housing in Chicago, 1940–60* (New York: Cambridge Univ. Press, 1983), 16; Hirsch, "'Containment' on the Home Front," 167.

9. Hirsch, "'Containment' on the Home Front," 167–68.

10. "Any Way You Turn You're Wrong," *Chicago Defender*, December 9, 1950; Hirsch, *Making the Second Ghetto*, 41; Chicago Commission on Human Relations, press release, June 14, 1951, NAACP Papers, II:A130; *Chicago Defender*, December 2, 1950, 1, June 23, 1951, 4.

11. Homer Jack, "Cicero Nightmare," *Nation*, July 28, 1951; "New Disgrace for Cicero," *Life*, July 23, 1951, NAACP Papers, II:A130; Walter White, "Disgrace in Cicero," *New York Herald Tribune*, July 23, 1951.

12. Report of the secretary to the board of directors for the months of July and

August 1951; WFW, "Disgrace in Cicero"; NAACP press release, August 8, 1951, NAACP Papers, II:A130.

13. Arnold Hirsch, "Choosing Segregation: Federal Housing Policy between *Shelley and Brown*," in Bauman et al., *From Tenements to the Taylor Homes*, 217–18; Hirsch, "'Containment' on the Home Front," 168.

14. WFW, telegram to (listed) branches, September 19, 1951; NAACP, press releases, September 20, 1951, October 11, 1951, December 13, 1951, NAACP Papers, II:A131; *Chicago Defender*, October 6, 1951, 1, October 13, 1951, 1, November 3, 1951, 11, January 14, 1952, 10, June 14, 1952, 1; Hirsch, *Making the Second Ghetto*, 16.

15. WFW, "New Leader," outline re Cicero case, NAACP Papers, II:A130; NAACP Legal Defense and Education Fund, Inc., report of March 1953 Conference Committee on Racial Discrimination in Housing, NAACP Papers, II:B77.

16. Dalfiume, *Desegregation of the U.S. Armed Forces*, 175–96, 219.

17. William Bowers, William Hammond, and George Macgarrigle, *Black Soldiers, White Army: The 24th Infantry Regiment in Korea* (Washington, DC: Center for Military History, 1996), 67–79, 93; "NAACP Alarmed by Smears on Negro Troops," *Chicago Defender*, November 18, 1950, 12.

18. Thurgood Marshall, address to forty-second annual convention of the NAACP, June 28, 1951; *Chicago Defender*, May 5, 1951, 1; *New York Times*, April 6, 1951, 27.

19. *New York Times*, April 12, 1951, 1; Arthur Shores to TM, April 12, 1951, NAACP Papers, II:B130; Dalfiume, *Desegregation of the U.S. Armed Forces*, 210–19.

20. Minutes, board of directors, January, March, April, September, November, 1951. Palmer Weber on "surrender to the Dixiecrats," minutes, board of directors, March 1951, NAACP/mf, p1-supplement r1.

21. Berman, *Politics of Civil Rights*, 180, 183–84; WFW, report on 1951 to the annual meeting, January 1952; minutes, board of directors, February 1952, NAACP Papers, I:A6; Roy Wilkins, keynote address to forty-second annual convention of the NAACP, Atlanta, June 26, 1951, NAACP Papers, II:A45.

22. WFW, report on 1951 to the annual meeting, January 1952; minutes, board of directors, September 1951, NAACP/mf p1-supplement r1; report of the administrator of finance, November 1951; Roy Wilkins to board of directors, memorandum on finances, November 12, 1951; WFW, address to forty-third annual convention of the NAACP, Oklahoma City, June 29, 1952, NAACP Papers, II:A48. Clarence Mitchell was often referred to as the 101st senator, a tribute to his mastery of the legislative process and his long tenure as the leading lobbyist for civil rights legislation. Watson, *Lion in the Lobby*, 13, 350–51.

23. Tuck, *Beyond Atlanta*, 72–80; Fairclough, *Race and Democracy*, 329–30; Emmons, "Flame of Resistance," 158–66; Arthur Shores to Hon. John D. Hill, April 5, 1949; E.D. Nixon to James Folsom, June 6, 1949, *Birmingham Post*, June 2, 1949, NAACP Papers, II:B131; "Zoning of More Acres for Negroes Is Urged," August 15, 1949; "Connor Sees Dark Era Unless Zoning Is Upheld," *Birmingham Post*, Septem-

ber 29, 1949; TM to Arthur Shores, October 7, 1949; Shores to TM, October 10, 1949; TM to Arthur Shores, May 15, 1950; "NAACP Hails Voiding of Birmingham Zoning," press release, December 15, 1950; "Negro Home Is Dynamited Here," *Birmingham Post-Herald*, December 22, 1950; Arthur Shores to George Triedman, Civil Rights Section, Dept. of Justice, December 23, 1950; TM to Arthur Shores, December 27, 1950, NAACP Papers, II:B130; Mississippi State Conference of Branches, press release, November 2, 1952, NAACP Papers, II:C98; Ruby Hurley to TM, May 8, 1951, NAACP Papers, II:C221; minutes, board of directors, June 28, 1951, NAACP/mf p1 supplement r1; TM, quoted in report by Ruby Hurley, June 4, 1951, NAACP Papers, II:A587.

24. Ben Green, *Before His Time: The Untold Story of Harry T. Moore, America's First Civil Rights Martyr* (Gainesville: Univ. Press of Florida, 1999), 83–108; *Pittsburgh Courier*, March 24, 1951, 12, April 14, 1951, 1; *New York Times*, April 10, 1951, 1.

25. TM, legal report for 1951; Eric W. Rise, "Race, Rape, and Radicalism: The Case of the Martinsville Seven, 1949–1951," *Journal of Southern History*, 58 (August 1992), 467–68, 472–88; on Mack Ingram case: *Pittsburgh Courier*, July 21, 1951, 27, November 24, 1951, 9, March 7, 1953; *Chicago Defender*, November 22, 1952.

26. Thurgood Marshall, address at forty-second annual convention of the NAACP, June 28, 1951; Roy Wilkins, keynote address at forty-second annual convention of the NAACP, June 26, 1951; report of Committee on Branches and Fieldwork, minutes, board of directors, November 1951, NAACP/mf p1 supplement r2. Estimated national membership numbers from 1951 to 1953 fluctuated from 162,926 to 155,617 to 176,184, report of the secretary, November 1951, October 1952, November 1953, NAACP/mf p1-supplement r2.

27. Ruby Hurley, interviewed by John H. Britton, January 26, 1968, Ralph Bunche Oral History Collection, MSRC; Gloster Current to Ruby Hurley, March 19, 1951; Ruby Hurley to Bobbie Branch, "Tuesday"; Ruby Hurley to Lucille Black, April 6, 1951; Hurley to Gloster Current, April 7, 1951; Ruby Hurley to TM, May 8, 1951, NAACP Papers, I:C221.

28. Ruby Hurley interview; Ruby Hurley, itinerary, April 21–May 20, 1951; Report from Workshop of Tennessee NAACP Branches, May 13, 1951; Ruby Hurley, memorandum to branches in southern Georgia re Cordele Conference, June 22, 1951, NAACP Papers, II:C221.

29. Bender had helped recruit a plaintiff for the teachers' salary case in Jackson and promoted voter participation in the 1946 primary; he was hired as a field-worker on the recommendation of Thurgood Marshall. Marshall told the New York staff, "The only way to do a good job in Mississippi is to have someone who knows Mississippi and . . . the people. There are places in Mississippi where they will not talk to anyone . . . who is from outside the state." Bender had good contacts in the state, and, Marshall added, he had "guts." TM to WFW, July 13, 1950; TM to Gloster Current, August 28, 1950; membership status of Mississippi branches, October 30, 1952, NAACP Papers, II:C98; Ruby Hurley to Gloster Current et al., report from meeting of Mississippi state conference, May 7, 1951, NAACP Papers, II:C98.

30. Legal Department annual report, 1951; Gloster Current to Ruby Hurley, September 18, 1951, NAACP Papers, II:C221; Ruby Hurley interview.

31. Roy Wilkins, address to the forty-second annual convention of the NAACP, Atlanta, June 26, 1951, NAACP Papers, II:A45; Gavins, "The NAACP in North Carolina," 116–18; Ruby Hurley, memorandum to branches in southern Georgia; resolutions adopted by the sixth annual convention of the Mississippi state conference of branches, November 3–4, 1951, NAACP Papers, II:C98.

32. Legal Department annual report, 1951; Wilkins address to forty-second annual convention, June 26, 1951; *New York Times*, June 8, 1950, 1, September 6, 1950, 47; Ruby Hurley to Gloster Current, April 7, 1951, NAACP Papers, II:C221; "Fielding Wright Vows to Fight for Segregation," *Atlanta Daily World*, April 8, 1951, 1; "Governor Wright Becomes Third Bitter Ender," *Chicago Defender*, April 14, 1951, 1.

33. Carter-Kluger interview; Carter, *A Matter of Law*, 97–98; Robert Carter, interviewed by author, December 10, 2008; Rev. Joseph DeLaine, interviewed by Richard Kluger, *Brown v. Board* Collection.

34. Carter, *A Matter of Law*, 99.

35. Kluger, *Simple Justice*, 317–21; Kenneth Clark, interviewed by Richard Kluger, November 4, 1971, Thurgood Marshall, interviewed by Richard Kluger, December 28, 1973, *Brown v. Board* Collection.

36. Kluger, *Simple Justice*, 328–31; Clark-Kluger interview; Ted Posten, interviewed by Richard Kluger, July 22, 1971, *Brown v. Board* Collection.

37. Kluger, *Simple Justice*, 346–47; Posten-Kluger interview.

38. Kluger, *Simple Justice*, 347–50.

39. Ibid., 337, 353–58, 361–63; Robert Carter's report on the trial, minutes, board of directors, June 1951, NAACP Papers/mf, p1-supplement r1.

40. Kluger, *Simple Justice*, 345, 359–60; Carter, *A Matter of Law*, 103–4.

41. Kluger, *Simple Justice*, 363–65.

42. Minutes, board meeting, June 1951; Thurgood Marshall, address at the forty-second annual convention of the NAACP, June 28, 1951.

43. Kluger, *Simple Justice*, 365–66.

44. Yarbrough, *A Passion for Justice*, 195–96, 210–11.

45. Jack Greenburg, *Crusaders in the Courts: How a Dedicated Band of Civil Rights Lawyers Fought for the Civil Rights Revolution* (New York: BasicBooks, 1994), 26, 42–46, 87–89, 126–28; *New York Times*, August 10, 1950, 29; Carter, *A Matter of Law*, 113–14.

46. Kluger, *Simple Justice*, 374–95, 401.

47. Ibid., 400–23.

48. Ibid., 424.

49. Ibid., 423–24; Carter-Kluger interview; Greenburg, *Crusaders in the Court*, 130.

50. Thurgood Marshall, address at the forty-second annual convention of the NAACP, June 28, 1951.

51. Kluger, *Simple Justice*, 452–56, 464–67; Bob Smith, *They Closed Their School:*

Prince Edward County, Virginia, 1951–1964 (Chapel Hill: Univ. of North Carolina Press); John A. Stokes with Lois Wolfe, *Students on Strike: Jim Crow, Civil Rights and Me* (Washington, DC: National Geographic, 2008), 44–51.

52. Stokes, *Students on Strike*, 54–68; Kluger, *Simple Justice*, 469–72.

53. Stokes, *Students on Strike*, 69–84; Kluger, 476–79.

54. Minutes, board of directors, November 1951; *Atlanta Daily World*, July 22, 1951, 1, August 7, 1951, 3; Stokes, *Students on Strike*, 102–3; Kluger, *Simple Justice*, 527;

55. Emmons, "Flames of Resistance," 157–58, 163–73, 176–77; Green, *Before His Time*, 134–44.

56. Minutes, board of directors, November 1951; "Guard NAACP Chief," *Pittsburgh Courier*, December 22, 1951, 1. Walter Irvin was tried in February 1952, with Marshall leading the defense. He was found guilty by an all-white jury and sentenced to death. The NAACP appealed the case to the Supreme Court twice, but the Court declined to hear it. In 1955, Governor Leroy Collins commuted Irvin's sentence to life in prison. Irwin was paroled in 1969 and died a year later. Green, *Before His Time*, 191–92, 206–7; Kluger, *Simple Justice*, 561.

57. Green, *Before His Time*, 164–71; Marjorie McKenzie, *Pittsburgh Courier*, January 5, 1952, 6; *Atlanta Daily World*, December 28, 1951, 6; *Washington Post*, December 28, 1951, 19; "Terror in Florida," *Washington Post*, December 29, 1951, 8.

58. Emory Jackson, "Delegates Pledge to Carry on Moore's Work at NAACP Meeting," *Atlanta Daily World*, January 22, 1952, 1; Emory Jackson, "NAACP Delegates Combine Efforts to Fight for Security in the South," *Atlanta Daily World*, February 1, 1952, 6.

59. Report from Political Action Institute, Atlanta, April 19–20, NAACP Papers, II:C222; Steven F. Lawson, *Black Ballot: Voting Rights in the South, 1944–1969* (Lanham, MD: Lexington Books, 1999), 129–39; Ruby Hurley to Gloster Current, July 14, 1952, NAACP Papers, II:C222.

60. Kluger, *Simple Justice*, 446–50, 506.

61. Charles H. Thompson, "Introduction: The Present Status of and General Outlook for Racial Integration in Education in the United States," *Journal of Negro Education: Special Issue on The Courts and Racial Integration and Education* (Summer 1952): 231–33. The special issue includes papers presented and transcripts of discussions at the April 1952 meeting; "Marjorie McKenzie in Challenge to Legal Tactics," *Pittsburgh Courier*, July 7, 1951, 6; Marjorie McKenzie, "Pursuit of Democracy," *Pittsburgh Courier*, July 28, 1951, 20.

62. James Nabrit, "An Appraisal of Court Action as a Means of Achieving Racial Segregation in Education," 421; Harry Ashmore, "Racial Integration with Special Reference to Education in the South," 250–255; John P. Frank, "Can the Court Erase the Color Line," 304–16, (all in) *Journal of Negro Education* (Summer 1952).

63. *Journal of Negro Education*, 238 (Johnson), 327 (Marshall), 429 (Nabrit), 440 (Horne).

64. Ibid., 239 (Johnson), 246–50 (Bond), 335–37 (Marshall), 395 (Hill), 425, 429 (Nabrit).

65. Ibid., 235 (Johnson), 326 (Marshall), 333–34 (Robinson), 425–26 (Nabrit).

66. Kluger, *Simple Justice*, 537–40.

67. *Washington Post*, December 10, 1952, 1; *New York Times*, December 10, 1952, 1; "Segregation on Trial," *New York Times*, December 14, 1952; "Jim Crow and the Supreme Court," *Chicago Defender*, December 20, 1952, 10; "Drama in the District," *Pittsburgh Courier*, December 20, 1952.

68. Kluger, *Simple Justice*, 543–81, 513–16.

69. Ibid. 617–45; Franklin, *Mirror to America*, 156–58.

70. Kluger, *Simple Justice*, 667–78.

71. Ibid., 702–8.

72. *Atlanta Daily World*, May 18, 1954, 1, 3; *Pittsburgh Courier*, May 22, 1954, 9; *Los Angeles Sentinel*, May 20, 1954, A1; Pauli Murray to Caroline Ware, May 18, 1954, in Anne Firor Scott, ed., *Pauli Murray and Caroline Ware: Forty Years of Letters in Black and White* (Chapel Hill: Univ. of North Carolina Press, 2006), 87–90; Avon Kirkland, comments at screening of *Simple Justice*, *Brown v. Board of Education* Fiftieth Anniversary Symposium, Univ. of South Carolina, April 23, 2003.

73. *Washington Post*, May 18, 1954, 2; *Los Angeles Times*, May 18, 1954, 6; *Atlanta Daily World*, May 18, 1954, 1.

74. Carter, *A Matter of Law*, 112; *The Crisis*, June-July, 1954, 352–53, 358–59; "Desegregation Goes Ahead," *The Crisis*, October 1954, 484–85; "Report on Desegregation," *The Crisis*, December 1954, 612–13; *The Crisis*, January 1955, 36–39, June-July 1955, 354–57.

75. Arkansas, Florida, Maryland, North Carolina, Oklahoma, and Texas submitted briefs. Kluger, *Simple Justice*, 724–25.

76. "Ruling on Relief," May 31, 1955, in Waldo E. Martin, ed., *Brown v. Board: A Brief History with Documents* (Boston: Bedford/St. Martin's, 1998), 194–98; Thurgood Marshall and Roy Wilkins, "Interpretation of Supreme Court Decision and NAACP Program," *The Crisis*, June-July 1955, 329–33; "Statement of the Emergency Southwide NAACP Conference, Atlanta, June 4, 1955," *The Crisis*, June-July 1955, 337; "Directives to the Branches Adopted by Emergency Southwide NAACP Conference," *The Crisis*, June-July 1955, 339–40, 381.

77. *Orangeburg (SC) Times & Democrat*, July 14, 1955, 1, July 31, 1955, 1; Cecil Williams, *Out-of-the-Box in Dixie* (Orangeburg, SC: Williams Assoc., 2006), 97–101; Democratic Party Platform of 1956, August 13, 1956, John T. Woolley and Gerhard Peters, The American Presidency Project, Univ. of California, Santa Barbara.

78. Numan V. Bartley, *The Rise of Massive Resistance: Race and Politics in the South During the 1950s* (Baton Rouge: Louisiana State Univ. Press, 1969), 82–107, 116–17.

79. Bartley, *Rise of Massive Resistance*, 62–63; Steven M. Gillon, *Politics and Vision: The ADA, Liberalism and American Liberalism* (New York: Oxford Univ. Press, 1988). 84, 94, 97, 101; Democratic Party Platform of 1956, August 13, 1956, John T. Woolley and Gerhard Peters, The American Presidency Project, Univ. of California, Santa Barbara.

80. "Segregated Transportation," *The Crisis*, October 1955, 500–502; Rosa Parks interview, in *Will the Circle Be Unbroken: An Audio History of the Civil Rights Movement in Five Southern Communities and the Music of Those Times* (Atlanta: Southern Regional Council, 1997) Disc 4, Part 7; Stewart Burns, ed., *Daybreak of Freedom: The Montgomery Bus Boycott* (Chapel Hill: Univ. of North Carolina Press, 1997), 1–27.

81. Bartley, *Rise of Massive Resistance*, 217–18, 230–31.

82. Ibid., 211–32; Larissa M. Smith, "Black Lawyers and Civil Liberties: Fighting Massive Resistance in Virginia, 1956–1963," paper given at the Southern Historical Association meeting, Atlanta, Georgia, November 2005; Roy Wilkins to Medgar Evers, December 21, 1955, in Myrlie Evers-Williams and Manning Marable, eds., *The Autobiography of Medgar Evers* (New York: Basic Civitas Books, 2006), 43–44; Peter F. Lau, "From the Periphery to the Center: Clarendon County, South Carolina, *Brown*, and the Struggle for Democracy and Equality in America," in Peter F. Lau, ed., *From the Grassroots to the Supreme Court:* Brown v. Board of Education *and American Democracy* (Durham, NC: Duke Univ. Press, 2004), 118–21.

83. Evers-Williams and Marable, *The Autobiography of Medgar Evers*, 1–42, 54–56, 61–65, 80–84, 89, 90, 92–97, 124.

84. Watson, *Lion in the Lobby*, 336–94; Norrell, *Reaping the Whirlwind*, 111–16; John Doar, "The Work of the Civil Rights Division in Enforcing Voting Rights Under the Civil Rights Acts of 1957 and 1960," *Florida State University Law Review*, Fall 1997, 1–2; Bob Moses, presentation to 2008 National Endowment for the Humanities Summer Institute, W.E.B. Du Bois Institute, Harvard University, July 2008.

85. Johanna Miller Lewis, "Implementing *Brown* in Little Rock," in Brian J. Daugherity and Charles C. Bolton, *With All Deliberate Speed: Implementing* Brown v. Board of Education (Fayetteville: Univ. of Arkansas Press, 2008), 12–13; Julian Bond, interviewed by author, December 15, 2008.

86. Smith, *They Closed Their Schools*, 151–52; Lau, "From the Periphery to the Center," 118–20; Fairclough, *Race and Democracy*, 234–51; *Southern School News*, April 1960, 1, September 1960, 1. In April, 1960, the *Southern School News* reported that Washington, D.C., and West Virginia "have complete integration in their school systems." According to the September 1960 report, 1 of 67 districts in Florida was desegregated; 8 of 173 in North Carolina school districts had desegregated, and only 11 out of 128 school districts in Virginia were desegregated.

87. Virginia Durr to Clark Foreman, April 7, 1960, in Patricia Sullivan, ed., *Freedom Writer: Virginia Foster Durr, Letters from the Civil Rights Years* (New York: Routledge, 2003), 205. Donald S. Strong, *Negroes, Ballots, and Judges: National Voting Rights Legislation in the Federal Courts* (Tuscaloosa, AL: University of Alabama Press, 1968), 4–5.

88. John Doar and Dorothy Landsberg, "The Performance of the FBI in Investigating Violations of Federal Laws Protecting the Right to Vote, 1960–67," 23–31, 59–61, unpublished article in author's possession; author interview with John Doar, September 5, 2008.

89. Gretchen Cassel Eick, *Dissent in Wichita: The Civil Rights Movement in the Midwest*, (Urbana: Univ. of Illinois Press, 2001), 1–33; Doar and Landsberg, "Performance of the FBI," 23–31; Evers-Williams and Marable, *Autobiography of Medgar Evers*, 89, 96; Taylor Branch, *Parting the Waters: America in the King Years* (New York: Simon and Schuster, 1988), 272–84; Ransby, *Ella Baker*, 237–47; Arsenault, *Freedom Riders*.

Epilogue

1. James Weldon Johnson, address at NAACP annual meeting, January 3, 1923, in Sondra Kathryn Wilson, ed., *In Search of Democracy: The NAACP Writings of James Weldon Johnson, Walter White, and Roy Wilkins, 1920–1977* (New York: Oxford Univ. Press, 1999), 101.

2. Bob Moses, telephone interview with author via telephone, December 7, 2008.

3. Report of the National Advisory Commission on Civil Disorders (New York: Bantam Books, 1968), 1.

4. Carter, *A Matter of Law*, 165–203.

5. Lyndon B. Johnson, "To Fulfill these Rights," commencement address at Howard University June 4, 1965, in *Public Papers of the Presidents of the United States: Lyndon B. Johnson, 1965*, vol. 2 (Washington, D.C.: Government Printing Office, 1966), 635-40; Gary Orfield, *Reviving the Goal of an Integrated Society: A 21st Century Challenge* (Los Angeles: The Civil Rights Project/Projecto Derechos Civiles at UCLA, 2009), 13–14. *New York Times*, February 28, 2008 (on incarceration rates); John Hope Franklin, *The Color Line: Legacy for the Twenty-first Century* (Columbia: Univ. of Missouri Press, 1993), 74.

6. Charles H. Houston, Our Civil Rights, *Baltimore Afro-American*, January 29, 1949.

Index